$222.00

WORLD of FORENSIC SCIENCE

WORLD of FORENSIC SCIENCE

VOLUME 1
A-L

K. Lee Lerner and Brenda Wilmoth Lerner EDITORS

GALE
CENGAGE Learning

Detroit • New York • San Francisco • New Haven, Conn • Waterville, Maine • London

World of Forensic Science

K. Lee Lerner and Brenda Wilmoth Lerner, Editors

Project Editor
Elizabeth Manar

Editorial
Luann Brennan, Meggin M. Condino, Kathleen J. Edgar, Madeline Harris, Melissa Hill, Kristine Krapp, Paul Lewon, Kimberley A. McGrath, Heather Price, Lemma Shomali, Jennifer York Stock

Editorial Support Services
Andrea Lopeman

Indexing
Synapse, The Knowledge Link Corporation

Rights and Acquisitions
Margaret Abendroth

Imaging and Multimedia
Emma Hull, Lezlie Light, Denay Wilding

Product Design
Michelle DiMercurio

Composition
Evi Seoud, Mary Beth Trimper

Manufacturing
Wendy Blurton, Dorothy Maki

LIBRARY OF CONGRESS CATALOGING-IN-PUBLICATION DATA

World of forensic science / K. Lee Lerner and Brenda Wilmoth Lerner, editors.
   p. cm.
     Includes bibliographical references and index.
     ISBN 1-4144-0294-5 (set : hardcover : alk. paper) —
     ISBN 1-4144-0295-3 (v. 1) — ISBN 1-4144-0296-1 (v. 2)
     1. Forensic sciences—Encyclopedias.
     2. Criminal investigation—Encyclopedias.
     I. Lerner, K. Lee. II. Lerner, Brenda Wilmoth. III. Title.
HV8073.W674 2005
363.25'03—dc22   2005006921

This title is also available as an e-book.
ISBN: 1414406118 (set)
Contact your Gale sales representative for ordering information.

Printed in the United States of America
4 5 6 7 8 9 14 13 12 11 10 09 08

CONTENTS

ACKNOWLEDGMENTS

In compiling this edition, we have been fortunate in being able to rely upon the expertise and contributions of the following scholars who served as academic and contributing advisors for *World of Forensic Science*, and to them we would like to express our sincere appreciation for their efforts to ensure that *World of Forensic Science* contains the most accurate and timely information possible.

Contributing Advisors

Susan Aldridge, Ph.D.
London, United Kingdom

Brian Cobb, Ph.D.
Institute for Molecular and Human Genetics
Georgetown University, Washington, D.C.

Nicolas Dittert, Dr. rer. Nat.
University of Bremen
Bremen, Germany

Brian D. Hoyle, Ph.D.
Microbiologist
Nova Scotia, Canada

Alexandr Ioffe, Ph.D.
Russian Academy of Sciences
Moscow, Russia

Pamela V. Michaels, M.S.
Forensic Psychologist

Eric Stauffer, MS, F-ABC, CFEI
Senior Forensic Scientist
MME Forensic Services
Suwanee, GA

Because they are actively working in criminal investigations, some advisors, contributors, and biographical subjects requested the release or inclusion of a minimum of personal information.

Special Thanks

In addition to our academic and contributing advisors, it has been our privilege and honor to work with the following contributing writers, and scientists: Janet Alred, William Arthur Atkins, Juli Berwald, Ph.D., Robert G. Best, Ph.D., Sandra Galeotti, M.S., William Haneberg, Ph.D., Agnieszka Lichanska, Ph.D., Adrienne Wilmoth Lerner, Eric v.d. Luft, Ph.D., M.L.S., Holly F. McBain, Caryn Neumann, Ph.D., Michael J. O'Neal, Ph.D., Mark H. Phillips, Ph.D., and Jennifer M. Rossi, Ph.D.

Many of the advisors or contributors to *World of Forensic Science* authored specially commissioned articles within their fields of expertise. The editors would like to specifically acknowledge the following contributing advisors for their special contributions:

Ed Friedlander, M.D.
Autopsy

Antonio Farina, M.D., Ph.D.
Gestational age, forensic determination

Nancy Masters
Friction Ridge Skin and Personal Identification: A History of Latent Fingerprint Analysis

The editors would like to extend special thanks to Connie Clyde for her assistance in copyediting. The editors also wish to specially acknowledge Jenny Long for her diligent and extensive research related to the preparation of sensitive biographical entries.

The editors gratefully acknowledge the assistance of many at Gale for their help in preparing *World of Forensic Science*. The editors wish to specifically thank Ms. Meggin Condino for her help and keen insights while launching this project. Special thanks are also offered to Gale Senior Editor Kim

McGrath for her timely and friendly guidance through various project complexities. Most directly, the editors wish to acknowledge and offer both professional and personal thanks to our Project Manager, Ms. Elizabeth Manar, for her thoughtful and insightful sculpting of *World of Forensic Science*. Her good nature and keen eye kept *World of Forensic Science* on course throughout a hectic production schedule.

INTRODUCTION

World of Forensic Science portrays the vast scope and influence of modern forensic science. From its origins in pre-scientific human fascination with the causes, manner, and circumstances of death, to the increasingly vital role of forensic science in law, security, and global economic and health issues, *World of Forensic Science* contains articles dedicated to providing insight into the science, applications, and importance of forensics.

To cover a topic of such scope and impact as forensic science is a daunting task. Interest in forensics spans human history, impacts philosophical and religious thoughts about death, and now, fueled by television and movies, is reflected in popular culture. Human interest in forensics dates to our earliest recorded histories. Egyptian Pharaohs first appointed officials to make inquiries into questionable deaths as early as ca. 3000 B.C., and accounts of ancient Roman law include references to the use of forensic experts in legal proceedings. Medieval English Common law, upon which portions of modern United States law is based, called for forensic determinations in the handling of estates.

Forensic science also has played—and in some cases continues to play—an important part in philosophical and religious thoughts about death. In some religions, for example, the determination of the manner of death may impact whether a body is fit for burial in certain grounds. Religious beliefs can also impact forensics, as there are still areas of the world and groups that consider autopsies as desecration.

As a formal science, forensics grew lockstep with advances in many branches of science during the nineteenth and twentieth centuries. The interval from scientific invention to forensic application narrowed as forensic scientists borrowed from the latest innovations of virtually every field of science to solve mysteries. However, just as advances in microscopes and atomic science allowed forensic applications to aid in the investigation of crimes at the most minute molecular and cellular level, the breadth of applications of forensic science underwent exponential expansion. In modern times, in addition to solving local crime, the next global pandemic or bioterrorist attack might well be first detected by a forensic scientist initially investigating a mysterious death.

World of Forensic Science is a collection of nearly 600 entries that evidence the wide diversity of forensic science. Articles on topics such as art forgery and wine authenticity indicate the far-reaching economic impact of forensic science. Heart-wrenching applications of forensic science, from uncovering the mindsets, methods, and motives of modern terrorists to discovering the far-reaching extent of natural disasters, are discussed in articles ranging from the "Identification of Beslan victims in Russia" to "Identification of tsunami victims"

Articles on a number of topics related to genetics, DNA fingerprinting, and microbiology show how recent advances in research quickly find their way into forensic application. A range of articles related to basic science reflects the fact that modern forensic investigators must be able to understand and properly apply tools from virtually every scientific discipline.

Nature is often innately tricky enough to confound scientists seeking to uncover its mysteries, but forensic scientists must also pit their skills against those deliberately trying to conceal or mislead. The importance of skill and experience to the forensic investigator is evidenced in the authoritative writing of many articles, including Ed Friedlander's article on autopsy procedures and Nancy Master's article on latent fingerprint analysis. (Friedlander serves as chairman, Dept. of Pathology, Kansas City University of Medicine and Biosciences, is board-certified in anatomic and clinical pathology, and has conducted an estimated 700 autopsies. Masters is the 2004 Dondero Award winner for identification in forensics.)

While selected topics acknowledge the relationship of forensic science to history and culture, and others describe the brutal realities of sensational crimes involving serial murders, ritual killers, or bombers, it was our intent to keep *World of Forensic Science* focused on science. The editors hope that *World of Forensic Science* serves to inspire a new generation of forensic scientists and investigators. It is also our modest wish that this book provide valuable information to students and readers regarding topics often in the news or the subject of civic debate.

K. Lee Lerner & Brenda Wilmoth Lerner
Editors
Santa Rosa Island, Pensacola, FL, and London, U.K.
April 2005

How to Use This Book

The articles in the book are meant to be understandable by anyone with a curiosity about topics in forensic science. Cross-references to related articles, definitions, and biographies in this collection are indicated by **bold-faced type**, and these cross-references will help explain and expand the individual entries. *World of Forensic Science* carries specifically selected fundamental topics in genetics, anatomy, physiology, microbiology, and immunology that provide a basis for understanding forensic science applications.

This first edition of *World of Forensic Science* has been designed with ready reference in mind:

- **Entries are arranged alphabetically**, rather than by chronology or scientific field.
- **Bold-faced terms** direct the reader to related entries.
- "See also" references at the end of entries alert the reader to related entries not specifically mentioned in the body of the text.
- A **sources consulted** section lists the most worthwhile print material and web sites we encountered in the compilation of this volume. It is there for the inspired reader who wants more information on the people and discoveries covered in this volume.
- The **historical chronology** includes many of the significant events in the advancement of forensic science.
- A **comprehensive general index** guides the reader to topics and persons mentioned in the book. Bolded page references refer the reader to the term's full entry.

Although there is an important and fundamental link between the composition and shape of biological molecules and their detection by forensic testing, a detailed understanding of chemistry is neither assumed or required for *World of Forensic Science*. Accordingly, students and other readers should not be intimidated or deterred by the complex names of chemical molecules. Where necessary, sufficient information regarding chemical structure is provided. If desired, more information can easily be obtained from any basic chemistry or biochemistry reference.

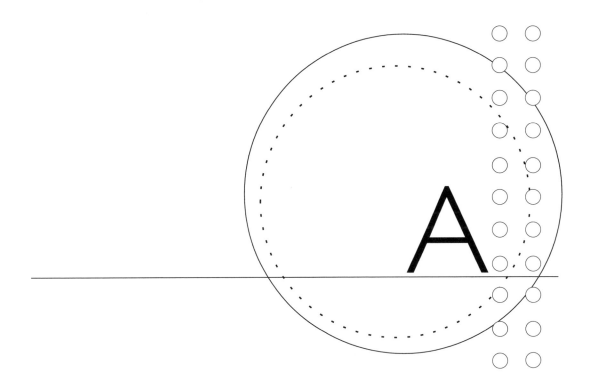

Accelerant

An accelerant is a substance that is used to cause the rapid spread of a fire. An example of a commonly used accelerant is petroleum distillate, the liquid that is collected from the vaporization of petroleum-containing liquids. This fire-starting fluid is sold in hardware stores and is utilized to rapidly ignite coals in a barbeque.

The accelerant used in a barbeque is deliberately applied. So it is with the accelerants that are of forensic concern. A fire in a building, vehicle, or other location can be deliberately set. This is known as **arson**. In an investigation of a fire whose origin is suspicious, a forensic investigator will be interested to find out how the fire started. As part of this investigation, the investigator will look for **evidence** of the presence or use of an accelerant.

During a fire, the fuel available for burning combines with the oxygen in the air in a reaction that is called combustion. Often, a fire will start in one location and subsequently spread. However, if an accelerant has been spread in an area, the pattern of the fire's origin can be different. The origin can be spread out more than is the case naturally. As well, the fire may start more explosively than would occur naturally. These differences can yield patterns that are distinctive to the trained eyes of the forensic investigator.

Once the origin of a fire has been determined, the area can be probed for the presence of residual amounts of the accelerant. This can be done using specially trained dogs that literally sniff out the chemical. In addition, samples of the scene can be collected and taken to a laboratory for analysis with specialized instruments.

For liquid samples, an instrument called a gas chromatograph is typically used. The liquid is heated to convert it to a mixture of gases. The identity of each of the gas components can be determined and this pattern will tell the investigators whether or not the liquid was an accelerant.

Similar analyses can be done on articles of clothing and even the skin of a suspect. Detection of traces of the accelerant on a person or their clothing can be powerful evidence linking them to the arson site.

SEE ALSO Accident reconstruction; Arson; Canine substance detection; Childers hostel blaze; Fire investigation.

Accident investigations at sea

Accidents can occur anywhere that there are people operating machinery. The world's oceans are no exception. Sea-going accidents have been a consequence of maritime tradition ever since boats put out to sea thousands of years ago.

Even in the early days of seafaring, there was interest in determining how an accident occurred and in seeking ways of preventing similar occurrences. These investigations eventually became official duties of the government, for example, in Britain formal marine accident inquiries were established approximately 150 years ago. Today, the investigations of sea accidents can reply on the skills of forensic scientists and the various technologies they can bring to bear.

When a seagoing accident involves an injury or fatality, an investigation can be very similar to that conducted on land. The object is to determine the cause of injury or death. Photographs of all the areas of the ship that are relevant in the investigation will be taken. The accident scene will be carefully scrutinized to recover any **evidence** and witnesses will be interviewed. All these steps help to piece together what occurred.

But an accident investigation conducted at sea presents some unique challenges. If the ship is still at sea, then the rapid transport of the samples to a laboratory for analysis may not be possible. In that case, the samples need to be stored so as to prevent tampering and deterioration. In the case of biological samples like tissues and **blood**, storage on ice at refrigerator or freezer temperatures can be options.

Other facets of an accident investigation are not concerned with injuries, but with the damage caused to the vessel. By analyzing the pattern of a fractured hull, for example, inspectors can gain an understanding of the cause of the damage. A gashed hull caused by a collision with an iceberg will be different than the damage caused by an impact with another vessel. A skilled forensic naval architect is able to examine a damaged vessel (a bent propeller shaft, for example) and determine the cause of the damage.

An accident investigation can involve the recovery of materials that have been dislodged from the vessel into the surrounding water, or of an entire sunken vessel. Some material may be floating on the surface. Then, recovery of the flotsam involves a surface search, usually by means of a search boat. Divers or submersible craft may also be used to locate debris that has sunk to the bottom of the ocean. In deep water, this process can be a very complex and dangerous activity.

In the investigation of an accident or crime on land, the investigative team often consists of more than one person. But, in the depth of the sea, only a single diver may be present. The diver must handle an object to identify it and determine its position on the sea floor. Once back at the surface, the diver must report on what was seen. The smallest detail can be important in guiding further recovery efforts and in piecing together the course of events. So, an investigative diver must be meticulous and attentive to detail.

Subsequent efforts can utilize sonar. This underwater version of radar sends out pulses of energy and displays the pattern of returning echoes to obtain images of underwater objects.

A critical facet of a marine accident investigation is collecting information on the weather patterns around the time of the accident. The value of this approach is exemplified by the investigation of the November 10, 1975, sinking of the freighter SS *Edmund Fitzgerald* in Lake Superior. The tragedy, which killed 29 mariners, formed the basis of a song by the Canadian singer/songwriter Gordon Lightfoot. By analyzing the ship's course and wind patterns, investigators determined that a shift of wind during a fierce mid-winter storm took the ship away from the protection of nearby land and put the vessel directly in the path of huge waves.

That investigation also exemplified the value of collecting and analyzing all communications that occur between the affected vessel and other vessels, aircraft, and the shore. In the case of the *Edmund Fitzgerald*, it was established that the captain was not aware of the severity of the threat until the ship became swamped with water and sank.

Simulations of the accident can be a useful way to reveal potential causes of an incident. Computer programs can be used to carry out simulations. As well, models of the affected vessel can be constructed and positioned in a specially constructed pool that can generate waves. The National Centre for Inland Waterways, located in Burlington, Ontario, Canada, has a pool where such testing can be carried out.

Another technology that has been advocated and is becoming more popular is the voyage data recorder. Akin to the flight recorders that are a standard on aircraft, a voyage data recorder provides information on various aspects of the ship during the voyage. A meeting of the International Marine Organization held in December 2004 was expected to pass amendments to the 1974 International Convention for the Safety of Life at Sea (SOLAS) requiring the presence of voyage data recorders on cargo ships.

SEE ALSO Accident reconstruction; Chemical and biological detection technologies; Drowning (signs of).

Accident reconstruction

Deaths from vehicle accidents declined in the years of the late twentieth century, thanks to the widespread use of seat belts and a decrease in persons driving while intoxicated. Cars are now manufactured to higher safety standards, with design features such as airbags and crumple zones to help reduce the impact of a collision. Airplanes and trains are equipped with numerous safety features and have established emergency procedures that protect passengers in case of a mishap. When an accident does occur, it is important to investigate it thoroughly, especially if someone has been injured or killed or if a crime has been committed. Reconstructing an accident is a key element of such investigations.

The police clear vehicular accidents away as soon as possible to stop blocking the highway. Investigators, therefore, may not have the chance to visit the accident site. Instead, they use **evidence** to create a reconstruction of the accident from which they can try to work out the cause. Investigators require access to: photographs of the accident site; the police accident report, including eyewitness reports; and the wreckage of the vehicles. These sources provide information on velocities and positions of the vehicles; skid marks; impact damage to the vehicles; condition of the vehicle, especially the tires; the weather conditions; and the condition of the drivers.

The investigators first put together a general reconstruction scenario and then fill in the details from the facts available. Because the final positions of the vehicles are usually well established, they might work backwards from this point. If there is also hard information on the initial velocities and conditions, perhaps from a speed camera or a reliable eyewitness, a beginning and end point of the collision might be established. Then the task is to work out what happened between these two points.

The majority of vehicle accidents involve collisions—with another vehicle, a stationary object like a wall or tree, or a pedestrian. Therefore, the focus of the investigation is usually to analyze the collision itself from the reconstruction so the cause of the accident can be determined. There are two physical laws that guide this analysis, the law of conservation of energy and the law of conservation of momentum. Used together, these can often provide a detailed analysis of a collision.

The law of conservation of energy states that energy can neither be created nor destroyed, but it can be converted into different forms. A moving object, such as a vehicle, has kinetic energy. When it comes to a stop, it has zero kinetic energy. Under normal conditions, this energy is converted into heat through the friction between the brakes and the road. In a collision, the kinetic energy is dissipated in two main ways, via a skid, and in deforming the vehicles

and their occupants on impact. A skid is an out-of-control type of braking and the analysis of any skid marks is a very important part of the accident reconstruction. Deformation of a metal object like a car involves work, the energy for which is the kinetic energy of the moving vehicle. Injuries to individuals are also brought about by transfer of kinetic energy.

Momentum is the product of the vehicle's mass and its velocity. A car traveling at 30 miles an hour has less momentum than one going at 40 miles an hour, and a truck generally has higher momentum than a car at the same velocity. When a collision occurs, the total momentum of the vehicles remains the same, but their individual momenta will change. If a car hits a stationary vehicle in a traffic queue (line), it will lose momentum, but the other vehicle will gain it. Overall, there is no alteration in momentum. The investigator can use the conservation of energy and momentum equations to try to establish facts such as initial velocity of the vehicles and so build a detailed picture of the collision.

The point of impact of the collision is an important factor and one that may be difficult to determine exactly. Tire marks, such as skids that suddenly change direction, however, can act as important clues. A head on collision might flatten the front tires, giving rise to a skid mark that suddenly terminates.

Examination of the vehicle wreckage, generally done off road, can also provide valuable information. For instance, under-inflated tires blowing out are an important cause of accidents. The blow point is often marked by a characteristic discoloration in the surrounding area. The hardness of the tire can also be measured using an instrument called a durometer. Its hardness profile shows if the tire has been run under-inflated. Metallurgic analysis of any fractures or dents in the car wreckage can give information on issues such as faulty welding or inferior repair work.

Accident reconstruction is particularly important in the case of large-scale accidents that involve many people, such as plane crashes, train wrecks, and even space shuttle disasters. The National Transportation Safety Board takes the lead in plane crashes and train collisions or derailings. Recovery of an airplane's black box, recording crew voices and instrument readings, is an important way to recover pertinent information about a plane crash. Conversations with air traffic controllers may provide information on what was happening on the plane at the time of impact. Witnesses may be asked to verify sounds or smoke coming from an airplane in trouble. These

A view of the floor of the Kennedy Space Center RLV Hangar showing a grid with outline of an orbiter and much of the space shuttle *Columbia* debris collected as of March 11, 2003, by the Columbia Reconstruction Project Team. Reconstruction of the orbiter helped to determine the cause of the *Columbia's* destruction. © NASA/CORBIS

investigations can be quite complex, and can take a year or more to complete, especially in high-profile cases.

The National Aeronautics and Space Administration (NASA), and sometimes an independent review board, investigates space shuttle accidents, such as the explosions of the *Challenger* in 1986 and *Columbia* in 2003. Although space shuttles are not equipped with black boxes, the crew members are in constant communication with NASA crews on the ground, and information from the shuttles' computers is constantly fed to ground control and recorded. This information becomes vital to an accident investigation and reconstruction process, should it become necessary.

Accident reconstruction is a complex matter. Not only does information from many sources have to be integrated, gathering this information is sometimes difficult, even traumatic. And however well the reconstruction has been put together, it is still only a model, and will often be subject to challenge from experts acting for parties to the accident.

SEE ALSO Airbag residues.

Adipocere

Also known as "grave wax," adipocere (from the Latin, *adipo* for fat and *cera* for wax) is a grayish-white postmortem (after death) matter caused by fat **decomposition**, which results from hydrolysis and hydrogenation of the lipids (fatty cells) that compose subcutaneous (under the skin) fat tissues.

Although decomposition of fatty tissues starts almost immediately after death, adipocere formation time may vary from two weeks to one or two months, on average, due to several factors, such as temperature, embalming and burial conditions, and materials surrounding the corpse. For instance, the subcutaneous adipose (fatty) tissue of corpses immersed in cold water or kept in plastic bags may undergo a uniform adipocere formation with the superficial layers of skin slipping off.

Several studies have been conducted in the last ten years to understand and determine the rate of adipocere formation under different conditions. Other studies also investigated the influence of some bacteria and chemicals, present in grave **soils**, in adipocere decomposition. Although this issue remains a challenging one, the purpose of such studies is to establish standard parameters for possible application in forensic analysis, such as the estimation of time elapsed since death when insect activity is not present. In forensics, adipocere is also important because preserved body remains may offer other clues associated either with the circumstances surrounding or the **cause of death**. The ability of adipocere to preserve a body has been well illustrated in exhumed corpses, even after a century.

Adipose cells are rich in glycerol molecules and are formed by triglycerols (or triglycerides). Bacterial activity releases enzymes that break these triglycerides into a mixture of saturated and unsaturated free fatty acids, a process known as hydrolysis. In the presence of enough water and enzymes, triglycerol hydrolysis will proceed until all molecules are reduced to free fatty acids. Unsaturated free fatty acids, such as palmitoleic and linoleic acids, react with hydrogen to form hydroxystearic, hydroxypalmitic acids and other stearic compounds, a process known as saponification, or turning into soap.

This final product of fat decomposition, or adipocere, can be stable for long periods of time due to its considerable resistance to bacterial action. This resistance allows for slower decomposition of those areas of a corpse where adipose tissues are present, such as cheeks, thighs, and buttocks. When a corpse is exposed to insects, however, adipocere probably will not be formed, as body decomposition will be much faster because of the insects' action. Animal scavenging of a dead body will also prevent adipocere formation.

SEE ALSO Decomposition; Entomology; Forensic science.

AFIS SEE Automated Fingerprint Identification System (AFIS)

Aflatoxin

A forensic investigation can often involve determining whether the victim was poisoned. Many different kinds of poisons exist. While some are synthetic, others are manufactured by living organisms. One example of the latter are aflatoxins.

Aflatoxins belong to a group of **toxins** called mycotoxins, which are derived from fungi. In particular, aflatoxins are produced by the soil-born molds *Aspergillus flavus* and *Aspergillus parasiticus* that grow on the seeds and plants. At least 13 aflatoxins have been identified, including B1, B2, G1, G2, M1, and M2. The B aflatoxins fluoresce blue and the G aflatoxins fluoresce green in the presence of ultraviolet light. The M aflatoxins are present in milk products. Aflatoxin B1 is the most ubiquitous, most toxic, and most well studied of the aflatoxins.

Afatoxins are so powerful that access to them is restricted and possession or handling of them by certain individuals constitutes a crime. The USA Patriot Act enacted on October 25, 2001 and signed into law (P.L. 107-56) by President George W. Bush is in effect as of January 2005 and contains a provision prohibiting possession or access to, shipment or receipt of, a "Select Agent" by "Restricted Persons" punishable by fines or imprisonment. Aflatoxins are considered select agents.

A restricted person is defined as someone who: (1) Is under indictment for a crime punishable by imprisonment for a term exceeding 1 year; or (2) Has been convicted in any court of a crime punishable for a term exceeding 1 year; or (3) Is a fugitive from justice; or (4) Is an unlawful user of any controlled substance (as defined in section 102 of the Controlled Substances Act (21 U.S.C. 802); or (5) Is an alien illegally or unlawfully in the United States; or (6) Has been adjudicated as a mental defective or has been committed to any mental institution; or (7) Is an alien (other than an alien lawfully admitted for permanent residence) who is a national of a country as to which the Secretary of State, has made a determination (that remains in effect) that such country has repeatedly provided support for acts of international terrorism (as of January 2005 these countries included Cuba, Iran, Iraq, Libya, North Korea, Sudan, and Syria); or (8) Has been discharged from the Armed Service of the United States under dishonorable conditions.

Aspergillus spp. contamination occurs as a result of environmental stresses on plants such as heat, dryness, humidity, or insect infestation. It can also occur if plants are harvested and stored in hot, humid environments. As a result, people who live in the regions of the world most prone to these conditions, such as sub-Saharan Africa and southeast Asia, are at highest risk for aflatoxin poisoning.

Aflatoxins were first identified in England in 1960 when more than 10,000 turkeys and ducks died within a few months. The disease contracted by these animals was called Turkey X disease and its cause was traced to *Aspergillus flavus* contamination of peanut meal that had originated in Brazil. The toxin was named for the shorthand of its causative agent: *A. fla.*

Aflatoxins are the most toxic naturally occurring carcinogens known. Aflatoxin B1 is an extremely hepatocarcinogenic compound, causing cancer of the liver in humans. Aflatoxin B1 exposure results in both steatosis (an accumulation of fat) and necrosis (cell death) of liver cells. Symptoms of aflatoxicosis are gastrointestinal, including vomiting and abdominal pain. Other symptoms can include convulsions, pulmonary edema, coma, and eventually death. Aflatoxins also pose a threat to developing fetuses and they are transferred from mother to infant in breast milk. Aflatoxins B1, G1, and M1 are carcinogenic in animals.

Poisoning due to aflatoxin occurs from ingestion of crops that have been infested with *Aspergillus* spp. or from eating animal products from animals that have ingested these crops. High concentrations of aflatoxins are most often found in plants with very nutritive seeds such as maize, nuts, and cereal grains in Africa and rice in China and Southeast Asia. In the United States, peanuts are routinely tested for aflatoxin concentrations, and contamination has also occurred in corn, rice, and cereal grains.

Most consider aflatoxins extremely dangerous and suggest that in human food they should have no detectable concentration. The maximum allowable concentration of aflatoxins set by the United States **FDA** is 20 parts per billion (ppb). Foreign markets usually reject grains with concentrations of 4 to 15 ppb. Acceptable levels of aflatoxins for animal consumption are up to 100 ppb. Because of the strict regulations regarding the permissible concentration of aflatoxin, exporting countries often reserve contaminated grains for consumption within their own country. Because *Aspergillus* spp. is usually colorless and does not break down during cooking, it is difficult to know whether or not people are consuming contaminated food.

SEE ALSO Biological weapons, genetic identification; Poison and antidote actions; Toxicology.

African Lemba tribe

The Lemba are a tribe of about 50,000 people living in South Africa and Zimbabwe who practice a religion that is strikingly similar to that of the Jews during Biblical times. Molecular genetics have provided the technology to compare genetic material of the Lemba people with that of modern Jewish people. The results show that the Lemba share several genetic characteristics with Jews including a particular marker on the Y-chromosome called the Cohen Modal Haplotype.

The Hebrew Bible tells the story of Jacob, the grandson of Abraham, who had 12 sons. Each of these sons became the leader of a tribe, collectively known as the twelve tribes of Israel. Historians date the origin of the twelve tribes to about 2,700 years ago. Over time, the twelve tribes became divided politically and geographically. The tribes of Judah and Benjamin lived in the southern part of Israel, while the other ten lived in the north. During the years 722–721 B.C.E., the Assyrians conquered Israel and exiled the ten northern tribes. Historians agree that the ten tribes were likely scattered and assimilated into local cultures to the east. Many groups from locations as disparate as Japan, China, India, and Ethiopia have claimed to be ancestors of the lost tribes, however the actual fate of these people is largely a mystery.

The Lemba of South Africa follow religious traditions that share many similarities with that of the Jews. They practice circumcision and ritual slaughter, scorn intermarriage, and have many similar food taboos, such as not eating meat from pigs. They follow a lunar calendar and celebrate holidays timed with the phases of the moon. Though they speak Bantu, their traditions vary greatly from that of other Bantu people. In addition, their oral tradition states that they came from the Middle East: "We came from the north, from a place called Senna. We left Senna, we crossed Pusela, we came to Africa and there we rebuilt Senna." Although many different lines of evidence point to a connection between the Lemba and the Jews, validating the relationship was never possible until the development of genetic testing.

The modern Jews are traditionally divided into three groups, essentially based on the oral traditions of their families. The Cohanim are thought to be descended from Moses' brother Aaron, who was the high priest of the Hebrew temple. Because Jewish tradition follows a paternal line of inheritance, all modern Cohanim share a paternally inherited priestly ancestor. The other groups are the Leviim, descended from the ancient tribe of Levi, and the Israelites, all non-Cohen and non-Levite Jews. In 1997, genetic researchers found that there is a specific marker on the Y-chromosome, which paternally passes through the genome, called the Cohen Modal Haplotype. This set of genetic markers is found in nearly 50% of all Jewish men who identify themselves as Cohanim. It is found with nearly the same frequency in both the Ashkenazic and Sephardic Cohanim, even though these two major groups of Jews have been geographically separated for hundreds of years. The Cohen Modal Haplotype is only found in about 10% of the Levites and Israelites. It is nearly non-existent in non-Jewish populations.

In 1999 genetic data on the Lemba was collected by Tudor Parfitt, director of the Center for Jewish Studies at the School of Oriental and African Studies in London. He and his collaborators took genetic samples from men of six Lemba clans whose geographic range was from South Africa to Zimbabwe. Of these six clans, the Buba are notable as being the priestly clan. The genetic material was analyzed for the genetic markers that have been found in the Jews. Similar to the general Jewish population, the Cohen Modal Haplotype was found in nearly 10% of all Lemba men. In addition, the Cohen Modal Haplotype was found in nearly half of the men in the Buba tribe.

Additional research by Parfitt identified a location in the Hadramaut region of Yemen as the Senna of the Lemba's oral history. In the past, Jewish communities thrived in Yemen. Parfitt found a town called Sena, which had been a vibrant community but had been almost completely abandoned nearly 1,000 years ago. The Lemba oral history stated that Senna was an extremely fertile place and that was irrigated as the result of a great dam. Parfitt found the remains of a dam in Sena and documented the rich history of the town. In addition, a valley called Wadi-al-Masila leads from Sena to a port city called Sayhut. Parfitt asserts that the Pusela of the Lemba oral tradition is the Masila valley near Sena. Under the right meteorological conditions, the winds could take a boat from Sayhut to South Africa in just over a week. Finally, the family names of the Lemba sound strikingly similar to names from the Hadramaut area.

While the Lemba cannot yet prove that they are one of the ten lost tribes of Israel, the scientific and ethnographic evidence shows that the Lemba of South Africa share a common ancestor with the Jewish people, and more specifically with an ancient priest. This has important implications, both historical and legal. Israeli law upholds the "right of return" that guarantees citizenship for any Jew. Jewish law, however, establishes Jewish identity maternally. Given that the Lemba have established their genetic heritage paternally, and that they practice a form of Judaism that is quite different from that practiced in Israel, there may still be controversy over the status of the Lemba in Israeli courts.

The ruins of Great Zimbabwe, discovered in 1867. Some scholars claim that the modern Zimbabwean Lemba tribe shares key genetic and cultural characteristics with descendents of an ancient Jewish people, and could be the creators of ancient Zimbabwe. © MARTIN HARVEY; GALLO IMAGES/CORBIS.

SEE ALSO DNA fingerprint; DNA sequences, unique; Genetic code; Y chromosome analysis.

Air and water purity

Humans are susceptible to contaminated air and water. Breathing in air that is laden with a noxious substance can cause illness or even death. Similarly, drinking water that contains an inorganic or organic poison, or an infectious microorganism can be debilitating or lethal.

Both water and air are particularly vulnerable to contamination by some bacteria and protozoa, and by their toxic products. While the contamination of air and water can be inadvertent, the noxious substances can also be introduced deliberately. Chemicals can also be dispersed in water and by air. A recent example occurred in 1995, when the Japanese cult Aum Shinrikyo released **sarin gas** into the Tokyo subway system. The poisonous gas attack killed 12 people and sickened 5,000.

As another example, in the months following September 11, 2001, there were several deliberate releases of **anthrax** spores into the air following the opening of contaminated letters. As well, the vulnerability of water supplies to contamination with a variety of infectious organisms has been recognized.

An amount as small as a glass of water can be contaminated with a quantity of organic or inorganic poison or microbe sufficient to cause harm. Even if the water has been chlorinated, disease causing microorganisms such as *Giardia* and *Cryptosporidium* are resistant to chlorine, as are bacterial **toxins**.

Technologies exist to kill the microorganisms that might be present (disinfection) or to completely remove the microbes and chemicals from the air or water (purification). These technologies, however, are usually designed to remove naturally occurring or polluting contaminants.

Groundwater or surface water treatment focuses on providing water that is fit to drink. Typically, the water is filtered to remove large debris. Some jurisdictions also pass the water through microfilters that remove objects as small as viruses from the treated water. Most drinking water is treated with chlorine or chlorine-containing compounds to kill any bacteria. Other treatments that are gaining widespread acceptance include the use of ultraviolet light, ozone, and other chemicals such as bromine. Water can also be purified by techniques involving reverse osmosis and steam distillation, although these techniques are not typically used, as they are expensive and purify relatively small volumes of water at one time.

Treatment and monitoring ensure that the water emerging from the treatment plant is safe to drink and that it remains that way all the way to the consumer's tap. However, these measures are not intended to thwart a deliberate contamination.

Yet for large surface water supplies, the volume of water alone makes the possibility of deliberate contamination remote. For example, it has been estimated that the contamination of the Crystal Springs Reservoir, which supplies some of the water for San Francisco, California, with enough hydrogen cyanide to harm anyone who drinks a glass of water would require over 400,000 metric tons of the poison. Similarly, huge amounts of bacteria or viruses would be required.

Technician taking a water sample. © JOHN ZOINER/CORBIS.

Air is vulnerable to contamination with a variety of bacteria, viruses, and fungi that are light enough to become dispersed in air currents. When inhaled, the microbes can cause infections. Chemicals and toxins can also float in the air, to be inhaled or settle onto exposed skin.

Air purification has long been possible using filters. Bacteria, viruses, and even some inorganic chemicals can be retained on specialized filters. These filters are mainly suitable for laboratories or relatively small, specifically designed ventilation systems. In large indoor environments such as malls or sizeable office buildings, and in the open air, air purification is virtually impossible.

Contamination of the open air poses a similar problem as the contamination of a large volume of water, namely the amount of poisonous agent that is required. For example, estimates are that hundreds of pounds of anthrax **spores** would be needed to achieve a massive contamination of the population of a large city.

The release of toxic agents into a more limited area such as an office building or a home is more plausible.

SEE ALSO Air plume and chemical analysis; Bioterrorism; Organic compounds; Toxins.

Air and water purity, forensic tests

Consumption of contaminated water or breathing in air that contains a noxious compound can be debilitating or lethal. Thus, forensic testing can include the testing of water or air to assess purity or impurity.

Many noxious gases can be transported in the air. For example, people are cautioned against leaving an automobile engine running in an enclosed space. This is because the tasteless, odorless, and colorless carbon monoxide (CO) emitted in the exhaust can cause illness or death, depending upon the concentration of the gas in the air. For example, at a concentration of 200 parts per million (ppm), CO produces a slight headache within hours. A concentration of 800 ppm causes nausea and convulsions (seizures) within 45 minutes of exposure, and can lead to unconsciousness, coma, and ultimately, death.

CO replaces oxygen in the bloodstream, by competing with oxygen molecules for the binding site in the transport compound of the blood called **hemoglobin**. As a result, the body becomes starved for oxygen.

As with gases, particulate material such as soot and asbestos can also be light enough to drift on currents of air. Microorganisms such as bacteria, viruses, and molds (and the **spores** produced by some strains) that dislodge from a surface can also drift on air currents.

The presence of these various agents in the air can be accidental. For example, the growth of molds and fungi in a damp wall of a house can lead to the aerial dissemination of spores. Of particular note, the fungus designated *Stachybotrys chartarum* produces spores that are toxic if inhaled. The fungus was implicated in the illness of 27 infants, nine of whom died, in Cleveland, Ohio, in 1993. All the infants lived in homes that sustained flood damage.

Besides *S. chartarum*, *Aspergillus versicolor* and several species of *Penicillium* are potentially toxic, and also thrive in damp environments.

Noxious agents have also been deliberately introduced into the air. For example, on March 20, 1995, the Japanese cult Aum Shinrikyo released sarin **nerve gas** in the Tokyo subway system, killing 10 people. And, at various times during the 1990s, the cult attempted to aerially disperse *Clostridium botulinum* spores.

Another form of spore is produced by the bacterium called *Bacillus anthracis;* the cause of **anthrax**. In the fall of 2001, a series of incidents occurred in the United States, in which letters containing a powdery form of anthrax spores were mailed to public figures including Senators Patrick Leahy and Tom Daschle and NBC news-anchor Tom Brokaw. Five people died after inhaling the spores released from tainted letters.

Water has been described as "the universal solvent." A huge number of **inorganic compounds** can dissolve in water. As well, microorganisms can be maintained in suspension and can survive for varying periods of time. The result if the water is used for drinking, washing food, bathing, and even recreation, can be illness or worse.

A particularly graphic example of the hazard posed by impure water occurred in the Canadian town of Walkerton, Ontario, in the summer of 2000. Contamination of one of the municipality's wells by a disease-causing (pathogenic) bacterium called *Escherichia coli* O157:H7 sickened over 2,000 people and killed seven. A number of those who recovered have been left with permanent kidney damage. Contamination of water and food by *E. coli* O157:H7 causes an estimated 73,000 illnesses and over 60 deaths in the United States each year, according to the **Centers for Disease Control and Prevention**.

Other bacteria including species of Salmonella, Vibrio and Shigella, which, like E. coli, normally dwell in the intestinal tract, can enter water when the water is contaminated by feces, as can intestinal viruses and protozoans. Contamination of drinking water by a protozoan called *Cryptosporidium* in 1993 produced a diarrhea-like illness in over 400,000 people in Milwaukee, Wisconsin.

Forensic testing of air and water is accomplished using the standard analytical procedures employed in other sectors. With air, for example, a device can be used that draws a defined amount of air through a filter. The size of the holes (pores) in the filter is big enough to allow the air molecules to pass, but restricts the passage of particulate material. Even viruses can be retained, if the filter's pore size is in the nanometer (10^{-9} meter) range.

The Simpson Tacoma Kraft Pulp Mill spews air pollution over the city of Tacoma, Washington, from its site on Commencement Bay in the shadow of Mount Rainier. © JOEL W. ROGERS/CORBIS.

The particles are subsequently recovered from the filters and analyzed. Analysis techniques include **spectroscopy**, electron microscopy, and the examination of genetic material. The latter can involve the use of a technique called **polymerase chain reaction (PCR)**, which greatly increases the number of copies of a selected target region of the deoxyribonucleic acid (**DNA**). The sequence of nucleotide building blocks that comprise the DNA can then be determined.

Water samples can also be filtered to recover particulates and suspended microorganisms. The above techniques can then be used to examine a sample. As well, particularly for bacteria, assays that rely on the growth of the organisms on an appropriate food source, first developed hundreds of years ago, are still an important means of identifying the bacterial cause of an illness.

The types of forensic air and water analyses that are performed rely on the skill of the forensic exam-

iner. Knowledge of the circumstances surrounding an illness or death, appearance of the scene, and the symptoms or behavior of the victim can provide clues suggestive of the involvement of a particular noxious agent.

SEE ALSO Aflatoxin; Air plume and chemical analysis; Biosensor technologies; DNA typing systems; *Escherichia coli*; Nerve gas; Pathogens; Sarin gas; Toxicological analysis; Water contamination.

Air Force criminal and forensic investigations

Forensic investigations are a part of the military as much as civilian life. Military investigations can take on added importance, since the use of **firearms**, **explosives**, and other high-risk tools are more prevalent than in civilian life. A military forensic investigation, such as in the U.S. Air Force, can help root out an anomaly, criminal or otherwise, that would otherwise threaten other service personnel.

A branch of the U.S. Air Force that is concerned with **forensic science** is the Air Force Office of Special Investigations. The AFOSI is the principal investigative service of the United States Air Force. Its ranks, which numbered over 2,500 in 2005, include active-duty Air Force personnel, reservists, and civilians.

Established in 1948 by then United States Secretary of the Air Force W. Stuart Symington, AFOSI is charged with investigating and preventing criminal activities by United States Air Force personnel, as well as by individuals outside the Air Force whose actions threaten the service's equipment, personnel, activities, or security.

Symington patterned the new office after the Federal Bureau of Investigation (**FBI**), and appointed Special Agent Joseph Carroll, assistant to FBI director **J. Edgar Hoover**, as the first AFOSI chief. Symington and Carroll developed an investigative service designed to provide unbiased information and operate independent of top air force command. To this end, the AFOSI included civilian personnel from the beginning.

Among the crimes addressed by AFOSI investigators are **murder**, robbery, rape, drug use and trafficking, black-market activities, and other unlawful acts committed by or against U.S. Air Force personnel. Economic crime, or fraud, is an area of investigation that places particularly large demands on AFOSI resources. AFOSI includes personnel with specialized missions and skills who fulfill functions ranging from that of polygrapher to computer expert to behavioral scientist.

SEE ALSO Aircraft accident investigations; Flight data recorders.

Air plume and chemical analysis

An air plume is a layer of warm air that immediately surrounds a person's body. It has also been referred to as a human thermal plume. An air plume carries chemical signatures that can be used to detect the presence of various compounds on a person.

While the security implications of this are immediately evident, for example if residue from **explosives** is in the air surrounding a person, an air plume can also be used in an investigation into a person's death. If an examination is conducted soon after death, the presence of a chemical residue may still be detectable in the air surrounding the body.

The skin's surface temperature is typically 33° Celsius, which is approximately nine degrees warmer than the surrounding air at a typical room temperature. The temperature difference causes heat to be lost from the entire surface of the skin to the surrounding air.

Because warm air rises, the plume rises up the body and flows off the top of the head and shoulders, instead of radiating outward to the surrounding air from all parts of the body. As the air moves up and away from a person, tiny bits of the skin and chemicals that were present on the skin's surface can also be carried upward. The presence of clothing has no effect on the upward movement of the air.

The presence of clothing also does not block the migration of chemicals from items being carried in the clothing. Particles of an explosive in a pocket, for example, will be able to pass through the pores of the fabric to the immediate vicinity of the skin. There, they will encounter the air plume and migrate upward with the airflow.

The chemicals that are carried in the air plume can be detected using sophisticated detection equipment. The chemical analysis of an air plume can detect explosives and even the aromas emitted by microorganisms.

The analysis of an air plume has grown out of studies that relied on the use of what is termed a *schlieren* system. The word schlieren is German for streaks, and describes the appearance of air in a special optical system. Schlieren optics measure air flow based on the scattering of light due to differences in density at the interface between moving air and relatively motionless air.

Scientists interested in imaging the schlieren patterns produced by people modified the small optical system so that it could be accommodated in a larger device. The device is similar in appearance to the walk through x-ray machines that are now commonplace in airport security areas.

When someone walks through the portal, the air plume is drawn into an analysis chamber positioned in the portal's archway. Any particles present are collected in a trap. As well, the vapors in the air plume can be condensed onto the trap. Chemical analysis is performed using a machine called an ion trap mobility spectrometer.

The trapping of particles and condensation of the vaporous air plume concentrates any compounds that are present. The trapped sample is delivered to a chamber that converts the sample molecules to ions. Typically, bombarding the sample atoms with electrons accomplishes this conversion. When an electron collides with a sample ion, an electron is dislodged from the sample atom, producing a more positively charged ion. As voltage is applied along the length of the chamber, the positively charged sample ions move toward the negatively charged cathode. Separation of the ions occurs based upon their different sizes and masses. For example, smaller ions move down the chamber faster than larger ions. As ions arrive at the cathode, a current is produced. The current can be amplified to produce a detectable signal. The different signals can be plotted to produce a spectrum. The different peaks in the spectrum can be related to known ions to determine the ionic composition of the sample.

The spectrometer is extremely sensitive and fast. Chemicals that are present in only a few parts per billion will be detected in about 10 seconds.

SEE ALSO Analytical instrumentation; Biodetectors; Gas chromatograph-mass spectrometer.

Airbag residues

Various residues (small particles) can attach to a person's body or clothing. These can be detected and analyzed to provide clues as to the person's involvement in a particular incident. **Evidence** of

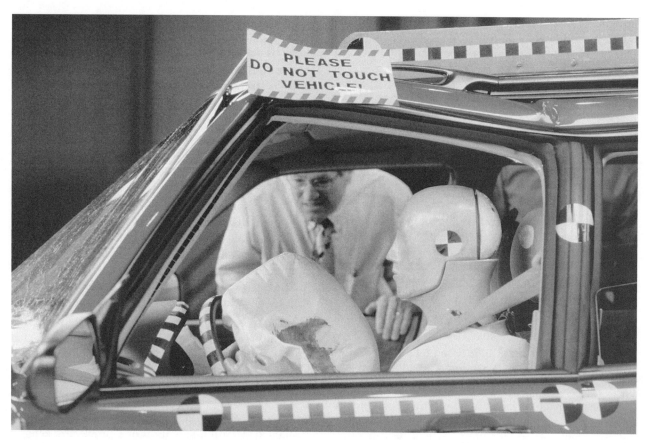

A researcher examines a crash dummy and deployed airbag after a test crash. A powdery substance helps many air bags deploy without sticking, and often leaves a residue that can be collected for evidence in a crash. © TIM WRIGHT/CORBIS.

involvement in a motor vehicle crash can be provided by the detection of the residue released when an airbag is deployed.

An airbag is essentially a pillow (albeit a specialized one) that is normally concealed. It is triggered to expand by the force of a collision.

Airbags first appeared commercially in automobiles in the 1980s. At that time, they were located only on the driver's side, and were concealed in a compartment in the middle portion of the steering wheel. Airbags have been standard equipment on the front passenger side of cars since the 1998 model year and on the trucks since the following year. Some cars now additionally offer side-mounted airbags that offer protection in the event of a side collision.

The deployment of airbags depends on momentum, which is the product of the mass and velocity of an object. When a car is moving forward, both the vehicle and all the objects inside the car, including the passengers, will tend to keep moving forward.

When the vehicle is rapidly stopped, as occurs in a collision, the passengers' momentum will continue to carry them forward. Typically, passengers are restrained by seatbelts. But, in a high-speed accident, or when a passenger is not buckled in, the forward movement can be so great that the passenger is propelled forward at great speed. The result can be catastrophic injury.

It is this injury that airbags are designed to prevent. The airbag inflates when an accelerometer detects a force equal to running into a brick wall at 10–15 miles per hour. This force causes a switch in the accelerometer to close, allowing the flow of electricity. This current activates the sensor, which in turn activates the airbag's inflation system.

It is the inflation system that proves to be of forensic significance. A gas generator inside the airbag contains sodium azide (NaN_3), potassium nitrate (KNO_3) and silica (SiO_2). Upon the signal from the sensor, heat is supplied, which is necessary to decompose NaN_3. A series of three chemical reactions occurs. In the first reaction, the breakdown of NaN_3 produces nitrogen gas (N_2) and sodium (Na). The sodium then reacts with KNO_3 to generate potassium oxide (K_2O), sodium oxide (Na_2O) and yet more nitrogen gas. Finally, the potassium and sodium oxides react with SiO_2 to produce alkaline silicate (glass).

The latter reaction is a safety measure. Potassium oxide and sodium oxide are very reactive substances and it is dangerous to have them as the end products of the airbag inflation.

Prior to inflation, the NaN_3 and KNO_3 are solids, typically pellets. Their subsequent reactions produce a large amount of nitrogen gas, which bursts the nylon or polyamide airbag from its storage compartment at upwards of 200 miles per hour to approximately the size of a couch decorative pillow.

The entire process, from detection of an impact to the deflation of the airbag, is approximately 170 milliseconds; literally, in the blink of an eye. The inflation of the airbag coincides with the forward movement of the driver or passenger, so by the time a person contacts the airbag, deflation has begun. In this way, the bag acts as a cushion and dissipates the passenger's forward momentum. Without this exquisite timing, a person would contact a rock-hard bag that could cause as much injury as a high-speed collision with the car's windshield.

During deflation, the nitrogen gas vents through very small holes in the bag. It is during this deflation that other contents of the bag can also be released. This residue contains alkaline silicate, but most typically consists of cornstarch or talcum powder. The latter two compounds are included to keep the airbag soft and lubricated while stored.

The deflation can produce a fine powdery cloud of residue that will settle on clothing, vehicle surfaces, hair, and exposed skin. The residue is dissipated very quickly from the airbag. Once the bag has deflated, no more residue is released.

The airbag residue is slightly corrosive and so can be a mild respiratory and skin irritant. The red skin that can result from surface contact with the residue or the mild airway and lung irritation produced upon breathing in the residue can be other forensic clues of a person's involvement in a vehicle collision.

Because of this irritation, forensic investigators wear gloves and goggles when near a deployed airbag and wash with soap and water afterwards.

SEE ALSO Accident reconstruction; Automobile accidents; Death, cause of; Trace evidence.

Aircraft accident investigations

Although flying is generally a safe method of transportation, accidents occasionally happen—whether through human error, mechanical failure, or criminal activity. Over the last two decades (1985–2005), there have been between 30 and 65 fatal aircraft accidents per year worldwide. These, and lesser accidents, have to be investigated scientifically in order to gain important lessons about aircraft performance and safety.

The International Civil Aviation Organization (ICAO) requires that a civil aircraft accident be investigated by an independent body belonging to the country where the accident took place. Each country has its own organization taking responsibility for this: in the United States, it is the **National Transportation Safety Board** (**NTSB**); in the United Kingdom, it is the Air Accidents Investigation Branch (AAIB). The NTSB investigates around 2,000 accidents and incidents a year. The purpose of the investigation is to find out why the accident happened and how similar events might be avoided in the future, rather than to apportion blame. The police will be involved in the investigation if sabotage or some other form of criminal activity is suspected, and the military generally looks into accidents involving service aircraft.

The ICAO sets guidelines on how an aircraft investigation is to be carried out. The first step is to report the aircraft accident or incident. An accident is an event involving death or serious injury, or severe damage to an aircraft. Missing or out-of-contact aircraft must also be reported. Incidents are not as serious; they are events best described as "near misses" involving problems such as forced landings, near collisions, or fires.

The investigation team consists of a permanent core group and outside scientific experts who are called on when needed. They respond immediately to the accident and go to the accident site. Each member will carry flashlights, tape recorders, camera and film, as well as any specialist tools. The investigation of the accident site and the wreck itself may take from several hours to a few days. During this time, the team works in small groups and gathers a wide range of data which may be relevant to the inquiry.

The history of the flight and the crewmembers' duties leading up to the accident are noted. Careful documentation is made of the wreckage and accident scene, with calculation of the impact angles so that the pre-accident flight path can be determined. The experts will also examine the engines and propellers,

Forensic experts inspect some of the wreckage on July 26, 2000, after the crash of an Air France Concorde which ditched in a field outside Paris shortly after takeoff, killing its 109 passengers and crew. © REUTERS/CORBIS.

together with all details of the electrical, hydraulic, and pneumatic systems of the craft and the flight control instrumentation. The investigation is extended beyond the aircraft itself, to the weather prevailing at the time of the accident and the air traffic control instructions given to the plane. Crewmembers are interviewed to look at possible human error factors, such as medical history, fatigue, **training**, workload, working environment, and drug and alcohol abuse. If survivors are involved, the team will document injuries, offer support, and arrange evacuation and rescue efforts.

A vital part of the aircraft accident investigation in the case of larger planes is recovery and examination of the flight recorder, also known as the black box. Airplanes usually have two types of flight recorders, the flight data recorder (FDR) and cockpit voice recorder (CVR).

The FDR is a digital recorder which may use magnetic tape to record, although solid-state devices are now available which can store data on memory chips. The flight data recorder records various flight parameters; the basic ones include: altitude, airspeed, direction, acceleration, and microphone keying, that is, the timing of radio transmissions made by the crew. Modern jet aircraft can record far more data than this with the most advanced logging up to a thousand different parameters, covering every aspect of the flight. The FDR records on an endless loop principle and contains data from the last 24 hours of the flight.

The cockpit voice recorder (CVR) records not only the voices of the crew in conversation or making radio transmissions, but any noise within the cockpit such as alarms, control movements, switch activations, and engine noise. Data from the CVR is correlated with that from the FDR by the microphone keying mentioned above. The CVR may be an analogue recorder using magnetic tape, although, as with FDRs, there are now solid-state devices that store the audio data in digitized form on memory chips. The CVR also operates on an endless loop principle and carries the last 30 minutes of audio information.

Analysis of data from the flight recorders may be the only way of establishing what happened in some aircraft accidents, particularly if they occur at night or where there is little recoverable wreckage. They are also very useful when a sudden event, such as a change in wind speed or direction, is the prime cause of an accident.

Photographs such as this, showing the Concorde's left wing bursting into flame upon takeoff, helped experts determine the probable cause of the 2000 crash—engine contamination from a blown tire caused by a small piece of metal on the runway. © BUZZ PICTURES/CORBIS SYGMA.

Flight recorders are built to protect the data from both high-speed impact and any fire that may occur after impact. They are usually located near the aircraft's tail, because past experience has shown that this is the area that generally suffers least damage in an accident.

Recovering the flight recorders after an accident can, however, be challenging. In the VH-IWJ Westwind 1124 accident, which occurred on October 10, 1985, an aircraft crashed into the sea off Sydney, Australia, shortly after takeoff. The pilot and co-pilot, who were the plane's only occupants, were killed. Three months passed before the flight recorders were discovered on the seabed. Analysis of the CVR at the Australian Transport Safety Bureau (ATSB) labs showed that the pilot was testing the co-pilot and

simulating emergency instrument flight conditions. The FDR revealed a loss of control at 5,000 feet which caused the plane to crash.

The flight recorders are analyzed in specialized audio laboratories. The black box data can be integrated with that from other sources, including ground-based radar recorders, wreckage analysis, and eye-witness reports. Advanced computer graphics can be applied to create a graphical reconstruction or video of the sequence of events leading up to the accident or incident.

The mission of the investigative team is to produce an interim report within four to eight weeks that will be sent to all the interested parties for their comments. Safety recommendations are always given priority, so that any changes can be put into place as soon as possible. A final report will appear some time after the investigation and will be published on the website of the investigative organization. This final report includes all the factual information collected in the course of the investigation, an analysis of the information, and a conclusion which gives the cause of the accident or incident and any safety recommendations arising.

Aircraft accident investigations cover events from the crash of light aircraft flown by one person to major disasters such as the terrorist attacks of September 11, 2001. One example, which illustrates many of the aspects of accident investigations described above, is the investigation into the loss of Pam Am Flight 103 over Lockerbie, Scotland, on December 21, 1988. None of the 259 crew members and passengers on board the Boeing 747 survived and eleven people on the ground were also killed. The US-based plane was bound for New York, but it was the United Kingdom's AAIB which carried out the investigation—starting on the day of the crash and reporting in 1990. The plane was brought down by a bomb that had been placed in one of the overhead luggage lockers. The criminal aspects of the event were investigated separately, as were issues of airport security.

The flight recorders were found just east of Lockerbie, about 15 hours after the accident. These showed nothing unusual, stopping suddenly at the moment when the bomb exploded. Investigation of the crew and the aircraft's technical history ruled out human error or technical failure. Weather conditions were unremarkable and the air traffic control records were consistent with the sudden loss of the plane as shown by the flight recorders.

The plane disintegrated in mid-air, creating 1,200 significant items of debris requiring investigation.

Larger items, such as the engines and the aircraft wings, fell on the town of Lockerbie, producing a fireball. Lighter debris was scattered for many miles.

Forensic scientists discovered traces of explosive material in the debris and were able to reconstruct the explosion and the impact it had on the plane. Postmortem examination of the victims revealed they died of multiple injuries consistent with a mid-air explosion followed by impact on the ground.

The loss of Pam Am Flight 103 was a tragedy with far reaching legal and political implications. But for AAIB, the priority was aircraft safety. The report recommends developing the facility for a flight data recorder to record the pressure changes associated with explosions. It also suggests that aircraft should be designed to better withstand the impact of an explosion.

SEE ALSO Explosives; Flight data recorders.

Alcohol testing SEE Breathalyzer®

Alternate light source analysis

A forensic examination that is conducted only using the visible light wavelengths that are emitted from conventional bulbs may not reveal all the **evidence** present. Depending on the composition of the evidence or the material it is in contact with, its presence may be poorly revealed, if at all, by conventional light. The use of what has been termed alternate light sources can reveal otherwise hidden evidence.

The use of alternate light sources in forensic investigations was pioneered by the Royal Canadian Mounted Police in the 1970s. Then, the units were typically water-cooled argon-ion lasers. These large and expensive machines could not be transported to the scene. Rather, samples needed to be brought to a laboratory equipped with the **laser**.

Portable lasers capable of delivering a single wavelength of light were developed in the late 1980s. In the 1990s, the development of a high-intensity incandescent bulb allowed a wider range of wavelengths to be generated, from the ultraviolet range of the light spectrum to the near infrared. Modern alternate light sources can be less than 20 pounds and are easy to operate.

In general, an alternate light source consists of the light itself (such as a laser or incandescent bulb),

a filter or combination of filters that enable all but the selected wavelengths of light to be screened out, a device to deliver the light to the area being examined and appropriate viewing accessories (such as protective goggles, if the wavelengths of light being used are potentially harmful, or goggles equipped with a filter to further screen the incoming light).

Since alternative light source examinations are typically done at the scene of the accident or crime, the light-delivering device needs to be rugged and portable. Typically the light will be equipped with a wheel containing a half dozen or so filters, which can be rotated to bring a different filter into the light path. Another alternate light source design utilizes a flexible fiber-optic cable, which is advantageous in examining confined spaces.

The key to the use of alternate light sources is **fluorescence**; the absorption of light at one wavelength and the emission of light at a longer wavelength. The emitted light can be detected by use of the screening filters, which block out the other wavelengths of light.

Most organic materials can be made to fluoresce. As an example, a **fingerprint** can be invisible to the naked eye. But, when illuminated using an intense blue-green light from a laser or incandescent source, the organic materials in the fingerprint will fluoresce yellow. The fluorescence is visible without the addition or powders or dyes.

The same principle applies to other organic samples including **semen**, **saliva**, **fibers** from materials, and ink. Furthermore, different organic materials will absorb light and fluoresce at different wavelengths. This means that evidence such as a fingerprint or a bite mark can be detected on materials as diverse as skin, paper, rubber, and cloth fabric.

This sort of differentiation requires a skilled operator, since the color of the illuminating light is critical to elicit the maximum fluorescence from the evidence while minimizing the background fluorescence from the supporting material. As well, the selection of the filter(s) is important, since it will block all but the desired wavelengths of the illuminating light while not blocking the wavelengths of the emitted fluorescent light (which is generally much less intense).

One use for alternate light sources is the examination of a weapon such as a gun or knife. Finger and palm prints are nearly invisible on such metal surfaces when examined under room light. But, when viewed under a green light and observed through an orange filter, the prints can easily be seen. Similar

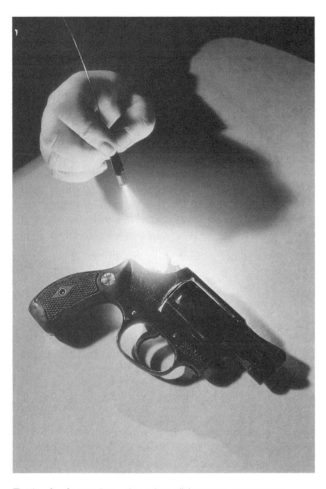

Testing for fingerprints using a laser lightsource. © CHARLES O'REAR/CORBIS.

lighting conditions and special film can be used to photograph prints.

Body **fluids** can be detected using alternate light sources. For example, the use of near-ultraviolet light can readily reveal the presence of semen stains. Other body fluids that can be detected include saliva, **blood**, urine, and vaginal secretions.

Gunshot residue can also be readily observed using the appropriate illumination. Small bits of paint, fiber, hair, **glass**, crystals, and other "trace evidence," which can be physically difficult to find at a crime or accident scene, can be located using alternate light. Moreover, the differing chemistries and shapes of the objects can produce different patterns of fluorescence, allowing different objects to be coincidentally detected.

As a final example, **document forgery** can be detected using alternate forensic light sources, since differences in ink composition and the differing per-

iods of time that the ink was in contact with the paper will produce detectable changes.

SEE ALSO Crime scene investigation; Document forgery; Fingerprint; Fluorescence; Luminol; Polarized light microscopy; Trace evidence.

American Academy of Forensic Sciences

The American Academy of Forensic Sciences (AAFS) is a non-profit, professional organization founded in 1948 in an effort to improve the effectiveness of justice through the application of scientific expertise to the legal process, **evidence** gathering, and crime investigation. AAFS is also dedicated to educating the law enforcement, legal, and scientific communities about the many scientific disciplines that have given rise to modern **forensic science**, and the application of scientific forensic techniques. The term forensic means "pertaining to the forum" (e.g., to a legal public court of justice). The forensic sciences, therefore, apply the knowledge of a variety of scientific disciplines to achieve optimum accuracy in legal investigations and the establishment of sound evidence to be used in civil legal disputes or in criminal courts. AAFS has achieved international prestige and recognition, presently counting more than 5,600 members from 50 different countries worldwide. These professionals represent different fields of expertise such as **medicine** (legal medicine, public health, **autopsy**, **toxicology**, **pathology**, **epidemiology**, genetics, infectious disease), physical **anthropology**, jurisprudence, **criminology**, sociology, **psychiatry** and behavioral sciences, molecular biology, chemistry, engineering, education, archeology, **geology**, and **odontology**. Additionally, other persons with technical expertise, such as document analysis and graphology, are important members of the forensic sciences community.

AAFS is dedicated to the promotion of **training** programs for professionals, the exchange of information among the scientists of the above disciplines, the development of new forensic techniques, the advancement of forensic sciences, the support of new research, and the development of emerging forensic techniques and disciplines. Among the latter, examples are techniques involving **photography** superposition, forensic **skull** reconstruction, computer image enhancing, voice and diction analysis, account auditing, and improved polygraph examinations. Another AAFS goal is to preserve and impart ethical standards of professional conduct among its members.

AAFS publishes the *Journal of Forensic Sciences*, and holds an annual scientific meeting along with several regional seminars. The Academy also provides educational information to the general public and to those considering pursuing a career in one of the many fields of the forensic sciences. Programs of continuing education and accreditation in forensics for professionals and college graduates are another service under the responsibility of the following AAFS sections: **criminalistics**, engineering sciences, general, jurisprudence, odontology, pathology and biology, physical anthropology, psychiatry and behavioral science, **questioned documents**, and toxicology.

SEE ALSO Civil court, forensic evidence; Evidence; Expert witnesses; Federal rules of evidence; Forensic science; Medical examiner; Polygraphs; Professional publications; Toxicology; Voice analysis.

Ammunition and weapons, examination and identification
SEE Ballistics

Ammunition size SEE Caliber

Amphetamines

Amphetamines are a family of chemical compounds that are indirect stimulants of the central nervous system (CNS). Amphetamines cause the increased release into the brain of dopamine and norepinephrine, two endogenous (produced by the body) chemical messengers, which in turn stimulate the nervous system. Many drug abusers seeking a boost of physical energy and mental stimulation consume amphetamines due to their cocaine-like behavioral effects. Determining the presence or absence of amphetamines in the **blood** is included in most forensic drug screening tests.

Effects of amphetamines that may be experienced include: increased alertness, appetite inhibition, insomnia, decreased fatigue, and emotional euphoria. In high doses, amphetamines can induce delirium, panic attacks, confusion, aggressiveness, and suicidal tendencies. Chronic users sometimes

develop a state of amphetamine-induced psychosis that shares similarities with an acute schizophrenic crisis. Drug abusers usually inject amphetamines intravenously or inhale them by smoking.

MDMA (Methylenedioxymethamphetamine), an amphetamine derivative also known as Ecstasy, is swallowed in tablets or capsules, in doses ranging from 60–120 milligrams, usually in association with alcoholic drinks. Drug abusers in general tend to consume these stimulants together with alcohol or marijuana, whose alkaloids further enhance the effects of amphetamines. The amphetamine-induced euphoric state lasts an average of 4–6 hours, which is more than twice the time of cocaine effects.

Like cocaine, some amphetamines also cause addiction and progressive tolerance within a few weeks of use, leading its users to increase doses to achieve the same initial effects. Other physical effects of amphetamine abuse are cardiac arrhythmias, dangerously high blood pressure, chest pain, circulatory collapse, chills, excessive perspiration, and headaches. Nausea, anorexia, diarrhea, vomiting and abdominal cramps, and coma may also occur. A national survey by the Drug Abuse Warning Network under commission of the Substance and Mental Health Services Administration, reported that between 1999 and 2001, more than 86% of all life-threatening cases of intoxication recorded by hospital emergency services in the U.S. were associated with the use of MDMA in combination with either alcohol, marijuana, cocaine, or heroin.

The U.S. Department of Justice, Drug Enforcement Administration (**DEA**), classifies both illegal and controlled substances under five levels of Schedules, I to V. Most amphetamines are categorized in Schedule I, along with other substances such as LSD, marijuana, peyote, mescaline, heroin, etc. A drug or substance scheduled at level I is thus classified because the drug has a high potential for abuse, has no currently accepted medical use in treatment in the United States, and there is a lack of accepted safety for use of the drug. Therefore, amphetamine parent chemicals scheduled under level I cannot be prescribed by physicians in the United States.

Other amphetamine derivatives such as methamphetamine, phenmetrazine, and methylphenidate are under Schedule II, along with cocaine. Schedule II drugs are described as drugs with a high potential for abuse and physical or psychological dependence, but with currently accepted medical uses in the United States with severe restrictions. Schedule II drugs are tightly regulated and require a written prescription from a licensed physician.

Schedule III–V amphetamines also require prescription by a physician, but their manufacture and supply are less controlled and the potential for abuse is less. Therapeutic drugs such as some appetite suppressants and some drugs prescribed for attention deficit disorder fall into this category. Some amphetamines are approved by the Food and Drug Administration either as ingredients of pharmaceutical drugs or as a one-salt drug, such as methylphenidate, used in the treatment of narcolepsy, a clinical condition that induces patients to an uncontrollable state of sleepiness that leads to suddenly falling asleep anywhere and at any time.

SEE ALSO FDA (United States Food and Drug Administration; Illicit drugs; Narcotic; Nervous system overview; Neurotransmitters.

Analytical instrumentation

Forensic science can involve determinations of the presence or absence of compounds or materials. For example, if a victim has died of a stab wound, then noting that a knife was found near the body can be an important piece of **evidence** in trying to decipher the details of the death.

This sort of presence or absence level of detail produces qualitative information. The data does not have an amount associated with it or information concerning the composition of a sample.

In contrast, other useful information can be gained by quantitative examinations; examinations that tell how much of a material is contained within a sample. For example, if the knife noted above has **blood** on the blade, a blood sample can be vital to learning the blood type and the composition of the **DNA** carried in the blood, as well as indicating the presence and amount of any **toxins** or chemical poisons.

For quantitative forensic analyses, specialized instruments are used. A variety of analytical instruments exist, which have their respective advantages depending on what is being examined and the potential target molecules that could be contained within it.

Another area of forensic analysis that uses analytical instrumentation is **gunshot residue** analysis. When a rifle or a handgun is fired, the residue that propelled the bullet out of the barrel is also propelled outward. The residue can attach to exposed skin or the clothing of the person who fired the gun, or on a nearby person or surface.

The residue contains spherical particles that are comprised of lead, antimony, and barium. The particles' shapes and elemental compositions mean that they can be detected using a scanning electron microscope equipped with an energy dispersive x-ray analyzer. The analyzer operates by trapping electrons from the scanning microscope that have bounced off of the sample surface. The surface interaction causes an energy loss. Depending on the nature of that surface, the electrons will lose a certain amount of energy. As well, some of the electrons that were part of the object's surface can be dislodged by the force of the bombardment. By analyzing the pattern of energy levels of the reflected and dislodged electrons, the instrument can be used to determine the elements that are present in the sample and even how much of each element is present. Also, the scanning electron microscope allows the spherical residue particles to be directly visualized. Some instruments are equipped to visually display the elemental pattern on the sample image.

The elemental pattern that is obtained consists of various peaks rising above the background signal. Each peak represents a single element. If the pattern obtained from a sample recovered from a person matches the pattern of a sample obtained from a suspect, then it can be powerful evidence linking the suspect to the fired weapon.

Another important facet of forensic science is the use of DNA typing to identify individuals. The subtle differences in the arrangement of DNA that exist from person to person are every bit as unique as a **fingerprint**, and so have the potential to identify a DNA sample as belonging to a particular individual.

An especially powerful DNA examination technique is known as the **polymerase chain reaction (PCR)**. The technique uses an enzyme (polymerase) to make many copies of a minute amount of target DNA. The amount of DNA that can be made permits other analyses to be done on material that otherwise would have been present in too low a quantity.

PCR allows DNA to be recovered and analyzed from samples such as cigarette butts, the sealing flaps of envelopes, or pieces of hair and bone, even if the samples have been exposed to the environment or are contaminated with other compounds or microorganisms.

Another analytical instrument, the **gas chromatograph-mass spectrometer**, is adept at analyzing fluid samples. Separation of the various compounds that make up the fluid is accomplished by the gas chromatograph. The sample is injected into the machine and is immediately vaporized. The now-vaporized chemicals are carried through the **chromatography** column by a non-reactive gas such as helium. Depending on the chemical properties of the column, different compounds move at different rates of speed and so appear at the other end of the column at different times. This allows the different compounds to be separated from each other.

The separated compounds are then analyzed by the mass spectrometer. The sample's molecules are hit by a beam of electrons, which causes some of the sample's electrons to be dislodged (ionization). The ionization pattern can be used to identify the molecules and even to determine the mass of the compounds.

Databases that contain the mass spectrometric information on thousands of compounds exist in various state and federal law enforcement agencies. This information can be accessed to help identify the composition of a sample mixture with great precision.

SEE ALSO Air plume and chemical analysis; Biodetectors; Chemical and biological detection technologies; DNA fingerprint; Gas chromatograph-mass spectrometer; Laser ablation-inductively coupled plasma mass spectrometry; Micro-fourier transform infrared spectrometry; Mitochondrial DNA analysis; PCR (polymerase chain reaction); Visible microspectrophotometry.

Anatomical nomenclature

Over the centuries, anatomists developed a standard nomenclature, or method of naming anatomical structures. Terms such as "up" or "down" obviously have no meaning unless the orientation of the body is clear. When a body is lying on its back, the thorax and abdomen are at the same level. The upright sense of up and down is lost. Further, because anatomical studies, and particularly embryological studies, were often carried out in animals, the development of the nomenclature relative to comparative anatomy had an enormous impact on the development of human anatomical nomenclature. There were obvious difficulties in relating terms from quadrupeds (animals that walk on four legs), who have abdominal and thoracic regions at the same level, to human bipeds in whom an upward and downward orientation might seem more obvious.

In order to standardize nomenclature, anatomical terms relate to the standard anatomical position. When the human body is in the standard anatomical position it is upright, erect on two legs, facing frontward, with the arms at the sides with each rotated so that the palms of the hands turn forward.

In the standard anatomical position, *superior* means toward the head or the *cranial* end of the body.

The term *inferior* means toward the feet or the *caudal* end of the body.

The frontal surface of the body is the *anterior* or *ventral* surface of the body. Accordingly, the terms "anteriorly" and "ventrally" specify a position closer to—or toward—the frontal surface of the body. The back surface of the body is the *posterior* or *dorsal* surface and the terms "posteriorly" and "dorsally" specify a position closer to—or toward—the posterior surface of the body.

The terms *superficial* and *deep* relate to the distance from the exterior surface of the body. Cavities such as the thoracic cavity have internal and external regions that correspond to deep and superficial relationships in the midsagittal plane.

The bones of the **skull** are fused by sutures that form important anatomical landmarks. Sutures are joints that run jaggedly along the interface between the bones. At birth, the sutures are soft, broad, and cartilaginous. The sutures eventually fuse and become rigid and ossified near the end of puberty or early in adulthood.

The sagittal suture unties the parietal bones of the skull along the midline of the body. The suture is used as an anatomical landmark in anatomical nomenclature to establish what are termed *sagittal planes* of the body. The primary sagittal plane is the sagittal plane that runs through the length of the sagittal suture. Planes that are parallel to the sagittal plane, but that are offset from the midsagittal plane are termed *parasagittal planes*. Sagittal planes run anteriorly and posteriorly and are always at right angles to the coronal planes. The *medial plane* or *midsagittal plane* divides the body vertically into superficially symmetrical right and left halves.

The medial plane also establishes a centerline axis for the body. The terms *medial* and *lateral* relate positions relative to the medial axis. If a structure is medial to another structure, the medial structure is closer to the medial or center axis. If a structure is lateral to another structure, the lateral structure is farther way from the medial axis. For example, the lungs are lateral to the heart.

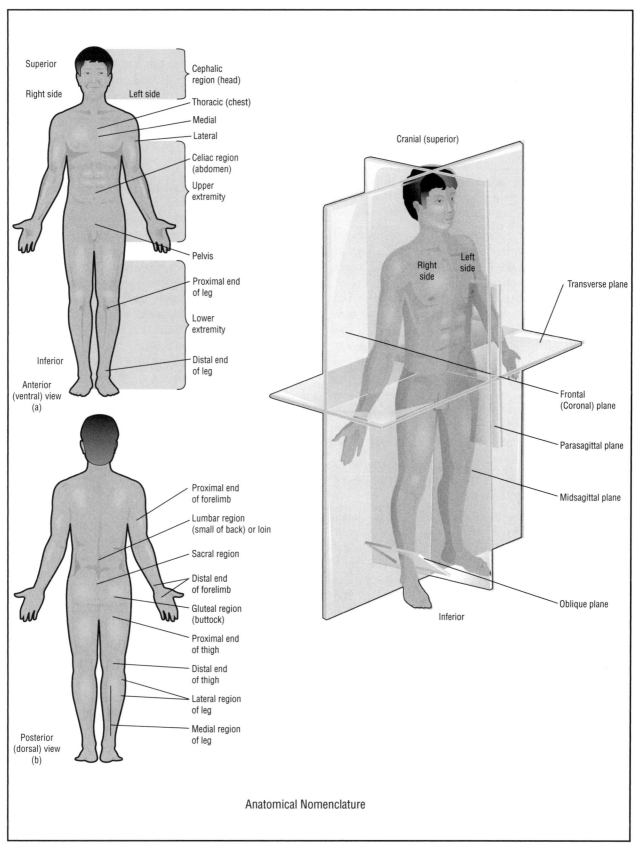

Anatomical Nomenclature

Three views of anatomical nomenclature (clockwise), anterior (ventral) view, cranial (superior) view, posterior (dorsal) view, illustration
ILLUSTRATIONS CREATED BY ARGOSY.

The coronal suture unites the frontal bone with the parietal bones. In anatomical nomenclature, the primary *coronal plane* designates the plane that runs through the length of the coronal suture. The primary coronal plane is also termed the *frontal plane* because it divides the body into frontal and back halves.

Planes that divide the body into superior and inferior portions, and that are at right angles to both the sagittal and coronal planes are termed transverse planes. Anatomical planes that are not parallel to sagittal, coronal, or transverse planes are termed oblique planes.

The body is also divided into several regional areas. The most superior area is the *cephalic region* that includes the head. The *thoracic region* is commonly known as the chest region. Although the *celiac region* more specifically refers to the center of the *abdominal region*, celiac is sometimes used to designate a wider area of abdominal structures. At the inferior end of the abdominal region lies the *pelvic region* or *pelvis*. The posterior or dorsal side of the body has its own special regions, named for the underlying vertebrae. From superior to inferior along the midline of the dorsal surface lie the *cervical*, *thoracic*, *lumbar* and *sacral* regions. The buttocks are the most prominent features of the *gluteal region*.

The term *upper limbs* or *upper extremities* refers to the arms. The term *lower limbs* or *lower extremities* refers to the legs.

The *proximal* end of an extremity is at the junction of the extremity (i.e., arm or leg) with the trunk of the body. The *distal* end of an extremity is the point on the extremity farthest away from the trunk (e.g., fingers and toes). Accordingly, if a structure is proximate to another structure it is closer to the trunk (e.g., the elbow is proximate to the wrist). If a structure is distal to another, it is farther from the trunk (e.g., the fingers are distal to the wrist).

Structures may also be described as being medial or lateral to the midline axis of each extremity. Within the upper limbs, the terms radial and ulnar may be used synonymously with lateral and medial. In the lower extremities, the terms fibular and tibial may be used as synonyms for lateral and medial.

Rotations of the extremities may be described as medial rotations (toward the midline) or lateral rotations (away from the midline).

Many structural relationships are described by combined anatomical terms (e.g. the eyes are anterio-medial to the ears).

There are also terms of movement that are standardized by anatomical nomenclature. Starting from the anatomical position, *abduction* indicates the movement of an arm or leg away from the midline or midsagittal plane. *Adduction* indicates movement of an extremity toward the midline.

The opening of the hands into the anatomical position is *supination* of the hands. Rotation so the dorsal side of the hands face forward is termed *pronation*.

The term *flexion* means movement toward the flexor or anterior surface. In contrast, *extension* may be generally regarded as movement toward the extensor or posterior surface. Flexion occurs when the arm brings the hand from the anatomical position toward the shoulder (a curl) or when the arm is raised over the head from the anatomical position. Extension returns the upper arm and or lower to the anatomical position. Because of the embryological rotation of the lower limbs that rotates the primitive dorsal side to the adult form ventral side, flexion occurs as the thigh is raised anteriorly and superiorly toward the anterior portion of the pelvis. Extension occurs when the thigh is returned to anatomical position. Specifically, due to the embryological rotation, flexion of the lower leg occurs as the foot is raised toward the back of the thigh and extension of the lower leg occurs with the kicking motion that returns the lower leg to anatomical position.

The term *palmar surface* (palm side) is applied to the flexion side of the hand. The term *plantar surface* is applied to the bottom sole of the foot. From the anatomical position, extension occurs when the toes are curled back and the foot arches upward and flexion occurs as the foot is returned to anatomical position.

Rolling motions of the foot are described as *inversion* (rolling with the big toe initially lifting upward) and *eversion* (rolling with the big toe initially moving downward).

SEE ALSO Anthropometry; Autopsy; Biometrics; Pathology; Skeletal analysis; Skeletal system overview (morphology).

Ancient cases and mysteries

Modern **forensic science** has provided historians, archeologists, and anthropologists with new tools to investigate mysteries whose roots extend back hundreds, even thousands, of years. **DNA** analysis, for example, has shed light on such cases as that of the **Peruvian Ice Maiden**, the 500-year-old mummified body of a young girl sacrificed to the gods by Incan priests, discovered in 1995. It has also identified with certainty the skeletal remains of the Romanovs, the Russian royal family killed by revolutionaries in 1918. In 2005 Spanish researchers hope to use DNA analysis to settle a dispute over whether the remains of explorer Christopher Columbus are buried in Spain or the Dominican Republic.

Forensic scientists have unlocked the secrets of human remains, such as the mummy of ancient Egyptian king Tutankhamen. The discovery of King Tut and his tomb in 1922 was the most significant archeological find of its generation. The burial chamber, which had survived intact for over 3,000 years, was filled with gold, ivory, and carved wooden treasures, including a now-famous funerary mask. But some features of the tomb puzzled archeologists. The burial chamber's small size suggested that it was built for a non-royal. It appeared to be unfinished and to have been hastily decorated, with paintings marred by splotches of paint that were never cleaned up. The tomb's artifacts were originally marked with other people's names, which were rubbed out and replaced with Tut's name. These features suggested that King Tut, who died at the early age of eighteen and who was the son of a controversial, and by some, hated, leader, may have died unexpectedly and of unnatural causes. Further, buckets of unguents dumped over the mummy raise the question of whether an attempt was made to cover up a **murder**.

In 1968 researchers from the University of Liverpool x-rayed the King Tut mummy and found a sliver of bone in the brain cavity and an area at the base of the **skull** that may have been a blood clot, clues suggesting that the king may have died from a lethal blow to the back of his head. Later, medical experts examined the x rays and spotted more clues. They found abnormalities in the bones above the king's eye sockets, consistent with injuries that occur when a head strikes the ground sharply in a backward fall and the brain snaps forward. Additionally, the vertebrae in the king's neck were fused, **evidence** of a condition called Klippel-Fell syndrome that makes a person highly susceptible to serious injury from a fall or a push. If Tut was murdered, suspects include Maya, his royal treasurer; Horemheb, his military commander; Ankhesenamen, his wife; and Ay, his prime minister, who assumed the throne after Tut's death. Additional forensic evidence was gathered in 2005, when Tut's mummy was removed from his tomb and scanned in a CT scanner. The resulting evidence may never solve the crime, but it may

establish whether or not a crime took place. In March 2005, scientists were also considering the possibility that Tutankhamen could have died from complications of a fracture, when the CT results revealed evidence of a broken left thighbone.

Other forensic scientists focus not only on a body, but also on the physical environment in which a historical person died, searching for clues as to the **cause of death**. Such is the case with French emperor Napoleon, who in October 1815, after the Battle of Waterloo, was exiled by the British to the island of Saint Helena, where he died on May 5, 1821. The official cause of death was listed as a perforated stomach ulcer that had turned cancerous. In 1955 though, the diaries of his valet, Louis Marchand, were published. Marchand's descriptions of the emperor and his behavior in the months before his death created suspicion that he had been poisoned to death with arsenic administered over a long period of time.

In 2001 the Strasbourg Forensic Institute in France bolstered this suspicion by examining a lock of the emperor's hair. Arsenic, usually in the form of white arsenic, or arsenic oxide, works as a poison by binding with sulfur atoms in proteins and enzymes, interfering with their ability to regulate body chemistry. The protein keratin, found in hair, contains sulfur atoms, so evidence of arsenic poisoning will survive in the hair. What's more, because hair grows, a histogram of segments of the hair, created by subjecting the hair sample to x-ray **fluorescence spectroscopy**, can show how arsenic levels changed over time. The Strasbourg researchers concluded that during the time in which the sample of hair grew, Napoleon's body contained arsenic concentrations of seven to thirty-eight times higher than normal.

The central question is: Was Napoleon deliberately poisoned to death, perhaps by his captors, by a disgruntled staff member, or by French Bourbons who wanted to ensure that he never resumed the throne? Some researchers say no. The head of the **toxicology** department for the Paris police noted that hair samples from 1805 and 1814 show similar concentrations of arsenic. If arsenic had caused the emperor's death, he would have died much earlier. Further, arsenic was at the time a common ingredient in some medicines and in hair tonics.

In the nineteenth century, mysterious cases of arsenic poisoning were turning up in Europe, but it was not until 1893 that an Italian chemist named E. Gosio worked out what was happening: that when wallpaper containing a particular pigment became damp and moldy, the mold converted a compound in

View of King Tutankhamun's tomb and wall paintings near Cairo, Egypt. In early 2005, researchers briefly removed King Tut's mummy for a CT scan in order to determine Tut's age at the time of his early death, along with the cause of death. © ROYALTY-FREE/CORBIS

the pigment, copper arsenite, into a vaporized form of arsenic. Anyone who breathed the vapor would get a form of arsenic poisoning that came to be called Gosio's disease. The pigment in question, called Scheele's Green, had been developed around 1770 by a Swedish chemist and was used widely in fabrics and wallpapers. Historical investigation showed that the wallpaper in the drawing room of Napoleon's house indeed was colored with Scheele's Green and that the house had a tendency to be damp. Further, the island's governor, Sir Hudson Lowe, was worried that the emperor would try to escape, so he posted sentries around the house. In an effort to avoid their watchful eyes, Napoleon spent more and more time in the house, especially the drawing room, where he inhaled the arsenic vapor as he spent hours looking out the windows

or through holes that he had bored in the shutters. Thus, modern investigators conclude that the likely source of the arsenic in Napoleon's system was his wallpaper, not a murderer.

Forensic investigation has also proven useful in authenticating or disproving claims made about artifacts. One is the Shroud of Turin, a 14-by-3 1/2-foot (4.27-by-1-meter) bloodstained burial cloth that shows faint images of a man who appears to have been tortured and crucified. The cloth came to light in 1204, when the Crusaders sacked the city of Constantinople. The cloth had been removed from the Middle Eastern city of Edessa in 944, where it had been discovered in 544. It was displayed in Lirey, France, in the 1350s but later moved to Chambery, France, where it was almost destroyed by fire in 1532. Many scientists assert that the Edessa Cloth and what is today called the Shroud of Turin (in Turin, Italy) are one and the same. Many people believe that the shroud is the burial cloth of Jesus Christ and that the images are his; some believe that the images are the product of a miracle.

The Shroud of Turin has intrigued modern forensic scientists, especially chemists, whose central question is whether the shroud could have been Christ's burial shroud—that is, whether it was a Greco-Roman burial shroud that can be placed in Jerusalem two thousand years ago. The nature of the cloth, the presence of travertine aragonite limestone dirt particles on it, and pollen grains, some from species now extinct, support claims that the shroud was in the environs of Jerusalem. In 1988 carbon-14 dating apparently proved that the cloth dated from the medieval period, and was hence a fake. More recent studies insist that the carbon-14 sample used in those tests was invalid, contaminated by a later repair patch, and that the cloth dates from an earlier century. The image shows coins on the man's eyes, a common burial practice at the time, and evidence suggests that the coins were struck during the first century A.D.

Scientists have also probed the images on the cloth, subjecting them to a panoply of scientific tests, including visible and ultraviolet spectrometry, infrared spectrometry, x-ray fluorescence spectrometry, thermography, pyrolysis-mass-spectrometry, lasermicroprobe analyses, and microchemical testing. Such tests reveal that the images were not formed by dyes or pigments, meaning that they were not somehow "painted" onto the cloth. Rather, the images are superficial (200–600 nanometers thick) and fully contained in a layer of starch and saccharides (simple sugars) coating the outermost layers of the fabric. Further, a faint image on the reverse side of the cloth corresponds exactly with the image on the outside. Analysis shows that this image, too, is superficial, meaning that nothing soaked through the cloth from the inside to form the image on the outside. The color, often described as caramel-like, was likely the result of a complex chemical reaction, called a Maillard reaction, between amines, or ammonia derivatives, that are released by decaying bodies, and saccharides in a carbohydrate residue covering the **fibers** of the shroud and likely originating with soap that was used to clean the cloth. Put simply, the images appear to have a natural explanation and are not the result of fakery. Despite these tests, the debate continues, and the Shroud of Turin remains a chief exhibit in the debate between faith and science.

SEE ALSO Infrared detection devices; Mummies; Paint analysis; Peruvian Ice Maiden; Skeletal analysis; Spectroscopy.

Animal evidence

Evidence of animals, especially animal hair, is often discovered at crime scenes. Pet or other animal hairs can be found on the clothes of the victim or on other items of **physical evidence** collected at the crime scene. The **identification** and analysis of human and animal hairs from a crime scene can indicate physical contact between the victim and a suspect, or provide other investigative leads. Transferring of pet hairs to the victim, to a suspect, or to the crime scene may happen when the perpetrator is a pet owner (or when the victim owns a pet), or when the crime was committed in a place where animals are kept, such as barns, stables, basements, or transport vehicles.

Through microscopic analysis, hairs can be identified as belonging to a particular species of animal. In the case of a known suspect, animal hair identified on the victim's clothing can be compared to hairs found either in the suspect's home, car, or clothing in search of a match. If the pet of the victim or of the suspect is available, further forensic analysis can be made to confirm whether that particular pet is the source of the hair in question. The pet's bed or brush can also provide samples for such identification.

When human remains are found outdoors, forensic procedures are conducted to establish whether the **cause of death** was due to homicide, suicide, accident, animal attack, or natural illness (i.e., heart attack, stroke, or other pathological condition). Perforation wounds, bullet holes, blunt force injuries, and other lesions normally point to a criminal act as the cause of death. However, animal access to corpses may cause such destruction of the remains that the real cause of death can be impossible to determine in certain cases. Animals feeding on a dead body leave distinct marks on bones and tissues. The signs of wild carnivores and scavenger birds, for instance, are recognizable through characteristic marks left on the bones and soft tissues by claws, fangs, and beaks. Nevertheless, even bodies found in urban areas or inside doors can suffer animal destruction by rodents and domestic animals, such as dogs and ferrets.

Forensic anthropologists are experts in determining the gender, race, and age of unrecognizable remains (usually by studying the bones) and in identifying what kind of animal activity was responsible by the destruction of those remains. Bodies of drowned individuals found on seashores or riverbanks can also display signs of animal activity, such as from crabs or fish.

Animal evidence in human remains has been systematically registered and studied since 1943, including the action of a variety of species, such as wild dogs, large cats, bears, cows, horses, poisonous snakes, marine animals, constricting snakes, rodents, birds, and domestic dogs. The types of injuries and typical feeding behaviors of various species are also well documented. One of the indications of animal scavenging on human remains involves bones or body parts that are scattered, such as a **skull** found some distance from the body, with teeth lost after death. This is common in bodies left on the surface or buried on shallow graves in woods or country areas. Missing body parts or bones are often retrieved from dens of coyotes, foxes, or skunks along tracks and pathways used by these animals.

The types of postmortem marks left on human remains by animals allow the identification of the species involved because of the known specific anatomical features and feeding behavior of each species. Seagulls, crows, owls, and other carrion-eating birds leave puncture wounds in the flesh, caused by their hard sharp bills. Vultures damage bones with their talons and beaks as they remove the flesh. Coyote, fox, and other wild and domestic canids puncture, tear, and crush the soft tissues by gnawing and shaking their heads, splintering bones, and leaving jagged bone edges through the action of their posterior teeth. Rodents have sharp paralleled incisors that leave parallel furrows in flesh and bones, with a pattern of layered destruction of tissues. Big cats leave v-shaped punctures from their canine teeth, claw slashes, and abrasions, and great amounts of crushed and splintered bones. Big cats, wolves, and wild dogs have a preference for eating the internal organs first, therefore eviscerating the body. Domestic dogs also can eat human remains when they are hungry, causing great destruction of the corpse. Such situations can pose extra challenges to forensic investigators in determining the circumstance, time, and real cause of death.

SEE ALSO Anthropology; Crime scene investigation; Death, cause of; Evidence; Microscope, comparison; Skeletal analysis; Taphonomy.

Animal poaching (forensic detection) SEE Wildlife forensics

Animation

In movies, computer animation has become astonishingly adept at mimicking reality. The animation power of computers and computer-aided design (CAD) software is now being exploited as a forensic tool.

Forensic animation seeks to produce images that recreate eyewitness accounts of crime scenes, vehicle accidents, and other events. The animation is intended primarily for a jury in a courtroom trial. Instead of relying solely on a verbal account of an eyewitness, jury members can watch a recreation of the testimony.

As an example, animation can recreate the weather conditions visible from the inside of a moving car on the night of a motor vehicle accident, to provide the viewer with a much better appreciation of what a driver faced than what could be realized from verbal testimony.

In another example, an animated reconstruction can be made of a crime scene. The simulation can duplicate the appearance of the scene. In addition, the view of the crime scene can be shifted from a ground level to an overhead view. This can provide a much richer appreciation of the crime scene than would listening to testimony alone or even looking at a series of photographs.

In one real-life example, animation was used in a liability suit in Iowa over a 1993 collision that killed University of Iowa basketball player Chris Street. In the accident, Street was struck and killed by an oncoming snowplow when he pulled out to pass a truck. The driver of the truck acknowledged that he was speeding 10 miles per hour over the speed limit at the time of the crash.

The driver's admission was key to the US$14-million lawsuit filed against him by Street's parents, who contended that his negligence resulted in the death of their son.

The animation formed part of the defense. Using reports from the police, an accident investigator who reconstructed the incident, and measurements of the actual braking distances required for the snowplow at various speeds, two computer animations were created. The first displayed the accident when the snowplow was traveling at 55 miles per hour in the 45 miles per hour zone. In that animation, as in the real-life accident, the snowplow struck the center of the car.

In the second animation, the snowplow was traveling at the speed limit. Then, the plow still struck the car, this time at the rear of the vehicle. The defense argued that, despite the different impact points, the crash that likely would have occurred at the legal speed limit would still have been fatal. In viewing the animations, the jury decided that the accident was caused by Street's failure to properly assess traffic conditions before pulling out in front of the truck.

In another example, an animated recreation of the shooting death of a Scraton, Pennsylvania woman was a vital piece of **evidence** that led to the conviction of her husband for **murder**. The man, a former police officer with a history of domestic violence, had claimed that he shot his wife in self defense as she tried to attack him with a knife.

Based on the photographic information gathered at the crime scene by forensic investigators, an animation was created that presented a three-dimensional view of the room. The detail and multi-perspective view of the scene was used convincingly by the prosecution to argue that the **blood** pattern on the victim was not consistent with her husband's explanation of the death.

Implicit in the above examples is the accuracy of the information that forms the database of the animation file. The intent of forensic animation is to accurately present the testimony of eyewitnesses or experts to a jury, not to create a situation that is not based in reality.

Similar concerns have been voiced in the past about the reliance on expert testimony and the use of other forensic reconstructions that attempt to indicate what a long-missing person might appear like in the present day.

The normal sharing of information by prosecution and defense will hopefully circumvent this recognized risk that animation could be misused to create a fictitious reality. For example, in the Chris Street case, the opposing attorneys were able to view the animations prior to their presentation in court, giving them time to formulate their response strategy. As well, an animation can be presented frame-by-frame, with questioning and expert commentary provided for each frame.

Another concern surrounding forensic animation, exemplified by the above example, is the cost of producing an animation. The high cost of producing a high quality animation, in the tens of thousands of dollars, is often beyond the budget of a defense team.

SEE ALSO Accident reconstruction; Computer forensics; Crime scene staging.

Antemortem injuries

Antemortem injuries are those injuries a body has received before death. They may be a contributing factor in the death or even its cause. On the other hand, they may have occurred many years ago. During an **autopsy**, the pathologist assesses the age of antemortem injuries, as well as distinguishing them from postmortem injuries—that is, injuries occurring after death. Postmortem injury can come from various sources such as deliberate mutilation of a body by a murderer following a homicide, predation by wild animals, or careless handling in the mortuary. Postmortem injuries can cause confusion over the manner and **cause of death**.

One major difference between an antemortem and a postmortem injury is the presence of signs of bleeding. While the person is still alive, the blood is circulating and any injuries such as cuts or stabs will bleed. After death, the body usually does not bleed. However, there are exceptions. For instance, when a person drowns, their body usually floats face down and this results in the head becoming congested with blood. If the cadaver receives a head injury by being buffeted around in the water and colliding with boats or propellers, then there could be some **evidence** of bleeding. Scalp wounds sustained after death may also leak some blood.

It can be especially difficult to distinguish between injuries inflicted in the very last few minutes of life and those caused postmortem. If the person collapses, there may be areas of laceration (cuts or scrapes) to the head and scalp which may be very hard to interpret.

After death, the blood stays liquid in the vessels and no longer clots. Careless handling of a cadaver may produce some post-mortem bruising which may need to be distinguished from antemortem bruising. Blood also tends to pool under gravity after death, causing a bruised appearance in the lower limbs, arms, hands, and feet known as **lividity**. Some of the smaller vessels may even hemorrhage under the pressure of this pooled blood. These bruises could be confused with ante-mortem bruising.

Recent research has focused on improved techniques for distinguishing between an antemortem and a postmortem injury by analyzing damaged tissue. Antemortem injuries show signs of inflammation, while postmortem injuries do not. Chinese scientists have found that tissue from antemortem injuries contains a chemical involved in inflammation leukotriene B4 (LTB4). Postmortem injuries were found to have no LTB4. This could help the pathologist classify injuries more accurately.

SEE ALSO Blood; Body marks; Pathology; Wound assessment.

Anterior SEE Anatomical nomenclature

Anthrax

Forensic science can involve the investigation of an outbreak of illness or the death of an individual that is caused by a microorganism. Some microbes are especially toxic, and so are of forensic concern. A good example is anthrax.

While anthrax is an ancient bacterial disease, the disease again sprang to prominence following the September 11, 2001, terrorist attacks on the World Trade Center buildings in New York City and the Pentagon in Washington, D.C. In the months following these attacks, letters containing a powdered form of *Bacillus anthracis*, the bacteria that causes anthrax, were mailed to representatives of the U.S. government and the media, among others. Five people who acquired the disease died.

Bacillus anthracis can enter the body via a wound in the skin (cutaneous anthrax), via contaminated food or liquid (gastrointestinal anthrax), or can be inhaled (inhalation anthrax). The latter in particular can cause a very serious, even lethal, infection.

The disease has been present throughout recorded history. Its use as a weapon stretches back centuries. Hundreds of years ago, bodies of anthrax victims were dumped into wells, or were catapulted into enemy encampments. Development of anthrax-based weapons was pursued by various governments in World Wars I and II, including those of the United States, Canada, and Britain.

Humans naturally acquire anthrax from exposure to livestock such as sheep or cattle or wild animals. The animals are reservoirs of the anthrax bacterium.

While all three types of anthrax infections are potentially serious, prompt treatment usually cures the cutaneous form. Even with prompt treatment, the gastrointestinal form is lethal in 25%–75% of those who become infected. The inhaled version of anthrax is almost always lethal.

When *Bacillus anthracis* is actively growing and dividing, it exists as a large "vegetative" cell. But, when the environment is threatening, the bacterium can form a spore and become dormant. The spore form can be easily inhaled. Approximately 8,000 **spores**, hardly enough to cover a snowflake, are sufficient to cause the inhalation form of anthrax when the spores resuscitate and begin growth in the lungs.

The growing *Bacillus anthracis* cells have several characteristics that make them so infectious. First, the formation of a capsule around the bacterium can mask the surface from recognition by the body's **immune system**. The body can be less likely to mount an immune response to the invading bacteria. Also, the capsule helps fend off antibodies and immune cells that do respond. This protection can allow the organism to multiply to large numbers.

The capsule also contains a protein that protects the bacterium. This protective **antigen** dissolves other protein molecules that form part of the outer coating of host cells. This allows the bacterium to evade the host's immune response by burrowing inside host cells such as the epithelial cells that line the lung.

A toxic component called lethal factor actively destroys the host's immune cells. Finally, another toxic factor called the edema factor (edema is the build up of fluid in tissues) disables a host molecule called calmodulin. Calmodulin regulates many chemical reactions in the body.

With the various toxic factors, *Bacillus anthracis* is able to overcome the attempts of the host to deal with the infection. Bacterial **toxins** enter the bloodstream and circulate throughout the body. The destruction of blood cells and tissues can be lethal.

The early symptoms of anthrax infections are similar to other, less serious infections, such as the flu. By the time the diagnosis is made, the infection can be too advanced to treat. This can make the recognition of a deliberate anthrax attack difficult to recognize until large numbers of casualties have resulted. While the bacteria can be killed by

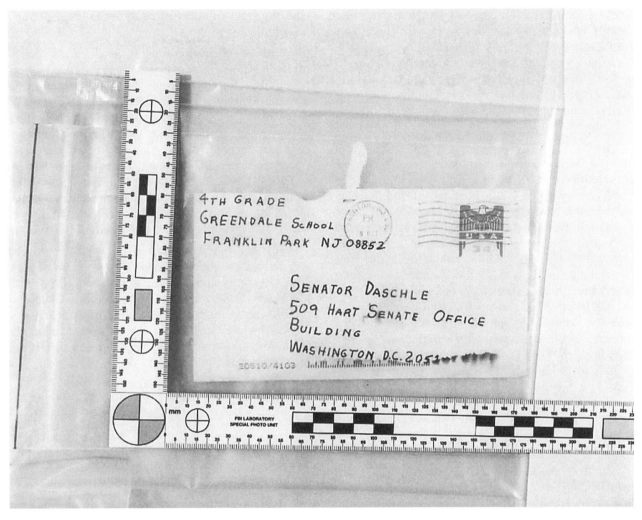

Envelope in which an anthrax-laced letter was sent to Senate Majority Leader Tom Daschle, in Washington D.C., October 23, 2001. © REUTERS/CORBIS.

antibiotics, in particular an antibiotic called ciprofloxacin, the antibiotic needs to be administered early in an infection.

A vaccine to anthrax does exist, although the possibility of serious side effects has limited its use to only those at high risk for infection (i.e., soldiers, workers in meat processing plants, anthrax researchers). Vaccine researchers are exploring the possibility that the edema factor and the capsule could be exploited as targets of **vaccines**. The idea is that the vaccines would stop the bacteria from getting into host cells. This would make it easier for the immune response to kill the invading bacteria.

SEE ALSO Antibiotics; Biological warfare, advanced diagnostics; Biological weapons, genetic identification; Bioterrorism; Vaccines.

Anthrax, investigation of 2001 murders

The 2001 **anthrax** letter attacks brought the first known deaths ever caused by **bioterrorism** in the United States. The fear that subsequently paralyzed the nation focused attention on the new field of microbial forensics, which is responsible not only for tracing outbreaks of microbial diseases but also on collecting data that must meet legal standards for **evidence**.

The anthrax attacks began with the illness of Robert Stevens, a sixty-three year old British immigrant employed as a photo editor at the *Sun*, a supermarket tabloid newspaper published by American Media, Inc. in Boca Raton, Florida. Stevens became ill on September 29 while vacationing with his wife in

North Carolina. Initially, he felt fatigued and weak. Later, he became feverish and had trouble breathing. He then began vomiting and became delirious. Stevens, having driven home, was admitted on October 2 to JFK Medical Center in the West Palm Beach, Florida suburb of Atlantis. The presumptive diagnosis was meningitis, an inflammation of the membrane covering the brain.

In the United States, only eighteen cases of anthrax from inhaled **spores** were recorded in the twentieth century. Despite the rarity of anthrax, Stevens' physician, Dr. Larry Bush, suspected the bacteria. He had a sample of Stevens' **blood** sent to Anne Beall, the lead medical technologist at Integrated Regional Laboratories in Ft. Lauderdale. To detect anthrax, Beall conducted a series of tests. She first determined the motility of the bacteria or whether they were capable of spontaneous movement. Motility can be observed through the microscope or, occasionally, through the spread of growth in a **culture** medium. Beall then checked the action of the bacteria upon red blood cells. When placed in a medium containing red blood cells, some bacteria destroy the cells in a process called hemolysis. The tests took hours to complete because quantities of bacteria had to first be grown for the procedures. The bacteria taken from Stevens were nonmotile and nonhemolytic. These are characteristics of anthrax bacteria.

In 1999, the Centers for Disease Control established a bioterrorism preparedness and response program. The Florida State Laboratory in Jacksonville, part of the **CDC** network, received the Stevens' samples according to protocol. Dr. Philip Lee, Florida's biological defense coordinator, examined the bacteria according to CDC procedures for suspected anthrax.

Lee conducted three tests: capsular staining, a polysaccharide test of the cell wall, and a gamma phage test. Capsular staining identifies whether the bacillus has a capsule, a thick outer coating. The test by itself is not conclusive for anthrax because some other bacteria are also encased in capsules. The polysaccharide test checks to see whether the cell wall contains a specific sign, a polysaccharide, which is specific to anthrax and a few other bacteria. A positive result is not a confirmation of anthrax. However, if both the capsular and polysaccharide tests are positive, the bacteria are almost certainly anthrax. The gamma phage test is based on the knowledge that certain viruses, known as phages, can enter and infect bacteria. A gamma phage can infect anthrax. The test involves introducing gamma phages to suspected anthrax. If the bacterial cells split open, or lyse, they are virtually certain to be anthrax. All three tests indicated anthrax.

With anthrax confirmed, the CDC needed to determine how Stevens became exposed to the bacteria and to identify other possible cases. Stevens, who died on October 5, never recovered sufficiently to assist in the investigation. Investigators initially suspected that he had encountered anthrax, which typically strikes animals, by drinking from a stream in North Carolina. CDC-organized teams of federal, state, and local investigators interviewed people, swabbed surfaces, and collected samples for testing at the places where Stevens worked, lived, shopped, fished, hiked, and visited in Florida and North Carolina.

At this point, American Media employees recalled that a mailroom clerk had gone home sick with symptoms similar to those of Stevens. The clerk had entered a Miami hospital on October 1 and had received large doses of the antibiotic ciprofloxacin or Cipro. The clerk survived. Cipro, more than any other antibiotic, is effective against a large variety of anthrax strains.

Preliminary testing indicated that *Bacillus anthracis* was present in samples taken from the American Media building where Stevens worked and the computer keyboard that he used. There was no reason why anthrax should be present in these areas. Investigators concluded that Stevens had been deliberately exposed. Jean Malecki, director of the Palm Beach County Health Department, ordered the American Media building closed. It has never reopened. About 1,000 people who were considered at risk of developing anthrax by being present in the building some time since August 1 had their nostrils swabbed to test for the presence of anthrax, and were given a ten-day supply of **antibiotics**.

The ill mailroom clerk indicated the mode of transmission of anthrax into the American Media building. Some *Sun* employees recalled a trifolded letter containing powder and a small, plastic, gold-colored Star of David charm. They were uncertain of the text of the letter. Stevens had taken the letter and sat down at his keyboard with it on September 19.

On October 15, the Florida Department of Health announced that anthrax had been found in the Boca Raton post office. Spores were found in an area where mail was sorted for pickup by American Media.

Meanwhile, an NBC employee in New York City received a diagnosis of cutaneous anthrax (anthrax lesions of the skin) on October 12. By October 25, nasal swabs had been taken from 2,580 people in

New York City and preventive Cipro had been given to 1,306. All seven confirmed cases were connected to the media: two at NBC, three at the *New York Post*, and one each at ABC and CBS.

Health authorities recovered the letter sent to NBC. Addressed to anchorman Tom Brokaw, it contained hand-printed capital letters that stated, "This is next. Take precautions now. Death to America. Death to Israel. Allah is Great." Three other anthrax letters were later found and all were postmarked Trenton, New Jersey, the imprint made at the large postal sorting and distribution center on Route 130 in Hamilton Township, ten miles from Princeton. Investigators swabbed 561 mailboxes and delivered the cotton tips to state laboratories. Only one mailbox, on a street corner in Princeton, tested positive for anthrax.

On October 15, anthrax was found in letters sent to prominent U.S. Senators Tom Daschle (D-South Dakota) and Russell Feingold (D-Wisconsin). Twenty members of Daschle's staff were exposed, as were two Feingold workers and six responders from the Capitol Hill Police. The Hart Office Building, home to Daschle and Feingold, was ordered closed on October 16 and would not open again until January 2002, when decontamination had been completed. The Capitol and all five remaining Congressional office buildings were also closed for screening. In subsequent weeks, suspicions of anthrax prompted closings throughout the Washington, D.C. area, including parts of the Federal Reserve Building, the U.S. Supreme Court, the Pentagon, and the State Department.

The mail processing facility that served Congress is located on Brentwood Road in Washington, D.C. Four of the Brentwood employees became ill with inhalation anthrax and two died. In a postal center, anthrax spores might settle not only in the nasal passages or skin of workers but also on sorting machines and other mail. Each newly infected piece of mail could become a potential anthrax carrier. Inhalation anthrax, apparently spread through cross-contaminated mail, killed Kathy Nguyen, a Vietnamese immigrant hospital supply worker in Manhattan on October 31 and Ottilie Lundgren, an elderly rural Connecticut woman on November 21.

Naming the anthrax investigation "Amerithrax," the Federal Bureau of Investigation released a profile of the suspect on November 9. According to the **FBI**, the anthrax mailer was likely an adult male with a scientific background or a strong interest in science. He had access to a source of anthrax, knew how to refine it, and had familiarity with the Trenton, New Jersey area. A non-confrontational person and a loner, the mailer probably tended to hold grudges for a long time.

Some scientists and journalists publicly speculated that the anthrax mailer had ties to the government since anthrax is not easy to obtain. The anthrax that had been discovered in the New York City and Washington, D.C. letters belonged to the Ames strain of anthrax. First acquired by the U.S. army for vaccine research at Fort Detrick, Maryland, Ames anthrax was discovered when it infected some cows in Texas in 1981. When samples were later sent to other military and civilian labs, the strain was named "Ames" after the return address label of a government lab in Ames, Iowa. Some samples of the Ames strain were sent to allies overseas, including one batch that went to the British biological defense establishment at Porton Down.

The timing of the anthrax attacks, right after the September 11 terrorist attacks on the Pentagon and World Trade Center, also raised suspicions that foreign terrorists were responsible. Two of the September 11 hijackers had lived in South Florida, not far from American Media headquarters, and one was reportedly treated for cutaneous anthrax. The FBI, preferring the theory of a lone domestic terrorist, continues to pursue leads as of 2005.

SEE ALSO Anthrax; Antibiotics; Bacterial biology; Bacteria, classification; Biological weapons, genetic identification; Bioterrorism; Criminal profiling; Cross contamination; FBI (United States Federal Bureau of Investigation); Mail sanitization; September 11, 2001, terrorist attacks (forensic investigations of).

Anthropology

Anthropology is the study of the behavior, origin, and physical and social development of humans. The term forensic refers to the gathering of scientific **physical evidence** for use in a court of law. Thus, forensic anthropology is the use of anthropology to gather and examine scientific **evidence**. Forensic anthropologists use a blend of sciences, such as biology, chemistry, physics, and anatomy to aid in the investigation of crimes.

One of the primary roles of a forensic anthropologist at a crime scene is to identify human remains. A forensic anthropologist uses scientific methods and technologies to answer key questions about the crime such as: how many victims are present? Who are they? When did they die? How did they die? Most of

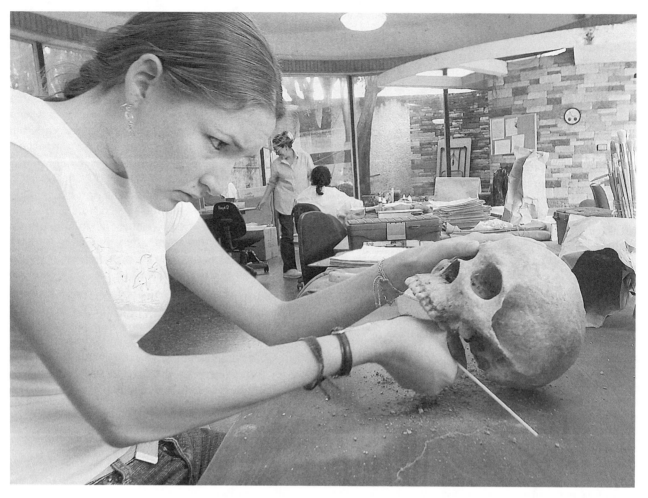

A member of the Guatemalan Forensic Anthropology Unit cleans a human skull in 2004 that was exhumed from a mass grave after a decades-long armed conflict in Guatemala left a toll of 500,000 people killed and 250,000 still missing. © CARLOS LOPEZ-BARILLAS/CORBIS

the answers to these questions come from studying human skeletal remains.

The **skull** provides the most information for physical anthropologists. Craniosacral, or skull measurements (especially between the eye sockets and the jaw bone,) often help forensic anthropologists determine the race, age, and sex of a body. Forensic anthropologists can sometimes recreate the likeness of a person from skeletal measurements. Teeth can be compared to dental records as a means of **identification**. Holes, fissures, stains, and other abnormalities indicate trauma and may help to determine **cause of death**.

Forensic anthropologists also look at the size and shape of the pelvis, as well as signs of wear in the hip joint, to help determine the age and sex of remains. They can tell whether a broken bone happened before, during, or after death. Evidence of

bones that were broken during childhood and later healed may help identify an adult body.

Forensic anthropologists may even be able to determine what kind of career a victim may have had by examining skeletal remains. Ridges that form where muscle tissue attaches to bone indicate that a person's job required physical labor. Ridges may also indicate if a person was right or left handed. Looking at microscopic lines in bone fragments yields clues about the overall health of person before death.

Often, physical anthropologists must work with badly decomposed, charred, or damaged remains instead of well-preserved, whole skeletons. When working with fragments, forensic anthropologists employ technologies such as CAT scans and x rays. They may attempt to gather **DNA** evidence to identify remains.

Forensic anthropology is not only used to investigate present-day crimes, but is also applied to examine historical events. For example, forensic anthropologists have played a significant role in identifying the remains of wartime military personnel, even decades after the event. This type of forensic anthropology is sometimes referred to as forensic **archaeology**.

SEE ALSO Ancient cases and mysteries; Anthropometry; Archaeology; Careers in forensic science; DNA mixtures, forensic interpretation of mass graves; Identification of war victims in Croatia and Bosnia; War forensics.

Anthropometry

The measurement of the human body, its component parts and relative dimensions, such as body weight, height, length of limbic bones, pelvic bones, **skull**, etc., is known as anthropometry. The word anthropometry comes from the Greek *anthropos*, meaning man, plus the word *metron*, meaning measure. Anthropometry is a scientific tool presently used in several fields including **medicine, anthropology**, archeology, and **forensic science** to study and compare relative body proportions among human groups and between genders. For instance, by comparing relative body and bone proportions between two groups of children of the same age, under normal and abnormal conditions, physicians can determine the impact of malnourishment upon the physical development during childhood. Anthropologists compare cranial and body proportions to identify sets of characteristics common to individuals of a given race and the morphological differences among races. Paleontologists are able to tell historical periods using anthropometry—such as whether a set of skeletal remains pertains to a Neanderthal (man, woman, or child) or to a *Homo Sapien.*

Anthropology is the discipline that has developed anthropometrical comparison studies into a set of reliable standardized data and mathematical formulae, which are now useful for both modern forensic science and archeology. Presently, anthropometry is a well-established forensic technique, which uses anthropological databanks to calculate computational ratios of specific bones and skull features associated with differences between genders and with specific races. For instance, the size and conformation of pelvic bones and skull structures can indicate gender; the length of the long bones of limbs allows

the estimation of height. The metric proportions of skull features, given by the size, shape, and relative position of structural bones such as the temporal bones and the mastoid process, superciliary ridge, supraorbital foramen, zygomatic bone, nasal bone, mandible, ocular orbits, etc., may indicate race (Caucasian, Asian, African, or Native American), age (fetus, newborn, child, young adult, etc.), and gender.

When a complete skeleton is available, the level of reliability in establishing sex, age, and race through anthropometrics is almost 100%. Pelvic bones alone offer a 95% reliability, while pelvic bones plus the skull result in an accurate estimation 98% of the time. Sex can be determined by studying the size and shape of some skull bones and by comparing them with the well-established dimorphisms (differences in shape) between human male and female skulls. For instance, the mastoid process, a conic protuberance forming the posterior part of the right and left temporal bones, is large enough in males for the skull to rest on it on the surface of a table. In the female skull, however, the mastoid process will tilt backward to rest on the occipital area or other portions of the skull. This happens because the mastoid process in the female skull is not large enough to keep it in a balanced position on a flat surface. Gender dimorphisms are also found in many other human bones.

Forensic anthropometry may also indicate the nutritional status of an individual, along with existing degenerative diseases or infections at the time of death. Such information may be combined with other kind of circumstantial and forensic data to identify human remains and to determine the **cause of death**.

Anthropometry was not always considered a true science, however, because it initially gave rise to several political and social pseudo-scientific assumptions, and even to some poorly based medical theories, especially during the nineteenth and early twentieth centuries. Cesare Lombroso (1836–1908), an Italian physician, published a series of essays, "The Criminal Man" (1875), "Algometrics of the Sane and the Alienated Man" (1878), "The Delinquent Man" (1897), and, in 1900, "The Crime, Causes and Remedies," stating that two types of criminal temperaments existed, the criminoid and the natural-born criminal. Lombroso claimed that some specific anthropometrical body proportions were associated with each type of criminal. According to Lombroso, the natural-born criminal, whose urge to commit crimes was beyond his own will due to a hereditary psychological illness and compulsion, had prominent, long jaws and low eyebrows. The criminoid type of criminal, such as

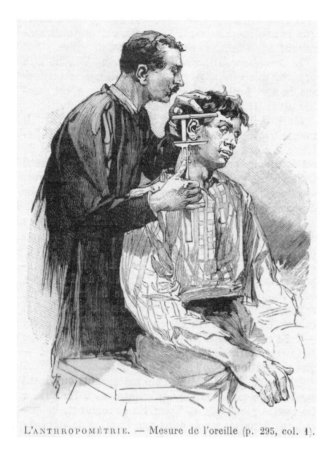

L'ANTHROPOMÉTRIE. — Mesure de l'oreille (p. 295, col. 1).

Engraving ca.1885-1900 of a man taking measurements of a criminal's ear according to an anthropometrical system for criminal identification developed by Alphonse Bertillon. © BETTMANN/CORBIS.

pickpockets and petty thieves, had long narrow fingers and scanty beards. Through facial, skull, and hand anthropometrics, Lombrose developed what came to be known as these Lombrosian Types.

Paul Broca (1824–1880), a French surgeon interested in brain morphology, published his anthropometrical studies in his essays "General Instructions for the Anthropological Investigation" and "Craniological and Craniometrical Instructions." Broca declared that women should be denied higher education because their cranial volume was smaller than a man's. According to Broca, the reduced cranial volume of women indicated that human females were less intelligent than males.

Another example of pseudo-scientific use of anthropometrics involved claims by Nazi scientists during World War II (1939–1945) that they could establish racial profiles of pure Aryan populations, along with profiles of non-Aryans that they considered inferior, on the basis of measurements of skull and facial proportions and other body characteristics.

These unfounded misuses of anthropometrics gave way to more sound scientific approaches after 1950. Besides forensics, anthropometrics are now also used in industry for sizing clothing, machines, and other products to fit the people who use them.

SEE ALSO Anthropology; Osteology and skeletal radiology; Pathology; Pseudoscience and forensics; Sex determination; Sexual dimorphism.

Antibiotics

A variety of infectious diseases are caused by bacteria. Some bacterial infections can be treated using compounds that are collectively known as antibiotics. Antibiotics act only on bacteria, and are not effective against viruses.

The presence of antibiotics in **blood** or tissue samples obtained after death (post-mortem samples) can be an important clue to the presence of an infection in the deceased.

The unique chemical structure of an antibiotic, relative to the natural tissue, can allow the compound to be detected. For example, cephalosporin antibiotics have been successfully detected in post-mortem samples using the technique of high-pressure liquid **chromatography**, which separates compounds based on their differing rates of movement through a porous support material.

Antibiotics can be naturally produced. For example, the first antibiotic discovered (penicillin; discovered in 1928 by Sir Alexander Fleming) is produced by a species of a mold microorganism. There are a variety of different naturally produced antibiotics, while many other antibiotics have been chemically produced.

Prior to the discovery of penicillin there were few effective treatments to battle or prevent bacterial infections. Pneumonia, tuberculosis, and typhoid fever were virtually untreatable. And, in those persons whose immune systems were not functioning properly, even normally minor bacterial infections could prove life-threatening.

In nature, antibiotics (or antimicrobials) help protect a eukaryotic cell (i.e., plant cell) or bacteria from invading bacteria (in some environments, bacteria may be in competition). In the laboratory, this protective advantage is evident as the inhibition of growth of bacteria in the presence of the antibiotic-producing species. Screening for antimicrobial activity is done on preparations that are obtained from a variety of sources (soil, water, plant extracts). This screening can be automated so that thousands of samples can be processed each day.

The chemical synthesis of antibiotics is now very sophisticated. The antibiotic can be tailored to affect a specific target on the bacterial cell. Three-dimensional modeling of the bacterial surface and protein molecules is an important aid to antibiotic design.

Penicillin is in a class of antibiotics called beta-lactam antibiotics. The name refers to the chemical ring that is part of the molecule. Other classes of antibiotics include the tetracyclines, aminoglycosides, rifamycins, quinolones, and sulphonamides. The action of these antibiotics is varied. The targets of the antibiotics are different. Some antibiotics disrupt and weaken the cell wall of bacteria (i.e., beta-lactam antibiotics), which causes the bacteria to rupture and die. Other antibiotics disrupt enzymes that are vital for bacterial survival (aminoglycoside antibiotics). Still other antibiotics target genetic material and stop the replication of deoxyribonucleic acid (**DNA**) (i.e., quinolone antibiotics).

Antibiotics can also vary in the bacteria they affect. Some antibiotics kill only a few related types of bacteria and are referred to as narrow-spectrum antibiotics. Other antibiotics such as penicillin kill a variety of different bacteria. These are the broad-spectrum antibiotics.

Following the discovery of penicillin, many different naturally occurring antibiotics were discovered and still many others were synthesized. They were extremely successful in reducing many infectious diseases. Indeed, in the 1970s the prevailing view was that infectious diseases were a thing of the past. However, beginning in the 1970s and continuing to the present day, resistance to antibiotics is developing.

As of 2005, the problem of antibiotic resistance is so severe that many physicians and scientists think that the twenty-first century will initiate the "post antibiotic era." In other words, the use of antibiotics to control infectious bacterial disease will no longer be an effective strategy.

Resistance to a specific antibiotic or a class of antibiotics can develop when an antibiotic is overused or misused. If an antibiotic is used properly to treat an infection, then all the infectious bacteria should be killed directly, or weakened such that the host's immune response will kill them. However, if the antibiotic concentration is too low, the bacteria may be weakened but not killed. The same thing can happen if antibiotic therapy is stopped too soon. The surviving bacteria may have acquired resistance, which can be genetically transferred to subsequent generations of bacteria. For example, many strains of *Mycobacterium tuberculosis*, the bacterium that causes tuberculosis, are resistant to one or more of the antibiotics currently used to treat the lung infection. Some strains of the *Staphylococcus aureus* bacteria that causes boils, pneumonia, or bloodstream infections, are resistant to most (and with one strain, all) antibiotics.

SEE ALSO Anthrax; Bioterrorism; L-Gel decontamination reagent; Pathogens.

Antibody

Among the many techniques used in **forensic science** are those that involve the specific immunological recognition of a protein (the **antigen**). The protein molecule that recognizes an antigen is called an antibody.

An antigen-antibody reaction is exquisitely specific. This permits the unequivocal detection of a protein. As well, some antigen-based methods are highly sensitive, and so permit the quantification of very small amount of the protein antigen.

Antibodies are also referred to as immunoglobulins (Igs). Specific genes for antibodies direct the construction of antigen specific regions of the antibody molecule. Such antigen-specific regions are located at the ends of the arms of the Y-shaped immunglobulin molecule. The central core of the immunoglobulin is more constant in construction. Genetic engineering and the use of various mutational mechanisms allows the construction of a vast array of antibodies (each with a unique genetic sequence).

There are five different antibody types (Ig G, A, M, D, and E), each with a different Y-shaped configuration and function.

IgG is the most common type of antibody. It is the chief Ig against microbes. It acts by coating the microbe to hasten its removal by other **immune system** cells. It gives lifetime or long-standing immunity against infectious diseases. It is highly mobile, passing out of the blood stream and between cells, going from organs to the skin where it neutralizes surface bacteria and other invading microorganisms. This mobility allows the antibody to pass through the placenta of the mother to her fetus, thus conferring a temporary defense to the unborn child.

The antibody responsible for allergic reactions, IgE, acts by attaching to cells in the skin called mast cells and basophile cells (mast cells that circulate in the body). In the presence of environmental antigens like pollens, foods, chemicals, and drugs, IgE releases histamines from the mast cells. The histamines cause the nasal inflammation (swollen tissues, running nose, sneezing) and the other discomforts of hay fever or other types of allergic responses, such as hives, asthma, and in rare cases, anaphylactic shock (a life-threatening condition brought on by an allergy to a drug or insect bite). An explanation for the role of IgE in allergy is that it was an antibody that was useful to early man to prepare the immune system to fight parasites. This function is presently overextended in reacting to environmental antigens.

The presence of antibodies can be detected whenever antigens such as bacteria or red blood cells are found to agglutinate (clump together), or where they precipitate out of solution, or where there has been a stimulation of the plasma complement system. Antibodies are also used in laboratory tests, including the analysis of forensic samples, for blood typing and for the **identification** of target microorganisms or **toxins**.

The use of antibodies in forensic investigations is also called forensic **serology**. Blood typing is a common example of forensic serology. Here, antibodies against the A or B proteins that can be present on the surface of a blood cell are used to differentiate the four types of blood (A, B, AB, and O). If blood cells have only the A antigen present, then in the presence of the anti-A antibody, the cells can agglutinate. However, in the presence of anti-B antibody, which does not recognize the antigen, the cells will not agglutinate.

Antibodies are also used to discriminate blood from someone with a blood-related malady (i.e., sickle-cell anemia), based on the presence or one or more abnormal enzymes in the blood.

Other forensic serology applications include the detection of drugs, noxious compounds like toxins, and past exposure to specific microorganisms.

SEE ALSO Analytical instrumentation; Antigen; Biosensor technologies; Immune system.

Antigen

Antigens, which are usually proteins or polysaccharides, stimulate the **immune system** to produce antibodies. The antibodies inactivate the antigen and help to remove it from the body.

This ability of antigens to stimulate **antibody** production is very useful in forensic analyses. Detection of an antibody to a target molecule (**botulinum toxin**, for example) provides powerful evidence that a victim or suspect had been exposed to the particular antigen. In the case of a death, this evidence can help determine the course of events.

By definition, anything that makes the immune system respond to produce antibodies is an antigen. Antigens are living foreign bodies such as viruses, bacteria, and fungi that cause disease and infection. Or they can be dust, chemicals, pollen grains, or food proteins that cause allergic reactions.

Antigens that cause allergic reactions are called allergens. A large percentage of any population, in varying degrees, is allergic to animals, fabrics, drugs, foods, and products for the home and industry. Not all antigens are foreign bodies. They may be produced in the body itself. For example, cancer cells are antigens that the body produces. In an attempt to differentiate its "self" from foreign substances, the immune system will reject an organ transplant that is trying to maintain the body or a blood transfusion that is not of the same blood type as itself.

There are some substances such as nylon, plastic, or Teflon that rarely display antigenic properties. For that reason, nonantigenic substances are used for artificial blood vessels, component parts in heart pacemakers, and needles for hypodermic syringes. These substances seldom trigger an immune system response, but there are other substances that are highly antigenic and will almost certainly cause an immune system reaction. Practically everyone reacts to certain chemicals, for example, the resin from the poison ivy plant, the venoms from insect and reptile bites, solvents, formalin, and asbestos. Viral and bacterial infections also generally trigger an antibody response from the immune system. For most people penicillin is not antigenic, but for some there can be an immunological response that ranges from severe skin rashes to death.

Another type of antigen is found in the tissue cells of organ transplants. If, for example, a kidney is transplanted, the surface cells of the kidney contain antigens that the new host body will begin to reject. These are called human leukocyte antigens (HLA), and there are four major types of HLA subdivided into further groups. In order to avoid organ rejection, tissue samples are taken to see how well the new organ tissues match for HLA compatibility with the recipient's body. Drugs will also be used to suppress and control the production of helper/suppressor T-cells and the amount of antibodies.

Red blood cells with the ABO antigens pose a problem when the need for blood transfusions arises. Before a transfusion, the blood is tested for type so that a compatible type is used. Type A blood has one kind of antigen and type B another. A person with type AB blood has both the A and B antigen. Type O blood has no antigens. A person with type A blood would require either type A or O for a successful transfusion. Type B and AB would be rejected. Type B blood would be compatible with a B donor or an O donor. Since O has no antigens, it is considered to be the universal donor. Type AB is the universal recipient because its antibodies can accept A, B, AB, or O.

SEE ALSO Analytical instrumentation; Antibody; Anthrax, investigation of 2001 murders; Biosensor technologies; Immune system.

Archaeology

Forensic archaeologists use archaeological techniques to help solve or study crimes. The term forensic relates to the law, often describing material appropriate for presentation in court. Archaeology is the scientific study of the past through the analysis of materials (artifacts) and remains within their context, or surrounding area. Using a blend of many sciences, forensic archaeologists examine human skeletal remains and other materials to gather **physical evidence**. Not all sites examined by forensic archaeologists are linked to a crime or a court case.

A forensic archaeologist who is examining a site attempts to gather **evidence** about the events that took place at that site. They may seek answers to questions such as: who is buried here? Did the person die here or somewhere else? How many people were here? What materials did they leave behind? How old is this site? Is it related to another historical or criminal event? What other activities happened here?

Investigating both recent and historical events, the work of forensic archaeologists aids both law enforcement and historians. When studying historical sites, forensic archaeologists use many of the same investigative techniques as they do when examining present-day crime scenes. Forensic archaeologists have located sites of mass murder in Rwanda and the former Yugoslavia. They have investigated historical sites associated with the Holocaust. Law enforcement employed forensic archaeologists to investigate the World Trade Center site of the September 11, 2001, terrorist attacks in New York.

Forensic archaeologists employ in the field many of the same techniques that forensic anthropologists use in the lab. Often, forensic archaeologists work to recover information from the smallest of materials, such as a single hair, tooth, clothing fiber, or bone fragment. Modern medical and scientific investigative technologies aid their research. A forensic archaeologist may use CAT scans or x rays to examine ancient remains, such as **mummies**, without destroying them. **DNA** analysis is used to determine if or how remains found in close proximity are related to each other. They study human skeletal remains and teeth for clues about age, sex, health, trauma, and date and manner of death. For example, a forensic archaeologist may examine damage to a **skull** to determine that the victim died from a trauma to the head. They may even be able to tell what kind of weapon, from an ancient projectile point to a modern gun, inflicted the injury.

Forensic archaeologists also carefully scrutinize the area that surrounds remains. The relationship between remains and the environment in which they are found is known as context. They may use complex **remote sensing** technologies to look below ground and locate burials or other sites. Alternatively, a forensic archaeologist may use classical archaeological techniques such as using probes to feel for loose dirt, observing patterns of discolored surface soil, or surveying an area for abnormal surface features, like shallow depressions or small mounds.

SEE ALSO Ancient cases and mysteries; Anthropology; Careers in forensic science; Crime scene investigation.

Architecture and structural analysis

Since the collapse of the World Trade Towers in New York on September 11, 2001, there has been greatly increased emphasis on studies of structural analysis and the design of architecture able to withstand acts of terrorism. Historically, structural analysis has also been employed in the construction of biochemical, petrochemical, and industrial plants, in order that they might withstand accidental chemical explosions.

Since 9/11, buildings, and the sites upon which they are constructed, have become increasingly designed to withstand and minimize the devastating effects of terrorist weapons and bomb blast loads. In addition, emphasis has been placed on retrofitting existing structures, in order to make them less vulnerable to terrorist attack. Much structural analysis research (also called blast mitigation research) has been done since 9/11, with the goal of understanding the mechanisms and factors that cause structural damage in a blast, minutely characterizing the sequence of structural responses during a blast, and quantifying the likely effects on the human inhabitants of the building in the event of a blast. There are a variety of means of gathering this data: extensive study of the aftereffects of actual terrorist events (such as the World Trade Towers, the Murrah Building in Oklahoma City, the Pentagon, and the Khobar Towers bombing in Saudi Arabia), assessment of existing architecture, creating controlled explosions in experimental structures, and the use of **computer modeling** sequences.

There has been much forensic, architectural, and structural analysis of the debris remaining after the collapse of the World Trade Towers, in part because there was a general expectation that the structures should have been able to withstand the impact of the aircraft. The Towers were built between the mid-1960s and the early 1970s, and were intended as a model of modern architecture. They utilized modular construction, and were comprised of very lightweight materials. The World Trade Towers were squared; the width of each face measured 64 meters (209.97 feet). They spanned 411 meters (1348.43 feet) above street level, and were placed on foundations that reached 21 meters (68.90 feet) below the ground. The height to width ratio of the Towers was 6.8. Each Tower weighed approximately 500,000 tons (1,000,000,000 pounds), and was built to stand firm against hurricane wind force of 225 kilometers per hour (139.81 miles per hour) and to withstand a wind load of 2 kilopascals (41.77 pounds per square foot) and a lateral wind load of 5,000 tons (10,000,000 pounds). In order to meet all of the structural integrity requirements, the architecture comprised a "perimeter tube" design, containing 244 exterior columns of 36 centimeter square (1.18 feet) steel box sections on 100 centimeter (3.28 feet) centers. Inside each perimeter tube was a 27-meter (88.58 feet) by 40-meter (131.23 feet) core, which was designed to support the weight of the Tower. The elevators, stairwells, mechanical risers, and the utilities were also housed within the core. The core was attached to the perimeter at each floor level by web joists that were 80 centimeters (2.62 feet) tall; these were covered with concrete slabs used to create the floors of the structures.

This type of building design is often referred to as an egg crate structure; it is actually about 95% air and 5% solid material. In comparison, most other buildings constructed during the same era contained massive columns seated on 5 meter (16.40 feet) centers, with enormous amounts of masonry designed to carry the brunt of the structural load.

The "airiness" of the Towers was the reason that the rubble and debris left by the buildings' collapse only rose a few stories above the ground. The strength of the structures resulted from their redundancy; that is, the architecture was such that if a few columns were destroyed, the load would redistribute among the remaining columns, with no appreciable loss of structural integrity.

Each Tower contained more than 1,000 times the mass of the aircraft that crashed into it, and had been constructed to be able to withstand steady wind loads of 30 times the weight of each plane. Had the blasts been confined only to impacts, with no resultant fires, the Towers could probably have remained standing. The Towers' collapse resulted from the fires caused by the explosion, and resultant ignition, of approximately 90,000 liquid gallons of jet fuel. Initially, it was hypothesized that the heat of the fire melted the steel girders in the structures, causing the Towers to collapse. After forensic investigation and structural analysis, that was found to be incorrect. The fire caused by the blast was characterized as "diffuse and fuel-rich," meaning that the fuel and air mixed together in unpredictable and uncontrolled ways after the blast, and there was more fuel than there was fire. In fuel-rich fires, the excess fuel is heated, but unburned. This was apparent in the Trade Tower fires because of the copious amounts of thick, black smoke given off; which was a by-product of incompletely burned fuel. The structural analysts estimated that the temperature during the fire was in range of 750°C–800°C (1382°F–1472°F), which is generally too low to melt steel (requiring a minimum of 1,500°C or 2732°F). Structural steel starts softening at about 425°C (797°F), and its strength is halved at 650°C (1202°F). However, even loss of half their structural steel strength should not have caused the Towers to collapse. The critical issue was the uncontrolled nature of the fire: it caused differential buckling and structural distortion in some areas, leading to the buildings' collapse.

As the structural analysts reconstructed the scenario, using both direct examination of rubble and structural steel, computer modeling, and simulation scenarios, the perimeter tubes of the World Trade Towers were able to withstand the initial impacts of

Remains of the World Trade Center in New York after the September 11, 2001, terrorist attack. Scientists studied the remaining structural beams to help determine the mechanism of the buildings' collapse. © PAUL COLANGELO/CORBIS

the aircrafts, shifting loads from severed or damaged columns to those left standing. The extraordinary speed of the fire's spread generated very high heat, causing weakening, softening, twisting, and buckling of structural steel. The Towers' most vulnerable points were deemed by the analysts to be the angle clips connecting the floor joists between the core structure and the columns on the perimeter walls. As the joists fell away on the most seriously burned floors, the outer box columns began to bow outward. The outward bowing caused the affected floors to collapse and fall downward; it also caused the floors above them to implode downward, setting in motion a domino effect that caused the Towers to collapse vertically within approximately 10 seconds, hitting the ground at a velocity of about 200 kilometers (124.27 miles) per hour.

Overall, the analysts deemed the Towers did not contain structural defects; they were simply not created to withstand the intentional impact of airliners filled with incendiary jet fuel. Their conclusion: the buildings were impossible to save; rather than attempting to build terrorist impervious structures,

it is more practical to focus on creating better emergency preparedness (communications, emergency response, and evacuation) systems.

SEE ALSO Aircraft accident investigations; Building materials; Computer modeling; Endothermic reaction; Exothermic reactions; Explosives; Fire debris; First responders; NTSB (National Transportation Safety Board).

Arson

Arson is typically defined as the malicious burning of property. It is important to understand that arson is a legal term, and the definition varies from one country to another or even between different states within a country. The Uniform Crime Report (UCR) of the Federal Bureau of Investigation defines arson as: "any willful or malicious burning or attempt to burn, with or without intent to defraud, a dwelling house, public building, motor vehicle or aircraft, personal property of another, etc." When a fire occurs, fire investigators, crime scene investigators, or forensic scientists are called to the scene to determine the origin and cause of the fire and the potential of arson.

The general definition of arson means that somebody deliberately or intentionally set fire to a property in order to destroy it, with a criminal intent. The person who decides to burn dead leaves in a backyard is normally not charged with arson, as it is his/her own property and there is no criminal intent. Criminal intent can be very broad. It includes gain of profit, fraud, persecution, or causing injury. The crime of arson is a very serious offense, punishable by several years of imprisonment. Also, there are some state's statutes, such as those in Georgia, which extend the crime of arson to fires that are accidentally created during the execution of a **felony**. These recent statutes were created in order to respond to the accidental fires and explosions that took place in neighborhood drug laboratories, such as methamphetamine labs. With these new statutes, law enforcement agencies and prosecutors can, for example, charge a criminal with arson if a house was burned down due to an accidental fire started during the manufacturing of methamphetamine. In intentional burnings, the charge of arson can extend in some states to the person who ordered the burning and not only to the person who actually performed the act of setting the property on fire.

Individuals who commit arson (arsonists) can be characterized in a variety of ways. About 90% of arsonists are men and about 50% are younger than 18 years old. Juvenile fire setters are a great concern, and several programs have been created in the United States to identify these juveniles and address their problem behaviors. There are different motives for committing arson and they are usually classified into categories, such as profit, spite, excitement, crime concealment, and vandalism.

Arson for profit includes all arsons committed with the expectation of obtaining a gain from the perpetrator (arsonist). It is important to note that the perpetrator does not necessarily need to obtain gain, but to show the intent that gain was going to be obtained. The gain can be direct or indirect. An example of direct gain would be the collection of the insurance money for the replacement of a burned house. Indirect gain would be an increase of business by eliminating (burning) the competitor who was doing business across the street. One of the most important arsons for profit committed in the United States is insurance fraud. This kind of criminal act is relatively widely spread in the United States. Some arsonists found it easier to burn their homes rather

than to invest money to repair them. Also, when a vehicle arrives at the end of a lease and the mileage is excessive, arsonists have burned the car, simulating an accidental fire, rather than paying for the extra mileage.

Arson for spite is also known as arson for revenge. This type of arsonist wants to take revenge against a person, a group of persons, an organization or institution, or against society, in general. Some activist organizations for peace, or groups who fight violence against animals, for example, have regularly committed arson and destroyed laboratories or headquarters of research facilities for the sake of their cause.

Arson for excitement is committed by people who are bored, in need of attention, or sexually stimulated by the crime of arson. These criminals are considered dangerous, as they do not have a particular target, and will burn any place or thing that would fulfill their need for excitement, attention, or get them the recognition they think they deserve. Because of the random nature of excitement motivated arsons, when one arsonist commits several burning acts, they are often difficult to profile.

Arson for crime concealment is performed when criminals try to hide another crime. For example, after murdering an individual, the house is set on fire, destroying the body and much of the **evidence** of the **murder** activities. In some instances, a vehicle that was stolen for a joy ride or to commit another crime, such as a robbery, is set on fire in order to destroy evidence that would link the authors to the theft. Criminals are aware that fire is a powerful weapon to achieve destruction of evidence. Fortunately, there are many forensic techniques that have been developed throughout the years to retrieve different evidence, such as **blood** patterns or fingerprints, after a fire.

Arson for vandalism is typically performed by young criminals or juvenile fire setters for no apparent reason. Schools or educational facilities are often the target of such crimes.

In the United States, the crime of arson is typically first investigated by the fire department. The fire department is the first agency to be on scene to proceed with extinguishing the fire. The fire chief usually determines if the fire occurred among suspicious circumstances and if arson investigator needs to be called. If the fire is considered as arson, either the fire department pursues the investigation, or other law enforcement agencies are contacted for assistance. Most states have state fire marshal offices that specialize in arson investigation. Also, at the federal level,

Arson is a serious problem in many countries and more particularly in the United States. This is reflected in local and national statistics. In 2003, there were 37,500 structure fires reported as arson in the U.S. These fires resulted in 305 deaths and 692 million dollars in damage. They represented approximately 3% of all structure fires that occurred in 2003 in the United States. In addition, there were about 30,500 vehicle fires reported as arson that resulted in a dollar loss of approximately 132 million dollars. Fortunately, these figures are in regression for the last ten years as there were 90,500 structure fires in the United States for the year 1995, resulting in 1.6 billion dollars of direct loss. The UCR reports approximately the same number of offenses for 2003, but adds the proportion of cleared offenses, which is 16.7%. It also specifies that arson occurs at the rate of 30.4 offenses per 100,000 inhabitants.

There are several organizations that provide programs and information or **training** to fight against the crime of arson. The National Fire Protection Association (NFPA) provides training documents and statistics for fire and arson investigators. The National Insurance Crime Bureau (NICB) provides statistics and training. The Insurance Committee for Arson Control (ICAC) provides publications and seminars to increase public awareness of the arson problem and help insurance companies fight the problem of arson.

SEE ALSO Accelerant; Fire debris; Profiling.

Students at Centenary College (Hackettstown, New Jersey) observe burning patterns in several staged fires during an arson investigation course, taught by former Somerset County arson investigator Professor Norman Cetuk, March 4, 2004. AP/WIDE WORLD PHOTOS. REPRODUCED BY PERMISSION.

the Bureau of Alcohol, Tobacco, Firearms (**ATF**), is also involved in arson investigation and has the greatest number of arson investigators at the federal level. The ATF also has several National Response Teams (NRT), which can travel to assist other law enforcement agencies. While most fires are in the jurisdiction of local authorities, there is one exception to this rule: church fires. In 1996, in order to respond to an increase in the number of deliberate church fires, President Bill Clinton formed the National Church Arson Task Force (NCATF). The goal of the NCATF was to allocate federal resources to the investigation of church fires around the country. The ATF and the **FBI** are the main agencies that investigate these fires. The NCATF coordinated investigations of 945 church arsons or bombings that occurred between January 1, 1995, and August 15, 2000, which led to the arrest of 431 suspects in connection with 342 incidents. This represents a clearance rate of about 36%, more than twice than the national average.

Art forgery

The imitation of works of art, from paintings to sculpture, has been carried out for hundreds of years. Students and followers have always made copies of the works of master artists as part of their instruction. There are many artists, both amateur and professional, who like to paint or draw in the style of those they admire. There is nothing morally wrong or illegal with this kind of copying or imitation. Art forgery, however, is different. It involves passing a copy of the artist's work off as created by the original artist, usually for financial gain. Where fraud or deception is involved, establishing whether a work of art is a forgery becomes a forensic investigation.

Art forgery can be extremely difficult to detect and investigate. There may be many forged works of art in museums and galleries around the world, and in private collections. Experts may be unaware if the forgery is accomplished cleverly, of the existence of a

Four old frescoes adorning the walls of St. Mary's Church in Luebeck, Germany, are considered expertly painted and "aged" forgeries. A German artist, Lothar Malskat, claimed they were painted by him in the 1950s. © BETTMANN/CORBIS

themselves away even before laboratory analysis of their work begins. They often add an element of their own natural style, or they may unknowingly include some contemporary period detail that the historian will notice immediately. Art experts also comment on a "lack of freedom" to many forgeries, as the forger sometimes uses more rigid brush strokes or lines to capture details of the original work. After all, the thought processes of a grand master creating a work of art is quite different from those of someone far less talented who is merely trying to imitate him or her. Often this difference will spill out into the work, although the forger may not be aware of it.

A full analysis of a possible forgery, however, must rely on more than the expert opinion of an art historian. A laboratory analysis of the materials used to create the work is required, using techniques such as X-radiography and infrared reflectography. Modern artistic materials, such as paper, inks, and paints are different in composition today from those used hundreds of years ago. It is true that old materials can be re-created and used today, so one could, theoretically, fake a Rembrandt in the twenty-first century using seventeenth century style materials. However, the presence of acrylic paints, which first became available in the 1930s, would readily give away a Rembrandt fake. Rembrandt remains one of the most imitated artists of all time. To complicate matters, his signature is often found on works done by lesser artists. Works of art also age from the moment they are created owing to exposure to the atmosphere, handling, and other factors. The expert forger may try to artificially age his or her work to make it look as if it was created long ago.

Although many types of artwork are forged, the examination of a typical oil painting illustrates many of the general principles of detecting a forgery. A painting is composed of four layers: support, ground layer, paint layer, and varnish. The support is often made of wood or canvas. The analysis of a wood support can be very informative because modern fakes are often painted on older wood panels to make them look authentic. **Dendrochronology**, the examination of growth ring patterns, can sometimes be used to age the wood itself. X rays will penetrate to the wood layer and reveal the construction of a panel, including features like saw marks. Manual saws were used to make artists' supports before the introduction of mechanical saws during the nineteenth century Industrial Revolution. Manual saws leave characteristic uneven marks. If the investigator finds regular saw marks on a painting claimed to be of seventeenth century origin, this will be a strong indication of a fake.

forged artwork, or they may be reluctant to admit they have been deceived. Sometimes the forger is more interested in getting the better of a dealer or collector than they are in their own financial gain. In such cases, transactions may be covered up and it is difficult to prove whether a criminal act has actually taken place.

For instance, the Spanish surrealist painter Salvador Dali (1904–1989) gave away around 20,000 blank sheets of paper with his signature, triggering a flood of forged Dali prints. Dealers would pay $2,000 to $20,000 for these fake prints. The art world also abounds with fake Picasso, Chagall, and Miró prints—to the extent that some experts are now reluctant to authenticate prints from certain modern artists because of the sheer volume of work it involves.

Distinguishing an authentic work of art from a forgery requires a blend of technical expertise and a profound knowledge of art history and the work of individual artists. Forgers do, however, often give

The investigator might focus on the edge of the painting, using a special magnifier or infrared light to detect the nature of the ground layer. Such testing is non-destructive to the painting. Sometimes an invasive test might be carried out. This is not quite a bad as it sounds; a tiny pinprick is made in the painting, perpendicular to its surface and the sample extracted. If the sample is taken at the edge of a painting, or at an area that is already damaged, the harm done to the work is minimal. This cross-sectional sample can then by studied by x-radiography or microscopy to reveal all four layers and their composition. These can be compared with cross sections of authenticated work from the artist to see if there is a resemblance.

A technical examination of the paint layer can help to confirm a work's age and authenticity. The investigator will look at the materials themselves and how they were handled, which may be characteristic of the individual artist. The pigments that give paints their color have evolved over time and this history is quite well known. Earth colors, derived from **minerals** such as iron oxide came first, followed by greens (malachite), blues (azurite), and black (charred animal bone). Animal and vegetable dyes such as indigo and saffron also have a long history. The nineteenth century saw the introduction of synthetic dyes such as the anilines. These were far more chemically and physically stable. Analysis by visible **spectroscopy** can reveal the chemical composition of an organic pigment and x-ray analysis might be used for inorganic pigments such as titanium dioxide. If the pigments prove too modern for its alleged date, then there are various possibilities. The work may be a forgery, a genuine painting which has been touched up, or the dating may be in error.

Examination and **photography** of the paint layer with a microscope or magnifying glass, perhaps using light directed at an angle, is important. Surface irregularities may be observed, as well as features such as tiny particles arising from the use of hand-mixed pigments. Ready-mixed pigments, which have a smoother appearance, are a more modern development. Examination of the paint layer in ultraviolet light can show re-painted areas as dark spots. A re-paint is not necessarily a sign of forgery; some artists re-painted as a matter of course. If a re-paint is found in the work said to be of an artist who did not alter their work, then it is cause for suspicion. This may be a sign of a forger trying to correct a mistake. Similarly, infrared reflectography can reveal underdrawings in a painting. The paint layer is transparent to infrared light that passes through, but is absorbed by drawing lines beneath and reflected by the rest of the ground layer. This creates an image of the underdrawings in infrared light that can be photographed. While some artists would begin their work with a sketch used as a basis for the painting, others never did. The investigator would be alerted if an underdrawing was revealed in work alleged to come from one of the latter. Conversely, the lack of an underdrawing might be indicative of forgery, if it was said to come from an artist who never did them.

The aging of paint shows itself by a characteristic cracking pattern known as craquelure. Examination of the surface of the paint with a magnifying glass will reveal whether the extent of the craquelure matches the alleged age of the painting. Many paintings are varnished to protect them and enhance their appearance. Like paint, different varnishes have evolved over time. Ultra-violet light can distinguish between varnishes. Synthetic varnish gives a clear or lavender **fluorescence** (emission of light), while shellac fluoresces orange. Varnish discolors with time and this can also help date a painting.

Besides examining the four layers of a painting, the investigator will also look out for other significant signs of authenticity. Some manufacturers of artists' material marked their products with a stamp and there are databases giving information, including dates, of these stamps. The presence of collectors' marks or other signs that a painting has been owned, sold, exhibited, or framed can help establish the history of a work of art. Some artists signed their work and the forger may attempt to forge their signature. Strange as it may sound, a forger may create a copied artwork, complete with the artist's signature, quite legitimately. It is only when they offer this work for sale at an inflated price and attempt to represent the work as an original, that they enter the realms of forgery. The law on selling, buying, and owning forged works of art varies from country to country. Therefore, the amount of criminal investigation that will be carried out into a particular work depends upon context and circumstances. However, the forging of a certificate of authenticity to accompany the work of art is always considered a criminal offense, and can also be investigated by a forensic document examiner.

SEE ALSO Art identification; Document forgery; Paint analysis.

Art identification

The **identification** of works of art follows the same general procedures as detecting a forgery or determining the treatment needed to restore a damaged item. The technical specialist works with the art historian or curator to discover who was the actual executor of a particular painting, drawing, or sculpture. This kind of work is particularly significant when large sums of public money are to be committed to a major purchase for an art gallery. The question is often whether a newly discovered work, typically a painting, is really that of a well-known artist. It is not uncommon for such finds to be made in an antique shop or someone's attic. Determining their authenticity is a significant challenge for the investigating team. Often the claim proves to be unsubstantiated, but there is always a chance of discovering a lost or previously unknown Grand Master.

It is important to determine the history of the artwork under question in as much detail as possible. Sometimes this is difficult. Families may pass art collections down through generations and accompanying documentation can be lost. Paintings are stolen or lost and can disappear for many years. For instance, the upheavals of World War I and World War II led to the dispersal of many valuable artworks by looting. Some may have since been acquired by art dealers, museums, and private collectors, but questions remain as to their authenticity.

An important task in art identification is to compare the questioned item with examples from the artist's main body of work. This falls to the art historian, who has specialist knowledge of the artist's approach, themes, favorite materials, and techniques. The extent of technical examination needed depends very much on the context and circumstances—it can be relatively easy to disprove or prove authenticity in some cases, but other cases may be more challenging. The investigation begins with a visual investigation of the painting, accompanied by **photography** in normal, infrared, and ultraviolet light. Photographs are taken in front of the painting with both normal illumination and tangential illumination, the latter revealing surface irregularities.

A painting is generally made up of four distinct layers: the support; the ground, which serves as a foundation for the paint; the paint itself; and varnish. The materials used in each layer are often characteristic of the time of creation of the painting. Most old materials can be re-created, so their presence alone cannot confirm a painting's age. However, the presence of acrylic paint means a work that has been made in the twentieth or twenty-first century.

The support is usually made of wood or canvas. The age of wood such as oak can readily be determined by **dendrochronology**, which is the examination of tree rings. Canvas age can be solved by carbon-14 dating. When it comes to pigments, the presence of lead-tin yellow can always exclude the nineteenth century. This pigment was widely used in the fifteenth, sixteenth, and seventeenth century, but disappeared completely around 1850. It was rediscovered in 1941. Another yellow pigment that has been used in identification is cadmium yellow, which was introduced about 1800. In 1942, the St. Louis Art Museum bought a still life said to be by the Spanish master Francisco de Zurbaran (1598–1664). However, the discovery of cadmium yellow in the painting meant it could not date back to the seventeenth century.

The presence of underdrawings, as revealed by infrared reflectography, is an interesting aid to identification. The paint layer is transparent to infrared light, but it is absorbed by lines drawn on the ground layer. The rest of the infrared is reflected back by the ground. Thus an infrared photograph reveals any underdrawing that the artist may have done. The absence of underdrawings may be indicative of a forgery, because they may not be necessary if someone is just making a copy.

X-radiography can also reveal what is beneath the surface of a painting. The technique is not unlike the x rays that are used to examine the human body. Most elements of the paint layer are transparent to x-radiation, save for white pigments containing lead and vermilion, a red that contains mercury. X-radiography can show revisions and additions to the painting if these have been done with lead or mercury-containing pigments. It can also reveal the structure of the support, showing any marks that have been made in its construction.

In one well-known case, a painting long assumed to be a copy was identified as being authentic, thanks to technical testing. A small panel of the Virgin and Child first attributed to Jan Gossaert (1478–1532) had been consigned to the storerooms of the National Gallery in London because it had been decided it was only a copy, probably made in the eighteenth or nineteenth century. Further testing in 1994 involved studying the surface and cross-section samples in ultraviolet light. This showed re-painting and addition of a varnish layer had been done in the nineteenth century. However, there were older paint layers containing a red pigment from the sixteenth century. Dendrochronology showed the support to be equally old. Removal of the later paint and varnish restored the original Gossaert, which matched an engraved copy from 1589. The painting was the original in a group of six closely related paintings which survive.

SEE ALSO Art forgery; Holocaust, property identification; Paint analysis.

Artificial fibers

Investigation of a crime or accident scene involves the collection of **evidence**. This collection must be scrupulous; every piece of evidence is important in deciphering the course of events, identifying the victim, and in implicating a suspect.

One piece of evidence that can be important is **fibers**; the material that makes up clothing and other material. Even wigs may be comprised of fibers.

Fibers can be made of a natural material (i.e., wool) or a synthetic compound or blend. The differentiation of these fibers types can be important. For example, if a suspect was wearing rayon trousers, then it would be of interest to determine if the fibers found at the scene were rayon.

Most synthetic fibers are polymer-based, and are produced by a process known as spinning. This process involves extrusion of a polymeric liquid through fine holes known as spinnerets. After the liquid has been spun, the resulting fibers are oriented by stretching or drawing out of the fibers. This increases the polymeric chain orientation and degree of crystallinity, and has the effect of increasing the modulus and tensile strength of the fibers.

Fiber manufacture is classified according to the type of spinning that the polymer liquid undergoes: melt spinning, dry spinning, or wet spinning.

Melt spinning is the simplest of these three methods, but it requires that the polymer constituent be stable above its melting temperature. In melt spinning, the polymer is melted and forced through the spinnerets, which may contain from 50 to 500 holes. The diameter of the fiber immediately following extrusion exceeds the hole diameter. During the cooling process, the fiber is drawn to induce orientation. Further orientation may later be achieved by stretching the fiber to what is known as a higher draw ratio.

Melt spinning is used with polymers such as nylon, polyethylene, polyvinyl chloride, cellulose triacetate, and polyethylene terephthalate, and in the multifilament extrusion of polypropylene.

In dry spinning, the polymer is first dissolved in a solvent. The polymer solution is extruded through the spinnerets. The solvent is evaporated with hot air and collected for reuse. The fiber then passes over rollers, and is stretched to orient the molecules and increase the fiber strength. Cellulose acetate, cellulose triacetate, acrylic, modacrylic, aromatic nylon, and polyvinyl chloride are made by dry spinning.

In wet spinning, the polymer solution is spun into a coagulating solution to precipitate the polymer. This process has been used with acrylic, modacrylic, aromatic nylon, and polyvinyl chloride fibers. Viscose rayon is produced from regenerated cellulose by a wet spinning technique.

In a forensic examination, fibers are most easily collected using adhesive tape. The collected fibers are separated based on color and other appearance characteristics (i.e., wooly versus string-like).

Forensic analysis of fibers is conducted in several ways. Synthetic fiber polymers can be suited to examination using infrared **spectroscopy**. Specified guidelines exist for this type of examination, which makes the technique standard and so more easily legally admissible.

The constituents of the dye that has been used to color fibers can be separated using **chromatography**, which can separate compounds based on differences of size or charge.

Artificial fibers can also act as lenses, by virtue of the drawing out process of manufacture. Based on the optical properties of a fiber, shining a light on it will either focus the light towards the center or the edge of the fiber. This can aid in identifying the nature of a fiber sample.

SEE ALSO Crime scene investigation; Evidence; Fourier transform infrared spectrophotometer (FTIR).

David Robinson Ashbaugh

3/11/1946–
CANADIAN
FORENSIC SPECIALIST, POLICE OFFICER

David R. Ashbaugh has spent his career in the fields of law enforcement and **forensic science**, working as a sergeant and forensic identification specialist in Canada. He has focused his research and expertise on the science of ridgeology, a term Ashbaugh coined in 1982. He has written, lectured, and consulted extensively on ridgeology, and wrote a fundamental text on the subject, *Quantitative-Qualitative Friction Ridge Analysis*.

For more than thirty years, Ashbaugh has worked in law enforcement, most recently as a staff sergeant for the Royal Canadian Mounted Police and the detachment commander in Hope, British Columbia. In addition, he has worked for more than twenty years as a certified forensic identification specialist. Over these years, Ashbaugh has conducted extensive research on the science behind friction ridge identification. As a result, he is considered an expert in the field and has lectured and consulted on the topic internationally.

In 1983, Ashbaugh published the article "Ridgeology: Our Next Evaluative Step," in the *Royal Canadian Mounted Police Gazette*. With the article, he was using the word ridgeology for the first time. By Ashbaugh's definition, ridgeology was the process of friction ridge identification based on quantitative-qualitative analysis. The article marked the first of many papers and books Ashbaugh has written on the subject of ridgeology.

In 1999, Ashbaugh wrote and published *Quantitative-Qualitative Friction Ridge Analysis: An Introduction to Basic and Advanced Ridgeology*, a book considered to be an essential resource for latent print examiners. The book gives an overview of the history of friction ridge identification, as well as detailed discussions of ridgeology methods, including poroscopy, edgeoscopy, pressure distortion, and problem print analysis. Ashbaugh also includes the methodology he developed for palmar flexion crease identification.

Ashbaugh also serves as director of Ridgeology Consulting Services, a firm that provides friction ridge identification **training** for law enforcement officials. Among his many professional affiliations, he is a distinguished member of the **International Association for Identification**, a fellow of the Fingerprint Society of the United Kingdom, and an editorial board member of the *Journal of Forensic Identification*.

SEE ALSO Fingerprint analysis (famous cases); Ridge characteristics.

Aspermia

Aspermia, put plainly, describes the condition where there are no **sperm** present in the male **semen**. In fertile males with a completely functional reproductive system, the testes constantly produce sperm. Sperm cells are collected in the epididymus (a small sac connected to each testicle) and stored there until a later time when the male reaches orgasm and ejaculates. During the process of ejaculation, a thick, highly concentrated mass of sperm cells (approximately 100 million cells) from the epididymus travels through the vas deferens, a tubular passageway connecting the testicles to the prostate gland. In the prostate gland, sperm are mixed with a more fluid secretion from the prostate gland, seminal vesicles, and Cowper's gland, resulting in the ivory colored fluid (semen) that is released from the penis during ejaculation.

The function of the sperm cells is to provide male germ cells capable of fertilizing an egg. By far, the vast majority of cells present in semen are sperm cells from the testicles. The function of the glandular fluid is to provide a medium for transporting the sperm and an ideal environment in which the sperm cells can swim toward the egg.

From birth through early childhood, the testes naturally do not produce sperm. After the onset of puberty during adolescence, the sperm-producing cells of the testes normally become active, and remain active throughout most of adulthood.

Two common causes of aspermia in males are mechanical obstruction (usually in the vas deferens) and lack of sperm production in the testes. When the passageway between the testes and prostate gland is in some way disrupted, the testes may continue to produce sperm, but there is no physical means for the sperm to mix with glandular **fluids** and enter the ejaculate. Males may have natural obstructions or be born without a functional passageway joining the testes and the prostate gland. The vas deferens may intentionally be cut surgically in a procedure called a vasectomy as a means of birth control. Some mechanical forms of aspermia can be corrected surgically, and vasectomy is often reversible. In some males, sperm production never begins, or it may cease after a relatively short period of time.

The result of aspermia is that the semen does not contain any significant amount of cellular material and is therefore incapable of causing fertilization of an egg. Since the ejaculate in males with aspermia is not cellular, there is also very little **DNA** present that might be used in forensic testing. Males with aspermia are generally able to reach orgasm and ejaculate, however, and are typically, therefore, sexually active.

At **autopsy**, aspermia may provide clues to death caused by prolonged exposure to some **toxins**, such as thallium, which was used in rodenticides (rat poisons) before being banned. Also, aspermia identified

Man with his dead cattle after volcanic activity under Lake Nyos in Cameroon produced a cloud of carbon dioxide that asphyxiated 1,746 villagers and many animals in 1986. © PETER TURNLEY/CORBIS

in seminal fluids may help to exclude individuals in paternity issues, and can sometimes provide preliminary information about possible assailants in cases of rape.

SEE ALSO Paternity evidence.

Asphyxiation (signs of)

Asphyxiation is a term that describes death that occurs due to the lack of oxygen. This lack of oxygen affects the functioning of the brain, which in turn catastrophically affects the functioning of the remainder of the body.

Asphyxiation can be caused by a number of events. Strangulation, the deliberate squeezing of the neck, can cut off oxygen to the brain. Other accidental or deliberate means of asphyxia include suffocation, where air movement into the body through the nose and mouth is restricted. The classic

movie murder image of someone being smothered by a pillow is an example of suffocation.

Another cause of asphyxiation is drowning, where the air in the lungs is replaced by water. The airway can also be blocked when a victim chokes on an object such as a small toy or piece of food. Finally, the airway can also be physically be blocked by hanging, when a person is suspended in the air by a rope or other object wrapped around their throat. Asphyxiation from hanging can occur quickly if the trachea is compressed, or can occur as a result of strangulation if the carotid arteries are compressed.

When investigating a suspected case of asphyxiation, a forensic investigator will look for telltale signs. For example, in the case of strangulation, neck injury could be evident when an **autopsy** is done on the victim. The squeezing of the neck, whether manually or via an object tied around the neck, can produce distinctive injuries. So will larynx injury resulting from blows to the neck.

Signs of suffocation-related asphyxiation such as strangulation can include bruises and fingernails scratches on the neck, bleeding around the throat, and in some cases, the fracture of the U-shaped hyoid bone at the base of the tongue. **Evidence** of suffocation may include small red or purple splotches in the eyes and on the face and neck as well as the lungs (petechial hemorrhages).

Asphyxiation may also produce foam in the airways as the victim struggles to breathe and mucus from the lungs mixes with air. This is especially typical in drowning. Other changes can include an enlarged heart and an altered **blood** chemistry.

By assessing these types of external or internal injuries, the forensic scientist can gain a better understanding if death resulted from asphyxiation and whether the asphyxiation was deliberate or accidental.

SEE ALSO Choking, signs of; Death, mechanism of; Hypoxia.

Assassination

Assassination is a sudden, usually unexpected, act of **murder**, typically with a political or military leader as its target. The practice of assassination goes back to ancient times, and extends into the present day. Assassinations have occurred throughout history, in places all over the globe. At one time, the most widely used tool for assassination was a knife or dagger. Modern day assassinations more often use guns, bombs, poisons, and biological agents such as **toxins**.

In the United States, the President has been a frequent target. In 1865 Abraham Lincoln became the first American president killed by an assassin's bullet, followed by James A. Garfield in 1881, William McKinley in 1901, and John F. Kennedy in 1963. Unsuccessful attempts were made on Franklin D. Roosevelt, Harry S Truman, Gerald Ford, and Ronald Reagan.

The assassination of Austrian Archduke Francis Ferdinand in 1914 precipitated World War I, and, 30 years later, the attempted assassination of Adolf Hitler by his generals very nearly ended World War II. In India, not only Mohandas K. Gandhi in 1948, but Prime Minister Indira Gandhi (no relation) in 1984, and her son and successor, Rajiv Gandhi in 1991, fell victim to assassin's bullets. Leaders in various countries throughout the Middle East have been killed by assassins: King Abdullah of Jordan in 1951, President Anwar Sadat of Eygpt in 1981, and Israeli Prime Minister Yitzhak Rabin in 1995 were all victims of assassination. Interestingly, all of these leaders were killed by extremists on their own political side. On

the other hand, extremist leaders are as likely as any to become targets of assassins. Senator Huey Long of Louisiana was assassinated in the 1930s and Nation of Islam leader Malcolm X was killed 30 years later. George Lincoln Rockwell, leader of the American Nazi Party, and Pim Fortuyn, founder of a Dutch radical anti-immigrant party, were also slain by assassins.

Targets of assassination are not necessarily national leaders, formal office-holders, or even political leaders. When a Turkish assassin attempted to shoot Pope John Paul II in 1981, it was clearly a political act even though the pope was not a political leader per se. Martin Luther King and Robert Kennedy, both assassinated in 1968, were political leaders, but King held no formal office and Kennedy, although he was a senator and presidential candidate, symbolized a larger cultural atmosphere of optimism and activism. Furthermore, his status as John F. Kennedy's brother added greatly to the symbolic impact of the event.

In the aftermath of any assassination, **forensic science** may be used to try to determine the method of death and to identify those responsible. Forensic science is not concerned with the aims or the political implications of assassinations. Rather, the battery of tests and skills of the forensic investigators are geared toward deducing how the murder was carried out.

Even in an obvious case of an assassination by means of gunshot, a forensic investigation can possibly identify the firearm that was used. Furthermore, **ballistics** and **gunshot residue** studies can be used to implicate a suspect.

Forensic **identification** techniques for poisonous **inorganic compounds** and biological agents such as bacterial toxins can be valuable in unraveling the nature of assassinations that involve these harder to detect weapons.

SEE ALSO Assassination weapons, biochemical; Assassination weapons, mechanical; Kennedy assassination; Lincoln exhumation; Ricin; Sarin gas.

Assassination weapons, biochemical

Assassination is usually defined as politically inspired **murder**. The term is probably derived from the Arabic word for hemp (Hashish), which was apparently used by Hasan-ban-Sabah (c.1034–1124) to induce motivation in his followers. These "hashishins" or assassins were assigned to carry out political and other murders, usually at the cost of their own lives. Thus, at the etymological level, there is already a connection between assassination and compounds derived from nature.

Forensic science is often a part of the follow-up investigation in an assassination. The various forensic techniques and skills of the investigators are utilized to try to unravel the nature of the assassination. Their efforts may involve determining if a biochemical agent was involved and how the agent was delivered.

Knowledge of the possible biochemical agents that can kill someone are helpful in such an investigation. Various agents will have different physiological effects.

Biochemicals in the context of assassination involve mostly plant-derived drugs or **toxins**. They can be **organic compounds** such as alkaloids, diterpenes, cardiac and cynogenic glycosides, nitro-containing compounds, oxalates, resins, certain proteins, and amino acids. A selection of these biochemicals was effectively used in assassination attempts throughout history.

The ancient civilizations of the Near East, Greece, and Rome developed the use of poisons in political homicide to a high degree of efficiency. In classical Rome, mushroom poisons were expertly administered by Agrippina (A.D. 16–A.D. 59), wife of the Emperor Claudius and mother of Nero. She successfully disposed of several political rivals, including Marcus Silanus, who was to succeed Claudius, and eventually Claudius himself. Agrippina probably employed the properties of Amanita species, which contain amanitin polypeptides that produce degenerative changes in the liver, kidney, and cardiac muscles. In ancient Egypt, Queen Cleopatra, in her search for a suitable suicide compound, became familiar with the properties of henbane (*Hyoscyanus niger*) and belladonna (*Atropa belladonna*), although she judged death by these plants to be rapid, but painful. Cleopatra was also disappointed with *Strychnos nux-vomita* (a tree whose seeds yield strychnine). Strychnine causes stimulation of the central nervous system, produces generalized convulsions, and distorted facial features at death. The latter did not suit Cleopatra, who eventually settled for the bite of an asp (Egyptian cobra), which produced a more serene and prompt death worthy of a queen.

Hemlock is another notorious biochemical used in political murders. The hemlock plant contains coni-

ine, an alkaloid, and was used to execute the Greek philosopher Socrates (c.479 B.C.–399 B.C.). The drug causes progressive motor paralysis extending upwards from the extremities until death results from respiratory failure. Some of the deadliest political poisons were concocted by the alchemists of the Middle Ages. La Cantrella was a secret assassination weapon used by Cesare Borgia (1476–1507) and Lucrezia Borgia (1480–1519) to dispatch their enemies. Even today its exact composition is not known, but it was most probably a mixture of naturally derived copper, arsenic, and crude phosphorus.

In later times, cyanide became more widely used as a homicidal poison. Today, cyanide is usually derived in large quantities from industry, but it has its source in biochemical processes involving cyanogenic glycosides. Amygdalin is one of the most widely distributed glycosides, yielding hydrocyanic acid (HCN) as a product of hydrolysis. It is present in the Rosaceae plant family and found in the seeds of apples, cherries, peaches, and plums. HCN inhibits the action of the enzyme cytochrome oxidase and prevents the uptake of oxygen by cells. As little as 0.06 g can cause death in humans. Consumption of a lethal dose of HCN is usually followed by collapse and death within seconds. As an assassination weapon, it was famously employed in the killing of the Russian monk Gregory Efimovich Rasputin (c.1872–1916). Legend has it that Rasputin's unnaturally strong constitution allowed him to ingest enough cyanide to kill six men, yet he continued to breathe and eventually received his *coup de grace* from a gun shot.

Ricin is found in the shell casing of castor beans and is easily produced, thus having the potential to be a large-scale murder weapon. Ricin came to public attention in 1978 when it was used in the assassination of Bulgarian dissenter Georgi Markov in the United Kingdom. Markov worked as a broadcaster for the British Broadcasting Corporation, and relayed pro-Western material to his communist homeland. Markov died several days after being jabbed by an umbrella at a bridge in London. The poison-tipped umbrella injector was designed by the Soviet intelligence agency KGB, whose Bulgarian agent carried the umbrella and delivered the ricin to the victim. An **autopsy** revealed that a platinum-iridium pellet the size of a pinhead had been implanted in Markov at the site of his injury. The pellet was cross-drilled with 0.016-inch (0.4-mm) holes to contain the ricin.

Ricin is an extremely toxic poison, and thus can kill even if applied in a small amount. The chemical is particularly deadly because it can be inhaled, ingested, or swallowed and is quickly broken down in the body and is virtually undetectable. There is currently no antidote to ricin, although a prospective vaccine has been developed that has been successfully tested in mice.

In the 1950s and 1960s Sidney Gottlieb (1918–), a talented chemist and poisons expert, worked for the United States Central Intelligence Agency (CIA). He also operated under the name Joseph Scheider. In the 1960s, Gottlieb was involved in various chemical and biochemical projects, none of which were apparently successful. Gottlieb created devices that could deliver poisons by which the CIA could carry out assassinations of political leaders who were assumed to be a threat to U.S. national security. One of these leaders was Fidel Castro, whose liking for Havana cigars was considered to be a possible means of administering poison pellets. Gottlieb is thought to have inserted poison into Havana cigars that were sent to Castro, but the cigars were somehow intercepted and never arrived. Gottlieb then tried to create a poisoned wetsuit, which Castro never wore. Another assassination attempt involving Gottlieb was planned by the CIA on General Abdul Karim Kassem of Iraq by planting a poisoned handkerchief in his suit pocket, but this plan also failed. Gottlieb adopted a slightly different tactic in the planned assassination of African leader Patrice Lumumba, the left-wing Prime Minster of the Congo (now Zaire). In September 1960, he constructed an assassination package that included a biological agent able to induce **tularemia** (rabbit fever), brucellosis (undulant fever), **anthrax**, **smallpox**, tuberculosis, and Venezuelan equine encephalitis (sleeping sickness). This agent was mixed with toothpaste and placed in a tube that could be slipped into Lumumba's traveling kit. Gottlieb delivered this package to Lawrence Devlin, the CIA station chief, instructing him to kill Lumumba. However, the operation also did not achieve its aim, as Lumumba's enemies in the Congo murdered him first in January 1961.

SEE ALSO Assassination weapons, mechanical; Kennedy assassination; Lincoln exhumation; Ricin; Sarin gas.

Assassination weapons, mechanical

The deliberate **murder** of a political leader, figurehead or other important person can be accomplished using the variety of weapons. Some means of **assassination** involve biological agents. Others use the brute mechanical force of guns, knives, and other hardware.

In the aftermath of an assassination, **forensic science** can be valuable in establishing the nature of the weapon used. For example, the trauma inflicted by a bullet and the chemical traces left by the residue are easily distinguished from a knife wound and its effects, such as the scouring of bone by the knife blade.

The various analytical forensic analysis techniques and skills of the forensic investigator can be used to ferret out the details of the assassination, such as the type of bullet used and the firearm that the bullet came from.

A forensic investigator can also benefit from knowledge of the operative principles of the various mechanical means of assassination. To varying degrees, all of these use the mechanical principles of force, pressure, and momentum, which are related through various ratios involving the fundamental physical interactions of mass, length, and time. Additionally, several are variations on the three classic "simple machines" of classical mechanics: the inclined plane (knife), the lever (the firing mechanism of a pistol), and the hydraulic press (some types of firing devices other than pistols).

Firearms also employ chemical properties. The gunpowder in a bullet undergoes a chemical, rather than a merely physical change. A physical change, such as the freezing of water, is reversible, but once gunpowder has chemically been altered by the addition of heat and the process of combustion brought about by interaction with oxygen, it turns into fire, smoke, and ash—and a fraction of it becomes energy—such that it can never become gunpowder again.

Mechanical firing devices can also be a means of deploying a poison. A classic example is the poison pen, most effectively employed by the Soviet KGB. Disguised as an ordinary writing pen, one such device fired hydrocyanic acid in the form of gas. Another KGB pen used as a weapon fired pellets of **ricin**, a poison long favored by agents in the assassination squad known as SMERSH.

SMERSH used variations on this technique to eliminate several Bulgarian dissidents living abroad in the 1970s. The most famous example of this occurred in London, where SMERSH caught up with journalist Georgi Markov in September 1978. As an unsuspecting Markov stood waiting in a crowd for a bus at Waterloo Bridge, a man walked past him and jabbed him in the thigh with the pointed end of his umbrella. Within a few days, Markov was dead. The man with the umbrella was a SMERSH assassin, and the pointed tip of his umbrella had fired a platinum pellet containing ricin. So clever was this method of murder that it took some time before Western intelligence operatives realized what had happened, and arranged for Markov's body to be exhumed. Only then did they discover the pellet.

In this and other such cases, a biochemical agent actually caused death, yet the method of delivery was mechanical. In the same way, poison that passes through a syringe (a hydraulic pump) into the victim's body is a biochemical weapon delivered by mechanical means. By contrast, when the Aum Shinrikyo cult employed ricin to kill 12 commuters, and injure thousands more, in a Tokyo subway in 1995, they used it in the form of gas—an almost purely biochemical technique. Victims inhaled the gas, which went to work immediately on their systems.

More conventional mechanical assassination weapons include bludgeons; knives and other sharp objects; guns and other firing devices; and miscellaneous weapons. An encyclopedic treatment of such weapons would fill an entire book, especially where guns are concerned. Therefore, the focus here is confined to weapons noted for their clever design or means of concealment that were developed by and for covert action organizations or similar groups. Even then, it is possible only to touch on a few notable examples.

Bludgeons and blunt instruments are used to deliver a blow when the victim and assassin are very close together. Forensically, the injury would be evident as a fractured **skull** or other signs of blows to other parts of the body.

Another mechanical weapon is a knife, edge weapon, or pointed instrument. All can deliver a cut or slash or sever a vital artery. Such assassination technology can be quite sophisticated. British special forces in World War II, for example, used the push dagger and the thrust weapon, both sharp instruments that are more like stakes or spikes than knives. Other British forces, serving as commandos in North Africa, employed a combination of knife and brass knuckles, by which the user could first stun the victim before using the knife.

As with most assassination weapons, concealment is a key issue. Hence, many units responsible for special operations in World War II used thumb knives, which were so small they could only be gripped with the thumb and forefinger. Their size made them easy to hide in the user's clothing, or even

in a closed hand. Also during the war, the British Special Operations Executive (SOE) designed an ingenious knife kit for the U.S. Office of Strategic Services (OSS), the forerunner of CIA. The kit, made to fold up and fit neatly in a pocket, contained a plethora of knives and sharp instruments, ranging from a tiny knife painted a nonreflective black to a fierce-looking open-handled dagger.

There are also miscellaneous assassination devices that either combine aspects of the bludgeon and edge weapon, or use strangulation as a means of killing. A notorious example of the latter is the garrote, typically used when the killer is able to approach the victim unexpectedly from the back. Consisting of two handles joined by a thin, strong wire a little longer than a man's shoulders, the garrote is a highly effective low-tech weapon. Again, a pattern of injury that is produced that is distinctive to the instrument used. This can aid a forensic investigator in identifying the weapon utilized.

SEE ALSO Assassination weapons, biochemical; Kennedy assassination; Lincoln exhumation; Ricin; Sarin gas.

ATF (United States Bureau of Alcohol, Tobacco, and Firearms)

United States federal agencies, like The Bureau of Alcohol, Tobacco, and Firearms, and Explosives (ATF or BATF), can provide useful information in a forensic investigation. The ATF is responsible for enforcing federal law with regard to the sale and use of alcohol, tobacco, firearms, and explosives. In accordance with the Homeland Security Act of 2002, on January 24, 2003, the ATF was transferred from the Department of the Treasury to the Department of Justice. Though the Bureau has had authority over explosives since 1972, its name did not reflect this until its transfer in 2003; it still retains the initials ATF.

Although the ATF itself was created in 1972, at that time making it the youngest tax-collecting office of the Treasury Department, its roots go back to the founding days of the Republic. The order of items in its name corresponds to the order in which Treasury began to assume control over the items themselves: alcohol in the post-Revolutionary War era, tobacco around the time of the Civil War, and firearms during the Great Depression.

Alexander Hamilton, the first Secretary of the Treasury, suggested that Congress impose a tax on imported spirits to pay a portion of the debt incurred

Three Bureau of Alcohol, Tobacco and Firearms (ATF) agents, from left, Walter Dandridge, Joe Anarumo and Steve Gerido, display rifles as examples of the type of guns that could have been used in the Maryland sniper shootings, Rockville, Maryland, 10/04/2002. AP/WIDE WORLD PHOTOS. REPRODUCED BY PERMISSION.

in the War of Independence. Congress passed a resolution calling for such a tax, and in 1789 gave Treasury responsibility for collecting it. An Act passed in 1862 created the Office of Internal Revenue, whose responsibilities included the collection of taxes on spirits and tobacco products. Renamed the Bureau of Internal Revenue (BIR) in 1877, in 1886 it established a laboratory that in time would assume responsibility for analyzing a variety of alcohol and tobacco products, as well as firearms and explosives.

Following the passage of the Eighteenth Amendment, which banned the sale, distribution, and consumption of alcohol, Treasury in 1920 established the Prohibition Unit. The deeds of "revenuers" and "T-men" such as Eliot Ness in the years that followed would become legendary, as would the less admirable exploits of gangsters such as Al Capone. Nationwide concern over the violence associated with organized crime led to the passage of the National Firearms Act in 1934. Four years later, Congress

passed the Federal Firearms Act, and BIR became responsible for collecting taxes on firearms.

After a number of changes in the section of BIR concerned with alcohol taxes, in 1940 this division became the ATU, or Alcohol Tax Unit. In 1942 Congress gave ATU responsibility for enforcing the Firearms Act.

Throughout much of the preceding century, BIR had included a Miscellaneous Tax Unit (MTU), which had responsibility for tobacco taxes and, between 1934 and 1942, taxes on firearms. In 1952, MTU was dismantled, and its firearms and tobacco tax functions fell under ATU. At the same time, BIR received a new name, one familiar to millions of Americans today: the Internal Revenue Service (IRS). ATU then came under IRS control as the Alcohol and Tobacco Tax Division, an arrangement that lasted for two decades.

In 1968, when Congress passed the Gun Control Act, the old BIR/IRS laboratory became responsible for analyzing firearms and explosives, and the Alcohol and Tobacco Tax Division became the Alcohol, Tobacco, and Firearms (ATF) Division. The 1970 passage of the Organized Crime Control Act made the role of the ATF Division more explicit, and signaled a shift away from IRS purview. On June 1, 1972, the Treasury Department issued Order No. 120-1, which separated the ATF from the IRS.

The order gave the new bureau authority not only over the three items listed in its name, but also over explosives. During the 1970s, ATF and its laboratory became involved in **arson** investigations, and in 1982, Congress amended Title XI of the Organized Crime Control Act to make arson a federal crime and formalize the ATF's role in investigating it.

During the 1990s and the beginning of the twenty-first century, the ATF undertook a number of new efforts toward fighting and investigating crime. Among these was the Integrated Ballistic Identification System, a computerized program for matching weapons and ammunition fired from them. In the mid-1990s, after its abortive 1993 raid on a Waco, Texas, compound controlled by the Branch Davidian cult, the bureau became the focus of hostility on the part of fringe right-wing groups.

By the turn of the twenty-first century, the ATF annually collected more than $13 billion in revenue for the federal government.

SEE ALSO Integrated Ballistics Identification System (IBIS).

Athletic souvenirs SEE Souvenirs from athletic events

Audio tape analysis SEE Tape analysis

Automated Fingerprint Identification System (AFIS)

The Automated Fingerprint Identification System (AFIS) is a computerized storage system for tens of millions of fingerprint images. The database picks out the most likely matches to the new print being fed into the system, narrowing the search parameters for investigators. Final analysis of the print and the retrieved images is done by AFIS Technicians to ensure accuracy of identification. The comparison

takes the computer only minutes to do a job which would have taken weeks before computerization of the system.

Prior to the 1970s, trained officers analyzed inked fingerprints and various items were noted. Minutiae details, such as ridge endings, ridge dots, bifurcations, and enclosures would be coded and the fingerprint cards filed according to patterns (whorls, loops, arches) from the Henry classification system. This method meant that it could take weeks or months for a fingerprint to be processed, as the prints would have to be analyzed at a central fingerprint bureau.

In the late 1970s and early 1980s, an analog system combined manual coding with filing codes on computers. Trained staff would then check the current print against a short computer-generated list of hard-copy inked images. Still the process was laborious and only relieved when the AFIS database was released commercially to agencies in 1986. A barrage of private software vendors marketed their AFIS products, resulting in incompatible databases and a confused market. By 2005, a small number of companies had developed universal standard applications to bring together national databases for comprehensive libraries of prints, making the selection of software upon which to run the AFIS database easier for agencies.

Simon A. Cole, author of *Suspect Identities: A History of Fingerprinting and Criminal Identification* (2001) explains that the AFIS can work in three ways. Ten-prints (prints of all digits from one individual) lifted from a crime scene or a body can be checked against the database of catalogued ten-prints; a single latent print can be checked against the ten-print catalogue; and a ten-print from a scene can be checked against single latent prints stored in the database. "Unsolved" fingerprints can be stored in the AFIS system and automatically checked against with each new entry.

Fingerprint identification has become more scientific with the use of computers and portable scanners (the no-ink solution to fingerprint collection) than prior to the 1970s. The AFIS is an effective system for identifying people and establishing the criminal history of offenders. However, automated identification methods are not foolproof, and it still takes at least two experienced pairs of eyes to positively match current fingerprints with stored images.

SEE ALSO Fingerprint; Identification; Integrated automated fingerprint identification system; Latent fingerprint.

Automobile accidents

Automobile accidents are still a major source of injury to pedestrians, drivers, and passengers, although mortality has gone down owing to the introduction of seat belts and other safety measures such as air bags. The forensic investigator is usually called in when a crime, such as a hit and run incident, speeding, drunk driving, or even homicide, is suspected. An investigation is also necessary when insurance claims for damages by the injured parties arise from the accident. A medical examination and assessment of the injuries sustained in an automobile accident form a vital part of the total investigation of an automobile accident. The medical and **pathology evidence** can be integrated into **physical evidence**, such as tire marks or impact damage, at the scene of the accident to help reconstruct what happened before, during, and after the accident.

An automobile may collide with another vehicle or with a stationary object like a wall, lamppost, or a pedestrian. The amount of damage inflicted depends on many factors such as the weight, velocity, and condition of the vehicle; the state of the road; and the condition of the driver. Injuries occur when the momentum and kinetic energy of the vehicle are brought to zero on impact, since the energy is transferred to the skeleton and surrounding tissues of the victim(s). There are three types of victims in an automobile accident: pedestrians; cyclists (motor or pedal); and the occupants of the vehicle, be it the driver or front or back seat passenger(s). Most often, it is the pedestrian who is most vulnerable to injury in an automobile accident, particularly in areas where potential contact between pedestrians and vehicles is high, such as at crossings or in built-up areas. Pathologists note characteristic patterns of injuries in these different victim groups that can be very revealing about the circumstances of the accident.

Pedestrians generally suffer two kinds of injuries when they come into contact with moving vehicles. Primary injuries arise from contact with the vehicle itself. Secondary injuries occur when the impact with the car forces the pedestrian into contact with some other object or surface, such as the road itself. Often it is the secondary injuries that do the most damage and which are the cause of most fatalities arising from automobile accidents.

For an adult hit by a car, the bumper generally strikes them first, around knee level at the front, side, or back of the leg, depending on their location relative to the vehicle. Further contact, generally with the hood of the car, produces injuries further up the body, usually to the pelvis, thigh, or hip. If victims are hit by a larger vehicle, such as a truck, the corresponding primary injuries will be higher up the body. If a child is hit, then the primary injury pattern is also higher up the body. Older people and children are more vulnerable to being hit by a car because the former tend to be less mobile and the latter may not be sufficiently vigilant or able to judge the speed of an oncoming vehicle. What happens after the initial impact depends on how fast the vehicle is going. Up to 10 mph, the pedestrian will likely be thrown off the hood of the car onto the road. If the car is traveling up to 35 mph—just beyond the speed limit for most built-up areas—then the victim tends to pitch forwards on the hood and the victim's head may strike the windshield. At higher speeds, the victim may be flung into the air, over the car, and hit the road with some considerable force. A pedestrian who may survive a 30 mph impact with a car could well be killed if that same vehicle is traveling at 40 mph. The pathologist's evidence can be vital in accidents caused by speeding.

Automobile accidents produce a wide range of secondary injuries to pedestrians. Skidding across the road will produce extensive abrasions. Direct contact often causes fractures of the **skull**, spine, and limbs. It is usually the internal damage associated with such fractures that is lethal rather than the fracture itself. Brain damage, even without a skull fracture, is common if the moving head hits a road surface.

Being "run over" by a car is actually quite unusual. When it does occur, though, injuries can be very extensive. Their nature depends on what part of the body is involved, the speed of the vehicle, and its weight. The skull may be crushed, and internal organs disrupted. If the car runs over the victim's chest, there will be multiple fractures to the ribs. Sometimes the rotation of the wheel will strip off a huge area of the skin, giving rise to a characteristic "flaying" injury. Occasionally, someone is run over deliberately, but more often it happens when someone is knocked down accidentally and then run over if the car cannot stop in time.

Most automobile accidents involve the front or front sides of the vehicle. Those occurring by impact from behind or from the side, which may cause the car to roll over, are somewhat less common. The front seat occupants, if unrestrained by a seat belt, will continue moving as the car decelerates on

Kansas Highway Patrol troopers and Olathe firefighters work at the site of a fatal accident, near State Routes 10 and 7. AP/WIDE WORLD PHOTOS. REPRODUCED BY PERMISSION.

impact. The head and face hit the windshield, possibly causing skull fractures and brain damage. The driver's chest and abdomen can hit the steering wheel, causing damage to the ribs, heart, and liver. The force of impact may even tear the body's main artery, the aorta, an injury that is generally fatal. The impact of the crash on the legs is transmitted upwards, potentially causing multiple fractures of the legs and pelvis. On very severe impacts, the front occupants may even be flung through the windshield to hit the road and sustain secondary injuries. On a fast-moving highway, such victims may be in danger of being run over by other vehicles. The back seat occupants are prone to similar, but usually less severe, injuries through impact with the front seats and the front seat occupants. If the impact is very severe, they may be flung through the windshield.

Seat belts, worn by both front and back seat occupants, have undoubtedly reduced fatalities from road traffic accidents. They work by preventing contact between the occupant's body and forward obstructions like the steering wheel and windscreen. They also spread the force of impact on the body and increase deceleration time slightly so that the force per unit area of body is less, which reduces the severity of any injuries. A seat belt also stops an occupant from being flung out of any doors or windows that burst open on impact. Airbags, a more recent development, provide a "cushion" between

the vehicle and any object with which it collides. This also protects front seat occupants from injury. However, some critics have argued that the presence of an airbag produces a sense of complacency among drivers, making them less careful than they should be because they assume the air bag will protect them in the event of an accident.

Motorcyclists generally fall from their machine onto the road when in collision with another vehicle or object. This causes, at the very least, severe abrasions. Injuries to the limbs, chest, and spine are also common when the motorcyclist becomes entangled with the machine, which may fall on top of the motorcyclist, or with another object. Head injuries are a common cause of injury and death among motorcyclists involved in an accident, even if a helmet is worn. In many countries, a helmet is compulsory and its presence or absence may be a factor in any criminal case or litigation. But, protective clothing and a good helmet can go a long way to reducing the severity of injury to motorcyclists in an accident.

Most bicycles travel at relatively low speeds, which means that most injuries sustained in an accident are mild to moderate. However, collision with a vehicle traveling at low speed may well produce fatal injuries if the cyclist is thrown against the vehicle and then falls onto the road. Cycles are inherently unstable and even the most gentle of collisions is likely to make the rider fall off, potentially into the path of a moving vehicle, when they may be "run over" and sustain severe, and potentially fatal, internal injuries.

Whatever the type of victim, be it pedestrian, car occupant, or cyclist, the principles of the forensic medical exam are the same. The investigator will first, of course, offer medical assistance to living victims. Then an external exam is done to note all the injuries, recording, measuring them with a ruler and taking photographs. Sometimes tire marks are present in the form of bruising or abrasions and these can be helpful in identifying the vehicle used by a hit and run driver. The victim's clothing should also be examined for **trace evidence**, such as **glass**, paint, or rust, which might help identify the vehicle involved. It is always possible that alcohol or drugs have contributed to the accident and **blood** samples are often taken from the victim and drivers, if they are present, for laboratory analysis.

SEE ALSO Accident reconstruction.

Automobile crash investigations
SEE Airbag residues

Autopsy

Autopsy means "see for yourself." It is a special surgical operation, performed by specially trained physicians, on a dead body. Its purpose is to learn the truth about the person's health during life, and how the person died.

There are many advantages to getting an autopsy. Even when the law does not require it, there is always something interesting for the family to know—something worth knowing that wasn't known during life is often found. Even at major hospitals, in approximately one case in four, a major disease is found that was unknown in life. Giving families the explanations they want is often stated as one of the most satisfying things that a pathologist does. A pathologist is a physician with a specialty in the scientific study of body parts. This specialty always includes a year or more learning to do autopsies.

Under the laws of most states, an autopsy can be ordered by the government. The job of **coroner** is a political position, while a **medical examiner** is a physician, usually a pathologist. Exactly who makes the decisions, and who just gives advice, depends on the jurisdiction. Autopsies can be ordered in every state when there is suspicion of foul play. In most states, an autopsy can be ordered when there is some public health concern, for example a mysterious disease or a worry about the quality of health care. In most states, an autopsy may be ordered if someone dies unattended by a physician (or attended for less than 24 hours), or if the attending physician is uncomfortable signing the death certificate. If autopsy is not required by law, the legal next-of-kin must sign an autopsy permit.

When a loved one dies, a family can ask the hospital to perform an autopsy. If the family prefers, a private pathologist can do the autopsy in the funeral home. It does not matter much whether the body has been embalmed first. Whoever does the autopsy, there should not be a problem with an open-casket funeral afterwards. This is true even if the brain has been removed and the dead person is bald. The pillow will conceal the marks.

Most religions allow autopsy. If the body is that of an Orthodox Jew, pathologists are happy to have a rabbi present to offer suggestions. Many Muslims prefer not to autopsy.

Here's how an autopsy is done. In this example, there are three pathologists working together.

The body has already been identified and lawful consent obtained.

The procedure is done with respect and seriousness. The prevailing mood in the autopsy room is curiosity, scientific interest, and pleasure at being able to find the truth and share it. Most pathologists choose their specialty, at least in part, because they like finding the real answers. Many autopsy services have a sign, "This is the place where death rejoices to teach those who live." Usually it is written in Latin: *Hic locus est ubi mors gaudet succurrere vitae.* Autopsy practice was largely developed in Germany, and an autopsy assistant is traditionally called a "diener," which is German for "servant."

The pathologist first examines the outside of the body. A great deal can be learned in this way. Many pathologists use scalpels with rulers marked on their blades. The body is opened using a Y-shaped incision from shoulders to mid-chest and down to the pubic region. There is almost no bleeding, since a dead body has no blood pressure except that produced by gravity. If the head is to be opened, the pathologist makes a second incision across the head, joining the bony prominences just below and behind the ears.

When this is sewn back up, it will be concealed by the pillow on which the dead person's head rests.

The incisions are carried down to the **skull**, the rib cage and breastbone, and the cavity that contains the organs of the abdomen. The scalp and the soft tissues in front of the chest are then folded back. Again, the pathologist looks around for any abnormalities.

One pathologist prepares to open the skull using a special vibrating saw that cuts bone but not soft tissue. This is an important safety feature. Another pathologist cuts the cartilages that join the ribs to the breastbone, in order to be able to enter the chest cavity. This can be done using a scalpel, a saw, or a special knife, depending on the pathologist's preferences and whether the cartilages have begun to turn into bone, as they often do in older people. The third pathologist explores the abdominal cavity. The first dissection in the abdomen usually frees up the large intestine. Some pathologists do this with a scalpel, while others use scissors.

The skull vault is opened using two saw cuts, one in front, and one in back. These will not show through the scalp when it is sewn back together. The top of the skull is removed, and the brain is very carefully cut free of its attachments from inside the skull.

When the breastbone and attached rib cartilages are removed, they are examined. Often they are fractured during cardiopulmonary resuscitation. Freeing up the intestine takes some time. The pathologist carefully cuts along the attachment using a scalpel.

The chest organs, including the heart and lungs, are inspected. Sometimes the pathologist takes blood from the heart to check for bacteria in the blood. For this, he or she uses a very large hypodermic needle and syringe. The team may also find something else that will need to be sent to the microbiology lab to search for infection. Sometimes the pathologist will send blood, urine, bile, or even the fluid of the eye for chemical study and to look for medicine, street drugs, alcohols, and/or poisons.

Then the pathologist must decide in what order to perform the rest of the autopsy. The choice will be based on a variety of considerations. One method is the method of Virchow, which is removing organs individually. After the intestines are mobilized, they are opened using special scissors. Inspecting the brain often reveals surprises. A good pathologist takes some time to do this. The pathologist examines the heart, and generally the first step following its removal is sectioning the coronary arteries that supply the heart with blood. There is often disease here, even in people who assumed their hearts were normal.

After any organ is removed, the pathologist will save a section in preservative solution. Of course, if something looks abnormal, the pathologist will probably save more. The rest of the organ goes into a **biohazard bag**, which is supported by a large plastic container.

The pathologist weighs the major solid organs (heart, lung, brain, kidney, liver, spleen, sometimes others) on a grocer's scale. The smaller organs (thyroid, adrenals) get weighed on a chemist's triple-beam balance. The next step in this abdominal dissection will be exploring the bile ducts and then freeing up the liver, usually using a scalpel. After weighing the heart, the pathologist completes the dissection. There are a variety of ways of doing this, and the choice will depend on the case. If the pathologist suspects a heart attack, a long knife may be the best choice.

The liver has been removed. In our example of a fictitious autopsy, the pathologist finds something important. It appears that this man had a fatty liver. It is too light, too orange, and a bit too big. It is possible that this man had been drinking alcohol heavily for a while. The liver in this case weighs much more than the normal 49.4 ounces (1400 gm).

The pathologist decides to remove the neck organs, large airways, and lungs in one piece. This requires careful dissection. The pathologist always examines the neck very carefully. The lungs are almost never completely normal at autopsy. These lungs are pink, because the dead man was a nonsmoker. The pathologist will inspect and feel them for areas of pneumonia and other abnormalities. The pathologist weighs both lungs together, then each one separately. Afterwards, the lungs may get inflated with fixative. Dissecting the lungs can be done in any of several ways. All methods reveal the surfaces of the large airways, and the great arteries of the lungs. Most pathologists use the long knife again while studying the lungs. The air spaces of the lungs will be evaluated based on their texture and appearance.

The liver is cut at intervals of about a centimeter, using a long knife. This enables the pathologist to examine its inner structure.

The rest of the team continues with the removal of the other organs. They have decided to take the

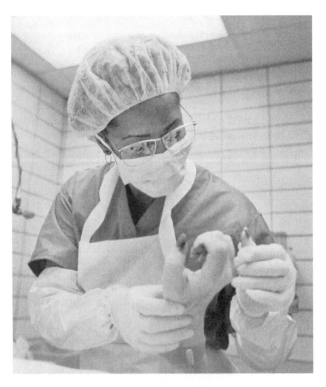

A chief medical examiner in Texas performs an autopsy, initially searching for signs of external injury, providing a physical description of the body, and documenting any external substances collected for further testing. © SHEPARD SHERBELL/CORBIS SABA

urinary system as one piece, and the digestive system down to the small intestine as another single piece. This will require careful dissection. One pathologist holds the esophagus, stomach, pancreas, duodenum, and spleen. He will open these, and may save a portion of the gastric contents to check for poison. Another pathologist holds the kidneys, ureters, and bladder. Sometimes these organs will be left attached to the abdominal aorta. The pathologist will open all these organs and examine them carefully.

Before the autopsy is over, the brain is usually suspended in fixative for a week so that the later dissection will be clean, neat, and accurate. If no disease of the brain is suspected, the pathologist may cut it fresh.

The kidneys are weighed before they are dissected.

When the internal organs have been examined, the pathologist may return all but the portions they have saved to the body cavity. Or the organs may be cremated without being returned. The appropriate laws and the wishes of the family are obeyed.

The breastbone and ribs are usually replaced in the body. A pathologist prepares a large needle and

thread used to sew up the body. The skull and trunk incisions are sewed shut ("baseball stitch"). The body is washed and is then ready to go to the funeral director.

The pathologists will submit the tissue they saved to the histology lab, to be made into microscopic slides. When the slides are ready, the pathologists will examine the sections, look at the results of any lab work, and draw their final conclusions.

The only finding in this imaginary autopsy was fatty liver. There are several ways in which heavy drinking, without any other disease, can kill a person. The pathologists will rule each of these in or out, and will probably be able to give a single answer to the police or family.

A final report is ready in a month or so. The glass slides and a few bits of tissue are kept forever, so that other pathologists can review the work.

SEE ALSO Anatomical nomenclature; Body Farm; Coroner; Death, cause of; Death, mechanism of; Decomposition; Identification; Medical examiner; Pathology; Pathology careers; Rigor mortis; Time of death; Toxicological analysis.

Autorad

Autorad is short for autoradiograph, the final result in a **DNA** analysis. An autorad resembles a bar code or a ladder and each different DNA sample will give a different pattern on an autorad. Therefore, an autorad can be an important piece of **identification evidence** in a forensic investigation. Autorads are also sometimes known as DNA fingerprints.

The procedure for creating an autorad has to be meticulously followed if the end result is to be of value in identification of a criminal. Thanks to advances in DNA technology, it is now possible to extract meaningful results from even tiny samples of DNA. The first step is to use specific chemical reagents to remove the DNA from the sample, be it **blood**, hair, or some other tissue. This depends on breaking down cell membranes and digesting proteins in the cell so the DNA can be released in a "clean" form ready for analysis.

DNA is a very long molecule and its analysis depends on chopping it into segments of a more manageable size. This is done using enzymes that produce a mixture of segments that are characteristic of the DNA in the sample. DNA from suspect A will give a mixture of segments of different lengths from the DNA of suspect B. The segments are then separated by first applying the mixture of segments to a slab of gel to which an electric current is applied. Shorter segments move faster through the gel than do longer segments. This creates the bar code pattern, but at this stage it is still invisible.

The pattern on the gel is transferred to a nylon membrane that is then exposed to radioisotopes. These attach to the DNA segments. The nylon membrane is now placed between two sheets of x-ray film and photographed. The segments now show up dark, through exposure to the film, and the familiar bar code pattern can be clearly seen. To make a comparison, DNA from a sample from the scene of the crime would be placed on the gel alongside DNA taken from a suspect, from their **saliva** or blood, for example, as well as with reference lab samples of DNA. The samples run in parallel. If the crime scene DNA is that of the suspect, then the two corresponding autorads will appear identical. If they do not, then this piece of evidence, at least, eliminates the suspect, although there may be other evidence linking the suspect to the crime.

SEE ALSO DNA fingerprint; DNA isolation methods; DNA profiling.

Aviation security screeners, United States

Forensic investigations attempt to determine the cause of accidents and even to reconstruct (at least conceptually) the course of events leading up to and including the incident. In the case of an aircraft accident, where much of the **evidence** may be destroyed or damaged by a crash, the task is particularly challenging. Analysis of all data complied before and during the flight is useful in piecing together what occurred.

Analysis of the flight data recorder that is installed on many aircraft is a well-known forensic tool. However, air travel security technologies, which are in place principally to thwart aircraft high-jacking and terrorist opportunities, can also provide information useful to a forensic investigation.

One such technology involves the security screening that is a part of the pre-flight process. Aviation security screeners focus on both the passenger and luggage. Airline passengers are familiar with

walking through a metal detector and having security personnel examiner them more closely using a hand-held metal detector. More recently, a walk-through machine has been introduced that can analyze the air flowing off of a person's body. The air can be rapidly analyzed, enabling the detection of non-metallic chemicals, which would otherwise escape the metal detector. The odor of the chemicals wafts off of the body along with the plume of heated air. Suspicious chemicals, such as those in plastic **explosives**, may be detected in this way.

Another routine part of air travel is the examination of carry-on and shipped baggage using an x-ray machine. The high energy x rays are able to penetrate through the suitcase to reveal the outline of the objects inside. A skilled operator is able to assess the contents based on their shape and translucency and focus on suspicious objects.

Chromatography is also routinely used to survey personal computers to verify that the computer case is not in fact housing an explosive. The object to be examined is swabbed using a fabric, which is then inserted into the chromatograph. The analysis takes only a few seconds to complete.

Documentation is another aspect of security screening. For example, passports provide an officially sanctioned photographic record and other information from a person. Concerns about the falsification of passports has led to the adoption of other documentation systems, including **fingerprint** and retinal scans.

Prior to the terrorist attacks of September 11, 2001, security screening at the more than 400 major commercial airports around the United States was the work of personnel employed by private firms that contracted with airlines. One outcome of the attacks was the Aviation and Transportation Security Act (ATSA), signed into law by President George W. Bush on November 19, 2001, which placed security screeners under the control of the newly created Transportation Security Administration (TSA). Early assessments of the new program were uneven, and TSA has encountered a number of challenges in what has proven to be one of the largest mobilizations of a civilian agency in U.S. history.

The fact that ATSA was written and passed just two months after the terrorist attacks serves to indicate the intensity of concern over air safety that prevailed in early fall of 2001. In fact, the bill would have passed even more quickly if it had not been for the thorny question of whether the government or private enterprise should control security screeners—and,

A security screener stands by a detection unit at JFK Airport in New York that provides explosive detection via a walk-through portal. The unit can detect particles and vapors of explosive materials by passing air over a person to release such particles. © RAMIN TALAIE/CORBIS

assuming government control, whether Transportation or Justice was the department better suited for this task.

As of January 2002, TSA had just 13 employees, but by November 2002, a year after the passage of ATSA, there were 47,000 newly trained federal security screeners at airports nationwide. TSA spokesman Robert Johnson compared the mobilization to the rush of enlistees that followed U.S. entry into World War II in December 1941. Others were not as sanguine in their appraisal. Representative Harold Rogers (R-KY) maintained that the average screener at his home facility, Kentucky Bluegrass Airport in Lexington, processed just four people per hour.

All checked bags are supposed to be screened for bombs by TSA workers as of December 31, 2002. Screeners earlier began a practice of matching bags to passengers—that is, ensuring that for each name

listed as the owner of the bag, there was a passenger with that name. Bag matching had been a practice on international flights since the 1980s, but many critics maintained that it would do nothing to stop suicide bombers such as those who perpetrated the September 11, 2001, attacks.

Much of the information used for aviation security screening is part of databases. Proof of citizenship is one well-known example. As well, the data collected in luggage and passenger pre-boarding security checks can be maintained for a set period of time. If the latter records are still available, a forensic inspector is able to trace the pre-boarding history of each passenger.

SEE ALSO Air plume and chemical analysis; Aircraft accident investigations; Biometric eye scans; Explosives; Flight data recorders; Gas chromatograph-mass spectrometer; Metal detectors.

Bacteria, classification

The shapes of bacterial cells, often of keen interest to forensic investigators, are classified as spherical (coccus), rodlike (bacillus), spiral (spirochete), helical (spirilla), and comma-shaped (vibrio) cells. Many bacilli and vibrio bacteria have whiplike appendages (called flagella) protruding from the cell surface. Flagella are composed of tight, helical rotors made of chains of globular protein called flagellin, and act as tiny propellers, making the bacteria very mobile. On the surface of some bacteria are short, hairlike, proteinaceous projections that may arise at the ends of the cell or over the entire surface. These projections, called fimbriae, facilitate bacteria adherence to surfaces.

Other proteinaceous projections, called pili, occur singly or in pairs, and join pairs of bacteria together, facilitating transfer of **DNA** between them.

Oxygen may or may not be a requirement for a particular species of bacteria, depending on the type of metabolism used to extract energy from food (aerobic or anaerobic). Obligate aerobes must have oxygen in order to live. Facultative aerobes can also exist in the absence of oxygen by using fermentation or anaerobic respiration. Anaerobic respiration and fermentation occur in the absence of oxygen, and produce substantially less ATP than aerobic respiration.

During periods of harsh environmental conditions some bacteria can produce within themselves a dehydrated, thick-walled endospore. These endospores can survive extreme temperatures, dryness, and exposure to many toxic chemicals and to radiation. Endospores can remain dormant for long periods (hundreds of years in some cases) before being reactivated by the return of favorable conditions.

Pathogens are disease-causing bacteria that release **toxins** or poisons that interfere with some function of the host's body.

An understanding of the basic classification of bacteria found at crime scenes and taken from bodies at **autopsy** is critical to forensic investigators (including forensic epidemiologists) attempting to identify bacteria. The **identification** schemes of *Bergey's Manual* are based on morphology (e.g., coccus, bacillus), staining (gram-positive or negative), cell wall composition (e.g., presence or absence of peptidoglycan), oxygen requirements (e.g., aerobic, facultatively anaerobic) and biochemical tests (e.g., which sugars are aerobically metabolized or fermented).

Another important identification technique is based on the principles of antigenicity—the ability to stimulate the formation of antibodies by the **immune system**. Commercially available solutions of antibodies against specific bacteria (antisera) are used to identify unknown organisms in a procedure called a slide agglutination test. A sample of unknown bacteria in a drop of saline is mixed with antisera that has been raised against a known species of bacteria. If the antisera causes the unknown bacteria to clump (agglutinate), then the test positively identifies the bacteria as being identical to that against which the antisera was raised. The test can also be used to distinguish between strains of slightly different bacteria belonging to the same species.

SEE ALSO Anthrax; Bacterial biology; Bacteria, growth and reproduction; Bacterial resistance and response to antibacterial agents; Biological weapons, genetic identification; Biosensor technologies; Bubonic plague; Decontamination methods.

Bacteria, growth and reproduction

Forensic scientists often **culture** and grow bacteria found at crime scenes or extracted from remains. This process is often necessary to achieve a large enough population of bacteria upon which tests can then be performed.

An understanding of how bacteria grow, multiply, and change over time also helps explain many field or **autopsy** findings.

A population of bacteria in a liquid medium is referred to as a culture. In the laboratory, where growth conditions of temperature, light intensity, and nutrients can be made ideal for the bacteria, measurements of the number of living bacteria typically reveals four stages, or phases, of growth, with respect to time. Initially, the number of bacteria in the population is low. Often the bacteria are also adapting to the environment. This represents the lag phase of growth. Depending on the health of the bacteria, the lag phase may be short or long. The latter occurs if the bacteria are damaged or have just been recovered from deep-freeze storage.

After the lag phase, the numbers of living bacteria rapidly increases. Typically, the increase is exponential. That is, the population keeps doubling in number at the same rate. This is called the log or logarithmic phase of culture growth, and is the time when the bacteria are growing and dividing at their maximum speed.

The explosive growth of bacteria cannot continue forever in the closed conditions of a flask of growth medium. Nutrients begin to become depleted, the amount of oxygen becomes reduced, the pH changes, and toxic waste products of metabolic activity begin to accumulate. The bacteria respond to these changes in a variety of ways to do with their structure and activity of genes. With respect to bacteria numbers, the increase in the population stops and the number of living bacteria plateaus. This plateau period is called the stationary phase. Here, the

number of bacteria growing and dividing is equaled by the number of bacteria that are dying.

Finally, as conditions in the culture continue to deteriorate, the proportion of the population that is dying becomes dominant. The number of living bacteria declines sharply over time in what is called the death or decline phase.

Bacteria growing as colonies on a solid growth medium also exhibit these growth phases in different regions of a colony. For example, the bacteria buried in the oldest part of the colony are often in the stationary or death phase, while the bacteria at the periphery of the colony are in the actively-dividing log phase of growth.

Culturing of bacteria is possible such that fresh growth medium can be added at rate equal to the rate at which culture is removed. The rate at which the bacteria grow is dependent on the rate of addition of the fresh medium. Bacteria can be tailored to grow relatively slow or fast and, if the set-up is carefully maintained, can be maintained for a long time.

Bacterial growth requires the presence of environmental factors. For example, if a bacterium uses organic carbon for energy and structure (chemoheterotrophic bacteria), then sources of carbon are needed. Such sources include simple sugars (glucose and fructose are two examples). Nitrogen is needed to make amino acids, proteins, lipids and other components. Sulphur and phosphorus are also needed for the manufacture of bacterial components. Other elements, such as potassium, calcium, magnesium, iron, manganese, cobalt and zinc are necessary for the functioning of enzymes and other processes.

Bacterial growth is also often sensitive to temperature. Depending on the species, bacteria exhibit a usually limited range in temperatures in which they can grow and reproduce. For example, bacteria known as mesophiles prefer temperatures from $20°C–50°C$ ($68°F–122°F$). Outside this range growth and even survival is limited.

Other factors, which vary depending on species, required for growth include oxygen level, pH, osmotic pressure, light, and moisture.

The events of growth and division that are apparent from measurement of the numbers of living bacteria are the manifestation of a number of molecular events. At the level of the individual bacteria, the process of growth and replication is known as binary division. Binary division occurs in stages. First, the parent bacterium grows and becomes larger. Next, the genetic material inside the bacterium uncoils from the normal helical configuration and replicates.

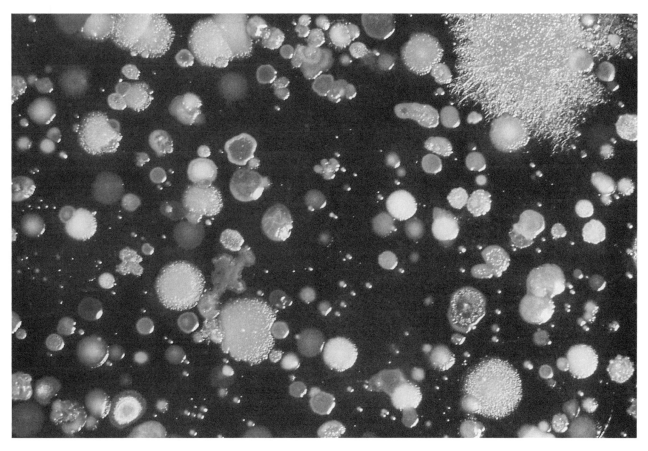

Blood agar culture plate showing anthrax growth. © CDC/PHIL/CORBIS

The two copies of the genetic material migrate to either end of the bacterium. Then a cross-wall known as a septum is initiated almost precisely at the middle of the bacterium. The septum grows inward as a ring from the inner surface of the membrane. When the septum is complete, an inner wall has been formed, which divides the parent bacterium into two so-called daughter bacteria. This whole process represents the generation time.

Bacteria can exchange genetic material via conjugation. Genetic recombination between bacteria (or protists) occurs via a cytoplasmic bridge between the organisms. A primitive form of exchange of genetic material between bacteria involving plasmids also can occur. Plasmids are small, circular, extrachromosomal DNA molecules that are capable of replication and are known to be capable of transferring genes among bacteria. For example, resistance plasmids carry genes for resistance to **antibiotics** from one bacterium to another, while other plasmids carry genes that confer pathogenicity (the ability to cause disease). In addition, the transfer of genes via bacteriophages—viruses that specifically parasitize bacteria—also serves as a means of genetic recombination.

Bioengineering uses sophisticated techniques to purposely transfer DNA from one organism to another in order to give the second organism some new characteristic it did not have previously. For example, in a process called transformation, antibiotic susceptible bacteria that are induced to absorb manipulated plasmids placed in their environment can acquire resistance to that antibiotic substance due to the new genes they have incorporated. Similarly, in a process called transfection, specially constructed viruses are used to artificially inject bioengineered DNA into bacteria, giving infected cells some new characteristic.

Evolution has driven both bacterial diversity and bacterial adaptation. Some alterations are reversible, disappearing when the particular pressure is lifted. Other alterations are maintained and can even be passed on to succeeding generations of bacteria.

SEE ALSO Anthrax; Bacterial biology; Bacteria, classification; Bacterial resistance and response to antibacterial agents; Biological weapons, genetic identification; Biosensor technologies; Bubonic plague; Decontamination methods.

Bacterial biology

The Dutch merchant and amateur scientist Anton van Leeuwenhoek was the first to observe bacteria and other microorganisms. Using single-lens **microscopes** of his own design, he described bacteria and other microorganisms as "animacules."

An understanding of the fundamentals of bacterial biology is critical to bacteriologists and other forensic investigators attempting to identify potential biogenic **pathogens** that may be exploited by bioterrorists. In addition, the reaction of the body to bacteria and the type of bacteria present often offer invaluable clues to forensic investigators.

Bacteria are one-celled prokaryotic organisms that lack a true nucleus (i.e., a nucleus defined by a membrane). Bacteria maintain their genetic material, deoxyribonucleic acid (**DNA**), in a single, circular chain. Bacteria also contain DNA in small circular molecules termed plasmids.

In addition to not being contained in a membrane bound nucleus, the DNA of prokaryotes is not associated with the special **chromosome** proteins called histones, which are found in higher organisms. In addition, prokaryotic cells lack other membrane-bounded organelles, such as mitochondria.

Although all bacteria share certain structural, genetic, and metabolic characteristics, important biochemical differences exist among the many species of bacteria. The cytoplasm of all bacteria is enclosed within a cell membrane surrounded by a rigid cell wall whose polymers, with few exceptions, include peptidoglycans—large, structural molecules made of protein carbohydrate. Bacteria also secrete a viscous, gelatinous polymer (called the glycocalyx) on their cell surfaces. This polymer, composed either of polysaccharide, polypeptide, or both, is called a capsule when it occurs as an organized layer firmly attached to the cell wall. Capsules increase the disease-causing ability (virulence) of bacteria by inhibiting **immune system** cells called phagocytes from engulfing them.

During the 1860s, the French microbiologist Louis Pasteur studied fermenting bacteria. He demonstrated that fermenting bacteria could contaminate wine and beer during manufacturing, turning the alcohol produced by yeast into acetic acid (vinegar). Pasteur also showed that heating the beer and wine to kill the bacteria preserved the flavor of these beverages. The process of heating, now called pasteurization in his honor, is still used to kill bacteria in some alcoholic beverages, as well as milk.

Pasteur described the spoilage by bacteria of alcohol during fermentation as being a "disease" of wine and beer. His work was thus vital to the later idea that human diseases could also be caused by microorganisms, and that heating can destroy them.

The first antibiotic (a substance designed to kill bacteria) was penicillin, discovered in 1928 by Sir Alexander Fleming. Since then, a myriad of naturally occurring and chemically synthesized **antibiotics** have been used to control bacteria. Introduction of an antibiotic is frequently followed by the development of resistance to the agent. Resistance is an example of the adaptation of the bacteria to the antibacterial agent.

Bacteria can multiply and cause an infection in the bloodstream. The invasion of the bloodstream by the particular type of bacteria is referred to as a bacteremia. If the invading bacteria also release **toxins** into the bloodstream, the malady can also be called blood poisoning or septicemia. *Staphylococcus* and *Streptococcus* are typically associated with septicemia.

The bloodstream is susceptible to invasion by bacteria that may gain entry in several ways, including: via a wound or abrasion in the protective skin overlay of the body; as a result of another infection elsewhere in the body; following the introduction of bacteria during a surgical procedure; or via a needle during injection of a drug.

Depending on the identity of the infecting bacterium and on the physical state of the human host (primarily with respect to the efficiency of the immune system), bacteremic infections may not produce any symptoms. However, some infections do produce symptoms, ranging from an elevated temperature, as the immune system copes with the infection, to a spread of the infection to the heart (endocarditis or pericarditis) or the covering of nerve cells (meningitis). In more rare instances, a bacteremic infection can produce a condition known as septic shock. The latter occurs when the infection overwhelms the ability of the body's defense mechanisms to cope. Septic shock can be lethal.

Septicemic infections usually result from the spread of an established infection. Bacteremic (and septicemic) infections often arise from bacteria that are normal residents on the surface of the skin or internal surfaces, such as the intestinal tract epithelial cells. In their normal environments the bacteria are harmless and even can be beneficial. However, if they gain entry to other parts of the body, these so-called commensal bacteria can pose a health threat. The entry of these commensal bacteria into the bloodstream is a normal occurrence for most people. In the majority of people, however, the immune system is more than able to deal with the invaders. Yet if the immune system is not functioning efficiently, the invading bacteria may be able to multiply and establish an infection. Examples of conditions that compromise the immune system are another illness (such as acquired immunodeficiency syndrome and certain types of cancer), certain medical treatments such as irradiation, and the abuse of drugs or alcohol.

Examples of bacteria that are most commonly associated with bacteremic infections are *Staphylococcus, Streptococcus, Pseudomonas, Haemophilus,* and **Escherichia coli**.

The generalized location of bacteremia produces generalized symptoms. These symptoms can include a fever, chills, pain in the abdomen, nausea with vomiting, and a general feeling of ill health. Not all these symptoms are necessarily present at the same time. The nonspecific nature of the symptoms may not prompt a physician to suspect bacteremia until the infection is more firmly established. Septic shock produces more drastic symptoms, including elevated rates of breathing and heartbeat, loss of consciousness, and failure of organs throughout the body. The onset of septic shock can be rapid, so prompt medical attention is critical.

As with many other infections, bacteremic infections can be prevented by observance of proper hygienic procedures including hand washing, cleaning of wounds, and cleaning sites of injections to temporarily free the surface of living bacteria. The rate of bacteremic infections due to surgery is much less now than in the past, due to the advent of sterile surgical procedures, but is still a serious concern.

Bacterial infection does not always result in disease—even if the pathogen is virulent (able to cause disease). The steps of pathogenesis (the process of causing actual disease), can depend on a number of genetic and environmental factors. In some cases, pathogenic bacteria produce toxins released extracellularly (exotoxins) that migrate from the actual site of infection to cause damage to cells in other parts of the body.

Evidence of bacteremic infections can provide forensic investigators with valuable clues about the nature of wounds, the time wounds were inflicted, and even specifics about wound care after injury.

SEE ALSO Anthrax; Bacteria, classification; Bacteria, growth and reproduction; Bacterial resistance and response to antibacterial agents; Biological weapons, genetic identification; Biosensor technologies; Bubonic plague; Decontamination methods.

Bacterial resistance and response to antibacterial agents

An understanding of how bacteria adapt to their environment and how certain agents interact with bacteria is essential for forensic investigators and those charged with the ultimate cleaning of crime scenes. The condition of bacteria often yields important clues as to the treatment of a body after death and can even play an important part in the determination of the **cause of death**.

Bactericidal is a term that refers to the treatment of a bacterium so that the organism is killed. A bactericidal treatment is always lethal and is also referred to as sterilization. Bacteriostatic refers to a treatment that restricts the ability of the bacterium to grow.

Bacteria can develop resistance to agents intend to kill them. For example, antibiotic resistance can develop swiftly. In fact, resistance to penicillin (the first antibiotic discovered) was recognized almost immediately after introduction of the drug. As of the mid 1990s, almost 80% of all strains of *Staphylococcus aureus* were resistant to penicillin. Meanwhile, other bacteria remain susceptible to penicillin. An example is provided by Group A *Streptococcus pyogenes*.

The adaptation of bacteria to an antibacterial agent such as an antibiotic can occur in two ways. The first method is known as inherent (or natural) resistance. Gram-negative bacteria, which possess two membranes that sandwich a thin, supporting structure called the peptidoglycan (Gram positive bacteria have only one membrane and a much thicker peptidoglycan) are often naturally resistant to penicillin, for example. This is because these bacteria have another outer membrane, which makes the penetration of penicillin to its target more difficult. Sometimes when bacteria acquire resistance to an antibacterial agent, the cause is a membrane alteration that has made the passage of the molecule into the cell more difficult. This is adaptation.

The second category of adaptive resistance is called acquired resistance. This resistance is almost always due to a change in the genetic make-up of the bacterial genome. Acquired resistance can occur because of mutation or as a response by the bacteria to the selective pressure imposed by the antibacterial agent. Once the genetic alteration that confers resistance is present, it can be passed on to subsequent generations. Acquired adaptation and resistance of bacteria to some clinically important **antibiotics** has become a great problem in the last decade of the twentieth century.

Bacteria adapt to other environmental conditions as well. These include adaptations to changes in temperature, pH, concentrations of ions such as sodium, and the nature of the surrounding support. This adaptation is under tight genetic control, involving the expression of multiple genes.

Bacteria react to a sudden change in their environment by expressing, or repressing the expression of, a variety of genes. This response changes the properties of both the interior of the organism and its surface chemistry.

Another adaptation exhibited by a great many bacteria is the formation of adherent populations on solid surfaces. This mode of growth is called a biofilm. Bacteria within a biofilm and bacteria found in other niches, such as in a wound where oxygen is limited, grow and divide at a far slower speed than the bacteria found in the test tube in the laboratory. Such bacteria are able to adapt to the slower growth rate, once again by changing their chemistry and **gene** expression pattern. When presented with more nutrients, the bacteria can often very quickly resume the rapid growth and division rate of their test tube counterparts.

The phenomenon of chemotaxis is a further example of adaptation, whereby a bacterium can sense the chemical composition of the environment and either moves toward an attractive compound, or shifts direction and moves away from a compound sensed as being detrimental. Chemotaxis is controlled by more than 40 genes that code for the production of components of the flagella that propel the bacterium along, for sensory receptor proteins in the membrane, and for components that are involved in signaling a bacterium to move toward or away from a compound.

Bactericidal methods include heat, filtration, radiation, and exposure to chemicals. The use of heat is a very popular method of sterilization in a microbiology laboratory. The dry heat of an open flame incinerates microorganisms like bacteria, fungi, and yeast. The moist heat of a device like an autoclave can cause deformation of the protein constituents of the microbe, as well as causing the microbial membranes to liquefy. The effect of heat depends on the time of exposure in addition to form of heat that is supplied. For example, in an autoclave that supplies a temperature of 121° F (49.4° C), an exposure time of 15 minutes is sufficient to kill the so–called vegetative form of bacteria. However, a bacterial spore can survive this heat treatment. More prolonged exposure to the heat is necessary to ensure that the spore will not germinate into a living bacteria after autoclaving. The relationship between the temperature and the time of exposure can be computed mathematically.

A specialized form of bactericidal heat treatment is called pasteurization, after the inventor of the process, Louis Pasteur. Pasteurization achieves total killing of the bacterial population in fluids such as milk and fruit juices without changing the taste or visual appearance of the product.

Another bactericidal process, albeit an indirect one, is filtration. Filtration is the physical removal of bacteria from a fluid by the passage of the fluid through the filter. The filter contains holes of a certain diameter. If the diameter is less than the smallest dimension of a bacterium, the bacterium will be retained on the surface of the filter it contacts. The filtered fluid is sterile with respect to bacteria. Filtration is indirectly bactericidal since the bacteria that are retained on the filter will, for a time, be alive. However, because they are also removed from their source of nutrients, the bacteria will eventually die.

Exposure to electromagnetic radiation such as ultraviolet radiation is a direct means of killing bacteria. The energy of the radiation severs the strands of deoxyribonucleic acid in many locations throughout the bacterial genome. With only one exception, the damage is so severe that repair is impossible. The exception is the radiation resistant bacterial genus called *Deinococcus*. This genus has the ability to piece together the fragments of **DNA** in their original order and enzymatically stitch the pieces into a functional whole.

Exposure to chemicals can be bactericidal. For example, the gas ethylene oxide can sterilize objects. Solutions containing alcohol can also kill bacteria by dissolving the membrane(s) that surround the contents of the cell. Laboratory benches are routinely "swabbed" with an ethanol solution to kill bacteria that might be adhering to the bench top. Care must be taken to ensure that the alcohol is left in contact with the bacteria for a suitable time (e.g., minutes).

Otherwise, bacteria might survive and can even develop resistance to the bactericidal agent. Other chemical means of achieving bacterial death involve the alteration of the pH, salt or sugar concentrations, and oxygen level.

Antibiotics are designed to be bactericidal. Penicillin and its derivatives are bactericidal because they act on the peptidoglycan layer of Gram-positive and Gram-negative bacteria. By preventing the assembly of the peptidoglycan, penicillin antibiotics destroy the ability of the peptidoglycan to bear the stress of osmotic pressure that acts on a bacterium. The bacterium ultimately explodes. Other antibiotics are lethal because they prevent the manufacture of DNA or protein. Unlike bactericidal methods such as the use of heat, bacteria are able to acquire resistance to antibiotics. Indeed, such resistance by clinically-important (i.e., capable of causing disease) bacteria is a major problem in hospitals.

Bacteriostatic agents prevent the growth of bacteria. Refrigeration can be bacteriostatic for those bacteria that cannot reproduce at such low temperatures. Sometimes a bacteriostatic state is advantageous as it allows for the long-term storage of bacteria. Ultra-low temperature freezing and lyophilization (the controlled removal of water from a sample) are means of preserving bacteria. Another bacteriostatic technique is the storage of bacteria in a solution that lacks nutrients, but which can keep the bacteria alive. Various buffers kept at refrigeration temperatures can keep bacteria alive for weeks.

SEE ALSO Anthrax; Bacterial biology; Bacteria, classification; Bacteria, growth and reproduction; Biological weapons, genetic identification; Biosensor technologies; Bubonic plague; Decontamination methods.

Michael Baden

1934–
AMERICAN
FORENSIC PATHOLOGIST

Michael Baden, a longtime **medical examiner** for New York City, has helped publicize the work of forensic pathologists through his books and television appearances. Baden has focused particularly on the need for physicians trained in **pathology** to conduct autopsies and the importance of developing national standards for investigating unnatural deaths. He has served as an expert witness in several high-profile cases, including the examination of the remains of Tsar Nicholas of Russia, the death of comedian John Belushi, and the re-autopsy of civil rights leader Medgar Evers.

Baden was born in the Bronx section of New York City to Jewish immigrants from Russian Poland. A troubled juvenile, he was sent away at the age of six to live at the Hawthorne Reform School in Westchester County, New York. His housemother worked at the Bellevue Psychiatric Hospital and she impressed the boy by telling him that Bellevue was a place were great people cured the less fortunate. After paying a visit to Bellevue in 1947, Baden decided to become a physician.

As a medical student at the New York University School of Medicine, Baden planned to become an internist. The New York City Medical Examiner shared the morgue next door to Bellevue. Advised by a professor to examine the bodies, Baden began to assist in autopsies. Few other medical students had an interest in forensic pathology, which was widely regarded in the medical profession at the time as a refuge for alcoholics and others who could not meet the grade. Following his 1959 graduation, Baden interned in New York City hospitals while moonlighting as a medical examiner.

From 1961 to 1986, Baden worked as forensic pathologist in the Office of the Chief Medical Examiner in New York City. He and his colleagues examined the causes of death from auto accidents, which helped to demonstrate that seatbelts were important for preventing fatal injuries. Baden also helped to establish how suicides in jails, the most frequent **cause of death** there, could be prevented. Most jailhouse suicides were accomplished by hanging; Baden recommended putting up bars that would collapse under weight and taking away shoelaces and belts from prisoners.

Baden is one of only about three hundred fulltime forensic pathologists in the country. He served as the Chief Medical Examiner of New York City from 1978 to 1979. Conflict ensued in this capacity when Baden envisioned the office as scientific and apolitical, and the District Attorney considered the medical examiner an important arm of the prosecution.

Most coroners are untrained in medicine. Most jurisdictions require only that a **coroner** be an American citizen and over 21 years of age. Additionally, there are no national standards for investigating unnatural deaths and for protecting, documenting, and collecting **evidence** at the crime scene. The lack of standards has led to cases such as that of President John F. Kennedy, who was examined by hospital pathologists who had no **training** or

Michael Baden, New York police's forensic pathologist, examines evidence from a crime: a 9mm semiautomatic with bullets, a skull, and x rays. © NAJLAH FEANNY/CORBIS SABA

experience with gunshot wounds. Baden became the first forensic pathologist to examine Kennedy's wounds via photographs as the chairman of the Forensic Pathology Panel of the U.S. Congress Select Committee on Assassinations that investigated the deaths of President John F. Kennedy as well as the **murder** of Dr. Martin Luther King, Jr.

Baden has conducted more than 20,000 autopsies during his career. From 1981 to 1983, he was employed as the Deputy Chief Medical Examiner for Suffolk County in New York. He is currently co-director for the Medico-legal Investigative Unit of the New York State Police. As a forensic pathologist with a private practice, Baden travels around the country providing expert witness testimony. He testified for the defense in the case of Claus Von Bulow, accused of murdering his wife with an injection of insulin, and the trial of actor Marlon Brando's son Christian, who shot his sister's lover. He participated in the **exhumation** of the body of civil rights worker Medgar Evers when

Mississippi decided to re-open the murder case thirty years after Evers' 1963 killing by a white supremacist. Baden's popular reputation has given him a second career as a media star. He has authored two popular books on pathology for a lay audience and regularly appears on **television shows** devoted to autopsies.

SEE ALSO Autopsy; Crime scene investigation; Expert witnesses; Kennedy assassination; Pathology.

Matthew Baillie

10/27/1761–9/23/1823
SCOTTISH
PHYSICIAN

Over the course of his career, Matthew Baillie worked as a physician, lecturer, and author. While he worked at both St. George's Hospital and in his own private practice, he also served as the physician for many members of the royal family, including King George III.

Born in Lanarkshire in 1761, Baillie attended the University of Glasgow. In pursuit of a career in **medicine**, he moved to London to live with and study under his uncle William Hunter, the celebrated anatomist. At Hunter's home Baillie attended public lectures and was given private instruction by his uncle. In London he also attended Balliol College, Oxford, graduating in 1786. Three years later he received an M.D. from the school as well, and became a fellow of the Royal College of Physicians.

In 1787 Baillie was hired as a physician at St. George's Hospital, where he worked for a number of years. During this time, he also gave many lectures on various medical subjects. At the age of 36, Baillie left St. George's and devoted himself exclusively to his private medical practice. In this capacity, he became the physician of King George III, Princess Amelia, and Princess Charlotte. Baillie also continued to serve both wealthy and poor patients alike.

Baillie is perhaps best known as the author of *The Morbid Anatomy of Some of the Most Important Parts of the Human Body*, published in 1793. The book is credited with establishing morbid anatomy as an independent science. In it Baillie provides the first clinical descriptions of cirrhosis of the liver, gastric ulcers, and chronic obstructive pulmonary emphysema, and gives one of the clearest descriptions written about the pulmonary lesions of tuberculosis.

SEE ALSO Careers in forensic science.

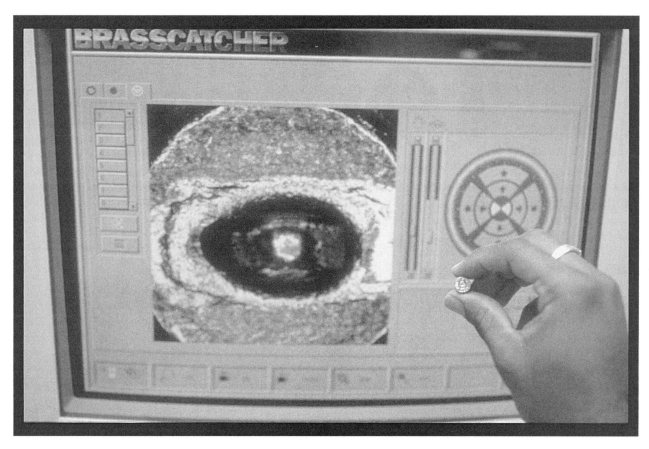

A technician at the Bureau of Alcohol, Tobacco, and Firearms uses computer assisted technology to identify the patterns made by a particluar type of bullet. © STEVE LISS/CORBIS SYGMA

Ballistic fingerprints

A ballistic fingerprint is the unique pattern of markings left by a specific firearm on ammunition it has discharged. The technique has been used in **forensic science** to match a bullet obtained from a victim to a particular gun. This can help determine the **cause of death** as well as being instrumental in criminal prosecutions.

In 1997, the National Integrated Ballistics Identification Network, established by the Federal Bureau of Investigation and the Bureau of Alcohol, Tobacco, and Firearms, made 8,800 ballistic fingerprint matches, which resulted in the linking of 17,600 crimes. As of 2000, two states—Maryland and New York—had passed laws requiring the ballistic fingerprinting of weapons. Upon selling a firearm, a dealer was required to provide the state with a spent round from the gun, so as to establish a permanent record of the gun's ballistic fingerprint. Other states followed suit.

Despite this, the use of ballistic fingerprinting as a tool of forensics is controversial. On the one hand, many law-enforcement officials insist that ballistic fingerprints are as useful as ordinary fingerprints in linking a round of ammunition to a specific gun. Police used ballistic fingerprints, in part, to link the shootings of numerous people in the Washington, D.C., area during the fall of 2002 to the accused "Beltway snipers," John Muhammad and John Lee Malvo. The case brought ballistic fingerprinting to national attention.

On the other hand, many advocates of gun-owners' rights maintain that these fingerprints change so much over time that they are largely useless as a means of matching a spent round to a firearm.

Criminologist Daniel W. Webster, director of the Center for Gun Policy and Research at Johns Hopkins University in Baltimore, is an advocate of ballistic fingerprints as a tool of forensics. In *Comprehensive Ballistic Fingerprinting of New Guns*, Webster cited research suggesting that although ballistic fingerprints change over time, these changes do not prevent authorities from establishing a match between a firearm and a spent round.

However, technical factors may limit the current use of ballistic fingerprinting in forensic science. An independent study contracted by the California Department of Justice and conducted by the National Institute for Forensic Science reported in early 2003 that ballistic fingerprinting was impractical. Testing revealed that the computer software used to match the discharge pattern on a bullet with a specific firearm was too inaccurate to be reliable.

SEE ALSO Ballistics; Bomb damage, forensic assessment; Crime scene investigation; Firearms; Gunshot residue.

Ballistics

When a forensic investigation involves a shooting, ballistics becomes an important facet of the investigation. Ballistics is a term that refers to the science of the flight path of a bullet. The flight path includes the movement of the bullet down the barrel of the firearm following detonation and its path through both the air and the target.

Tracing the path of a bullet is important in a forensic examination. It can reveal from what direction the bullet was fired, which can be vital in corroborating the course of events in the crime or accident.

It is an obvious truism that the distance that a bullet can travel depends on its speed. A higher speed imparts more energy to the bullet. The frictional resistance of the air and the downward pull of gravity will take longer to slow the bullet's flight, as compared to a bullet moving at a lower initial velocity.

Generally, a bullet fired from a rifle will carry more energy than a bullet fired from a handgun. This is because the stronger firing chamber of a rifle is able to withstand the increased explosive power of a larger quantity of powder that would likely rupture the barrel of the handgun. Detonation of the powder in a rifle or handgun supplies the thrust to propel the bullet down the barrel.

Expansion of the exploding gunpowder generates pressure, which is measured as the force of the explosion that pushes on the area of the bullet's base. This area is essentially the diameter of the barrel of the firearm, which remains constant. Thus, the explosive energy that passes to the bullet depends on the mass of the bullet multiplied by the force of the explosion multiplied by the time that the force is applied (i.e., the time the bullet is in the barrel). A longer barrel will produce a faster moving bullet.

Once a bullet leaves the rifle or gun barrel, the aforementioned frictional and gravitational forces begin to slow its speed, producing a downward arc of flight. The frictional force is affected by the bullet's shape. A blunt shape will present more surface area to the air than will a very pointed bullet.

Another factor that affects the flight of a bullet is called yaw. As in an orbiting spacecraft or a football tossed through the air, yaw causes a bullet to turn sideways or tumble in flight. This behavior is decreased when the object spins as it moves forward (the spiraling motion of a football). The barrel of a rifle or gun contains grooves that cause the bullet to spin. More damage results from a bullet that is tumbling rather than moving in a tight spiral.

The shape of a typical bullet—much like a football with one end blunt instead of tapered—is a compromise that reduces air resistance while still retaining the explosive energy that allows the bullet to damage the target.

The composition of a bullet is also important. Lead is commonly used to form the core of bullets. However, because it tends to deform, the blending in of other metals (typically antimony and copper) produces a bullet that can withstand the pressure of flight and impart high energy to the target upon impact.

Copper is often used to jacket the inner lead core of a bullet. However, some bullets are deliberately made without this full metal jacket. Instead, the bullet has a tip made of lead or a tip that is hollow or very blunt. These bullets deform and break apart on impact, producing more damage to the target than is produced by a single piece of metal. This is because the bullet's energy is dissipated within a very short distance in the tissue.

Forensic and medical examiners are able to assess the nature of tissue damage in a victim and gain an understanding of the nature of the bullet used.

A bullet produces tissue damage in three ways. First, a bullet can shred (lacerate) or crush tissue or bone. Bullets moving at relatively low velocity do most of their damage this way. Fragmentation of bone can cause further damage, as the bone shards themselves become missiles.

The second form of damage is known as cavitation. This damage is produced by the forward movement of air or tissue in the wake of the bullet. The wound that is produced by the bullet is destructively broadened by the force of the moving air or tissue. In a tissue, this produces even more structural damage.

Third, the air at the front and sides of a very fast moving bullet can become compressed. The explosive relaxation of the compression generates a damaging shock wave that can be several hundred atmospheres in pressure. Fluid-filled organs such as the bladder, heart, and bowel can be burst by the pressure.

Recovery of bullets can be a very useful part of forensic ballistics. A variety of bullet designs exist, some that are specific to the firearm. Furthermore, the scouring of a bullet's surface as it encounters the grooves of the firearm barrel can produce a distinctive pattern that enables a bullet to be matched with the firearm. A weapon recovered from a suspect can be test fired and the bullet pattern compared with a bullet recovered from the scene to either implicate or dismiss involvement of the firearm in the crime.

This aspect of ballistics was crucial in convicting John Allen Muhammad and John Lee Malvo of the 10 sniper murders and the wounding of three others in the Washington, D.C. area that occurred during three weeks in October of 2002.

SEE ALSO Bullet lead analysis; Bullet track; Crime scene investigation; Gunshot residue; Firearms.

Victor Balthazard

1/1/1872–1950
FRENCH
PROFESSOR IN FORENSIC MEDICINE

In the early 1900s, Victor Balthazard worked as a professor in forensic medicine at the Sorbonne University in Paris, France. Together with the French physicist Pierre Curie (1859–1906) and his Sorbonne colleague Charles Bouchard (1831–1915), they collaborated on the physiological action of radium (radon) emanation on mice and guinea pigs.

At this time, the Canadian physician Wilfred Derome (1877–1931) worked as director of laboratories at the Notre Dame Hospital in Montreal, Quebec, in close proximity to the courthouse where he was frequently summoned to provide expert testimony. Recognizing his need for more training, Derome traveled to France in 1909 to obtain a diploma in forensic medicine at the Sorbonne under professor Balthazard. Because of Balthazard's interest in firearms, Derome also became competent in this discipline and, upon his return, he successfully lobbied the Attorney General of Quebec on the importance of the new specialty of forensics. In July 1914, the Premier announced the establishment of the Laboratoire de Recherches Medico-Légales (research laboratory for forensic medicine).

Body hair carries pieces of circumstantial forensic evidence. Examining hair under an optical or an electronic microscope can help identify the nature of a crime, and its condition reveals information on the circumstances of a crime. Thus, the identification of a person might eventually be possible through particular characteristics such as hair dyes or hair diseases. The first forensic hair studies are recorded by the German physician Rudolph Virchow (1821–1902). In 1910, however, Victor Balthazard and Marcelle Lambert published the first comprehensive hair study "Le poil de l'homme et des animaux" ("The hair of man and animals"), which includes numerous microscopic studies of hairs from most animals. As a result, during one of the first legal cases ever involving hairs, French citizen Rosella Rousseau was prompted to confess to murder in 1910.

Victor Balthazard is credited for his statistical model of fingerprint individuality, published in 1911. His model is simplistic and ignores relevant information, but is the foundation for later improved statistical models. Balthazard's work was the basis for Locard's Tripartite Rule, referring to statistical models supporting quantifiable thresholds for friction ridge individualization.

In 1912 Balthazard asserted that machine tools used to make gun barrels never leave exactly the same markings. After studying images of gun barrels and bullets, he reasoned that every gun barrel leaves a signature set of etched grooves on each bullet fired through it. Another milestone in firearms identification history occurred when Balthazard devised a number of procedures to match fired bullets to the firearms from which they were fired by taking an elaborate series of photographs of test fired bullets from the firearm as well as evidence bullets. The photographs were then carefully enlarged, and the observed markings compared. Balthazard applied these same specialized photographic techniques to the examination and identification of cartridge casings using firing pin, breech face, ejector, and extractor marks, too, and he was among the first to attempt to individualize a bullet to a weapon.

It took Balthazard another decade to advance ballistics, i.e. the study of the functioning of firearms, the flight of the bullet, and the effects of different types of ammunition. In the early 1920s, Balthazard's work had evolved so much that court cases and literature continued at a fast pace. In 1922 two articles were published in the recognized French *Comptes Rendus de l'Académie des Sciences* describing the perfected technique for determination of the identification of projectiles. One year later, other articles appeared in the French journal *Annales de Médicine Légale* investigating fissures of the **skull** by revolver bullets at short range, and the identification of fired bullets and shells. Eventually, ballistics was formally established in 1923 in crime investigation, and the United States Bureau of Forensic Ballistics was established in 1925.

SEE ALSO Ballistic fingerprints; Ballistics; Bullet track; Civil court, forensic evidence; Computer modeling; Fingerprint; Firearms; Hair analysis; Identification; Locard's exchange principle; Medicine; Photography.

Barbiturates

The term barbiturate is a name given to a group of drugs that function by depressing the activity of the central nervous system. Their principal effect is to reduce stress and bring the user a feeling of calm. Often, this sedation can help someone fall asleep. This is why barbiturates are often termed sleeping pills.

Barbiturates were first made over a century ago by the Bayer laboratories in Germany. They take their name from barbital, which was the first barbiturate used medically, in the first decade of the twentieth century.

Aside from their stress relief, the nervous system alteration induced by barbiturates can also be beneficial in the management of diseases like **epilepsy**.

Of the dozen or so barbiturates still in common medical use, the speed at which the effects are produced and the length of time the effects persist are the distinguishing features between the drugs.

Some barbiturates produce an effect within seconds of being taken. Others require more time to act but last longer. Finally, those used for sedation before an operation can last for hours.

Barbiturates are important to forensic scientists when they are present in **blood** samples in excess amounts. This can occur accidentally, since the effective dose of many of the drugs is not too different from a dose that causes harm. One well-known victim of an accidental overdose of sleeping pills was the musician Jimi Hendrix. As well, a barbiturate overdose can be deliberately administered. When present in excessive amounts, the drugs can cause debilitating changes. Sedation can even be so severe that coma and death result.

Forensic investigators can be interested in determining if barbiturates were a factor in someone's illness or death. Recollections of the victim's behavior can be helpful in determining the involvement of barbiturates. For example, side effects of an overdose include slurred speech and unsteady balance. Admittedly, these are also symptoms of excessive alcohol consumption.

More definitive evidence of barbiturate use comes from the chemical demonstration of the drug in tissue samples. Because most barbiturates tend to accumulate in fat deposits in the body, to be released at varying rates depending on the specific drug, a barbiturate may be detectable in tissue specimens recovered even some time after death.

SEE ALSO Amphetamines; Analytical instrumentation; Autopsy; Death, cause of; Narcotic; Psychotropic drugs.

John G. Bartlett

2/12/1937–
AMERICAN
PHYSICIAN

John G. Bartlett is known as one of the founding directors of the Center for Civilian Biodefense Strategies in 1997. Under the guidance of Bartlett and D.A. Henderson, the Center's objective is to stop the development and use of biological weapons and to minimize the consequences to victims if such weapons are used. Today, Bartlett is a Stanhope Bayne-Jones professor of **medicine** and chief of The Johns Hopkins University (Baltimore, Maryland) School of Medicine, Division of Infectious Diseases, Department of Medicine.

In 1959 Bartlett was awarded an undergraduate degree at Dartmouth University in Hanover, New Hampshire. From there, he received his doctor of medicine (M.D.) degree in 1965 from Upstate Medical Center School of Medicine in Syracuse, New York. For the next three years, Bartlett performed his residency **training** in internal medicine, first at the Peter Bent Brigham Hospital in Boston, Massachusetts (1966–1967) and then at the University of Alabama, Birmingham (1967–1968). He began, in 1968, his fellowship training in infectious diseases at UCLA (University of California, Los Angeles) School of

Medicine and the Wadsworth Veterans Administration Hospital (Los Angeles).

Bartlett became a faculty member at UCLA and the School of Medicine, Tufts University (Boston) in 1970. Ten years later, in 1980, Bartlett transferred to The Johns Hopkins University to assume the positions he presently holds: professor in the School of Medicine (and joint appointment in the Epidemiology Department) and chief of the Infectious Diseases Department. From 1980 to today, Bartlett has performed research within the areas of anaerobic infections, antibiotic-associated colitis, diarrhea, human immunodeficiency virus (HIV)/acquired immune deficiency syndrome (AIDS), pathogenic mechanisms of *Bacteroides fragilis*, and pneumonia, with clinical interests in infectious diseases, HIV primary/managed care, and HIV and hemophilia.

Members of the Center for Civilian Biodefense Strategies, with past affiliation to The Johns Hopkins University and current affiliation, as of November 1, 2003, to the University of Pittsburgh Medical Center, have used their expertise to: build a world network to improve biosecurity communications; provide independent research and analysis for the bioscience, government, national security, medicine, and public health sectors; propose, design, build, and promote systems to manage the consequences of biological attacks; promote responsible use of bioscience/biotechnology; and develop **bioterrorism** scenarios. In 2001, the Center co-sponsored the "Dark Winter" scenario at Andrews Air Force Base (Maryland), where participants responded to a hypothetical **smallpox** attack on the United States.

As the author of 41 editions of 13 books, more than 300 articles, and over 300 chapters, reviews, and letters, one of Bartlett's more recently authored books is *PDR Guide to Biological and Chemical Warfare Response*. Bartlett currently chairs the Antimicrobial Availability Task Force for the Infectious Diseases Society of America. He has been a member of such organizations as the American Society for Clinical Investigation, Anaerobe Society of America, Society of Critical Care Medicine, American College of Physicians, and Institute of Medicine. Bartlett has been on the editorial boards of such publications as *Infectious Diseases in Clinical Practice, Clinical Infectious Diseases, Medicine, American Journal of Medicine*, and *Journal of Clinical Illness*.

SEE ALSO Biological warfare, advanced diagnostics; Bioterrorism.

William Bass III

AMERICAN
FORENSIC ANTHROPOLOGIST

William ("Bill") Bass, professor emeritus of the University of Tennessee and one of the world's most renowned forensic anthropologists, is perhaps best known as the (former) custodian of "The Body Farm," also known as the University of Tennessee's Anthropology Research Facility. The **Body Farm**, as it is commonly known, is the world's only research facility dedicated solely to studying the **decomposition** of human bodies. Bill Bass started the research center with one corpse and a small piece of land in 1971.

Bass retained directorship of the University's Forensic Anthropology Center after achieving emeritus status. He has continued an active forensic consulting practice, with particular areas of expertise in estimating **time of death** and victim **identification**. He has remained a sought-after forensics public speaker well into his retirement from academia.

The Body Farm encompasses three barbed wire encircled acres not far from the University of Tennessee's Medical Center. At any given time, about forty bodies are being studied as they decompose under varying conditions; some hang from scaffolds; some are left in cage-like enclosures; some are in car trunks; some lie in the sun; some are in the shade; some are barely covered by leaves and forest debris; some are covered with brush; some are submerged in ponds; and some even occupy shallow graves.

Throughout the United States, law-enforcement agencies and graduate students of forensic anthropology have sent students and staff to the Anthropology Research Facility (informally called ARF, but publicly known as the Body Farm, particularly by readers of Patricia Cornwell's Kay Scarpetta series). The **FBI** conducts short-course trainings at the ARF each year, teaching Special Agents what to look for when they excavate areas to search for bodies. Agents learn which insects feed on human bodies, and how their activity can suggest time of death (or, more accurately, time since death).

Eventually, the skeletal remains of the Body Farm's inhabitants are collected and cleaned; sorted by age, gender, and race; numbered; and stored in boxes in an indoor lab, where they are used during student research.

Bass's work has been lauded in worldwide media; he has been profiled by CNN, featured in the *American Bar Association Journal*, the

Philadelphia Inquirer, and Reuter's News Service, among many others. Bass estimates that he has personally been involved in the **training** of at least 65% of the forensic scientists in the United States. William Bass continues to be intrigued by the study of decomposition of human bodies, and believes that much is yet to be learned. Bass views his life's work not as the study of death, but as an intriguing science experiment. Bass sees his job as marshalling all of his abilities and his knowledge, striving to see the corpse as an individual, and trying to determine exactly what happened to him or her.

SEE ALSO Ancient cases and mysteries; Anthropology; Decomposition.

Bathymetric maps

A bathymetric map represents ocean depths depending upon geographical coordinates, in much the same way a topographic map represents the altitude of the Earth's surface in given different geographic points. Bathymetric maps have provided useful forensic **evidence** in court when certain types of crimes involving the sea are committed, or disputes arise about fishing boundaries or national boundaries at sea. Bathymetric maps have also been used by treasure-seekers when investigating the sea floor to identify the most likely areas to seek sunken ships, and aided in the search for the H.M.S. *Titanic* in the 1980s.

The most common type of bathymetric map displays lines called isobaths that indicate ocean depths. Like geographical maps of the Earth's surface, bathymetric maps are usually constructed in Mercator projection. Mercator projection is a mathematical method for displaying the surface of the Earth on a flat sheet of paper or computer screen. Mercator projection maps have been used for centuries in constructing sea charts that are used for sailing in all latitudes except the polar regions. Mercator projections are not used at extreme northern and southern latitudes because of the increasing degree of map distortion (the difference between map depiction and geographical reality) as one nears the poles.

The creation of a bathymetric map for a given region depends on the amount of depth measurement data for that region. Since before the invention of the echo sounder (an instrument that uses sound waves to gauge the depth of a body of water or of objects below the surface) in the 1920s, ocean (sea) depth measurements were quite rare; these measurements were made only in isolated points, and the creation of a bathymetric map was practically impossible. Thus, the structure of the ocean floor was unknown. It should be noted, for example, that the most important structure in the Atlantic Ocean—the Middle-Atlantic ridge—was discovered and began to be studied only after World War II (1939–1945). Another important factor for creating bathymetric maps lies in the determination of the geographical coordinates of the point where the depth measurement is made. In order to produce precise maps, precise geographical determinations are needed. GPS (Global Positioning System) technology is usually used for determining the coordinates of measurement points in bathymetric mapping.

Bathymetric maps of a country's continental shelf (the gradually sloping seabed around a continental margin) are important due to the special legal status of sea areas. These maps are important not only for defining territorial waters; they are also important because the shelf is home for intensive mineral deposits and mineral output, such as oil from beneath the sea floor off the coasts of the United Kingdom, Norway, and Mexico.

The United Nations Convention on the Law of the Sea (1982) states that, "The fixed points comprising the line of the outer limits of the continental shelf on the seabed...either shall not exceed 350 nautical miles from the baselines from which the breadth of the territorial sea is measured or shall not exceed 100 nautical miles from the 2,500 meter isobath, which is a line connecting the depth of 2,500 meters." It is clear that this statement implies that bathymetric maps are essential to draw precise boundaries of continental shelves. The Law of the Sea also determines that the foot of a continental slope will be set as the point where the slope's gradient change at its base is the greatest. A gradient is the maximum angle of the surface of a slope at a given point, and on the sea floor, a gradient can only be determined with bathymetric mapping.

When constructing topographic land maps, one can always measure the altitude of any point of the surface precisely. However, when constructing bathymetric maps, it is practically impossible to determine the depth of any one point on the ocean bottom. Obviously, bathymetric maps are more precise when more depth measurements per surface area unit in the given region are available. The most precise and detailed bathymetric maps are constructed using data provided by multi-beam echo sounding. The multi-beam echo sounder is a special kind of sonar located on board the research vessel that measures the depth

Wreckage of the Russian nuclear submarine *Kursk* in dry dock at Murmansk, Russia, 2001. Explosions caused the submarine to sink in 2000 in 355 feet (108 meters) of water in the Barents Sea. © REUTERS/CORBIS

simultaneously in several points of the ocean bottom, creating a swath of data. Depth determination by this method is performed regularly every few seconds while the vessel is in motion.

Bathymetric maps are finding more and more use both for practical forensic and scientific purposes. They have documented evidence that has resulted in laws to protect the environment of a given area (for example, locating areas of the sea and estuaries stressed by pollution off South Florida in 1999). In 1997, also in South Florida, bathymetric maps served as evidence of environmental compliance violations when they illustrated detrimental changes in submerged wetlands after sea grass was removed by illegal dredging.

Bathymetric mapping is also important for projects conducted in port territories; in these cases, usually a very detailed bathymetric map is constructed. Besides their uses in international courts, bathymetric maps are important for scientists who study the development of the Earth, the formation of seas and oceans, and the changing sea floor.

SEE ALSO Accident investigations at sea; Remote sensing.

Henri-Louis Bayard

1812–10/12/1852
FRENCH
FORENSIC PATHOLOGIST

Henri-Louis Bayard was one of the earliest practitioners of legal **medicine**, known today as **forensic science**. Born in 1812 in Paris, Bayard received his medical degree in 1836, studying medicine under the well-known forensic scientist Charles Prosper Ollivier d'Angers. When d'Angers died in 1845, Bayard inherited much of his forensic practice.

Bayard's work in Paris in the years prior to 1848 was extensive, and he was highly respected as a "legal physician." In addition to his own practice of forensic science, Bayard also wrote extensively. His published works include an analysis of juvenile murders, volumes championing the importance of forensic medicine as a field of study, and a biography of his mentor. Bayard also served as co-editor of *The Annals of Public Health and Legal Medicine*, an early French professional journal in the field. Some of Bayard's publications are still valuable today; a first edition example of his 1845 work *Manuel Pratique Medicine Legale* (Manual of legal medical practices) was offered in early 2005 at an online antique book dealer for $150.00.

Bayard's most notable scientific achievements were in the realm of microscopy. While microscope pioneer Antony van Leeuwenhoek first observed and identified **sperm** cells in the seventeenth century, the use of sperm analysis in forensic science remained error-prone, with numerous techniques being practiced and no standard criteria for acceptance or rejection of findings. This led another forensic writer of the day to warn that numerous other items could resemble detached sperm heads, hence intact sperm should be considered the "gold standard" for evidentiary use. In the face of numerous, often unreliable methods, Bayard's research in microscopy led to the first reliable procedure for detecting sperm. Bayard also contributed substantially to the understanding of fiber characteristics and their use in criminal cases by documenting the distinct characteristics a wide variety of fabrics.

The overthrow of the monarchy in Paris and the accompanying unrest during 1848 spelled the end of Bayard's stay in the city, and he relocated to Chateau-Gontier, a regional capital in western France. While there he divided his time between practicing medicine and overseeing his mining interests. He died at the age of 40.

SEE ALSO Fibers; Microscopes.

Frank Bender

AMERICAN
FORENSIC SCULPTOR

Frank Bender is a man of many talents. He is a painter, a sculptor, and a forensic artist. Bender is expert at the evaluation and authentication of fine art paintings for insurance purposes. He also creates architectural models for government and agency use. In forensics, Bender is adept at traffic accident scene model reconstruction; he is an expert witness with local, state, and federal courtroom experience; he is an expert at facial reconstruction of homicide victims from **skull** to full three-dimensional face and head; he is the co-founder of The Vidocq Society, which is an international society of forensic experts dedicated to the solution of "cold cases"; he is expert at creating sculptures in order to facilitate **identification** of crime victims whose bodies are no longer recognizable; and he is perhaps best known for his age-progressed three-dimensional sculptural renderings of fugitives.

The most well known case in which Frank Bender was involved was that of John List. In November of 1971, List shot and killed his wife, his mother, and his three children. He made no effort to hide the crime, and left several notes stating that he felt a need to "free his family's souls." It took the police about a month to discover the bodies, and the only clue as to List's location was the discovery of his car in the parking lot of a nearby airport. Eventually, it was learned that List had lost his job and was feeling considerable anxiety and shame over financial pressures. Rather than choosing to deal with his difficulties and facing the consequences thereof, List opted to **murder** his entire family.

List successfully eluded capture until 1989, when the television show *America's Most Wanted* planned to air an episode about the List murder. The show's executives approached Frank Bender, and asked him to create a strong visual representation of what John List would look like 18 years after the crime. Although Bender had considerable experience in aging faces, he felt that this case also required psychological insight in order to estimate how List might look—how he might have chosen to alter his appearance after the crime; how his personality traits might have affected the aging process and his appearance across time; and, generally, how to make the sculpture "come alive." Bender enlisted the aid of criminal psychologist Richard Walter, and they collaborated on the creation of a "profile" to assist in the generation of List's age-progressed appearance.

Ultimately, they created a psychological portrait of a man who would alter his appearance very little, who would try to re-create his former life as much as possible (to include re-locating to an area less than 300 miles from his original home, although he might have traveled some distance immediately after the murders), and who would have opted not to hide a potentially identifying surgical scar behind his right ear. They decided that he would probably be a bit paunchier, have drooping jowls, deep worry lines, and a receding hairline, and they incorporated those features into the final List sculpture. The bust was completed and aired during the proposed television program. Within days of the broadcast, a call was received from a female former neighbor of a man named "Bob Clark," who felt that he might be List, and was able to offer a number of striking details. Less than two weeks after the call, **FBI** agents arrested "Clark" at his office, which was located less than 250 miles from the murder site. Bender learned that List largely resembled the bust that he had created, and was quite similar to the profile generated by he and Walter. Ultimately, List was convicted of five counts of first-degree murder and sentenced to life in prison.

SEE ALSO Ancient cases and mysteries; Art identification; Cold case; Composite drawing; Crime scene reconstruction.

Alphonse Bertillon

4/24/1853–2/13/1914
FRENCH
CRIMINOLOGIST

The French criminologist Alphonse Bertillon is often cited as a pioneer in the arena of **forensic science** and is known as the inventor of the first scientific method of identifying criminals.

Alphonse Bertillon was born in Paris, the son of Louis Adolphe Bertillon, a physician and statistician. Because of Alphonse's poor scholarship, his father sent him to Great Britain, where he was forced to rely on his own resources. Returning to France, he was inducted into the army.

In 1879, having completed his military service, Bertillon took a position as a minor clerk with the Paris Prefecture of Police. One of his duties was to copy onto small cards the recorded descriptions of the criminals apprehended each day. Bertillon realized that the short descriptions were practically useless for the purpose of identifying recidivists, or criminal repeaters. He had a general familiarity with anthropological statistics and anthropometric techniques because of the work of his father and his elder brother Jacques, also a doctor and statistician.

Bertillon devised a system of **identification** of criminals that relies on 11 bodily measurements and the color of the eyes, hair, and skin. He included standardized photographs of the criminals to his anthropometric data. He first described his system

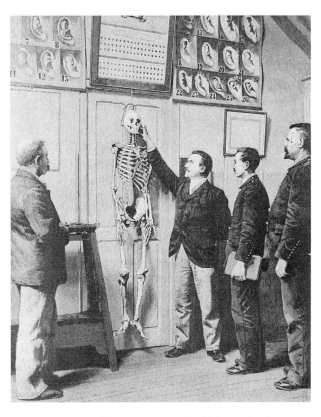

1899 photograph of French criminologist Alphonse Bertillon demonstrating his system of identifying criminals based on anthropometric measurements at police headquarters, Paris, France. © BETTMANN/CORBIS.

in *Photography: With an Appendix on Anthropometrical Classification and Identification* (1890). The Bertillon system proved successful in distinguishing first-time offenders from recidivists, and it was adopted by all advanced countries.

It is commonly believed that Bertillon was the first to recognize the value of fingerprints. Actually, that achievement must be associated with Sir **Francis Galton**, Edward Henry, and **Juan Vucetich**. However, Bertillon was the first in Europe to use fingerprints to solve a crime.

In 1888, the Department of Judicial Identity was created for the Paris Prefecture of Police; Bertillon became its head. He invented many techniques useful to criminologists. His use of **photography** was especially effective, and he did much to improve photographic techniques in **criminology**. Around the turn of the century, fingerprinting began to replace the Bertillon system and has now superseded it throughout the world.

Bertillon died Paris at the age of 60. His anthropometric method of identifying recidivists represented a first step toward scientific criminology. It is said that his work played an important role in inspiring greater confidence in police authorities and in establishing a more favorable sense of justice toward the end of the nineteenth century.

SEE ALSO Anthropometry; Automated Fingerprint Identification System (AFIS); Criminology; Photography.

Marie François Xavier Bichat

11/11/1771–7/2/1802
FRENCH
ANATOMIST, PATHOLOGIST, PHYSIOLOGIST

The French anatomist, pathologist, and physiologist Marie François Xavier Bichat was a pioneer in the field of **forensic science**. He was the founder of animal histology, the microscopic study of animal tissues.

Bichat was born in Thoirett, France. His father, a physician, was his first teacher of anatomy. He studied anatomy and surgery at Montpellier and Lyons and later served as an assistant to P. J. Desault, a famous physician at the Hôtel-Dieu, a hospital in Paris. In 1799, Bichat, after the death of Desault, became physician at the Hôtel-Dieu. From 1800 onward, he abandoned surgery and did only research in anatomy, performing as many as 600 autopsies in a single year. He investigated the structure of the body generally, rather than studying particular organs as separate entities. He broke down the organs into their common elemental materials, for which he introduced the term "tissues."

Bichat rejected the notion of iatrochemistry, the assumption that disorders in human health were caused by an imbalance in the chemical relations of fluids in the body. He also rejected Stahl's animism, which maintained that there is a special spirit of life. Bichat was a follower of Albrecht von Haller's philosophy of vitalism, which states that the body possesses some truly vital functions such as motion, communication, and sensibility, while other characteristics of the body are not vital. In other words, he rejected the old theory that life is a collection of subtle fluids and maintained rather that life is a result of a combination of vitality and the vital functions of various tissues of the body. Bichat also rejected the reductionist philosophy, which states that all biological phenomena have to be reducible to the laws of physics and chemistry—an attitude prevalent in his own time. Bichat's definition was that life consists of the sum of functions by which death is resisted. One

of his most interesting works is *Physiological Researches on Life and Death*.

Bichat's experimental work had great influence and was long quoted as a model of experimental exactitude and penetrating insight. In this context it is interesting to note that Bichat steadfastly refused to make use of the most advanced experimental tool for anatomy, namely, the microscope. His frenetic activity weakened him, and in 1802, after a fall from the Hôtel-Dieu's staircase, he contracted a fever and died on July 22; he was only 31 years old.

SEE ALSO Anatomical nomenclature; Autopsy; Pathology.

Bindle paper

Bindle paper is one of the tools that has long been used by forensic examiners to collect **evidence** and transport the evidence so that none of the contents are lost or contaminated. While many sophisticated techniques of forensic analysis and detection have emerged, the simple use of bindle paper remains an important part of an examiner's repertoire.

Typically, bindle paper is used for so-called **trace evidence** such as **fibers**, hair, paint chips, crystallized or dust-like material such as drugs, or other tiny particles. This material is light and can be difficult to see, which increases the chances that it can go missing if not carefully stored.

Bindle paper is nothing more than a clean sheet of paper that is folded in a defined manner in a series of steps. An 8 x 12 inch sheet of paper is a convenient size to use. And can be easily transported to the scene of the accident or crime.

In order to house (place) the evidence, the flat sheet of paper is first lightly folded in thirds horizontally and vertically to create nine similarly sized squares. Next, the vertical creases are folded, with the left hand side of the paper folded first, followed by the right hand side. The bottom square is folded upward. At this point the evidence is placed into the opening at the top edge of the paper. The top square is then folded down and the edge is inserted into the opening present in the lower folded square.

If done correctly, the evidence is secured inside the folded paper, which is then secured shut with tape. The package is never stapled shut, as this introduces holes through which the evidence might escape or contaminating air or moisture can enter.

At this point the bindle paper package can be put into an envelope for transport to the forensic laboratory. The folding design of bindle paper is preferred over an envelope. The manufactured corners, folds, and opening of the latter can all be places where evidence can be lost. Furthermore, the use of paper for trace evidence is preferred over plastic containers for evidence that can pick up an electrostatic charge, is moist, or which may require genetic analysis.

Biodetectors

Biodetectors, which are used to detect the presence of biological material, can be used in forensics to detect microorganisms or some of their components in material and tissue recovered after death (post-mortem samples).

More specifically, biodetectors are analytical devices that combine the precision and selectivity of biological systems with the processing power of microelectronics. These detectors typically consist of a biological recognition system, usually enzymes or binding proteins immobilized on a surface acting as a physico-chemical transducer. One typical example of a biodetector is the immunosensor, which uses antibodies as the biorecognition system. In addition to enzymes and antibodies, the recognition systems can consist of nucleic acids, whole bacteria and other single-celled organisms, and even tissues of higher organisms. Specific interactions between the target molecule or analyte and the complementary biorecognition layer produce a detectable physico-chemical change, which can then be measured by the detector.

The detection system can take many forms, depending upon the parameters being measured. Electrochemical, optical, mass, or thermal changes are the most common parameters providing both qualitative or quantitative data.

In recent years, the emphasis on measures to combat terrorism has led to the development of techniques that could be useful in **forensic science**. For example, a microarray of fluorescent labeled nucleic acids immobilized on a support has been developed by researchers at Argonne National Laboratory. The intended application for the "bacillus microchip" is the detection of *Bacillus anthracis* (the **anthrax** agent). It would distinguish *B. anthracis* from other related bacteria, such as *B. thuringiensis*, *B. subtilis*, and *B. cereus* and also indicate whether the organism is alive or dead by detecting **DNA** when there are no RNA matches. However, the same technique could be applied to the detection of other microorganisms in post-mortem samples.

A number of new fast, reliable, and portable DNA detection devices have been developed that can prepare and test samples within a very short time. Devices consisting of cell disruptors, capable of breaking bacterial **spores** and extracting DNA that is then used to identify the species of organism, are being tried. Some companies have incorporated an automated sample preparation scheme and coupled it with a microfluidic "lab on a chip" device for detecting microorganisms on the basis of their DNA sequence. The system can reduce a laboratory preparation procedure that can take six hours to just 30 minutes. The chip contains tiny channels, valves, and chambers through which milliliters of sample can be pumped and concentrated into a microliter volume. Any bacterial cells are broken ultrasonically and their DNA is extracted, amplified by **PCR (polymerase chain reaction)** and sequenced.

A DNA-based biochip designed by Northwestern University detects DNA sequences that are specific for pathogenic microorganisms. The chip initially contains very short single strands of DNA between two small electrodes. The DNA strands are complementary to DNA sequences from a specific pathogen. When DNA from that pathogen comes into contact with the chip, it hybridizes with the DNA on the chip. To detect the hybridization, further pieces of DNA are added to the system and these are complementary to the sections of pathogen DNA that have not hybridized. The additional DNA pieces contain gold particles that, on successful hybridization, form a bridge of conducting metal linking the two electrodes. The bridge completes an electrical circuit and triggers a signal.

SEE ALSO Anthrax, investigation of the 2001 murders; Bacterial biology; Biosensor technologies; Pathogens; RFLP (restriction fragment length polymorphism).

Biohazard bag

A biohazard bag is a specially designed plastic or paper bag that is used to collect and transport **evidence** from a crime or accident scene to another site, such as the laboratory, where subsequent analyses can be done.

Samples such as **blood**, fabric, bullets, and other pieces of evidence cannot be analyzed at the scene. But if the transport to the laboratory alters the

Military personnel in hazmat suits handle a biohazard bag between the Longworth and Rayburn House Office Buildings on Capitol Hill in Washington, 2001, after the buildings were swept for anthrax. © REUTERS/CORBIS

sample composition (i.e., contamination, **decomposition**) then the value of the sample as a legally admissible piece of evidence is destroyed.

The use of a biohazard bag prevents such contamination of a sample. As well, in the case of a potentially contaminated or poisonous sample, the handler is kept safe.

Biohazard bags vary in their dimensions and capacity. Typical dimensions are 6 x 9, 8 x 10, and 12 x 15 inches. However, several features are often preserved. They are similar to the kitchen-variety sandwich bag, in having a "zip-lock" type of closure. This eliminates the need for an external enclosure and allows a bag to be closed when a handler is wearing gloves.

Similar to some household plastic sealable bags, biohazard bags can have plastic strips positioned above the zip-lock. They provide material that the user can grasp when opening the bag, without having to handle the actual storage area. This allows a bag to be easily and repeatedly opened, especially when the user is wearing gloves, and lessens ripping of the bag.

A common feature of biohazard bags is their rugged construction. In contrast to the single layered sandwich bags, biohazard bags can have three layers of polypropylene or other plastic polymer. This reduces the chance of leakage and puncture.

Most biohazard bags will have a roughened portion on the surface that allows for writing on the surface. Written **identification** of all retrieved evidence is essential. Bags can also have an external pouch to house related paperwork.

Sharp objects that could puncture plastic will typically be stored first in a paper bag or other receptacle instead of a plastic bag. Biohazard bags made of Kraft paper are commercially available.

The choice of paper instead of plastic can be advantageous in other ways. Paper allows a sample to remain dry during transport. In contrast, condensation that can form in a plastic bag transported at a warm temperature can be deleterious to, for example, blood-stained fabric.

SEE ALSO Crime scene investigation; Evidence.

Biological warfare, advanced diagnostics

Forensic analysis techniques are often used for other applications. For example, various chromatographic techniques can be used to examine an array of materials, including **blood** and other forensically-relevant samples.

Technologies that are used to detect biological warfare agents can be relevant to forensic analyses. These include the detection of living bacteria, based on the metabolic conversion of one compound to another by the organisms. Indeed, one novel technology can detect the distinctive aromas emitted by bacteria when they metabolize certain compounds.

Toxins that are produced by bacteria including *Bacillus anthracis* (the agent of **anthrax**) and *Clostridium botulinum* (which causes the food-borne illness of botulism) can be detected using antibodies targeted specifically for the particular toxin protein. Other poisons (such as **ricin**) are likewise detectable.

In the United States, the development of diagnostic capabilities for biological warfare is a government concern. The Advanced Diagnostics Program is funded by the Defense Advanced Research Projects Agency of the United States government (DARPA). Its objective is to develop tools and medicines to detect and treat biological and chemical weapons in the field at concentrations low enough to prevent illness. Challenges to this task include minimizing the labor, equipment, and time for identifying biological and chemical agents.

One area of interest includes development of field tools that can identify many different agents. To accomplish this goal, several groups funded under the advanced diagnostics program have developed field-based biosensors that can detect a variety of analytes, including fragments of **DNA**, various hormones and proteins, bacteria, salts, and antibodies. These biosensors are portable, run on external power sources, and require very little time to complete analyses.

A second focus of the advanced diagnostics project is the **identification** of known and unknown or bioengineered **pathogens** and development of early responses to infections. Many viruses act by destroying the ability of cells to replicate properly. One group funded under the advanced diagnostics program is studying the enzyme inosine 5′-monophosphate dehydrogenase (IMPDH), which produces products that are required for synthesizing nucleic acids, such as RNA and DNA, both of which are essential for proper cell replication. This group seeks to develop novel drugs based on IMPDH, which can cross into cells and thwart viral infection.

A final goal is to develop the ability to continuously monitor the body for **evidence** of infection. Researchers are addressing this goal in two ways. The first involves engineering monitoring mechanisms that are internal to the body. In particular, groups funded under the initiative are developing bioengineered white blood cells to detect infection from within the body. Often genetic responses to infection occur within minutes of infection, so analysis of blood cells provides a very quick indication of the presence of a biological threat. The second method involves the development of a wearable, non-invasive diagnostic device that detects a broad-spectrum of biological and chemical agents.

SEE ALSO Aflatoxin; Bacterial biology; Bioterrorism.

Biological weapons, genetic identification

The ability to use microorganisms and their components as weapons has been a reality for decades. Individual countries and organizations such as the United Nations have mounted efforts to detect the use and presence of microbial weapons. A recent example is the effort by United Nations and United States inspectors to detect **evidence** of microbial weapons in Iraq in the aftermath of the two Gulf Wars.

Initiatives like the aforementioned represent the use of **forensic science**. Traditional forensic investigations relied on the use of techniques that required the growth of the target microorganism. This approach has limitations. For example, the growth conditions selected might not be suitable to permit the growth of the target microbe. Furthermore, the laboratory facilities required, especially for the **culture** of highly infectious organisms, may not be widely available.

The use of genetic techniques of **identification** represents a promising forensic approach. Genetic technologies can be useful in the detection of biological weapons. Of particular note is the **polymerase chain reaction**, or **PCR**, which uses select enzymes to make copies of genetic material. Within a working day, a target sequence of genetic material can be amplified to numbers that are detectable by laboratory tests such as gel **electrophoresis**. If the target sequence of nucleotides is unique to the microorganism (e.g., a **gene** encoding a toxin), then PCR can be used to detect a specific microorganism from among the other organisms present in the sample.

Hand-held PCR detectors that have been used by United Nations inspectors in Iraq during their weapons inspections efforts of 2002–2003 purportedly can detect a single living *Bacillus anthracis* bacterium (the agent of **anthrax**) in an average kitchen-sized room.

The sequence of components that comprise the genetic material (genome) of a microorganism can also be deduced using techniques such as electrophoresis. Once a sequence is known, it can be compared to the many bacterial, viral, protozoan, and other microbial sequences in databases in order to determine if the deduced sequence resembles a catalogued sequence.

SEE ALSO Anthrax, investigation of the 2001 murders; Biosensor technologies; Chemical and biological detection technologies; Nucleic Acid Analyzer (HANAA); PCR (polymerase chain reaction); RFLP (restriction fragment length polymorphism); STR (short tandem repeat) analysis; Toxins.

Biometric eye scans

The **identification** of a victim or suspect of a crime can result from comparison of information collected during a forensic examination with information residing in various data bases. One example includes fingerprints. The **Integrated Automated Fingerprint Identification System** that is maintained by the Federal Bureau of Investigation is a repository for millions of **fingerprint** patterns and other information. Another example is the pattern obtained from a scan of the retina and iris, both parts of the eye.

The retina is the neural part of the eye responsible for vision. The pattern of blood vessels serving the retina is unique to an individual, and is as unique as fingerprints. The chance that two people will have the same iris pattern is estimated to be one in 10^{78}.

The technology that scans the retina is known as retinal scanning. The true target for the scan is the capillary pattern in the retina. The process relies on generating images of the retina using a low intensity light source. In 1930s retinal capillary patterns were suggested to be unique, but the technology to use this

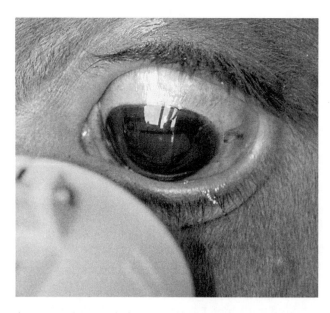

A steer receives a retinal scan used by a meat company to better track the cow's life history to assure consumers that the beef the company processes is safe to eat. AP/WIDE WORLD PHOTOS. REPRODUCED BY PERMISSION.

information was developed much later. Although military and high-security use of photographic retinal scans began decades earlier, by 1985, retinal scan technology became available for computerized biometric identification and commercial security use.

Retinal scans are just one of the biometric methods using the eye for personal identification. Two years after the first retinal scanner was developed, in 1987, Leonard Flom and Aram Safir patented the use of iris patterns as a personal identifier. However, it was not until 1994 when John Daugman developed the technology for iris scanning. Since then iris scanning technology began to challenge the retinal scans. Currently a number of companies claiming that they perform retinal scanning, in reality are performing iris scans.

Retinal scans are based on the presence of the fine network of capillaries supplying retina with oxygen and nutrients. These vessels absorb light and can be easily visualized with proper illumination. Retinal scans require close contact of user and scanner, a perfect alignment of the eye with a scanner, and no movement of the eye. The examiner is required keep the subject's eye within half an inch (1 cm) of the instrument. The subject must focus on a little green light (to properly align the eye) and avoid blinking. A low intensity coherent light is then transmitted through the eye and the reflected image of the retinal capillary pattern is recorded by the computer.

A frequent flyer has his iris scanned at Boston's Logan Airport in a 2004 trial program allowing frequent fliers to cut down on their airplane boarding times, after submitting to fingerprinting, iris scanning, and a background check. AP/WIDE WORLD PHOTOS. REPRODUCED BY PERMISSION.

Although retinal patterns are generally thought to be constant during a person's life, they can change in case of diabetes, glaucoma, retinal degenerative disorders or cataracts. Therefore, although retinal scans are nearly 100% accurate, they cannot be used as a universal security measure without making allowances for normal age-related physiological changes.

An initial scan (enrollment) takes a minimum of five scans and lasts approximately 45 seconds; subsequent authentication scans are faster and take only 10–15 seconds. An acquired image containing 320–400 reference points is converted to a map of the retina and used to identify a match from the templates encoded in the scanner's software. Retinal images captured are extremely small, only 35 bytes in size.

The technology for retinal scans has changed in recent years. The initial large devices are being followed now by smaller and more accurate instruments. The first commercial retinal scanner was developed in 1984. One of the most recent developments in the area is a small mobile and easy to use retinal scanner. Although it was initially developed for diagnostic purposes, it will be available as a security tool as well.

Fooling the retinal scanner is very difficult, as it requires intact retina to complete a scan. Following death, the retina degrades very quickly and thus cannot be used in most cases for accurate post-mortem identification. Although often a popular movie special effect, using a retina detached from a cadaver would fail with modern scanning equipment. Likewise, surgical alteration of the retinal pattern would be not only a dangerous and extremely expensive process, but futile, as the changes introduced would be readily detected by modern scanning equipment.

Iris scans use characteristics more similar to fingerprints than to retinal vein pattern. The colored part of the eye appears to be as unique as fingerprints and retinas. Scanning technology takes advantage of crypts, furrows, ridges, striations, ligaments, and collarette. While 240 points are recorded, the image size is 512 bytes, over ten times larger than a retinal scan. The main advantage of the iris scans is the ability to perform them from a distance of up to three feet and short time of scan of only 20 seconds initially, with subsequent identification requiring only two seconds. Glasses and contact lenses do not interfere with the scanning process and identification.

In contrast to the retinal scanners, iris scanners are of two main types: active and passive. The active system works from 3–14 inches (7.5–35 cm) and also requires the user to move forward and backward so the camera is adjusted properly. In contrast the passive system can work over longer distance from one to three feet (0.3–1 m).

Biometric techniques are used in identification and authentication. The features used for the two processes can overlap, or can be different. Authentication requires high accuracy to ensure restricted access. Retinal and iris scans offer high accuracy, and the primary users of retinal scans are military and government facilities, such as CIA, **FBI**, and NASA. Scans are used to control access to high security areas.

An acceptance is growing for the iris recognition systems and they are now used by government agencies, commercial companies, and also in the public sector. Among the government users are the U.S. Congress, and Departments of Defense, State, and Treasury. Some of the commercial companies that protect themselves by using iris recognition are Bank United, GTE, Hewlett Packard, Lockheed Martin, and British Telecom.

Scanning is also being implemented at airports as an added security feature. For example, as of 2005, eight of the largest Canadian airports (Toronto, Vancouver, Ottawa, Montreal, Halifax, Winnipeg, Calgary, and Edmonton) have, or are planning to install, systems that will be part of the U.S. Customs inspection process.

SEE ALSO Fingerprint; Identification.

Biometrics

Biometrics refers to the measurement of specific physical or behavioral characteristics and the use of that data in identifying subjects. With wide application,

biometric-based **identification** techniques are increasingly an important part of **forensic science** investigations because biometric data is difficult, if not impossible, to duplicate or otherwise falsify. Examples of such data include retinal or iris scans, fingerprints, hand geometry, and facial features. Accordingly, biometric systems offer highly accurate means of comparison of measured characteristics to those in a pre-assembled database.

Biometric identification points include gross morphological appearance that is most often subjectively interpreted upon superficial examination (e.g., gender, race or color of skin, hair, and eye color). Other gross biometric data can include more quantifiable—and therefore less subjective—data (e.g., weight, height, location of scars or other visible physical markings). Some biometric data is easily changeable and therefore not reliable (e.g. presence of facial hair, wearing of glasses, etc.).

Because even objective features such as weight can change over time, systems of identification that rely on changeable or gross features are not as reliable as biometric systems that measure more stable anatomical and physiological characteristics such as fingerprints, retinal blood vessel patterns, specific **skull** dimensions, dental and skeletal x rays, earlobe capillary patterns, and hand geometry.

The most specific and reliable of biometric data is obtained from **DNA sequencing**.

More controversial and, at present, less reliable biometric studies seek to enhance quantification of social behaviors, voice characteristics—including language use patterns and accents—handwriting, and even keystroke inputs patterns.

Biometric data can be encoded into magnetic stripes, bar codes, and integrated circuit "smart" cards.

On a global scale, biometric data interchange and interoperability standards are at present fragmented into different measurement and input format schemes. The Common Biometric Exchange File Format (CBEFF), in development by the International Biometric Industry Association (IBIA), seeks to integrate such measurement schemes to enhance reliability and use of biometric data. Other integration efforts include the Biometric Application Programming Interface (BioAPI) specification program used by the United States Department of Defense. The Department of Defense has also established a Biometrics Management Office (BMO). BioAPI protocols are also being used by other governmental agencies and the financial service industry in the development of smart cards.

Britain's Prime Minister Tony Blair's demonstration biometric card is displayed at the Passport Office in central London during a biometrics enrollment trial, where records were taken of volunteers' facial identity, iris recognition, and fingerprints. © CHRIS YOUNG/POOL/REUTERS/CORBIS

The National Institute of Standards and Technology (NIST) also dedicates programs to biometric research and exchange. NIST developed the initial data protocols used in the Face Recognition Vendor Test (FRVT) and established the format for data collection used by most face recognition technologies.

Finally, reflecting the power of biometrics in forensic science, police forces are increasingly equipping themselves with the technical and personnel expertise to undertaken biometric examinations. These efforts are aided by the Internet, which allows police forces to access databases and share information on a global scale.

SEE ALSO Automated Fingerprint Identification System (AFIS); Digital imaging; DNA fingerprint; Fingerprint; Hair analysis; Handwriting analysis; Integrated Ballistics Identification System (IBIS).

Biosensor technologies

The detection of biological agents that pose a threat of disease has become an important facet of forensic investigations. A well-known example was the effort of United Nations inspectors to detect

microbiological weapons before and following the 2003 Gulf War between Iraq and coalition forces headed by the United States.

Part of these detection efforts involved the use of hand-held devices that could identify the presence of certain bacteria with great precision and sensitivity. These devices represent the cutting-edge application of what are known as biosensors.

Biosensor technology is also used more routinely, for example, in forensic investigations of an illness outbreak or death. The systems currently available for sensing biological analytes rely on two technologies: reporter molecules that attach to antibodies and give off fluorescent signals and the **polymerase chain reaction (PCR)** that amplifies suspect **DNA**. Because two steps are required to identify biological weapons, the procedure is both labor and time intensive. The Defense Advanced Research Projects Agency (DARPA) initiated the Biosensor Technologies program in 2002 to develop fast, sensitive, automatic technologies for the detection and **identification** of biological warfare agents. The program focuses on a variety of technologies, including surface receptor properties, nucleic acid sequences, identification of molecules found on the breath, and mass spectrometry.

A major thrust of the surface receptor research is to enhance or replace the chemical signal given off by antibodies to biological analytes. One such project has developed short polypeptides (4–5 amino acids long) that can bind to **anthrax spores**. A separate group has engineered aptamers, short strands of nucleic acid that specifically bind to the DNA of the bacteria that cause anthrax. Another research area involves using ion channels for amplifying the signal of a reporter molecule. This work includes the engineering of an artificial ion channel that is triggered by the binding of an **antibody** or other small molecules. Such engineered ion channels are sensitive to a single binding event, require no external energy, and can greatly amplify the chemical signal. Finally, converting phosphors as a replacement for fluorescent reporter molecules is being investigated.

The focus of the nucleic acid sequence technology is the development of a biochip that contains an array of engineered molecules that react with the genome of biological warfare agents or disease causing organisms of public health importance. The biochip is embedded in a platform that is portable, automated, and allows for direct sampling of the environment. A biochip platform to identify the anthrax bacteria is in the testing stages and additional biochips for identifying other harmful bacteria and viruses are in development.

SEE ALSO Antibody; Antigen; Anthrax; Bacterial biology; Biodetectors; Biological weapons, genetic identification; Fluorescence; PCR (polymerase chain reaction).

Bioterrorism

Bioterrorism is the use of a biological weapon against a civilian or military population by a government, organization, or individual. As with any form of terrorism, its purposes include the undermining of morale, creating chaos, or achieving political goals. Biological weapons use microorganisms and **toxins** to produce disease and death in humans, livestock, and crops.

Bioterrorism is viewed as a serious threat to national security and a range of experts, including forensic investigation teams, would be called on to deal with an incident involving biological weapons. For example, disaster scenarios created by United States government agencies predict that the release of a few hundred pounds of the **spores** of *Bacillus anthracis* (the bacterium that cause the disease called **anthrax**) upwind of Washington, D.C., could

sicken or kill hundreds of thousands to millions of people within 24 hours. Forensic scientists would likely respond by identifying the bacterium, tracing its source, and gathering and analyzing other **evidence** from the biocrime scene and the victims.

Bioterrorism can also be used as a weapon to damage or destroy the economy of the target nation. A report from the **Centers for Disease Control and Prevention (CDC)** estimates the cost of dealing with a large-scale anthrax incident is at least $26 billion per 100,000 people. Only a few such incidents would cripple the economy of any nation. Indeed, the few anthrax incidents that occurred following the September 11, 2001, terrorist attacks cost the United States government hundreds of millions of dollars in treatment, investigation, and other response measures.

Biological, chemical, and nuclear weapons can all be used to achieve similar destructive goals (i.e., massive loss of life). Relative to chemical and nuclear weapons, biological weapons are inexpensive to make. A sophisticated biological production facility can be set up in a warehouse or even a small house. Biological weapons are relatively easy to transport and can resist detection by standard security systems.

In general, chemical weapons act immediately, causing illness in minutes. For example, the release of **sarin gas** in the Tokyo subway in 1995 by the religious sect Aum Shinrikyo almost immediately killed 12 and hospitalized 5,000 people. In contrast, the illness and death from biological weapons can occur more slowly, with evidence of exposure and illness appearing over time. Thus, a bioterrorist attack may at first be indistinguishable from a natural outbreak of an infectious disease. By the time the deliberate nature of the attack is realized, the health care system may be unable to cope with the large number of victims.

The deliberate production and stockpiling of biological weapons is prohibited by the 1972 Biological Weapons Convention. The United States ceased offensive production of biological weapons in 1969, on orders from President Richard Nixon. The U.S. stockpiles were destroyed in 1971–1972. This measure has not stopped bioterrorists from acquiring the materials and expertise needed to produce biological weapons.

Genetic engineering can produce a wide variety of bioweapons including bacteria or viruses that produce toxins. More conventional laboratory technologies can also produce bacteria that are resistant to **antibiotics**.

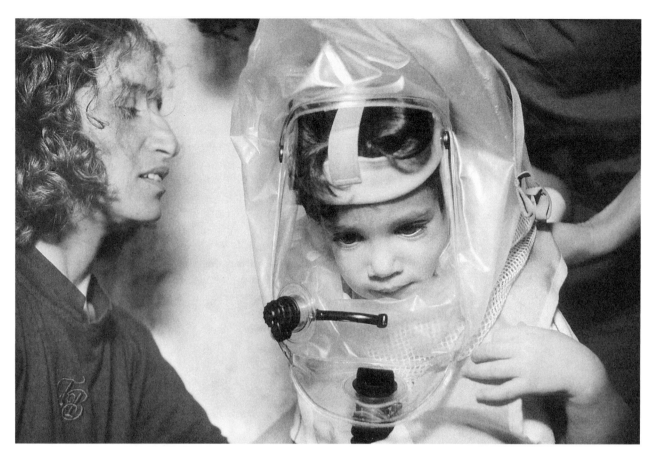

A young child tries on a gas mask designed especially for small children in Tel-Aviv, Israel. © JEFFREY L. ROTMAN/CORBIS

Examples of the bioterrorist weapons most likely to be used include **smallpox** (caused by the **variola virus**), anthrax (caused by *Bacillus anthracis*), and plague (caused by *Yersinia pestis*).

The last recorded case of smallpox was in Somalia in 1977. Today, only two facilities—one in the United States and one in Russia—are authorized to store the virus. In spite of international prohibitions, security experts suspect that smallpox viruses may be under development as biological weapons in other laboratories of many nations. As recently as 1992, Russia had the ability to launch missiles containing weapons-grade smallpox. A number of terrorist organizations, including Al Qaeda, have explored the use of biological weapons.

Bioterrorism may ultimately prove to be more destructive than conventional warfare because of the mobility of the weapons and their ability to spread infection through an entire population. An epidemic can spread a disease far from the point of origin of the illness.

Preparing a strategy to defend against biological warfare is challenging. Traditional identification of microorganisms such as bacteria and viruses relies on assays that detect growth of the microbes. Newer technologies detect microbes based on sequences of genetic material. The genetic technologies can detect microbes in minutes. However, these technologies are not available to any but the most sophisticated field investigative units.

Researchers are also working to counter bioterrorist attacks using several other technological strategies. For example, robots equipped with sensors or microchip-mechanized insects (with computerized circuitry that can mimic biological processes such as neural networks) are being refined. Bees, beetles, and other insects outfitted with sensors are used to collect real-time information about the presence of toxins or similar threats. These technologies could be used to examine a suspected biological weapon and spare exposing investigators to potential hazards. The robotics program of the Defense Advanced Research Project (DARPA) works to rapidly identify bio-responses to **pathogens**, and to effectively and rapidly treat them.

Research is also underway to find genetic similarities between the microbes that could be used by bioterrorists. A vaccine made to act on a protein that is common to several bacteria could potentially offer protection to the exposure any bacterium in the group, for example.

SEE ALSO Anthrax, investigation of the 2001 murders; Biological warfare, advanced diagnostics; Biological weapons, genetic identification; Chemical Biological Incident Response Force, United States; Pathogen transmission; Pathogens; Sarin gas; September 11, 2001, terrorist attacks (forensic investigations of); Smallpox; Vaccines.

Bite analysis

Bite marks may be found at the scene of a crime and their analysis has been used for many years as an aid in forensic investigation. Bite marks can occur on the skin of a victim or on other objects, including foods such as cheese, chocolate, or apples. Non-food items that may bear bite marks and are therefore worthy of investigation include chewing gum, bottle tops, masking tape, and pencils. The bite mark itself may be matched to the bite mark of a suspect. There is also the possibility of gathering **saliva** from the bite mark, which can then be used to identify a suspect through **DNA** analysis.

Bite marks tend to have a double horseshoe pattern showing the six central teeth of the upper jaw and the corresponding six teeth in the lower jaw. Those made in food are usually well defined; bite marks made in flesh are usually less defined. The analysis of a bite mark begins with photographing the **evidence** in both black and white and in color, and from several angles. It is important to take these photographs within eight hours of the injury being inflicted in the case of a victim. Inflammation tends to blur the pattern after this time if the victim is alive. If the mark is deep enough, then a cast can be made using dental processes similar to those used for making a tooth crown or a bridge. The next step is to make an image that can be overlaid on the bite mark of a suspect for comparison. The image can be made by manual tracing or by scanning into a computer and using a program that makes a picture on a transparent overlay sheet.

Bite marks reveal features such as gaps between the teeth, ridges on the biting surfaces of the teeth, rough fillings, as well as missing, broken, chipped, or distorted teeth. In fact, human teeth patterns are individual and careful expert analysis of a bite should be able to tie the mark to a suspect. **Identification** through bite mark analysis is given over to a forensic odontologist, who is a specialist in dental anatomy and its interpretation.

Flesh is elastic and stretches when it is bitten. A bite mark on a body, therefore, is somewhat different from a bite mark on an inanimate surface. A forensic pathologist will note a bruising pattern in the shape of two curved lines facing one another if the bite has been inflicted antemortem (before death). Bites inflicted on muscular tissue make a more distinct pattern than bites found on fatty tissue. Postmortem bites do not produce bruising. Particularly ferocious bites will produce lacerations. Bite marks on a victim tend to be specific to the nature of the attack. For example, bite marks on the neck, breasts, and shoulders are seen in some rapes, sexual assaults, or incidents of domestic violence. Multiple bites on the arms or buttocks are sometimes a feature of child abuse. Sometimes a victim may bite the suspect as a means of the defense using the teeth as a weapon; this tends to produce multiple bites, rather than single bites.

It is also important to take sterile swabs of the bite to collect traces of saliva. The presence of the enzyme amylase in the swab shows that saliva is present and the injury is indeed a bite. Microbiological evidence from the swab can also be informative if it corresponds to the microbial flora (microorganisms present) from the mouth of a suspect. It may also be possible to determine the **blood** group of the suspect from saliva analysis. This kind of evidence is useful for excluding a suspect, taken with the bite pattern analysis. If DNA can be extracted from the saliva as well, then the bite mark evidence for or against the suspect becomes even stronger.

One of the most famous cases involving bite analysis is that of serial murderer Ted Bundy. In 1978, a brutal attack at the Chi Omega sorority house at Florida State University left two young women dead and two others seriously injured. A fifth woman, who escaped, was able to describe her attacker. Bundy, an escaped prisoner, was caught and put on trial for the Chi Omega murders. A crucial piece of evidence for the prosecution was an enlarged photograph of a bite mark found on the left buttock of one of the victims. An image of the outline of Bundy's front teeth was created on a transparent overlay. Bundy's teeth were misaligned and chipped. According to the forensic odontologist, this matched perfectly with the photograph of the bite mark found at the scene. This helped identify Bundy as the attacker and he was found guilty and executed in 1989. Bundy confessed to up to 50 other murders.

SEE ALSO Body marks; Bundy (serial murderer) case; Odontology.

Edward T. Blake

7/31/1945–
AMERICAN
FORENSIC SCIENTIST

For more than thirty years, forensic scientist Edward T. Blake has been considered an expert in **DNA** analysis. He was the first to use **polymerase chain reaction** (**PCR**) based DNA testing in the United States, during the civil court case *People v. Pestinikas* in 1986. Since that time, he has worked as a consultant to analyze biological **evidence** in countless criminal cases, including work that has led to the exoneration of approximately fifty people wrongly accused of crimes.

Born in Honolulu, Hawaii, Blake early on was interested in the field of **forensic science**. He attended University of California, Berkeley (UCB), earning a bachelor's degree in **criminalistics** in 1968 and a doctorate of **criminology** in 1976. While in school, Blake worked at the Contra Costa County Sheriff's Office Criminalistics Laboratory, and served as a teaching assistant in the Forensic Science Program at UCB. After graduation, he immediately began his work as a consultant in forensic biology, and eventually opened his own consulting firm, Forensic Science Associates, in 1978.

With Forensic Science Associates, Blake conducts independent analysis of DNA and crime scenes, analyzing biological evidence such as **saliva**, **blood**, and **semen**. This analysis can take months, if not years, to perform. But through the use of PCR-based DNA testing, analysts can identify a genetic profile with incredible accuracy. While much of the work is conducted before or during a criminal trial, Blake's firm has earned national recognition as a source of post-conviction testing as well. As an advisor and consultant, Blake has taken part in hundreds of court cases, including such high-profile cases as the O.J. Simpson trial in California.

Since the 1970s, Blake has also been a regular contributor to many trade publications, including the *American Journal of Human Genetics*, the *New England Journal of Medicine*, the *Journal of Forensic Science*, and the *Banbury Report*. He has often written about the topics of genetic markers, DNA analysis, and PCR-based testing. He has also frequently spoken at conferences and seminars held by key professional societies and organizations, including the California Association of Criminologists, the **American Academy of Forensic Sciences**, and the Federal Bureau of Investigation.

SEE ALSO DNA evidence, cases of exoneration; PCR (polymerase chain reaction).

Blood

Frequently, the forensic analysis of a crime or accident scene will involve the analysis of blood. Whether in the form of fresh liquid, dried blood, jelly-like coagulated blood, or patchy drops or stains, blood can be a treasure trove of information. As one example, the pattern of a bloodstain can tell a forensic investigator much about the nature of the accident or crime. Just as important is the composition of the blood.

A typical human body contains approximately ten pints (4.7 liters) of blood. Depending on the severity of a wound, blood can be lost slowly or, as in the case of a severed artery, can spurt quickly out of the body. A forensic examiner can tell a great deal about the nature of the accident or crime from the pattern of the blood residue. Additionally, knowledge of the composition of blood and properties of these components is also valuable in identifying a victim or implicating an assailant.

Human blood is made up of several different types of cells. Each has a distinctive appearance and function.

Red blood cells are absolutely vital for life. Each drop of blood contains millions of these cells. In the body, the circulating red blood cells deliver oxygen to cells and transport waste material from the cells.

Red blood cells are round, smooth-edged, and saucer-like in shape, typically having a slightly depressed center. In a disease like anemia or sickle cell anemia, the cells can be present in reduced numbers or can adopt an abnormal sickle shape. This reduces the oxygen carrying capacity of the blood. The presence of such abnormalities can alert a forensic investigator or **medical examiner** to the presence of disease or poison, or lack of constituents, including iron, vitamin B_{12}, or folic acid, or other maladies.

The bright red color of a healthy red blood cell comes from the presence of an iron-containing compound called **hemoglobin**. The presence of iron makes hemoglobin an excellent molecule for the binding and transport of oxygen and carbon dioxide. As blood passes through the tiny channels that permeate the lung, the oxygen molecules that diffuse across the channel membrane bind to the hemoglobin. The oxygen is subsequently released to cells all through the body during the circulation of the red blood cells.

Once vacant, the binding site in the hemoglobin is able to accommodate the binding of carbon dioxides and other waste products of cellular metabolism. These products, which would become toxic to the cells if allowed to accumulate, are then transported away. As the red blood cells pass back through the lung, the carbon dioxide and other waste molecules are released from the hemoglobin and are exhaled.

Red blood cells are long-lived, but not immortal. The average lifetime is approximately 120 days. Although cells are continually dying and being replenished, the number of red blood cells remains constant in a properly-operating body.

In contrast to the smooth, plate-like red blood cells, white blood cells are spheres that have numerous knob-like projections sticking out from their surface.

White blood cells are part of the body's defense system against infection. When a microbial threat is recognized by the **immune system**, white blood cells are signaled and directed to the site of the threat. There, they attack the invading microorganisms, by producing antibodies directed against components of the microbe or by physically engulfing, ingesting, and dissolving the invader.

White blood cells are primed and ready for their defensive duties by means of a short life span. They live only a few days to several weeks.

Under normal conditions there are 7,000–25,000 white blood cells per drop of blood. The determination of this number can provide an indication of the presence of disease. For example, if a bacterial, viral, or parasitic infection proves resistant to eradication, an increased number of white blood cells will be recruited to do battle with the invader, reducing the white blood cell count in the blood. Conversely, cancer of the blood (leukemia) causes the numbers of white blood cells to increase markedly. A leukemia patient can display upwards of 50,000 white blood cells per drop of blood.

The bloodstain that confronts a forensic investigator at the site of an accident or crime may be the result of a catastrophic injury that the body was unable to repair. Normally, the cuts and scrapes that occur during the normal course of life can be addressed by sealing up the wound.

The patching of a wound is the task of the colorless blood cells called platelets. Platelets do not have a uniform shape. Rather, they are reminiscent of an amoeba, being blob-like, with long and thin surface projections.

Platelets are recruited to the site of a cut or wound. Their shape and sticky surface facilitates their clumping together, along with calcium, vitamin K, and a protein called fibrinogen. The clump is known as a clot.

Clot formation is a complicated process that involves a cascade of biochemical reactions. Without platelets, clotting would not occur. When in the vicinity of the open wound, and so in the presence of an increased concentration of oxygen, the platelets dissolve. A consequence of the dissolution is the conversion of fibrinogen to fibrin. The tiny thread-like fibrin molecules collect to form a mesh that entraps intact and dissolved blood cells and other constituents. As this mass hardens, the clot forms. A hardened clot is also called a scab.

This effective wound patching system does have its limits, however. In the case of a catastrophic injury such as a knife or bullet wound, bleeding may continue unabated. If not treated, such a wound can be fatal.

The various blood cells are suspended in a straw-colored liquid called plasma. Plasma is composed mainly of water. Physiologically-important ions including calcium, sodium, potassium and magnesium also comprise plasma.

Plasma provides the medium in which the blood cells are suspended and transported around the body. As well, the disease-fighting antibodies produced by the immune system are also ferried to where they are needed via the plasma.

Blood, specifically the red blood cells, are also a valuable resource for a forensic investigator, as the cells can be used to determine what is known as the blood type of the victim or assailant.

The chemical residues present on the surface of red blood cells are the basis of blood typing. These were first described early in the twentieth century by the Austrian-born American immunologist **Karl Landsteiner** (1868–1943), who subsequently developed the typing criteria. For his achievements, Landsteiner was awarded the 1930 Nobel Prize in Medicine.

Landsteiner noted the presence of two distinct molecules—protein antigens A and B—on the surface of red blood cells. Type A blood is comprised of red blood cells that have only the A molecule, whereas the red blood cells of type B blood have only the B molecule. The presence of both molecules occurs in type AB blood. Finally, red blood cells can be devoid of both molecules. This occurs in type O blood.

The determination of blood type can be easily done by mixing a sample of blood with antibodies to the A or B components. In the presence of the correct **antibody**, the blood cells will clump together, forming a visible precipitate.

Blood typing remains a powerful forensic tool in linking someone to the crime or accident scene. In addition, because blood type is a genetically acquired trait, blood typing can be useful in establishing familial relationships. However, because a great many people have the same blood type, this test alone is not a definitive **identification**.

Another very useful aspect of blood in forensic examinations involves a factor known as the Rh (for Rhesus) factor. The factor, which was also discovered by Landsteiner, derives its name from the Rhesus monkey, a species similar to us and so one that is used in medical studies. The Rh factor of human blood was discovered in blood comparisons between humans and the Rhesus monkey.

Rh factor is a protein that is present in the blood of some people (who are described as Rh positive, or Rh$^+$. Some people lack the blood protein, and so are described as being Rh negative (Rh$^-$).

The determination of the Rh status of a blood sample provides another piece of **evidence** that can help determine the identify of the victim or link someone to the crime or accident.

In addition to the A and B antigens and Rh factor, modern day blood typing includes over 150 blood-borne proteins and 250 enzymes located in blood cells.

This extensive form of blood typing, while still useful, is laborious and has been largely replaced by the molecular precision of genetic analysis.

As with every other cell in the body, blood cells contain genetic material in the form of deoxyribonucleic acid (**DNA**). DNA can be isolated and subjected to a variety of sophisticated analyses to determine the sequence of the nucleotide building blocks that comprise the structure. As well, small sequences that tend to vary from person to person can be quickly copied over and over again, using the **polymerase chain reaction** (**PCR**), to produce sufficient quantities for the sequence analysis. In this way, the pattern of DNA that is unique to an individual can be revealed.

Recovering the same DNA pattern in a blood sample of a suspect and from blood recovered at a crime scene is very powerful evidence tying the person to the crime scene. As seen in the trial of O.J. Simpson, however, even this evidence can fail to sway a jury if not convincingly presented or defended.

SEE ALSO Blood spatter; Bloodstain evidence; Blood volume test; Blood, presumptive test; Cast-off blood; DNA; Toxins; Wound assessment.

Blood, presumptive test

A forensic investigator can be confronted with a variety of **fluids** at a crime or accident scene. It is critical to determine the nature of each fluid.

While a detailed examination of a suspect bloodstain requires the equipment and technical expertise of an analysis laboratory, a fluid suspected of being blood can be examined at the scene to determine if it indeed could be blood. This examination is called a blood presumptive test.

Properly done, a blood presumptive test rules out the possibility that a fluid is blood. A blood presumptive test relies on the use of chemicals that will change color when in the presence of blood. As one common example, a solution of phenolphthalein, which is colorless, will turn an intense pink when added to a blood stain in the presence of hydrogen peroxide. The formation of a pink color indicates that the fluid could be, and indeed, likely may be, blood. However, confirmation requires the more detailed lab analyses.

Another chemical called o-tolidine can also be used in conjunction with hydrogen peroxide instead of phenolphthalein. Again, the formation of the characteristic color must be followed up by a more detailed and confirmatory examination of the sample.

When a blood presumptive test is done at a crime or accident scene, an investigator must include the use of controls to ensure the accuracy of the result. This is because a blood presumptive test can be subject to what is known as a false positive result. This is when the characteristic color reaction is produced by

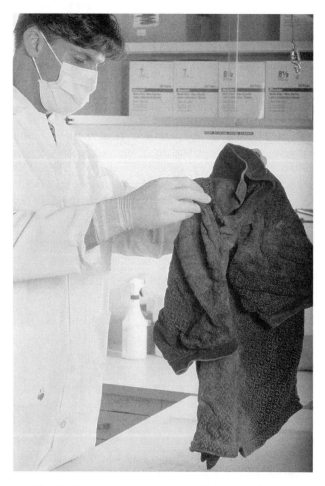

An FBI pathologist in a laboratory at the FBI Academy in Quantico, Virginia, inspects dried material on a jacket before performing a presumptive blood test. © ANNA CLOPET/CORBIS

Blood spatter

Blood spatter, or bloodstain pattern interpretation, is a technique that seeks to piece together the events that caused bleeding. Knowing how the blood got on the wall or other surface can be helpful in determining if a crime was committed and if the blood is **evidence** in that crime.

The blood spatter pattern can tell a trained investigator much about what crime may have been committed and rule out other types of crime. Together with other evidence, blood spatter can be very useful in piecing together what took place, identifying the victim, and determining who was responsible.

One of the first things that a forensic investigator needs to do when examining a blood spatter is to verify that the material is indeed blood. This can be determined by using tests that are portable enough to be used right at the scene. Later, tests will be done to determine if the blood is animal or human in origin and even to narrow down the people from whom the blood may have come.

In the actual spatter analysis, a forensic investigator determines the **trajectory** of the blood (where the blood came from and how it spread over the surface). By measuring the shape of the bloodstain on a surface, the direction of movement can be determined. As well, the speed at which the blood contacted the surface can be approximated. This can help distinguish, for example, between the rapid movement of blood that can be produced by a gunshot or the severing of an artery in opposition to the slower movement of blood from a minor cut.

If blood originated some distance away from a surface, the force of impact will cause the blood to break up into smaller drops. Thus, a blood spatter consisting of larger drops with a trail of smaller drops can tell an investigator much about how the blood got there and where the blood came from (i.e., near the floor, higher up in a room, near or far away from the surface).

The trained eyes of an experienced investigator remain one of the most powerful tools in blood spatter analysis. Specialized analytical computer programs are also available. Such detailed analysis can be important if the blood spatter is presented as evidence in a legal case.

a sample that is in fact not blood. As well, a false negative reaction is possible, where for some reason a blood sample does not produce the characteristic color change in the indicator chemical.

Standard procedures can rule out the possibility of a false positive or negative result. However, if these controls are not run, then the accuracy of the presumptive test can be questioned. In that case, the results would not be admissible in a court of law.

Presumptive blood tests are commercially available in a convenient form that is easily transportable to the crime or accident scene. Typically, a sample is placed in a sterile plastic bag or box to which are added the chemicals. Upon mixing, the solution is visually observed for the development of the target color. Other containers contain the positive and negative controls.

SEE ALSO Blood; Blood spatter; Bloodstain evidence; Blood volume test; Indicator, acid-base.

SEE ALSO Bloodstain evidence; Cast-off blood; Crime scene investigation.

Blood volume test

The forensic investigation of a crime or accident scene involves the collection and analysis of **evidence**, including any **blood** present at the crime scene. One facet of a forensic examination that concerns blood is known as the blood volume test.

A blood volume test is designed to determine the quantity of blood that has been shed in a particular area. As well, the test seeks to relate the shed blood to a blood stain on a surface such as a rug or floor, or a **blood spatter** pattern on a surface such as a wall. Finally, the blood volume test can provide information concerning the length of time that was needed to create the stain or spatter pattern.

The volume of blood that is present at a crime or accident scene can tell a forensic examiner a great deal about the origin of the blood. For example, a small quantity of blood is typically produced by a relatively insubstantial cut, whereas a copious quantity of blood is more characteristic of a severe cut such as a deep stab wound, bullet impact or the severing of an artery.

Blood is sometimes collected directly from a person. As in a hospital, this collection involves drawing the blood from the person into a sterile container (Vacutainer) that is specifically designed to hold blood.

Blood that has collected on surfaces can be collected in a clean unused plastic container. It is likely that not all the blood will be collected. But, enough can be retrieved to discriminate between a small or copious blood spill. Once collected, the blood volume test should be refrigerated, transported to the laboratory, and analyzed as soon as possible, to prevent contamination of the specimen or destruction of blood cells.

The retrieval of dried blood is more complicated. The area containing the dried blood can be scrapped or cut free of the surrounding fabric. Sometimes, dried blood can be lifted off a surface by applying sticky tape (fingerprint tape is typically used), or absorbing the blood onto a pre-moistened thread or cotton square.

The collected dried blood can subsequently be reconstituted into a known volume of liquid for the determination of the blood volume.

Determination of the volume of the sample occupied by blood cells is not complicated. Each sample is spun in a centrifuge, which causes the heavier blood cells to move to the bottom of the tube. The tubes have gradations that allow the packed volume of the blood cells to be measured, relative to the total volume of the cells and liquid (plasma).

SEE ALSO Blood; Blood, presumptive test; Blood spatter; Crime scene investigation.

Bloodstain evidence

Bloodstains are an important piece of **evidence** in a forensic examination. The pattern of a stain and the quantity of **blood** present can be important clues to the nature of the accident or crime. Moreover, detailed analysis of the blood obtained from a stain can reveal genetic and other information that can help identify a victim or implicate the person responsible.

Analysis of bloodstains can also help reveal the nature of the injury and even the order that the wounds were received. The pattern of the bloodstain, which is also referred to as **blood spatter**, can be important in identifying the weapon used to inflict the injury, and help determine if the victim was moving or motionless when injured.

When initially dealing with a bloodstain, a forensic investigator will seek to obtain as much information as possible without disturbing the scene. This can involve recording the bloodstain by means of a sketch, video camera, or digital camera. As well, a chemical called **luminol** can be sprayed over the area of the bloodstain. Under ultraviolet illumination, the luminol that has bound to blood will fluoresce, which can reveal small quantities of blood that might otherwise escape detection.

When establishing the extent and pattern of a bloodstain, the use of sufficient illumination is important, to avoid shadows that might contribute to misleading shapes to blood drops, since the shape of a drop can indicate the direction and speed of impact of the drop with the surface.

The pattern of a bloodstain can tell a lot about the origin of the blood. For example, blood can drip or ooze out of a cut or bullet wound, spurt out at much higher speed from a severed artery, or be flung off a weapon as a blow is delivered. The resulting patterns will differ. Indeed, the pattern of **cast-off blood** from a weapon can even be used to determine if the assailant was right- or left-handed.

A drop of blood falling from 5–6 feet (1.5–2 m) above a floor will splash upon impact, while a drop falling several feet straight down will tend to be

Bloodstains on lyrics of a song about peace carried by former Israeli Premier Yitzhak Rabin on the day he was assassinated in 1995.
© REUVEN KASTRO/CORBIS SYGMA

somewhat circular but with a wavy edge. A drop oozing out of a cut that is just a few inches above a floor likely will be circular.

In another example, the high impact of a gunshot wound can send blood away from a body at high speed. If the blood impacts a wall at an angle, the blood drop will assume more of a teardrop shape than if the blood impacts the wall straight on. Moreover, the orientation of several of the teardrop-shaped bloodstains will allow a forensic investigator to apply trigonometric functions to produce a three-dimensional recreation of the area that the blood came from.

A smeared bloodstain around a body can be evidence that the body was dragged to that position. Similarly, a trail of blood drops leading to a body can be evidence that the person was moving while bleeding, or was being carried by someone else.

A skilled forensic investigator is often able to trace these patterns back to their origin; literally, to the scene of the crime.

Bloodstains can also be a treasure trove of other information. If someone walked through a bloodstain on the floor, an impression of the sole of the shoe may have been left. This piece of evidence can help match someone to the scene of the crime or accident. The blood may also have carried bits of skin, hair, or clothing with it. All these materials can be recovered and analyzed to provide more information about the victim or the assailant.

Blood naturally carries the genetic information of the person from which it originated. Blood cells will contain deoxyribonucleic acid (**DNA**). The DNA can be enzymatically digested into many differently sized fragments and the fragments can be analyzed to deduce the sequence of building blocks (bases) that comprise the DNA. Small stretches of DNA that are of particular interest can be obtained in large quantities using a procedure known as the **polymerase chain reaction (PCR)**. Essentially, PCR makes a copy of the target region, uses those copies to make more copies, and so on. The number of copies grows at a logarithmic rate to quickly generate millions of copies of the target region. The unique region can then be studied.

In this way, an individual's DNA sequence can be found. This sequence, like a fingerprint, can be almost unique to the individual. DNA sequence analysis, if properly done, can be a powerful piece of evidence.

Such was the case in the O. J. Simpson murder trial. The DNA pattern obtained from blood at the scene of the double **murder** matched the patterns obtained from blood found in Simpson's vehicle and from a blood sample obtained from Simpson himself. The odds that the blood was Simpson's and not someone else's were astronomically high. However, Simpson's lawyers were able to create doubt in the juror's minds concerning the way the blood samples were collected. The result, despite this overwhelming evidence, was an acquittal.

A bloodstain can also be tested to determine the blood type. There are four possible blood types: A, B, AB, and O. These various types can be distinguished from one another by virtue of the different proteins (antigens) on the surface of the blood cells. The different antigens can be recognized by specific antibodies.

Blood typing can be another powerful means of linking someone to a crime or accident scene, or exonerating them. For example, if a bloodstain at a crime scene contains Type A blood and a suspect has Type O blood, then the blood did not come from the suspect. However, because many people have the same blood type, blood typing alone cannot implicate someone.

Blood also can possess another **antigen** group called the Rh factor. Individuals who produce the Rh antigen have Rh positive blood. Those who do not produce Rh antigen have Rh negative blood.

Bloodstain analysis is now recognized as a vital facet of a forensic examination. This importance is exemplified by the Royal Canadian Mounted Police (RCMP), who maintain a Crime Scene Bloodstain Section in their Forensic Support Services. This section is one of the most advanced in the world, and is the only agency that specifically trains investigators to do bloodstain analyses at a crime scene.

SEE ALSO Blood, presumptive test; Blood spatter; Blood volume test; DNA fingerprint; Indicator, acid-base; Simpson (O. J.) murder trial.

Bloody Sunday inquiry in Northern Ireland

The Bloody Sunday inquiry in Northern Ireland examined the events surrounding the killing and wounding of Catholic civil rights protesters by British soldiers on January 30, 1972. The violence that day formed the latest episode of a decades-long resistance by Catholics against Protestants supported by the British government. The turbulent atmosphere demanded an impartial investigation. The refusal of the investigators to consider all forensic **evidence** led many Catholics to conclude that they could not obtain justice from the British government.

The Northern Ireland city of Derry, known to Protestants as Londonderry, was one of the centers of the Catholic civil rights movement. In the winter of 1972, the Northern Ireland Civil Rights Association (NICRA) informed British authorities that it intended to stage a protest march in Derry. Scheduled for Sunday, January 30, the march protested against the policy of the internment without trial instituted the previous year.

A crowd estimated to be between 10,000–25,000 strong turned out on the sunny January day. The atmosphere was relaxed and jovial, but the history of sudden violence in the region prompted the British government to expect trouble. The 1st Battalion of the British Parachute Regiment was assigned to conduct scoop-up operations against rioters. The regiment, trained to shoot to kill when confronted with a threat to life or personal safety, had the reputation of being among the toughest in the British Army. To later critics, this particular regiment had supposedly been chosen specifically to kill Catholics.

Initially, the marchers, many of whom were children with their parents, seemed intent on avoiding a direct confrontation with the army. When the march reached army barricades, the protesters turned and walked away. At this point, the army proceeded through one barricade in a convoy of ten vehicles, while soldiers walked through another barricade. The protesters began to jeer and throw stones. The soldiers responded, as was typical in past erupting protests, with spray from water cannons and rubber bullets. Much of the crowd dispersed.

The commander in charge of the British forces, defying a specific instruction not to conduct a running battle with Catholic protesters, deployed a unit to arrest and disperse the remaining rioters. In the space of about ten minutes, thirteen civilians were shot dead and another thirteen were wounded. No

Chairman of the Bloody Sunday Inquiry, Lord Saville, at the Inquiry in Londonderry, Northern Ireland in 2004, after Britain's Prime Minister Tony Blair ordered a fresh probe into the killing of 13 civilians by paratroopers in Northern Ireland in 1972.
© PAUL MCERLANE/REUTERS/CORBIS

guns were recovered from any of the victims. Four nail bombs were recovered on one body in circumstances that suggested that they could have been planted. Forensic tests conducted on all of the deceased proved negative for handling bombs or carrying explosive residue. Five of the dead also tested negative for **firearms** handling with the tests on the remaining suspects proving inconclusive.

The British government appointed an inquiry commission on January 31, headed by the Lord Chief Justice of England, Baron John Widgery. The tribunal conducted seventeen public sessions between February 21 and March 14, 1972, in which it heard 117 witnesses. Three further sessions were held from March 16 to March 20 to hear closing speeches. The tribunal's report, issued on April 10, 1972, blamed those who had organized the illegal march for creating a highly dangerous situation in which a clash between the demonstrators and the British forces was almost inevitable. Catholics condemned the report as a biased and unabashed attempt to protect the army against any claims of serious wrongdoing.

The problems with the Widgery Inquiry began with Lord Widgery. As a former officer in the British Army, he had an interest in maintaining the reputation of the army. Widgery did not interview the wounded that were still hospitalized, and he refused to accept over 700 eyewitness statements made to NICRA on the grounds that the statements were an attempt to embarrass him. Widgery also refused to consider some evidence damaging to the army because it did not satisfy the technical rules governing the admission of evidence in a court of law, although the inquiry was not a court of law. He did not visit the scene of any of the shootings and did not commission diagrams of the shootings.

The evidence that Widgery did accept included over two hundred statements and a large number of photographs. The soldiers stated that they had been attacked by gunfire, nail bombs, acid bombs, gasoline bombs, and various other missiles. No photographs showed gunmen or bombers. Civilians and journalists claimed that the soldiers fired at unarmed civilians.

Given the tense political situation in Northern Ireland, it is unlikely that the Widgery inquiry would have satisfied everyone. However, Widgery's refusal to consider all forensic evidence injured Northern Ireland Catholic faith in the British justice system. The release of the Widgery report was marked by rioting and a jump in the membership of the Irish Republican Army.

SEE ALSO Explosives; Firearms; Gunshot residue; Trace evidence.

Blunt injuries, signs of

The signs of blunt injuries (also called blunt trauma or blunt force trauma injuries) include lesions such as abrasions (scrapes), contusions (bruises), and lacerations (cuts), but can also include bone fractures and organ ruptures. Blunt injury lesions occur when the skin of the human body makes contact with a blunted object in the form of a crushing impact or penetrating blow. For the investigations performed by forensic scientists, lesions are usually found to result from assaults and beatings of a victim often in the form of hitting, kicking, punching, or clubbing; but they can also occur from accidents such as falls. The general form of such lesions usually assumes the pattern or characteristic of the impacting blunt object. For the most part, blunt injuries to the human body cause pain and discomfort. If severe enough, however, blunt injuries sustained to the head can cause death primarily due to blood clots in the lungs that cause blockage of the major pulmonary arteries or foreign objects that flow to the brain.

Abrasions normally include only external injuries. These injuries result when the skin is rubbed away by contact with a blunt object (such as a block of wood) or rough surface (such as being dragged across a concrete floor). The signs of abrasions usually appear as lines of scraped skin with small areas of bleeding.

Contusions usually include either external or internal injuries. These injuries are the result of powerful trauma that injures an internal bodily structure (such as the rib cage) without actually breaking the skin. Contusions can be caused by blows to the abdomen, chest, or head with a blunt object such as a fist. The signs of contusions appear as a bruise beneath the skin or may not appear at all, only showing up through the use of **imaging** examinations. The injury occurs when the small blood vessels located beneath the skin are damaged. As a result, the unbroken skin surrounding the fragmented blood vessels swells and turns dark shades of blue, red, and purple as blood runs into neighboring tissues. The amount and degree of such discolorations can vary by the victim's weight, where obese people show color more than lean people. Initially, victims may feel weakness and pain, and show signs of perspiration. Signs of brain contusions are less noticeable and, thus, more difficult to analyze. The severity of brain trauma is usually more obvious on the opposite side of impact because, upon contact with a blunt object, the brain will slide to the opposite side of the **skull**.

Lacerations (or open wounds), such as tears, generally include either external or internal injuries. The injury results in an irregular break or opening in the skin, sometimes called a separating wound. The edges of the wound may be dirty, jagged, or bleeding. These injuries are caused by a large force against the body. Lacerations usually affect only the skin, but may damage deeper tissues of the body such as bones, fat, muscles, and tendons.

SEE ALSO Pattern evidence; Puncture wound.

Body Farm

The Body Farm is more correctly known as the University of Tennessee Forensic Anthropology Research Facility. It was established in 1980 by the pioneering forensic anthropologist William Bass and is dedicated to the study of the rate of **decomposition** of the human corpse under various conditions that are relevant to crime investigation. Many hallmark scientific papers have come out of the research at the Body Farm and this new knowledge has been crucial in driving forensic investigation into unsolved deaths.

Bass had long experience as a "bone detective," as forensic anthropologists were previously known, and knew that there were many unsolved scientific problems in this area. A major issue was estimating the **time of death** of a body that is discovered, and this remains a challenge today in difficult cases. The human body undergoes many changes after death. It is colonized by bacteria and insects, the skin falls off, decomposition occurs, and all of this is dependent upon both the circumstances of any crime that has been committed and on the environment into which the body has been placed.

Research at the Body Farm has increased scientific understanding of what happens to the human body after death and this new knowledge has been used in court to convict the guilty in many of the cases that Bass describes. The Body Farm is a research facility close to the forensic labs at the University of Tennessee, where human bodies are allowed to decompose under various different environmental conditions that are relevant to the investigation of crime. The work involves the smell of decomposing bodies and dealing with maggots and flies, but the scientists who work at the Body Farm are dedicated to science and solving crime.

The facility began as a piece of waste ground close to the University of Tennessee in Knoxville. From 1980, Bass and his team began to prepare the site and, in 1981, received their first body for examination. There are two kinds of bodies donated to the Body Farm, with the consent of their next of kin. The first are bodies donated to medical research and the second are corpses that have been involved in crime of some kind. Whatever the cause and circumstances of the death, the mere presence of a corpse at the Body Farm allowed the researchers the first opportunity to study what happens to the human body after death in a controlled fashion. As Bass describes, it took only two weeks for the first body received by the facility to undergo dramatic change. The **skull** had become bone. The hair slid off in a mat that lay in a greasy pool, while the initially bloated abdomen had collapsed to leave a shrunken belly clinging to the rib cage. This marked a clear transition that was already known; a dead body does initially swell up with gas because of bacterial action, but afterwards it starts to shrink and decompose. At the Body Farm, these changes were observed, documented, and categorized in a scientific manner.

One of the main research aims of the Body Farm is to make it easier for pathologists to determine the time since death when a corpse is discovered. When someone dies, their body starts to decompose and eventually it will become a skeleton. However, the rate at which a body decomposes varies widely. A thin person, especially a child, decomposes more slowly than an obese or older person. Much also depends on climate, geography, and season. In the summer heat of Tennessee, where the Body Farm is situated, a body can become a skeleton in as little as two weeks.

Researchers who have worked at the Body Farm have begun to contribute information that aids in determining time of death with precision. For example, the role of insects in corpse decomposition has been investigated by Bill Rodriguez. His observations back in the early days of the Body Farm showed that blowflies come to a body within minutes of death and feed on bloody areas, where wounds have been inflicted, or on moist areas like the mouth. After this, they go through their life cycle, feeding on the body, and producing eggs and maggots. This kind of **evidence** can be used in a forensic investigation, but had not been much researched before the advent of the Body Farm. A paper on this work published by Rodriguez in the *Journal of Forensic Sciences* in 1982, went on to become one of the most cited articles in the field.

Decomposing corpses are consumed by bacteria as well as flies and other predators. Other research carried out by Arpad Vass and colleagues at the Body Farm has shown how bacterial action on a corpse could be used as a forensic clock. As a body decays, a succession of different bacteria preys upon it. Different species have their own feeding requirements. A fresh corpse may not appeal to one bacterial species, but once it is three weeks old, they may start to invade. Bacteria, like all other living things, excrete waste products to the environment. In the case of bacteria feeding on a corpse, this means that analysis of the surrounding soil can be revealing.

Bacteria work inside the body, and more recent research has focused on examining their products in tissues from the decomposing brain, liver, and kidneys. This can help pinpoint the time of death in an even more accurate way, within hours if the corpse is a few weeks old. This type of research is now looking at ways of measuring the distinctive odor of death, that is, the molecules that signify death and decay. It may be possible in the future to transfer this knowledge to portable systems that forensic investigators could use when investigating a burial ground.

It is well known that a body kept in cold conditions is going to decompose slower than one kept at a higher temperature. This makes estimating time of death rather tricky. However, the Body Farm research has come up with a way of controlling for this. A measure called the accumulated degree days, or ADDs, is a method of accounting for the number of days of decomposition at a particular temperature. A measure of 700 would give a specific set of signs of decomposition, but it would have occurred at a certain number of days at one temperature and fewer days at a higher temperature, where the rate of decay would be accelerated. In Body Farm experiments, ADDs were measured from the moment of death, which was known, of the bodies donated to the facility. When a body was being investigated, this knowledge was applied using local climate data and the state of the body. This kind of data helps reveal time of death in the circumstances of the crime.

Despite the unique scientific work it accomplishes, a facility like the Body Farm does not exist without some controversy. Some are concerned that the work does not show proper respect to the dead, although the bodies have always been given to the research with full consent, and are solemnly buried after the conclusion of observations. In the early days, it was local residents who objected to the existence of the Body Farm. If they got close, they could see the bodies decomposing. However, the local community came round when the scientific importance of the work was publicized.

In 1993, novelist **Patricia Cornwell**, who has a background in **forensic science**, came to the Body Farm with the intent of trying to have experiments carried out that would help her latest book. *The Body Farm* was, by 1996, one of the best-selling detective stories of all time. This meant massive publicity for the Body Farm, which was featured in the book. It helped raise awareness of the importance of forensic anthropology and the emerging science of **taphonomy**, which is concerned with what happens to a person's body when they die.

The work at the Body Farm is immensely important to forensic investigations. The research that has been done there helps establish time of death more accurately, although it is still hard to be exact. With a time of death, witness and suspect alibis and statements have much more meaning. Further work at the Body Farm, and elsewhere if the facilities can be established, can help set the forensic clock for any body that is discovered under suspicious circumstances.

SEE ALSO Adipocere; Decomposition; Entomology; Taphonomy.

Body marks

External examination of either a corpse, injured victim, or suspect includes a careful verbal and visual record of any body marks. These include features such as birthmarks, moles, body piercings, tattoos, and scars. Body marks can be characteristic of an individual and can be used to support an **identification**, in conjunction with medical or police records and with identification given by family members.

Tattoos are patterns on the skin formed by injection of dyes into a pattern of prick marks. The presence of tattoos can signify a number of meanings—sometimes people are tattooed with the name of a loved one, or it may be a sign of belonging to a gang. There are even a few remaining instances of tattoos from World War II (1939–1945) concentration camps among elderly victims or suspects. Semipermanent make-up is another form of tattoo that might be used for identification purposes. It is sometimes possible to link a tattoo to a particular tattoo artist by analyzing the materials used in creating the tattoo. The chemical composition of the dyes can be determined by extracting a small amount from the tattoo and subjecting it to **thin layer chromatography** or high performance liquid **chromatography**. Generally, a tattoo is a permanent feature and it might be possible to identify a suspect by looking for a record of the tattoo in police records. A tattoo might also be mentioned in a missing person's record that could help identify a victim or suspect. Tattoos survive partial **decomposition** of the body; they can still be seen even if the outer layer of the skin has been sloughed off.

Body piercing is fashionable and related items of jewelry like earrings can be used as **evidence**, possibly aiding identification via the evidence from relatives. The site and number of piercings may be matched to existing records if they have been present for some time. Birthmarks are another important body mark. Birthmarks are benign tumors involving the blood vessels just under the skin. They are often present at birth, as the name suggests, although they may fade with time. They are sometimes known as strawberry marks or port wine stains and these names are very characteristic of their appearance. The shape and positioning of a birthmark can be important in helping identify an individual involved in a crime. Moles and warts are other important skin features, although they are more common and less individual than a birthmark.

Scars are another important type of body mark. A scar is a healed wound and it may arise from surgery, accident, or assault. Needle tracks in drug users make characteristic scars that may be informative in the context of many crimes. Severe acne during adolescence may leave scars that persist into adult life and may be a useful identification aid. Many people have scars from common operations such as appendix or gall bladder removal. The dates of such operations should be in the person's medical records and the **medical examiner** will try to relate this to the age of the scar. The internal examination will relate the scar to the operation because the relevant organ will be missing. Operation scars are an aid to identification, but are not usually sufficient alone for identification as they are fairly similar and common. It is also possible to remove some scars with modern laser surgery, so expected scars may no longer be present.

Any wound, however it was acquired, follows the same course of healing. Serious **knife wounds**, deep or jagged accidental cuts, and surgical wounds need stitches to repair them. For several months after the wound was inflicted, a telltale pattern from the stitches will be apparent and this can help age the wound. The healing process involves tiny blood vessels supplying the wounded area with blood and this gives a characteristic pink to reddish brown color to the wound. Later, the body will create scar tissue by laying down collagen, a protein found in connective tissue. This makes the scar fade and shrink. Four to six months after the wound occurred, it will have the appearance of a faint white line. After this, the appearance of the scar won't change much, although it will still be present. This means it is possible to be precise about recent surgery, accidents, or assaults. However, older wounds cannot be dated with much precision although the presence of a scar can still be a useful aid to the identification of an individual.

It is important that the pathologist distinguishes between body marks and injuries that have been sustained during the crime. Often the difference between new and old injuries is obvious. If a body is partially decomposed, dating body marks and assessing their significance may be more of a challenge.

SEE ALSO Autopsy; Wound assessment.

Bomb damage, forensic assessment

Fires and explosions are closely related phenomena in physical and chemical terms. Appropriately, bomb-damage assessment is an aspect of **forensic science** closely related to **arson** investigation.

Explosions can be accidental, such as the rupture and ignition of a propane tank, yet they can also be the deliberate result of the detonation of a bomb. In assessing a crime scene, forensic scientists look for the telltale signs of the cause of the bomb damage.

Such forensic investigations can take place at the municipal and state level, if the involved agencies have the capability to conduct the investigations. Certainly, such capability exists at the national level. In the United States, the two agencies most concerned with bomb-damage assessment at the federal level are the Bureau of Alcohol, Tobacco, and Firearms (**ATF**), and the Explosives Unit of the Federal Bureau of Investigation (**FBI**).

Explosions involve a physical change in materials. A solid or a liquid is converted into a gas or, given the tremendous force of some bombs, directly into energy. Both processes must take place in the presence of oxygen, which is among the most reactive of the chemical elements, meaning that it is highly likely to bond with atoms of other elements.

During the process of oxidation, an element bonding with oxygen loses electrons, while the oxygen gains electrons, a process chemically known as reduction. The world is full of oxidation-reduction reactions, some of which include the rusting or corrosion of metals, the metabolism of food and other biological processes, and combustion. The last of these is commonly known as the process by which materials catch fire, and explosion is simply a fast form of combustion. In the combustion process, chemical bonds are broken quickly, releasing energy that is experienced in the form of heat. In the case of explosion, these bonds are broken even more quickly, producing even more heat and more kinetic energy, which propels objects outward from the center of the blast with greater force.

The investigator of a scene where a bombing has taken place must be schooled in basic physics and chemistry and in forensic science. An initial concern is to ascertain how the explosion occurred and what caused the explosion.

Some bombs are relatively unsophisticated. One example is a pipe bomb, which is typically little more than a metal pipe containing shotgun powder.

Much more complex are explosives using trinitrotoluene (TNT) or nitroglycerin. The latter is a component of dynamite, which combines sodium nitrate and inert compounds to generate the explosive punch. One notorious variety of an explosive is ammonium nitrate. This common ingredient found in fertilizer was used in the 1993 World Trade Center bombing and the 1995 Oklahoma City bombing. Combined with fuel oil, it produces a foul smelling and lethal ammonium nitrate and fuel oil (ANFO) sludge.

One difference between lower-level explosives and their more sophisticated cousins is the fact that the latter requires a detonator or blasting cap, a device to make it active. Investigators will, therefore, seek not only the telltale physical and chemical residue that will lead to a determination of the type of bomb used, but also for **evidence** of detonators

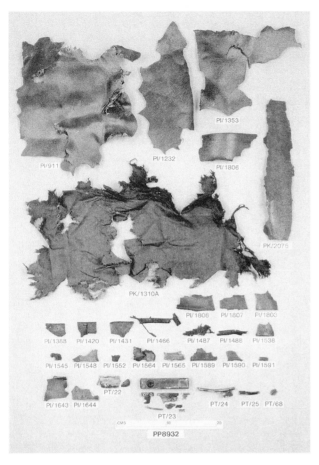

A forensic explosives laboratory photograph shows recovered fragments of a suitcase containing a bomb that exploded aboard the Pan Am airliner above Lockerbie in December, 1988. © REUTERS/CORBIS

teams, which may include civilians. Such was the case in the investigation of the scene in Bali, Indonesia, where Islamist terrorists detonated a bomb that killed several hundred people in October 2002.

SEE ALSO Accelerant; Architecture and structural analysis; Bomb detection devices; Bomb (explosion) investigations; Explosives.

Bomb detection devices

Forensic investigations often involve determining the nature of damage caused to property and people. Various means of destruction impart telltale signs that an expert forensic scientist can unearth.

A related part of forensics can be the detection of the destructive device before it can do its damage. Various bomb detection devices are part of **forensic science**.

Bombs are capable of enormous power and devastating damage. When detonated in strategic, population-dense, or confined spaces, bombs are especially destructive. For example, a bomb planted by political terrorists in a suitcase was responsible for the explosion of Pan Am Flight 103 over Lockerbie, Scotland, on December 21, 1988, that claimed 270 lives. Given the devastation that bombs can cause, and the risk they pose to national security, the detection of bombs is a important priority in airports and elsewhere.

Despite the fact that x-ray examination may not detect some bombs, the technique is still a mainstay in bomb detection. For example, x rays are the best way to reveal the presence in luggage of suspicious shapes. A drawback is that plastic **explosives** can be molded to resemble common objects. Also, explosives are not metallic, and so will escape metal detection. A well-trained operator is a key part of this bomb detection strategy. A newer version of the x-ray examination places a reflector on the opposite side of an object from the x-ray beam. As the rays are scattered back, they are analyzed by a sophisticated computer program, which can reveal differences in the outgoing and incoming beams that were caused by passage of the beams through suspicious material.

Another version of the x ray—dual energy technology—sends two x-ray beams through the object at the same time. One of the beams distinguishes organic material (i.e., food, leather objects, paper) and displays them as red. The other beam distinguishes inorganic objects (i.e., metal clips, umbrellas, metal pens) as green or blue. The color difference helps the operator

and other components such as tapes, wires, timers, switches, and batteries.

ATF agents investigating the first World Trade Center bombing, which killed six people, found a great deal of chemical evidence in the aftermath, ranging from a lingering acrid and acidic aroma to the presence of specific types of molecular residues. There was also **physical evidence** that identified the perpetrators' van as the site from which the blast originated: among the items noted were "feathering," blast-related stretching; "bluing," exposure to welding-torch-like heat; and "dimpling," whereby the metal close to the blast liquefied and shot out, colliding with nearby objects and leaving tiny craters on their surfaces.

In addition to the ATF, the FBI operates a laboratory to which other law-enforcement agencies submit materials for investigation. At the international level, bomb damage assessment may be performed by security services of various nations, or even by international quickly scan packages and baggage for objects that are suspicious by their shape or chemistry. A similar method, which uses radio waves instead of x rays, is called quadrupole resonance technology.

Another optical device is computer tomography, a technique that has been adapted from the CAT scan x-ray technology used in the medical operating room. In tomography, an object is scanned and then a computer analyzes the x-ray image. If areas of the package have not been adequately revealed, the x-ray source can be rotated so as to produce a detailed view of the specific area. In this way packages and baggage can be examined in great detail.

Some bomb components can leave a scent. Until a few decades ago, specially trained dogs were a mainstay of bomb detection squads. Specially trained dogs are still used today to check out packages or locations that are difficult to examine using a machine. A dog's nose is actually a bit more sensitive than the sensitivity of detection machinery that is currently available. However, a dog and handler team costs approximately $50,000 a year, whereas a piece of detection equipment represents a one-time cost of $20,000 to $40,000. Thus, machines are becoming more prevalent.

One such technology utilizes gas **chromatography** and a property called chemiluminescence. In gas chromatography, chemicals of different composition can be separated from each other based on their differing speeds in a stream of gas (selection of the gas can determine the rate of movement of different compounds). A compound in the gas, which will then glow, will recognize an isolated compound that has a certain chemical group in its structure. The glowing (chemiluminescence) registers on an optical detector, revealing the presence of the explosive chemical.

Devices known as sniffers detect vapor given off by certain explosives. Chemicals such as nitroglycerin are readily detected. But, a sniffer can miss explosives such as plastic explosives that do not readily vaporize. Thus, a sniffer should be used only as part of a bomb detection forensic regimen that involves other detection techniques.

Another forensic device detects chemicals present in bombs by concentrating the air collected from a target location. The air is drawn through a filter, where explosive chemicals collect, due to their tendency to be heavier than the air molecules around them. The filter is analyzed using ion mobility spectrometry.

The spectrometric technique is very sensitive. Less than a nanogram (10^{-9} gram) of explosives resi-

PackBots like this one, demonstrated by an iRobot executive in 2004, are currently being used by the U.S. military in Iraq and Afghanistan for reconnaissance and bomb detection and detonation. © BRIAN SNYDER/REUTERS/CORBIS

due can be detected. To put this into perspective, a **fingerprint** on a luggage handle left by someone who had been handling explosives will typically contain 100,000 times more of the residue.

SEE ALSO Accelerant; Architecture and structural analysis; Bomb (explosion) investigations; Explosives.

Bomb (explosion) investigations

The investigation of explosions has a long history in **forensic science** and covers incidents ranging from accidents in the home or workplace to major terrorist attacks. An explosion is a sudden release of physical or chemical energy, carried on a high-pressure wave, and generally accompanied by an emission of heat, light, and sound. An explosion may result from a criminal act involving a bomb, but it can also occur by accident—if a spark ignites a leak of domestic gas, for example. Establishing the nature of an explosion can be a significant challenge to the forensic investigator. The high-pressure wave of an explosion can be extremely destructive, both to bystanders and any objects of materials in the vicinity. Analyzing this kind of **evidence** can be a very difficult task, particularly as an explosion is often followed by a fire. This causes complications for the investigators as much valuable evidence is then destroyed. There are also potential hazards to the investigators themselves in investigating a bomb site. There may be structures in danger of imminent collapse as well as exposure to dangerous materials such as broken **glass**, flammable or toxic vapors, or asbestos. In the case of a bombing, there is always a possibility that a second device has been placed to kill or maim those who respond to the explosion.

Explosions are an example of the Law of Conservation of Energy, which states that energy can neither be created nor destroyed, but it can be converted from one form into another. The two main classes of explosions are chemical and physical. When a bomb explodes, for instance, the chemical energy stored in the molecules of the explosive making up the device is converted into kinetic (movement) energy, heat, light, and sound. This is an example of a chemical explosion—probably the class of most interest to the forensic scientist. Physical explosions are the other main class requiring investigation. A typical example of a physical explosion is the sudden release of gas from a container of pressurized gas or liquid if it becomes overheated.

An explosive is a substance that can produce an explosion through a chemical reaction. When it is used illegally and to cause harm it is generally known as a bomb. Legitimate **explosives** include fireworks and blasting materials used in quarrying. Explosives generally contain fuel and an oxidant and it is the chemical reaction between them which releases stored chemical energy.

There are two types of explosions due to chemical reactions, which is reflected in the type of damage they cause at the scene. In a detonation, the speed at which the chemical reaction moves though the explosive is greater than the speed of sound in that material. The resulting pressure wave may move at up to 8,500 meters per second (9,296 yards per second). High explosives, such as dynamite, generally undergo detonation and have a characteristic shatter-

ing effect on their surroundings. A deflagration occurs when the speed of the chemical reaction of the explosion travels through the explosive slower than the speed of sound in the material. This creates a pressure wave moving at 1,000 meters (1094 yards) per second or less. The impact of low explosives, such as a mixture of air and gasoline vapor or sugar and potassium chlorate, is best described as pushing, rather than shattering, although they can still produce an enormous amount of damage. Depending on their nature, explosives may or may not need an initiating material, called a detonator, to set them off. A useful distinction can also be made between condensed explosives, which are solid or liquid, and dispersed explosives, consisting of aerosol or gas.

Investigation of the scene of an explosion aims to discover whether an explosion actually took place and, if so, whether it was an accident or a bomb. The forensic scientist will then try to find out what kind of explosion occurred, the materials involved and, in the case of a criminal act, they will work with the police to find out who was responsible. Examination of the scene and witness reports can establish whether an explosion has happened. Loud bangs, flashes, violent eruption of debris, shattering of nearby objects and formation of a crater where the event occurred are all indicative of an explosion. The investigator will look for evidence of a possible accident, such as a gas leak or creation of a cloud of flammable gas at the scene. If it looks as if a bomb caused the explosion, then the explosive device must found. This involves searching for the device itself and any detonator fragments which may be scattered among the debris. There may have been a timing device to allow the bomber time to get away, which would consist of electronic circuitry, wires, and batteries. The remains of the device will probably contain some residue from the explosive and may even bear fingerprints from the perpetrators. The construction of the device and how it was triggered may also be deduced from examination of these fragments.

The investigator will probably have to search far and wide at the scene of the explosion to recover bomb fragments. Some may be embedded in the bodies of victims, and here medical staff will need to carry out x rays to identify any evidence and, if possible, recover it for forensic investigation. A suicide bomber is, of course, an important source of such evidence. Suspect surfaces must be swabbed with various solvents to extract invisible chemical traces of explosive residue. There is nearly always a part of the bomb that did not explode and these residues can be very informative. Small items that

Rescue workers and crash investigators search the area around the cockpit of Pan Am flight 103 that crashed east of Lockerbie, Scotland in 1988, killing 270 people. Investigators found the aircraft was downed by a Libyan planted bomb exploding in mid-air.
© REUTERS/CORBIS

may bear explosive residue can be placed in a beaker and agitated with a suitable solvent. The solvent has to be chosen to match the explosive—diethyl ether may be used for organic materials, while water dissolves inorganic materials such as potassium chlorate.

Once the samples are back in the laboratory, there are many sensitive analytical techniques, such as high performance liquid **chromatography** and **thin layer chromatography**, that can be used to assess the chemical nature of explosives and identify the **trace evidence**, comparing it with reference samples of explosives. Similar techniques can be used to sample for traces of explosives on suspects' hands and clothing. Comparison may be sufficient to link a suspect with a crime scene. The analysis of traces of explosives has to be done with great care and expertise because there is ample opportunity for

cross contamination to occur. This means taking scrupulous care with the collection of the trace evidence and then using **control samples** throughout the analysis. If the explosive can be identified, the police investigation will look for buyers and sellers of that particular material.

Explosions often cause characteristic damage to nearby surfaces through a combination of the high temperature generated and the high pressure wave. A mottled irregular appearance, known as gas wash, results from a combination of melting and erosion of the surface material. Textiles may undergo characteristic clubbing damage as the polymer melts and then re-solidifies. On metal surfaces, microcraters may be visible on microscopic examination. Soot deposits on more distant surfaces, such as window frames, are also characteristic of an explosion.

The pattern of damage at the scene of an explosion will help the forensic scientist to determine what happened. The location and depth of any crater or the nature of structural damage such as broken windows can all help to locate the actual seat of explosion, for instance. The scene can also be very informative about the nature of the explosion too, as different combinations of explosive and explosion can give rise to characteristic types of damage. Detonation of a condensed explosive tends to produce a huge crater and very severe damage that involves pulverizing and shattering of nearby objects, even if they are made of tough materials like steel. A deflagration in a condensed explosive produces intense heat and could bend or melt objects rather than cutting them. Detonation is rare with dispersed explosives, but deflagration gives a pattern in which most of the damage may occur some way from the explosion itself owing to a pushing out effect. In one example, a natural gas explosion caused only superficial burns to two people in the basement underneath the room where it occurred, yet the incident was violent enough to blow furniture out of the building.

Some explosions are of a mixed type. Petrol (gasoline) bombs are often used by terrorists and typically involve using a small charge of high explosive to disperse and ignite petrol, which is a flammable liquid. This event involves detonation of a high explosive and deflagration of a dispersed explosive. The detonation will produce damage close to the point where the bomb was set off, while the deflagration will produce damage further away.

SEE ALSO Accelerant; Bomb damage, forensic assessment; Bomb detection devices.

Robert Borkenstein

8/31/1912–8/10/2002
AMERICAN
ALCOHOL/DRUG RESEARCHER, TRAFFIC
SAFETY INVENTOR

Known for contributions in the area of chemical tests for blood and breath alcohol, Robert F. Borkenstein was the scientist who invented in 1954 the first practical, hand-held breath-alcohol-measuring device called the **Breathalyzer®**. Based on Borkenstein's groundbreaking invention, police officers use such devices today as a simple but accurate way to determine a driver's level of intoxication. By taking a sample of expelled breath when a driver is stopped, police officers are able to calculate the amount of alcohol as a percentage of blood. Borkenstein was also instrumental in founding and developing the International Council on Alcohol, Drugs and Traffic Safety (ICADTS), an independent, nonprofit organization whose purpose is to reduce injury and death caused by the abuse of drugs and alcohol while operating motor vehicles.

Borkenstein was born in Fort Wayne, Indiana. With an early interest in criminal justice and traffic safety, Borkenstein began his career in 1936 as a police photographer. He advanced quickly to criminal justice technician for the Indiana State Police, and completed his 22-year career as captain in charge of the Indiana State Police Forensics Laboratory. Borkenstein completed a bachelor's of arts degree in 1958 from Indiana University (IU) in Bloomington. Upon graduation, he became an IU professor and the chairman of the university's newly created Department of Police Administration, a position he held until his retirement in 1983. During his tenure, Borkenstein expanded the department so that today it offers masters and doctor of philosophy (Ph.D.) degrees. In 1963, Borkenstein received an honorary doctor of science degree from Wittenberg University in Springfield, Ohio. Then, in 1971, Borkenstein became the director of the IU Center for Studies of Law in Action. Today, the Center offers a one-week course (twice a year)—the "Robert F. Borkenstein Course on Alcohol and Highway Safety: Testing, Research, and Litigation"—for professionals in criminal justice, **forensic science**, law, and law enforcement. Indiana University bestowed Borkenstein with a honorary doctor of laws degree in 1987.

Because Borkenstein felt so strongly about reducing drunk driving, the use of breath samples for the enforcement of blood alcohol concentration (BAC) limits has been adopted in many countries around the world. Borkenstein's invention also allows for a larger percentage of impaired driving arrests by police officers because it eliminates the need to call a specially trained technician to take blood samples and the consequential delays for laboratory results. It also enables a greater number of convictions by prosecutors because the accurate breath samples are allowed as forensic **evidence** in court.

In 1950 Borkenstein attended the first meeting for the organization that would eventually become the ICADTS. Largely due to his early organizing efforts and his monetary contributions, the ICADTS became an international organization of professionals from such fields as economics, law, law enforcement, government, **medicine**, and public health. Borkenstein also helped to establish the Widmark Award, which is presented to individuals and organizations—such as the U.S. National Safety Council and Mothers Against Drunk Drivers—who have made outstanding contributions to reducing impaired driving.

During the 1960s, Borkenstein led a research team in the "Grand Rapids" study, which determined the relative risk of motored vehicle crashes due to BAC levels. The study was one of the earliest and largest studies of its kind and had a strong influence on strengthening the impaired driving laws around the world.

SEE ALSO Automobile accidents; Breathalyzer®; Chemical and biological detection technologies; Sobriety testing.

Botany

Soil, plant fragments, and pollen, maybe in trace amounts, are often left behind at the scene of a crime. Most people entering a house will bring in some soil or mud from outside. Even if they take off their shoes, their clothing may contain tiny smears of mud where they have been splashed or come into contact with a surface. Tools like shovels might also contain significant traces of mud. An expert in botany, the science of plants, can often help unravel the identity and significance of such **trace evidence**. Soil and mud, in particular, are often present in footprints or **tire tracks** and can help link a suspect to the scene of a crime. The pattern of mud on clothing can also be significant.

Soil is a mixture of mineral, plant, and animal matter that is often characteristic of a particular area and may reveal something about a suspect's movements. Often soil also contains some man-made products such as **glass** or paint. The forensic scientist is interested in the patterning of soil and mud staining and how it might relate to the circumstances of a crime. For instance, if an assault takes place out-of-doors, then the mud staining of a suspect's clothes could naturally be revealing.

The visual and chemical analysis of a soil trace can often link it to a particular geographical region. This, in turn, can help to track the movements of a suspect if he or she has traveled to the area where the crime was committed. If a body has been moved for burial, then soil or plant material in a vehicle could be important.

The forensic botanist, first with the naked eye, looks at any soil or mud and assesses its color and texture. Microscopic examination reveals more about the content of the soil and the range of particle sizes it contains. Large samples might be sieved to separate them into different portions, depending upon particle sizes. Then these can be further examined to give more information.

Chemical analysis using advanced techniques like atomic absorption **spectroscopy** will give the mineral composition of a soil sample, such as chalk or clay, which is often characteristic of the area it came from. The acidity of the soil is also measured, as this varies greatly with place of origin. Thermal analysis of the soil, heating it in an oven till it decomposes, is also often characteristic of its origin. There may be dramatic color change or the soil may absorb heat in a characteristic way.

Suspects and victims also, often unknowingly, carry various items of plant debris on their bodies and clothes such as flower petals, seeds, and pollen. These are often native to a specific area. For instance, if pine needles are found around a victim who seems to have perished in an area where there are no evergreens, it may tell the investigators something important and specific about the suspect and his or her movements. The botanist can investigate what species carries these particular needles and so help link the perpetrator to a specific source.

Pollen grains are tiny and are not usually noticed by those involved in a crime. Pollen is often found almost everywhere—in hair, on surfaces, and on paper. If pollen is found on the envelope of a threatening letter or a ransom note, for instance, it may provide a valuable link to the suspect. There are pollen databases which can show the investigators where a particular pollen sample may have come from.

When a body is left out in the open or in a shallow grave, plant debris, including leaves and needles, may cover the remains. Analysis of this growth can often help establish the time and season of death and burial.

In one British case from 1887, a 15-year-old boy was found drowned in a ditch. Footprints led down the bank of the ditch. Sand grains were found on the suspect's trousers and matched to the ditch. Mud on the clothing of the suspect's daughter, who turned out to be an accomplice, was examined microscopically. Hairs from the seeds of the groundsel plant were found. This mud matched samples taken from the part of the ditch where the body was found, but not mud found from other areas. If botany helped solve a case so long ago, it can be even more powerful today with modern analytical techniques.

SEE ALSO Geology; Geographic profiling; Minerals; Pollen and pollen rain; Soils; Spores.

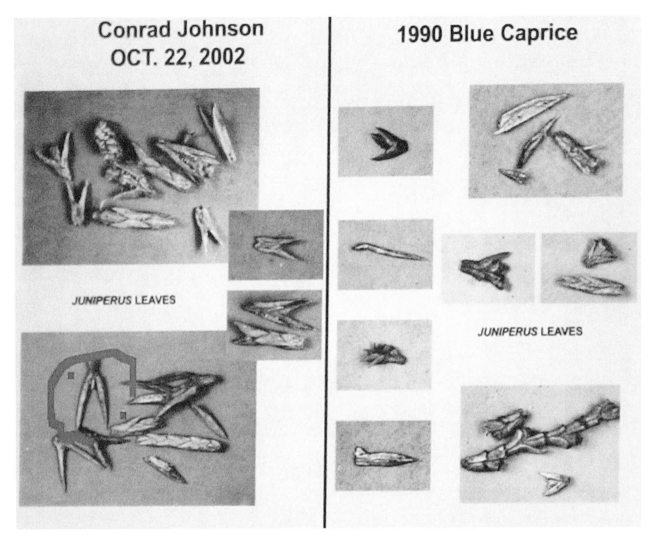

Magnified plant material was displayed on a screen during the testimony of Bureau of Alcohol, Tobacco, and Firearms (ATF) forensic chemist Edward C. Bender during the trial of convicted sniper suspect John Allen Muhammad in 2003. © DAVE ELLIS/POOL/CORBIS

Botulinum toxin

Clostridium botulinum is a spore-forming bacterium. Like the well-known **anthrax** bacillus, the **spores** of *Clostridium botulinum* can persist in the environment for many years and, when conditions become more favorable (i.e., in a wound, food, and the lungs) the spore can germinate and free the toxin.

There are at least seven structurally different versions of botulinum toxin. The type designated as type A is responsible for some botulism food-borne outbreaks in the United States and elsewhere. Improperly canned foods are a particular threat.

Botulinum toxin is among the most poisonous substances known in the natural world. The toxin, which can be ingested or inhaled, and which disrupts transmission of nerve impulses to muscles, is natu-

rally produced by the bacterium *Clostridium botulinum*. Certain strains of *C. baratii* and *C. butyricum* can also be capable of producing the toxin.

Botulinum toxin acts by preventing the transmission of nerve signals between the nerves that connect with muscle cells. Progressive functional deterioration of the affected muscles occurs. Symptoms of botulism intoxication include dizziness, blurred or double vision, nausea, vomiting, diarrhea, and weakness of muscles in various areas of the body. The muscle failure can be so severe as to lead to coma and respiratory arrest. Even in those who survive exposure to the toxin, complete recovery can take months.

The damage and lethality that can be inflicted by the toxin makes this agent important in **forensic science**. If botulism toxin poisoning is suspected, a

Clostridium botulinum (Type E) colonies grown on a 48-hour egg yolk agar plate. © CDC/PHIL/CORBIS

forensic scientist can check for the presence of the bacterial spores.

The sometimes deliberate use of the toxin is also forensically relevant. Contamination of food is one route for infection with the toxin. This can occur naturally, via the bacterial contamination of the food. On the other hand, food can be deliberately contaminated. As well, the toxin can also be released into the air. The latter is invariably deliberate. For example, on at least three occasions between 1990 and 1995, while experimenting with biological warfare agents, the Japanese cult Aum Shinrikyo released botulinum **toxins**, but failed in attempts to spread them.

SEE ALSO Biodetectors; Bioterrorism; Nervous system overview; Pathogens; Toxins.

Bovine spongiform encephalopathy SEE Mad cow disease investigation

Brain wave scanners

The term brain wave scanners, in the context of law enforcement, particularly concerning forensic investigations, encompasses an array of research and technological developments that seek to electronically determine whether a statement is true or false.

It has been demonstrated that brain patterns are altered when a lie is being told. Moreover, using a technique called magnetic resonance **imaging** (MRI), the alteration can be visualized as a lie occurs (commonly referred to as "real-time"). Simply put, a lie can be seen.

The concept of a brain wave scanner is not unlike that of a polygraph. Whereas a polygraph measures fluctuations in heart rate and breathing, a scanner measures brain responses to stimuli. It could be more effective, because a person adept a telling a lie may experience little excitement in the circulatory system. However, even this individual would be required to expend extra energy on the thought necessary to tell a lie, and it is this energy that a brain wave scanner may be able to measure.

When one is asked a question to which one knows the true answer, that answer comes first to mind automatically. Even if the individual has already prepared and rehearsed a lie, it is still necessary to think past the true answer and access the lie. This extra activity is easily measured on a brain scan.

After the September 11, 2001, terrorist attacks, a number of government agencies began to take a new look at brain scanning technology as a means of security screening. In 2002, officials of the National Aeronautics and Space Administration reportedly informed airline officials that they were developing brain-monitoring technology for use in screening airline passengers. Such activity, along with an increase of interest in brain-wave scanning by the Federal Bureau of Investigation, has raised concerns among civil-libertarians, who view brain-wave scanning as a particularly objectionable invasion of privacy in the service of public security.

SEE ALSO Epilepsy; Neurotransmitters; Polygraphs; Radiation, electromagnetic radiation injury.

Breathalyzer®

Accidents or crimes can occur when one or more of those involved are intoxicated. Impaired driving is the obvious example. In the United States, at least 25,000 people die in alcohol related traffic accidents each year, representing about 500 people each week. In fact, alcohol-related traffic accidents are the leading **cause of death** among Americans aged 16–24.

Alcohol can also fuel domestic disturbances and other altercations between people that result in injury and death.

Traffic accidents and violent incidents can lead to a forensic investigation. Thus, alcohol is closely tied to **forensic science**.

The determination of alcohol level can be an important part of an ongoing investigation. Returning to the example of a traffic accident, one of the early facets of an investigation can be the determination of the alcohol level of a driver. Often a police officer needs to ascertain whether a person is legally impaired. Several tests of coordination (i.e., walking a straight line, touching the tip of the nose with a finger) can be helpful indicators. But, determination of blood alcohol levels via a Breathalyzer® test is a critical part of the assessment of sobriety.

An initial Breathalyzer® measurement is often conducted at the scene of the accident, since normal metabolic processes in the body will reduce the alcohol level within hours.

Measurements of alcohol level are most conveniently taken by monitoring expired air. The Breathalyzer® is one of three different devices that can be used. It is the most popular device for portable, at-the-scene use. The instrument uses a color reaction to detect alcohol; the degree of color change is related to the alcohol level in the breath.

The result is typically expressed as the blood-alcohol concentration (BAC), which represents the grams of alcohol per 100 milliters of blood. The legal BAC limit can vary between jurisdictions; 0.08% is a typical limit. So, for example, if a suspect's breathalyzer reading was 0.15%, they would be legally impaired. If they were driving a vehicle, they would be charged with driving while impaired (DWI) or driving under the influence (DUI).

The development of the devices that could monitor alcohol in the breath dates back to the 1940s. In 1954, Dr. Robert F. Borkenstein of the Indiana State Police invented the modern-day Breathalyzer®.

The Breathalyzer® relies on the fact that, when consumed, alcohol is not altered in the bloodstream and on the volatility of the compound (the tendency of the compound to evaporate from solution). The latter is important when alcohol-laden blood passes through the tiny channels in the air sacs of the lungs. There, alcohol's volatility encourages its passage across the channel membranes into the lung, where it can be exhaled.

A Breathalyzer® detects this expired alcohol. When someone blows into a Breathalyzer®, the device detects both the volume of air expired and, as described below, the amount of alcohol present. The ratio of the amount of alcohol in the breath to the blood alcohol level is 2,100:1. By determining the amount of alcohol in the volume of expired air, a calculation of blood alcohol concentration can be made. This calculation is done as described below.

When air is blown into a Breathalyzer®, it bubbles through a mixture of potassium dichromate, sulfuric acid, silver nitrate, and water. The sulfuric acid acts to remove the alcohol from the air into the aqueous solution. In the solution, the silver nitrate acts as a catalyst (a compound that speeds up the rate of reaction without directly participating in the reaction) in the reaction that follows.

In this reaction, the alcohol (ethanol) reacts with the reddish-orange potassium dichromate to produce

A Santa Monica police officer tests a man on a breath analyzing machine to determine alcohol levels in his bloodstream.
© SHELLEY GAZIN/CORBIS

the greenish-colored chromium sulfate, potassium sulfate, and acetic acid. The degree of the color change corresponds to the amount of alcohol that is present.

To determine the degree of the color change, and so calculate the alcohol level, it is necessary to compare the test solution to an unreacted solution. The latter control solution is contained in another compartment in the Breathalyzer®. The control solution is in a photocell; an electric current that is produced causes a needle in the device to move from its resting place. The operator then turns a knob to move the needle back to its resting place and then records the alcohol level from the position of an indicator on the knob relative to a scale.

Other versions of Breathalyzers® can perform the calculations automatically and display the alcohol level as a digital read-out. With improvements in technology, the Breathalyzer® has become smaller. Some models are so small that they can be attached to a key chain. Forensically-approved versions are larger, but are still portable enough to be taken to the scene of an investigation.

Two other alcohol detection devices can be used. They do not detect ethanol in the color-dependent fashion of a Breathalyzer®. An Intoxilyzer® detects alcohol using infrared **spectroscopy**, while an AlcoSensor® detects alcohol based on its use as fuel in another type of chemical reaction.

SEE ALSO Crime scene investigation; Evidence; Indicator, acid-base.

Pat Brown

AMERICAN
INVESTIGATIVE CRIMINAL PROFILER

Pat Brown is a prominent investigative criminal profiler whose company, the Pat Brown Criminal Profiling Agency, specializes in providing scene analyses and behavioral **profiling** to defense attorneys, prosecutors, the judicial system, and to international clients. She is also the C.E.O. of The Sexual Homicide Exchange (SHE), which was created in 1996 in an effort to provide a broadened approach to police **training**, homicide investigation, criminal justice, advocacy, and community involvement. SHE provides *pro bono* (at no cost) investigative and criminal profiling services to the families of homicide victims, as well as to law enforcement agencies. A central focus of SHE is the investigation and profiling of **cold case** homicides.

Through SHE, Pat Brown is piloting the CAPTURE (Coalition for Apprehending Predators through Utilizing Resources Effectively) Program, a serial homicide investigation methodology and training program for law enforcement personnel, the goal of which is to increase the efficiency of homicide investigations and thereby increase the rate of serial killer arrests (and significantly decrease the number of **serial killers** at large).

As an investigative criminal profiler, Pat Brown makes herself (and her team of profilers) available to assist law enforcement agencies without charge. Although their profiling work may sometimes serve merely to validate the work of the ongoing homicide investigation and to provide reassurance to the families of victims that the criminal justice system is doing all it can to solve the crime, they can sometimes offer new ideas and provide alternative directions for the investigation to take. In suspected serial homicides, investigative profiling may be used to narrow investigative focus or, alternatively, to broaden the base of possible leads; it may be used as a tool for linking crimes together.

Brown views investigative criminal profiling as a dynamic process that does not conclude until a suspect is arrested and convicted. She deems it a support process for the criminal investigative team, made up of a combination of four skills: investigation, forensic analysis, psychological assessment, and the application of cultural anthropology. Brown considers this type of profiling to be a real-time, speculative process requiring ongoing checking to avoid missing any significant data, and should never be done in isolation, but rather as one piece of the entire criminal investigative process.

Pat Brown, through her commonsense, straightforward law enforcement training programs, her media commentary work, her development of the CAPTURE program, and the evolution of SHE, has done much to contribute both to the solution of cold cases and ongoing investigations.

SEE ALSO Anthropology; Cold case; Crime scene reconstruction; Crime scene staging; Serial killers.

Richard L. Brunelle

AMERICAN
FORENSIC CHEMIST

Richard L. Brunelle worked for both the government and the private sector as a forensic chemist for almost forty years, specializing in document authentication and **ink analysis**. Brunelle's expertise led him to write two successful books on the subject. He also served as a consultant on many criminal cases. In addition, Brunelle is responsible for founding the Society of Forensic Ink Analysts.

Brunelle began his career as a forensic chemist for the Forensic Science Laboratory at the U.S. Bureau of Alcohol, Tobacco, and Firearms (**ATF**). He worked with the ATF for twenty-eight years, holding various positions including the chief of the Forensic Science Laboratory. During this time Brunelle conducted extensive research in the area of ink analysis, including work with chemist Antonio Cantu to develop new methods for chemically determining the relative age of ballpoint pens. Additionally, Brunelle was consulted on document fraud cases across the country and wrote articles for a number of **professional publications**.

Brunelle is perhaps best known for the two major books he co-wrote on the subject of ink analysis. The first was the 1984 *Forensic Examination of Ink and Paper*, written with Robert W. Reed. The text details the history, properties, and composition of writing inks and paper, as well as the forensic examination and court acceptability of said products. In 2003, Brunelle and fellow forensic scientist Kenneth R. Crawford wrote *Advances in the Forensic Analysis and Dating of Writing Ink*. In this book, the authors outline laboratory procedures used in examining and dating inks, and discuss the techniques' applications in civil and criminal cases. They focus on advances made within the last twenty years, including relative age comparisons and accelerated aging of inks.

After his retirement from the ATF, Brunelle started his own forensic science firm, Brunelle Forensic Laboratories. There he specialized in dating inks on **questioned documents**. He also was responsible for establishing the Society of Forensic Ink Analysts. It was the first professional association for forensic ink chemists, created to advance the science of forensic ink analysis such as ink comparisons, ink **identification**, and ink dating. Brunelle was awarded the 1972 John A. Dondero Award from the **International Association for Identification**, given in recognition of outstanding contributions in the field of scientific identification.

SEE ALSO Careers in forensic science; Document forgery.

Bubonic plague

Bubonic plague is an infectious disease. Thus, it is a concern in **forensic science** as a possible **cause of death** during an occurrence or outbreak featuring an unknown pathogen (illness-causing agent).

The bacterium that is responsible for bubonic plague is *Yersinia pestis*, named after one of its co-discoverers, Alexandre Yersin, and is also known as *Pasteurella pestis*. Typically, the bacterium is passed from rodents to other animals and humans via the bite of a flea. The flea acquires the bacterium as it lives on the skin of the rodent. Humans can also acquire the disease by direct contact with infected tissue or **fluids**.

Pneumonic plague (infection with *Yersinia pestis* bacteria in the lungs) results from inhaling minute droplets of moisture in the air that are contaminated with the bacteria, usually from being near another person with pneumonic plague who is coughing.

With bubonic plague, *Yersinia pestis* invades the lymphatic system. Bubonic plague is named because of the symptoms. The bacterial infection produces a painful swelling of the lymph nodes. These are called buboes. Often, the first swelling is evident in the groin. During the Middle Ages, a large epidemic of bubonic plague was referred to as the Black Death, because of the blackening of the skin due to the dried blood that accumulated under the skin's surface.

The bubonic plague has been a significant cause of misery and death throughout recorded history. The Black Death was only one of many epidemics of plague that extend back to the beginning of recorded history. The first recorded outbreak of bubonic plague was in 542–543. This plague destroyed the attempts of the Roman emperor of the day to re-establish a Roman empire in Europe. This is only one example of how bubonic plague has changed the course of history.

The plague of London in 1665 killed over 17,000 people (almost twenty percent of the city's population). This outbreak was quelled by a huge fire that destroyed most of the city.

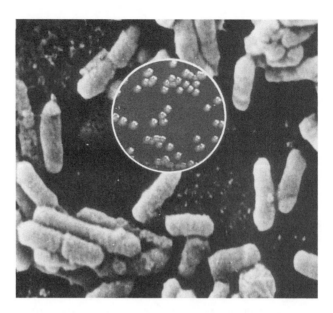

Microscopic section showing plague bacteria. © CORBIS SYGMA

The disease remains present to this day. In North America, the last large epidemic occurred in Los Angeles in 1925. With the advent of the antibiotic era, bubonic plague has been controlled in the developed world. However, sporadic cases (e.g., 10–15 cases each year) still occur in the western United States. In less developed countries (e.g., in Africa, Bolivia, Peru, Ecuador, Brazil), thousands of cases are reported each year.

The infrequent outbreaks of bubonic plague do not mean the disease disappears altogether. Rather, the disease normally exists in what is called an enzootic state. That is, a few individuals of a certain community (e.g., rodents) harbor the disease. Sometimes, however, environmental conditions cause the disease to spread through the carrier population, causing loss of life. As the rodent populations dies, the fleas that live on them need to find other food sources. This is when the interaction with humans and non-rodent animals can occur. Between outbreaks, *Yersinia pestis* infects rodents without causing much illness. Thus, the rodents become a reservoir of the infection.

Symptoms of infection in humans begin within days after contamination with the plague bacterium. The bacteria enter the bloodstream and travel to various organs (e.g., kidney, liver, spleen, lungs) as well as to the brain. Symptoms include shivering, nausea with vomiting, headache, intolerance to light, and a whitish-appearing tongue. Buboes then appear, followed by rupture of blood vessels. The released blood can coagulate and turn black.

If the infection is untreated, the death rate from plague in humans approaches 75%. Prompt treatment most often leads to full recovery and a life-long immunity from further infection. Prevention is possible, since a vaccine is available. Unfortunately, the vaccine is protective for only a few months. Use of the vaccine is usually reserved for those who will be at high risk for acquiring the bacterial infection (e.g., soldiers, travelers to an outbreak region). **Antibiotics** such as tetracycline or sulfonamide are used more commonly as a precaution for those who might be exposed to the bacterium. Such use of antibiotics should be stopped once the risk of infection is gone, to avoid the development of resistance in other bacteria resident in the body.

The most effective way to prevent bubonic plague is the maintenance of adequate sanitary conditions. This acts to control the rodent population, especially in urban centers.

SEE ALSO Biodetectors; Bioterrorism; Nervous system overview; Pathogens; Toxins.

Bugs (microphones) and bug detectors

A forensic investigation typically involves the examination of items at the scene of the crime or accident. Fabric, bloodstains, and food are examples. In addition, an investigator will make use of recording devices that were in place prior to the incident. One example is a security camera. Another example involves the various forms of technology that allow voice conversations to be recorded. Microphones (bugs) can be installed in a room or even within a telephone.

Hand-in-hand with the development of bugs came technologies designed to detect the devices (bug detectors). Bug detectors are a very useful forensic tool, enabling a crime or accident scene to be scanned for the presence of recording bugs.

A typical electronic bug consists of a microphone and a radio transmitter. The microphone receives sound waves and either vibrates a thin membrane called a diaphragm (a dynamic microphone) or a thin metal ribbon suspended in a magnetic field (a ribbon microphone). Vibration of the diaphragm produces an electrical signal. Vibration of the metal ribbon produces a voltage change, which can be converted to an electrical signal.

The electric signals are then beamed out of the transmitter portion of the bug to a receiver. The conversation transmitted by the bug to the receiver can be recorded or listened to directly. Other types of bugs exist. For example, radio frequencies passing through the electrical wiring of a building can be intercepted. Bugs can also intercept the electrical transmissions from portable phones, wireless computers linked to a network, and even from a computer monitor.

The designation of secret listening devices as bugs is entirely suitable, given their small size. Modern bugs can be concealed in pens, calculators, and even buttons (although the latter need to be replaced frequently, as their power supply is so small).

The miniaturization of electronics has made it possible to pack more devices into the small package. For example, video equipment can be contained in a bug, enabling sight as well as sound surveillance.

Up to the 1980s, bugs operated using very high frequency, or VHF, radio waves. However, the development of mobile communications technology, particularly digital telephones, paved the way for the development of bugs that operate using ultrahigh frequency wavelength or microwaves. This has made the detection of bugs more difficult than simply detecting the output of radio waves. Some modern bugging devices can also disguise the output signal or vary the frequency of the signal, which can thwart detection.

Some bugs contain voice-activated recorders that are capable of storing up to 12 hours of conversation. The information can then be rapidly sent to a receiver in a "burst" transmission. Because detection of the bug is geared toward the frequencies emitted during transmission, the detection of these bugs is difficult. Counter systems are designed to try and activate the bug and then detect it. The transmission range of bugs has improved from mere yards to miles. Some bugs can even transmit to satellites, making monitoring from thousands of miles away feasible.

Another surveillance option is the use of a microphone. Conventional microphones operate electronically; the electrical signals representing the converted sound waves are passed through a wire to a receiving device located elsewhere. Microphones that operate using magnetic fields also exist.

Shotgun microphones equipped with a parabolic reflector can record conversation outside at a distance. Electronic filters screen out extraneous background noise in order to enhance the sensitivity of the microphone.

Laser microphones bounce a laser beam off of an object that is near the conversation. The object must be something that resonates, or is able to move as pressure waves created by noise in the room encounter it. As the object vibrates back and forth due to the sound waves from the conversation in the room, the distance traveled by the laser beam will become slightly shorter and longer. These length differences can be measured over time, and the pattern of the vibrations translated into the text of the conversation.

Microphones are extremely hard to detect, especially when used in a room where other electrical appliances (i.e., computers, telephones) are operating.

Bugs are detected by virtue of the frequencies they emit. Essentially, a bug detector is a receiver. When brought near an operating bug, the detector will collect and amplify the bug's transmission. Bug detectors are now portable enough to be carried in a "sweep" of a room.

Bugs and microphones have moved from the arena of political espionage to the boardrooms of corporate offices and police surveillance operations. Recognizing the prevalence of electronic eavesdropping devices and their threat to privacy, the United States Congress passed the Electronic Communication Privacy Act in 1986, which made bugging illegal. Nonetheless, the use of eavesdropping devices and detectors is widespread in the intelligence and business communities. One estimate places the annual sales of such devices in the United States alone at $888 million.

SEE ALSO Crime scene investigation; Evidence; Telephone recording system; Telephone tap detector.

Building analysis SEE Architecture and structural analysis

Building materials

Sometimes a burglar or assailant enters or leaves premises through a window, via a roof or ceiling, or by breaking down or forcing a door. This can produce a range of wide range of **trace evidence** derived from the building materials used in that particular dwelling. Trace **evidence** is often invisible and will adhere to the clothing, hair, skin, and footwear of a suspect without the person being aware of it. Foren-

sic examination of the suspect may produce evidence that can link the person to the scene of the crime through the presence of tiny amounts of building materials.

Forensic analysis of building materials covers a wide range of substances, such as brick, plaster, slate, loft insulation, **glass**, and wood. The broad principles for collecting and examining such materials are the same. The evidence has to be collected from around the site of entry or escape from the scene of the crime, by brushing, taping, picking with tweezers, or vacuuming. The samples need to be stored in a separate unused container and transferred to the forensic laboratory through a careful **chain of custody**. Examination of the suspect and his or her clothes for matching trace evidence of building materials has to be done with great care and preferably not by the same investigator who was at the scene of the crime. Otherwise, fragments of brick dust or glass, for instance, could be unknowingly transferred to the suspect.

Most building material trace evidence is in the form of **fibers** or dust. For instance, loft insulation is composed of glass fibers. The first step is to examine the material by eye, in good lighting, and then under a microscope. Various microscopic techniques are used to establish the nature of the material. In comparison microscopy, the sample is compared to known reference samples of various types of brick or plaster. The exact color of the sample can be established by microspectrophotometry.

There are various analytical techniques that can determine the chemical composition of a building material. Forensic scientists may use infrared **spectroscopy**, neutron activation analysis, or x-ray diffraction as appropriate. The analysis of building material evidence may tell the investigators a great deal about how an entry or exit to a building was made by a suspect. This provides a vital link in reconstructing the events before and after the crime took place.

SEE ALSO Crime scene investigation; Crime scene reconstruction; Glass; Paint analysis; Physical evidence.

Bullet lead analysis

Crime scene bullets are sometimes too mutilated or fragmented to be useful for normal **ballistics** analysis—that is, the bullet has no markings that investigators can compare with those produced by a gun connected to a suspect. Bullet lead analysis, sometimes called compositional bullet lead comparison or comparative bullet lead analysis (CBLA), allows forensic investigators to identify the elemental composition and characteristics of a bullet. This information can show if the bullet matches that of a bullet whose source is known, whether two bullets likely came from the same source (a single manufacturer's lot), or possibly even the same box. CBLA is widely accepted in the courts to show that a bullet recovered from a crime scene matches other bullets found in the possession of a suspect, strongly suggesting that the suspect fired the bullet in question. CBLA can also be used to exclude suspects.

The procedure, which is generally carried out by the Federal Bureau of Investigation (**FBI**), was developed in the 1960s by researchers under a federal grant to develop uses for neutron activation analysis (NAA). With the aid of a nuclear reactor, these researchers were able to show that a billet, or ingot, of lead poured from a pot of molten lead was homogenous in its elemental composition. Thus, any bullets manufactured from that ingot were analytically indistinguishable. Conversely, bullets manufactured from billets poured from different pots of molten lead were analytically distinguishable because the concentrations of elements in them were different. Since about 1995, researchers have replaced NAA with a process called inductively coupled plasma-optical emission **spectroscopy** (ICP-OES). This process enables researchers to measure the concentrations of up to 70 elements simultaneously. The relevant elements in bullet lead are antimony, arsenic, copper, bismuth, silver, tin, and cadmium.

Bullets are generally manufactured from lead obtained from secondary lead smelters, which obtain most of their lead from recycled automobile batteries. The smelter separates the lead and melts it in kettles with a capacity of up to 100 tons, often supplementing the recycled lead with virgin lead. Elements such as antimony may be added to produce hardened lead, which is generally used in non-jacketed bullets. Soft lead, generally used in jacketed bullets, contains little or no antimony. Other elements are likely to be present in varying trace amounts. The lead is then processed into ingots ranging in weight from 65–80 pounds (29.5–36.2 kilograms); billets, from 100–300 pounds (45.3–136 kilograms); or sows, which weigh a ton. The bullet manufacturer then re-melts the lead, often adding scrap lead. The lead is then poured into a mold, where it is allowed to cool and harden before being extruded into "wires" that are cut into slugs, which are then formed into bullets by a process called swaging, then tumbled to make them smooth, and

Bullet fragments found on the front seat of John F. Kennedy's presidential limousine. Included as an exhibit for the House Assassinations Committee formed in 1976. © CORBIS

loaded into cartridges with gunpowder. The cartridges are then placed into boxes, which are stamped with a packing code or lot number.

CBLA is regarded as reliable forensically because each batch of lead that comes from secondary smelters is unique in its elemental composition. Differences in composition are tolerated as long as they are within acceptable quality limits. At the bullet manufacturer, rejected bullets, rejected lead from previous runs, trimmings, and any other source of lead may be recycled into a particular batch, creating similar variances that give each batch a unique elemental fingerprint. The result is that each batch, and the bullets manufactured from it, is homogeneous, while elementally distinguishable from all other batches. The FBI states that ICP-OES technology is able to detect narrow compositional ranges of 0.01–0.05 percent of each of the seven relevant elements. The result is that ICP-OES can detect millions of distinguishable lead compositions.

The scientific validity of CBLA has been challenged in the courts. Specifically, defense attorneys have challenged the "same composition, same molten lead" theory of CBLA under Rule 702 of the **Federal Rules of Evidence**, claiming that the premises of CBLA—that lead and bullet samples are representative and that lead sources are compositionally uniform and unique—have not been sufficiently tested. CBLA has withstood these challenges, notably in *United States v. Jenkins* (1997) and in a 1998 New York case, *People v. McIntosh*. CBLA is likely to come under increased scrutiny as a result of a 2004 report released by the National Research Council of the National Academies of Science (NAS). The report was the result of a 12-month study conducted by the Committee on Scientific Assessment of Bullet Lead Elemental Composition Comparison, which found weaknesses in the research base that underpins CBLA. Following release of the report, though, the FBI maintained that CBLA "will still be useful in linking individuals to a crime as well as to exclude others."

SEE ALSO Ballistics; FBI crime laboratory; Federal Rules of Evidence; Laser ablation-inductively coupled plasma mass spectrometry; Spectroscopy.

Bullet track

When a bullet is fired from a gun, its **trajectory** or journey to its final destination is divided into three parts. The internal part of the trajectory concerns what happens from pulling the trigger to the bullet leaving the gun. The external trajectory involves the journey from the gun to the target. The final part of bullet's journey, from the target to the place where it comes to rest, is called the terminal trajectory. When a human being is the target, the forensic investigator gets involved. In such cases, the terminal trajectory leaves a bullet track inside the victim.

When someone is hit by a bullet, there will always be an entry wound. There may or may not be an exit wound, depending upon the track taken by the bullet and the way it is fired. Whether a bullet actually passes through the body depends on many factors such as the range of firing, whether it was with the gun in direct contact with the skin or from a distance. It also depends on the type of gun and bullet used. The forensic pathologist will examine the entry wound and note its shape and edges. Sometimes the edges are blackened and there may be some degree of ballooning if the gases from the bullet explosion enter the body. A shooting at close range will burn the skin on entry.

The exit wound of a bullet is generally somewhat bigger than the entry wound. However, if the victim is wearing tight clothing this may provide a constraint that makes the entry and exit wound look similar. Certainly no assumptions should be made by the investigator until he or she has all the information possible about the incident.

The internal effects of a bullet in the body, whether it exits or is left there, depend upon the kinetic energy it carries. Low velocity, low-energy bullets, as those fired from air rifles and some

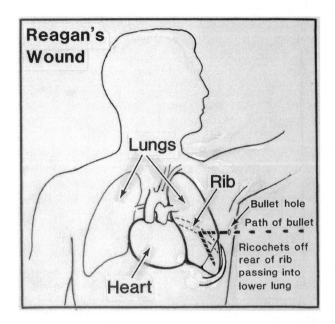

Diagram of the path of a bullet fired at close range at President Ronald Reagan during an assassination attempt in 1981. © BETTMANN/CORBIS

revolvers, just cause a mechanical disruption, pushing tissue aside. A high-velocity bullet from a shotgun or machine gun would transfer large amounts of energy to tissues or organs. This typically forms large and destructive cavities within organs such as the liver or brain that may prove lethal.

SEE ALSO Ballistics; Gunshot residue.

Bundy (serial murderer) case

Ted Bundy was responsible for a series of brutal sex murders in the Pacific Northwest, Utah, and Colorado between 1969 and 1975. The law graduate was a handsome, charming young man who did charity work and volunteered for political candidates. In his early years, however, he had been unsettled and insecure. He had a history of repeated petty theft and found it difficult to make friends, suggestive of psychopathic tendencies.

Bundy's trick was to feign injury and ask for help to lure women to his car, an old Volkswagen Beetle. He had already claimed several victims in Seattle when, on November 8, 1974, he approached Carol DaRonch in Salt Lake City, posing as a policeman. He managed to persuade her into his car, despite her suspicions. Bundy then tried to handcuff her and pulled a gun, but she managed to escape.

Theodore Bundy (center) confers with his defense attorneys during his murder trial in 1979. Bundy was later convicted, then executed in 1989. © BETTMANN/CORBIS

Seventeen-year-old Debbie Kent wasn't so lucky; Bundy killed her later that night.

Eventually, in August 1975, Bundy was caught, but not before he had committed more brutal murders. Carol DaRonch picked him out in an identity parade (line-up) and he was convicted of kidnapping her and jailed for 15 years. The Colorado authorities also wanted him for the **murder** of Caryn Campbell. However, Bundy escaped from prison twice, once only briefly before recapture. The second time he adopted a false name and lived by theft. On January 15, 1978, in the dead of night, he traveled to Florida, where he broke into the Chi Omega sorority house at Florida State University. Here Bundy attacked four students, raping Lisa Levy, 20, and then killing her by beating her about the head with a log. Margaret Brown 21, was strangled, but not sexually assaulted. Another student, Nita Neary, saw him fleeing the scene and was later able to identify him.

A month later, Bundy sexually assaulted and strangled his last victim, 12-year-old Kimberley Leach. Bundy was finally caught driving a stolen car, by which time he was wanted for murder in several states. In the car was telling evidence—handcuffs and a crowbar. At the trial, Bundy insisted on conducting his own defense. No **fingerprint evidence** was found at the scene of the Chi Omega murders. However, there was a bite mark on the buttocks of Lisa Levy and another on the nipple, a common finding in violent rape. The first mark was photographed and a transparent overlay created. Bundy was forced by court order to give a dental impression. Forensic dentist Richard Souviron declared the outline of Bundy's front teeth, which were chipped and misaligned, an exact match to the pattern on the transparent overlay. This proved to be a major piece of evidence for the prosecution.

Bundy was found guilty of the murder of the two Chi Omega students and sentenced to death. He spent ten years on Florida's Death Row, using legal tactics to gain a reprieve. At first he insisted on his innocence. Later, though, he admitted to the murders of up to 50 women. Those who have studied this case suggest he could have been responsible for as many as 100 deaths. The true number will probably never be known. In these confessions, he always referred to himself in the third person, claiming an entity inside drove him to kill.

Bundy admitted to becoming obsessed with hard-core pornography involving sadomasochism, a tendency completely at odds with his clean-cut appearance and demeanor. Psychologists who had examined him during his first stay in prison suggested he was neither psychotic nor a sexual deviant. However, he was very dependent on women and feared humiliation in his relationships. He admitted enjoyment of the power he had over his victims. The primary motive in his crimes was, he said, always rape. He then felt compelled to murder his victims to prevent them giving evidence against him. It is interesting that all the victims bore a striking resemblance to one another, having dark hair parted in the middle. This suggests a female fantasy figure that was central to his sexual crimes. Bundy was finally executed in the electric chair on January 24, 1989.

SEE ALSO Bite analysis; Odontology; Serial killers.

Bureau of Alcohol, Tobacco, and Firearms SEE ATF (United States Bureau of Alcohol, Tobacco, and Firearms)

Ann Wolbert Burgess

AMERICAN
FORENSIC PSYCHIATRIC NURSE

Ann Wolbert Burgess is one of the foremost experts in **forensic nursing** in the continent of North America. She is a respected author, educator, advanced practice psychiatric nurse, and researcher who has been a pioneer in the rapidly expanding field of forensic nursing. She earned her bachelor's and doctoral degrees in nursing from Boston University, and her master's degree from the University of Maryland. In the mid-1970s, Lynda Lytle Holmstrom and Ann Burgess were the co-founders, at Boston City Hospital, of one of the first hospital-based crisis intervention programs for victims of rape. In 1974, the early results of their research at that program resulted in establishment of the validity of the rape trauma syndrome, which has since gained admissibility in more than 300 appellate court decisions.

Since 1972, Burgess has been actively involved in research on issues of child and adult sexual assault, battering, stalking, identifying markers for elder sexual abuse, and rape. Her forensic and other clinical research interests have expanded through the years to include heart attack victims and return to work, the use of children in pornography, sexual homicide, crime scene patterning, crime scene investigations, the use of children as witnesses in child sexual abuse trials, AIDS, infant kidnapping, and forensic markers in elder sexual abuse. With the **FBI**, she has studied serial perpetrators of sexual homicide, rape, and child sexual offenses, as well as the possible relationship between child sexual abuse and exploitation, juvenile delinquency, and eventual expression of criminal behavior.

Burgess has written or co-authored numerous textbooks in the fields of psychiatric nursing and crisis intervention. Her works have included books on the assessment and treatment of child, adolescent, and adult survivors of sexual assault, and texts concerning serial offenders: rapists, abductors, child molesters, and murderers. Among her best-known works in this area is the award-winning *Crime Classification Manual*. She has co-authored nearly 150 articles, book chapters, and monographs on rape victimology, child sex rings, adolescent victims of rape, adolescent runaways, child abductors and molesters, infant abduction, and juvenile prostitution.

Burgess continues to play a pivotal role in the advancement of **forensic science** through her continuing research, her prolific writings, and her prominence as an expert courtroom witness.

SEE ALSO Contact crimes; Criminal profiling; Expert witnesses; Forensic nursing; Pattern evidence.

John J. Buturla

AMERICAN
TERRORISM AND SECURITY EXPERT

Over the course of his career, John J. Buturla turned his interest in and experience with **forensic science** and law enforcement into one of the highest ranking roles in state security, as Director of Homeland Security for the state of Connecticut. Under his leadership, the state took part in one of the largest terrorism drills ever attempted.

Buturla pursued a career in law enforcement by becoming a police officer in the town of Trumbull, Connecticut, in 1979. During that time, he also attended Sacred Heart University, where he earned a bachelor's degree in criminal justice. In 1982 Buturla joined the Connecticut State Police. While working on the state level, he rose to the rank of Major and held numerous posts, including Chief of Staff for the State Police and Commanding Officer of Major Crime. He also returned to school, and in 1988 he earned a master's degree in forensic science from the University of New Haven.

In 1999, Buturla graduated from the **FBI** National Academy Program in Quantico, Virgina. Two years later, he moved into the position of Deputy Director of Homeland Security for the state of Connecticut. In this role he worked directly with the Federal Department of Homeland Security, developing a unified security plan for the state. In 2004, he took over the role of Director. That same year, Buturla led Connecticut in the execution of an international terrorism drill, in conjunction with the state of New Jersey and the United Kingdom. It involved a fictional terrorist organization, volunteers posing as victims at local hospitals, and federal officials tracking down leads regarding the fictional attack.

Buturla has also contributed to the literature of forensic science, as a contributing author of *Forensic Aspects of Chemical and Biological Terrorism*. Written for public health and safety workers, the book addresses the roles and responsibilities of these officials in the event of a terrorist attack.

In 2005 Buturla returned to the Connecticut State Police, overseeing the operations of its forensic lab. He also continued to work as an adjunct professor at the University of New Haven, instructing students in the Graduate Program in National Security.

SEE ALSO September 11, 2001, terrorist attacks (forensic investigations of).

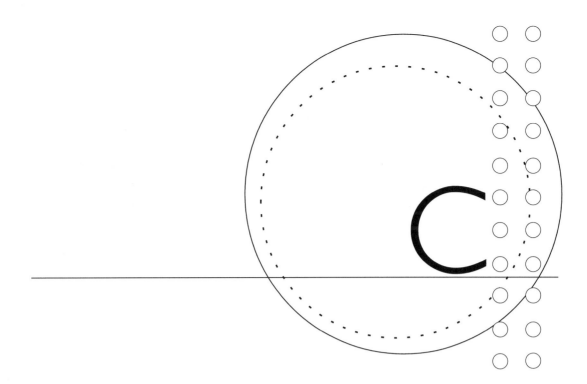

Caliber

There are two recognized definitions of caliber that differ slightly. First, there is the factual term caliber that is defined as the internal diameter of the barrel of a firearm. Second, the nominal caliber of a bullet refers to its nominal diameter and the characteristics of the cartridge. In many instances, the numerical value of the nominal caliber corresponds to the factual caliber, but this is not always the case, as some variations might appear.

The caliber of a cartridge can usually be determined from the size, weight, and shape of the bullet. Once the caliber of a cartridge is known, it is possible to obtain a list of **firearms** capable of firing such a caliber. In addition, by looking at other characteristics imprinted on the bullet, it is possible to further narrow the possibilities. This is extremely important **evidence** in a forensic investigation. With one bullet found at a crime scene it is possible to determine which firearms could have fired the bullet, and therefore, enhance the search for a suspect.

Calibers are usually expressed in hundredths of an inch or thousandths of an inch in the United States and in Great Britain. In many other countries, these are expressed in millimeters. For example, the .25 Auto is equivalent to the 6.35 Browning, the .32 Auto is equivalent to the 7.65 Browning, and the .30 Luger is equivalent to the 7.65 Para. This can be confusing if the conversion is unknown.

Calibers range from very small to very large. Among the commonly known calibers, one of the smallest is the .117 or 4.5 mm and one of the largest is the .700 Nitro Express. Some well-known calibers are the .22 LR (long-rifle), 9 mm Para, .38 Special, .357 Magnum, 10 mm Auto, and .45 ACP (automatic Colt pistol).

The term gauge instead of caliber is used with smooth-bore firearms such as shotguns. In this case, the gauge number corresponds to the number of identical spherical balls of pure lead fitting the gun's diameter that could be made from one pound of lead. For example, a 20-gauge shotgun has a diameter of 15.6 mm, meaning that one pound of pure lead can make up 20 identical balls of a diameter of 15.6 mm each. Gauge numbers range from 4 to 26, which corresponds to 23.4 mm and 10.2 mm, respectively.

SEE ALSO Ballistics; Crime scene investigation; Microscope, comparison.

Cameras

A classical image of a crime or accident investigation involves an investigator photographing the scene. Cameras are vital to **forensic science**, providing a visual record of the scene. For example, a picture of a **blood spatter** can be used to help determine the cause of the spill long after the stain itself has been cleaned away.

A visual image is an ideal way to preserve a record of a scene before items are disturbed. Pictures are admissible as legal **evidence**, providing the

A Western .38 Special stamp marks a bullet used in forensics tests during the Kennedy assassination investigation. © CORBIS

prosecution or jury members with an evocative image of the scene. Visual images can aid in reaching a verdict on a crime.

A traditional camera functions by focusing light through a lens onto a surface coated with light-sensitive chemicals. Digital cameras have internal processors that record images in an electronic form, converting wave-like analog information into digital information represented by bits. The concept of the camera dates back to the Renaissance idea of the camera obscura, a small, dark chamber into which light was permitted only through pinholes. During the early nineteenth century, inventors perfected the camera obscura to make the prototype of the modern camera, but early **photography** was a cumbersome affair characterized by large, boxy cameras and slow exposures.

Surveillance cameras, which have long been an espionage tool, can also be a useful forensic tool. According to the Security Industry Association, by 2003 there were some two million **closed-circuit television** systems in operation, most of them operated by private businesses for security purposes, in the United States. Many households are also equipped with surveillance cameras.

A forensic investigator can gain legal access to the recordings made by a security camera. This can provide vital information of events before, during, and following the crime or accident.

Increasingly, municipalities are installing surveillance cameras at traffic intersections to monitor the license plate numbers of traffic violators. Such data can be useful forensically.

Virtually all traditional cameras have at least one glass lens, and one with a zoom or telephoto lens typically has three: front and rear convex lenses, with a concave one in between. Though zoom lenses clearly have an application in the world of law enforcement, they can also provide long-distance photos that are useful in a forensic investigation. Miniature and subminiature cameras are usually for photographing images at close range. Typically they would have only a single lens, perhaps with a coating to reduce reflections or glare.

In place of lenses, a pinhole camera uses tiny apertures, or openings, so small that they are known as pinholes. The value of a lens lies in its ability to focus and thus photograph distant objects or ones close by, depending on the settings. By contrast, the value of a pinhole camera is precisely the fact that it does not have lenses, and therefore can produce images of distant and nearby images equally well.

Forensic photography is typically the responsibility of a skilled photographer. The photographer will be careful to photograph the subject from a variety of angles and to use lighting conditions that will emphasize all the detail of the object.

Digital cameras can be useful, since the digitized information can be downloaded to a database for further scrutiny. But, even traditional film photographs can be digitized for electronic storage and analyses.

SEE ALSO Crime scene investigation; Evidence.

Canine substance detection

An important aspect of a forensic investigation can be the determination of the presence and location of compounds of interest. Probably the best example is the need to establish where illicit chemicals and agricultural plants are present.

Sophisticated detection equipment such as gas and gas-liquid chromatographs can detect extremely small levels of a variety of compounds. Their portability, however, can be limited. Fortunately, the detection sensitivity of these instruments is rivaled by the nose of a dog. Dogs play a central role in some forensic operations.

John Long and his bomb-sniffing dog Coby check luggage as they go through a drill at Lackland Air Force base in San Antonio, Texas, in February 2002. AP/WIDE WORLD PHOTOS. REPRODUCED BY PERMISSION.

Canine substance detection involves the use of specially trained dogs, commonly golden or Labrador retrievers, for the detection of illegal substances. Dogs are now being used in settings that include workplaces, airports, and schools to detect weapons, contraband, **narcotic** drugs, medications, beverage alcohol, **firearms**, and **explosives**.

Dogs trained to detect the scent of illegal substances are useful as they can utilize their acute sense of smell to penetrate many hiding places which are inaccessible to other detection methods. A dog has about 200 million sensitive cells in its nose, compared to approximately five million in a human being, producing a detection sensitivity that outrivals us by some 40-fold. A dog's sense of smell is made even keener by an organ in the roof of the mouth that is not found in the human olfactory system. This organ enables it to "taste" a smell, in essence amplifying a weak signal into a stronger, more easily detectable signal.

This sensitivity enables a trained dog to be able to discriminate one odor from another, even when the latter is more intense. For example, drug-sniffing dogs can be trained to detect the odors of heroin, marijuana, and cocaine even when these items are concealed in a suitcase containing perfume.

Not surprisingly, canine detection of substances like drugs is a routine part of forensic investigations aimed at curbing the illicit traffic of drugs. Canine drug detection is a common sight at areas of cross border travel such as border crossings, airports, bus stations, and ports.

Some dogs are specially trained to detect the acidic smell of nitroglycerin and the sulfur in gunpowder for work with explosives detection. Forensic investigators use **arson** dogs to help in criminal investigations in the aftermath of fires. These dogs locate minute traces of gas or other flammable liquids in situations where arson is suspected. Arson dogs are trained in such a way that they can accurately detect traces of chemicals at the parts-per-million or even billion levels. This detection sensitivity rivals and can even exceed that achievable using electronic detectors.

SEE ALSO Analytical instrumentation; Bomb detection devices; Illicit drugs.

Carbon monoxide poisoning

Carbon monoxide, with chemical formula CO, is a compound of carbon (C) and oxygen (O_2). It is a colorless, odorless, and tasteless gas that in appropriate amounts is poisonous to human beings and, for that matter, to all warm-blooded animals and many other life forms on Earth. Carbon monoxide is poisonous when, as a result of being inhaled into the lungs, it combines with the blood's **hemoglobin**, which then prevents the absorption of oxygen into the respiratory system of the body. Carbon monoxide poisoning results when the human body is consistently denied essential oxygen. A person without sufficient oxygen in the blood stream will initially feel dizziness, fatigue, headaches, nausea, and shortness of breath, which will eventually lead to unconsciousness and eventually to asphyxiation and death.

Carbon monoxide is a component of air pollution, both as an intentional or accidental side product, that results from many natural and artificial products, materials, and processes such as gasoline-powered vehicles, furnaces, manufacturing plants, and forest fires. The identification of carbon monoxide poisoning is important to forensic scientists because carbon monoxide can be the primary or secondary cause of such investigations as accidents, homicides, and suicides, or can be used as a deceptive tactic by criminals to hide other causes of crimes. For example, a forensic investigator might examine three unrelated dead bodies inside automobiles within three different closed garages and find (1) one body with carbon monoxide in the blood stream, but without any other suspicious **evidence** (which indicates a suicide), (2) another body with carbon monoxide in the blood, but with greasy fingers and clothing (which indicates an accidental death), and (3) a third body with blunt injuries to the head and only a small amount of carbon monoxide in the body (which indicates a homicide).

In order to determine the level of carbon monoxide within the blood stream of a deceased person, the accurate measurement of the blood pigment carboxyhemoglobin is required. Carboxyhemoglobin is

hemoglobin that is saturated with carbon monoxide. Several detection methods are used for the measurement of carbon monoxide including CO-Oximeter, flame ionization, infrared spectrophotometry, syringe capillary, thermal conductivity, ultraviolet spectrophotometry, and Van Slyke. In ultraviolet spectrophotometry, for example, carbon monoxide is expelled from the blood stream and is then measured when exposed to ultraviolet radiation.

SEE ALSO Asphyxiation (signs of); Hemoglobin; Poison and antidote actions; Toxicological analysis; Toxicology.

Careers in forensic science

A forensic scientist works in one of several scientific fields used in a court of law. He or she helps improve public health and safety by using scientific knowledge to contribute to a court proceeding and determine the facts in a given case. Thus, a career in **forensic science** combines science and public service. A forensic scientist may work for a law enforcement agency, uncovering **evidence** for the prosecution of a crime, or he or she may work for a law firm, detecting evidence for use in a criminal defense. However, not all forensics personnel are scientists. There are many careers in forensics that relate to non-science careers such as administrative, legal (non-jurisprudence), and security related fields. Most forensic professionals find jobs with police agencies, government agencies, universities, federal agencies, armed forces, and law offices.

Forensics professionals have two main objectives: to detect **physical evidence** and to link this evidence to the crime scene and a suspect. This requires the joint effort of many professionals with specific backgrounds. A crime has many aspects and several forensics professionals will often work on a case, each studying the aspect of the crime that relates to their particular specialty. Physical evidence is usually handled by the criminalist, whose chief role is to first identify the evidence, then coordinate the appropriate analysis of the evidence.

The criminalist uses results from all analyses of physical evidence to recreate the details of a crime scene. Physical evidence can be very small, such as a drop of **blood** or a hair follicle; it can also include toolmarks, footprints, a piece of clothing, or a distinct odor. A criminalist, therefore, must exercise a broad range of skills with the ability to apply various scientific and analytical approaches to answer questions related to a criminal investigation. They must also be able provide interpretations that non-scientists, such as members of the jury and court, can understand. Most criminalists have a strong scientific background with, minimally, a bachelor's of science degree in chemistry, molecular biology, or physics. Specific courses in forensic science targeted at preparing students for the American Board of Criminalistics certification test are also offered. Criminalists are usually employed by government forensics laboratories that are part of police departments or federal agencies, such as the Drug Enforcement Administration (**DEA**) or the Central Intelligence Agency (CIA). They are also employed by medical examiners offices, private companies, and to a lesser extent, universities.

A criminalist will often require the expertise of a forensic engineer to help recreate details in a crime scene. A forensic engineer is responsible for applying fundamentals of engineering to help understand aspects in a court case, particularly for civil suits, but also for regulatory or criminal proceedings. Since engineering specialties can vary considerably, the expertise required in each case also varies. For example, a forensics engineer that understands the physics of a firearm might be required to determine which gun was used during a crime, how it was fired and from where it was fired. A broad based repertoire of practical experiences and a strong engineering background is necessary for this type of position. Credentials for such a position are not yet systematic, and therefore, must be achieved separately with a moderate level **training** in legal and criminal coursework. Many of the engineers serve in forensics-related positions as consultants.

Many forensics specialties require strong backgrounds in the biological sciences. There is an increasing need for forensics scientists with molecular biology backgrounds. This is because **DNA** based analyses have revolutionized the capacity to identify and convict criminals by linking suspects to the scene of the crime or to physical evidence. For example, in cold cases (cases that have gone unsolved for several years) DNA matching has lead to reversing charges for wrongfully convicted individuals. Experience in DNA extractions from all types of samples is very important in the training of a molecular biologist that wishes to specialize in forensics. Specialty training in mitochondrial genetics is helpful for understanding techniques to use for paternity testing, matching a sample to a suspect, or screening DNA samples from a database of criminals. These individuals usually work in or direct crime labs in conjunction with state, local, or federal organizations. They

can also be private companies that offer a service to federal or state investigations.

Forensic **odontology** (dentistry) is an important subspecialty in forensics that is usually associated with coroner's or medical examiner's offices, although many serve as specialized consultants. These professionals can use dental or cranial examinations to provide information regarding human remains including **identification** of missing persons, victims from catastrophic events (plane crashes, etc.), postmortem examination with searchable database record keeping, dental injury analysis in potential abuse cases, and examination of bite marks in assault or rape cases. A forensic odotonologist must obtain a doctor of dental science (DDS) degree and have considerable experience in the field of dentistry prior to transitioning or consulting in forensics applications. The American Society of Forensic Odontology is an organization that offers comprehensive courses to prepare dentists for a role in forensics specialization.

For applications that involve tissue evaluation beyond the scope of odontology, forensic anthropologists are helpful. Their expertise is usually related to direct skeletal examinations. By using archeological methods, bones and remains can be carefully extracted from precarious surroundings, without compromising the integrity the sample. If the skeletal sample is compromised, anthropologists can be helpful in recreating the skeletal configuration of the remains. They are also trained to examine the insect remains to determine the state of body **decomposition**, especially in cases that involve a considerable amount of decomposition. A forensic anthropologist should have a doctorate in **anthropology** and certification through the American Board of Forensic Anthropology.

Other medical professionals are also in demand in the field of forensics. Psychiatrists are medical doctors that, with specialized forensic training, can help the forensics team understand pathological and criminal behavior. They can help predict and prevent repetitive crimes by, for example, **serial killers**. They can also help explain complicated crimes or cases that involve psychiatric patients by using behavioral patterns to uncover concrete motives in a crime. **Pathology** is another medical specialty that has forensic applications. Pathologists can perform microscopic **autopsy** evaluations of tissues, body **fluids** (blood, urine, skin), and organs to discover the **cause of death** in cases that involve, for example, poisoning or unusual injuries of unclear origin. They can be also help determine the **time of death** by evaluating the extent of tissue deterioration or obtaining tissue samples. Recently, forensic pathologists have been instrumental in coordinating medically related investigations of possible exposure to biological weapons such as **anthrax**. Pathologists require forensics specialty training and board certification. They are typically employed by the Centers for Disease Control, as well as medical examiners offices and hospitals. All medical professionals that serve in forensics careers can also serve to provide the courts with expert testimonials.

Sometimes a pathologist needs to send tissue samples to a toxicologist for further study. A toxicologist specializes in the medical and scientific study of poisons. Toxicologist are often involved in forensics cases by evaluating tissue samples for possible chemical exposures such as illicit drug use. Toxicologists can have a M.S. or a Ph.D. degree in **toxicology** with certification in both the American Board of Forensic Toxicology and the Forensic Toxicology Certification Board.

Not all forensics professionals are scientists or physicians. Trial lawyers that have forensics training can be valuable to criminal and civil court cases. Not only can forensic knowledge can help lawyers determine the admissibility of evidence, but it can also help them review the credentials of **expert witnesses**, understand the techniques and analysis that the expert employs, and cross-examine the expert witness. A law degree is required and positions can be found in both private practice as well as in state and district offices.

The subspecialties discussed here represent only a portion of the career paths available in forensics. Clinical personnel, computer programmers, accountants, archeologists, sculptors, coroners, **ballistics** experts, marine biologists, environmentalists, social workers, and nurses are all fields that can be useful in forensic science. All forensics professionals that have the appropriate credentials can serve as expert witnesses during court proceedings. The field of forensics is growing, and job vacancies in most areas of forensic science are expected to increase until at least the year 2012.

There are several professional organizations in forensic science. One such organization is the **American Academy of Forensic Sciences** (AAFS), a professional society that offers membership to a wide range of forensic specialties. The AAFS is dedicated to improving accuracy, precision, specificity, and sensitivity of forensic sciences by promoting educational resources in the form of meetings, training, and seminars. There are currently over 5,600 members, which

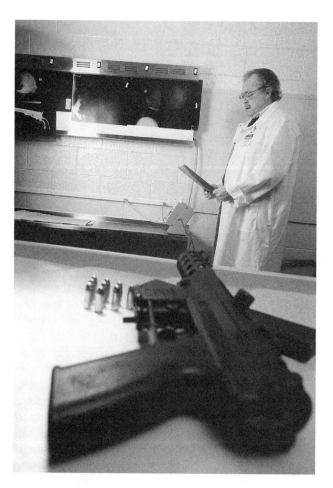

A nine millimeter semiautomatic gun lies before forensic physician Michael Baden as he examines evidence on an x-ray sheet. © NAJLAH FEANNY/CORBIS SABA

include (but are not limited to) individuals with a variety of education backgrounds including physicians, attorneys, criminalists, engineers, toxicologists, dentists, and anthropologists. Representation spans the United States, Canada, and 50 additional countries worldwide. The AAFS hosts an annual scientific meeting, and produces an internationally recognized scientific journal (*Journal of Forensic Sciences*), which are both utilized by a wide variety of scientists and educators from various forensic specialties.

SEE ALSO Anthropology; Coroner; Criminalistics; Entomology; Epidemiology; Forensic accounting; Forensic nursing; Geology; Linguistics, forensic stylistics; Medical examiner; Pathology; Psychiatry; Toxicology; Wildlife forensics.

Cases and mysteries, ancient SEE Ancient cases and mysteries

William E. Cashin

1/19/1904–
AMERICAN
FINGERPRINT IDENTIFICATION EXPERT

William E. Cashin served the New York State Police Department in various positions for almost 45 years, most notably in the role of Director of the Division of Criminal Identification. Under his leadership, the division made groundbreaking strides in advancing the technology available for criminal investigations. Cashin also introduced a new system for searching latent prints. Officials from countries around the world came to New York to study and observe the new technologies Cashin's team was using. For his work, Cashin received numerous awards from various professional organizations.

Born in New Jersey in 1904, Cashin was fascinated with horses and became a trick rider as a youth. When he chose his career, he picked one that involved his equestrian interests, and joined the New York State Police. There he was able to trick ride as part of his job. But in 1926, he fractured his pelvis and had to give up riding. During his recovery, he became interested in **fingerprint** identification, and sought tutoring to help him learn about the field. When he returned to work, Cashin established a Bureau of Identification for his division and became a fingerprint instructor at the State Police School.

During the next phase of his career, Cashin moved up the ranks in his division and continued to study and research the area of fingerprints and personal identification. In 1936, he became the Director of the Division of Criminal Identification. In this role, he installed the first automated fingerprint searching machines and a machine that searched through files of physical descriptions. He also started a new system of searching latent fingerprints. Because of these advances, fingerprint experts from around the world came to study Cashin's department and observe the new technology at work.

In 1960, Cashin retired from New York State and accepted a position with the U.S. State Department, where he worked as an identification advisor in countries such as Brazil, Venezuela, and the Philippines. For his visionary leadership, Cashin received the 1956 Governor Charles E. Hughes Award, and the 1960 John A. Dondero Award from the **International Association for Identification**, given in recognition for those who have made substantial contributions to the science of forensic identification.

SEE ALSO Careers in forensic science; Technology and forensic science.

Casting

Casting is the process used to replicate three-dimensional prints or marks. It is widely used to obtain the exact replicate of toolmarks, **tire tracks**, **shoeprints**, and sometimes teeth. Casting is of paramount importance in forensic sciences as it allows a crime scene investigator to collect an identical copy of a mark or print from a scene, which can then be compared to a seized tool, shoe, or tire in order to establish a link between a suspect and a crime scene.

Casting can only be accomplished on three-dimensional marks or traces. In the case of toolmarks, for example, casting can be used to obtain the perfect copy of the mark of a screwdriver used to force open a door during a burglary. With a shoeprint, it allows for the shoeprint of a thief that was left in the soil outside the window of the apartment he or she exited to be preserved as **evidence**. A vehicle used to flee the scene of a murder could leave tire tracks in the snow, which can be recorded and saved for later comparison with a suspicious vehicle. Casting is also used to record dental characteristics of a body and compare these characteristics with known dental records in order to make a proper **identification**.

The choice of casting material depends on the mark to be copied and the surface on which it is found. For most toolmarks, a dental cast polymer is used. It consists of two pastes mixed together right before the cast is taken. Once mixed together, the paste is applied onto the mark and allowed to dry before being removed. With tire tracks or shoeprints, usually a plaster, such as plaster of Paris, is used. This kind of casting material does not provide as many details as the dental polymer, but can cover a bigger surface and will dry very well over surfaces such as soil. On snow, the use of plaster is not ideal, and molten sulfur offers a much better cast. Sulfur is heated until it liquefied and then poured onto the trace. As soon as the sulfur touches the cold snow, it immediately hardens and takes the shape of the print.

SEE ALSO Crime scene investigation; Microscope, comparison.

A plaster cast of the remains of a child incinerated in a garden after Vesuvius's eruption in 79 A.D. in Pompeii, Italy.
© JONATHAN BLAIR/CORBIS

Cast-off blood

A moving source of **blood**, such as a bleeding victim or a blood-stained weapon, can give rise to cast-off blood—that is, droplets of blood flung from the object so as to make a trail of blood where it lands. Such bloodstain patterns can be very informative about the nature of an attack. Forensic scientists distinguish two types of cast-off blood dependent on the kind of movement producing it. In swing cast-off, the blood droplets come from an arcing motion of a weapon like a piece of wood or maybe the bloody hands of the attacker or victim. Cessation cast-off arises when the motion of a source of blood is suddenly arrested; the impact of a weapon with the victim is a typical example.

The laws of physics account for the phenomenon of cast-off blood. Wet blood tends to move to the end of an object, where it pools. Depending on the shape of the object, there may be one or more pools of blood ready to be cast off. If the momentum—product of mass and velocity—of the object can overcome the surface tension making the pool of blood cling to the surface, then the blood is cast off in a series of spherical droplets.

Swing cast-off is, in theory, more likely to occur during a forward swing because more momentum is gathered during this phase of motion than in the backward swing. But the situation is a bit more complex than this; in practice, more cast-off is seen in a backward swing, simply because more blood is available. Once the forward swing begins, most of the blood has already been cast-off. In cessation cast-off, the deceleration of the arresting impact transfers force to the blood. It is then cast-off in a pattern not unlike that seen in impact spatter, which is caused by a force such as kicking or beating applied directly to wet blood.

The size of the droplets of cast-off blood depends upon many factors such as the shape and surface of the object, its velocity, and the amount of blood it is carrying. Long, relatively light weapons create more cast-off staining than shorter, heavier weapons. The blood is usually flung away from the arc of movement, which means that it tends to land on nearby surfaces, rather than on the attacker. The resulting **cast-off trails** may help the investigator to deduce how the attack took place.

SEE ALSO Blood; Blood spatter; Bloodstain evidence.

Cast-off trails

Cast-off trails are the bloodstain patterns that are created by **cast-off blood**. When a **blood** source moves, drops slide towards its end and may be flung off if the object is moving fast enough. This is called cast-off blood and it moves away from its source as a spray of droplets. When these land on a nearby surface, a cast-off trail is formed. Analysis of the trails may tell the forensic investigator some key facts about the nature of the attack.

When droplets of cast-off blood land on a surface, they do so in a linear trail described as in-line staining. The actual size of the spherical splashes depends on many factors such as the size and shape of the blood source, which is often the weapon, as well as its velocity and the amount of blood it produces.

Cast-off trails occurring some way from the presumed attack, such as on a ceiling, may be indicative of the use of a long, relatively light weapon. Droplets cast-off from a forward swing of a weapon tend to be smaller than those from a backward swing. Pronounced cast-off, consisting of large drops at some distance from the attack, often indicates the end of a backswing from a weapon. This is a point at which particularly large forces are applied to any cast-off blood.

The physics of the trajectory of cast-off blood is quite complex. Generally, the droplets are flung at any angle from radial to tangential to the arc along which the source is moving. This means that the cast-off trail is usually found outside the arc of swing and the attacker is protected from it. One exception can occur, however, when the attacker is kneeling, and cast-off trails might be found on the lower leg. Sometimes cast-off trails are also found on the attacker's back.

There are so many factors affecting the nature of a cast-off trail that the investigator has to take great care in its interpretation. Nevertheless, the patterns can often provide some useful information. For instance, the minimum number of blows in an attack might be estimated from looking at the number of trails of in-line staining on a surface. Geometric analysis of the trails might also help assess the location of the attack.

SEE ALSO Blood; Blood spatter; Bloodstain evidence.

Catalyst

A catalyst is any agent that functions to speed up a reaction or process without being used up or changed itself.

In chemical reactions, molecules are changed by moving or rearranging atoms or clusters of atoms. For each reaction, to achieve these chemical transitions from one molecule to an altered molecule, a certain amount of energy is normally required to prepare the molecule to undergo change. This is referred to as the activation energy. Activation energy can be thought of as a barrier that prevents molecules from changing from one form to another.

In a chemical reaction, catalysts function to hold a molecule in a certain position or influence the strength of the individual chemical bonds that undergo change during the reaction. Catalysts speed up reactions by lowering the activation energy necessary for the reaction to take place. In living systems, most chemical reactions are catalyzed by proteins called enzymes.

Catalysts can be homogeneous or heterogeneous. A homogeneous catalyst is one that exists in the same phase (gas, liquid, or solid) as the reacting chemical. In biology, for example, enzymes are distributed in the liquid environment inside of cells, and the reacting chemicals are dissolved in the liquid state there as well. In contrast, heterogeneous catalysts exist in a different physical state than the reacting chemicals. For example, in automobiles, the catalytic converter is a solid phase platinum-based catalyst found in the exhaust system, but the reacting chemicals are found in the exhaust gases that pass through after combustion of the gasoline.

Catalysts can be slowed when various inhibitors or poisons are present. Inhibitors are agents that physically interact with the surface of a catalyst to slow or interfere with a chemical reaction. Often, molecules that act as inhibitors for a certain catalyst have shapes and structures very close to the chemical that normally interacts with the catalyst. The inhibitors differ chemically from the reacting chemical, however, so that they are unable to be chemically altered by the normal action of the catalyst. In the case of enzymes, specific inhibitors may often be used in drugs, such as the popular statin drugs used to lower cholesterol. In the example of the catalytic converter, heavy metals such as lead function as poisons by irreversibly combining with the catalytic surface of the platinum, destroying its catalytic properties.

Among the many catalysts used in forensic testing, scientists use inorganic catalysts in the analysis of paint samples and biological catalysts when analyzing **DNA**.

SEE ALSO Chemical equations; Endothermic reaction; Exothermic reactions.

CCTV SEE Closed-Circuit Television (CCTV)

CDC SEE Centers for Disease Control and Prevention (CDC)

Centers for Disease Control and Prevention (CDC)

The Centers for Disease Control and Prevention (CDC) is a federal agency primarily focused on protecting public health and safety. The CDC was founded in 1946 and is organized under the U.S. Department of Health and Human Services. The agency's headquarters are located in Atlanta, Georgia. Various programs of the CDC are directed toward disease prevention, controlling the spread of disease, promotion of good health practices, and public education to improve health. More recently, preparedness for health threats and **bioterrorism** have become key activities of the CDC. Forensic scientists are involved in almost all departments of the DCD, from identifying the **cause of death** during a disease outbreak, to supplying data and testimony at legal proceedings about injury trends and environmental or other health hazards.

The annual budget for operations within the CDC is just under $8 billion, including approximately $5 billion for primary CDC activities, and an additional $3 billion for the Agency for Toxic Substances and Disease Registry (ATSDR), childhood **vaccines**, and terrorism programs. Two broad areas of spending are in health promotion and prevention of disease, and in preparedness for health threats and terrorism.

The CDC employs more than 8,500 people within the United States, approximately 65% of whom are located in the Atlanta area with less than 20% at the primary headquarters. More than 100 employees of the CDC are stationed overseas in 45 different countries at any given time.

There are seven different National Centers within the CDC including:

- The National Crenter on Birth Defects and Developmental Disabilities provides national leadership for preventing birth defects and developmental disabilities and for improving the health and wellness of people with disabilities.
- The National Center for Chronic Disease Prevention and Health Promotion works toward prevention of premature death and disability from chronic diseases and promotion of healthy lifestyles.
- The National Center for Environmental Health focuses in the prevention and control of disease and death resulting from environmental agents.
- The National Center for Health Statistics is a key national resource that provides statistical information to guide actions and policies to improve health.
- The National Center for HIV, STD, and TB Prevention engages in prevention and control of human immunodeficiency virus infection, sexually transmitted diseases, and tuberculosis.
- The National Center for Infectious Diseases is primarily concerned with the prevention of illness, disability, and death caused by infectious agents (bacteria, viruses, and other organisms) in the United States and around the world.
- The National Center for Injury Prevention and Control works to prevent death and disability from injuries that are not work-related, including both acts of violence and unintentional causes.

The CDC also operates a National Immunization Program (NIP), providing leadership for planning, organizing, and implementation of immunization activities across the country. Primary activities within the NIP include consultations, training, statistical support, promotion, education, health monitoring, and technical services to assist health departments with immunization related services.

The Epidemiology Program Office at the CDC operates to strengthen the public health system through health monitoring, and provides national and international support for such public health efforts through scientific communications, consultation in epidemiology and statistics, and by training experts in disease surveillance, epidemiology, applied public health, and prevention effectiveness.

The Public Health Practice Program Office at the CDC attends primarily to four elements of public health practice: the public health workforce, organi-

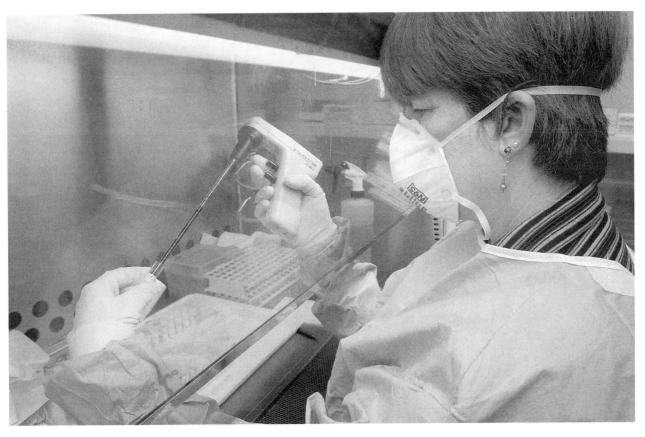

Scientist at the Special Pathogens Branch of the Center for Disease Control processes SARS specimens. The CDC is part of a global collaboration to address the continuing emergence of the SARS virus. © CDC/PHIL/CORBIS

zational effectiveness, the scientific capacity of public health laboratories, and the systems that manage public health information and knowledge.

The National Institute for Occupational Safety and Health (NIOSH) is an institute within the CDC that serves as the primary government-sponsored agency responsible for conducting research and making recommendations for the prevention of work-related injuries and illnesses. Occupational injuries number in the millions each year in the United States, and thousands of deaths due to occupational injuries occur each year, with an annual cost of $40 billion. Additionally, work-related diseases result in nearly 50,000 deaths each year. NIOSH, and its sister organization in the Labor Department, the Occupational Safety and Health Administration (OSHA), were created by the U.S. Congress in 1970. While OSHA plays a more regulatory role in monitoring and enforcing safety standards, NIOSH provides research, training, education, and information directed toward the improvement of occupational safety and **identification** of potential hazards.

The Agency for Toxic Substances and Disease Registry (ATSDR) is an adjunct CDC agency focused on critical health assessment work related to toxic waste sites, and improving the health consequences of related exposures. ATSDR serves the public by using the best science, taking responsive public health actions, and providing trusted health information to prevent harmful exposures and disease related to toxic substances.

The CDC has identified a number of challenges and future programs will be developed to meet these challenges. This includes enhancing the extent to which science is applied to improving health, prevention of violence and unintentional injury, health and safety needs of a changing workforce, utilization of new technologies to provide credible health information, protection against the threats of bioterrorism and newly emerging infectious diseases, elimination of racial and ethnic health disparities, fostering safe and healthy environments, and promoting good health globally.

SEE ALSO Bioterrorism; Epidemiology; Toxicology.

A 10-pound, battery-powered hand-held detector that brings state-of-the-art radiation spectrometry anywhere radioactive materials are found, including inside a dirty bomb. © REUTERS/CORBIS

Chemical and biological detection technologies

A well-recognized national security issue is the detection of chemicals and either biological agents or their components (i.e., **toxins**). For example, the inability to rapidly inspect mailed letters for the presence of **anthrax spores** provided a route for the targeting of the mail with infectious microorganisms in the United States in 2001. This demonstration has spurred development of more sophisticated, accurate, and rapid detection technologies. Aside from national security concerns, detection of chemical and biological compounds is important in a forensic investigation.

X-ray examination has long been of value in scanning luggage at airports. The same technology can be used locate objects hidden inside other objects. As well, newer x-ray technology enables the discrimination of organic from inorganic objects. Most of the x-ray beam is reflected back immediately upon encountering an object. Some of the radiation, however, passes through the object. By analyzing the beams that actually penetrate through an object, information on the object's composition is provided. Another version sends two different x rays of different wavelengths through an object. The different beams can distinguish between organic objects, such as food and paper, and inorganic objects.

A chemical detection technology known as gas **chromatography** has been sped into routine use in airports since the U.S. terrorist attacks of September 11, 2001. The different chemicals present on a cloth that is swiped over an object can be separated based on their different preference for the gas mixture that is pumped through the sample chamber. A target chemical (i.e., an explosive) is detected within seconds.

Chemical detection technologies have also been adapted for use "in the field," such as by United Nations inspectors deployed in Iraq beginning in November 2002, to the presence of missiles that were supposedly destroyed by the Iraqi government in the mid-1990s. These portable technologies are beginning to find their way into forensic use.

Sound can also be used to detect chemicals. For example, the acoustic wave sensor uses a quartz surface to convert incoming sound waves into electrical signals. Over a dozen different chemicals can be detected within seconds, even from biological sources. In another sound-based technique, called acoustic resonance, the pattern of vibrations when sound waves are sent inside an object can reveal whether the object is filled with a solid or a liquid, and even the type of chemical present.

Light is another means of chemical detection. The use of light is called **spectroscopy**. Mass spectroscopy determines the mass of proteins, which is important in determining the identity of the chemical or biological agent. Matrix-Assisted Laser Desorption/Ionization Mass Spectroscopy (MALDI-MS) can identify proteins that are unique to *Bacillus anthracis* (the cause of anthrax) and *Yersinia pestis* (the cause of plague). Raman spectroscopy measures the change in the wavelength of a light beam by the sample molecules. Optical spectroscopy measures the absorption of light by the chemical groups and the subsequent emission of light by the same groups as the identification method.

The ability to detect genetic sequences that are unique to certain bacteria (**gene** probing) has been exploited to develop genetically based microbial detection methods. The best example of gene probing is the **polymerase chain reaction** (**PCR**), which can enzymatically detect a target stretch of genetic material and rapidly amplify that region to detectable levels. Handheld PCR detectors (i.e., Handheld Advanced **Nucleic Acid Analyzer**, or HANAA), used in the 2002–2003 inspections of Iraqi facilities by United Nations officials, are already being exploited in law enforcement.

Biological detection devices can monitor the surrounding air at regular intervals. Air is automatically drawn into the device and analyzed for target genetic sequences using the PCR technology. The results can be electronically relayed to a central database for analysis and shared with other law enforcement agencies.

Another biological technology utilizes antibodies that are produced in response to the presence of a specific microorganism. Tests are available that detect *Bacillus anthracis*, *Clostridium botulinum*, viruses (e.g., **smallpox**), and chemicals (e.g., **ricin**) in minutes.

Some older biological detection technologies still prove reliable in forensic analyses. Growth of microorganisms on artificial food sources (media) produces populations called colonies. A medium can be selected that produces colonies that have a distinctive appearance and color. Gel **electrophoresis** separates differently sized pieces of genetic material or other microbial components (e.g., protein) into bands. The banding pattern can be used to identify the microorganism. Finally, chromatography separates compounds from one another based on their differing speed of movement through a gas or a liquid mixture.

SEE ALSO Aflatoxin; Bacterial biology; Bioterrorism; Chemical warfare.

Chemical Biological Incident Response Force, United States

The Chemical and Biological Incident Response Force (CBIRF) is a unit of the United States Marines devoted to countering chemical or biological threats at home and abroad. Activated in 1996, the unit serves a number of protective functions. Since the terrorist bombings of September 11, 2001, its prominence has increased dramatically. Now part of the 4th Marine Expeditionary Brigade (MEB), it has performed homeland security functions that included the removal of suspected toxic agents from House and Senate office buildings during a rash of **anthrax** incidents that followed the September terrorist attacks in 2001. CBIRF is a precursor to investigative efforts of forensic experts.

Chemical agents have been a widespread threat since 1915, when first used by German forces on the Eastern Front in World War I. Soon the British developed their own chemical weapons, and the age of **chemical warfare** began, forever altering the battlefield equation. Both military and civilian personnel are increasingly vulnerable to chemical attacks, as evidenced by use of chemical weapons by Saddam Hussein on Kurdish civilians, use by both Iran and Iraq during their prolonged war in the 1980s, and use during the 1994 and 1995 attacks by Aum Shinrikyo (a Japanese cult) that released deadly **sarin gas** into the Tokyo subways, the latter of which killed 12 civilians.

U.S. Marines participate in a biochemical attack simulation in conjunction with the New York Fire Department, 2003.
© RAMIN TALAIE/CORBIS

On June 21, 1995, partly in response to the Aum Shinrikyo attacks, as well as the Oklahoma City bombing on April 19 of that year, the administration of President William Jefferson Clinton issued Presidential Decision Directive 39, United States Policy on Counterterrorism. The directive called for a number of specific efforts to deter terrorism in the United States, as well as that against Americans and allies abroad. In response to the need for a response team to deal with chemical and biological threats, the United States Marine Corps established the Chemical Biological Incident Response Force (CBIRF) on April 4, 1996.

In a 1999 article in the Marine Corps magazine *Leatherneck*, the CBIRF was described thus: "It's new, it's unique to the Armed Services, and right now, it's the only quick reaction force in the world equipped to help in the aftermath of a chemical, biological, or radiological (nuclear) attack." In the words of a force protection element commander for CBIRF, "We are a consequence management force.

Our mission is to respond, to come in and save lives. We bring the full package: self-contained, expeditionary, and task-organized."

During the spring and early summer of 1996, CBIRF was deployed for **training** in a variety of environments throughout the United States. Its members closely studied the bombing that took place at Centennial Olympic Park in Atlanta on the night of July 27, and practiced coordinating a response with local fire and police. They also undertook an experiment at The Citadel, a military college in Charleston, South Carolina, where CBIRF personnel acted to control lethal agents released by a mock chemical weapons plant. Moving beyond training to real-world situations, CBIRF provided security for President Clinton's second inauguration in January 1997, and for the Summit of Eight in Denver, Colorado, that following summer.

In the aftermath of the September 11, 2001, terrorist attacks on the United States, CBIRF's mission became incorporated into the 4th MEB, along with the Marine Security Force Battalion, the Marine Security Guard Battalion, and the new anti-terrorism battalion. (The latter had evolved from the 1st Battalion, 8th Marines, that had been hit in the 1983 terrorist bombings of United States Marine barracks in Lebanon.) In December 2001, CBIRF sent a 100-member initial response team into the Dirksen Senate Office Building alongside Environmental Protection Agency (EPA) specialists to detect and remove anthrax. A similar mission was undertaken at the Longworth House Office Building in October, during which time samples were collected from more than 200 office spaces.

SEE ALSO Anthrax, investigation of the 2001 murders; Chemical warfare; Oklahoma bombing (1995 bombing of Alfred P. Murrah building); Sarin gas; September 11, 2001, terrorist attacks (forensic investigations of).

Chemical equations

Chemistry is a part of **forensic science**. By studying the reactions that occur during various tests, the forensic scientist can receive clues about the nature of the compound under study. Often, knowledge of the nature of the chemical reactions is helpful. This knowledge comes from the chemical equation that describes the reaction.

Chemical equations reveal the chemical species involved in a particular reaction, the charges and weight relationships among them, and how much heat a reaction generates. Equations define the beginning compounds, called reactants, and the ending compounds, called products, and which direction the reaction is going.

It is fairly difficult to take a few chemical compounds and derive chemical equations from them, because many variables need to be determined before the correct equations can be specified. However, to look at a chemical equation and know what it really means is not as difficult.

In general, reactants are placed on the left-hand side of the equation, and the reaction products are shown on the right. The symbol "→" indicates the direction in which the reaction proceeds. If the reaction is reversible, the symbol "⇌" should be used to show that the reaction can proceed in both the forward and reverse directions. Δ means that heat is added during the reaction, and not equal implies that heat escapes while produced. Sometimes, Δ is replaced by "light" (to initiate reactions) or "flame"

(for combustion reactions.) Instead of showing the symbol Δ, at the same place we may just indicate the operating temperature or what enzymes and catalysts are needed to speed the reaction.

Each chemical species involved in an equation is represented by chemical formula associated with stoichiometric coefficients (numerical measures showing relationships between reactants and products in a chemical reaction). For instance, a, b, c, and d are the stoichiometric coefficients for A, B, C, and D, respectively.

The chemical equation needs to be balanced, that is, the same number of atoms of each "element" (not compounds) must be shown on the right-hand side as on the left-hand side. If the equation is based on an oxidation-reduction reaction which involves electron transfer, the charges should also be balanced. In other words, the oxidizing agent gains the same number of electrons as are lost by the reducing agent. For this reason, we must know the oxidation numbers for elements and ions in chemical compounds.

Because the stoichiometric coefficients are unique for a given reaction, chemical equations can provide us with more information than we might expect. They tell us whether or not the conversion of specific products from given reactants is feasible. They also tell us that explosive or inflammable products could be formed if the reaction was performed under certain conditions.

SEE ALSO Analytical instrumentation; Inorganic compounds.

Chemical Safety and Hazard Investigation Board (USCSB), United States

The United States Chemical Safety and Hazard Investigations Board (USCSB) is a federal agency formed to identify the causes of chemical accidents. In the event of a fatality (or fatalities) caused by a chemical incident, a forensic investigation often includes experts from this agency.

Created in 1990 as part of an amendment to the Clean Air Act, the USCSB did not begin functioning until it received funding in 1998. Although its purpose overlaps that of other federal agencies, notably the Occupational Safety and Health Administration (OSHA), the Environmental Protection Agency (EPA), and the **National Transportation Safety Board** (**NTSB**), the USCSB differs from these organizations in that it does not have the power to make or enforce rules affecting the routine day-to-day activities of businesses. Instead, the USCSB makes a unique contribution to the protection of workers, the public, and the environment by investigating chemical accidents in the country and attempting to prevent future mishaps. The only regulations put into place by the fact-finding agency involve the reporting of chemical incidences.

The establishment of the Washington, D.C.-based USCSB is a result of the belief that existing hazard investigation agencies, like OSHA, EPA, and NTSB, focus on violations of existing rules while ignoring factors that contribute to a chemical accident, but which do not constitute a violation of existing rules and regulations. By creating this independent, scientific, investigatory agency and modeling it after the NTSB, Congress hoped to produce fuller accident reports that could then be used to formulate new regulations and policies to prevent future dangerous chemical spills and explosions. The amended Clean Air Act of 1990, which gave birth to the USCSB, directs the board to investigate and report on the circumstances and the probable causes of chemical incidents resulting in a fatality, serious injury, or substantial property damages; to recommend measures to reduce the likelihood or the consequences of such accidents and propose corrective measures; and, lastly, to establish regulations for reporting accidental releases. The board has no enforcement authority, does not issue fines or penalties, and essentially plays a very limited regulatory role.

Accidental releases of toxic and hazardous chemicals occur frequently and often have serious consequences. The USCSB is notified of every chemical release in the country and then decides which accidents to investigate. The agency is required to coordinate its activities with OSHA, NTSB, and EPA. However, when an accident involves transportation, NTSB is the lead agency. Board members, appointed by the president to five-year renewable terms and confirmed by the Senate, are ultimately responsible for the conduct of investigations and the content of accident reports. Staffers and contractors conduct the actual investigations, which typically involve extensive site visits, **evidence** collection, and analytical work. Investigators may issue brief summaries or detailed investigative reports. Some investigations may conclude without the issuance of any report. Accident reports must be approved by a majority vote of the five board members before they are issued. Initially, the USCSB issued only a handful of reports, in part because of insufficient staffing but also as a result of serious

disagreements among board members. Staff levels have since been raised and the board has established a more harmonious working arrangement. The agency is in the process of developing the Chemical Incidents Reports Center, an online database of chemical incidents that have occurred worldwide, in the hopes that the site may inspire researchers to investigate the incidents that the USCSB cannot examine for lack of resources.

The rise in global terrorism and the corresponding fear of a terrorist attack that utilizes chemicals makes the USCSB an important component of the United States Department's Homeland Security agency. It also provides **training** for forensic investigators.

By identifying hazardous practices, the agency promotes preventive actions by the public and private sectors that may make it more difficult for terrorists to create chemical incidents.

SEE ALSO Chemical and biological detection technologies; Chemical Biological Incident Response Force, United States; Chemical warfare; NTSB (National Transportation Safety Board).

Chemical warfare

Chemical warfare involves the aggressive use of bulk chemicals that cause death or grave injury. These chemicals are different from the lethal chemical compounds that are part of infectious bacteria or viruses. The latter constitute biological warfare.

Forensic examinations are a part of chemical warfare, especially when the nature of the attack is unclear. Examination of the scene of the incident and of the victims provide clues that are used to determine the nature of the attack.

A number of compounds cause choking or irritation of lung tissue. Examples include chlorine, phosgene (carbonyl chloride), diphosgene, chloropicrin, ethyldichloroarsine, and perflurorisobutylene.

Chlorine gas is suffocating and quickly burns tissues in the nose, mouth, and lungs. The burned tissue can die and slough off, causing lasting damage. Chlorine gas dissipates in the air very quickly. If exposure is not too long, than damage can be minor. In contrast, the compound called disphosgene is a liquid at room temperature, and so persists much longer.

Blister agents cause the formation of large and painful blisters on the skin. Eye and lung tissue can also be damaged. A well-known example of a

German storm troopers emerging from a thick cloud of phosgene gas laid down by German forces as they attack British trench lines.
© HULTON-DEUTSCH COLLECTION/CORBIS

blistering agent dating from World War I is **mustard gas**. The damage to cells of the skin cause blistering up to 24 hours after exposure to mustard gas. These blisters take a long time to heal and can send the body into a lethal shock reaction.

Other examples of blistering agents include nitrogen mustard, lewisite, and phenyldichloroarsine. The latter compound is a liquid, which can be sprayed onto an enemy or released from a balloon, helicopter, or airplane.

Blood agents interfere with the body's ability to transport oxygen in the bloodstream. This is done by either blocking the use of oxygen by cells in the body or by blocking the ability of the blood to take up the oxygen. Examples include hydrogen cyanide (also called prussic acid), cyanogen chloride, arsine, carbon monoxide, and hydrogen sulfide.

Hydrogen cyanide is initially a liquid at room temperature, but it quickly evaporates. This compound is noteworthy in recent world history, as it was used by Iraq in 1988 on an attack on the Kurdish town of Halabja during the Iran-Iraq war. Because of

its past use by Iraq, hydrogen cyanide was one of the major concerns of United Nations inspectors who inspected various facilities in Iraq during the winter of 2003.

Compounds such as arsine and carbon monoxide destroy the ability of the **hemoglobin** component of the blood to bind oxygen. Arsine does this by destroying the red blood cells. Carbon monoxide binds to hemoglobin, blocking the binding of oxygen.

Nerve agents interfere with the body's transmission of nerve impulses. This is done by disrupting the activity of a chemical called acetyl cholinesterase, which functions to bridge the gap between adjacent nerve cells, permitting an electrical nerve signal to pass from one nerve cell to the next.

Nerve agents were first developed in 1936, following the development of organophosphate types of pesticides. The first nerve agent that was made is called **tabun**. It is a member of what is known as the G series of nerve agents. Other G series members are sarin and soman. Sarin is particularly lethal; a small amount absorbed through the skin can kill

During the 1990 Persian Gulf War, a soldier from the 7th Naval Expeditionary Brigade carries a bag of anti-chemical warfare equipment during a chemical warfare simulation. © JACQUES LANGEVIN/CORBIS SYGMA

someone within two minutes. When inhaled, death occurs within 15 minutes. Sarin is infamous as the gas released into the Tokyo subway system by the fringe group Aum Shinrikyo in 1995.

Another series of nerve agents are called the V series. Members of this series—which are commonly abbreviated according to their chemical composition—are more potent than the agents of the G series. As well, they persist longer in the environment. They can, for example, be applied to surfaces like roads as a slime.

Examples of V series agents include VX, VE, VG, and VM. VX is extremely potent; a drop of the liquid absorbed through the skin is lethal within a few hours if treatment is not provided.

Herbicides are chemicals that kill vegetation. Such chemicals are often used in everyday life to keep lawns free of weeds (although more environmentally-friendly alternatives are becoming popu-

lar). When used in war, herbicides are weapons of mass destruction to foliage. Destruction of plants and the resulting loss of leaf cover remove much of the concealment for an enemy in a forested area. These philosophies lead to the massive use of Agent Orange by the United States in the Vietnam War in the 1970s. Since that war, the damaging effects of herbicides like Agent Orange and paraquat on the human nervous and immune systems have become evident.

Incendiaries are chemicals that cause fires. In warfare, they are also used to remove vegetation. An infamous incendiary is napalm. Napalm is a mixture of naphthenic acid, coconut fatty acids, and palm oil. In addition to its highly flammable property, napalm absorbs into exposed skin, where it can cause severe burns if ignited.

SEE ALSO Chemical and biological detection technologies; Water contamination.

Childers hostel blaze

In June 2000 the century-old Palace Backpackers Hostel in Childers, Queensland, Australia, was burned to the ground. Fifteen young people of various nationalities lost their lives in the blaze. According to fire and explosion forensic expert Dr. John De Haan, the fire was not accidental.

The chief suspect was Robert Long, an itinerant fruit picker and former hostel resident with a history of mental illness who was said to despise backpackers. He disappeared after the fire and, when police found him hiding in the bush, Long attacked two dog handlers and a police dog with a knife. At the trial, survivors said Long had made various threats during the weeks leading to the fire, including a boast that he would burn the hostel down. One even saw him pour a liquid into a rubbish bin in the vicinity less than two hours before the fire, although this **evidence** was later called into question.

A forensic police officer said he was not able to determine the cause of the fire, but his tests suggested no accelerants had been used. A fire investigator hired by the insurers of the hostel said that in his expert opinion, the speed and intensity of the blaze made it unlikely that electrical malfunctioning or a smoldering cigarette was responsible. But, under cross-examination by Long's lawyer, he did admit that maybe an electrical fault could not be ruled out as the cause.

Firemen inspect the rear of a backpackers' hostel after a fire killed 15 backpackers and left three unaccounted for in Childers in the state of Queensland, Australia, in 2000. © REUTERS/CORBIS

According to Dr. De Haan, the blaze was caused by several fires, lit around the same time, in the television and lounge room of the hostel. Most likely, he said, the fire was started by direct ignition of furniture in the room by an open flame, which could have been a match, cigarette lighter, or candle. Long was found guilty of **arson** and two counts of **murder**.

However, Long was not the only guilty party in this case. Those of the 88 inhabitants of the hostel who survived were fortunate to do so. The old wooden building did not have sprinklers or fire extinguishers, nor were there plans to fit them. The fire alarm system was faulty and had been turned off. Dr. De Haan pointed out that in the first floor room where several of the fatalities occurred, the doors through which escape might have been possible were blocked by bunk beds, a clear fire hazard. Important lessons were learned from the Childers hostel fire requiring the hostel industry to take measures to reduce casualties in case of fire, and stricter safety regulations for backpackers hostels were enacted.

SEE ALSO Accelerant.

Choking, signs of

Determination of the **cause of death** is an important facet of a forensic investigation. Some causes of death are easily apparent. A gunshot wound or stab wound are two such examples. Other causes of death, such as poisoning and choking, can be less obvious. To a skilled investigator, even the less than obvious causes of death will leave telltale clues. Choking is defined as the complete obstruction of the airway. Choking can occur when an excessively large piece of solid food such as a piece of meat is swallowed. The object can become lodged in the airway, plugging the flow of air. Even reflexive gagging may be insufficient to free the obstruction.

Food is a common cause of choking. As well, especially when the victim is in a supine position, vomit can puddle in the airway in sufficient quantity to block air flow. Unless the obstruction can be cleared, air cannot enter the lungs and death can ensue within about four minutes.

Signs of choking are obvious in a conscious person. A victim may be unable to talk, cry out, breathe, or cough. Initially, a person may grasp at their throat, in an instinctive although futile attempt to clear the blockage. As the full comprehension of what is happening dawns, a person can become very anxious and even panicked in behavior. As oxygen limitation becomes accentuated, skin color can change from the normal pinkish hue to blue or dusky. Finally, a loss of consciousness can occur.

Once a person is unconscious and unable to communicate their plight, recognition of the severity of the situation and the application of emergency relief becomes more difficult. All the while, however, oxygen deprivation is causing a loss of brain function. If the airway obstruction is not soon removed, death will result.

In an unconscious or dead victim, another sign of choking is the inability to push air into the lungs when artificial respiration is attempted. This failure is evident by the inability of the lungs to artificially inflate with air and visibly expand when air is blown into the mouth.

In a deceased person, the task then becomes to establish that choking did occur. A forensic investigator will search out eyewitnesses to the choking event. Recollections of the aforementioned behaviors by eyewitnesses provide a clue as to what might have happened. Additionally, a change in skin pallor associated with oxygen deprivation may still be evident in a corpse, such as a bluish tint around the lips.

Observation of the scene around the victim can provide clues. For example, choking may lead to loss of consciousness, causing the victim to fall. A resulting blow to the head on a table or other object can occur. A cut on the scalp, bloodstain near the head, and signs of impact with furniture can all be clues to choking.

A prudent investigator would look for signs of a meal such as food or food debris, plates, and cutlery. Observation of vomit should be taken as at least a suspicion that choking occurred.

When someone is unconscious but still alive, clearance of the airway, either by sweeping of the mouth or modified Heimlich maneuver, is essential. As well, a forensic investigator who suspects choking will attempt to identify and recover the blocking object from the airway.

In both cases the procedure is the same. The mouth is opened by grasping the tongue and lower portion of the jaw between the thumb and fingers, then lifting. With the jaw elevated, the upper portion of the airway is visible. An obstruction in the upper airway can sometimes be swept out of the airway using a hooked index finger.

In the case of a forensic examination of a corpse, if choking is suspected but no object is recovered, it is prudent to probe for an obstruction deeper within the airway upon **autopsy**. **Imaging** techniques such as x rays or CT scanning can also confirm an airway obstruction in a deceased person.

SEE ALSO Antemortem injuries; Asphyxiation (signs of); Crime scene investigation; Death, mechanism of; Hypoxia; Lividity.

Chromatography

Chromatography is a family of laboratory techniques for separating mixtures of chemicals into their individual compounds. The basic principle of chromatography is that different compounds will stick to a solid surface or dissolve in a film of liquid to different degrees. Chromatography is used extensively in forensics, from analyzing body **fluids** for the presence of **illicit drugs**, to fiber analysis, **blood** analysis from a crime scene, and at airports to detect residue from **explosives**.

When a gas or liquid containing a mixture of different compounds is made to flow over such a surface, the molecules of the various compounds will tend to stick to the surface. If the stickiness is not too strong, a given molecule will become stuck and unstuck hundreds or thousands of times as it is swept along the surface. This repetition exaggerates even tiny differences in the various molecules' stickiness, and they become spread out along the "track," because the stickier compounds move more slowly than the less sticky ones do. After a given time, the different compounds will have reached different places along the surface and will be physically separated from one another. Or, they can all be allowed to reach the far end of the separation surface and be detected or measured one at a time as they emerge.

Using variations of this basic phenomenon, chromatographic methods have become an extremely powerful and versatile tool for separating and analyzing a vast variety of chemical compounds in quantities from picograms (10^{-12} gram) to tons.

Chromatographic methods all share certain characteristics, although they differ in size, shape, and configuration. Typically, a stream of liquid or gas (the mobile phase) flows constantly through a tube (the column) packed with a porous solid material (the stationary phase). A sample of the chemical mixture is injected into the mobile phase at one end of the column, and the compounds separate as they move along. The individual separated compounds can be removed one at a time as they exit (or "elute from") the column.

Because it usually does not alter the molecular structure of the compounds, chromatography can provide a non-destructive way to obtain pure chemicals from various sources. It works well on very large and very small scales; chromatographic processes are used both by scientists studying micrograms of a substance in the laboratory, and by industrial chemists separating tons of material.

The technology of chromatography has advanced rapidly in the past few decades. It is now possible to obtain separation of mixtures in which the components are so similar they only differ in the way their atoms are oriented in space, in other words, they are isomers of the same compounds. It is also possible to obtain separation of a few parts per million of a contaminant from a mixture of much more concentrated materials.

In gas-liquid chromatography (now called gas chromatography), the material that separates components is chemically bonded to the solid support, which improves the temperature stability of the column's packing. Gas chromatographs can be operated at high temperatures, so even large molecules can be vaporized and progress through the column without the stationary phase vaporizing and bleeding off. Additionally, since the mobile phase is a gas, the separated compounds are very pure; there is no liquid solvent to remove.

The shapes of chromatographic columns, originally vertical tubes an inch or so (2–3 cm) in diameter, became longer and thinner when it was found that this increased the efficiency of separation. Eventually, chemists were using coiled glass or fused silica capillary tubes less than a millimeter in diameter and many yards long. Capillaries cannot be packed, but they are so narrow that the stationary phase can simply be a thin coat on the inside of the column.

A somewhat different approach is the set of techniques known as "planar" or "thin layer" chromatography (TLC), in which no column is used at all. The stationary phase is thinly coated on a glass or plastic plate. A spot of sample is placed on the plate, and the mobile phase migrates through the stationary phase by capillary action.

In the mid-1970s, interest in liquid mobile phases for column chromatography resurfaced when it was discovered that the efficiency of separation could be vastly improved by pumping the liquid through a short packed column under pressure, rather than allowing it to flow slowly down a vertical column by gravity alone. High-pressure liquid chromatography, also called high performance liquid chromatography (HPLC), is now widely used in industry. A variation on HPLC is supercritical fluid chromatography (SFC). Certain gases (carbon dioxide, for example), when highly pressurized above a certain temperature, become a state of matter intermediate between gas and liquid. These "supercritical fluids" have unusual solubility properties, some of the advantages of both gases and liquids, and appear very promising for chromatographic use.

All chromatographs must have a detection device attached, and some kind of recorder to capture the output of the detector—usually a chart recorder or its computerized equivalent. In gas chromatography, several kinds of detectors have been developed; the most common are the thermal conductivity detector, the flame ionization detector, and the electron capture detector. For HPLC, the UV detector is standardized to the concentration of the separated compound. The sensitivity of the detector is of special importance, and research has continually concentrated on increasing this sensitivity, because chemists often need to detect and quantify exceedingly small amounts of a material.

Within the last few decades, chromatographic instruments have been attached to other types of **analytical instrumentation** so that the mixture's components can be identified as well as separated (this takes the concept of the "detector" to its logical extreme). Most commonly, this second instrument has been a mass spectrometer, which allows **identification** of compounds based on the masses of molecular fragments that appear when the molecules of a compound are broken up.

Absorption chromatography (the original type of chromatography) depends on physical forces such as dipole attraction to hold the molecules onto the surface of the solid packing. In gas chromatography and HPLC, however, the solubility of the mixture's molecules in the stationary phase coating determines which ones progress through the column more

After contaminated cattle feed was traced through the food chain in the Midwest in 1986, a scientist prepares to test a tube of mother's milk by gas chromatography to determine if the amount of Heptachlor in the milk is sufficient to harm babies. © BETTMANN/CORBIS

slowly. Polarity can have an influence here as well. In gel filtration (also called size-exclusion or gel permeation) chromatography, the relative sizes of the molecules in the mixture determine which ones exit the column first. Large molecules flow right through; smaller ones are slowed down because they spend time trapped in the pores of the gel. Ion exchange chromatography depends on the relative strength with which ions are held to an ionic resin. Ions that are less strongly attached to the resin are displaced by more strongly attached ions. Hence the name ion exchange: one kind of ion is exchanged for another. This is the same principle upon which home water softeners operate. Affinity chromatography uses a stationary phase composed of materials that have been chemically altered. In this type of chromatography, the stationary phase is attached to a compound with a specific affinity for the desired molecules in the mobile phase. This process is similar to that of ion exchange chromatography, and is used mainly for the recovery of biological compounds. Hydrophobic interaction chromatography is used for amino acids that do not carry a positive or negative charge. In this type of chromatography, the hydrophobic amino acids are attracted to the solid phase, which is composed of materials containing hydrophobic groups.

Chemists choose the mobile and stationary phases carefully because it is the relative interaction of the mixture's compounds with those two phases that determines how efficient the separation can be. If the compounds have no attraction for the stationary phase at all, they will flow right through the column without separating. If the compounds are too strongly attracted to the stationary phase, they may stick permanently inside the column.

SEE ALSO Analytical instrumentation; Gas chromatograph-mass spectrometer.

Chromosome

A chromosome is a threadlike structure found in the nucleus of most cells. It carries genetic material in the form of a linear sequence of deoxyribonucleic acid (**DNA**). In prokaryotes, or cells without a nucleus, the chromosome represents circular DNA containing the entire genome. In eukaryotes, or cells with a distinct nucleus, chromosomes are much more complex in structure. The function of chromosomes is to package the extremely long DNA sequence. A single chromosome (uncoiled) could be as long as three inches and therefore visible to the naked eye. If DNA were not coiled within chromosomes, the total DNA in a typical eukaryotic cell would extend thousands of times the length of the cell nucleus.

DNA is the genetic material of all cells and contains information necessary for the synthesis of proteins. DNA is composed of two strands of nucleic acids arranged in a double helix. The nucleic acid strands are composed of a sequence of nucleotides. The nucleotides in DNA have four kinds of nitrogen containing bases: adenine (A), guanine (G), cytosine (C), and thymine (T). Within DNA, each strand of nucleic acid is partnered with the other strand by bonds that form between these nucleotides. Complementary base pairing dictates that adenine pairs only with thymine, and guanine pairs only with cytosine (and vice versa). Thus, by knowing the sequence of bases in one strand of the DNA helix, you can determine the sequence on the other strand. For instance, if the sequence in one strand of DNA were ATTCG, the other strand's sequence would be TAAGC.

DNA functions in the cell by providing a template by which another nucleic acid, called ribonucleic acid (RNA), is formed. Like DNA, RNA is also composed of nucleotides. Unlike DNA, RNA is single stranded and does not form a helix. In addition, the RNA bases are the same as in DNA, except that uracil replaces thymine. RNA is transcribed from DNA in the nucleus of the cell. Genes are expressed when the chromosome uncoils with the help of enzymes called helicases and specific DNA binding proteins. DNA is transcribed into RNA.

Newly transcribed RNA is called messenger RNA (mRNA). Messenger RNA leaves the nucleus through the nuclear pore and enters into the cytoplasm. There, the mRNA molecule binds to a ribosome (also composed of RNA) and initiates protein synthesis. Each block of three nucleotides, called codons, in the mRNA sequence encodes for a specific amino acid, the building blocks of a protein.

Genes are part of the DNA sequence called coding DNA. Noncoding DNA represents sequences that do not have genes and only recently have been found to have many new important functions. Out of the 3 billion base pairs that exist in the human DNA, there are only about 40,000 genes. The non-coding sections of DNA within a **gene** are called introns, while the coding sections of DNA are called exons. After transcription of DNA to RNA, the RNA is processed. Introns from the mRNA are excised out of the newly formed mRNA molecule before it leaves the nucleus.

The human genome (which represents the total amount of DNA in a typical human cell) has approximately 3×10^9 base pairs. If these nucleotide pairs were letters, the genome book would number over a million pages. There are 23 pairs of chromosomes, for a total number of 46 chromosomes in a diploid cell, or a cell having all the genetic material. In a haploid cell, there is only half the genetic material. For example, sex cells (the **sperm** or the egg) are haploid, while many other cells in the body are diploid. One of the chromosomes in the set of 23 is an X or Y (sex chromosomes), while the rest are assigned numbers 1 through 22. In a diploid cell, males have both an X and a Y chromosome, while females have two X chromosomes. During fertilization, the sex cell of the father combines with the sex cell of the mother to form a new cell, the zygote, which eventually develops into an embryo. If the one of the sex cells has the full complement of chromosomes (diploidy), then the zygote would have an extra set of chromosomes. This is called triploidy and represents an anomaly that usually results in a miscarriage. Sex cells are formed in a special kind of cell division called meiosis. During meiosis, two rounds of cell division ensure that the sex cells receive the haploid number of chromosomes.

Chromosomes can be visible using a microscope just prior to cell division, when the DNA within the nucleus uncoils as it replicates. By visualizing a cell during metaphase, a stage of cell division or mitosis, researchers can take pictures of the duplicated chromosome and match the pairs of chromosomes using the characteristic patterns of bands that appear on the chromosomes when they are stained with a dye called giemsa. The resulting arrangement is called a karyotype. The ends of the chromosome are referred to as telomeres, which are required to maintain stability and recently have been associated with aging. An enzyme called telomerase maintains the length of the telomere. Older cells tend to have shorter telomeres. The telomere has a repeated sequence (TTAGGG) and intact telomeres are important for proper DNA replication processes.

Karyotypes are useful in diagnosing some genetic conditions, because the karyotype can reveal an aberration in chromosome number or large alterations in structure. For example, Down's syndrome is caused

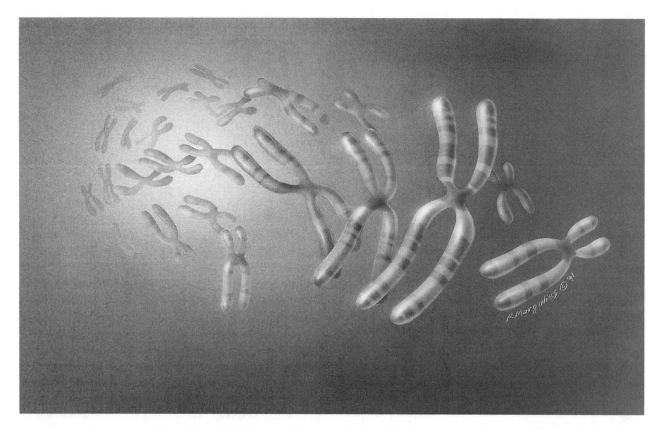

Chromosomes are a group of thread-like structures contained in the nucleus of a cell and composed primarily of genes, or DNA. Human cells normally have 23 pairs of chromosomes. © R. MARGULIES/CUSTOM MEDICAL STOCK PHOTO. REPRODUCED BY PERMISSION.

by an extra chromosome 21, called trisomy 21. A karyotype of a child with Down's syndrome would reveal this extra chromosome.

A chromosome usually appears to be a long, slender rod of DNA. Pairs of chromosomes are called homologues. Each separate chromosome within the duplicate is called a sister chromatid. The sister chromatids are attached to each other by a structure called the centromere. Chromosomes appear to be in the shape of an X after the material is duplicated. The bottom, longer portion of the X is called the long arm of the chromosome (q-arm), and the top, shorter portion is called the short arm of the chromosome (p-arm).

DNA in chromosomes is associated with proteins and this complex is called chromatin. Euchromatin refers to parts of the chromosome that have coding regions or genes, while heterchromatin refers to regions that are devoid of genes or regions where gene transcription is turned off. DNA binding proteins can attach to specific regions of chromatin. These proteins mediate DNA replication, gene expression, or represent structural proteins important in packaging the chromosomes. Histones are structural proteins of chromatin and are the most abundant protein in the nucleus. In fact, the mass of histones in a chromosome is almost equal to that of DNA. Chromosomes contain five types of these small proteins: H1, H2A, H2B, H3, and H4. There are two of each of latter four histones that form a structure called the octomeric histone core. The H1 histone is larger than the other histones, and performs a structural role separate from the octomeric histone core in organizing DNA within the chromosome.

The octomeric histone core functions as a spool from which DNA is wound two times. Each histone-DNA spool is called a nucleosome. Nucleosomes occur at intervals of every 200 base pairs of the DNA helix. In photographs taken with the help of powerful **microscopes**, DNA wrapped around nucleosomes resembles beads (the nucleosome) threaded on a string (the DNA molecule). The DNA that exists between nucleosomes is called linker DNA. Chromosomes can contain some very long stretches of linker DNA. Often, these long linker DNA sequences are the regulatory portions of genes. These regulatory portions switch genes on when certain molecules bind to them.

Nucleosomes are the most fundamental organizing structure in the chromosome. They are packaged into structures that are 30 nanometers in size and called the chromatin fiber (compared to the 2 nm DNA double helix, and 11 nm histone core). The 30 nanometer fibers are sometimes then further folded into a larger chromatin fiber that is approximately 300 nanometers thick and represented on of the arms of the chromsome. The chromatin fibers are formed into loops by another structural protein. Each loop contains 20,000–30,000 nucleotide pairs. These loops are then arranged within the chromosomes, held in place by more structural proteins. Metaphase chromosomes are approximately 1400 nm wide.

Chromosomes in eukaryotes perform a useful function during mitosis, the process in which cells replicate their genetic material and then divide into two new cells (also called daughter cells). Because the DNA is packaged within chromosomes, the distribution of the correct amount of genetic material to the daughter cells is maintained during the complex process of cell division.

Before a cell divides, the chromosomes are replicated within the nucleus. In a human cell, the nucleus just prior to cell division contains 46 pairs of chromosomes. When the cell divides, the sister chromatids from each duplicated chromosome separate. Each daughter cell ends up with 23 pairs of chromosomes and after DNA replication, the daughter cells have a diploid number of chromosomes.

In meiosis, the type of cell division that leads to the production of sex cells, the division process is more complicated. Two rounds of cell division occur in meiosis. Before meiosis, the chromosomes replicate, and the nucleus has 46 pairs of chromosomes. In the first round of meiotic cell division, the homologous chromosomes pairs separate as in mitosis (a stage called meiosis I). In the second round of cell division (meisosis II), the sister chromatids of each chromosome separate at the centromere, so that each of the four daughter cells receives the haploid number of chromosomes.

SEE ALSO DNA; DNA databanks; DNA fingerprint; DNA mixtures, forensic interpretation of mass graves; DNA profiling; Evidence; Gene; STR (short tandem repeat) analysis; War forensics.

Circumstantial evidence

Jurisprudence defines **evidence** as any written or oral testimony given under-oath, including documents, records, or physical objects admissible in a court of law, according to established rules of evidence, either to prove or disprove the authenticity of alleged facts, claims, or accusations. Circumstantial evidence is indirect information or secondary facts that allow the reasonable inference of the principal fact, without actually proving that such inference is true. Therefore, circumstantial evidence ideally requires further corroboration through other forms of evidence to prove a fact. All presented evidence will be considered by a jury, or by a judge, depending on the nature of the legal process, to test its relevancy and level of reliability, including the credibility of witnesses. In the United States, until 1975, the decision about which evidence was admissible in court was decided on the basis of judicial precedent (e.g., prior court decisions in similar cases). In the absence of a statutory law on a particular matter, the judge would make the rules. This common law jurisprudence descends from the colonial British legal system.

California was the pioneer American state in the creation of four statutory codes (in 1872): the Civil Code, the Code of Civil Procedure, the Penal Code, and the Political Code, in which the Code of Evidence was also implemented, establishing the necessary standard criteria of importance, validity, and legal weight of different types of evidence for civil and criminal courts. The California Evidence Code has inspired both the federal and other state legislations, in varied degrees, since then. However, only in 1974 did the Congress approve the implementation of the **Federal Rules of Evidence**, proposed by the U.S. Supreme Court in the preceding years.

The purpose of evidence in courts is to prove or disprove the existence of a fact. The level of proof or evidence presented must be solid enough to convince the court that such fact is true beyond a reasonable doubt, especially in **criminal trials**. In **civil trials** however, the standard of proof is often based on whether the true existence of the fact is more probable than not. Circumstantial evidence, therefore, carries different weight in criminal and civil trials.

Circumstantial evidence, in spite of its indirect nature, may be of great value, for instance, in highlighting inconsistencies between the behavior of a suspect and his allegations, thereby "filling in the blanks" of a probable crime scenario. For instance, although a suspect was unseen at the crime scene, the tire prints found on the scene match those of his car and a similar car was seen in the vicinity of the crime scene around the time the crime was committed. Or, sometime before the crime, the victim may have told a friend that they were afraid of the suspect, or a neighbor overheard a bitter and violent argument between the victim and the suspect in the recent past. Circumstantial evidence may be presumptive and inconclusive, admitting rebuttal by the other part, or, on the contrary, its quantity and pattern may be strong enough to substantiate a prosecution where other types of evidence are scarce and by themselves inconclusive.

One recent example of use of circumstantial evidence was the trial of Scott Lee Peterson, where the evidence presented was essentially circumstantial. A day after reporting that his eight-months pregnant wife was missing (December 23, 2002), Peterson was considered a suspect, because investigators found he had several extra-marital affairs since his marriage, and had recently been in a relationship with another woman. Petersen alleged that at the time of his wife's disappearance he was fishing at the Berkeley Marina, and was innocent. In April 2003, the remains of an unborn baby and the partial remains of a woman were found on the shores of the San Francisco Bay. **Autopsy** and other forensic tests identified the remains as those of his wife and her baby, although where, how, and when she died was not specifically determined. The **FBI** and forensic teams conducted extensive investigations at the Petersons' house, as well as searching Scott Peterson's boat, truck, toolbox, clothes, and personal objects, in search of forensic evidence of violence such as bloodstains or weapons. No physical piece of forensic evidence was identified that could link Peterson to the **murder** of his wife.

Although the prosecution could not present any **physical evidence** of Peterson's involvement with the crime, and the defense tried to defuse the circumstantial evidence, in November 2004, the jury convicted Scott Peterson of first degree murder for killing the wife "with special circumstances," and of second degree murder for killing his unborn baby. That December, the jury recommended a death sentence for Scott Peterson. In a press conference, the jurors declared that they had found Peterson guilty, in part, because of his demeanor. Circumstantial evidence including Peterson's change in haircut and color immediately after the crime, buying a car in his mother's name, and testimony by his ex-lover that he frequently lied and said he was a widower previous to the crime, weighed heavily with the jury.

One case where forensic evidence supported circumstantial evidence was California vs. Orenthal James Simpson in 1995. Nicole Brown, the ex-wife of famous football player and actor O. J. Simpson,

was killed with her friend Ronald Goldman, on June 12, 1994. Evidence from the crime scene pointed to Simpson as a suspect, and he was later arrested for the crime.

The prosecution relied on forensic physical evidence along with circumstantial evidence to build the case against Simpson. Circumstantial evidence included footwear prints at the crime scene that matched Simpson's size, failure to keep an arranged appointment with the police to turn himself in, initiating a two-hour-long highway journey in a white Ford Bronco with police in pursuit, a left-handed glove found among Simpson's belongings that matched a bloody right-handed glove found at the crime scene, a documented history of domestic abuse against Brown, previous telephone calls made by the victim in which she relayed fears of being physically injured by Simpson to the police, and a letter from Simpson given to a friend that indicated an intention to leave the country in disguise.

Forensic evidence supported much of the circumstantial evidence. More than 40 bloodstains were tested for **DNA** fingerprinting, and each could be linked with either the victims and/or to Simpson. These samples were taken from the primary crime scene area, the secondary scene area, Simpson's Ford Bronco, and from Simpson's home. DNA profiles that matched the victims were found in **blood** taken from the crime scene and from Simpson's Bronco.

In spite of the circumstantial evidence, often supported with forensic evidence, the jury declared O. J. Simpson not guilty of murder in 1995. A civil jury, however, used much of the same evidence to convict Simpson on a civil court in 1997, and awarded the victim's families over 30 million dollars in damages.

In some countries, circumstantial evidence in the absence of other more solid testimonial and material evidence is not admissible in criminal courts. Circumstantial evidence is considered relevant to a case as an explanatory complement to existing testimonial and/or forensic evidence of indisputable accuracy. Controversy about the two cases above described continues among jurists and other experts, due to the perceived quality and relevance of evidence presented in each of those trials.

SEE ALSO Artificial fibers; Blood; Bloodstain evidence; Civil court, forensic evidence; CODIS: Combined DNA Index System; Crime scene investigation; Crime scene reconstruction; DNA fingerprint; DNA profiling; DNA sequences, unique; DNA typing systems; Evidence; Expert witnesses; Federal Rules of Evidence; Fibers; Hair analysis; PCR (polymerase chain reaction);

RFLP (restriction fragment length polymorphism); Statistical interpretation of evidence; U.S. Supreme Court (rulings on forensic evidence).

Civil court, forensic evidence

Civil lawsuits in civil courts often seek redress (financial compensation or repayment) to recover or restore loss due to damages inflicted by the defendant (lost wages, costs related to damage of property, financial compensation for pain and suffering, etc.)

The United States court system contains two separate but parallel systems, the state and federal courts. Each of these courts has criminal and civil court divisions. Each of the court systems in the United States is governed and operated by means of specific sets of rules. In particular, the use of forensic **evidence** is dictated by the type of court (that is, federal criminal court, federal civil court, state criminal court, state civil court).

Civil courts deal with non-criminal matters and, although many of the procedures and rules are similar, there are fundamental differences in the burden of proof required for a verdict of guilty in a criminal trial as opposed to a verdict of "liable" in a civil trail. Because the defendant does not risk imprisonment in a civil court proceeding, the Constitutional protections afforded a defendant at civil trial are often less than those enjoyed in criminal court. For example, in a criminal trial, a suspect being tried cannot be called against their will to the witness stand to present testimony that may prove to be incriminating. According to the Constitution, a person may not be compelled to testify at his or her own criminal trail unless he or she makes an informed choice to do so. In a civil court proceeding, the plaintiff (the victim, or party making allegations against the defendant) can usually compel the perpetrator to testify under oath both before and during the trial.

Civil lawsuits may be filed regardless of the outcome of an associated criminal prosecution or lack of prosecution. A victim can sue in a civil court even if the alleged perpetrator was found "not guilty" in a criminal court.

One of the most famous examples of this involved former professional football star O. J. Simpson. Simpson was acquitted of **murder** charges at the state criminal court level in 1995, and later held liable for the deaths of his wife and a friend of his wife at a civil trial. In Simpson's civil trial, there was not only a lower threshold for proof of liability, Simpson was required to take the witness stand and offer testimony (something he was not required to do at his criminal trial). In the O. J. Simpson civil case the jury was unanimous in declaring Simpson liable, and he was ordered to pay penalties of roughly $8.5 million.

Civil penalties may consist of more than financial damages; the defendant may be required perform a specific action (such as community service) or refrain from a specific action (for example, not being permitted to practice **medicine** in a particular state). Either party has the right to appeal a civil verdict.

In criminal courts, the prosecution (the state or federal government) must prove the defendant guilty beyond a reasonable doubt. In civil court, the plaintiff need only prove that the defendant is liable by a "preponderance of evidence" (a greater of amount of evidence indicating liability than non-liability).

A civil action begins with a complaint sworn by the plaintiff, in which he or she makes a claim against another person (the defendant). The defendant must admit or deny every allegation made by the plaintiff, and then mount a defense against them (the allegations). A defendant may also choose to counter the plaintiff's claim with a claim of his or her own, or request the court to dismiss the suit for lack of valid proof. The next phase of a civil action involves discovery, a process in which either party may ask and answer questions, provide evidence, request documentation from other relevant sources (usually via subpoena), and/or be required to undergo physical or psychological evaluation or assessment.

During the discovery phase, lawyers may question potential witnesses under oath (a deposition) including forensic experts. The goal of such depositions is to examine potential testimony, or, in some special cases, preserve the testimony of individual who may later not be able to appear at trial.

With regard to rules of evidence that include the use of forensic evidence, however, many of the same standards apply to both criminal and civil cases (rules of admissibility related to **chain of custody**, etc.).

The **Federal Rules of Evidence** are used as the standard by which the federal court system makes decisions about evidentiary admissibility (including the rules regarding the use of forensic evidence). These rules govern the introduction of evidence in proceedings, both civil and criminal, in federal courts. While they do not directly apply to suits in state courts, the rules of many state courts (both criminal and civil) are often closely modeled on federal rules.

There is discretionary ability to either set individual rules of evidence (including rules for forensic evidence) for each state or to choose to follow some, or all, of the federal rules. Generally, individual state rules of evidence are created or determined by the state legislature and then imposed on the state courts.

There are three areas of evidentiary law (rules related to the admission of evidence at trial) in which the states generally draw heavily upon text and logic set forth in the federal rules of evidence, relevancy, shared burden of proof, and admissibility of oral testimony. In determining admissibility of evidence, many of the rules look first to the concept of relevancy. Some of the tests of relevancy are: does this expert's testimony or this opinion relate to the basic questions to be answered at this trial? Is the experience of this purported expert germane to the areas of law being examined in this case? Does the admission of this piece of material evidence have direct bearing on the outcome of the case, or is there some other underlying motive by the plaintiff's or the defendant's legal counsel in bringing it forward? Does it speak to the issues at hand, or is there some reason to exclude it?

Just as in criminal cases, during a civil proceeding forensics investigators or experts may be called to offer testimony or offer expert opinion as to the collection and handling of forensic evidence or testimony related to the findings and meaning of subsequent forensic tests.

SEE ALSO *Frye* standard; Trials, civil (U.S. law); Trials, criminal (U.S. law); Trials, international.

Civil trials SEE Trials, civil (U.S. law)

Closed-circuit television (CCTV)

Part of a forensic investigation can be to record the events that take place at a scene. If for example, a suspicious fire takes place at a factory, forensic investigators could examine tapes from surveillance **cameras** to see if anyone was on the property near the time of the fire. Thus, closed-circuit television (CCTV) can play an important role in **forensic science**.

CCTV involves the use of video cameras to produce images for display on a limited number of screens connected directly to a non-broadcast transmission system. Commercial cable TV is, technically, an example of CCTV, but the term "closed-circuit TV" is generally reserved for systems serving a small number of screens that are monitored for security purposes.

CCTV is a ubiquitous feature of institutional security systems. It is employed by prisons, banks, urban police forces, airports, military organizations, utilities, large corporations, various other organizations, and wealthy individuals. Examples include:

- X ray baggage-inspection devices at airports.
- Remote viewing of dangerous industrial processes, rocket liftoffs, and other operations.
- Perimeter security around power plants, military installations, warehouses, police stations, and other defended facilities.
- Intrusion or theft monitoring of secure spaces, whether indoors (halls, lobbies, specific doors and rooms, etc.) or outdoors (parking lots, automatic teller machines, loading docks, etc.).
- Monitoring of vehicular traffic for traffic-control purposes or detection of illegal activity.
- Identity-checking of persons desiring entry into a building.
- Computerized recognition of individual faces, with possible **identification** of "wanted" persons.

Prior to CCTV, in order to secure the perimeter of an area, it was necessary to post guards in such a way that their collective line of sight covered the entire circumference of the area. With CCTV, it is possible to reduce the number of personnel needed to secure a perimeter by placing TV cameras at strategic points and transmitting the resulting images to a control room where a few guards can monitor many screens. Ideally, these observers will note any suspicious event on their screens and alert a response team. CCTV has, thus, for decades been a component of the typical perimeter intrusion detection system (PIDS), which combines CCTV with devices designed to detect intrusion by other means, including ultrasonic motion detectors and window alarm-contacts.

CCTV technology, however, has not proved as effective in PIDS applications as was once hoped. As vigilance studies by psychologists confirm, guards who spend hours "screen gazing" at static scenes (>20 minutes, in tests) tend to become bored and less efficient, and are then likely to miss low-frequency events, such as a figure running up to and climbing over a fence.

Starting in the 1980s, designers sought to combat the bored-guard effect by using automatic video motion detectors (VMDs). These devices are designed to automatically detect scene action by comparing successive image-frames for changes. When change is detected that exceeds a predeter-

A British police CCTV (closed circuit television) image shows Southampton and Charlton Athletic soccer fans clashing in 2002 near Maze Hill train station in south London. © HANDOUT/REUTERS/CORBIS

mined threshold, an alarm is sounded. A guard then judges whether the alarm is false or valid.

VMDs, however, have not turned out to be a security panacea. There are too many sources of image change, especially in outdoor scenes, for a simple circuit to distinguish meaningful intrusions from nuisance alarms. VMD use is therefore restricted to artificially-lighted indoor spaces or to expensive systems that employ computer processing to reduce the false-alarm rate.

SEE ALSO Aviation security screeners, United States; Cameras; Fire investigation.

Codes and ciphers

Forensic analyses can be concerned with unraveling the true meaning of communications. This is particularly relevant in **forensic accounting**, where the trail of funds from person to person or within an organization is established. In the computer age, forensic accounting can involve the search of computer hard drives that have been seized as part of an investigation. An examiner may encounter information that has been converted into an unreadable format, at least until an algorithm is applied that unscrambles the information to a readable form.

From the beginnings of communication, there has been a need for secrecy. Codes and ciphers are a means of producing secret communications. Codes and ciphers are forms of cryptography, a term from the Greek *kryptos*, hidden, and *graphia*, writing. Both transform legible messages into series of symbols that are intelligible only to specific recipients. Codes do so by substituting arbitrary symbols for meanings listed in a codebook; ciphers do so by performing rule-directed operations directly on original message text. Because codes can only communicate concepts that are listed in their codebooks, they have limited flexibility and are not much used today. Rather, modern cryptography relies almost entirely on ciphers implemented by digital computers.

A code is a set of symbolic strings ("code groups") that are listed, along with their assigned meanings, in a code book.

Either a word or a number can be used as a code group. Code groups that are words are termed code words and those that are numbers are termed code numbers. Note that a single code group can encode a single word ("king") or an entire phrase ("deliver the films to agent number 3"). A coded message may, therefore, be shorter than the original message. It can also be made as long as or longer than the original message, if the codebook provides lengthy code phrases for single concepts or nonsense code groups for padding purposes. Such techniques can be used to make encoded messages harder for opponents to read.

A cipher uses a system of fixed rules (an "algorithm") to transform a legible message ("plaintext") into an apparently random string of characters ("ciphertext"). For example, a cipher might be defined by the following rule: "For every letter of plaintext, substitute a two-digit number specifying the plaintext letter's position in the alphabet plus a constant between 1 and 73 that shall be agreed upon in advance."

Incorporation of a variable term into a fixed algorithm is typical of real-world ciphers. The variable component is termed a key. A real key would be longer and would have a more complex relationship to the cipher algorithm than the key in this example, but its basic role would be the same: a key fits into an algorithm so as to enable enciphering and deciphering, just as a physical key fits into a lock to enable locking and unlocking. Without a key, a cipher algorithm is missing an essential part. In fact, so important is the concept of the key that in real-world ciphering it is not algorithms that are kept secret, but keys. Cipher designers assume that their algorithms will always become known to their opponents, but design the relationship between key and algorithm so that even knowing the algorithm it is almost impossible to decipher a ciphertext without knowing the appropriate key. Before a cipher can work, therefore, a key or set of keys must be in the possession of both the sender and the receiver.

If the key were always the same, it would simply constitute a permanent part of the algorithm, and keying would have no special advantage over trying to keep one's algorithm secret to begin with. Keys must, therefore, be changed occasionally. A new key may be employed every day, for every message, or on some other schedule.

Codes have the advantage of simplicity. No calculations are required to encode or decode messages, only lookups in a codebook. Further, because a code uses no fixed system for associating code groups with their meanings (even the amount of meaning assigned to a code word can vary, as seen above), a code may fail gracefully—that is, the meaning of a few code groups may be discerned while others are not. In contrast, a cipher produces ciphertext from plaintext (and vice versa) according to a fixed algorithm. Thus, if an enemy determines the algorithm and steals or guesses a key, they can at once interpret all messages sent using that key. Changing the key may restore cipher security, unless the enemy has developed a system for guessing keys. One such system, always possible in theory, is to try all possible keys until one is found that works.

Codes, however, have two great disadvantages. Users can only send messages that can be expressed using the terms defined in the codebook, whereas ciphers can transmit all possible messages. Additionally, all codes are vulnerable to code book capture. If a codebook is captured, there is no recourse but to distribute new codebooks to all users. In contrast, the key–algorithm concept makes cipher secrecy dependent on small units of information (keys) that can be easily altered.

Secure ciphers, however, entail complex calculations. This made the use of complex ciphers impractical before the invention of ciphering machines in the early twentieth century; codes and simple ciphers were the only feasible methods of ciphering. Yet, a

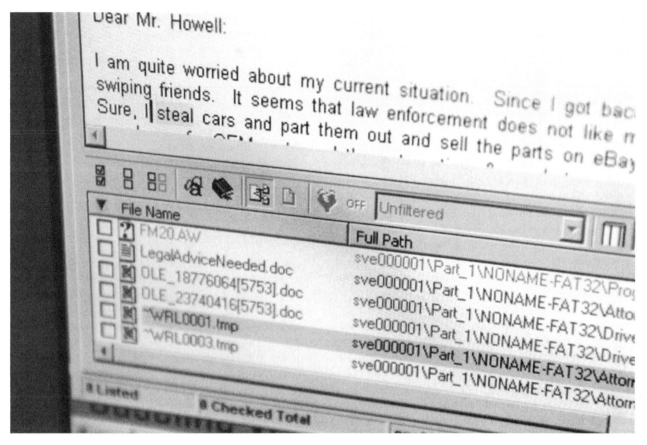

Scientists at the Silicon Valley Regional Computer Forensics Lab in Menlo Park, California, used various software tools to recover encoded evidence from data files, such as this e-mail message in 2005. © KIM KULISH/CORBIS

cipher that is simple to implement is proportionately simple to crack, and a cracked cipher can be disastrous.

Codes can be generally divided into *one-part* and *two-part* codes. In a one-part code, the same codebook is used for encipherment and decipherment. The problem with this system is that some systematic ordering of the code groups and their assigned meanings must be made, or it will be difficult to locate code groups when enciphering or their meanings when deciphering. (A randomly ordered list of words or numbers thousands of terms long is difficult to search except by computer.) Thus, code groups tend to be arranged in alphabetic or numerical order in a one-part code, an undesirable property, since an opponent seeking to crack the code can exploit the fact that code groups that are numerically or alphabetically close probably encode words or phrases that are alphabetically close. To avoid this weakness, a two-part code employs one codebook for encipherment and another for decipherment. In the encipherment codebook, alphabetically ordered meanings (e.g., A, ABDICATE, ABLE) are assigned randomly

ordered code groups (e.g., 6897, 1304, 0045). In the decipherment code book, the code groups are arranged in order (e.g., 0045, 1304, 6897), for easy location.

Code security can be improved by combining ciphering with coding. In this technique, messages are first encoded and then enciphered; at the receiving end, they are first deciphered and then decoded. A standard method for combining coding and ciphering is the "code plus additive" technique, which employs numbers as code groups and adds a pseudorandom number to each code group to produce a disguised code group. The pseudorandom numbers used for this purpose are generated by modulo-arithmetic techniques closely related to those used in stream ciphering.

Ciphers that encrypt whole blocks of characters at once—sush as 10 letters at a time, or 128 bits—are termed block ciphers. Block ciphers have the advantage that each character in each ciphertext block can be made to depend complexly on all characters of the corresponding message block, thus scrambling or smearing out the message content over many characters of ciphertext. The widely used Digital Encryption Standard (DES) is a block cipher that employs a 56-bit key to encrypt 56-bit blocks. In DES, the key and each message block are used as inputs to a complex algorithm that produces a 56-bit block of ciphertext. The same key is used to decode the block of ciphertext at the receiving end.

Stream ciphers operate upon series of binary digits ("bits," usually symbolized as 1s and 0s), enciphering them one by one rather than in blocks of fixed length. In stream encipherment, a series of bits termed the key-stream is made available by some means to both the sender and receiver. This stream is as long as the message to be sent. At the sending end, the key-stream is combined with the message-stream in a bit-by-bit fashion using the EXCLUSIVE OR operation of Boolean algebra, producing the ciphertext. At the receiving end, the same key-stream is combined again with the ciphertext to recover the message stream. This system of ciphering is unbreakable in both theory and practice if the key-stream remains secret. Ongoing breakthroughs in quantum cryptography may soon make perfectly secret key-streams available by exploiting certain properties of photons. If these techniques can be made technologically practical, truly unbreakable cipher systems will have become available for the first time in history.

All ciphers require the use of a secret key. Public-key ciphers (those ciphers that are sent with a key that is not secret) first developed in the late 1970s, are no exception. However, public-key ciphers have the important advantage that the key possessed by the sender need not be the same secret key possessed by the receiver; thus, no secure transfer of keys between the sender and receiver is ever necessary. Software for a powerful public-key cipher algorithm known as Pretty Good Privacy (PGP) is downloadable for free from many sites on the Internet.

Codes and ciphers can be attacked by two basic means. The first is theft of codebooks or keys—espionage. The second is cryptanalysis, which is any attempt to crack a code or cipher without direct access to keys or codebooks. Cryptanalysis may proceed either by trial and error or by systematic analysis of plaintext and ciphertext. The analytic approach may involve both looking for patterns in ciphertext and solving mathematical equations representing the encryption algorithm.

Cryptanalysis by trial and error usually means guessing cipher keys. A cipher key can be guessed by trying all possible keys using a computer. However, designers of encryption systems are aware of this threat, and are constantly employing larger and

larger keys to keep ahead of growing computer speed. Systematic cryptanalysis may seek patterns in ciphertext, either by itself or in conjunction with a known plaintext (the so-called "known-plaintext attack").

SEE ALSO Computer forensics; Computer hardware security; Computer software security; Cryptology and number theory; Decryption.

CODIS: Combined DNA Index System

CODIS, or the Combined DNA Index System, is a database and electronic search engine that allows crime laboratories throughout the United States to exchange DNA information about criminals, suspects, and victims of crime. CODIS is operated by the U.S. Department of Justice through the Federal Bureau of Investigation.

The CODIS project began in 1990 as a collaboration among 14 forensic laboratories. The DNA Identification Act of 1994 authorized the use of DNA data for forensic analysis and formalized CODIS. By October 1998, CODIS became operational on a national level. As of 2004, all 50 states along with Puerto Rico, the U.S. Army and the **FBI** were CODIS participants.

CODIS has a three-tiered hierarchical structure. DNA information originates at the local level (LDIS, Local DNA Index System), where biological samples are taken at police departments and sheriffs' offices. Data from the LDIS then flows into the state (SDIS, State DNA Index System) and the national (**NDIS**, National DNA Index System) databases. SDIS provides a means for local crime labs within a state to exchange information. The NDIS allows for the exchange of DNA profiles on the broadest scale at the national level. The hierarchical nature of CODIS allows investigators to use their databases according to the specific laws under which they operate.

CODIS consists of two major indexes. The Forensic Index contains DNA information from the crime scene, including DNA information found on the victim. The Offender Index contains DNA profiles of convicted felons. Most states require all people convicted of sexual offenses, as well as many convicted of violent crimes, to provide genetic information to CODIS. As of December 2004, CODIS contained 2,132,470 DNA profiles. The large majority, about 2 million, were made up of DNA profiles from convicted offenders and were included in the

Offender Index. The Forensic Index contained approximately 100,000 samples.

In addition, CODIS contains ancillary information that provides additional information for investigators to use in order to solve crimes. One index catalogues information collected from unidentified human remains and another collects DNA profiles voluntarily donated by the relatives of missing persons. CODIS also includes a population file consisting of anonymously donated DNA profiles. This file is used to quantify the statistical significance of a match.

Information entered into the Forensic Index from different locations in the United States can help link crimes together. For example, if the DNA profile taken from a crime scene in Tallahassee matches that taken from a crime scene in Miami, then there is **evidence** that the same person committed the crimes. This allows investigators to develop more leads and coordinate investigations. When a DNA profile from the Forensic Index matches one from the Offender Index, a suspect can be identified. After CODIS provides investigators with a potential match, experts in crime labs are always consulted for verification.

A DNA profile that is entered into CODIS consists of information that is gathered from stretches of the **chromosome** that are highly variable between different people. These variable regions are called polymorphisms. One type of polymorphism is a very short sequence of nucleotides, the building blocks of DNA, which repeats itself many times. This type of sequence is called a short tandem repeat, or STR. STRs are usually between two and five nucleotides long, and CODIS profiles specifically catalogue those that are four nucleotides long. STRs that are four nucleotides in length are referred to as tetramers. For example, the sequence of nucleotides "CGAAC-GAACGAACGAACGAA" represents five copies of the tetramer "CGAA." The number of times that "CGAA" repeats itself at a given location on the chromosome will vary from person to person. The CODIS core profile consists of STR information gathered from 13 different loci, or positions, on the chromosomes.

CODIS has been an extremely successful system that has aided in solving a variety of investigations. As of December 2004, CODIS produced more than 19,000 hits, which are defined as matches between suspect and crime that would not have been made without CODIS. CODIS has also assisted in solving 20,700 criminal cases in 47 states. Many of the investigations aided by CODIS have developed leads against sexual offenders. For example, in 1999, Virgi-

nia police received a phone call from a woman who had been stabbed and raped. By the time they arrived on the scene, the woman had bled to death. After gathering biological evidence from the woman's body, investigators developed a DNA profile of the suspect. Using CODIS, they produced a match in the Offender Index to a rapist who had been imprisoned in Virginia in 1989, but who had served out his term and been released. In another case, in 1996, two rapes occurred at in distant parts of St. Louis, both involving young girls who had been waiting at bus stops. The St. Louis Police Department was unable to solve the crimes. In 1999, they reanalyzed DNA evidence from the crimes and were able to generate a hit through CODIS to an offender in another rape case. He was eventually identified as the offender in both of the bus stop crimes. CODIS also played a role in the September 11, 2001 attacks. In the days following the attacks, the company that helped develop the CODIS software worked with the FBI and the New York Police Department to modify the software so that it could be used to identify the remains of those killed in the attacks.

SEE ALSO FBI crime laboratory; FBI (United States Federal Bureau of Investigation); Identification.

Coffin birth

Coffin birth (first defined by the German term *sarg geburt*) is the phrase used by coroners to explain the medical phenomenon when a pregnant woman spontaneously delivers her child after her own untimely death. The spontaneous birth happens when naturally expanding gases, built up in the abdominal and pelvic areas of a decomposing (pregnant) corpse, place sufficient pressure on the mother's uterus to force an unborn baby through the birth passageway and out the vagina. Coffin births have occurred throughout human history, with paleopathologic scientists discovering instances of coffin birth in ancient countries of what is now called the continent of Europe. However, with modern embalming techniques, the occurrence of coffin birth is very rare. On the other hand, coffin births still happen when (for example) accidental deaths and murders occur or in the unlikely situation where incorrect embalming procedures are performed. (As of the beginning of the twenty-first century, the term coffin birth has rarely appeared in medical literature for about twenty-five years due to its infrequency of occurrence.)

In April 2003 the chief **medical examiner** of San Francisco, California, along with other forensic investigators, initially stated that coffin birth was a possible reason as to why the decomposed bodies of an adult (pregnant) woman and an infant boy washed ashore separately (about a mile apart near Point Isabel Regional Shoreline) south of the city of Richmond, which is located northeast of San Francisco Bay. The media promoted such a theory during the coverage of the incident, but most scientists agreed at the time that coffin birth was only a possibility, one of many possible reasons why the pair was discovered apart. Forensic experts state that a coffin birth, sometimes called a postmortem birth, could take weeks or months to happen, depending on external factors such as outside temperature. It was later learned that the female corpse, Laci Peterson, was about seven and one half months pregnant and due to deliver a baby boy, Conner, on or about February 10, 2003, when she apparently disappeared from her Modesto, California, home on Christmas Eve 2002. Her husband, Scott, was convicted in March 2005 and sentenced to death for the murders of both his wife and unborn son.

SEE ALSO Decomposition.

Cold case

A cold case is any criminal investigation by a law enforcement agency that has not been solved for (generally) at least one year and, as a result, has been closed from further regular investigations. A cold case may be closed for various reasons such as: previously available technology was not able to adequately analyze the **evidence** in order to form a conclusion; witnesses were hostile and uncooperative; various time constraints hindered the investigation; the originally assigned detectives had a heavy workload; a lack of worthwhile leads stalled the case.

Almost assuredly, every law enforcement agency in the United States and in foreign countries has cold cases on their books that could be reopened and solved. However, since agencies have limited amounts of manpower and resources, usually only the most terrible cold cases such as violent crime are reopened. Plus, violent crimes such as homicides and sexual assaults are well matched to being reopened as cold case reviews because such cases generally produce the most evidence. However, the decision to reopen a cold case is also dependent on many other factors including: the overall severity and cruelty of the crime; cooperativeness, whereabouts, and number of witnesses; age of the crime; amount and condition of the inventory (including **physical evidence**) relevant to the case; whereabouts of previously identified suspects; and new technologies and tools that may help to determine evidence previously unable to be solved. Oftentimes, cases are reviewed and prioritized according to the likelihood of an eventual solution, with the highest priority cases given to those in which new witnesses, information, and evidence can now identify suspects.

Usually only the most talented and experienced law enforcement investigators are assigned to cold cases because of the thoroughness, persistence, and high motivation necessary to review the large numbers of detective notes, patrol reports, photographs, electronic information, laboratory documents, crime scene drawings and diagrams, witness lead sheets, and suspect information. Important characteristics required of cold crime members include: strong communication and interpersonal skills, seniority, strong research skills and deductive reasoning, creativity, patience, and enthusiasm. Sometimes a special "Cold Case Squad" may be organized, either temporarily or permanently, to deal solely with cold cases, especially when current cases prevent such older cases from being worked. In nearly all scenarios, cold case investigations present many varied and intense challenges to any law enforcement agency.

SEE ALSO Cold hit; Physical evidence.

Cold hit

A cold hit refers to an instance where one or more connections are made between a crime victim, a perpetrator, and/or a crime scene in the absence of a current investigative lead (i.e., a **cold case**).

In October of 1998, the **FBI** established the National DNA Index System (**NDIS**), the primary purpose of which was to make it possible for public sector forensic laboratories throughout the United States to electronically share and compare DNA samples and profiles. The overarching goal of this linkage system is to connect unsolved serial violent crimes to one another and to known violent offenders (particularly to known sex offenders).

In July of 1999, the FBI announced that the new system had produced its first successful cold hit, linking six unknown subject sexual assault cases in Washington, D.C. with three sexual assault cases then being investigated by the Sheriff's Office in

Jacksonville, Florida. Shortly thereafter, the forensic laboratory of the Florida Department of Law Enforcement announced that it had positively identified Leon Dundas (deceased) as the perpetrator in all six cases, based on their DNA analysis of a sample of the offender's **blood**.

CODIS, an acronym for the FBI Crime Laboratory's Combined DNA Index System, provides the framework for the Cold Hit programs. CODIS combines computer technology with **forensic science** to create a highly effective tool for linking, and potentially solving, violent crimes. Through CODIS, local, state, and federal forensic laboratories can compare and exchange DNA profiles.

The federal government established a series of grants for individual states' development of cold hit programs, in order to facilitate intra-state DNA database development and to defray equipment, administrative, and human resource costs during lab set up. In addition, forensic labs are funded in order to compensate for costs involved in screening external (not from within their own labs) DNA profiles for comparison with existing **evidence** and confirming hits on unsolved or suspectless sexual assault cases or violent crimes.

In addition to CODIS and NDIS, a website system within each state and across the nation exists for tracking the progress of each evidence kit from the time it enters the DNA analysis system through resolution. The Cold Hit Website system, which can be accessed by individual forensic labs, can be used to generate statistical reports as well as to track case status. Currently, forensic laboratories across all 50 states, Puerto Rico, and the U.S. Army participate in NDIS and the Cold Hit Program.

SEE ALSO Blood, presumptive test; Bloodstain evidence; Chemical and biological detection technologies; Cold case; Commercial kits; Decomposition.

Commercial kits

Commercial kits are used by forensic pharmaceutical or biochemical laboratories to make human **identification** possible through the use of **DNA profiling**. Commercial kits make use of standardized combinations of short tandem repeat loci (sequences of genetic material, also known as STR) in specific types of polymerase chain reactions (also known as **PCR** technology), which results in human identifications made with an extremely high degree of certainty. By using commercial kits with PCR

technology, **DNA** profiles can be generated from exceedingly small, very old, badly preserved, or partially decomposed samples.

The **FBI** is a world leader in the development of DNA typing technology and the **CODIS** system, used to identify the perpetrators of violent and serial crimes. In 1997, the FBI announced the isolation and selection of thirteen STR loci that would form the core of the CODIS database (national DNA database). The thirteen specific STR loci used by the FBI in the CODIS system are: D3S1358, vWA, FGA, TH01, D21S11, D8S1179, D18S51, TPOX, CSF1PO, D16S317, D5S818, and D7S820. The thirteenth STR locus is used for gender determination on the X and Y chromosomes.

Because the CODIS system is widely available, and the 13 FBI-recommended STR have been standardized, it is relatively simple to use the CODIS system with a commercial kit in order to make a highly accurate identification.

The advantages of using STR loci, PCR technology, and commercial kits are:

- The CODIS system is available worldwide.
- Using commercial kits, STR alleles can be very rapidly determined.
- STR alleles (one member of a pair or series of genes at a specific location on a specific **chromosome**) are standardized and behave according to scientific principles which are well known and understood.
- The data are ideally suited to use within computerized database systems.
- Forensic laboratories all over the world are adding to the known DNA database.
- STR profiles require very minute samples for accurate determination of identification.

DNA samples can be obtained from nearly any human tissue, and are typically deposited at crime scenes in the form of **blood**, **semen**, tissue from the victim, hair follicles, and **saliva**. DNA samples are extracted from these (or other similar) items of **evidence** and compared to DNA extracted from reference samples from known individuals (either offenders or member's of the victim's biological family).

Commercial kits have done much to advance the speed and accuracy with which forensic scientists can use DNA technology to make human identifications.

SEE ALSO Ancient cases and mysteries; Blood; Cold case; Cold hit; Decomposition; Electrophoresis.

Competency to stand trial

Persons accused of criminal activities must be competent to stand trial; that is, must be capable of understanding the purposes and aspects of the legal proceedings held against them and must have the ability to contribute to their own defense. The mental capability of the accused only matters during the period of time it takes to prosecute the person, as the act of taking legal action against a debilitated person is a violation of the U.S. laws of due process. According to the justice system, any accused person who becomes mentally incompetent before or during the events of a legal proceeding, including after a conviction is made, may not be subjected to the criminal penalties and punishments implemented by the court. However, the accused and/or convicted person may be held and confined to a mental hospital or facility for their own protection and for the protection of the general public.

When determining the competency of a person to stand trial one psychiatrist (or several psychiatrists with different concentrations) may be used to decide if the accused is competent. A psychiatrist will consider several psychological disorders when determining a person's mental state. The major disorders that are generally considered include: (1) mental retardations (often caused by congenital conditions, brain injuries, or infections), (2) neuroses (repeated anxiety, depression, and various maladjustments, but without psychotic symptoms), (3) organic brain syndromes (physical defects or diseases such as those found within elderly persons in the form of, for example, hardening of the arteries and within the general population in the form of, for example, brain tumors and multiple sclerosis), (4) personality disorders (inabilities to conform to socially accepted behaviors such as antisocial personality), and (5) psychoses (derangements of personality and loss of contact with reality such as with manic depressive illnesses).

The examination performed by the psychiatrist on the accused includes a physical examination (to learn about behavior, emotional state, and general appearance), a check of family and personal background (to identify mental illness history), psychological tests (to show specific mental states, including intelligence tests and psychomotor tests for conceptual thinking and memory), and personality tests (to detect the presence of psychopathologic characteristics). The psychiatrist also possesses the ability to use the concept of diminished responsibility (sometimes called diminished capacity or partial insanity). The concept permits the justice system to take into account the impaired mental state of the accused even though the specific impairment does not qualify as being incompetent to stand trial under the tests performed by the psychiatrist.

SEE ALSO Psychology; Psychopathic personality.

Composite drawing

Composite drawing is the most widely known application of forensic art. Composite drawing uses descriptions given by witnesses to create a drawing that is a useful tool for identifying or eliminating a suspect. A composite drawing is not intended to be a portrait of an individual, but more of a two-dimensional likeness that is a visual record of the witness' recollections.

Creating a composite drawing requires skill that goes beyond the technical. The artist must also be able to interview and relate to the witness, eliciting valuable information that will form the basis of the drawing. A composite drawing is made in three stages. First, the artist will block out the facial proportions—whether the suspect has a long chin, for instance, or a wide forehead. Then they will fill in shapes of facial characteristics, such as a bulbous nose or thin lips. Finally, shading is used to create facial form and texture.

Composite drawing is a two-way process. The artist encourages the victim or witness to look at the drawing at all stages of its progress. Not until they are satisfied that the drawing is the best possible representation of their recollections can it be considered completed. Sometimes, the very process of talking to the artist will bring up other important facts and memories from the witness. The drawing can be a powerful corroboration of a witness statement.

The advantage of a composite drawing is that it can be widely circulated—in newspapers, on message boards, or by fax or email to interested individuals. Composite drawings help involve the public in the search for a missing person, a suspect, or a fugitive. In one example, Stephen Mancusi, an experienced forensic artist with the New York Police Department, worked with a rape victim who had been attacked in the lobby of her apartment building. It was thought the attacker was a serial rapist loose in Manhattan who had attacked four women in their twenties at knife point. Mancusi and the fourth victim together produced a sketch of the suspect that was widely distributed throughout the city. A Bronx Assistant District Attorney saw the poster a short

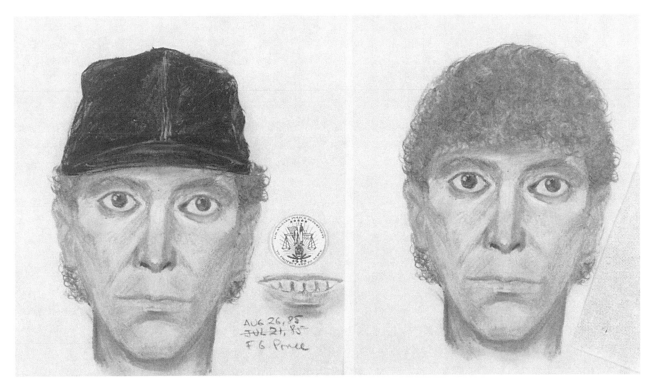

Police composite drawing of Richard Ramirez, the Los Angeles "Night Stalker" killer. © BETTMANN/CORBIS

time later and immediately recognized it as a relative. The assailant was tracked down to Florida and found to have a long history of sex offences. Put on trial, Anthony Mane admitted his crimes and was sentenced to 40 years in jail.

Composite drawings can be applied to a wide range of crimes—from shoplifting to homicide. Often kits are used to create the drawing. The Identikit approach uses a collection of noses, eyebrows, and other facial features to get the best fit to the witness description. Photofit pictures are created by putting together a picture from facial features drawn from a photographic library. The witness can pick out facial features of their suspect, including those from individuals of various ethnic origins, from such library collections. Advanced computer techniques allow synthesis of information from several witnesses, even those who only had a partial view. However the picture is generated, it is the skill and experience of the forensic artist, along with their empathy with witnesses that are still the keys to the success of the technique.

Composite drawing relies upon witness statements, but there are related techniques that use skeletal remains or photographs. There are computer programs that can create two or three-dimensional likenesses from **skull** bones. This helps identify missing people and murder victims. Photographs and

sketches can also be aged. A photo of a child who went missing or was abducted many years ago can be used to create a picture of how they may look in the present day. To do this, the forensic artist uses knowledge of the complex patterns of craniofacial growth to reveal how the child turns into an adult.

Similar techniques can be applied to the aging of adults to help identify fugitives, using anatomical knowledge of how the human face ages. It is also possible to change features such as hair color and add spectacles or facial hair in case the individual is in disguise. In 1991 forensic artist Karen Taylor used aging of a picture to help catch the Cuban fugitive Virgilio Paz Romero, who had been on the run for 15 years. He was wanted for the murder of the Chilean ambassador Orlando Letelier. When he was caught, he was even wearing the red shirt that Taylor had predicted.

SEE ALSO Anthropology; Anthropometry; Missing children.

Computer forensics

Computers are often used in crime, whether to plot a terrorist attack, contact children for sexual abuse, commit bank or credit card fraud, or other

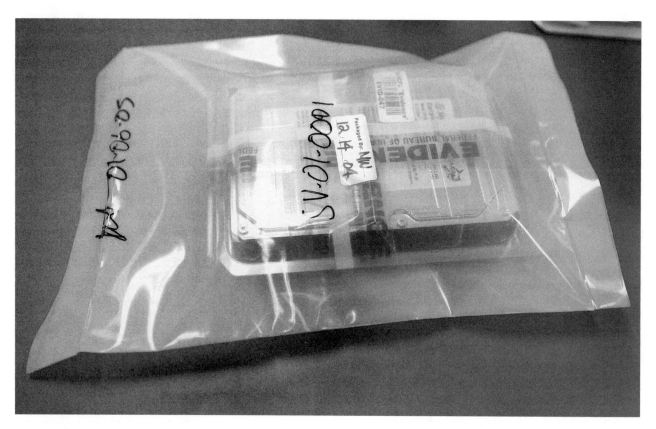

A hard drive taken as evidence at the FBI's Silicon Valley Regional Computer Forensics Lab in Menlo Park, California. The lab recovers digital evidence in a way that is legally acceptable to the courts. © KIM KULISH/CORBIS

crimes. Some crimes cannot actually be committed without a computer, such as hacking into company records. Others are just made easier by using a computer, such as sexual predators who can anonymously search for under-age victims on Internet chat sites. Whatever role the computer played, the machine can be seen as a crime scene in its own right. The police will often seize a computer if they suspect it holds **evidence** of an illegal act. They will then take it to a specialized forensic laboratory for examination. Computer forensics is a relatively new area of **forensic science** and one that requires considerable expert knowledge of operating systems, computer hardware and software, and the workings of the Internet.

As with any other crime scene, suspects leave behind **trace evidence** of their actions when using computers to commit a crime. Gathering evidence from a computer can be challenging, but valuable, because every operation that an individual carries out on a computer leaves behind a record that is usually dated. However, computer traces can also be fragile and, without the proper approach, files containing valuable evidence can be lost. Since

1990, guidelines on computer forensics have evolved by using the input of authorities around the world.

Generally the investigator is careful to do nothing that would alter the original data on the computer. Usually this means taking a copy of the hard disk for investigation, rather than the original data. Should it be necessary to look at original data, experts are consulted and only they are permitted access to data stored on hard drives. All processes involving the investigation of computer-based evidence is carefully recorded and examined and reproduced by an independent third party.

The first step in the forensic examination of a computer is to determine the condition of the computer, noting whether it is turned on, plugged in, connected to a network, or to the Internet. Then, modem or network connections should be unplugged so the computer's owner cannot access the machine remotely to destroy evidence. Note-taking and **photography** are used to record all the connections and any screen display. The computer is usually turned off by simply pulling the plug, as some computer criminals will manipulate the usual orderly shutdown process to destroy evidence. The next task is to create two physical backups of the hard drive, one for analysis and the other for evidence.

Further investigation of a computer crime scene involves looking at many different components and data, including compact disks (read only, read-write, and write-only), hard disks, and digital video disks. A hard disk is divided into various segments. Unallocated space on the hard disk, for instance, can be a rich source of forensic information as this is where files that the suspect believes deleted may be stored. Passwords and identifications sometimes appear in a part of the hard disk called slack space. Retrieving this kind of information may require specialist forensic software and, if the suspect is a computer expert, he or she may be one step ahead of the forensic investigator.

The Internet is another important source of evidence. Investigators will track a suspect's e-mail messages, their contributions to newsgroups, bulletin boards, and chat rooms. The websites accessed by a suspect can also be valuable evidence, especially when sexual crime is involved. Web browsers such as Netscape® and MS Internet Explorer® create cache files to improve performance. These show which sites have been visited recently. Although they are difficult to view, there are utilities that can allow their contents to be revealed, showing if a suspect has been indulging in incriminating use of the Internet, such as visiting child pornography, or terrorist or racist web sties.

Computer forensics can provide key evidence in both civil and criminal investigations. For example, sometimes employees from a large organization want to break away and set up a rival company. To do this, a dishonest employee could break into the organization's network and steal information about clients. In many cases, the suspects have been taken by surprise when a manager called in a computer forensic expert to examine their machines. Inappropriate use of the Internet in the workplace, for instance to access pornographic websites, can also be uncovered by this type of investigation. Computer forensics is one of the most challenging branches of forensic science. It is not just computer technology that moves fast, but also the criminals who exploit it. Keeping up or even outpacing them can be a source of satisfaction to the computer forensic expert.

SEE ALSO Computer hardware security; Computer security and computer crime investigation; Computer software security.

Computer fraud and abuse legislation

Forensic science relies on data. Using the global resources of the Internet, forensic scientists can probe databases to sift out information. Furthermore, much information they gather, such as digital images and reports, is preserved as computer files. This reliance on computer technology comes at a price. The data is vulnerable to theft or alteration by those who can gain access to the files. Federal forensic science data falls under the protective umbrella of legislation that was created several decades ago. Such legislation also provides a set of laws under which forensic investigators can act to develop **evidence** in cases where computers (and other devices housing digital information) are used or are compromised in violation of law.

The United States Computer Fraud and Abuse Act of 1986 served to define criminal fraud and abuse for computer crimes on the federal level. The act specified a **misdemeanor** crime for the trafficking and misuse of passwords. Two **felony** offenses were specified by the act for unauthorized access to federal information systems and private computers deemed to have a "federal interest." The act removed several legal ambiguities that surrounded computer information theft, such as the lack of specific legislation mentioning computers and the slightness of legal precedence in such cases.

Computer data systems of varying sorts had been used by the United States government since the 1960s. This is certainly true for forensic science, with national and international databases available for information on fingerprints, **ballistics**, felons, and genetic sequences of disease causing microorganisms.

In the early 1980s, the first computers for business and home use were available in the marketplace. This expanse of the computer-owning and software-literate population forced the government to begin finding ways to protect data, either through encryption or protective barrier mechanisms around certain files. With the advent of intranets and computer-to-computer communication through telephone lines, hacking, or the breaking into other computer systems, became more commonplace. In 1981, a computer-savvy 24-year-old named Ian Murphy hacked into several government systems, including the White House switchboard. Murphy used the switchboard to order various products before turning his attention to cracking the **codes** protecting sensitive military files. Murphy was arrested, but prosecutors did not have the legal recourse to try him for computer crimes, as no such laws existed. Murphy was eventually convicted of theft and knowingly receiving stolen goods.

By 1982, Congress began collecting data on computer crime, and gathering testimony from computer fraud victims. Most of the victims were major corporations who did not want their security breaches and vulnerability to become public knowledge. Not only was it easy for random hackers to crack a system, but also corporations could hack into the data systems of rival companies, engaging in corporate espionage. After five years, Congress introduced the Computer Fraud and Abuse Act of 1986. The bill passed decisively. That same session, the Electronic Communication Privacy Act of 1986 was passed, criminalizing the seizure and interception of digital messages and communication signals.

In January of 1989, Herbert Zinn was the first person to be convicted under the Computer Fraud and Abuse Act. As a teenager, Zinn broke into computer systems at the Department of Defense, wreaking havoc with several hundred files. Zinn was sentenced to nine months in prison and fined; he would have possibly received a harsher judgment if he had been over eighteen years-old at the time of the crime.

Since its inception, the Computer Fraud and Abuse Act has weathered changing technology and the development of the Internet. However, computer crime is once again on the rise, and only a fraction of victims report these crimes. Subsequent court proceedings and legislation such as the Computer Abuse Amendments Act of 1994 have provided specific wording criminalizing the promulgation of computer viruses and other damaging code.

In 1996, the act was amended, extending the "federal interest" to include any computer that is connected to the Internet. Appropriately, the phrase "federal interest" was replaced by the broader phrase "protected computer." Thus, the act that originally applied just to computers directly associated with federal functions now potentially applies to any computers that are involved in interaction with the federal government.

The United States Patriot Act was signed into law on October 25, 2001. The act, which was designed to strengthen the country's ability to withstand terrorist action, affected the Computer Fraud and Abuse Act. The Patriot Act specifically addressed the concept of "damage" in the act, providing more substance of what constituted damage and loss in a computer hacking incident. An individual can now be prosecuted for deliberately attempting to cause damage, even if no damage resulted from the hacking. Whether these amendments stand up to legal scrutiny awaits court challenges.

SEE ALSO Computer hackers; Computer hardware security; Computer keystroke recorder; Computer modeling; Computer security and computer crime investigation; Computer software security; Document destruction.

Computer hackers

Forensic science utilizes the global resources of the Internet to access databases and to communicate with concerned experts. This form of communication, however, can make forensic databases and files vulnerable to deliberate sabotage. Computer hackers are people who gain remote access (typically unauthorized and unapproved) to files stored in another computer, or even to the operating system of the computer. In the 1950 and 1960s, hackers were motivated more by a desire to learn the operating characteristics of a computer than by any malicious intent. Indeed, in those days hackers were often legitimate computer programmers who were seeking ways of routing information more quickly through the then-cumbersome operating systems of computers.

Since then, however, computer hacking has become much more sophisticated, organized, and, in many cases, illegal. Some hackers are motivated by a desire to cripple sensitive sites, make mischief, and to acquire restricted information.

In the late 1990s, several computer hackers attempted to gain access to files in the computer network at the Pentagon. The incidents, which were dubbed Solar Sunrise, were regarded as a dress rehearsal for a later and more malicious cyber-attack, and stimulated a revamping of the military's computer defenses. In another example, computer hackers were able to gain access to patient files at the Indiana University School of Medicine in February 2003.

One well-known hacker is Kevin Mitnick. Beginning in the late 1970s and continuing through the late 1980s, Mitnick was apprehended at least five times for hacking into various computer sites. Indeed, his lenient one-year jail sentence and subsequent

Convicted computer hacker Kevin Mitnick declining questions as he reads statement in improvised news conference after being released from Federal Correction Institute, Lompoc, California. AP/WIDE WORLD PHOTOS. REPRODUCED BY PERMISSION.

counseling was based on his defense that he suffered from a computer addiction. In 1989, he vanished, only to reappear in 1992, when police became suspicious of tampering with a California Department of Motor Vehicles database. Mitnick was arrested in 1995 and remained in prison until his release in 2002. He was barred by law from using a computer until January 21, 2003 and later published *The Art Of Intrusion: The Real Stories Behind The Exploits Of Hackers, Intruders, And Deceivers* in 2005.

The U.S. Patriot Act was signed into law on October 26, 2001. The intent of the act was to curb the danger posed to the country by terrorism. Computer hackers did not escape the legislative crackdown, since hacking represents a potential national security threat.

Under the act's provisions, the power of federal officials in criminal investigations involving hacking activities has been increased. These increased and somewhat secretive powers were among the contentious issues debated in 2005 as provisions of the Patriot Act come up for renewal.

Indeed, the threats to civilian privacy and national security from computer hackers was deemed so urgent that the U.S. government further enacted the Cyber-Security Enhancement Act in July 2002, as part of the Homeland Security measures in the wake of the terrorist attacks on September 11, 2001. Under this legislation, hackers can be regarded as terrorists, and can be imprisoned for up to 20 years. In seeking to prosecute a suspected hacker, investigators have the power to conduct Internet searches or telephone taps without court-sanctioned permission.

One tool that a hacker can use to compromise an individual computer or a computer network is a virus. Depending on their design and intent, the consequences of a virus can range from the inconvenient (i.e., defacing of a web site) to the catastrophic (i.e., disabling of a computer network). Within a few years during the 1990s, the number of known computer viruses increased to over 30,000. That number is now upwards of 100,000, with new viruses appearing virtually daily.

Despite the threat that they can pose, computer hackers can also be of benefit. By exposing the flaws in a computer network, hackers can aid in the redesign of the system to make information more inaccessible to unauthorized access.

SEE ALSO Computer hardware security; Computer keystroke recorder; Computer security and computer crime investigation; Computer software security.

Computer hardware security

A phenomenal amount of information now resides on computers. Individual computers, computers that communicate with each other in geographically-restricted local networks, and computers that communicate globally via the Internet contain billions of pages of text, graphics, and other sources of information. Without safeguards, this information is vulnerable to misuse or theft.

This is true for computers used in **forensic science**, which help with the acquisition, storage, and analysis of data. As with any data stored on a computer, there are vulnerabilities. **Computer security** provisions are a prudent facet of any top-quality forensic science operation.

Computer security can take two forms. Software security provides barriers and other cyber-tools that protect programs, files, and the information flow to and from a computer. Hardware security protects the machine and peripheral hardware from theft and from electronic intrusion and damage.

Physical on-site security can be as easy as confining mission-critical computers to a locked room, and restricting access to only those who are authorized. This also holds for servers, which are computers that function as a central routing point for information to and from the networked computers and the Internet. Many personal computer users pay to have this service provided by an Internet service provider (ISP). However, having an outside provider can generate security threats and can be disruptive if the ISP ceases operation. Nowadays, many corporations opt to establish an in-house ISP. In this way the security of the corporate server is under direct control.

Computers also have an internal form of a lock and key. A security password that is needed to gain access to all of a computer's functions can be stored on a chip known as the BIOS chip. Unfortunately, a dedicated thief can easily circumvent this hardware security feature, by removing the hard drive and putting it into another computer with a different BIOS chip.

With the exploding popularity of the Internet, hardware security has been extended to this electronic realm. Computers that are connected to the Internet are vulnerable to remote access, sabotage, and eavesdropping unless security measures are in place to buffer the computer from the outside electronic world.

Many corporations whose computers are linked to one another employ a local version of the Internet. An intranet or local area network (LAN) allows the exchange of information between the linked computers, while at the same time enabling the erection of hardware and software (i.e., firewalls) that screen information flowing to and from the Internet. Remote users of the internal network, such as telecommuting employees, can be protected through what is known as a virtual private network (VPN). A VPN establishes a protected communications link across a public network between the remote computer and the computers physically linked in the local network.

The individual computers that are linked in a network, and the dedicated devices that route information back and forth, are also known as nodes. The security measures that have been discussed above also function to safeguard nodes.

At the core of a network is a physical device called the hub. The hub exchanges the information between all of the connected computers. As such, it is key to a network. A hub should be kept away from high traffic areas, and preferably in a secure room. This restricts tampering.

While a hub relays information indiscriminately from computer to computer, a device called a switch is more selective. Information can be sent to one user computer but not to another. The use of a switch allows a network administrator to control the information flow to authorized viewers, which can be a security issue.

Fluctuations in the power supply can play havoc with computers. For example, a blackout or brownout can cause a computer to shut down abruptly. Information that is stored only in short-term memory will be lost. As well, the fluctuation can physically damage computer components. The use of a surge protector can guard against electrical spikes and drops. An uninterruptible power supply (UPS) can also be hooked up to a computer. A UPS is essentially a battery that will power the computer in the event of a power outage. This can provide time for information to be saved and for a computer to be shut down correctly.

SEE ALSO Computer hackers; Computer keystroke recorder; Computer software security.

Computer keystroke recorder

In isolation or linked globally via the Internet, computers contain billions of pages of text, graphics, and other sources of information. Without safeguards to the computer hardware and software, this information is vulnerable.

This use and vulnerability of computers holds true for **forensic science**. Like other computer-intensive operations, safeguards that can monitor the activity of computer users can be a wise provision in forensic science.

One such safeguard is known as the computer keystroke recorder. As its name suggests, a computer keystroke recorder is a device for sequentially recording all the keys pressed on a computer keyboard. Numerous versions of keystroke recorders are available commercially, but much more sophisticated devices are used by government agencies such as the Federal Bureau of Investigation (**FBI**).

Also called a keystroke logger, key logger, or keylogger, a computer keystroke recorder is a program that runs in the background as the computer operates, recording all key depressions or strokes. Some such devices are plugged in manually, but the more effective types operate by means of a computer program. The latter may be introduced to the computer by means of a Trojan horse, a remotely inserted program that operates much like a virus.

An example of an FBI keystroke-recording Trojan is Magic Lantern, which made it possible to log keystrokes by means of a **computer virus** sent to a remote user's machine. The revelation of the device's use, reported by MSNBC News on December 12, 2001, invoked the ire of civil libertarians, as well as computer companies whose assistance the government sought. According to the MSNBC report, vendors of anti-virus software refused to cooperate with FBI requests to bypass special government-created Trojans and viruses used for security purposes.

The FBI and its computer keystroke recording technology also made the news in late 2001 due to its involvement in *United States vs. Scarfo*. The first known case of its kind, *Scarfo* involved a request by the defense to allow analysis of the keystroke recording technique used to gather **evidence** against the defendant. The government claimed protection of classified information under the Classified Information Procedures Act (CIPA), and the court granted the government's motion.

The remote use of programs like Magic Lantern has been encouraged by the passage of the U.S. Patriot Act in 2001 and the Cyber Security Enhancement Act of 2002. These legislations, which were prompted by security concerns in the United States in light of the September 11, 2001, terrorist attacks, have given government authorities far-reaching powers of access to any computer that is attached to the Internet. In some cases, the security procedures do not require court approval before being carried out.

SEE ALSO Computer hackers; Computer hardware security; Computer software security.

Computer modeling

Computer modeling is a general term that describes the use of computers to simulate objects or events. As such, it is sometimes known as computer simulation. Forensic applications of computer modeling can produce purely graphical results (for example, the face of an unknown murder victim reconstructed from a **skull**) or mathematical idealizations of physical, chemical, biological, or geological processes (for example, calculations performed to estimate the speed of a vehicle before an acci-

dent). Most forensic computer models are extensions of graphical and mathematical techniques that have been used by forensic scientists for many years, but which have become much more complicated and visually compelling because of continuing advances in computer technology.

Craniofacial reconstruction (re-building the shape of the skull and face) is one example of a purely empirical graphical forensic technique that is adaptable to computer modeling. The traditional approach is to shape layers of clay placed on a cast of a skull in order to produce a likeness of an unknown person. The thickness of clay on different parts of the skull is constrained by information from tissue thickness databases, which were originally obtained from cadavers but now measured using techniques such as computerized tomography (CT) scans, magnetic resonance **imaging** (MRI), or ultrasound imaging of living subjects. This has been an important advance, because cadaver measurements represented only a small segment of the general population. In computer-assisted craniofacial reconstruction, a virtual representation of the skull is created using a **laser** scanner or stereo **photography** to produce a three-dimensional mesh of points. Tissue thickness at selected points on the skull is specified mathematically, often using statistical relationships derived from large CT scan or MRI database, and the shape of the face is modeled as a smooth three-dimensional surface that passes through the measurement points. The main weakness of any craniofacial reconstruction technique is that the soft tissue thickness is always an estimate and it is difficult to infer facial characteristics reflecting age, weight, sex, and ethnicity from skull shape (although this information can be inferred from a complete skeleton). Superficial characteristics such as hair color and skin texture are impossible to infer from skull shape and are only artistic embellishments. Therefore, a general resemblance between a craniofacial reconstruction and a deceased person is the best that can be achieved.

Process-based forensic computer models combine equations describing physical or chemical processes with empirical information in order to reconstruct sequences of events. One widely used computer program for automobile **accident reconstruction**, known as SMAC (Simulation Model of Automobile Collisions), was originally developed by the National Highway Traffic Safety Administration. It uses Newton's laws of force and motion to simulate colliding automobiles as moving bodies in much the same way that one might simulate the collision of billiard balls. Factors such as road condition and tire type are incorporated using empirical coefficients, and the model input is adjusted until the output agrees with observations made at the accident site. Whereas this kind of computer model might calculate the energy at impact, it would not explicitly simulate the crumpling and deformation of the automobiles. Computer **animation** can be used to visualize the results of process-based models by depicting the automobiles as specific makes, models, and colors rather than nondescript masses or by incorporating realistic topography and scenery to simulate the accident scene. This kind of animation, in which variables such as vehicle position and speed are the result of scientific analysis and inference, is known as forensic animation.

A more sophisticated kind of process-based computer modeling involves the detailed simulation of physical or chemical processes in two or three dimensions (and often over time) in order to reconstruct an event or process. For example, a sophisticated accident model might simulate the bending and buckling of each structural member in an automobile rather than just the total amount of energy absorbed by one moving mass colliding with another. Another example is the use of computer models to simulate the two and three-dimensional movement of chemicals contaminating an aquifer. In order to obtain accurate results using this kind of model, geologists must collect detailed information about the materials comprising the aquifer by drilling test wells, taking samples of the aquifer materials, and conducting a variety of tests. The velocity and chemical composition of the groundwater are then calculated at many thousands, and perhaps even millions, of points within the simulated aquifer and the model is calibrated by adjusting the input until the results agree with observed conditions. Experts can use this kind of model to infer the source of the contaminants or the time that they entered the aquifer, which can be important in legal proceedings such as the well-known lawsuit concerning groundwater contamination in Woburn, Massachusetts. Fire scientists likewise use computational fluid dynamics models to simulate the spread of fires in buildings, and other computer models can be used to simulate the mechanics of solid objects, the flow of fluids, and chemical reactions. As computer models become more complicated, however, they also become more difficult to apply because the quality and quantity of input increase dramatically. As is the case for simple process-based models, the results of multidimensional can be visualized using static and animated computer graphics.

SEE ALSO Accident reconstruction; Aircraft accident investigations; Crime scene reconstruction; Fire investigation.

Computer security and computer crime investigation

Computer crime, or cyber crime as it is often known, is the fastest-growing type of criminal activity in the world today. As more advanced computers are manufactured, the more sophisticated the cyber criminals become. Computer crime covers a large range of illegal activity, including bank and credit card fraud, computer hacking, industrial espionage, organized pedophilia, and terrorism. What is more, computer crime has no national boundaries. Investigators face many technical and legal barriers when it comes to trying to identify perpetrators of cyber crimes. Yet there have been some successes, and **computer forensics** is becoming an increasingly important part of **forensic science**.

Much undesirable, if not actually illegal, computer activity happens in the workplace. A recent survey carried out by the Federal Bureau of Investigation showed that most organizations have found security breaches of their computer networks. The most serious outcome was theft of confidential information, costing millions of dollars to companies as a whole. Almost all companies had had viruses infecting their computers with loss or potential loss of valuable data. Another major form of unwanted computer activity consisted of defacement of the company's website. There was also widespread reporting of abuse of computer privileges by employees by downloading pornography or pirated software.

Hacking is the most common form of computer crime. It is defined as willful penetration of a computer system for malicious purposes. All computer users are vulnerable to hacking, regardless of how secure they assume they are through anti-virus software, firewalls, and password protection. It happened to software giant Microsoft after all, so it could potentially happen to anyone. Sending a virus, a small program that acts on the victim's computer, is one of the main ways in which hackers operate. There are many types of viruses. They do not all destroy data; some viruses are designed to send valuable data back to the hacker. Trojan horse viruses, for example, consist of hidden instructions in e-mails or software which, when opened, will damage, modify, or send important data. Another is the aptly

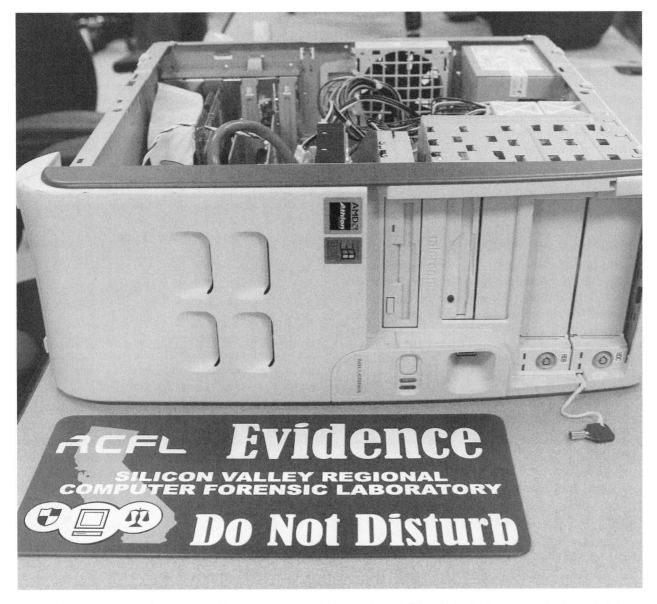

Photo of a computer opened on a exam table to retrieve data evidence at the FBI's Silicon Valley Regional Computer Forensics Lab on January 7, 2005, in Menlo Park, California. © KIM KULISH/CORBIS

named logic "bomb" that only takes effect a while after it has been sent, allowing the perpetrator ample time to clear away the **evidence**.

Once a hacker has access to a computer, he or she has access to much of the information inside it, such as bank details, credit card numbers, and passwords. On a personal scale, this kind of identify theft can be disastrous. For a company, it can lead to loss of revenue, delays, and loss of customers. Another growing form of computer nuisance is the sending of spam, or unsolicited e-mail. Measures are underway in many countries to make spam illegal, because it threatens to destroy people's ability to send and receive e-mail.

Investigating and stopping computer crime is difficult. Hacking is often not difficult to accomplish and the tools required to hack are freely available. Many hackers argue that hacking is often a victimless crime. Additionally, the Internet is international and the hacker is anonymous, which makes it hard to pursue and catch them. One answer is to step up computer security but, in reality, anti-virus software can only, by definition, deal with known viruses and so the software is always one step behind the inventive hacker.

Investigation of computer crime is also challenging because it can be hard to prove that a crime has actually been committed. Data can be manipulated after the event, because the hacker is rarely caught soon after the crime. Successful prosecutions are rare and punishments tend not be severe.

While computer forensics and approaches to investigation continue to develop, it is up to the individual and organizations to find ways of improving their computer security. Sometimes crimes are committed just by guessing someone's password. Longer passwords are harder to guess, therefore, most security experts recommend using passwords of at least 6–8 characters where possible. It may also help to get the hackers to turn their talents to helping the people they once attacked, by pointing out the weak points in their systems.

Despite the challenges, there have been some successful prosecutions of computer criminals. Recently, the U.S. government caught up with 19 individuals who ran one of the world's largest online centers for trafficking in stolen identities and financial fraud. The team, from the U.S. and several other countries, ran a site called Shadowcrew with 4,000 members dedicated to computer hacking for obtaining counterfeit documents, as well as stealing credit and debit card numbers. The U.S. Secret Service spent a year tracking down the gang. While operating, the gang had trafficked in at least 1.7 million stolen credit cards, causing losses in excess of four million dollars. In short, the site acted as a "one stop shop" for **identity theft**. They will trade no longer, and the successful conclusion of this case gives investigators renewed confidence in the fight against computer crime.

SEE ALSO Computer forensics; Computer hackers; Computer hardware security; Computer forensics; Computer virus; Identity theft.

Computer software security

Computers are an important facet of **forensic science**. Individual computers as well as computers that are electronically connected via the Internet house text, graphics, and other sources of forensic information.

This information can be vulnerable to unauthorized scrutiny, outright tampering, theft or misuse.

As with many other computer operations, computers that are critical to a forensic science operation ought to be equipped with a variety of hardware and software security features that help safeguard the information.

Software can prevent damage to computer files, programs, and operating systems, as well as to monitor a personal computer (PC) or laptop for theft.

A recommended feature for any computer that is connected to the Internet is software that protects the computer from viruses. Like biological viruses, computer viruses need the machinery of another host, in this case a computer, to make new copies of themselves and infect another host computer. There are upwards of 100,000 known viruses, with new viruses being detected literally every day.

Some viruses are hidden inside a program that appears safe. Once the program is downloaded into a computer and executed, the "Trojan" virus can enact great damage. Another type of virus called a worm usually is ferried into a computer via e-mail. The virus can then be emailed out to everyone in the computer's email address book. Thus, the virus can spread very widely and very quickly.

An infamous example is the "Love" virus, which infected millions of computers worldwide within hours of its release in May 2000. This virus was also a Trojan because it was contained in an innocuous appearing email attachment.

There are a wide variety of anti-virus software programs available that will recognize, quarantine and destroy many of these viruses. Anti-virus programs need to be updated frequently (often accomplished automatically "on-line" with some vendors products) to keep pace with the appearance of new viruses.

Next to viruses, theft represents the biggest security issue for computer users. Various hardware options are designed to lessen the chance of theft. Anti-theft software is also available. There are several software programs that aim to lessen the usability, and so the appeal, of a stolen computer (particularly laptop computers). In one setup, a registered identifier number is beamed out when the stolen computer is hooked up to the Internet. Proprietary software can detect and even track the location of the sending computer. Another strategy uses motion-sensing software that is adjusted to the motion patterns of the normal user. A different range of motions that are uncharacteristic of the principal user can trigger an audio alarm. As well, the computer is triggered to shut down and reboot. The user then needs to supply a complicated password to use the computer and even to read the scrambled files (see below) from the hard drive. This protection occurs even when the computer is shut off.

Another software security option is known as encryption. Encryption is the scrambling of the data into an undecipherable format. Encryption programs can scramble the data that is resident in the computer as well as data sent to another computer via email. The message can be reassembled to the original format if the receiving computer has an encryption program installed.

Computers connected to the Internet are often equipped with software known as a firewall. The firewall functions to monitor incoming transmissions and to restrict those that are deemed suspicious. It is a controlled gateway that limits who and what can pass through. A number of vendors offer firewall programs. Like anti-virus software, these programs can and should be frequently updated, since those who seek to maliciously gain remote access to computers are constantly developing methods to thwart the firewall barrier.

SEE ALSO Computer hackers; Computer hardware security; Computer forensics; Computer security and computer crime investigation; Computer virus; Document destruction.

Computer virus

As with other computer-based applications, **forensic science** can be compromised by agents that alter or disable computers, such as computer viruses.

A computer virus is a program or segment of executable computer code that is designed to reproduce itself in computer memory and, sometimes, to damage data. Viruses are generally short programs; they may either stand alone or be embedded in larger bodies of code. The term virus is applied to such code by analogy to biological viruses, microorganisms that force larger cells to manufacture new virus particles by inserting copies of their own **genetic code** into the larger cell's DNA. Because DNA can be viewed as a data-storage mechanism, the parallel between biological and computer viruses is remarkably exact.

Many viruses exploit computer networks to spread from computer to computer, sending themselves either as e-mail messages over the Internet or directly over high-speed data links. Programs that spread copies of themselves over network connections of any kind are termed worms, to distinguish them from programs that actively copy themselves only within the memory resources of a single computer. So many worm/virus hybrids have appeared that any distinction between them is rapidly disappearing.

A program that appears to perform a legitimate or harmless function, but is in fact designed to propagate a virus is often termed a Trojan Horse, after the hollow, apparently-harmless, giant wooden horse that was supposedly used by the ancient Greeks to sneak in inside the walls of Troy and overthrow the city from within. Chain letters have also been used as carriers for executable viruses, which are attached to the chain letter as a supposedly entertaining or harmless program (e.g., one that will draw a Christmas card on the screen).

The first wild computer viruses, that is, viruses not designed as computer-science experiments but spreading through computers in the real world, appeared in the early 1980s and were designed to afflict Apple II personal computers. In 1984 the science fiction book *Necromancer* by William Gibson appeared; this book romanticized the hacking of giant corporate computers by brilliant freelance rebels, and is thought by some experts to have increased interest among young programmers in writing real-world viruses. The first IBM PC computer viruses appeared in 1986, and by 1988 virus infestations on a global scale had become a regular event. An anti-virus infrastructure began to appear at that time, and anti-virus experts have carried on a sort of running battle with virus writers ever since. As anti-virus software increases in sophistication, however, so do viruses, which thrive on loopholes in software of ever-increasing complexity. As recently as January 25, 2003, a virus dubbed SQL Slammer (SQL Server 2000, targeted by the virus, is a large software package run by many businesses and governments) made headlines by suspending or drastically slowing Internet service for millions of users worldwide. In the United States alone, this caused some 13,000 automatic teller machines to shut down for most of a day.

All viruses cause some degree of harm by wasting resources, that is, filling a computer's memory or, like SQL Slammer, clogging networks with copies of itself. These effects may cause data to be lost, but some viruses are designed specifically to delete files or issue a physically harmful series of instructions to hard drives. Such viruses are termed destructive. The number of destructive viruses has been rising for over a decade; in 1993 only about 10 percent of viruses were destructive, but by 2000 this number had risen to 35 percent.

Because even non-malicious or non-destructive viruses may clog networks, shut down businesses or websites, and cause other computational harm (with possible real-world consequences, in some cases), both the private sector and governments are

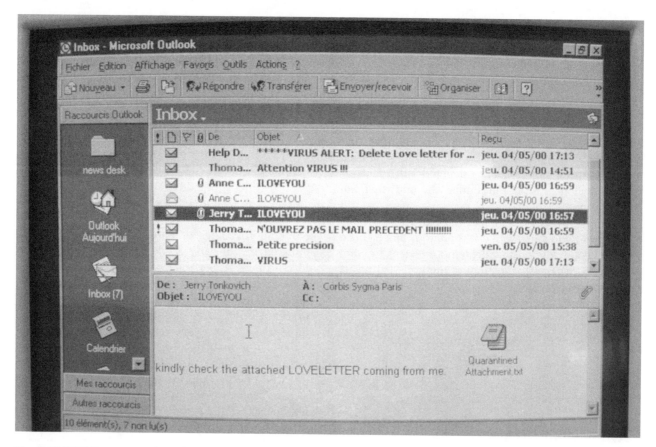

The "ILOVEYOU" computer virus cyber greeting as it appeared as an e-mail message. © SERRA ANTOINE/CORBIS SYGMA

increasingly dedicating resources to the prevention, detection, and defeat of viruses.

The first virus designed to be mass propagated, and perhaps the most famous virus to date, is a virus dubbed Melissa. The virus' creator, David Smith, initially unleashed the virus as part of an attachment in a file posted to a pornographic news group. The popularity of the group ensured a swift spread. For his dubious efforts, Smith was ultimately sentenced to 20 months in federal prison and fined $5,000.

Another infamous virus is the Michelangelo virus. Having infected a computer's hard drive, the viral program can wipe out information on the drive. The viral destruction is triggered by a certain date (March 6, presumably the birthdate of the Italian Renaissance artist and inventor Michelangelo Buonarroti). While some viruses are rather innocuous, the Michelangelo virus is malicious. Fortunately, the threat posed by this virus has passed.

An exhaustive list of current viral threats is essentially impossible. Twenty to 30 new viruses are identified every day, and over 50,000 viruses have been detected and named since the early 1980s, when

computers first became integrated with the world economy in large numbers.

Most viruses are written merely as egotistical pranks, but a successful virus can cause serious losses. The ILOVEYOU virus that afflicted computers globally in May 2000 is a dramatic recent case that illustrates many of the properties of viruses and worms.

The ILOVEYOU virus was so named because in its most common form (among some 14 variants) it spread by looking up address-book files on each computer it infected and sending an e-mail to all the addresses it found, including a copy of itself as an attachment named LOVE-LETTER-FOR-YOU.TXT.VBS. ("VBS" stands for Visual Basic Script, a type of file readable by World Wide Web browsers.) If a recipient of the e-mail opened the attachment, the ILOVEYOU virus code would run on their computer, raiding the recipient's address book and sending out a fresh wave of e-mails to still other computers.

The ILOVEYOU virus first appeared in Asia on May 4, 2000. Designed to run on PC-type desktop computers, it rapidly spread all over the world, infecting computers belonging to large corporations, media outlets, governments, banks, schools, and other groups. Many organizations were forced to take their networks off line, losing business or suspending services. The United States General Accounting Office later estimated that the losses inflicted by the ILOVEYOU virus may have totaled $10 billion worldwide. Monetary losses occurred because of lost productivity, diversion of staff to virus containment, lost business opportunities, loss of data, and loss of consumer confidence (with subsequent loss of business).

National security may also be threatened by computer viruses and similar software objects. During the ILOVEYOU incident, the U.S. Department of Health and Human Services was disrupted for many hours. An official of the department stated that if a biological outbreak had occurred simultaneously with this "Love Bug" infestation, the health and stability of the Nation would have been compromised with the lack of computer network communication.

The U.S. National Security Agency has stated that at least 100 governments are developing viruses and other cyberweapons, as well as terrorist groups. To counter such threats, the U.S. government has established a National Infrastructure Protection Center in the Federal Bureau of Investigation to coordinate information on threats to infrastructure, including threats (such as viruses) to computers and telecommunications networks.

SEE ALSO Computer hackers; Computer hardware security; Computer keystroke recorder; Computer modeling; Computer software security.

Confocal microscopy

The examination of samples obtained from an accident or crime scene can be a sophisticated process. Some of these examinations can determine the presence of certain compounds or materials. Various microscopic methods can be used to visually examine samples. The choice of the microscopy technique can be determined in part by the size of the target. For example, **gunshot residue** may be too small to be seen using a visible light microscope. Rather, the increased magnification available through the use of electrons or **laser** light is needed to resolve the residue.

Another sophisticated form of microscopy that is useful in forensic analyses is called confocal microscopy. As one example, the technique has been used to visualize the marks on bullets and cartridge cases

that were otherwise not easily seen using conventional light microscopy

In confocal microscopy, the source of illumination is laser light. A laser light wave can be focused to a very small area on a specimen, which permits very detailed examinations on a sample to be done.

As well, the wavelength of light used can be specifically selected. This is advantageous because some molecules and stains that can be applied to a sample will fluoresce when exposed to the particular wavelength. **Fluorescence** occurs when the sample molecules acquire more energy when they absorb the laser light. This energy increase is transient, and some energy is subsequently emitted. The emitted energy is the fluorescent light.

When a solid sample is examined, the confocal microscope can be equipped with detectors to capture the light that is reflected back off of the surface and the fluorescent light that is emitted. This information can be analyzed using a computer that is connected to the microscope and a very detailed image of the specimen can be produced.

If a specimen is transparent to the laser light, then the light beam can be progressively focused at different depths through the thickness of the specimen. The information collected from the reflected light at each of these so-called optical planes can be stored in the computer. Subsequently, each image can be analyzed separately to assess the composition and structure of the specimen throughout its depth. As well, the collected images can be merged together to produce a three-dimensional image of the specimen.

When confocal **microscopes** first appeared in the 1980s, they were expensive and beyond the range of many labs. However, now they are quite affordable and have become a popular addition to a forensic laboratory.

SEE ALSO Analytical instrumentation; Crime scene investigation; Fluorescence; Imaging; Scanning electron microscopy.

Contact crimes

As it is defined in the United States, a contact crime is one in which the perpetrator is known to the victim, or the victim and perpetrator repeatedly encounter each other through everyday activities, such as working in the same environment or riding the same subway train. A contact criminal is one who knows his victim (the term "he" is used as a convention throughout, as the majority of contact and other criminals are male). Most contact crimes involve some form of sexual assault, and the preponderance of sexual assault victims are female. More than 70% of contact murders are committed against females, and more than 80% of nonlethal contact crime victims are female.

A contact criminal need not be well known to the victim. Some contact criminals use the same location or environment in the perpetration of their crimes. Others seek out and get to know their victims, while still others place themselves in locations where they will encounter and desensitize potential victims (build an acquaintance-type relationship, creating a semblance of trust in the potential victim). According to the Bureau of Justice Statistics on victims of crime, nearly 70% of all reported female rape victims were acquainted with, related to, or intimately knew their assailants. Of young children murdered, approximately one fifth were killed by family members; adolescents (ages 15–17) were most likely to be murdered by an acquaintance or a friend.

A by-product of contact crime is its low incidence of reporting and successful prosecution. According to statistics released by the United States Senate Judiciary Committee, less than 10% of all violent contact crimes are actually reported to the police. Of those violent crimes reported, less than 1% result in a conviction involving incarceration. Some social scientists characterize the justice system as viewing contact crimes as less serious than other crimes, where the assailant is a stranger to the victim.

Contact crimes are often considered difficult to prosecute because there are rarely any witnesses, the victims do not always seek immediate medical assistance, appropriate forensic **evidence** is not always collected when the offense is promptly reported, and perpetrators rarely confess voluntarily. A significant deterrent to the reporting of contact crimes is the perception that the negative attention generated could make victims seem as much on trial as the alleged assailants. When children are the victims of contact crime, they are statistically unlikely to report it voluntarily, often as a result of intimidation by the perpetrator. Children are often not considered either accurate historians or reliable witnesses. Contact crimes against children are infrequently successfully prosecuted without ample **physical evidence** or eyewitness testimony.

SEE ALSO Expert witnesses; Gang violence, forensic evidence; Illicit drugs; National Institute of Justice; PERK (physical evidence recovery kit).

Control samples

Control samples are any type of well-known forensic samples used to assure analyses are properly performed so that results are reliable. Also called controls, known samples, and knowns, these control samples are fully known to the forensic community with respect to composition, identification, source, and type. Examples of control samples include known combustible substances used for **arson** cases, known drug samples for suspected illegal drug samples, known **blood** types in violent crime investigations, and known **DNA** types for **trace evidence** cases.

Control samples are an important part of quality control and assurance procedures that forensic scientists use to eliminate the inaccuracy of laboratory results. Without control samples such scientific results could yield false positives (any result that is true when in reality it is false) and false negatives (any result that is false when in reality it is true). For example, a forensic scientist tests a control sample along with a suspect sample when conducting DNA analysis. The control sample is collected before the suspect sample to reduce the possibility of contamination.

Control samples are acquired through any source that is considered completely reliable and whose identification has been verified through proper authorities. These sources include commercial vendors and manufacturers for such items as ammunition, **fibers**, and paints. The Forensic Science Service (FSS) in England, for example, examines fibers and paints recovered from crime scenes with microspectrophotometers. These sophisticated devices measure the spectra of a single suspect sample for comparison with the spectra of a control sample. Because the FSS is recognized internationally as a leader in applied forensic technology, its complex comparisons of suspect (or crime scene) samples and control samples are regularly used as **evidence** in courts of law.

Another often used type of control sample is one that contains nothing, a blank. In these cases, the control sample is known not to contain whatever substance is being considered. The idea behind a blank sample is to verify that the test instruments, equipment, or other implements are not contaminated with the substance being considered (which would lead to a false positive result). As an example, if an instrument has been used to test an illegal drug, then it is necessary to make sure that the instrument has been sterilized. When a blank sample is tested on the instrument, one that is known to be free of that illegal drug, a positive result will identify a contaminated instrument and require that the instrument be sterilized before proceeding with analysis.

SEE ALSO Forensic Science Service (U.K.); Quality control of forensic evidence.

Patricia Cornwell

6/9/1956–
AMERICAN
WRITER

Patricia Cornwell is an award-winning novelist of forensic mysteries and police procedurals that focus on medical autopsies and investigations. Her novels are characterized by the graphic authenticity of their detail and their compelling psychological studies of law enforcement and forensic professionals at work.

Cornwell has helped expand the role of the female detective in the mystery genre with her two recurring heroines—medical examiner Kay Scarpetta and police chief Judy Hammer. Her books' accurate detail is based upon research Cornwell did while a journalist working the beat in the Virginia medical examiner's office, where she witnessed scores of autopsies. Cornwell has also gone on police homicide runs. Cornwell's books regularly debut on the *New York Times* bestseller list and have a reputation for confronting readers with the occasional stomach-turning passage due to their graphic descriptions of dismemberment, murder, autopsies, and forensic **pathology**.

Cornwell was born in Miami, Florida, to Sam and Marilyn Zenner Daniels. Her parents divorced when Cornwell was five years old, and her mother moved her daughter and two sons to Montreat, North Carolina. By the time Cornwell was nine years old her mother was suffering from severe clinical depression. Unable to cope, she turned her children over to her Montreat neighbors, the Reverend and Mrs. Billy Graham. Ruth Graham put the children into foster care with a missionary couple who had recently returned from the Congo. It was Ruth Graham who encouraged young Cornwell to pursue writing. In high school Cornwell earned top grades, but pushed herself in other areas as well, battling anorexia and bulimia. She was briefly hospitalized for depression in the same facility where her mother had once stayed.

With Mrs. Graham's ongoing encouragement, Cornwell returned to school at Davidson College in North

Patricia Cornwell holds a knife that was available in England when "Jack the Ripper" went on his killing spree. AP/WIDE WORLD PHOTOS. REPRODUCED BY PERMISSION.

Carolina, majoring in English. After graduation she married Charles Cornwell, one of her former professors, and began working as a crime reporter for the *Charlotte Observer*. In 1980, Cornwell received an investigative reporting award from the North Carolina Press Association for a series she did on prostitution. At a time when Cornwell felt her career was getting underway, her husband decided that he wanted to become a minister, and the couple moved to Richmond, Virginia, where Charles Cornwell attended Union Theological Seminary. During this period, Cornwell began working with her husband to expand a newspaper profile she had written on Ruth Graham into her first book, *A Time for Remembering: The Story of Ruth Bell Graham*.

The book was such a success, Cornwell decided to try writing crime novels with the information she had gathered as a reporter. To make her murder plots seem more believable, she engaged in in-depth research. For advice and information, she turned to the deputy **medical examiner** at the Virginia Morgue, pathologist Dr. Marcella Fierro. Cornwell soon became a regular visitor at the forensic center and also took on technical-writing projects for the morgue to absorb more of the forensic knowledge she craved. The result was *Postmortem,* the first in a series of mysteries chronicling Cornwell's fictional investigative forensic pathologist, Dr. Kay Scarpetta. *Postmortem* focuses on the rape and murder of several Richmond women by a serial killer.

In subsequent novels of the series, Cornwell introduces Temple Gault, a serial killer whose intelligence matched that of Scarpetta. Gault, who specializes in the murder of children, only narrowly escapes being captured by Scarpetta herself in Cornwell's 1993 novel, *Cruel and Unusual.* Scarpetta faces Gault again in *From Potter's Field,* published in 1995 and set in New York City.

In 1996, Cornwell signed a contract with publisher Penguin Putnam, reportedly in the realm of $24 million for three books. *Cause of Death,* which appeared in 1996, was her first for the publisher. Her impressive sales figures continued with *Unnatural Exposure* in 1997, *Point of Origin,* published in 1998, and with her new, lighter series of crime fiction featuring Andy Brazil, a young police detective with a journalism background. *Hornet's Nest, Southern Cross,* and *Isle of Dogs* belong to this second series. Cornwell has also penned a novelette centered on a holiday-season get-together, *Scarpetta's Winter Table,* as well as a cookbook, *Food to Die For: Secrets from Kay Scarpetta's Kitchen.*

Cornwell took some 13 months to research and write her nonfiction book *Portrait of a Killer: Jack the Ripper—Case Closed.* In the book she claims to have solved the mystery of Jack the Ripper's identity, which was still unknown a century after the mysterious killer committed a series of gruesome murders in London's East End. Cornwell came to believe that the respected British Impressionist artist Walter Sickert (1860–1942) was the real Jack the Ripper, and her book makes the case for this theory. Sickert's artwork provides one source of **evidence** for Cornwell, who claims that several of Sickert's paintings of nude women resemble the Ripper's victims. She also argues that letters supposedly written by Jack the Ripper to London newspapers match Sickert's handwriting and were written on stationery owned by Sickert. Cornwell asserts that she has also identified later victims of the Ripper, victims not before linked to the infamous killer. She also used the book to take the "opportunity to push **forensic science** to limits that it hasn't been pushed to before—for example, using **DNA** on a 114-year-old case."

Cuyahoga County Coroner Elizabeth Balraj talks Tuesday, Jan. 18, 2000, in Cleveland, Ohio, about the results of tests conducted on the exhumed remains of Marilyn Sheppard as part of the state's attempt to show that Dr. Sam Sheppard killed Marilyn in 1954. TONY DEJAK/AP/WIDE WORLD PHOTOS. REPRODUCED BY PERMISSION.

SEE ALSO Autopsy; Crime scene investigation; DNA databanks; Literature, forensic science in; Medical examiner.

Coronal plane SEE Anatomical nomenclature

Coroner

The coroner is the person who is responsible for the legal investigation of any unexplained or suspicious death occurring within their area of jurisdiction. It is the coroner's job to determine the manner and **cause of death**. The manner refers to whether the death occurred naturally or by another's hand or by accident. The cause is the medical reason for the death.

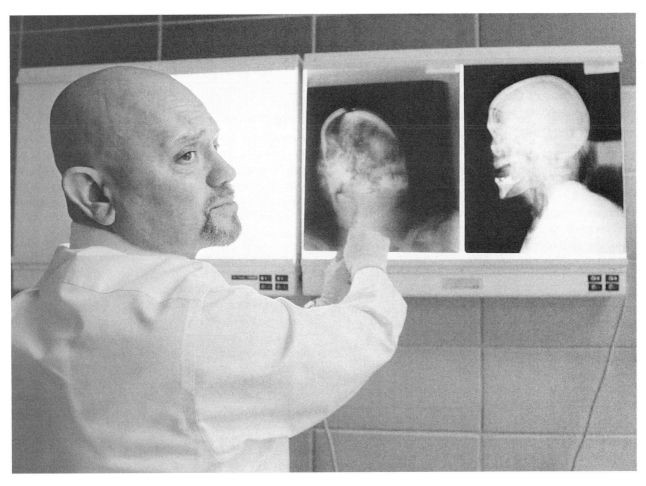

Las Vegas Coroner Michael Murphy looks over autopsy x rays on Jan. 27, 2004, of two recent self-inflicted gunshot deaths of visitors to Las Vegas. JOE CAVARETTA/AP/WIDE WORLD PHOTOS. REPRODUCED BY PERMISSION.

The coroner system has a long history in English speaking cultures, with the office existing in England before the tenth century. Indeed, the word coroner comes from the title of the person who crowned the king. Originally, the coroner was not required to have any particular **training** and many were not even qualified doctors. Coroners were appointed or elected to the position as to any other local political role. In the nineteenth century, when medical education became more formalized, coroners began to be replaced by medical examiners (MEs) in some states, beginning with Massachusetts. The change gathered pace through a series of scandals in New York City where deaths occurring through incompetent anesthesia were not, it was felt, properly investigated. Consequently, the New York administration required that deaths through surgery be examined by a medical practitioner. The ME is medically qualified, although their specialty is not necessarily forensic **pathology**, or even pathology. Some modern coroners are both lawyers and physicians, although

there are still some medically unqualified coroners in rural areas.

Today a coroner who is not medically qualified will consult an ME or forensic pathologist for carrying out autopsies, supervising the forensic laboratory, and testifying in court. The ultimate duties of the coroner include the **identification** of the deceased in a suspicious death, determination of the **time of death** (as well as its manner and cause), collection of **evidence** relevant to the death, and the certifying and signing of the death certificate.

The coroner or ME typically investigates any death that is traumatic, which might have arisen from accident, **murder**, or suicide. Deaths that are sudden, unusual, or unexpected will also be reported to the coroner. Any death that is unattended by a physician or which occurs within 24 hours of hospital admission or during a medical or surgical procedure will also be reported. Deaths in prison or in police custody are also brought to the coroner's attention. Perhaps a quarter of all deaths will be brought to a coroner's attention each year, although clearly this varies from time to time and from place to place. If there is cause for doubt, then the attending physician will not issue a death certificate, but will refer the matter to the coroner. The remainder of deaths are clearly from natural causes and the doctor can immediately sign the death certificate and release the body for burial or cremation.

Not all of the deaths reported to the coroner will justify an **autopsy**. The coroner will consult with the person's physician and may decide the death occurred through natural causes if there are no suspicious circumstances and the medical history of the deceased lends support to this view. If either party has any doubt, however, an autopsy and full investigation should be carried out. The rate of autopsy varies. Often a low autopsy rate occurs where it is the practice to have an ME perform an external examination on every corpse referred for investigation, as this measure alone is often sufficient to establish the manner and cause of death.

If the autopsy reveals death by natural causes, and sometimes this can only be determined by an internal examination, then the coroner can sign the death certificate and release the body to the family for burial or cremation. If the death was not by natural causes or if there is some public interest in it, then the coroner will hold an inquest, which is a public inquiry into the death. The inquest is not a trial; it seeks to find out who the victim is, where and when they died and, most difficult, how. There is a specific list of possible verdicts that can form the conclusion of an inquest. These include: unlawful killing, lawful killing, accident, suicide, natural causes, and an open verdict, where there is insufficient evidence to reach any other conclusion. Unlawful killing includes murder as well as **manslaughter** and death by dangerous driving. If the death is due to criminal activity, such as murder or manslaughter, then the inquest is usually adjourned if the police charge someone with causing the death.

SEE ALSO Autopsy; Careers in forensic science; Death, cause of; Medical examiner.

Counterfeit currency, technology and the manufacture of

In crimes involving counterfeit banknotes, a **forensic science** lab is often consulted to determine the presence of latent fingerprints and the origin of dyes and other materials used in producing the forged currency. Counterfeiters use a variety of methods to escape detection.

In the past, counterfeiters produced false banknotes with printing presses, and some of the more skillful counterfeiters went to great lengths to imitate the original. Today, sophisticated computer printers and copiers enable even unskilled would-be counterfeiters to produce notes that bear at least a superficial resemblance to real ones. However, the federal government continually works to stay a step or more ahead of counterfeiters, updating currency and making it ever more difficult to duplicate.

For virtually as long as there has been regular currency, there has also been false currency, which has provided a highly lucrative illegal trade to those who can successfully pass off false banknotes as the genuine article. The period since the middle of the twentieth century has seen two significant waves of counterfeiting. First, there was a surge in the illegal production of banknotes during the 1960s, when advances in printing and graphic arts technology enabled counterfeiters with the right equipment and skills to produce highly accurate copies of federal currency. By the 1990s, however, counterfeiting by means of the printing press had diminished in significance compared to a new variety of counterfeit currency manufacture, this one using computer printers.

The phenomenon of P-notes, or printer notes, first came to the attention of law enforcement in the early 1990s. In 1995, authorities made a total of 37 arrests nationwide in connection with the production and distribution of currency produced on ink-jet or laser-jet printers. By 2000, this number had skyrocketed to 4,500 arrests, and officials estimated that P-notes accounted for as much as 40% of the currency seized by the United States Secret Service (USSS) and other agencies annually.

The change in choice of technology also signaled a change in the profile of the average counterfeiter. The old variety of criminal operating in this field tended to be mature and skilled—a professional, highly trained practitioner who usually possessed, or at least had access to, printing equipment whose operation would require knowledge far beyond that of a novice.

The 1990's variety of counterfeiter, by contrast, fit a quite different profile. Rather than being professional counterfeiters, they were more likely to be drug dealers who used their P-notes in connection with other crimes, most notably the purchase of

A "100" visible only under ultraviolet light helps distinguish genuine German Mark currency from counterfeit bank notes.
© ROYALTY-FREE/CORBIS

drugs. Typically youthful (many were juveniles), these new counterfeiters lacked skills for counterfeiting. Whereas the old model at least required some degree of human ingenuity, the new type of counterfeiting was primarily a matter of possessing the right equipment.

Equipment loomed large in the old counterfeiting technology as well, but practitioners had to know how to use it. Counterfeiters of that era carefully studied currency, and made numerous photographs of it with graphic-arts **cameras** using different filters so as to break down the various stages of the printing process. Only after considerable trial and error could a workable set of printing plates be produced.

In contrast to this painstaking process, the new counterfeiting process required only that one use a high-quality scanner to obtain an image of a bill, then print that bill on a printer with high resolution. Given the ease of production, counterfeiting again became a growth industry during the 1990s, and in 2001, the federal government seized a record $47 million in counterfeit currency. By the following year, the figure had dropped to $43 million.

The fact that the value of counterfeit currency seized in 2002 had dropped by almost 10% is not an indication of looser standards in interdiction. Rather, after the September 11, 2001, terrorist attacks on the United States, the federal government was more likely to be aggressive in searching for counterfeiters, whose ranks could presumably include foreign operatives funding illegal operations while undermining the value of U.S. currency. The reduction in seizures is probably an indication of success in efforts by the federal government to make its currency more difficult to duplicate.

In 1996, partly as a response to the proliferation of P-bills, the U.S. currency underwent its first major redesign in 70 years. Already difficult to duplicate, the currency became much more so thanks to measures such as the use of optically variable ink (OVI). The latter contains tiny particles of special film such that it changes color depending on the angle from which it is viewed. Extremely expensive and therefore used in limited quantities, OVI is just one of several specialized varieties of ink used in producing currency. None are commercially available—another hurdle in the production of false currency.

A number of other features distinguish genuine currency from counterfeit. One of the most obvious ones is the paper itself. Every variety of national currency is made with a special type of paper (the Australian dollar is actually printed on very thin plastic), and U.S. currency uses a highly durable variety made from cotton pulp. Not only does it have a distinctive texture, it is far more resistant to tearing, deformation, moisture, or sunlight than most varieties of paper. Again, currency paper is not commercially available.

For the counterfeiter, a genuine banknote is a veritable minefield of potential pitfalls, and literally every square millimeter presents its own challenges. There are watermarks, embedded threads, see-through features, microprinting, holograms, latent images—even forms of embossing to facilitate recognition of various denominations by the blind and visually impaired. The printing of currency is also highly complicated, involving various processes at different stages. In addition to lithography, letterpress, and sometimes silkscreening, there is intaglio, an extremely expensive, technically difficult process in which the surface of the paper is deformed very slightly—another distinctive feature of official currency production.

Aside from these challenges to the would-be counterfeiter, there is also the problem of producing a usable serial number. Given these challenges, a drug dealer with a computer printer or copier is unlikely to enjoy long-term success in this illicit trade. For those using a copier, the problem is rendered even greater by additional measures. Most modern forms of currency have anti-copy features, tiny designs that have words such as *VOID* or *FAKE* embedded in them in such a way that they will be visible if copied.

Manufacturers of color copy machines have also implemented a number of measures to circumvent the use of their equipment for illegal purposes. Most modern copy machines carry and embed unique **codes**, invisible in ordinary light, such that their products are traceable to a specific machine. There is also technology that detects specific design elements of currency, and will cause the copier to shut down if is used for illegal purposes.

SEE ALSO Ink analysis; Latent fingerprint; September 11, 2001, terrorist attacks (forensic investigations of); Typewriter and printer analysis.

Crime scene cleaning

When a crime is committed, forensic investigators come in, survey the scene, collect the **evidence** they need, and then depart. Any bodies are, of course, removed. Crime, especially **murder**, suicide or robbery, is a messy business and the scene may be left in a state of some disarray. The next stage is crime scene cleaning, restoring the premises to the state they were in before the crime was committed. The police do not carry out crime scene cleaning. The job is usually assigned to a specialist technical company.

Crime scene cleaning is a specialized job employing highly trained technicians. First, the cleaners inspect the scene and make a written proposal of what needs to be done. Biohazardous waste, including **blood**, bodily excretions, and human tissue, is often present even after the forensic investigators have taken their samples. The technicians, dressed in surgical gloves and thick protective jumpsuits, will collect this waste, package it up, and have it disposed of through a licensed waste company. They also take up and remove soiled or stained material such as carpets and curtains. Cleaning companies follow guidelines issued by the health authorities for handling and disposing of biohazardous waste.

The site is then cleaned, disinfected and deodorized. This is particularly important if bodies have lain at the scene for some time. If there is structural damage, through breaking and entering for instance, the cleaners can repair, restore, and repaint. The technicians are also trained to preserve the scene should they discover additional evidence during their clean up.

There is a human side to this work too. Knowing they are not responsible for cleaning up the scene of a crime is important to a victim's relatives. A good clean up company will do the work for them in a safe and discreet manner. They will also be able to help the victims with work on any insurance claims arising from the damage done by the crime. At a time of distress this kind of support is often appreciated. Crime scene clean up may be an unpleasant job, but the people who are prepared to take it on do a valuable job for both the police and the victims of crime.

SEE ALSO Crime scene investigation.

Crime scene investigation

Scene **processing** is the term applied to the series of steps taken to investigate a crime scene. Although the methods and techniques may differ between the experts involved, their goals are the same: to reconstruct the exact circumstances of the crime through the identification of the sequence

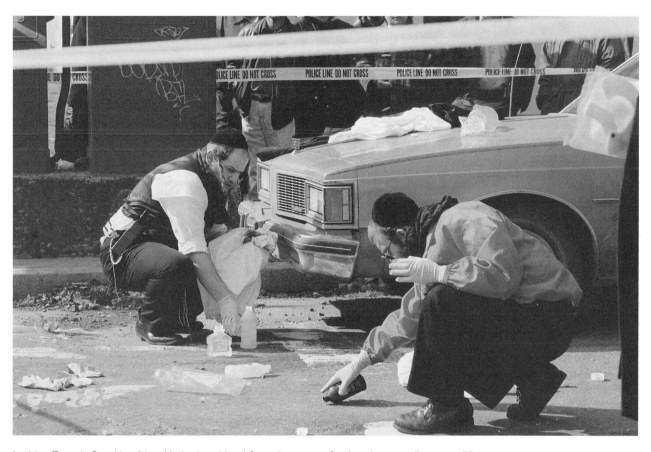

Jewish officers in Brooklyn, New York, clean blood from the scene of a shooting according to tradition. © MARK PETERSON/CORBIS

of events and to gather **physical evidence** that can lead to the identification of the perpetrators.

Crime investigation usually begins at the place where the crime was committed. The area must be isolated and secured to prevent the destruction of crucial physical **evidence** that can lead police to link the perpetrators to the victim. The size of the area to be isolated and secured varies with each case, and a series of protocols designed to secure and protect evidence are followed.

The first police officer on the scene is responsible for preventing other non-essential police personnel and civilians from entering the scene and often establishes a perimeter around the crime scene with ropes or tapes. If witnesses are present, they are identified and remain outside the perimeters of the crime scene while waiting for questioning by the investigation team. If a death has occurred, a **coroner**, a crime scene technician, and investigators are requested to the scene to assist the police.

The crime scene technician is an expert in finding and identifying physical evidence such as hairs, **fibers**, empty bullet capsules, bloodstained objects,

and body **fluids** which may be found in carpets, on furniture, on walls, etc. The scene and each piece of evidence is carefully photographed and then properly collected and conditioned to avoid contamination, to be later analyzed at the crime laboratory. This expert also writes a thorough report of the scene and describes the evidence found.

The investigator interviews witnesses, gathers information from the police on the scene, the crime scene technician, the coroner, pathologist, and other specialists that are present (such as a forensic anthropologist). The investigator is also responsible for the management of information given to the press, deciding what should or should not be initially disclosed to the public in order to not endanger the success of the investigation. The investigator will discuss with the prosecutor's office the available evidence and other information to determine the legal direction of the investigation, since both are responsible for the entire investigative process and for building a case when prosecuting persons charged with the crime.

The coroner or **medical examiner** on the scene instructs the pathologist as to what physical evidence

Police crime scene investigators look for clues and evidence at the burial site of a murder victim near the River Kent in Kendal, Cumbria, England, in 2004. © ASHLEY COOPER/CORBIS

should be collected from the corpse and determines how the victim was killed and what caused the death. The coroner or medical examiner is also the liaison person between the crime scene technician, the pathologist, and the investigators, providing useful information that can either identify the murderer or yield important leads. The pathologist collects physical evidence from the body, such as chemical or metallic residues, body fluids, hairs, or skin residues under the nails. **DNA** content from such organic samples may be compared against **CODIS** (the Combined DNA Index System) to verify whether it belongs to a known criminal, or it can be compared to other samples collected from specific suspects.

For investigative purposes, the area of a crime scene is always larger than the actual site or room where the crime occurred. Therefore, the first officer on the scene must be trained to identify and isolate the primary and secondary areas of the scene. If a body was found indoors, for example, the crime scene primary area is the room where it was found. The secondary crime scene perimeter is the remainder of the house or building, along with all the doors, windows, and corridors that give access to the pri-

mary area, including front and back yards. The secondary areas may contain important evidence of a fight, footwear prints, fingerprints, broken windows or doors, tire prints, or bloodstains.

In cases when a highly probable suspect is known, the suspect's house or car may also be treated as a secondary crime scene area, even when it is not located in the proximity of where the crime was committed. All physical evidence identified in both areas may help in the reconstruction of the chain of events of the criminal act.

The services of a forensic anthropologist are requested when highly decomposed or charred human remains are found, when difficulty in gathering physical evidence is experienced, or when the identification of the victim or the **cause of death** is not apparent. A series of physical changes and interactions with soil bacteria, insects, and animals takes place when humans are buried, especially in mass graves. In these cases, the anthropological analysis of hair, bones and soft tissues (if available) may reveal race, gender, stature, approximate age at the **time of death** and, often, the cause of death. The conduction of evidence gathering in these cases is a different procedure, usually not familiar to most crime scene technicians, and involves archeological techniques, soil analysis, identification of buried debris, recognition of buried marks of hands or footwear, and **animal evidence**.

Forensic anthropologists are often consulted for "cold case" investigations when human remains are unexpectedly found. These scenes should also begin with securing of the scene by the police, in case a determination is later made that a crime was committed. At least 10 yards around the spot where the remains are (or are believed to be buried) should be isolated. The anthropological gathering of evidence will take at least a full day, and when the remains are buried, two days. Only after this phase is completed can the remains be removed from the site. Forensic **anthropology** techniques may supply not only relevant physical evidence but also contextual information about the circumstances of the death, through the three-dimensional mapping and analysis of the scene, the location and interrelationship of physical evidence scattered around the remains, depth of the grave or pit, and geological characteristics of the soil.

SEE ALSO Analytical instrumentation; Animal evidence; Anthropology; Anthropometry; Artificial fibers; Autopsy; Ballistic fingerprints; Bloodstain evidence; Bite analysis; Crime scene reconstruction; CODIS: Combined DNA Index System; Death, cause of; Decomposition; DNA fingerprint; Entomology; Exhumation; Fingerprint; Hair analysis; Impression evidence; Pathology; Trace evidence.

Crime scene reconstruction

The process of working out the sequence of events before, during, and after a crime is known as crime scene reconstruction. It is perhaps one of the aspects of **forensic science** that fascinates the public most, featuring in most police dramas. Reconstruction requires not just a scientific approach but also logic, experience, and open-mindedness on the part of the investigating team who must be prepared to set aside any hypothesis that does not fit with the actual **evidence** presented to them.

Reconstruction starts when the investigator takes a first walk through the scene where the crime took place. Even at this stage, it may be possible to construct a rough hypothesis of what may have happened and how. A hypothesis is a set of ideas or a general picture of what may have happened. It does not become a theory until it fits all the available evidence and supporting information.

While the investigator is forming a first impression, others are recording the scene and gathering evidence. Crime scenes vary enormously, from a petty theft or break-in to violent crime that may involve fire or explosions. The principles of investigation remain the same, although the investment of time and energy into it will vary with the seriousness of the crime. The investigator will want to establish who was involved—that is, what are the identities of the victim, perpetrator, and witnesses. They also need to know where, when, how, and why the crime took place.

The crime scene is first documented through note-taking, video, **photography**, and sketching. The investigating team will then search for, record, collect, and take away various kinds of evidence such as toolmarks, hair, bloodstains, **fibers**, and footprints. According to **Locard's exchange principle**, every contact leaves a trace. That is, those involved in the crime always leave something behind or take something with them. Think of putting your hand on a patch of wet paint. The handprint may be clearly visible. You will also have paint stains on your hand. Evidence of this kind in a crime situation is known as **trace evidence** and consists of tiny amounts of substances like fibers, paint, mud, soil, or **blood**. Often is it only visible through a microscope and needs specialist laboratory investigation to assess its significance to the investigation.

To render trace and other types of evidence valid and admissible to the court, it is essential to have strict control of how the site is investigated to avoid undue interference or contamination. That is why access to the crime scene has to be limited and those involved will always proceed from the police cordon to the site of the crime itself down a common approach path, which will be set so as to allow minimal interference with any evidence.

Everyone who handles a piece of evidence is recorded and hands it on the next in line so that a tight chain of custody—from the scene to the laboratory and, eventually, the court room—is created. There are special ways of transporting evidence to protect it. Dry trace evidence, such as hairs and fibers, might be placed in druggists' folds, which are small, folded papers. Wet evidence, including bloody clothing, has to be allowed to air dry because moisture can attract molds that might decay the specimen, rendering it useless. After being placed inside an appropriate primary container, pieces of evidence are then placed inside a larger container, completely sealed with tamper-proof tape and carefully labeled.

Each item is packed separately to prevent cross-contamination, which could otherwise destroy the credibility of the evidence. In the case of toolmarks on points of entry, it may even be necessary to remove a whole door or window rather than attempt to excise the mark, which may damage it. Once in the forensic laboratory all the pieces of evidence are then analyzed and interpreted.

Bloodstain patterns are a vital aid to the reconstruction of a violent crime. When blood drips from wounds, weapons, or other objects, a splash or spatter pattern is created. The shape of the splash can show whether the source of the blood was moving and, if so, in which direction. Should the victim or perpetrator attempt to run away, the trail of blood will tell the investigator more details about the escape attempt because the shape of the blood drops will help reveal it. When someone is shot or hit with a blunt object, blood is projected from the wound and hits surrounding surfaces and objects. The resulting pattern can be analyzed to show how the weapon impacted the victim. There may be a break in the pattern; no blood where it would be expected on, for instance, a wall. This may suggest where the attacker was standing and whether the victim was struck or shot from the front or behind.

Blood is messy. During an attack it is also transferred to clothes, shoes, and hands and may leave behind bloody prints. Blood-soaked fabric makes marks with a characteristic weave pattern upon objects it comes into contact with, like a getaway car.

Some forensic tools are particularly important in crime scene reconstruction. Fluorescent light sources will glow when they are exposed to ultraviolet light. An important example is **luminol**, a chemical that reacts with **hemoglobin**, the red pigment in blood. Luminol detects blood at a concentration as low as one part in five to ten million or even lower. It is extremely valuable in revealing blood that the perpetrator believes he or she has cleaned away, such as bloodstains in a car used to remove the victim's body. However, luminol cannot detect bloodstains that have been wiped away with bleach. In such cases, fluorescein can be used as an alternative. In other words, fluorescent chemicals and light can be used to detect invisible trace evidence, giving a truer picture of the crime scene.

Footprints are a particularly rich source of evidence in a reconstruction because they can link a suspect to the crime scene. Even if a suspect says they were not there, their footprints, if matched, can tell a different story. Footprints have proved to be especially important in cases of homicide, assault,

robbery, or rape. When someone is at the scene of the crime, their soles come into contact with surfaces and leave an imprint, visible or not, which can be detected, examined, and assessed. Some prints, such as those made in the blood of a victim, are particularly obvious. If the print is in contact with a soft surface such as sand, soil, or snow, it will leave a three dimensional print. Should the contact be with a hard surface, the print is two-dimensional. Either the surface itself is removed and taken to the laboratory, or specialized photographs are made. The footprint can be linked to a particular kind of shoe by comparison with a footwear database. Individuals also wear down their shoes in a certain way, depending upon their gait. Other features such as scuffmarks can also be identified within the prints. Unless a suspect has had the foresight to destroy their footwear, examination of their shoes and comparison with footprints found at the scene can link them with the crime.

The investigators often carry out their own experiments to test the hypothesis. For instance, in establishing the relative location of victim and perpetrator in a shooting incident, it is important to know the distance between the gun and the point of impact. Was the victim shot from in front or behind? Was the suspect shooting at point blank range or from a distance? Simulation experiments to solve this question would involve shooting an identical weapon from different distances at a laboratory target. The resulting damage from the bullet could then be compared to that found at the actual scene of the crime.

The investigators must then relate all the evidence they have collected and analyzed with other information, such as **autopsy** reports and witness statements, continually refining or even rejecting their original hypothesis. The autopsy may show, for example, the **time of death** and whether the body has been moved. A witness statement may not be consistent with the evidence, which may provide a basis for further **interrogation** with questions directed by the interpretation of the evidence. This process will generate new information to be fitted into the hypothesis.

New information may continue to come in and must be examined to see if it is consistent with the hypothesis. A murder weapon or even a body may be found during the investigation. Maybe a witness will change or add to their statement. The final reconstruction is the investigator's presentation of the sequence of events before, during, and after the crime. It gives the location and position of everyone involved. More important, it tells how and why the crime occurred. The investigators can expect to be challenged in court, of course. While investigators

Henry Lee works with members of the Connecticut State Police forensic lab, using a dummy to reconstruct the crime scene where Officer Robert Allen shot and killed 14-year-old Aquan Salmon. AP/WIDE WORLD PHOTOS. REPRODUCED BY PERMISSION.

can never be sure of what actually happened at the scene of the crime, if they have used scientific principles and their experience in the reconstruction they can play a valuable role in explaining the crime and seeing that justice is done.

SEE ALSO Crime scene investigation; Crime scene staging; Evidence, chain of custody.

Crime scene staging

Sometimes a perpetrator will attempt to confuse the forensic investigators by staging a crime scene. This involves altering the scene to try to disguise what really happened. When reconstructing the crime scene, the investigating team must always be on the lookout for staging. Typically, **evidence** or bodies will be moved, or there will be signs of a break-in that did not actually happen.

A crime scene is often staged to make a **murder** appear like an accident or suicide. In historical cases, assailants have carefully placed a gun in the victim's

hand, but the nature of the victim's wounds were found not consistent with being self-inflicted. A murderer may move a body into the bathroom and pretend the victim fell when he or she got out of the bath or shower. Removing bloodstains with a cleanser like bleach is also not uncommon. However, invisible traces often remain which can be subjected to forensic analysis.

Staging a burglary on top of a murder is a common form of crime scene staging; the assailant may break a lock or a window, turn over drawers, and remove valuable items. Staged burglaries may also be set up as part of an insurance fraud where the owner pretends a valuable item has been stolen when he has actually removed it himself. Should they leave **trace evidence** from their own bodies or clothing at the break-in site, with no evidence present from the supposed robber, then the story will be called into question.

It takes a particular type of criminal to set up a successful staging. Sometimes the forensic psychologist can help with a profile of a suspect. A man who kills his wife in a fit of jealousy, for instance, and then tries to make it look like a burglary can give himself away unless he is calculating and careful. Crimes of passion often involve excessive violence, like multiple stabbings or gunshots. Most burglars are opportunists and will kill only if they panic. Such murders will generally not be as violent as those where anger against the victim is the motive. When a victim has died in a violent manner and it looks as if the motive is burglary, the investigator always considers the possibility that staging has taken place.

SEE ALSO Criminal profiling; Crime scene reconstruction.

Criminal profiling

Psychology can be applied to help catch criminals through the criminal **profiling** process. A perpetrator does not leave behind just **physical evidence** at the scene when he or she commits a crime. They also leave behind clues about their behavior and personality. Profiling was originally introduced to investigate violent **serial killers** where catching the perpetrator is a matter of great urgency.

The forensic psychologist, or specially trained officer, builds a criminal profile from crime scene **evidence** and **autopsy** data. The psychologist seeks to find out how the killer gained access to the victim, what was the killer's attraction to the victim, what did the assailant do to the victim, and whether the killer then tried to cover his or her tracks. Most important, the profiler wants to know what motives and fantasies drove the killer to the crime. The profile helps narrow down the search for suspects and also guides the **interrogation** process. Knowing what kind of person the investigators are dealing with helps officers better formulate their questions.

The profiler will be also interested in the suspect's modus operandi (MO), which describes the tools and strategies used to carry out the crime. This reveals aspects of the suspect's behavior, which in turn reflects upon the suspect's personality.

Forensic psychology has revealed three main types of offender. The organized offender plans the crime, sometimes meticulously, bringing tools and taking them away again. This type of offender will take care not to leave evidence behind and will also hide or dispose of the body. The organized offender is usually of average to high intelligence with a stable lifestyle, tending to be married and employed. The disorganized offender often leaves a mess behind. They don't plan or bring tools; instead, they use whatever they find at the scene to attack the victim. This type of offender generally lives alone or with a relative, may be unemployed and have a history of mental illness. The attacks by this type of offender are often accompanied by considerable violence. The third category is the mixed offender, who shows some characteristics of the first two types. While the approach may be carefully planned, the assault itself may be frenzied, showing a person losing control over deep-seated urges and fantasies.

Another important aspect of criminal profiling is looking at the suspect's signature, which is a feature of the crime unique to that individual. It bears no relation to how the crime is actually committed but is very revealing about personality and motive. Examples of signatures include torture and mutilation, having sexual intercourse with the corpse, using excessive violence, or posing the victim after death in a particular way. Sometimes, as part of their signature, killers take away a trophy or souvenir that they may use to relive the crime later on. In the mind of the offender, a trophy is taken as a symbol of accomplishment, while the souvenir is an object taken to remind him of the event. Such items are often of little value in themselves, but can be very revealing about the psychology of the serial killer.

Research on the psychology of serial killers has revealed further trends. Most are male and in their 20s or 30s. Most murders of this kind do not cross racial lines; whites tend to murder whites and blacks

murder blacks, etc. Most serial killers begin by hunting down victims close to home but, as their confidence grows, they may move further afield. Those with social skills, like Ted Bundy, may be able to trick their victims, while true loners tend to attack by surprise.

It can also be useful to profile the victim, to gain a full psychological picture of the crime. An understanding of the victim's lifestyle, habits, and behaviors may explain more about the suspect and why he chose this particular person to attack. Some victims are clearly at high risk of attack, if they meet many strangers, go out at night, and maybe if they make themselves vulnerable through drug or alcohol use or promiscuity. At the other end of the spectrum are low risk victims who stay close to home, do not venture out routinely at night, and have a steady routine job. Many people fall between these two categories. Whatever the type of victim, there is something about them that fulfils a serial killer's fantasies and then they are at great risk if they find themselves in the wrong place at the wrong time.

Criminal profiling was used to good effect to catch Carmine Calabro, who killed a young schoolteacher in 1979 with a pen and umbrella after raping her. Her mutilated body was placed in the shape of the Chai, which is the Jewish symbol of good luck. She was wearing a Chai pendant, which the killer seemed to have taken as a souvenir. This pointed to a disorganized killer driven by his own sexual fantasies. His profile would possibly be a person of low intelligence, with feelings of sexually inadequacy and a history of mental illness. This led the police to Calabro, an unmarried, unemployed 30-year-old whose father lived in the same apartment block as the victim. Calabro was undergoing psychiatric treatment at the time of the crime. Bites found on the body of the victim matched his dental anatomy and were instrumental in his conviction.

SEE ALSO Psychological profile.

Criminal responsibility, historical concepts

The precise definition of criminal responsibility varies from place to place but, in general, to be responsible for a criminal act implies the perpetrator must understand what they are doing and that it is wrong. Clearly, most young children are too immature to fully appreciate the difference between right and wrong. Most countries have fixed an age below which a child cannot be held criminally responsible for their actions. Commonly this is set at ten years, although the age of criminal responsibility can vary between six and 12 years.

An individual may also not be held responsible for their crimes on grounds of mental disorder. It has long been recognized that some people do not have control over or understanding of their actions and the issue of criminal responsibility has been a subject of debate since ancient times. A landmark case occurred in 1843, when Daniel M'Naghten shot and killed the secretary to Britain's Prime Minister Robert Peel. The medical **evidence** found M'Naghten to be insane. This led to the famous M'Naghten Rule where someone could evade criminal responsibility if it could be proved that they did not understand the "nature and quality" of the act they were committing. Equally, they were not held responsible if they did understand what they were doing, but did not appreciate that it was wrong.

Over the years, there has been much discussion over the meaning of these terms. In countries or states that do not have the death penalty, the difference between being found guilty and responsible and guilty and not responsible is a prison term or a stay in a mental institution. Where the death penalty applies, it may mean the difference between death and life. In March 2005, the United States Supreme Court ruled that while persons under the age of 18-years-old can be held responsible for crimes and punished by imprisonment, they are not subject to the death penalty for crimes committed while under the age of 18.

There are many situations in which someone may not be responsible for their actions. Psychosis may mean they were out of touch with reality at the time of the crime. Criminals suffering from schizophrenia may cite "inner voices" driving them to **murder** someone. Disorders of impulse control may mean someone is unable to stop himself or herself from attacking someone. People whose actions and judgment are affected by prescription drugs may also not be fully responsible. Crimes with no apparent or rational motive may also be committed by those who are not fully responsible for their actions.

The forensic psychiatrist will examine the accused and will also look for evidence of whether he or she understood what they were doing was wrong. Wearing gloves or a mask or giving a false alibi or name are all clear indicators of knowing a criminal act is being committed. Suspects who dispose of evidence, flee the scene, or lie to police are also likely to appreciate that they are doing wrong.

Some criminals can be very manipulative and may feign mental illness, thinking that a stay in a mental hospital is preferable to prison or, indeed, the death sentence. It is up to the forensic psychiatrist to examine all the evidence and the suspect and then to assess if the suspect is, or is not, responsible for the crime.

SEE ALSO Ethical issues; Psychological profile; Psychopathic personality.

Criminal trials SEE Trials, criminal (U.S. law)

Criminalistics

Criminalistics is one subdivision of forensic sciences. The terms criminalistics and forensic sciences are often confused and used interchangeably. Forensic sciences encompass a variety of scientific disciplines such as **medicine**, **toxicology**, **anthropology**, **entomology**, engineering, **odontology**, and of course, criminalistics. It is very difficult to provide an exact definition of criminalistics, or the extent of its application, as it varies from one location or country to another. However, the American Board of Criminalistics defines criminalistics as "that profession and scientific discipline directed to the recognition, **identification**, individualization, and evaluation of **physical evidence** by application of the physical and natural sciences to law-sciences matters." The California Association of Criminalistics provides a slightly different definition: "that professional occupation concerned with the scientific analysis and examination of physical **evidence**, its interpretation, and its presentation in court." These definitions are very similar to the ones used for forensic sciences, as both disciplines have as a goal to provide scientific analysis of evidence for the legal system.

It is also challenging to define a clear origin of criminalistics. The term comes from the German word *Kriminalistik*, invented by Austrian criminalist **Hans Gross** (1847–1915). While the field of criminalistics started long before Gross' time, the first serious and well-documented applications of scientific principles to a legal purpose, started in the middle of the nineteenth century. The famous novel hero Sherlock Holmes, invented by Sir **Arthur Conan Doyle**, was probably the first fictional founder of criminalistics. The real recognition of criminalistics as a science by itself can be attributed to Hans Gross who published his book *Handbuch fur Untersuchungsrichter als System der Kriminalistik* in 1899. The development of **anthropometry** (the study of human physical dimensions) by French anthropologist **Alphonse Bertillon** (1853–1914) and of **fingerprint** analysis in the same period by Scottish scientist **Henry Faulds** (1843–1930), English scientist **Francis Galton** (1822–1911), and English Commissioner Sir Edward Henry (1850–1931), also contributed to the reinforcement of criminalistics. The progress made in forensic **photography** by Swiss criminalist Rodolphe-Archibald Reiss (1875–1929) was also a major contribution to the world of criminalistics. Finally, the beginning of the era of modern criminalistics is attributed to French criminalist **Edmond Locard** (1877–1966) and some of his pupils such as Swedish criminalist **Harry Söderman** (1902–1956). In the United States, the work of American criminalist Paul Kirk (1902–1970) reinforced the predominant position of criminalistics in forensic sciences.

As an integral part of the forensic sciences, criminalistics encompasses the broadest variety of disciplines. These commonly include the examinations of **toolmarks**, **firearms**, fingerprints, **shoeprints**, **tire tracks**, soil, **fibers**, **glass**, paint, serial numbers, light bulbs, drugs of abuse, **questioned documents**, fire and explosion, biological **fluids**, and last but not least, crime scenes. Criminalistics also typically includes physical evidence that is not directly studied by another field of forensic sciences. The main goal of criminalistics is to apply the principles of sciences to the examination of evidence in order to help the justice system determine that a crime has been committed, to identify its victim(s) and perpetrators, and finally, determine the *modus operandi*, or **method of operation**. Criminalistics uses other scientific disciplines to examine physical evidence. Among these are chemistry, biology, physics, and mathematics. People performing criminalistics are referred to as criminalists.

Crime scene investigation consists of the detailed examination of a crime scene, and detection, recognition, and collection of pertinent evidence, as well as permanent documentation of the scene. Fingerprint examination consists of detection and revelation of fingerprints from different surfaces and comparison with other fingerprints, such as those provided by a suspect, in order to establish a link. Toolmarks, shoeprints, and tire tracks examination consists of recording and observing impressions in order to establish links with a potential tool, shoe, or tire. Drug analysis consists of the identification and

quantification of a drug of abuse. The examination of biological fluids, also referred to as forensic **serology**, consists in the detection, recognition, and collection of body fluids and their subsequent analyses in order to identify the person from whom they originate. **Trace evidence** encompasses a large variety of minute pieces of evidence such as fibers, glass, soil, and paints. Traces are examined and compared to potential sources of origin in order to identify their origin. Questioned documents consist of the examination of documents to determine their authenticity or to identify forgery or counterfeiting, and of handwriting and signature analysis to identify the person who wrote them. The examination of serial numbers consists of the determination of their authenticity and the restoration of the ones that have been erased. The study of light bulbs consists of determining if they were on or off at time of their breakage. This is particularly helpful in road accident investigation.

SEE ALSO American Academy of Forensic Sciences; Analytical instrumentation; Animal evidence; Anthropology; Anthropometry; Artificial fibers; Autopsy; Ballistic fingerprints; Bite analysis; Bloodstain evidence; Casting; CODIS: Combined DNA Index System; Crime scene investigation; Crime scene reconstruction; Death, cause of; Decomposition; DNA fingerprint; Entomology; Evidence; Exhumation; Fingerprint; Hair analysis; Impression evidence; Locard's exchange principle; Pathology; Quality control of forensic evidence; Trace evidence.

Criminology

Criminology was born as one of the theoretical fields of social sciences or sociology because crime and criminal behavior are social phenomena with direct impacts on societies. The efforts to understand not only the social determinants of criminality, but also the possible biological, moral, and psychological factors involved when someone commits a crime attracted researchers from other academic fields, such as **anthropology**, **medicine**, and **psychiatry**. As a consequence, a great variety of criminological theories have gradually developed in the last three centuries. In more recent years, criminology acquired an even wider scope, with the inclusion of new scientific fields such as **forensic science**, criminal **psychology**, and analysis of crime statistics.

The concept of crime is itself an object of study, as definitions of crime vary across cultures and change throughout history. For instance, for many centuries the practice of torture of prisoners, the destruction of civilian populations and cities by invading armies, child labor exploitation, and the capture and selling of human beings as slaves were almost universally practiced and accepted worldwide. These activities were part of the customs and values of previous times. As societies change and evolve, the moral standards also change to reflect the new social conventions. In consequence of such changes, some previously condemned behaviors may become accepted, whereas others, until then considered legally and morally justified, may be rejected as barbaric or criminal practices. Laws and penal codes reflect the values of a given historical period and tend to be amended or abolished to meet new emerging social and scientific consensus.

Criminological theories may be classified according to historical/cultural periods, or by the scope of their investigations. Some theories are developed around the psychological traits of criminal subjects, as well as the crime incidence among the general population or among a particular ethnic group or social strata. Other theories investigate the relation between socio-economic contexts and crime incidence, or between abuse and neglect in childhood and juvenile criminality, while others discuss the legal definition of crime, legal and social methods of punishment and rehabilitation, or means of crime prevention. The main theoretical schools of criminology are the classical school, positive school, and the Chicago school. However, criminological theories are more recently also classified according to scopes, such as biological, psychological, disorganization-ecological, learning, control, labeling, radical-conflict, feminist, middle-class, and integrated theories.

The classical school is considered the cradle of modern criminology, and was basically a product of philosophers and physicians of the seventeenth and eighteenth centuries. The classical school was a consequence of both the preceding Renaissance cultural movement and the social and humanistic ideals of the time, such as individual rights, egalitarianism, and democracy, which led to the American and French revolutions. Criminality was viewed as the result of free will and individual choice, as all human beings were considered to be endowed with natural rationality. The emphasis of the classical school was therefore, not the analysis of criminal behavior, but in the social and legal definition of crime, on the need of consensus between society's best interests, and the role of the state and laws in the protection of the common good.

The mainstream premise behind the Classical School was the existence of a natural and implicit social contract between the individuals of a society and their government. Cesare Beccaria (1738–1794), author of a seminal book of this school *On Crimes and Punishment* explained criminality as a consequence of bad and unjust legislation. Like Thomas Hobbes (1588–1679), Beccaria and others professed that men, in their natural state, are rational beings, always pursuing pleasure and self gratification and trying to escape suffering. Such pursuit inevitably led to the conflict between individuals' interests, thus preventing the maintenance of social peace and the individual fruition of happiness.

According to Hobbes, government was a natural necessity to protect society and to define the social common good and moral standards to be forcefully followed by all. In contrast to Hobbes, who was essentially a totalitarian (e.g., government dictates the rules), Beccaria insisted that governments should not suppress individual liberties but instead, be their guarantor. When government failed the expectations implied in the social contract or created oppression and injustice, social unrest and increased criminality would be the result. Beccaria declared that legal equality to all citizens was essential to the success of the social contract, but laws and regulations should be kept to an optimum minimum to avoid unnecessary restriction of individual liberties.

Another influential thinker of this school was Jeremy Bentham (1748–1832), with his utilitarian approach, in which individuals were believed to always consider the overall utility of government or of a law through the benefits it could yield in the present or in the future, weighted against those painful results or pleasures that could result from breaking the law or the social contract. The greater the benefits promoted by the government for the greater number of individuals, Bentham reasoned, the lesser the tendency of breaking the law among the population. Historical examples of the social contract application are the premises that justified the Declaration of Independence and the Constitution of the United States.

The positive school was born inside the positivist movement that rapidly dominated academic thought after the French Revolution, with the separation between science and religion. The positivist philosophy of Auguste Comte (1798–1857) was the cornerstone of this movement, whose emphasis was the systematization of scientific investigation, the consolidation of a scientific methodology, and the construction of rational hypothesis through the empirical observation, quantification, and analysis of facts or of natural phenomena. The positive school of criminology sought, therefore, to explain criminality as a human phenomenon whose probable causes were to be identified in both the human nature and/or in the social determinants. Cesare Lombroso (1835–1909), an Italian physician, is considered the founder of positivist criminology because he rejected criminality as a result of free will and rational decisions on the premises that criminal subjects should be studied in both their biological and social contexts. However, Lombroso assumed that biological diseases, such as **epilepsy** or some mental illnesses, were the main causes of criminal behavior, with socio-economic factors acting as secondary triggers. Lombroso and others studied the psychological and physical characteristics of thousands prisoners and mental hospital patients in an attempt to identify common features associated to criminal tendencies.

Lombroso described two main criminal types: the "born criminal type," whose compulsion to commit violent crimes was beyond the individual's control, and the "criminoid" type, a less dangerous (often harmless) and treatable and/or preventable pathological condition. Among the psychological features of born criminal types, Lombroso reported that they were incapable of remorse (an emotional process), displayed absence of moral values, lack of self-control, with many showing various degrees of mental illness. Therefore, Lombroso considered born criminals as psychopaths who needed to be isolated from society, as their condition was untreatable. Contrary to the general assumption, Lombroso never denied the social and cultural determinants, such as poverty, demographic density, educational deficiencies, childhood maltreatment and adolescence trauma, etc. as contributing factors or even direct causes to criminality, especially in the case of criminoid types. He also proposed several institutional solutions for the rehabilitation of criminoids, such as a reform in the prison system, with less emphasis on punishment and the introduction of educational and professional programs for those convicted of lesser crimes, along with social, medical, and educational policies to prevent criminality in problematic urban areas. However, his comparative anthropometrical study of physical morphological features between criminals and non-criminal individuals, a theory now widely discredited, is the best known and the most often cited of all Lombroso's theories.

The theory of social and environmental determinism (e.g., social conditions as the causal root) of criminal behavior gained force in the United States after 1910 with the Chicago school. This theory especially took hold after World War I. The concept of cultural relativism of moral values in opposition to the existence of human-inherent universal values was an emerging paradigm in American sociology as a result of immigration, fast and disorganized urban growth, economic crisis, and the industrialization boom, which attracted to the cities an ever-growing numbers of people from rural areas. These combined factors were seen as disruptive to the social organization of urban communities. Social organization was defined as a socially developed consensus about ethical norms and moral values that determined the regularity of behavior in a given community. The ensuing augment of crime incidence and the appearance of new types and styles of criminal behavior in certain "disorganized" local urban areas posed new questions to criminologists and sociologists.

Social scientists W. I. Thomas and Florian Znaniecki published in 1920 the result of a comparative social study between Polish rural populations and the process of cultural assimilation of Polish immigrants in the slums of Chicago. They concluded that in contrast to the older immigrants, who had lived in rural communities in Poland and whose social values and cultural traditions were well established and assimilated, the younger Polish generations in Chicago (who had never lived in those rural communities) were in a kind of socio-cultural limbo. They could not identify with the values of the older generation and were not assimilated by the socio-cultural values of their present urban environment and country. The authors associated this state of socio-cultural limbo to the increasing incidence of crime and delinquency among the Polish-descendant youth of Chicago.

Inspired by this study, social scientists created the Chicago concentric zone model of Chicago, dividing the city into five "natural urban areas," as follows: zone 1, the central business district; zone 2, the transitional zone (the area where recent immigrant groups lived in an environment of deteriorated houses and poor sanitation, among abandoned buildings, and factories); zone 3, the working class zone, where working families lived in apartment buildings at low rental rates; zone 4, the residential zone, where the middle class population owned single-family homes with garages, surrounded by back and front yards; and zone 5, the commuter zone, or suburbs. The scientists analyzed each zone in terms of family income, types of economic activities, community infrastructure and organization, and ethnic predominance. They called such sets of characteristics "the natural ecological habitat" of each of those populations. In other words, it was defined as the environmental conditions wherein a given urban community lived and related to one another. These social scientists established a direct relation between higher crime incidence, gang organization, and juvenile delinquency and the more impoverished and precarious urban environments. They proposed that as the residents of zone 2, for instance, progressed and moved to zone 3, other immigrants took their place in zone 2. As they moved farther from the center, crime incidence dropped.

The model was also used to study juvenile delinquency in the various zones of Chicago, when data was collected from 56,000 court records of juvenile delinquency between 1900 and 1933. The group also concluded that higher crime rates were associated to the more central zones, where immigrants, non-whites, and low-income families lived. These and other theorists of the Chicago school viewed poverty, population high density, and industrialization as the main factors inducing the deterioration of family ties and community relationships, which led to social isolation and juvenile delinquency. The group interpreted the results as showing that delinquency was the result of a defiant rejection of the established cultural norms and social values, which tended to grow through proximity and direct exposition of new individuals to delinquent groups.

Disorganization and criminality were, therefore, more prevalent in the central zones and tended to decrease with distance towards the suburban areas. In 1947, Edwin H. Sutherland published the theory of differential association, which he elaborated using elements from prior studies. Sutherland also introduced new data gathered from studies of patterns of learned behaviors through the relationship between the individual and his intimate group, which led him either to accept or reject criminal behavior, depending on which set of values is more emphasized by such influential groups or persons. In brief, Sutherland's theory proposed that: 1), criminal behavior is learned; 2), is learned through the interaction with other individuals or groups close or significant to the individual; 3) together with criminal behavior, individuals also learned techniques to commit specific forms of crime; 4), the choices, motivation, and preferences to commit certain types of crime derived from the quantity of exposition to accepted criminal behaviors in his/her relationships, whose definitions of behaviors that are justifiable, in spite of their illegality, and which are not justifiable, played an important role in criminal behavior.

Because human societies and human beings are both complex and dynamic entities, hardly a single-approach theory, or even a partially-integrated one, will offer the final answer to multi-sided human and social problems to which multiple contributing factors can be associated. Social theories tend in general to contain a variable degree of bias because the prevailing premises and implicit paradigms of their own cultural and personal backgrounds, as well as of their political beliefs in general influence the researchers of each generation. Theoretical criminology is a vast arena where a constellation of these and other recent studies, each tending to explain criminal behavior or its causes through different and often mutually excluding view points, are constantly fueling the academic debate.

SEE ALSO Anthropometry; Forensic science; Misdemeanor; Psychological profile; Psychopathic personality.

Cross contamination

Trace evidence like hair, **fibers**, paint, and **blood**, is by its very nature readily transferred from item to another. This raises the problem of cross contamination, where the source of trace **evidence** found on a significant item is uncertain. The trace evidence may have attached itself to a relevant item during the crime itself, in which case it becomes significant evidence. However, it is also possible that the evidence was transferred to the item via a third party during the investigation. This would be cross contamination, and such evidence is detrimental to an investigation. When a case comes to court, **expert witnesses** will always be on the lookout for the possibility of cross contamination, especially when a serious crime like **murder** or rape is involved. The only way of avoiding cross contamination is to follow strictly controlled forensic procedures during an investigation. This means making certain that the only way trace evidence could have arrived on an item is during the crime.

For instance, supposing fibers or hair from a victim are found on the clothing of a suspect. Such trace evidence could be highly incriminating. But what if an officer comes from the scene of the crime to the suspect's home and packs up his clothes for forensic examination? It is possible that the officer picked up trace evidence from the scene of the crime and acted as an intermediary, transferring it to the clothing of the suspect. Ideally, investigators would not attend more than one scene linked to the crime—in this case, the scene itself and the suspect's home—to avoid cross-contamination of this kind. Given there is a finite number of personnel available for each crime investigation, sometimes the same officer will be involved at more than one scene. In such cases, he or she must follow a strict decontamination process between attending different crime scenes. Careful records must also be kept of the movements of investigators between different scenes.

Cross contamination could also occur if packaging and re-packaging of items is not done correctly. It is essential to package each piece of evidence separately in an unused container. Obvious sources of cross contamination should always be kept well separated. For instance, the clothing of the suspect should never be packaged or handled in the same room as that of the victim and the investigators should be able to prove this procedure was followed. Only by following such procedures to prevent cross contamination can the true value of trace evidence be revealed in court.

SEE ALSO Evidence, chain of custody.

Jean Cruveilhier

2/9/1791–3/10/1874
FRENCH
ANATOMIST

Jean Cruveilhier was the first professor of **pathology** at the University of Paris. He introduced the descriptive method to the field of pathology, and this method was defined by the lithographs in his massive two-volume atlas, *Anatomie pathologique du corps humain (Pathological Anatomy of the Human Body)*.

Cruveilhier was born on February 9, 1791, in Limoges, France, as Léon Jean Baptiste Cruveilhier, the son of a career military surgeon. He was raised almost exclusively by his mother, as his father was usually away with the army during the French Revolutionary and Napoleonic Wars. Cruveilhier felt a calling to the Roman Catholic priesthood, but his father refused to allow it, insisting that he study **medicine** instead. He completed his secondary education at the College of Limoges in 1810, then moved to Paris, where his father had arranged for him to become the student of Guillaume Dupuytren, the most prominent French surgeon of the era.

Dupuytren struggled to turn his friend's son away from religion toward medicine and finally succeeded

in awakening his interest in pathology. After taking his M.D. degree in 1816, Cruveilhier sought only the simple life of an ordinary physician in his native town, but, goaded by his father's ambitious plans for him and failing, perhaps because of his father's machinations, to gain a staff position as hospital surgeon in Limoges, he returned to Paris in 1823. Dupuytren secured him a professorship in surgery at the University of Montpellier. Cruveilhier soon resigned, intending to go back to Limoges, but in 1825 he became professor of descriptive anatomy in Paris, where he spent the rest of his career.

By 1826, Cruveilhier was on the staff of most hospitals in Paris and had established a small but prestigious and successful medical practice. Charles-Maurice de Talleyrand-Périgord was among his patients. Cruveilhier took advantage of the death of René-Théophile-Hyacinthe Laënnec in 1826 to revive the Anatomical Society of Paris, which Dupuytren had founded in 1803 but which Laënnec, as president, had allowed to become dormant after 1808. Serving as its president until 1866, Cruveilhier broadened and solidified its publishing program.

Dupuytren died in Paris on February 8, 1835. His will stipulated that a chair of pathological anatomy at the University of Paris and a museum of pathological anatomy should both be established with funds from his estate and that Cruveilhier should occupy this chair. These bequests were honored. The toxicologist Mathieu Orfila founded the Musée Dupuytren in 1835; Cruveilhier assumed the professorship in 1836 and held it for the rest of his life. He published a short biography of Dupuytren in 1841.

The National Academy of Medicine elected Cruveilhier a member in 1836 and its president in 1839. Always concerned with medical ethics, he gave an important speech on November 2, 1836, at the public meeting of the Paris medical faculty, "On the Duties and the Morality of the Physician," which was published the following year.

Cruveilhier's first major publication was his doctoral thesis, *Essai sur l'anatomie pathologique en général (Essay on Pathological Anatomy in General)*, which appeared in 1816. He continued on this subject in his 1821 book, *Médecine pratiqueé éclairée par l'anatomie et la physiologie pathologiques (Practical Medicine Clarified by Pathological Anatomy and Physiology)*. In 1830 his textbook, *Cours d'études anatomiques (Course of Anatomical Studies)* appeared. His *Traité d'anatomie descriptive (Treatise of Descriptive Anatomy)* was published in four volumes from 1833 to 1836 and his *Traité d'anatomie pathologique générale (Treatise of General*

Pathological Anatomy) was published in five volumes from 1849 to 1864.

The subtitle of Cruveilhier's greatest work, the *Pathological Anatomy*, which he issued gradually in forty parts from 1829 to 1842, indicates that it contains "descriptions of the various morbid changes to which the human body is susceptible." Its text was quickly translated into English, German, Italian, Arabic, and Spanish and its plates were cheaply and sometimes poorly reproduced by either redrawing or transfer lithography. Cruveilhier's dissection of 54-year-old Louise Bonin, who died of uterine cancer in 1838, resulted in a section of the *Pathological Anatomy* that was long believed to be the first description of multiple sclerosis, but recent scholarship has established that Scottish pathologist Robert Carswell studied this disease before Cruveilhier.

Cruveilhier's contributions to **forensic science** predominantly involved developing precise methods of **autopsy** for determining the specific **cause of death**. His research into phlebitis, embolism, infarction, and other vascular disorders formed the basis of Rudolf Virchow's more significant work on these topics.

Cruveilhier lacked knowledge of chemistry, biology, histology, and several other disciplines that a medical scientist would normally be expected to have mastered. Yet, his observations of gross anatomy and lesions were so meticulous and his descriptions so clear and accurate that even the discerning neurosurgeon Harvey Cushing, a hundred years later, could not find fault with them. Cruveilhier died on March 18, 1876, at his country home near Limoges in Sussac, Haute-Vienne.

SEE ALSO Autopsy; Death, cause of; Pathology.

Cryptology and number theory

Forensic analyses can be concerned with unraveling the true meaning of deliberately convoluted communications. **Forensic accounting** can involve the search of seized financial and other paper and computer records. An examiner may encounter information that has been altered so as to be indecipherable. Understanding the nature of the informational alteration can permit descrambling strategies to be applied, rendering the information understandable.

Cryptography is a division of applied mathematics concerned with developing schemes and formula to enhance the privacy of communications through the use of **codes**. More specifically, cryptography is the study of procedures that allow messages or information to be encoded (obscured) in such a way that it is extremely difficult to read or understand encoded information without having a specific key (i.e., procedures to decode) that can be used to reverse the encoding procedure.

Cryptography allows its users, whether governments, military, businesses or individuals, to maintain privacy and confidentiality in their communications. The goal of every cryptographic scheme is to be "crack proof" (i.e., only able to be decoded and understood by authorized recipients). Cryptography is also a means to ensure the integrity and preservation of data from tampering. Modern cryptographic systems rely on functions associated with advanced mathematics, number theory that explores the properties of numbers and the relationships between numbers.

Encryption systems can involve the simplistic replacement of letters with numbers, or they can involve the use of highly secure "one-time pads" (also known as Vernam **ciphers**). Because one-time pads are based upon codes and keys that can only be used once, they offer the only "crack proof" method of cryptography known. The vast number of codes and keys required, however, makes one-time pads impractical for general use.

Many wars and diplomatic negotiations have turned on the ability of one combatant or country to read the supposedly secret messages of its enemies. The use of cryptography has broadened from its core diplomatic and military uses to become of routine use by companies and individuals seeking privacy in their communications. Governments, companies, and individuals require more secure systems to protect their databases and e-mail.

In addition to improvements made to cryptologic systems based on information made public from classified government research programs, international scientific research organizations devoted exclusively to the advancement of cryptography, such as the International Association for Cryptologic Research (IACR), began to apply applications of mathematical number theory to enhance privacy, confidentiality, and the security of data. Applications of number theory were used to develop increasingly involved algorithms (i.e., step-by-step procedures for solving a mathematical problems). In addition, as commercial and personal use of the Internet grew, it became increasingly important, not only to keep information secret, but also to be able to verify the identity of message sender. Cryptographic use of certain types of algorithms called "keys" allow information to be restricted to a specific and limited audience whose identities can be authenticated.

In some cryptologic systems, encryption is accomplished, for example, by choosing certain prime numbers and then products of those prime numbers as the basis for further mathematical operations. In addition to developing such mathematical keys, the data itself is divided into blocks of specific and limited length so that the information that can be obtained, even from the form of the message, is limited. **Decryption** is usually accomplished by following an elaborate reconstruction process that itself involves unique mathematical operations. In other cases, decryption is accomplished by performing the inverse mathematical operations performed during encryption.

In the late 1970s, government intelligence agencies, and Ronald Rivest, Adi Shamir, and Leonard Adleman, published an algorithm (the RSA algorithm) destined to become a major advancement in cryptology. The RSA algorithm underlying the system derives its security from the difficulty in factoring very large composite numbers. The RSA algorithm was the mathematical foundation for the development of a public two-key cryptographic system called Pretty Good Privacy (PGP).

Applications of number theory allow the development of mathematical algorithms that can make information (data) unintelligible to everyone except for intended users. In addition, mathematical algorithms can provide real physical security to data—allowing only authorized users to delete or update data. One of the problems in developing tools to crack encryption codes involves finding ways to factor very large numbers. Advances in applications of number theory, along with significant improvements in the power of computers, have made factoring large numbers less daunting.

In general, the larger the key size used in a system, the longer it will take computers to factor the composite numbers used in the keys.

Specialized mathematical derivations of number theory such as theory and equations dealing with elliptical curves are also making an increasing impact on cryptology. Although, in general, larger keys provide increasing security, applications of number theory and elliptical curves to cryptological algorithms allow the use smaller keys without any loss of security.

Advancements in number theory are also used to crack important cryptologic systems. Attempting to crack encryption codes (the encryption procedures) often requires use of advanced number theories that allow, for instance, an unauthorized user to determine the product of the prime numbers used to start the encryption process. Factoring this product is, at best, a time consuming process to determine the underlying prime numbers. An unsophisticated approach, for example, might be to simply to attempt or apply all prime numbers. Other more elegant attempts involve algorithms termed quadratic sieves, a method of factoring integers, developed by Carl Pomerance, that is used to attack smaller numbers, and field sieves, algorithms that are used in attempts to determine larger integers. Advances in number theory allowed factoring of large numbers to move from procedures that, by manual manipulation, could take billions of years, to procedures that—with the use of advanced computing—can be accomplished in weeks or months. Further advances in number theory may lead to the discovery of a polynomial time factoring algorithm that can accomplish in hours what now takes months or years of computer time.

Advances in factoring techniques and the expanding availability of computing hardware (both in terms of speed and low cost) make the security of the algorithms underlying cryptologic systems increasingly vulnerable.

These threats to the security of cryptologic systems are, in some regard, offset by continuing advances in design of powerful computers that have the ability to generate larger keys by multiplying very large primes. Despite the advances in number theory, it remains easier to generate larger composite numbers than it is to factor those numbers.

Other improvements related to applications of number theory involve the development of "non-reputable" transactions. Non-reputable means that parties cannot later deny involvement in authorizing certain transactions (e.g., entering into a contract or agreement). Many cryptologists and communication specialists assert that a global electronic economy is dependent on the development of verifiable and non-reputable transactions that carry the legal weight of paper contracts. Legal courts around the world are increasingly being faced with cases based on disputes regarding electronic communications.

SEE ALSO Codes and ciphers; Computer forensics; Computer hardware security; Computer security and computer crime investigation; Computer software security; Decryption.

Culture

One aspect of the forensic examination of samples or of a crime or accident scene can involve determining whether or not a particular microorganism is present. Disease-causing (pathogenic) microorganisms including bacteria and viruses are capable of causing illness and death, or may have contaminated a food or water source.

Modern techniques exist that rely on the detection of the genetic material of the microorganism and do not require the growth of the organism. Indeed, the organism can be dead and still remain detectable. However, the more traditional growth-dependent **identification** techniques are reliable, inexpensive, and are still widely used.

Bacteria require a food source to grow. Depending on the type of bacteria, the liquid or solid food source (growth medium) can be very general or highly specific, requiring the presence of certain types of amino acids, carbon sources, and other compounds. As well, some bacteria require the presence of oxygen (aerobic bacteria), while others require the complete absence of oxygen (anaerobic bacteria).

When the bacteria-containing sample is added to the medium in the step called inoculation, living bacteria will begin to assimilate the nutrients and use them to repair damaged components and construct new components. As a result, the bacteria will begin to grow and divide to produce two progeny bacteria.

Over the course of hours, the cycle of growth and division is repeated thousands of times. With each round of division, cell numbers double (i.e., growth is exponential). This rate of growth quickly leads to huge numbers of bacteria in the liquid medium or on the solid medium. This causes the liquid to become cloudy. On the surface, the countless growth and division cycles lead to the formation of a visible mound of bacteria that is known as a colony.

Bacteria can be cultured in different types of media and the various resulting biochemical reactions can be used to identify the type of organism that is present. Differing appearance of the colonies on the solid medium or the production of various compounds in the presence of specific nutrients can all be clues to the identity of the microoganism. Depending on the type of bacterium, culture-based identification can take from several days to weeks.

Viruses can also be cultured and identified (typically by their shape). However, since viruses cannot grow independently, they require the presence of a host cell. For example, poliovirus is cultured using cells found in eggs. Some viruses known as bacteriophages require a bacterial host.

SEE ALSO Bacterial biology; Bacteria, growth and reproduction; Biosensor technologies; Pathogens.

Brian E. Dalrymple

CANADIAN
FORENSIC ANALYST

For twenty-eight years, forensic analyst Brian E. Dalrymple worked for the Ontario Provincial Police, making significant contributions to the advancement of technologies used in its Forensic Identification Services program. Most notably, he conducted research that led to the use of lasers to detect fingerprints and other **evidence**. Dalrymple has since gone on to open his own forensic consulting firm, and has contributed numerous articles to industry magazines and journals as well as provided **training** to private investigators, attorneys, and police agencies.

In 1972, Dalrymple began working for the Ontario Provincial Police (OPP) as a forensic analyst. He excelled at **fingerprint** and footwear identification, forensic **photography**, computer enhancement, and body examination. In 1977, Dalrymple collaborated with the Xerox Research Centre to develop a method of using an argon **laser** to create a luminescent quality in fingerprints. The OPP became the first police agency in the world to regularly use this new technology. While the laser technique did not work on all fingerprints, it was often able to identify prints that could not be detected using conventional means. The technique was also non-destructive, allowing for other fingerprint identification techniques to be used afterwards.

In 1990, after ten years of research, Dalrymple again made an important advancement in technology with the application of computer enhancement technology to evidence images. Through computer enhancement, he found he could detect crucial details of evidence that traditional photographic and analog techniques couldn't reveal. His findings and their subsequent applications again made the OPP leaders in the field of **forensic science**.

Dalrymple retired from the OPP in 1999 to pursue forensic consulting work. He opened Brian Dalrymple & Associates, a firm that assists in computer enhancement techniques, fingerprint detection, forensic light source technology, and photographic evidence analysis for clients in Canada and the United States. He also has written articles for many industry journals, including the *Journal of Forensic Identification* and *Advanced Imaging*. In 1980, Dalrymple won the John A. Dondero Award from the **International Association for Identification**. He also earned the 1982 Foster Award from the Canadian Identification Society and the 1984 Lewis Marshall Award from the Fingerprint Society of the United Kingdom.

SEE ALSO Fluorescence; Technology and forensic science.

DEA (Drug Enforcement Administration)

The Drug Enforcement Administration (DEA) is the lead agency of the United States government for the enforcement of federal statutes on narcotics and controlled substances. Created in 1973, it is a division

Drug Enforcement Agency agents inspect chemicals removed from a home after St. Louis firefighters discovered items used to make methamphetamines in the house after responding to a small fire. © BILL GREENBLATT/CORBIS SYGMA

of the Department of Justice, with offices throughout the United States and in 56 countries. The DEA has numerous enforcement, education, and interdiction programs, an array as varied as the range of illegal drugs and the variety of groups to which they appeal.

Although it exists to enforce the drug laws of the United States, the DEA operates on a worldwide basis. It presents materials to the U.S. civil and criminal justice system, or to any other competent jurisdiction, regarding those individuals and organizations involved in the cultivation, production, smuggling, distribution, or diversion of controlled substances

appearing in or destined for illegal traffic in the United States.

The DEA's job is to immobilize those organizations by arresting their members, confiscating their drugs, and seizing their assets. Among its responsibilities are investigation of major narcotics violators operating at the interstate or international levels; seizure of drug-related assets; management of a national narcotics intelligence system; coordination with federal, state, and local law enforcement authorities, as well with counterpart agencies abroad; and **training**, scientific research, and information exchange in support of prevention and control of drug traffic. Part of these duties involves **forensic accounting** and forensic investigations of crime scenes.

Exemplifying this role, from its beginning, the DEA was concerned with the collection, analysis, and dissemination of drug-related intelligence through its Operations Division, which supplied federal, state, local, and foreign officials with information. Originally, the agency had just a few intelligence analysts, but as the need grew, so did the staff, such that by the end of the twentieth century, the DEA's intelligence personnel—both analysts and special agents—numbered nearly 700.

Along the way, demand for drug-related intelligence became so great that the DEA leadership, recognizing how overtaxed the operations division was, in August 1992, created the Intelligence Division. The latter consists of four entities: the Office of Intelligence Liaison and Policy, the Office of Investigative Intelligence, the Office of Intelligence Research, and the Electronic Privacy Information Center (EPIC). The last of these, located in El Paso, Texas, served as a clearinghouse for tactical intelligence (intelligence on which immediate enforcement action can be based) related to worldwide drug movement and smuggling. Eleven federal agencies participate at EPIC in the coordination of intelligence programs related to interdiction.

The DEA also creates, manages, and supports domestic and international enforcement programs aimed at reducing the availability and demand for controlled substances. Among its dozens of programs is Demand Reduction, a program operated by 22 special agents at 21 domestic field divisions to educate youth and communities as a whole, to train law-enforcement personnel, and to encourage drug-free workplaces.

Demand Reduction falls under the heading of the first of three goals the DEA established late in the twentieth century, and toward which it continued to work in the early twenty-first. That first goal is to educate and enable America's youth to reject illegal drugs as well as alcohol and tobacco products. Among the programs in the service of the second goal—to increase the safety of America's citizens by substantially reducing drug-related crime—are the Mobile Enforcement Teams, which work to dismantle drug organizations. The third goal, to break foreign and domestic drug sources of supply, places the DEA in collaboration with foreign governments and agencies through programs such as the Northern Border Response Force. The DEA also works with other federal agencies, including the Department of Justice National Drug Intelligence Center. DEA intelligence itself serves this third goal.

SEE ALSO Evidence; Illicit drugs.

Death, cause of

Cause of death is the generic term that refers to the conditions that lead to the death of a person or an animal. It is paramount to accurately determine the cause of death of an individual as part of crime investigation activities or when death is suspected to have been caused by a condition that has a strong genetic component. The determination of the cause of death is commonly the role of the death investigator, **coroner**, or forensic pathologist in collaboration with crime scene investigators and detectives. It is a complicated process that may require a lengthy period of time. In 2004 there were approximately 2.5 million deaths in the United States, including approximately 27,000 infants less than one year old. Autopsies to determine the precise cause of death were conducted in only about 10% of this group who died.

From a forensic perspective, there are four main categories of causes of death: homicide, suicide, accidental, and natural. Often, it is important to determine the cause of death for judicial reasons. If a homicide occurred, the perpetrator is ideally swiftly identified, arrested, and prosecuted. If a suicide took place, then documentation is necessary to alleviate the need for a criminal investigation. If an accident occurred, it is important to take preventive measures to ensure no further accidents will occur and to determine any legal repercussions. In some instances, a criminal will try to cover a homicide by making it looking like a suicide, but the reverse situation can also occur.

Homicide deaths include all the deaths that were deliberately carried out by an individual, or were due to an individual's negligent behavior. The number of homicides varies greatly from one country to another and from one region to another. In rural locations, homicide rates are usually lower, while in large cities, more homicides are likely to occur. In the United States, homicide represents slightly less than one percent of the total number of deaths. In 2003, the Federal Bureau of Investigation recorded 16,503 homicides in United States, which corresponds to 5.7 homicides per 100,000 inhabitants. Homicide deaths are further classified as caused by a particular condition such as by **firearms**, blunt injuries, sharp injuries, asphyxia, drowning, poisoning, or fire.

Suicide deaths include all deaths that were carried out by the deceased. Men are four times more likely to die from suicide than women. However, women are more likely to attempt suicide. The number of suicides also varies greatly from one country to another. In the United States, the rate of suicide is approximately double that of homicides, or 30,000 per year.

There are approximately 100,000 accidental deaths per year in the United States, which represents about 4% of the total number of deaths. Almost half of all accidental deaths are motor vehicle accident related.

Natural causes account for most of the deaths in the United States, accounting for approximately 90% of all deaths.

SEE ALSO Crime scene investigation; Crime scene staging; Autopsy.

Death, mechanism of

Death is defined as the complete and permanent cessation of all vital functions, such as lack of blood pressure and cardiac activity, absence of reflex response to stimuli, and cessation of spontaneous breathing. However, since some clinical pathological conditions may mimic some death characteristics, the certainty of death is achieved through the observation of the following negative vital signs: loss of consciousness, loss of sensibility, absence of motility or muscular tonus, cessation of blood circulation, and ultimately, absence of cerebral activity. Once all these criteria are met, an individual is declared dead.

From the biologic perspective, however, dying is a gradual process, with different organs and tissues halting their respective functions at different moments. Cells of the central nervous system need greater amounts of oxygen to survive than other cell types. Therefore, neurons in the brain can only live for three to seven minutes in the absence of oxygen, whereas epidermal cells (skin cells) can survive much longer, up to 24 hours or, depending on environmental conditions surrounding the corpse, even longer. Bone cells may survive for several days.

When the heart stops beating, blood is no longer pumped through the veins and arteries to be oxygenated by the lungs and further transported to cells.

The blood is drained from the capillary vessels into the larger veins present near the surfaces of the body, due to the collapse of arterial pressure (blood pressure). Therefore, cells no longer receive oxygen and muscle cells start the respiratory process known as anaerobic catabolism, whereby they break down complex chemical substances into simpler ones, in order to extract energy. Through anaerobic respiration, cells of some tissues and organs such as the heart, internal muscular fibers, and limb muscles are able to survive for a while after a heart failure. Anaerobic catabolism, also known as anaerobic glycolysis, causes the buildup of lactate in the muscular tissues that leads to lactic acidosis (high levels of lactic acid). High concentrations of lactic acid in the muscles cause muscular contraction and the body stiffens, losing all flexibility. This state is known in forensics as **rigor mortis** and occurs within three or so hours after death. The body remains in this state for approximately 36 hours. When muscle cells finally die, the rigor mortis ceases and the process of cellular **decomposition** begins. After death, the body tends to progressively lose heat, with the extreme parts such as feet, hands, and the face cooling first. However, the internal organs remain warm for about 24 hours. Environmental temperatures may accelerate or slow down the cooling process.

The above biological data, in combination with other information such as characteristics of the site where the corpse was found, environmental temperature, and presence or absence of insects, is used in forensic investigation to estimate the **time of death** in suspicious cases.

SEE ALSO Crime scene investigation; Death, cause of; Decomposition; Entomology; Time of death.

Death, time of SEE Time of death

Decomposition

The biological and chemical changes undergone by a body after death are known as decomposition. Decomposition is the continual process of gradual decay and disorganization of organic tissues and structures after death. Some tissues, such as bones, teeth, and hair, are more resistant to the action of microorganisms and other environmental factors and may last for centuries. Fossilized bones from animals and hominids, extinct millions of years ago, are studied today by paleontologists and anthropologists, thanks to such resilience.

Forensic **medicine** and forensic **anthropology** investigate the sequence and types of changes that affect decomposing bodies under different conditions and environments. A number of variables may affect both the rate and sequence of decomposition. Therefore, the estimation of time elapsed since death, known in forensics as the postmortem interval, takes into consideration the particular conditions associated with the decomposing body, such as temperature, level of humidity, and medium, such as exposure to preservatives, water, or soil.

For centuries, pigs were the animal model used to study both anatomy and the decomposition process due to their internal structural similarities to the human body. However, in 1980, the University of Tennessee at Knoxville began a research project on human decomposition with cadavers donated by the families of deceased persons or by the individuals who willed their bodies to science. In an area known as the Anthropological Research Facility, human bodies were laid to decompose in several different controlled conditions. These controlled experiments have significantly contributed to the better understanding of human decomposition and to new levels of accuracy of forensic reconstruction techniques, such as the circumstances of death, time and **cause of death**, and determination of age, race, and gender. The data collected from several types of experiments and the measurements of each skeleton are recorded in a computer data bank named ForDisc (Forensic Discrimination).

A general description of postmortem changes due to decomposition basically includes two stages of autolysis, and four stages of putrefaction, besides some conservative phenomena such as saponification or **adipocere**, natural mummification, calcification, etc. However, these latter events only occur in specific conditions. Autolysis consists of the fast and intense spontaneous self-destruction of tissues by the body enzymes present in the cells, without any bacterial interference. Once cells stop receiving nutrients and oxygen via blood circulation, they start anaerobic (without oxygen) "breathing", breaking ATP (adenosine tri-phosphate) into ADP (adenosine di-phosphate) to obtain energy. Anaerobic respiration lasts for a few hours, until all ATP reserves are exhausted. The anaerobic respiration induces the accumulation of lactic acid in cell tissues that disrupts cell function. Enzymes then collapse the cell nucleus and cell breakdown (necrosis) occurs.

Tissues rich in blood vessels (more dependent on oxygen and energy) are the first ones to suffer autolysis, whereas those poorly irrigated or deprived from blood vessels, like the ocular corneas, are not immediately affected by decomposition. Putrefaction (or breakdown by microorganisms) follows autolysis. With the exception of fetuses and newly born babies, the main source of these microorganisms in corpses is the right part of the large intestines. Microorganisms then invade the abdominal cavity, the chest, head, and limbs. The first visible signs of such activity are the greenish abdominal stains, accompanied by the initial odors of rotting flesh. The stains gradually expand to other parts of the body (thorax, head, and limbs) and change from light to dark green, then beginning to blacken. In people who have drowned, the greenish coloration starts on the face, progresses toward the thoracic area, and then to other parts, due to the position that drowned bodies assume in water, which facilitates putrefaction of the upper respiratory pathways first. In newly born infants, putrefaction agents (bacteria, fungi, etc.) invade the body through all cavities, especially through the respiratory pathways. The greenish stains appear in newly born babies first on the face, neck, and chest due to bacterial activity in the upper and lower respiratory pathways, and because their intestines are sterile. This phase of decomposition is known as the chromatic period.

Bacterial action destroys the structure of cells and soft tissues, releasing in the process body **fluids** in internal cavities such as chest, abdomen, and oral tract. Anaerobic microorganisms produce methane, hydrogen sulphide, and other gases responsible for the increasing stench that surrounds rotting organic matter. As gases accumulate inside the body, it starts to swell, forcing more fluids from organs to internal cavities and blood to the periphery of the body. This phase of decomposition is called the gaseous period.

Subcutaneous (under the skin) blisters containing a mixture of plasma, **hemoglobin**, and gases appear and a marbled-like pattern spreads through the skin. The outer layers of the skin (epidermis) begin to detach from inner layers of the skin (dermis) as the gaseous period progresses. The subsequent phase involves the process of liquid putrefaction, in which the soft tissues are gradually dissolved. The body loses its shape as tissue mass decreases and the separation of skin layers is completed. During this liquefaction period, gases are released and a putrefied creamy substance covers the skeleton. The next phase is known as skeletonization, with

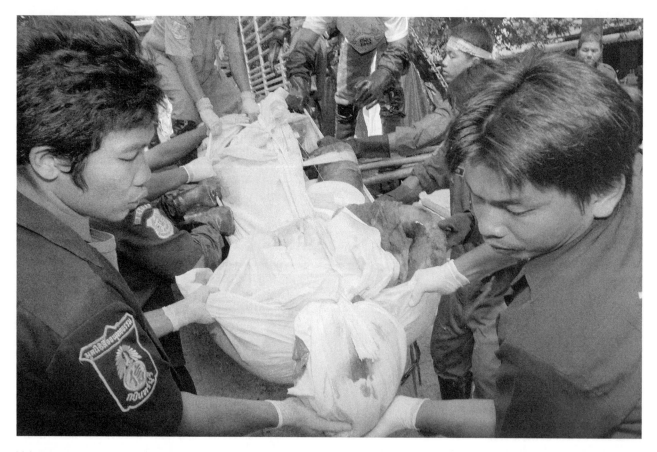

Volunteer rescue workers deliver a decomposed body to Wat Ban Muang temple in southern Thailand for identification after the tsunami of December 2004. © JAMES ROBERT FULLER/CORBIS

the environmental elements (e.g., larvae, worms, and sometimes insects) separating the skeleton from ligaments, which causes the detachment of the **skull**, the mandible, and long bones, with bones eventually collapsing apart. Bones become increasingly fragile and lighter over the years, and acidic **soils** eventually dissolve them.

Adipocere (a waxy substance formed after death by fatty tissues) formation is not a universal phenomenon during decomposition. It is more common in remains of children, women, and overweight people, requiring both adipose (fatty) tissues and contact with humidity in the soil, or immersion in water, or the prevention of body water evaporation. Collective burial graves, were bodies are piled together, are also favorable to adipocere formation. Adipocere is very rare in remains of slim individuals because it results from the spontaneous chemical transformation of fatty tissues into a grayish-white waxy matter. Coroners have a special interest in adipocere because of its preservation properties of other tissues underneath. Adipocere-conserved body

parts allow the performance of several forensic tests some months (and even years) after death. Examples are, the study of facial or neck lesions, toxicological tests, or the study of perforations caused by bullets.

Unborn fetuses that die between the sixth and the ninth months of pregnancy undergo a different process, known as maceration, due to prolonged exposure to the amniotic fluid. Fetal maceration external signs resemble in some ways those found in corpses immersed in water. However, the precise sequence of internal changes in fetal maceration is unique and offers three different well-defined phases or maceration degrees that allows the forensic determination of postmortem interval.

SEE ALSO Adipocere; Autopsy; Bacterial biology; Body Farm; Crime scene reconstruction; Death, cause of; Drowning (signs of); Entomology; Exhumation; Immune system; Medical examiner; Mummies; Osteology and skeletal radiology; Toxicology.

Decontamination methods

A crime or accident scene often contains **fluids**, including **blood**. These fluids could also contain noxious biological or **inorganic compounds**. It is necessary to carefully handle fluids when collecting **evidence** to avoid contamination. Additionally, after the survey of the crime or accident scene is complete, steps must be taken to decontaminate the site in order to remove any potential danger to others.

Human decontamination can involve removal of a contaminant from the skin. Usually such decontamination must be done quickly, since the contaminant may be absorbed through the skin where it can cause internal damage. Washing with regular hand soap or the antiseptic soap used in hospitals allows for the rapid removal of personal spills. Portable emergency response personal decontamination kits can also be carried to the scene.

Decontamination of an investigation scene often utilizes a variety of physical and chemical decontamination methods and strategies. The method selected depends on the nature of the contaminant. For example, vacuuming up a spill of a powdery chemical can be a prudent step, while the same technique might be inappropriate for a liquid spill.

Liquids such as blood are removed from inert surfaces or living surfaces (i.e., skin) by the use of sorbents. The sorbent can be a natural material, such as soil, diatomaceous earth, or activated charcoal, or can be synthetic (i.e., Amberlite XAD-2 and XAD-7 resins). Absorption involves the concentration of a substance from the liquid phase onto the surface of the adsorbent material due to the chemistry of the surface molecules.

The most recognizable solid absorbent is a clay material known as Fuller's Earth. This material is commonly found in cat litter. When solid absorbent materials like Fuller's Earth, soil, or diatomaceous earth are used, the contaminant is usually not altered. For example, petroleum products are readily absorbed, but are not changed in their character. Thus, the sorbent material becomes toxic and so must be collected and disposed of afterwards. Caution needs to be taken during the collection process, as fine dust or particles can be inhaled or stuck to exposed skin.

A different type of physical decontamination involves washing the contaminant away using another fluid like water, an alcohol, or freon. The aim here is to dilute the contaminant in the wash fluid, which should itself be collected for proper disposal. Washing is not a complete decontamination. Residual contaminant can remain behind in cracks or other hiding places. However, the use of high-pressure sprays can be an effective and rapid means of decontaminating surfaces like walls and floors.

Chemical decontamination goes further than merely removing a contaminant from the environment. Rather, in chemical decontamination the adsorbing chemical neutralizes a contaminant. One example of chemical neutralization is the adsorption of a contaminant by material that is impregnated with an alkaline chemical. Another general example is the use of chemically reactive compounds that interact with the contaminant and change its structure into a form that is non-toxic.

A popular chemical decontamination strategy relies on the use of oxidizing agents. Bleach is a well-known example of an oxidizing agent. The use of oxidizing compounds such as calcium hypochlorite or sodium hypochlorite inactivates a variety of chemical compounds as well as dangerous microorganisms such as bacteria and viruses.

Oxidizing agents can be wiped onto a spill and collected in an absorbent material. As well, some oxidizing agents can be incorporated into topical lotions, which are smeared onto the skin to help inactivate a chemical or biological spill.

A recent innovative example of an oxidizing agent is L-Gel. Developed at Lawrence Livermore National Laboratory, L-Gel uses potassium peroxymonosulfate to deactivate a variety of biological agents, including **anthrax spores** and *Yersinia pestis* (the bacterium that causes plague). The thick gel is able to cling to surfaces better than water, especially to steeply sloping surfaces like walls, which keeps the decontaminant in contact with the target longer than using a straight water-based decontaminant.

Strong bases, such as hydroxide forms of calcium, sodium hydroxide, and potassium, are other useful chemical decontaminants. These agents disrupt chemical bonds in the contaminant and so destroy the offending compounds' noxiousness.

Water is an ideal fluid for decontamination because a variety of chemically different detergents and soaps readily dissolve in water. These compounds can loosen or bind contaminants and so remove them from a surface. The friction of scrubbing also aids in decontamination of the skin during hand washing.

The different tendencies of chemicals to dissolve in water (a property known as solubility) affect the efficiency of a decontaminant. For example, a longer

An FBI team member is assisted by firefighters in the decontamination process at American Media, Inc. in 2001, a biohazard crime scene where federal agents gathered information into the death of a worker who died from exposure to anthrax. © REUTERS/CORBIS

period of decontamination is needed when using a compound that is not readily soluble in water. This problem can be somewhat overcome by the use of micro-emulsions, which are essentially very small droplets of the decontaminant. The droplet coat is a material that is less water-soluble. The effect is best seen when oil is added to water. Then, a sheen of oil appears on the water, rather than a homogeneous oil-water mixture. If a contaminant is not water soluble, it will quickly partition into the hydrophobic ("water-hating") decontaminant portion of a micro-emulsion. This can speed up the action of a decontaminant. Micro-emulsions can be applied to a contaminated surface as a spray, which can be washed off later.

SEE ALSO Anthrax, investigation of 2001 murders; Biohazard bag; Crime scene cleaning; L-Gel decontamination reagent; Pathogens; Toxins.

Decryption

Forensic analysis, in particular **forensic accounting** (the utilization of accounting, auditing, and investigation to assist in financial legal matters), can involve dealing with information that has been altered so as to be unreadable and impossible to understand without using decryption to convert it into readable material.

This scrambling of information is done in a controlled fashion, according to a pre-determined pattern. If this pattern can be understood, then the meaningless scramble can be reconverted to intelligible text.

Decryption is simply the reverse of encryption, the process by which ordinary data, or plain text, is converted into a cipher. A cipher, often incorrectly identified as a code, is a system in which every letter of a plain text message is replaced with another letter so as to obscure its meaning. To decipher a message requires a key, an algorithm that provides the method by which the message was encrypted.

Decryption operates in everyday life when financial information is sent over the Internet. During the electronic passage, the information is encrypted to make it meaningless if intercepted. At the other end of the electronic journey, the application of the decryption algorithm renders the message meaningful to those for whom it is intended.

In one of the earliest and simplest **ciphers**, Julius Caesar sent messages in which each letter was substituted by the letter three places after it in the alphabet. In place of *A*, then, one would use a *D*. The key for such a cipher would be simply, "Shift right by three," or something similar.

A key is an algorithm, or a method for solving a mathematical problem by using a finite number of computations, usually involving repetition of certain operations or steps. An excellent example of an algorithm is f(x) = y, a formula by which a relationship between two elements is shown on a Cartesian coordinate system. It is said that "y is a function of x," meaning that for every value of x, there is a corresponding value of y. Suppose it is established that $2x = y$; then the key for the function has been established, and all possible values of x and y can be mapped.

This is what occurs in decryption in a simplified form. The example shown is one that could easily be solved by what are called "brute-force" means. Brute force is a method of decryption in which a cryptanalyst, lacking a key, solves a cipher by testing all possible keys. This tends to be impractical for most ciphers without the use of a computer, and for the most sophisticated modern ciphers, brute force is all but impossible.

Suppose, however, one were shown a graph with the following coordinates for x and y: 1, 2; 2, 4; 3, 6; and so on. It would be fairly easy to determine from these values, using brute force, that $2x = y$, even if one did not have the key. This is an example of "weak" encryption. By contrast, some of the systems in use today for encryption of bank transactions or cellular phone communications and other purposes are extremely "strong". The ultimate example of strong encryption would be a situation in which decryption would be impossible without knowing the key.

Strong encryption is a controversial matter, due to the concerns of law-enforcement and intelligence authorities that such ciphers could be used by terrorists or other illegal groups. This has led to a move on the part of several governments, including that of the United States, to set up "key-escrow" arrangements, whereby all developers of ciphers would be required to give authorities a "back door" or key into the cipher. The government would maintain decryption keys in a secure location, and use them only when given a court order.

Forensic professionals can now use commercially available decryption software. Of course, updating of the software is vital to keep pace with newly devised ciphers. Many forensic officials will also have access to the state-of-the-art decryption software and expertise via organizations such as the Federal Bureau of Investigations and **Interpol**.

SEE ALSO Codes and ciphers; Computer forensics; Cryptology and number theory; Forensic accounting.

Defensive wounds

Defensive wounds are any type of injuries that result from an attempt, or repeated attempts, to defend against an assailant using such sharp edged weapons as knives or blunted instruments such as fists and clubs. Such wounds are usually deeply indented stab wounds, but can be either blunt or sharp in nature. Violent crimes involving defensive wounds can include criminal homicides, rapes, and robberies. Although defensive wounds can appear anywhere on the victim's body, they are generally found on the upper extremities of the human body including the back of the hands, the inside of the palms, and the inner side of the forearms. The different positioning and angles of the wounds indicate to the forensic examiner the exact way that the victim was trying to ward off and protect themselves against the attack.

In many cases, the victim will hold up hands and forearms in front of the body in a defensive, posturing position in order to protect the face and chest from injury during the assault inflicted by the perpetrator. In such a case, the victim may receive lacerations on the forearm when an assailant uses a sharp weapon such as a knife or multiple groupings of abrasions and bruises to both hands and forearms when fists or other blunt objects are used during the attack.

In a stabbing case, for example, slashing wounds on the hands of the victim may indicate that the victim grabbed the knife during the struggle only to have it pulled back by the assailant, thus inflicting more injuries to the victim. These wounds will usually be deep and focused around the palms and the undersurface of the fingers. Superficial cut and stab wounds to the back of the head, neck, and scalp, which are delivered at appropriate angles and positions with respect to both people, are indicative that the victim turned away from the attacker. In another example, a shotgun attack may show the presence of small, round pellets lodged within the hands or forearms of a victim, once again showing the victim was attempting to protect vital parts of the body against injury.

SEE ALSO Knife wounds.

Henry P. DeForrest

1864–1948
AMERICAN
PHYSICIAN

Henry Pelouze DeForrest (also deForest) is an important figure in the history of fingerprinting. Born in 1864, in Futon, New York, DeForrest was educated at Cornell University and received his medical degree from Columbia University. He became a surgeon and obstetrician in New York City. He was a surgeon with the New York City Police Department from 1902 to 1912, and was also the Chief Medical Examiner for the city's Municipal Civil Service Commission from 1912 to 1919. From 1903 to 1921, DeForrest was an associate professor of obstetrics at the New York Post Graduate Hospital and Medical School.

In 1902, while with the police department, DeForrest was asked to devise a system to scrutinize potential civil service employees to lessen the practice of having a person substitute for the actual candidate in the qualifying civil service exam. Drawing on the knowledge of the unique **identification** power of the **fingerprint**, DeForrest recommended the use of fingerprint identification. Beginning on December 19, 1902, the first person was fingerprinted in the new fingerprinting system that was subsequently complied.

This was actually the second use of fingerprinting in the United States. But DeForrest's accomplishment is significant, as it represented the first fingerprint file established in the United States, and the first use of fingerprinting by a U.S. government agency.

In 1903, spurred on by the success of the Civil Service experience, the systematic use of fingerprinting in criminal identification began in the United States, when the New York State Prison adopted the fingerprint system.

DeForrest's pioneering fingerprinting efforts paved the way for the subsequent widespread adoption of fingerprinting as an identification (and subseqently as a forensic identification) tool. In modern times, databases such as the **Integrated Automated Fingerprint Identification System** (IAFIS) maintained by the Federal Bureau of Investigation (**FBI**) houses millions of fingerprint patterns, which are available to law enforcement agencies worldwide.

DeForrest also invented the dactyloscope, a machine that records fingerprint patterns. The dactyloscope has found widespread use in fingerprint-based identification systems in airport customs facilities and in other applications where admittance or credit acceptance requires personal identification. DeForrest died in 1948.

SEE ALSO Fingerprint; Integrated automated fingerprint identification system.

Dendrochronology

Dendrochronology is the science of dating events and variations in environment in former periods by comparative study of growth rings in trees and aged wood. In scientific terminology, tree growth rings are used as proxy indicators for past environmental variations. The term dendrochronology is derived from the Greek terms *dendron* for tree, *chronos*, meaning time, and *logos* meaning the science of.

Dendrochronology is governed by a set of principles or scientific rules. These principles have their roots as far back as 1785 (the Principle of Uniformitarianism) and have continued to evolve as recently as 1987 with the Principle of Aggregate Tree Growth. Some are specific to dendrochronology, such as the Principle of Aggregate Tree Growth, while others, like the Principle of Replication, are basic to many disciplines. All tree-ring research must adhere to these principles, or else the research that results could be flawed.

Dendrochronology is an important technique in a number of disciplines, including archeology, paleontology, paleobotany, geomorphology, climatology,

A logger cuts pieces or samples from a fallen giant sequoia. Scientists study the tree rings to discover the sun cycles, amount of rainfall, the climate, and any fires during the lifetime of the tree. © JIM SUGAR/CORBIS

and ecology. Forensic applications concern the dating of wooden objects and matching objects with crime scenes using the wood's morphological features.

Plant anatomical features have long been used by archeologists and paleontologists to date and to characterize archeological sites. Since the 1930s they have become increasingly more common in forensic applications. The cell wall is particularly important for two reasons: it is not easily digested by most organisms and, therefore, persists when other plant features are destroyed, and the size, shape, and pattern of cell walls is often specific according to species.

Annual growth rings occur because the xylem cells become gradually smaller in radius as the growth season proceeds into the dormant season. There is an abrupt change in size from small, late season cells to the large, early season cells of the following spring. The approximate age of a temperate forest tree can be determined by calculating the annual growth rings in the lower part of the trunk.

The variation in ring width reflects environmental conditions. Wide rings signify favorable growing conditions, absence of disease and pests, and favorable climatic conditions. Ring patterns of several samples from a given geographic area subject to similar environmental conditions are cross-dated, giving standardized chronologies (curves) for different species in different areas, to which specimens of unknown origin can be compared. Tree rings record responses to a wider range of climatic variables, over a larger part of the Earth, than any other type of annually dated proxy record.

Tree ring analysis is a common technique for dating masterworks by European painters, many of which were painted directly on wood. If the samples are in good condition, analysts can pinpoint the exact year when the tree from which the wood for the painting was taken was cut down. For example, a Peter Paul Reubens painting originally dated 1616 was shown to be at least 10 years younger, and a painted wall panel recovered from a house in Switzerland in the 1970s was determined to have been painted on spruce harvested in 1497.

Likewise, dendrochronology techniques are useful in determining the provenance of wooden art objects and musical instruments. In one case, two violins forming part of an inheritance were purported to have been made by Antonio Stradivari. The sounding boards of the instruments were x-rayed and compared to standard curves for spruce from the Alpine region of northern Italy, where Stradivarius is known to have worked. The oldest rings from the samples dated to 1902 and 1894 respectively for the two violins. Furthermore, these oldest rings were not the outermost rings of the wood from which the violins were constructed. Allowing for a period of seasoning before the wood could be used to make the instruments, analyses showed that the violins could not have been made before 1910. Given that Stradivari did his best work at the turn of the 17th century, the instruments were deemed to be fakes.

It can be a challenge to estimate the time since death for a body when only bones remain. Plant roots, like their above-ground counterparts, exhibit annual growth rings that can be useful in pinning down the postmortem interval, or at least the time since the body came to be at the location where it was found.

In one criminal case, the discovery of human remains lying across a black spruce (*Picea mariana*) leader (branch) that subsequently grew up around the remains provided an opportunity to use the growth ring pattern to estimate the postmortem interval. These remains were discovered in an advanced state of **decomposition**, and it was clear that relevant insect **evidence** was not forthcoming. The asymmetrical growth of the leader resulted in a correspondingly asymmetrical pattern of its growth rings. As the date of cutting the leader was known, it was possible to evaluate the asymmetrical growth pattern to provide an estimation of the postmortem interval. Fine polishing of the cross section and computerized quantification of ring widths enabled an estimation of the displacement of the leader, and hence the time the decedent's body was so positioned. By charting the ring-width differential for the leader, the actual date of disappearance was confirmed.

SEE ALSO Crime scene investigation; Decomposition; Identification; Paint analysis.

Dial tone decoder

In the investigation of a crime, many experts are consulted, including forensic investigators and law enforcement agencies. All aspects of the crime are reviewed; in addition, investigators may dust for fingerprints, interview potential suspects, and wiretap telephones.

Telephone conversations are sometimes surreptitiously taped using microphones or other bugging devices. These devices run the risk of being detected. In some intelligence-gathering tapings, however, the contact telephone number may yield information that is as valuable as the actual conversation. If the content of a conversation is not essential, the contact telephone number can be obtained with a device called a dial tone recorder.

In a touch-tone telephone, each digit from 0 through 9 produces two tones when the particular key is pressed. Each tone has a particular wavelength (i.e., height of the peak and trough of the wave) and a frequency (i.e., the number of waves and troughs per unit area). One of the tones is from a low group, which represents the rows on the telephone keypad. The other tone is from a high group, which represents the columns on the keypad. The function of the dial tone decoder is to decipher the tone pairs and match up the combination with the row and column location on the telephone keypad. In an operating phone, this information is passed to a switch, which routes the signal to the phone line, allowing the call to proceed.

A dial tone decoder is also a standard feature of touch-tone telephones, and makes the phone capable of converting the numerical and symbolic information that is entered using the phone's keypad into a signal that can complete the transmission.

A decoder can also detect a busy signal. Dial tone decoders can also route the dial tones to a personal computer equipped with an infrared port, as the electrical impulses of the tones can be converted to infrared radiation. Thus, a computer can be used to record the activity of a telephone over time, including the numbers dialed during that period.

Instances of **assassination** via cellular telephones equipped with a decoder and an explosive device occurred in contested areas of the Middle East in the late 1990s. When the subject answered the telephone, a code was entered that triggered a blast. Detection of the code by the dial tone decoder triggers the explosive device. In this way, attacks were carried out from remote locations. Hamas, an Islamist militant group, orchestrated such an attack in July 2002, killing five Americans and four Israelis at the Hebrew University in Israel after a bomb placed in a backpack in the university cafeteria was remotely detonated by cell phone.

In police investigations, dial tone decoders are routinely used for intelligence gathering, and are also used by telephone repair crews to verify phone numbers.

SEE ALSO Bomb detection devices; Bomb (explosion) investigations; Telephone caller identification (Caller ID); Telephone recording system; Telephone tap detector.

Park Dietz

AMERICAN
FORENSIC PSYCHIATRIST

Park Dietz is one of the most well known forensic psychiatrists in the United States, and possibly in the world. Dietz earned an M.D. degree, a Master's in Public Health, and a Ph.D. in Sociology from Johns Hopkins University. Dietz's approach to forensic **psychiatry** is that of the rigorous scientist; he utilizes extensive and detailed study of the subject matter at hand in an effort to develop an understanding of the underlying patterns, whether the subject is serial killing, sexual sadism, spree killing, psychopathic crime, celebrity stalking, or **product tampering**. His case preparation style is somewhat unique. Dietz not only employs minutely detailed inspection and analysis of employment documents, such as military records; journals, diaries, books, and letters, photos, police reports, and crime-related information, he frequently examines the murder and burial sites as well. Dietz has earned a reputation as an expert who is able to relate information in layman's terms, comprehensible to the media, to juries, and to law enforcement personnel.

Some of the more high-profile cases in which he has been involved are the trial of Presidential shooter (and would-be assassin) John Hinckley, Jr., the trial of Unabomber Theodore (Ted) Kaczynski, the investigation of Tawana Brawley, the sieges at Waco and at Ruby Ridge, the trials of serial murderers Jeffrey Dahmer and Charles Ng, and the search for the Atlanta Olympics bomber. In the latter case, Dietz was able to tie the blast to two other explosions in Atlanta (one at an abortion clinic and one at a nightclub frequented by lesbians), and to one at a clinic in Birmingham, Alabama. Dietz developed a sufficiently detailed profile of the bomber that it helped lead to the **identification** of Eric Rudolph as a suspect; he later confessed to the crimes.

Park Dietz continues his work as a noted forensic psychiatrist through two different forums. Park

Dietz & Associates (PD&A) is a large forensic consulting firm whose specialty is a team approach to case evaluation and assessment; the Threat Assessment Group (TAG) is an expert **training** and consultation and firm dedicated to the prevention of school and workplace violence.

SEE ALSO Accident reconstruction; Autopsy; Criminal responsibility, historical concepts.

Digital imaging

Digital imaging is the electronic recording, processing, enhancement, and storage of visual information. Its applications in **forensic science** range from documenting crime scenes to enhancing faint or indistinct patterns such as partial fingerprints. Although digital imaging is often considered to be synonymous with digital **photography**, digital imagery can also be obtained by conventional x-ray radiography, computed tomography (CT or CAT scans), magnetic resonance imaging (MRI), **laser** scanning, and infrared photography.

Both digital and film photography employ lenses to focus light rays into a sharp image, with the size of the image controlled by the focal length of the lens. Lenses with long focal lengths produce larger images than those with short focal lengths, although the magnitudes of long and short are relative to the film or sensor size. Focal lengths are generally given in millimeters. A diaphragm within the lens (in combination with shutter speed) controls the amount of light entering the camera as well as the depth of focus in the image. In place of the film used in a digital camera, however, a digital camera uses a light-sensitive electronic sensor. Two sensor types are commonly used: CCD, or charged coupled device sensors, and CMOS, or complementary metal oxide semiconductor sensors. Both types of sensors are composed of rows and columns of photosites that convert light into an electronic signal. Each photosite is covered with a filter so that it is sensitive to only one of the three (red, blue, or green) components of visible light. Digital image processing techniques can also be applied to film negatives or positives if they are digitized using a high-resolution scanner that operates in much the same way as a digital camera.

Two primary measures are used to characterize digital images: resolution and size. Resolution refers to the ability of a sensor to represent details, and is generally specified in terms of pixels per inch (ppi).

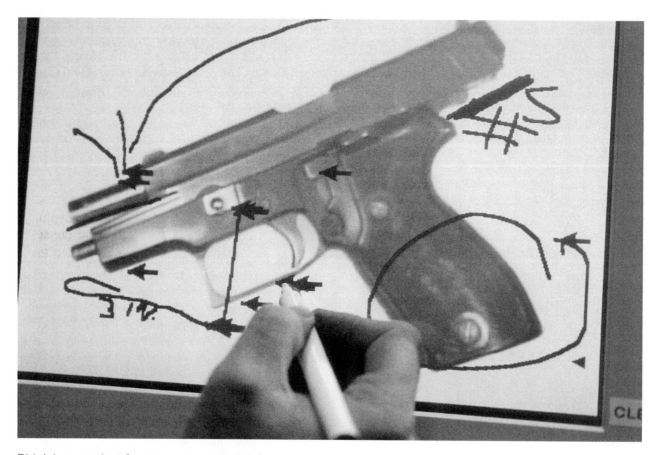

Digital demonstration of a gun. © ROYALTY-FREE/CORBIS

Image size refers to the total number of pixels comprising an image, and is typically given in terms of megapixels. A pixel is the smallest possible discrete component of an image, typically a small square or dot, and one megapixel consists of one million pixels. As of early 2005, the best commercially available digital **cameras** had resolutions of approximately 20 megapixels and many professional quality digital cameras had resolutions of 5 or 6 megapixels.

Regardless of its origin, once an image is available in digital form it can be modified or enhanced using digital image processing techniques. Common image processing techniques include contrast stretching to expand the tonal range of an image, edge detection to outline areas possessing similar textural or tonal properties, and unsharp masking to increase sharpness. Unsharp masking derives its unusual name from a film photography technique in which an original negative was combined with a deliberately blurred negative to produce a sharp print. Although these image processing techniques can do much to enhance subtle features of an image, they cannot create information that does not already exist.

One of the aspects that distinguishes forensic digital imaging from non-forensic digital imaging arises from legal considerations. Images that are destined for use in a court of law must be obtained and processed using carefully documented procedures if they are to be allowed as **evidence**. The documentation typically includes the name of the photographer, the date the image was obtained, the names of anyone who had access to the image before it was introduced in court, the names of anyone who enhanced or altered the image, and the details of any enhancement procedures. One issue that is a particular concern when an image is obtained with a digital camera is originality. Whereas traditional photography produces a film negative or positive that cannot be easily replaced without detection, digital cameras produce electronic files that can be modified and overwritten either accidentally or deliberately. It is possible to open a file, make modifications, and then save it with the same file name even though the image has been altered. Computer systems used to store forensic digital imagery must therefore be secure enough to prevent accidental modification of or deliberate tampering with original files.

The possibility of image tampering was raised during a 1995 **murder** trial in Seattle. The only evidence that linked the defendant to the crime scene consisted of a digitally enhanced image of a bloody palm print taken from a mattress pad. Prosecutors used a digital image that had been sharpened and filtered to remove the fabric texture, and the defense unsuccessfully claimed that the image could have been altered by the computer operator. The possibility of image manipulation was also raised in the O.J. Simpson murder trial, during which the Simpson defense suggested that photographs of him wearing a particular brand of shoes had been fabricated.

SEE ALSO Automated Fingerprint Identification System (AFIS); Cameras; Crime scene investigation; Evidence; Forensic science; Geospatial imagery; Photo alteration; Photography; Remote sensing; Simpson (O. J.) murder trial.

Disappeared children of Argentina

Between 1976 and 1983, Argentina was governed by a repressive military dictatorship. This government considered students, intellectuals, and politicians as dissidents and the dictatorial government severely censored and brutalized members of these groups. An estimated 30,000 people were kidnapped, tortured, and killed during these years. Because of these atrocities, the time period is often referred to as the "Dirty War." After people marked as dissidents were kidnapped from their homes, the government usually denied any information regarding their whereabouts; as such, the murdered people were referred to as "the disappeared."

A particular aspect of the terror involved kidnapping pregnant women and taking them to secret detention centers where they were held until they had their babies. After giving birth, the mothers were killed and the babies were given to families that wanted children and that had close ties to the government. The children of people deemed subversive by the government were also kidnapped. Approximately 220 babies were raised in adopted homes as a result of these brutal practices.

In 1977, a group of mothers and grandmothers of disappeared children began demonstrating in the Plaza de Mayo, which houses the capital building in Buenos Aires. Their peaceful march around the Plaza de Mayo with white headscarves eventually brought the attention of international aid groups, as well as reporters and journalists. This group became known as the grandmothers of the Plaza del Mayo (Abuelas de Plaza de Mayo). Although many of them believed that the government had killed their children, they hoped that their efforts would help them locate grandchildren.

In 1980, one of the Abuelas read an article describing a method for determining family relationships using biochemical markers on **blood** cells. She speculated that it might be possible to develop a test to prove that the Abuelas were the grandparents of children who had been adopted during the dirty war. They eventually enlisted the help of Mary-Claire King, an American geneticist from the University of California, Berkeley. King, in collaboration with Argentinean geneticist Ana Maria Di Lonardo, developed genetic tests to identify grandchildren of some of the Abuelas.

Political pressures removed the military government from power in 1983 and the newly elected president established a commission to investigate the fates of the disappeared and to prosecute those who committed crimes under the dictatorship. Part of the commission provided a structure for any children who were adopted under suspicious conditions during the period of the military government to have his or her **DNA** checked with the National Genetic Data Bank, which was run by Ana Maria Di Lonardo for the purpose of providing genetic **identification** for Argentinean citizens.

Four different types of genetic tests were developed that allowed grandparents to identify their grandchildren: HLA typing, Y-chromosome analysis, **mitochondrial DNA analysis**, and autosomal **STR (short tandem repeat) analysis**. HLA typing, or histocompatibility typing, was developed in the late 1980's and it was the original test used by King and Di Lonardo. HLA typing relies on identifying the genes that code for special molecules called antigens that are found on the surface of white blood cells. Since the Y-chromosome is inherited from the father, Y-chromosome analysis is used to determine paternity, or in the case of the children of the disappeared, grandpaternity. Mitochondrial DNA is inherited strictly from the mother, so mitochondrial DNA analysis is used to determine the identity of a mother or maternal grandmother. Autosomal **STR analysis** involves studying specific regions on the DNA found in the nucleus of a person's cells. These regions contain large numbers of repeating nucleotides, which are the building blocks of DNA. These repeating sequences are usually between two and five nucleotides long, and STR analysis often focuses on

Argentine forensic anthropologists exhume bones in 2002. The bones are suspected of belonging to children considered missing during Argentina's Dirty War dictatorship of the 1970s. © REUTERS/CORBIS

tetramers, which are four nucleotides long. The number of times these tetramers are repeated in a specific location on a **chromosome** will vary from person to person and will be inherited from a parent or a grandparent. Thus, the number of short tandem repeats in a certain location on a chromosome can be used to identify familial relationships.

As of 1996, 175 families and 2100 people provided genetic samples to the National Genetic Data Bank. Legislation passed in 1997 invalidated these adoptions and provided access to adoption records for these children. In all cases where identity of adoptive children was established, the courts considered the best interest of the child. In some cases, children remained with their adopted families; in others they returned to live with their grandparents, and in some cases the biological family was integrated into the life of the adopted family. By 2002, genetic tests proved the identities of 59 children who had been kidnapped and adopted during the military rule; 31 of the children were returned to their biological families.

SEE ALSO Gene; Mitochondrial DNA typing.

Distal **SEE** Anatomical nomenclature

Disturbed evidence

Evidence presented in court is only relevant if it can be shown to have been involved in a crime and to have survived intact until considered by the judge and jury. For example, if a gun, said to be a **murder** weapon, bears the fingerprints of an investigating police officer, then its value to the investigation is lost. Disturbed evidence refers to any item of evidence that has been interfered with in some way, whether intentionally or unintentionally. It is up to the crime scene investigators and the forensic analysts to make sure that none of their actions lead to a disturbance of evidence.

Before the investigators even arrive at the scene, however, there is already plenty of opportunity for perpetrators and witnesses to interfere with or dispose of evidence. They may carry out some form of **crime scene staging** to try to disguise what has really happened.

A common form of staging is trying to make a murder look like an accident or suicide. Perhaps a gun will be carefully placed in the victim's hand or beside the body. However, generally the pathologist will know that the nature of the wounds is not consistent with being self-inflicted. A murderer sometimes moves a body into the bathroom and pretends the victim fell after getting out of a bath or shower. Another type of staging is trying to blame a non-existent intruder for an attack. A man who murders his wife, for instance, may break a window, turn over jewelry boxes and drawers, and remove valuable items. Staged burglaries may also be set up as part of an insurance fraud; the owner removes an item and pretends it has been stolen.

Blood is, of course, one of the most significant forms of evidence. The pattern and nature of a blood-stain is not only revealing of the nature of the attack, it may also identify the perpetrator if there is blood on his or her clothing or if there has been a struggle in which his or her blood is left behind. Attackers may be surprised and panicked by the amount of blood some attacks can generate. They may assume that washing it away with a cleanser such as bleach will remove this most telling form of evidence. In fact, it is hard to remove all traces of blood, especially if the perpetrator is in a hurry to get away, and invisible traces nearly always remain. These can be visualized using a **luminol** spray, which fluoresces in ultra-violet light when it is sprayed on blood.

The first responder, that is, the first officer on the scene of a crime, may well find someone has tried to hide or destroy evidence. It is the officer's job to stop this from happening. Once the investigation team arrives, it becomes a case of ensuring that none of its actions destroy or compromise evidence. Establishing a common approach path or an agreed way of accessing and leaving the scene minimizes traffic of personnel at the scene. A policed cordon around the scene ensures that only those who really need to be there actually enter the scene, reducing the possibility of contaminating or destroying evidence.

Some items of evidence are, by their very nature, fragile, and the investigators must capture them as soon as possible by **photography**. Examples include **shoeprints** in snow or tire marks that could be washed away by rain. Sometimes evidence is destroyed by insects or predators. Insects will feed upon a body or lay their eggs in body tissues within hours of death. While their actions may provide valuable information on **time of death**, they may also render the body less amenable to pathological investigation. When **decomposition** is advanced, predators may scatter remains and bones, making it harder for a forensic pathologist or anthropologist to work out the identity of the deceased.

Once the investigators are on the scene, they must bear in mind that they are an intrusion and do their best not to degrade or destroy evidence.

According to **Locard's exchange principle**, everyone involved in a crime scene takes something from the scene, such as mud or blood, away with them, and leaves something of himself behind, like a **fingerprint**. This is as true of the investigators as it is of the perpetrator and witnesses. If they touch areas that are likely to bear fingerprints of suspects, they could contaminate them with their own fingerprints. Accordingly, investigators will wear gloves, masks, protective bodysuits, and overshoes. Evidence should be collected, if possible, on one occasion, which means it is better to collect too much evidence than too little. Returning to the crime scene to collect further evidence sometimes raises questions in court as to whether it was placed there since the crime occurred.

The possibility of cross-contamination is always a big issue when it comes to evaluating evidence. **Trace evidence**, like hair, **fibers**, paint, and blood, is by its very nature readily transferred from one item to another. If **cross contamination** occurs, the source of trace evidence found on a significant item is uncertain. It may have landed there during the crime itself, in which case it is significant and meaningful evidence. However, it is also possible that the evidence was transferred to the item via a third party during the investigation. The only way of avoiding cross contamination is to follow strictly controlled procedures during an investigation.

For instance, suppose hairs or fibers from a victim are found on the clothing of a suspect. Such trace evidence could be highly incriminating. However, an officer may come to the suspect's home from the scene of the crime after having had contact with the victim. Here the officer may pack up the suspect's clothes for examination. Should the suspect come to court, the defense will say that this officer picked up the hair or fibers from the scene of the crime and acted as an intermediary, transferring it to the clothing of the suspect. The investigating team must have procedures in place that ensure this does not happen. Ideally, officers would not attend more than one scene linked to the crime—in this case, the scene itself or the suspect's home—to avoid cross-contamination of this kind. Given there is a finite number of personnel available for each crime investigation, sometimes the same officer will be involved at more than one scene. In such cases, he or she must follow a strict decontamination process between attending different scenes. The cross-contamination charge can always be answered if careful records are kept of the movements of investigators between different scenes.

Once evidence has been collected, it must be handled, packaged, and transferred with scrupulous care to ensure it is not disturbed from its original state. Each piece of evidence is packaged separately in an unused container and then sealed into an outer container and labeled. Obvious sources of cross-contamination should always be kept well separated. For instance, the clothing of the suspect would never been packaged or handled in the same room as that of the victim and the investigators should be able to prove this. Only by following such procedures to prevent cross-contamination can the true value of trace evidence be revealed in court.

Perhaps the most powerful defense against evidence having been disturbed is the **chain of custody** protocol. Evidence found at the scene of a crime must eventually be presented and questioned in the courtroom. For the evidence to be of use in a trial, it must make the journey from crime scene to court in a validated and secure manner, so that all involved can be assured that it has not been contaminated and that it really is relevant to the crime investigation. That is why crime investigators must follow a routine commonly known as the chain of custody when it comes to collecting and handling evidence.

The first officer to collect an item of evidence, be it a fiber or a bullet, will sign and date either the item itself or its packaging. Clearly, marking an item ensures there is no ambiguity, as packaging could be separated from the evidence itself. However, some types of evidence, such as bullets, may be altered if someone marks them. Bloodstains and fingerprints, among the most valuable items of evidence, often cannot be collected directly, so it is a case of officers signing photographs or transfers and recording what has been done.

Evidence usually goes from the crime scene to the forensic laboratory for examination. The chain of custody does not end here, however. The receiving officer will sign for and date the evidence packages. Everyone who handles the evidence at any stage in the laboratory does likewise until the analysis is complete. After all, there are as many opportunities for compromising evidence in the laboratory as at the crime scene. Evidence may be stored at the wrong temperature or a label could go missing.

The analysis itself may disturb the evidence. Some experiments actually destroy evidence, so care must be taken that all other necessary tests, such as microscopy, have been done before, for instance, pyrolysis, which heats up a paint sample. Ideally, only a tiny sample would be taken for analysis, but if the evidence is only available in minute amounts, sampling may destroy it. Once laboratory investigations have been completed, the evidence will be handed over to the police for storage until its presentation in court.

The receiving police officer will sign for the evidence and it should be stored in a secure area to minimize the risk of interference or loss. The prosecuting lawyer is responsible for the evidence once the case arrives in court. He or she will sign to that effect, and is the last link in the chain of custody. The investigators should have been aware of any disturbance to the evidence before they arrived at the scene. Once they began work, they would have taken every care to protect fragile evidence and minimize any chance of cross-contamination. The chain of custody involves everyone with an interest in investigating the crime. If it has been followed correctly, then the case can proceed with all involved being aware of the precise journey the evidence took from crime scene to the court. This allows the court to judge the case on the basis of the evidence, assured that it has not been disturbed.

SEE ALSO Bindle paper; Control samples; Crime scene investigation; Cross contamination; Evidence; Evidence, chain of custody; Fibers; Quality control of forensic evidence; Trace evidence.

Bruce W. Dixon

AMERICAN
PHYSICIAN, EMERGENCY RESPONSE AND PUBLIC HEALTH EXPERT

Since the 1960s, Dr. Bruce W. Dixon has been working to improve the health and safety of the state of Pennsylvania. As a physician and professor, Dixon has treated patients and mentored medical students. As the director of the Allegheny County Health Department, he has instituted innovative health programs and made key moves to ready Pennsylvania for potential terrorist threats through disaster planning. Dixon also writes and lectures on **forensic science** and medical subjects.

Dixon attended the University of Pittsburgh, earning a B.S. degree in chemistry and then an M.D. After working and teaching at Duke University for a number of years, he returned to the University of Pittsburgh in 1975. In 1979, he became an associate professor, continuing to teach and practice **medicine**. He earned a reputation there for his approachability and enthusiasm for teaching. Dixon has also been a lecturer at the Cyril H. Wecht Institute of

Forensic Science and Law, at Duquesne University School of Law in Pittsburgh, speaking on subjects like the detection of biological and chemical weapons threats.

In 1992 Dixon was appointed as the director of the Allegheny County Health Department, in addition to his duties at the University of Pittsburgh. In the health department post he manages all health programs, including those affecting human health and environmental quality. He has seen to it that the state has been a leader in disaster planning and preparedness, creating an environment where emergency response workers can share knowledge and cooperate with each other. In 2000 Dixon helped form the Allegheny Correctional Health Services, Inc., a nonprofit organization that provides inmate medical services at the Allegheny County Jail. He was also involved with the Pennsylvania **smallpox** vaccination program, a preventative measure taken in 2003 when public health workers were vaccinated for the disease in response to the potential threat of terrorism.

In addition to his other achievements, Dixon contributes to journals and books on the subject of medicine and disaster response. He is a contributing author of *Forensic Aspects of Chemical and Biological Terrorism*, which is written for public health and safety workers, and addresses the roles and responsibilities of these officials in the event of a terrorist attack.

SEE ALSO Bioterrorism.

DNA

The deoxyribonucleic acid (DNA) of every human is unique. Furthermore, DNA is ubiquitous. These properties have made DNA an important tool for the **identification** of individuals, both in forensics and security applications.

DNA consists of two twisted strands of polymers, made up of mononucleotide units. Each nucleotide is composed of a 2-deoxyribose sugar ("2-deoxy-" because the hydroxyl or -OH group of the ribose sugar is missing from the second carbon position on the sugar ring), a phosphate, and one of the four bases: adenine (A), guanine (G), cytosine (C), thymine (T). The deoxyribose sugar and phosphate are linked by phosphodiester bridges in such a way as to form an unbranched polynucleotide chain.

According to the Watson-Crick model, which was published in 1953, the DNA molecule consists of two such polynucleotide chains which are complementary but not identical and which spiral around an imaginary common axis. The two strands are antiparallel, meaning that the phosphodiester links between the deoxyribose units read in opposite directions designated $5'$ to $3'$ on one chain and $3'$ to $5'$ on the other. The bases, which are perpendicular to the helix axis, protrude at regular intervals from the two spiral sugar phosphate strands, and reach into the interior of the helix. The strands are annealed together by hydrogen bonds between the bases of opposite strands. For correct annealing to occur, a purine (adenine or guanine) on one strand must pair with a pyrimidine (thymine or cytosine) on the other. Within the constraints of the double helix, hydrogen bonds can only form between adenine and thymine (A:T) and between guanine and cytosine (G:C). Through this pairing, the arrangement of bases along one strand determines that of the other, and the genetic information is thus coded in these base sequences.

The most commonly described DNA structure is that of the right-handed Watson-Crick double helix, also known as B-DNA, which has a diameter of 20å. The double helix is not symmetrical and has a broad groove (major groove) and a narrow (minor) groove between the chains. Adjacent bases are separated by 3.4å along the helix axis and related by a rotation of 36° which causes the helix structure to repeat after 10 residues on each chain; at intervals of 34å. DNA is, however, a dynamic molecule whose structure can vary and there are two other commonly found DNA conformations, each with slightly different dimensions.

Within a cell, DNA is organized into long strands called chromosomes. Each **chromosome** contains many thousands of different genes. A **gene** is a functional segment of DNA that codes for a specific protein. During protein synthesis, a portion of DNA is translated into a complementary strand of ribonucleic acid (RNA), which is further transcribed into a sequence of amino acids. A sequence of three nucleotides is required to code for one amino acid and chains of amino acids are further modified outside the nucleus of the cell into the proteins.

The **sequencing** of the human genome established that there are only about 30,000 different types of genes (and so proteins) encoded by the human genome. These proteins either perform tasks directly or synthesize molecules required for the biological activity that sustains life.

The DNA molecule is inherited by every cell and every individual. In asexual reproduction, the DNA in chromosomes is unwound and duplicated before the cell divides. Both daughter cells receive exact copies of the parent cell's DNA. In sexual reproduction, a portion of the DNA is inherited from both the female and the male parent. In humans, there are 23 pairs of chromosomes in the genome. During meiosis, which forms the sex cells or gametes (the egg in females and the **sperm** in males), the chromosomal pairs separate and each gamete receives 23 unpaired chromosomes. When a sperm fertilizes an egg, its 23 unpaired chromosomes are paired with the 23 unpaired chromosomes in the egg and the resulting zygote contains a unique set of paired chromosomes.

SEE ALSO Analytical instrumentation; Biological weapons, genetic identification; Chemical and biological detection technologies; DNA profiling; RFLP (restriction fragment length polymorphism); STR (short tandem repeat) analysis.

DNA banks for endangered animals

DNA banks for endangered animals consist of samples of **sperm**, ova, embryos, tissue samples, and **serum**. These biological materials are frozen in liquid nitrogen at $-196°C$ or $-373°F$, where they can be maintained indefinitely. About a dozen zoos and conservation groups around the world have begun collecting genetic material from endangered animals and preserving it. The goal of this type of collection is to preserve information stored in the genetic material of animals that may not exist in the future. This material contains information about the biochemistry, **physiology**, and even the environment in which the animals existed.

The material in DNA banks for endangered animals is usually collected during surgical procedures or soon after an animal dies. For example, before breeding season every year, veterinarians examine captive giant pandas to assess their health. At these times, gamete (sperm or ova) samples can be taken and stored in DNA banks. In instances when gametes cannot be obtained, tissue samples from skin cells or **blood** samples may be banked.

One of the challenges facing biologists building DNA banks for endangered animals is determining the best way to freeze, store, and then recover biological samples. Because animal cells are mainly com-

posed of water, when they are frozen, ice crystals destroy much of the cell. Therefore, the water in the cells must be removed and replaced with a cryoprotectant fluid, which protects the cellular structures and molecules. Scientists must develop special protocols to infuse the cells with this cryoprotectant, and these protocols vary from species to species. In addition, the rate at which genetic material is frozen and thawed may vary from species to species. In some species, special treatments may be needed after thawing occurs. Development of these sensitive procedures requires careful experimentation.

A variety of zoos and conservation groups have collected and stored genetic material from endangered species. The largest DNA bank for endangered animals is housed at the San Diego Zoo and is called the Frozen Zoo®. Between its establishment in 1975 and 2005, the Frozen Zoo collected samples from more than 7,000 threatened and endangered species, including more than 13,000 samples of **semen**, oocytes (eggs), and embryos. The Cincinnati Zoo and Botanical Garden holds genetic material for more than 60 animal species and 150 plant species. The Audubon Society maintains a DNA bank for at least 35 different animal species, most of which are endangered. In 2004, three British institutions, the University of Nottingham, the Institute of Zoology, and London's Natural History Museum, announced the formation of the Frozen Ark project, the purpose of which is to develop a genetic repository of all endangered species on the World Conservation Union's (IUCN) Red List, a list that totals more than 7,200 species.

Most of the DNA banks for endangered animals are focused on conservation. A major use for the genetic material stored in these banks is to increase the genetic diversity of species at risk of becoming extinct. As populations of endangered animals shrink, the gene pool of the animals becomes more limited. This leads to inbreeding, which increases the population's risk of disease, birth defects, and the inability to survive natural disaster. Material from DNA banks can be used to infuse small populations with new genetic material, increasing their chances of survival. Another goal of DNA banks is to increase the population size of endangered species by producing new individuals. In 1999 at the Audubon Center for Research of Endangered Species, a domestic housecat gave birth to an African wildcat kitten that had been frozen as an embryo in a DNA bank. This was the first example of interspecies birth. In 2000, the Center produced test-tube Caracal cats from

A Yacare caiman in Brazil. Forensic scientists provided DNA evidence that handbags and shoes imported through Kennedy Airport in New York were made from the skins of the endangered reptile. © STAFFAN WIDSTRAND/CORBIS

sperm that had been stored in their DNA bank. Material stored in DNA banks for endangered animals can also be used to understand animal physiology by analyzing the blood serum and tissue samples for hormones and other biochemical indicators. Information regarding the environment in which the animal lived may also be understood from biochemical markers, trace metals, and compounds from the environment found in tissue samples.

DNA banks are also used for forensic work with endangered animals. Between 1999 and 2001, researchers at the University of Trent in Ontario, Canada, developed DNA banks of endangered animals that are listed on the CITES (Convention on the International Trade of Endangered Species) list. They have developed a DNA bank of Gyrfalcons and Peregrine falcons so that wild birds can be distinguished from birds that have been bred in captivity. A DNA bank that includes genetic information of Amazon parrots helps to identify birds that are illegally traded. Genetic material from various species of sturgeon is also being deposited in DNA banks in

order to identify caviar that is from fish on the CITES list. DNA banks of tigers have also been developed to identify materials found in Asian medicines. Finally, DNA banks of North American endangered duck and goose species are used for **identification** and for population management.

SEE ALSO Gene; Wildlife forensics.

DNA databanks

With the advent of significant biotechnological advances in molecular biology, particularly with the completion of the human genome sequence, a better understanding of the genetic material that we inherit (**DNA**) has allowed scientists to utilize this information in a variety of applications. One of these ways has been to initiate and establish large-scale DNA databanks. A DNA databank is essentially a storage facility that maintains DNA extracted from a variety of sources from an individual including **blood**,

The Armed Forces Pathology Institute DNA Repository holds the DNA of all active Service men and women and civilians who work with the military in positions in which they might be killed. © KAREN KASMAUSKI/CORBIS

saliva, hair, skin, or other kinds of tissue (muscle, liver, etc). Since DNA in the proper storage conditions can be maintained indefinitely, creating DNA databanks can serve a variety of purposes that include screening for disease genes, paternity testing, identity matching for criminal investigations, and research-related studies.

The initial incentive for creating DNA databanks was to have a repository to send out samples for molecular genetics testing to screen for genetic predispositions to disease or inheriting disease genes. Currently, the United States lacks a DNA databank with a national, centralized repository system. Other countries such as Iceland, the United Kingdom, and Estonia have established large, centralized DNA databanks on a national level. An essential method to better understanding disease as it relates to the human genome has been to link DNA databanks to clinical information so that researchers can elucidate the mechanisms of heritable disease, susceptibility to disease, and identify ways to use the genome for therapeutic applications.

A national DNA databank in the United States has been controversial due to the ethical, legal, and social implications. These issues revolve around the fear that a national DNA databank will compromise an individual's privacy and give law officials too much accessibility to an individual's genetic information. Furthermore, having DNA stored in a national DNA databank risks misuse of the DNA in the future, even if initially there are carefully considered restrictions and the appropriate informed consent. Genetic information is analogous to anthropometric or biometric medical information. However, it is much more robust in terms of the information it contains.

Although a national DNA databank does not exist in the United States, most states collect DNA from convicted murderers or sex offenders. All states have a law regarding the storage of specific DNA information from any individual arrested or convicted of a **felony** in a database and a small percentage of states require the DNA profiles of all felons to be in this database. DNA has linked murderers to the crimes they committed retrospectively, in some cases decades after the **murder** was committed. In these cases, a national DNA databank would have significant ramifications in law enforcement. DNA identified at the scene of the crime could be matched to an individual within hours after the sample is analyzed. This would only be possible if the entire country underwent DNA fingerprinting and these findings were stored in a centralized database that law enforcement officers could use to match to DNA found at a crime scene. This would allow rapid **identification** of suspects and lead to a larger number of arrests. The cost for such a large-scale endeavor is considerable.

Currently, DNA databanks for forensic purposes utilize a standard DNA-typing system based on the Federal Bureau of Investigation (**FBI**) panel (13) of specific DNA markers called short tandem-repeat loci, or STRs. STRs are DNA sequences that are repeated a different number of times in different individuals. These repetitive sequences are inherited and can be used to identify an individual with a high degree of certainty. The DNA data is processed using a universal system known as the Combined DNA Index System, or **CODIS**. All states are expected to comply with this system and criminals who cross state lines, if their DNA information is stored in the database of genetic profiles, can be identified by any referral center that has the expertise and access to the system. The DNA information that stored is predominantly for the purposes of identification, no other genetic information is stored on the databases. CODIS DNA profiles are used for a dual law enforcement purpose. While one purpose is to store profiles of convicted felons based on states' requirements, the other is to collect and store unidentified DNA profiles that are from specimens obtained at crime scenes. Although the states maintain their own databanks, the FBI coordinates crosstalk between states through a searchable National DNA Index System, or **NDIS**.

CODIS is responsible for making over 500 matches, leading to arrests by establishing a connection between different violent crimes or by matching a suspect's DNA to DNA obtained from a crime scene using known convicted felons genetic profiles from the database. Over 1,000 crime investigations have benefited from CODIS since its inception. There are over 104 laboratories in 43 states and the District of Columbia. NDIS has assisted the FBI to link six sexual assault cases occurring in the District of Columbia to cases in Florida that otherwise would likely have remained unsolved. It is important to recognize that a significant percent of matches are linked to genetic profiles obtained from criminals arrested for crimes that are not felonies, suggesting that minor crimes are repeated with an increasing magnitude of offense.

SEE ALSO DNA fingerprint; DNA profiling; DNA sequences, unique; DNA typing systems; Mitochondrial DNA typing.

DNA evidence, cases of exoneration

When available and properly utilized, **DNA** is a powerful component of the **forensic science** and criminal justice systems; it can link seemingly unrelated crimes, resolve cold cases, track violent offenders both in and out of the penal system, solve crimes which would have been previously unsolvable, and prevent innocent people from going to prison. Currently, DNA is also being used to exonerate the innocent. Many people who were convicted of violent crimes and sentenced to lengthy periods in prison have continuously stated their innocence. DNA technology now makes it possible, in some cases, to prove or disprove their claims.

At present, there are more than 30 Innocence Projects headquartered at law and journalism schools across the United States, the goals of which are to overturn cases based on the introduction of compelling new **evidence** (frequently DNA-related). Attorney Barry Scheck started the first Innocence Project in New York in 1992; his goal was to be "the last word" for impoverished clients who maintained their innocence but had run out of other legal options. As of early 2005, nearly 160 people have been exonerated by the work of these groups. In addition to their goal of exonerating the wrongfully convicted, the Innocence Project is working to require states to pass legislation mandating that case evidence be preserved, and DNA testing be made readily available to those accused of crimes.

A parallel project was commissioned by the National Institutes of Justice and carried out by the Institute for Law and Justice in Alexandria, Virginia, in 1995. This project involved the study of cases in which post-conviction DNA analysis led to exoneration, as well as an in-depth investigation of DNA laboratories and testing processes. In her commentary on the release of the original report in 1996, former United States Attorney General Janet Reno said, "...DNA aids the search for truth by exonerating the innocent. The criminal justice system is not infallible, and this report documents cases in which the search for truth took a tortuous [twisting] path. With the exception of one young man of limited mental capacity, who pleaded guilty, the individuals whose stories are told in the report were convicted after jury trials and were sentenced to long prison terms. They successfully challenged their convictions, using DNA tests on existing evidence. They had served, on average, 7 years in prison."

DNA testing can be done on **blood**, **semen**, **saliva**, skin and tissue (buccal cells, or inner cheek scrapings, are frequently used), and hair. In one of the earlier recorded cases of the forensic use of DNA technology, in 1986 police in the United Kingdom requested that Alec Jeffreys of Leicester University verify the confession of a suspect in a case involving two rape-murders. DNA testing exonerated the suspect.

In 1987, Robert Melias was the first person in the United Kingdom to be convicted of a crime (rape) on the basis of DNA evidence. Also in 1987, one of the first uses of DNA technology to obtain a criminal conviction was reported in the United States; Tommy Lee Andrews was convicted of rape as a result of a DNA match between his blood sample and semen found in a victim.

One of the earliest recorded cases of DNA exoneration in the United States was that of Gary Dotson. On July 9, 1977, as she was walking home from work, the complainant alleged that she was abducted, forced into the back seat of a car, raped, assaulted, and pushed from the car onto the street. In July 1979, Gary Dotson was convicted of aggravated kidnapping and rape, and sentenced to 25–50 years in prison. The prosecution's evidence presented at trial was a police-drawn composite sketch of the defendant, with which the complainant had assisted; results of the victim's **identification** of Dotson from a book of mug shots and from a police line-up; testimony that a pubic hair removed from the victim's underwear was dissimilar to her own and similar to Dotson's; and the state serologist's report that semen on the woman's underwear came from a Type-B **secretor** (an individual who secretes the ABH antigens of the ABO blood group in saliva, semen, vaginal, and other bodily **fluids**), and that Dotson was a Type-B secretor. In 1985, the victim recanted her testimony and stated that it had been a fabrication to cover up a sexual encounter with her boyfriend. Dotson's attorneys contended that this recantation constituted grounds to vacate the original conviction. The judge hearing the motion (the same judge who presided over the original trial) refused to grant a new trial, because he

felt that the original testimony was more compelling than the recantation. In 1988, Dotson's new attorney (Dotson was released from prison in 1985, and was arrested several subsequent times for other infractions) had DNA tests conducted by Jeffreys of the United Kingdom and by Forensic Sciences Associates in California. These tests did not exist at the time of the original rape conviction. The DNA results indicated that the semen stains on the alleged victim's underwear could not have come from Gary Dotson, but could have come from her (alleged victim's) boyfriend. The chief judge of Cook County (Illinois) Criminal Court ruled that Dotson was entitled to a new trial. The State Attorney's office decided not to prosecute because of the DNA test results and the lack of credibility of the alleged victim. Dotson's conviction was overturned on August 14, 1989, after Dotson served eight years in prison as a result of the wrongful conviction.

Edward Blake, a noted forensic scientist from northern California, was the first to work with **PCR (polymerase chain reaction)**, which, in 1985, revolutionized the process of DNA testing. According to Blake, DNA testing as it is now done, strongly aids in the corroboration of the facts of a case, and the credibility of DNA evidence lies not just in the act of analysis, but also in the manner in which biological samples are collected, stored, processed, and transported. If there are any flaws in the process, it calls the final results of the DNA analysis into question.

One of the cases of exoneration to which Blake often refers is that of Earl Washington. Washington was a mildly retarded African-American farm hand from rural Virginia, who was convicted of rape and **murder**, and sentenced to die in the electric chair. In the spring of 1983, Washington had spent an evening drinking with friends, and got into a fight with his brother over a girl. The intoxicated Washington, angry and deeply distressed, ran next door to a neighbor's house to steal a gun with which to challenge his brother. When the elderly female neighbor attempted to prevent him from taking the gun, Washington hit her with a chair, took the gun, and ran back to his house (where he eventually shot his brother in the foot). When he was arrested soon after, he immediately confessed to shooting his brother and assaulting the neighbor. The police also questioned Washington about a number of unsolved crimes, including three rapes; he confessed to all of them. Next, the police questioned him about the rape and murder of Rebecca Williams, a 19-year old Caucasian mother of three small children. By that point, Washington was in tears, and he confessed to her rape and murder as well. The charges for the first three rapes were all dismissed when the victims came in and stated that Earl Washington was not the perpetrator. However, he was charged with capital murder in the Williams case, as there was no available witness. A primarily Caucasian jury heard Washington's case at trial; he was convicted after only 50 minutes of deliberation. An hour and a half later, the same jury recommended the death penalty.

The Virginia Supreme Court denied Earl Washington's appeal, and an execution date was set. Washington decided not to pursue the appeals process further, as he was not able to represent himself, as required, in a Habeas Corpus petition. In order to represent himself, he would have had to read the entire trial transcript, do his own research, write his own legal brief, and then represent himself before the hearing judge. A fellow death row inmate, with the help of the NAACP, successfully filed a civil rights suit charging that death row inmates who sought appeals should be entitled to free legal representation, and Washington's execution was stayed nine days before it was scheduled to occur, so that he might have the opportunity to pursue the appeal process. A Virginia defense attorney named Robert Hall took on Earl Washington's case, who argued that his client had been coerced by the police into making false confessions. Hall suggested that Washington had responded to the initial police questioning with answers based on the information supplied in their questions. When asked if the victim was white or black, he responded "black" (she was white); when asked if she was tall or short, he responded "kind of short" (she was tall). When the police asked him how many times he had stabbed her, he stated "once or twice," when she had died of multiple stab wounds. His responses to virtually every question were inaccurate.

When Hall examined the forensic reports, he noted that the genetic markers from the crime scene did not match those of Earl Washington. Even in the face of all of this information, it did not meet the criteria for reasonable doubt, and Washington was again facing the death penalty. As time went on, the hope for overturning Washington's conviction was shifted to the state crime lab and its ability to perform DNA analysis. Ten years after his arrest (1993), DNA testing done on a vaginal swab from Rebecca Williams indicated no link whatsoever to Earl Washington. His attorneys petitioned then-Governor Douglas Wilder for clemency and, on his last day in office, he offered Washington and his lawyers a deal: he could either accept life in

A Michigan man, Eddie Joe Lloyd, was freed with exonerating DNA evidence in 2002, after spending 17 years in prison.
© REUTERS/CORBIS

prison without parole, or take his chances with the incoming governor George Allen, who would have the authority to sign the death warrant. Washington opted to accept the deal that guaranteed him the ability to continue to live. Seven years later, another round of DNA testing conclusively exonerated him. Virginia Governor Jim Gilmore finally granted Earl Washington a full pardon and he was released from prison in 2001.

The Innocence Projects have encouraged the public to accept that fact that mistakes are made, and innocent people are sometimes convicted and imprisoned. Prosecutors, as well as defense attorneys, have begun to acknowledge a responsibility to find and free those who have been wrongly convicted. Thus far, DNA testing has resulted in thousands of convictions of guilty individuals, and the exoneration of more nearly 160 innocent people.

SEE ALSO Circumstantial evidence; Composite drawing; DNA fingerprint; DNA sequences, unique; Mitochondrial DNA analysis; *Frye* standard.

DNA evidence, social issues

The use of **DNA evidence** is a controversial issue from a social and ethical viewpoint. Although the techniques are widely understood by scientists and criminal investigators, the public in general does not have a deep understanding of the technology. Gone are the days of heated interrogations resulting in guilt or innocence and basic crime scene evidence. Investigations are now much more complex, using DNA evidence and trace samples. DNA databasing as an investigative tool is new (late 1990's), and the actual techniques of molecular biology are fairly recent (late 1970's). Thus, the vast majority of the population has yet to receive education on these topics. Uncertainty accompanies this lack of understanding, which can also be fuelled by sensationalism in news stories and coverage of trials where DNA evidence is utilized.

As with any new technology, a certain amount of speculation accompanies **DNA profiling** and databasing. Many people are concerned it is a fine line between developing a DNA database and violating civil liberties. DNA contains a wealth of information about not only an individual, but also can give information about family and ethnic background. Inappropriate use of DNA profiles in databases could lead to discrimination, so the proper degree of protection of the databases is essential.

There are two types of forensic DNA databases: the convicted offender database and the crime scene database. The convicted offender database is a log of STR (short tandem repeat) profiles. STR profiles utilize variability in the number of repeats at a given locus to differentiate among individuals. There are three major forensic DNA databases of individuals convicted of a crime: **CODIS** (Combined DNA Indexing System), which is maintained by the **United States Federal Bureau of Investigation**; the ENFSI (**European Network of Forensic Science Institutes**) DNA database; and the ISSOL (Interpol Standard Set of Loci) database maintained by Interpol. The type of offenses for which DNA is stored differs among countries and states. Initially, these databases contained only samples from violent offenders, those convicted of aggravated assault, rape, or **murder**. However, the value of obtaining DNA from offenders of less severe crimes has been recognized, as many small time criminals become repeat offenders and also more violent offenders. The power of a large bank of DNA samples extends to the possibility of it acting as a deterrent. A match of DNA evidence from a crime scene (which would then be logged in

the crime scene database) to one in the convicted offender database rapidly solves the crime, saving time, effort, and money. Conversely, the use of DNA evidence can immediately prove a suspect's innocence.

There are groups of people fervently opposed to DNA profiling for ethical and social reasons. Now that the complete human genome is sequenced, population genetics and other studies are ongoing that have linked genes to phenotypes, predisposition to disease, and predicted response to drug therapy. Should research establish a link between a particular genotype specific to offenders or violent criminals, this could potentially be used to profile potential criminals. In a world where one is guilty until proven innocent, what is the consequence of possessing a genetic profile suggesting that you may one day commit a crime? In society, this individual could potentially be convicted of a crime that he has never even committed. Thus, the opponents of DNA profiling argue, the use of databases to profile individuals for behavior types such as sex offender or violent criminal could affect human rights and civil liberties.

The potential for the criminal justice system to become more genetics-based is another concern. STR loci are based on non-coding sections of the human genome. There are several reasons for this; these regions of the genome tend to be highly variable and thus differ considerably among individuals. The result is a near impossible probability that when all STR loci are taken into account that the profile could belong to more that one human being. Secondly, by using non-coding regions, the STR profiles are not linked to any phenotype or human trait. However, if the genotype of other loci are utilized for analysis additional to STR database uses, it is possible that genetic-based profiling could occur.

Civil rights advocates are concerned that the DNA databases could one day be extended beyond that of criminal offenders to the point where genetic analysis or profiling could be used in a discriminatory manner. It is their intent to protect what exists currently in databases to ensure the DNA is not exploited in any manner that is unethical or violates human rights.

The cause for concern here is the fact that although STR profiles only are logged into the DNA database, be it CODIS, ENFSI, or ISSOL, if the sample is stored, it does include all other genetic information on that individual. Additionally, data obtained from a crime scene that would be entered into the crime scene database could first be utilized to provide a profile of the assailant. For example, DNA evidence left at the scene of a crime may not match any suspect in the criminal database. However, this DNA could potentially be used to obtain the person's sex, height, hair, and eye color and other such traits that may allow the police to generate a physical profile of the perpetrator. Thus, anyone matching this profile could become a potential suspect.

Further analysis of the STR profile via a DNA sample provided by a person under suspicion would easily rule that individual out if he was indeed innocent. However, this too, generates questions of human rights, as although the person is shown to be innocent, any negative consequences or publicity surrounding the investigation could be shown to violate that individual's human rights. Proponents of using genetics to generate a profile of the felon argue that constitutional rights are not violated as no particular group is singled out in such a profile. Furthermore, using such a method could actually decrease racial profiling, as disproportionate finger pointing toward a particular group would be avoided.

Legal implications are constantly considered in courts of law to assure adherence to the respective governing guidelines. In October 2004, President Bush signed into law the Justice for All Act. This law, part of the Advancing Justice Through DNA Technology Act of 2003, provides additional support for victims' rights, ensuring funding for victim's assistance programs. It also extends the DNA databases by providing funds to analyze samples in backlog and sets guidelines for the use of DNA testing post conviction for those who maintain their innocence. The Innocence Protection Act is part of the Advancing Justice Through DNA Technology Act of 2003 (HR 3214/S 1700), and is a United States Government initiative to utilize DNA and forensic evidence to prove the innocence of those wrongly convicted of a crime. It allows convicted individuals access to DNA evidence in order to demonstrate their innocence. Numerous people convicted of crimes, including some on death row, have been exonerated based on DNA evidence that either wasn't available or did not exist as an admissible courtroom technology at their time of conviction.

In Europe, Article 8 of the European Convention of Human Rights defines guidelines for the protection of individual rights. The use of forensic DNA databases has come into question under this law, but the proper use of DNA databases was shown not to be in violation. As the value of using forensic DNA databases across borders is realized, especially across Europe, human rights discussions become even more complex. Although most all European countries are governed by the European Convention of Human Rights, each individual country has its own additional guidelines and regulations when it comes to privacy rights, confidentiality of genetic information, and **crime scene investigation**. In order to address these concerns on a European basis, several councils and agencies are devoted to these tasks; examples include the Council of Europe convention for the protection of human rights with regard to the application of biomedicine, the United Nations outline for an International Declaration on genetic data, and the European Data Protection Commission.

The diversity of countries across Europe requires consideration of many social and ethical topics regarding forensic DNA databases. Some European Union member countries do not currently have a DNA database in existence. Different opinions exist across Europe concerning which crimes warrant taking a DNA sample. In addition, some countries require consent first, while others do not; and the length of time samples may remain in the DNA databank may be different from country to country. The Interpol DNA Monitoring Expert Group is committed to the development of a consolidated forensic DNA database across Europe as well as internationally. Part of this initiative includes promoting awareness of social, privacy, and **ethical issues**.

Clearly, social and ethical issues regarding DNA evidence will continue to be a topic of debate. Through education, legislation, and proper use of DNA forensic technologies and databases, the use of DNA evidence will continue to convict the appropriate offender and demonstrate the innocence of others.

SEE ALSO CODIS: Combined DNA Index System; DNA; DNA profiling; European Network of Forensic Science Institutes; Privacy, legal and ethical issues; Standardization of regulations; STR (short tandem repeat) analysis.

DNA fingerprint

DNA (deoxyribonucleic acid) represents the blueprint of the human genetic makeup. It exists in virtually every cell of the human body and differs in its sequence of nucleotides (molecules that make up DNA, also abbreviated by letters, A, T, G, C; or, adenine, thymine, guanine, and cytosine, respectively). The human genome is made up of 3 billion nucleotides, which are 99.9% identical from one person to the next. The 0.1% variation, therefore, can be used to distinguish one individual from another. It is this difference that can be used by forensic scientists to match specimens of **blood**, tissue, or hair follicles to an individual with a high level of certainty.

The complete DNA of each individual is unique, with the exception of identical twins. A DNA fingerprint, therefore, is a DNA pattern that has a unique sequence such that it can be distinguished from the DNA patterns of other individuals. DNA fingerprinting is also called DNA typing.

DNA fingerprinting was first used for sample **identification** after the geneticist Alec J. Jeffreys from the University of Leicester in Great Britain discovered that there are patterns of genetic material that are unique to almost every individual. He called these repetitive DNA sequences "minisatellites." The two major uses for the information provided by DNA-fingerprinting analysis are for personal identification and for the determination of paternity.

DNA fingerprinting is based on DNA analyzed from regions in the genome that separate genes called introns. Introns are regions within a **gene** that are not part of the protein the gene encodes. They are spliced out during processing of the messenger RNA, which is an intermediate molecule that allows DNA to encode protein. This is in contrast to DNA analysis looking for disease causing mutations, where the majority of mutations involve regions in the genes that code for protein called exons. DNA fingerprinting usually involves introns because exons are much more conserved and therefore, have less variability in their sequence.

DNA fingerprinting was originally used to identify genetic diseases by linking disease genes within a family based on the inheritance of the segregating markers and the likelihood that they would be in close proximity, but it also became used for criminal investigations and forensic science. In general, the United States courts accept the reliability of DNA analysis and have included these results into **evidence** in many court cases. However, the accuracy of the results, the cost of testing, and the misuse of the technique have made it controversial.

In forensics laboratories, DNA can be analyzed from a variety of human samples including blood, **semen**, **saliva**, urine, hair, buccal (cheek cells), tissues, or bones. DNA can be extracted from these samples and analyzed in a lab and results from these studies are compared to DNA analyzed from known samples. DNA extracted from a sample obtained from a crime scene then can be compared and possibly matched with DNA extracted from the victim or suspect.

DNA can be extracted from two different sources within the cell. DNA found in the nucleus of the cell, also called nuclear DNA (nDNA) is larger and contains all the information that makes us who we are. It is tightly wound into structures called chromosomes. DNA can also be found in an organelle within the cell called the mitochondria, which functions to produce energy that drives all the cellular processes necessary for life. Mitochondrial DNA (mtDNA) is much smaller, contains only 16,569 nucleotide bases (compared with nDNA, which contains 3.9 billion) and it is not wound up into chromosomes. Instead, it is circular and there are many copies of it.

Nuclear DNA is analyzed in evidence containing blood, semen, saliva, body tissues, and hair follicles. DNA from the mitochondria, however, is usually analyzed in evidence containing hair fragments, bones, and teeth. **Mitochondrial DNA analysis** is typically performed in cases where there is an insufficient amount of sample, the nDNA is uninformative, or if supplemental information is necessary.

Unlike nDNA, where one copy of a **chromosome** comes from the father and the other from the mother, mtDNA is exclusively inherited from the maternal side. Therefore, the maternal mtDNA should be the same as her offspring. This can be helpful in cases where it is not possible to obtain a sample from the suspect but it is possible to obtain a sample from one of the suspect's biologically related family members. By doing so, the suspect can be excluded as the culprit of a crime if the results indicate that the relevant family member's mtDNA does not match the mtDNA fingerprint from the sample.

Mitochondrial DNA can be informative in a different way than nDNA. Less than 10% of the mitochondrial genome is noncoding and localized in a region called the D-loop. In this region, there are sequence variations that are inherited that can be used for forensic purposes. These regions, called hypervariable regions, are broken down into two sections: HV1 and HV2. It is within these regions that inherited sequence variations can be identified.

One of the main reasons mtDNA analysis can be helpful to forensic scientists is that in some tissues, mitochondrial DNA is in excess compared to nDNA. As nDNA exists in chromosomes and there are only two copies of each chromosome (one inherited maternally, the other paternally) per cell, the nDNA copy number is much smaller. The mitochondrial genome can have a copy number of 2–10 per organelle and in some cases the number of organelles can reach the hundreds. For example, in muscle tissue, where the demand for energy is highest, there are a larger number of copies of the mitochondrial genome. Analysis of mtDNA, therefore, can be particularly helpful in forensic cases where sample integrity or size is compromised or when confirmation is needed.

There are many methods that forensic scientists use to determine the sample's DNA fingerprint. Once DNA is extracted, it can then be analyzed using a variety of molecular genetics techniques. In some cases, there is not enough DNA to directly evaluate it. If this occurs, a technique called the **polymerase chain reaction** (**PCR**) is used to amplify the genomic DNA from a sample. This procedure allows a scientist to amplify a specific sequence of DNA in the genome exponentially, so that it is in large enough quantities to be analyzed.

DNA analysis can be performed by **sequencing** the amplified DNA fragment using fluorescently labeled nucleotides and a **laser** that will recognize the nucleotide based on the fluorescent label to which it is attached. This technique is expensive, may not be informative, and is generally not the best approach to DNA fingerprint a sample.

If there is enough DNA, the DNA extracted from the sample can be cut or segmented using specific enzymes (proteins that speed up chemical reactions) called restriction endonucleases that act as molecular scissors by cutting specific sequences that they recognize. By cutting in the same sequence that is present in different locations throughout the genome, a pattern of fragments can be formed. Differences in the sequence patterns between two samples can be due to inherited variations in the DNA that can distinguish two different samples.

Once the DNA is cut, the segments are arranged by size using a process called **electrophoresis**, whereby an electrical field is generated, pulling the negatively charged DNA toward the positively charged end through a gel-like matrix. The segments are marked with radioactive probes and exposed on x-ray film, where they form a characteristic pattern of black bars. This pattern is called the DNA fingerprint. If the DNA fingerprints produced from two different samples match, the two samples are likely to have come from the same person.

DNA can also be processed and cut with restriction enzymes. If there is a variation in a particular sequence that results in the enzyme no longer recognizing and cutting the DNA (or a loss of the cut site), a larger fragment will be observed when running the DNA in a gel by electrophoresis. Using a chemical that binds to DNA (called ethidium bromide) and

fluoresces when it is excited by ultraviolet radiation, the fragments can be observed on a gel based on size. Bigger fragments will migrate more slowly in the gel. An individual with the sequence variation in which the enzyme does not cut would have a longer size fragment than the individual with the variation the enzyme does cut.

The original DNA fingerprinting procedure used Variable Number Tandem Repeats (VNTR), which are repetitive DNA sequences that are spread throughout the genome in noncoding regions. These targets are large, with repeat numbers that are variable from person to person and have a repeat size composed of hundreds of nucleotides which can be repeated a hundred times.

The biggest problem with using the VNTR-fingerprinting approach is that DNA extracted from samples in a crime scene, such as from a dried blood stain, is often broken up into tiny pieces due in most cases to natural DNA-degrading processes. This can make DNA analysis difficult, unless informative fragments remain intact. Additionally, the smaller the sample, the more likely it will be degraded. For example, a plucked hair might contain up to 30 nanograms (30 ng, or 30 billionths of one gram) of genomic DNA, but a hair shaft without the root might maximally only contain 0.1 ng of DNA. The integrity of the sample as well as the quantity, therefore, can make reliable and definitive identity determination difficult.

More recent approaches have circumvented the problem associated with degraded DNA. Shorter repetitive sequences, or short tandem repeats (STR), were later identified and found to contain repeat core units of three, four, or five nucleotides long and have a complete length of only 80–400 nucleotides. Due to the shortness of these sequences, only 50 pg of DNA (which is almost a 1000 times less than that found in a hair shaft without the root) is required. The discriminating power, when analyzing STRs at multiple locations with the genome, can match persons with a probability of 1 in 10^{15} to a stain. The DNA fingerprint using **STR analysis** can, therefore, be an extremely powerful technique in forensic sciences.

With the completion of the human genome sequence and the rapid post-genomic characterization of the sequences, it has become easier to analyze samples pertinent for forensic applications. In fact, forensic scientists have been able to link a suspect to the scene of a crime using dried chewing gum, the cells in the saliva from the butt of a cigarette, and cells found underneath fingernails. DNA fingerprinting, therefore, has revolutionized the forensic sciences by its use in investigations and prosecutions of active criminal cases, missing persons investigations, re-examining dead-end cases, post-conviction exoneration, and studies where maternal relatedness is in question.

SEE ALSO Analytical instrumentation; Chemical and biological detection technologies; DNA profiling; DNA recognition instruments; RFLP (restriction fragment length polymorphism).

DNA indexing SEE CODIS: Combined DNA Index System

DNA isolation methods

Deoxyribonucleic acid (**DNA**) isolation is an extraction process of DNA from various sources. Methods used to isolate DNA are dependent on the source, age, and size of the sample. Despite the wide variety of methods used, there are some similarities among them. In general, they aim to separate DNA present in the nucleus of the cell from other cellular components.

Isolation of DNA is needed for genetic analysis, which is used for scientific, medical, or forensic purposes. Scientists use DNA in a number of applications, such as introduction of DNA into cells and animals or plants, or for diagnostic purposes. In **medicine** the latter application is the most common. On the other hand, **forensic science** needs to recover DNA for **identification** of individuals (for example rapists, petty thieves, accident, or war victims), paternity determination, and plant or animal identification.

Presence of proteins, lipids, polysaccharides and some other organic or **inorganic compounds** in the DNA preparation can interfere with DNA analysis methods, especially with **polymerase chain reaction** (**PCR**). They can also reduce the quality of DNA leading to its shorter storage life.

Sources for DNA isolation are very diverse. Basically it can be isolated from any living or dead organism. Common sources for DNA isolation include whole **blood**, hair, **sperm**, bones, nails, tissues, blood stains, **saliva**, buccal (cheek) swabs, epithelial cells, urine, paper cards used for sample collection, bacteria, animal tissues, or plants.

It is quite clear that the extraction methods have to be adapted in such a way that they can efficiently purify DNA from various sources. Another important factor is the sample size. If the sample is small (for

example sperm, or a single hair) the method has to be different to the method used in isolating DNA from a couple of milligrams of tissue or milliliters of blood. Another important factor is whether the sample is fresh or has been stored. Stored samples can come from archived tissue samples, frozen blood or tissue, exhumed bones or tissues, and ancient human, animal, or plant samples.

The isolation of DNA usually begins with lysis, or breakdown, of tissue or cells. This process is essential for the destruction of protein structures and allows for release of nucleic acids from the nucleus. Lysis is carried out in a salt solution, containing detergents to denature proteins or proteases (enzymes digesting proteins), such as Proteinase K, or in some cases both. It results in the breakdown of cells and dissolving of membranes.

While the lysis of soft tissues or cells is easy, DNA also has to be isolated from hard tissues, such as bone, wood, and various plant materials. Most plant samples require freezing in liquid nitrogen and subsequently pulverizing the tissues to a fine powder. On the other hand, bones are highly mineralized and the ions have to be removed from the samples before extraction so they do not later interfere with PCR. Once the samples are partly processed they are then homogenized in lysis buffer using a mechanical homogenizer.

DNA isolation is a simple process and can be performed in a kitchen using household appliances and chemicals. Vegetables or meat can be homogenized with salt and water. After that, by application of a detergent, cellular proteins and lipids are separated away from DNA. Enzymes found in meat tenderizer or pineapple juice allow precipitation of proteins and free DNA into the solution. By adding alcohol to the mix, nucleic acid is brought to the top of the container and can be spooled onto a stick as a visible white string.

A number of commercial DNA purification kits use the very same principles as this household method, but different reagents. In a commercial kit the common lysis solutions contain: sodium chloride; tromethamine (also known as Tris), which is a buffer to retain constant pH; ethylenediaminetetraacetic acid (EDTA), which binds metal ions; and sodium dodecyl sulfate (SDS), which is a detergent. A common enzyme used in DNA extraction is Proteinase K.

The oldest methods of DNA purification in laboratories, still often used also by the **FBI**, rely on a mix of organic solvents. Lysed samples are mixed with phenol, chloroform, and isoamylalcohol for separation of DNA and protein. Proteins are denatured by the organic mixture. When the sample is centrifuged, DNA is retained in the aqueous (water) layer, phenol is at the bottom of the tube, and denatured proteins form a cloudy interface. This method is very efficient, but unfortunately it can only be used if the quantity of starting material is reasonably abundant. Moreover, the organic solvents used carry health and safety problems. The quality of the DNA from this procedure is usually not adequate for some more sensitive analytical techniques (especially **sequencing** and occasionally PCR).

A modification of the method uses high salt (sodium chloride, NaCl) concentration to bring down DNA. After the denaturation of cellular proteins using detergents and a protease for a few hours or overnight, salt is added and mixed with the solution. As a result, salt of nucleic acid is formed and in presence of alcohol can be recovered by centrifugation.

Occasionally, alkaline denaturation of the sample is used to release DNA from the cells. Buccal swabs and occasionally blood stains can be placed in small plastic tubes (eppendorfs) and subjected to denaturation with sodium hydroxide (NaOH). The solution is then re-equilibrated to neutral pH with a more acidic buffer solution and is ready for PCR. Although it is a quick and simple method, the quality of DNA is not always adequate for all applications.

A method similar to alkaline denaturation is heat denaturation, achieved by boiling samples. Heating of a sample to 100°C releases DNA into the solution but also denatures it by separating the two strands. In some cases this procedure gives adequate nucleic acid that can be amplified by PCR, however, most of the time there are remaining inhibitors in the form of degraded proteins, other **organic compounds**, or ions.

A related method used commonly in forensic laboratories utilizes Chelex ion exchange resin that binds multivalent metal ions and is particularly useful in removing inhibitors from DNA. It can be used with any type of sample, including whole blood, bloodstains, seminal stains, buccal swabs, or hair. The only difference from the previous method is the presence of resin, which binds the impurities from the solution, while DNA is being left in the solution. By centrifuging the samples, the resin is brought to a pellet and separated.

Another method similar to Chelex relies on the use of paramagnetic beads with DNA binding capacity. Samples are lysed and then the solid material is treated with Proteinase K. The lysates are then applied to the beads. Resin is subsequently washed and DNA is eluted of it at 65°C, magnetic beads are separated from the sample on a magnetic stand.

Other methods of DNA purification involve columns of various sorts, which are packed with ion exchange, or silica based resins or matrices. Ion exchange columns are generally positively charged to bind the negatively charged DNA; silica matrices are also charged and can also retain DNA. In such applications DNA from the cellular lysates is expected to bind to the column. These columns are then washed using salt solutions to remove unbound material. Nucleic acid is then recovered by applying water or a neutral pH salt solution to break down the resin-DNA bonding.

The use of columns allows increased throughput of samples, shorter time of isolation in comparison to traditional solvent based extraction, increased yield of recovered DNA, and improved quality of purified DNA.

In addition to columns and the previously described resins, there are also liquid resins that are used. The principle is the same as for magnetic beads, but at the final step the samples have to be spun to separate DNA from the resin.

All of these methods so far have dealt with simple, single samples. In some cases a sample consists of a mixture of cells, for example sperm cells and non-sperm epithelial cells. This extraction is based on differential properties of the two cell types. Sperm cells resist Proteinase K lysis; therefore the non-sperm cells are lysed first in its presence. When the tube is centrifuged, the solution contains epithelial DNA, while the pellet contains sperm cells. Sperm cells are subsequently lysed by adding dithiothreitol or DTT with Proteinase K. Any of the techniques mentioned before can be used to isolate the DNA from those differential lysates.

Although plants are not a common source of DNA for forensic investigation, analysis of their DNA is very common in science. Plants are more difficult to work with than many other materials for a couple of reasons. First, plant cells have a cell wall, which has to be at least partly destroyed before the cytoplasm with the DNA can be accessed. Second, plants often have high levels of sugars (for example starch or fructose) in their tissues or other organic compounds such as polyphenols.

Grinding of the samples in liquid nitrogen helps to destroy the cell wall, but the organic compounds including sugars still remain. As a result, methods were developed that use chloroform-octanol mix, hexadecyltrimethylammonium bromide (CTAB) with high salt to remove polysaccharides, and polyvinyl-pyrrolidone (PVP) to remove polyphenols.

All of these methods are successfully used in various laboratories and with various samples. The methods have to be properly selected to optimize the yield and quality of the DNA extracted.

SEE ALSO DNA; DNA profiling; DNA typing systems.

DNA mixtures, forensic interpretation of mass graves

War crimes are most often committed during conflicts between nations. Crimes against humanity, such as summary executions of civilians, are also not uncommon in situations of national armed conflicts, revolutions, or in totalitarian regimes. All of these events result in missing persons and often in undiscovered mass graves. Both are searched for and processed by forensic experts in the aftermath of the conflict. Legal **medicine** has greatly benefited from the development of molecular biology and its new analytical techniques, in particular **DNA** analysis, in the **identification** of highly decomposed human remains.

Terrorist attacks on densely populated areas or against large human gatherings, such as the 2001 attack on the World Trade Center and the 2002 Bali nightclub bombing, or mass disasters, such as the 2004 Indian Ocean earthquake and tsunami, also yield a tragically large amount of bodies to be identified. In some situations, such as after the conflict in Kosovo in the 1990s, the identification of human remains was possible in many cases by comparing medical and dental records of missing persons with findings at **autopsy** in cadavers rescued from mass graves. Mass graves containing a large amount of highly decomposed bodies and skeletal remains do pose specific challenges for forensic experts, especially when dental and medical records are not available, or when the grave is a secondary one, containing parts of bodies who were purposely removed and mixed by the perpetrators. The recent development of new DNA **sequencing** and profiling technologies, as well as the understanding of the uniqueness of certain DNA sequences among individuals, has become greatly useful for human identification in situations of mass casualty.

Discrete genetic variations among individuals in the population and among races are known as polymorphisms. The word polymorphism originates from the Greek *poly*, meaning several and *morphos*, meaning shape. Single nucleotide polymorphisms (SNP) are mutations of one base pair in the sequence of certain genes. Several polymorphisms are present in regions of DNA known as microsatellites, as well as in some types of repeated DNA sequences. Polymorphisms are of special interest in forensic investigation because they allow the identification of a person or suspect through the DNA extracted from a bloodstain by comparing it with another sample from the suspect, or the identification of a baby's mother or father, or of a murder victim through a bloodstain or **saliva** left at a crime scene, or the identification of unknown human remains by matching the DNA with that of a living relative. The latter procedure was frequently applied in the aftermath of the Asian tsunami in December 2004.

Most genes are inherited in two copies: one from the father and the other from the mother, which are respectively known as paternal and maternal alleles. Allelic comparison of certain genes is one of the identification techniques used in forensics. Conversely, DNA from cell organelles, the mitochondria, is only inherited from the mother (mtDNA), allowing the comparison of the mtDNA collected from a sibling, or from the mother with the mtDNA of a deceased person, to establish whether those remains belong to that family. The remains of an American soldier who served in Vietnam, for instance, were identified 24 years after his death through the mtDNA extracted from the bone marrow of his skeleton and samples donated from living relatives. Mitochondrial DNA does not identify an individual in particular, however, if more than one sibling is missing. When several members of a family are missing, other genetic and forensic tests may help to determine the identity of the remains found in a disaster area or in a mass grave.

Some specific repeating DNA sequences are also used for human identification. They are classified according to their characteristics, such as LINES (long interspersed sequences), SINES (short interspersed sequences), LTR (long terminal repeats), STR (short tandem repeats), and VNTR (variable number of tandem repeats, or microsatellite DNA). Short tandem repeats are used in tests of paternity and VNTR is used to identify victims and suspects.

Sir Alec Jeffreys, an English professor at Leicester University, was the first scientist to use DNA polymorphism tests in a forensic identity investigation in 1985. He chose a region of DNA known as VNTR because of its great variability (polymorphism) among individuals, which can only yield a perfect sequence match in cases of identical twins. Additionally, if two individuals do present a high degree of similarities (but not a perfect match) in their VNTR sequences, this indicates that they are related.

However, postmortem transformations quickly degrade DNA of soft tissues due to bacterial activity. Hochmeister and colleagues (Journal of Forensic Science, 1991;36:1649–1661) were the first to isolate DNA from the marrow of the human femur from a mummified body of an 11-year-old child and from a corpse that had been submerged in water for 18 months. They utilized two DNA analysis techniques to sequence VNTR from the bones: VNTR amplification by **PCR (polymerase chain reaction)** and **RFLP** (restriction fragment length polymorphisms), thus demonstrating that DNA is relatively well preserved in the marrow of long bones. In 1994 another group identified the Romanov family (the last Russian czar, his wife and three children killed in 1918), also using DNA extracted from their bones. Studies conducted by other researchers in 1996 found that even in bones DNA degrades differently in certain conditions, being best preserved in dry or arid environments such as deserts and worst degraded when the bone fragments were immersed in water. Teeth and dried **blood** stains however, even almost 100 years old, were found to be a good source of well preserved DNA for forensic identification of human remains.

Crime scenes, disaster areas, and mass graves often produce mixed biological samples containing genetic material from two or more individuals, such as mixed body **fluids**, bloodstains, or blood pools. In the 1994 murder case of Nicole Brown Simpson, for instance, the blood pool around the body of Nicole Simpson contained blood (and DNA) of both Nicole and her former husband, O. J. Simpson, who was charged and acquitted in criminal court and later found liable in civil court for her murder. When male and female cells are present in the same sample, the cells can be sorted by using a **laser** technique or **DNA profiling**. In mass graves or bombing scenes however, samples may contain DNA of several victims, rapidly degrading in tropical climates or due to moisture and soil conditions, all of which affect the STR sequences and other DNA loci used in human identification. Until recently, this constituted a serious obstacle to forensic interpretation. With the rapid evolution of genetic screening technologies, however, new test kits and software are being constantly developed. Some of these kits are more sensitive to low, degraded concentrations of DNA found in mixed samples than others.

Additionally, matches from DNA mixtures are also assessed against scientific profiles and probability or frequency estimates in order to establish the statistical significance of the match. These statistics serve to inform courts and jurors of the odds that a match can be common to more than one individual. In degraded DNA mixtures, the margin of error for minor STR components can be 10–33%, and the burial of several relatives with similar alleles in a mass grave can make individual identification of DNA from a mixture even more difficult. Statistical evaluation of DNA mixtures takes into account the match probability.

The International Commission on Missing Persons installed a forensic laboratory in Tuzla, Bosnia, in 2000 for the identification of victims of the war in Bosnia. The forensic team has chosen a more direct approach than DNA mixture analysis. Living relatives of missing persons donate blood samples for comparison with DNA extracted from the long bones and teeth of the exhumed human remains. In Bosnia, more than 30,000 people were reported missing, mostly Muslim men and boys. Mass graves were located and exhumed in nearby Srebrenica and other localities, but many mass graves are yet to be located and processed. To identify one corpse, this method requires samples from 3 relatives. Whenever nuclear DNA is not degraded, it is used in the tests, because the maternal and paternal alleles offer a unique profile for each individual. The other option is mtDNA profiling because mitochondrial DNA is usually better preserved and stays unaltered for longer periods than nuclear material.

ICMP is also profiling DNA from other mass graves in Croatia, Kosovo, and other former Yugoslavia territories. In Rwanda however, where more than 500,000 people were massacred in 3 months in 1994, due to the inexistence of automated DNA technologies and the rapid degradation of DNA because of the tropical heat and humidity, this task would have been impossible. In Brazil, collective summary executions occurred during the totalitarian military regime (1964–1985) and the location of many suspected mass graves remains unknown. Some were discovered in the 1990s. Legal physicians working in the identification of the human remains recovered from mass graves were faced with the same problems of DNA degradation common in other tropical countries. Nevertheless, DNA extracted from teeth and the application of other forensic identification techniques led to the successful identification of many of the victims.

A scientist uses blood samples taken from family members of people who disappeared during Chile's Augusto Pinochet's 1973–1990 dictatorship in an attempt to match DNA from people who disappeared during those years and were later uncovered in mass graves. © REUTERS/CORBIS

SEE ALSO Autopsy; Blood; DNA; DNA sequences, unique; DNA typing systems; Exhumation; Gene; Genetic code; Identification of the son of Louis XVI and Marie Antoinette; Laser; Medical examiner; Mitochondrial DNA analysis; Mitochondrial DNA typing; Mummies; Pathology; PCR (polymerase chain reaction); RFLP (restriction fragment length polymorphism); Skeletal analysis; War crimes trials; War forensics; Y chromosome analysis.

DNA profiling

DNA is the material within every cell of the body and represents the blueprint of life. It allows physical traits to be passed on from one generation to the next. Although the majority of the human genome (the complete set of genes for an individual) is the same across all ethnic populations, people differ in their genetic makeup by a minuscule amount, and thus have their own unique DNA pattern. DNA profiling, also referred to as DNA typing, is the molecular genetic analysis that identifies DNA patterns. In **forensic science**, DNA profiling is used to identify those who have committed a crime. It is estimated that roughly one percent of all criminal cases employ this technique; however, DNA profiling has been used to acquit several suspects involved in serious crimes such as rape and **murder** and it has been used to convict individuals of crimes years after investigators closed the unsolved case. Aside from identifying an individual responsible for violent crimes, the judicial system also can use DNA profiling to determine family relationships in the case of disputed paternity or for immigration cases.

DNA molecular analysis has also been used in the diagnosis of clinical disorders. Many genetic diseases are caused by mutations in DNA within regions of the genome that code for protein, and scientist look in these regions for mutations to determine if a patient is affected or is a carrier of a genetic disease. Unlike clinical molecular genetics, DNA typing for forensics takes advantage of locations within the human genome that do not code for protein. These locations typically involve repetitive DNA sequences that are polymorphic, or have a variable number of repeat sizes. Because non-protein-coding DNA is used, **DNA databanks** that contain DNA typing information do not reveal any information about an individual's health status or whether the individual has or is a carrier of a genetic disease.

The sensitivity of DNA profiling tests have dramatically increased over the last two decades. It used to be necessary to have a sample roughly the size of the ink in an ink pen, skilled forensic scientists can now obtain enough DNA from **saliva** left on the end of a cigarette to get a DNA profile result. The speed at which results can be obtained has also dramatically improved. This is all, in part, due to the discovery of the **polymerase chain reaction**, a technique that can amplify large amounts of specific small sequences of DNA from the human genome. It is also due to the advent of various DNA fingerprinting tools. The effect of these advances has broadened the sample size and quality required for analysis.

DNA profiling uses a variety of **DNA typing systems**, including: **restriction fragment length polymorphism** (**RFLP**) typing, short tandem repeat (STR) typing, single nucleotide polymorphism (SNP) typing, mitochondrial DNA (mtDNA) analysis, human leukocyte **antigen** (HLA)-typing, gender typing, and Y-chromosome typing.

The first approach to DNA typing used variable number tandem repeats, or VNTRs. VNTR's are repeating units of a DNA sequence, the number of which varies between individuals. They are analyzed as Restriction Fragment Length Polymorphisms (RFLPs). RFLPs are variations within specific regions of genomes that are detected by restriction enzymes. RFLP analysis originated in the 1970s after the discovery of restriction enzymes, or proteins that can cut DNA into smaller molecules (restriction fragments) based on specific DNA sequence recognition sites. A restriction enzyme recognizes and cuts DNA only at a particular sequence of nucleotides (the

components of DNA). VNTR's are 20–50 base pairs (pairs of nucleotides) long per repeat and a person can have anywhere from 50 to several hundred repeats. This repeat length is inherited. This DNA typing approach was first discovered by the British geneticist Alec Jeffreys in 1985 and is the principle behind today's DNA profiling systems.

The advantage of using a RFLP-based analysis for DNA profiling is that VNTR regions are highly variable in copy number from person to person. Therefore, it is highly unlikely that DNA profiles from unrelated individuals would be identical. However, there are also several drawbacks to this technique. Since these regions are large, it is often difficult to clearly separate the fragment using **electrophoresis**, which is a technique that uses a DNA sample loaded into a gel that migrates towards a positively charge electric field based on size. For example, larger fragments migrate slower than smaller fragments. This is problematic when the migration of one VNTR is indistinguishable from another VNTR, even if they differ in length. This is due to limited resolution of the gel matrix (only large differences can be detected). A larger amount of DNA (20 nanograms) of purified, high quality DNA is also required for this technique. Thus, DNA samples extracted from crime scene specimens may be not suitable in quality for this type of analysis. High purity in terms of DNA extractions can be compromised according to the source of the sample. If, for example, the sample is **blood** and is extracted from clothing, the dye from the cloth might alter the mobility of the extracted DNA in the gel, making the analysis difficult.

VNTR analysis has been replaced by Short Tandem Repeat (STR) analysis. STR regions are comprised of 2–4 base pair repeats that are repeated between 5 to 15 times. **STR analysis** is currently the standard approach to forensic DNA profiling. This is mainly because shorter repeat sequences are easier to analyze.

STR analysis is faster, less labor intensive, and can be automated. A single reaction can analyze 4–6 STR regions using very little DNA (only one nanogram is usually sufficient). If only a small amount of DNA is recovered or if it is degraded, it may be possible to use STR analysis, but not VNTR analysis.

Additionally, in VNTR analysis, genomic DNA is digested with restriction enzymes and then run on a gel. The fragments produced are transferred to a membrane and probed with a radiolabeled sequence of DNA that matches the VNTR sequence. The migration of the VNTR fragment on the gel determines their size and generates a pattern. The radiolabeled probe produces dark bands on x-ray film when exposed in a time-dependent and dose-dependant manner. Unlike VNTR analysis, STR analysis uses the polymerase chain reaction to amplify DNA in the region where the STR is located. These **PCR** products can then be run on a gel in the same manner as the VNTR fragment and using sophisticated computer software with **laser** controlled equipment, the migration of the PCR products can be compared to control DNA molecules that have a known size. If run together, the size of the unknown STR can be estimated. In this case, STRs are visualized by adding a DNA intercalator such as ethidium bromide into the gel, which intercalates into the DNA and fluoresces (emits) ultraviolet light.

STR analysis, however, is not without its drawbacks, as well. If very little DNA is recovered from a crime scene and it is degraded, not all regions in the genome will amplify, or there will be discriminatory amplification of DNA in only one chromosomal STR region, rather than both. This can significantly affect the results and lead forensic scientists to draw incorrect conclusions. Additionally, there may be substances in the sample that inhibit the PCR reaction. For these reasons, forensics scientists must use a standardized approach that is reproducible and includes all the necessary positive and negative controls for DNA profiling to be used as **evidence** during a court proceeding.

A significant problem in using DNA profiling as evidence in court proceedings is the possibility that a mistake was made in the sample extraction, preparation, or analysis. For this reason, investigators take precautions to reduce human error. Each forensics laboratory must maintain a high level of quality control and quality assurance standards to prevent this from happening. State and local mandates are being established to standardize these techniques.

Every cell, tissue, or organ in a person's body contains the same DNA pattern, so the United States law enforcement and armed forces has developed databases to collect information related to an individual's DNA identity. This information will be used for **identification** purposes in missing person cases or to identify the remains of deceased individuals. Other techniques previously used to identify individuals such as using dental records, dog tags, or blood typing have been superceded by DNA profiling, which provides more information and is more conclusive. For example, if two samples have the same blood type, it still is not clear that they came from the same person. Even dental records might not be helpful in cases where the integrity of the sample is compro-

mised to a degree that makes it difficult to match it appropriately. In DNA profiling, even if the deceased person was significantly disfigured, it would still be possible to analyze the sample.

SEE ALSO DNA databanks; DNA evidence, social issues; DNA fingerprint; DNA sequences, unique; DNA typing systems; Mitochondrial DNA typing.

DNA recognition instruments

With the advent of molecular detection techniques, the repertoire of forensic tools has grown considerably. The ability to detect deoxyribonucleic acid (**DNA**) and even to match the nucleic acid to its source can allow the forensic scientist to identify an individual, or to determine if the individual was at the scene of a particular investigation.

DNA recognition instruments allow rapid **identification** of the origin of DNA in an environmental or medical sample. Recognition of the source of DNA is important in pathogen (disease-causing agent) identification in various public health, diagnostic, and military forensic applications.

DNA recognition instruments utilize two main methods for detection and identification. These are nucleic acid hybridization and the **polymerase chain reaction** (**PCR**). Hybridization of nucleic acids allows differentiation of sequences that differ by as little as one base pair by using high temperature washes that remove partially matched DNA strands. Hybridization relies on the fact that single stranded DNA reforms a double stranded helix with a complementary strand. The method requires a single stranded target (unlabeled) and probe (labeled with a radioactive or fluorescent tag to detect signal). PCR-based detection in modern instruments is based on the specificity provided by primers required for DNA amplification and fluorescent probes to detect the product in real time.

Engineers and biologists are designing new technologies to make DNA recognition rapid and robust, with increased sensitivity of the assays and improved identification of positive samples. Optical identification methods are primarily used in PCR-based instruments; however, new magnetic and electrochemical methods were developed for hybridization-based assays.

Chip-based hybridization assays, where the target DNA is spotted onto a glass or plastic slide and a single stranded DNA probe is used to detect it, were developed recently by a number of companies. Technology allows placement of thousands of DNA molecules on the slide, but detection of the specific reaction is often lacking sensitivity. As a result, a number of research teams and commercial companies are researching better ways to identify a positive signal.

One breakthrough came with the implementation of electrical conductivity as a detection method. This method relies on the use of electrodes with gaps of 30–50nm in size, containing single stranded DNA molecules (oligonucleotides) immobilized on their surface (capture probes) and gold oligonucleotide nanoparticles allowing detection of electrical currents resulting from hybridization. Both oligonucleotides bind to the target sequence when the electrode is immersed in a solution containing target molecules.

Scientists at Northwestern University produced a modification of this method, called signal amplification, using a photographic developing solution. A salt wash before the addition of photographic developer removes mismatches and the silver coated gold particles can be easily visualized. The chip is then scanned using a flatbed scanner, removing the need for expensive equipment. This method is highly sensitive and very fast. It is able to detect concentrations of DNA (100 times more sensitive than conventional detection methods), in one to three minutes.

A further modification of this method was developed in 2002. It incorporates nanoparticle probes that in addition to gold particles, have Raman dye-label (for example Cy3, Cy5, or Texas Red). Detection of these probes can be either by Raman **spectroscopy** or by using a flatbed scanner to detect silver enhancement. By using multiple labels one is able to design chips detecting multiple target sequences (multiple **pathogens**).

The great advantages of hybridization-based instruments are that they do not require any DNA amplification, are highly sensitive, and give rapid results.

Scientists in industry are currently producing instruments that are based on measuring electrical conductivity. One is known as the eSensor. The system consists of bioelectronic chips, reader, and special software. The chips contain capture probes and signaling probes. After an interaction with a target sequence, signaling probes induce electric current, which is detected and interpreted by the sensor's software. This instrument can perform a number of assays simultaneously. A second instrument is directly based on the technology from the Northwestern University group, using a method of conductivity detection that

was modified to amplify the signal from gold particles by using a photographic developer solution to coat the gold particles. Although this instrument currently requires a large space, work is underway to design a hand-held device.

One company has licensed a Strand Displacement Amplification (SDA) method, and has devised an electrical method of binding DNA to silicon chips and performing hybridization. SDA oligonucleotides (probes) are localized to spots on the chip by charge and immobilized on the surface by chemical reaction. The sample is then added to the chip and by applying an electric current, the binding of the test to the probes is highly accelerated (one to three minutes). By reversing the charge, unbound molecules are removed and only perfect matches remain. The entire process takes about 15 minutes.

Chips for identifying pathogens such as the bacteria responsible for **anthrax** are under development.

The newest technologies in PCR-based instruments involve instrument miniaturization and methods for handling and detecting multiple pathogens in multiple samples. The ability to prepare clean PCR templates in a field is often difficult or limited. The presence of various chemicals can inhibit the amplification, giving false negative results and, in the case of an attempt to identify a biological threat, possibly endanger people's lives. As a result, a number of companies have started to offer sample preparation units with their PCR instruments.

The advanced nucleic acid analyzer (ANAA), developed in 1997, was the first DNA recognition instrument designed for work in the field. It was portable, but still large and was superseded by a hand-held ANAA (HANAA).

The major differences between the various instruments are in the proprietary heating and cooling systems, detection optics, and sample preparation and handling, as well as size. The speed of most of these instruments is similar to the typical sample analysis taking 7–20 minutes.

A different technology, but still PCR-based, uses a high-performance liquid **chromatography** to separate the PCR products and identify mutations. The advantage of the system is that it can detect mutations in any genes that could have been altered for designing biological weapons, thus, potentially complementing any other detection methods.

DNA recognition instruments are likely to be used in general monitoring of the environment, investigation

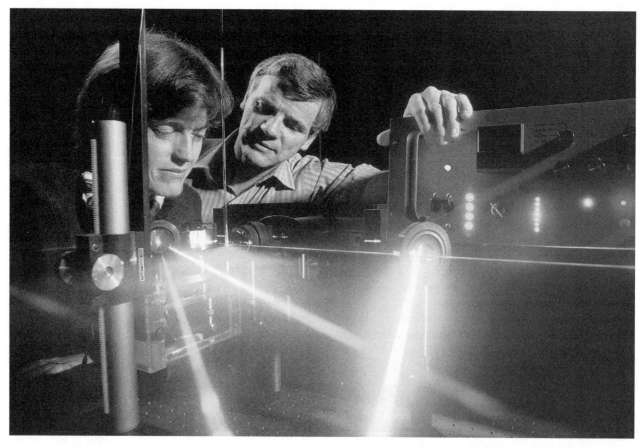

Biologists at the California Institute of Technology demonstrate a machine designed to read DNA sequences. The sequenator uses lasers, and is hundreds of times faster than human sequencers. © ROGER RESSMEYER/CORBIS

of suspicious objects, and in diagnostics. In all of these applications, detection must be rapid and accurate in order to introduce prevention measures or rapid treatment. Ease of use and result interpretation are important, as in the majority of cases users will be people with minimal laboratory **training**.

SEE ALSO Analytical instrumentation; Biological weapons, genetic identification; Chemical and biological detection technologies; DNA profiling; RFLP (restriction fragment length polymorphism); STR (short tandem repeat) analysis.

DNA sequences, unique

An increasingly important facet of **forensic science** is the use of techniques that detect and determine the structure of deoxyribonucleic acid (**DNA**). When the aim of the investigation is to identify an unknown person, the exploitation of unique portions of DNA can be very useful.

DNA contains genetic information that is unique to each organism. The entire cellular DNA of any organism, bacteria, plant, virus, or animal represents the genome. A DNA sequence is considered to be unique if it is present in only one copy in a haploid genome (that portion of DNA that contains only a single copy of each **chromosome**). In humans, for example, a haploid number of chromosomes is 23.

Not all of the DNA contained in the genome is unique; there are also various repetitive sequences present.

A DNA strand is composed of a strand of nucleotides (nitrogen-based building blocks of DNA and ribonucleic acid; RNA). Each nucleotide contains a phosphate attached to a sugar molecule (deoxyribose) and one of four bases, guanine (G), cytosine (C), adenine (A), or thymine (T).

It is the arrangement of the bases in a sequence, for example ATTGCCAT, that determines the encoded **gene**. This sequence allows scientists to identify organisms, genes, or fragments of genes.

One of the main characteristics of DNA is the fact that it forms double stranded molecules (helices) by forming hydrogen bonds between the complementary strands inside the helix and a sugar-phosphate backbone outside. This pairing is not random, A always pairs with T, and C pairs with G, therefore a sequence complementary to ATTCCGAT will be TAAGGCTA.

Genes are the sequences of encoded proteins, and, together with the surrounding regulatory sequences, are considered as unique genomic sequences, since they are present as single copies in a haploid genome. In contrast, some sequences are present in multiple copies. These represent repetitive fragments. The simplest genomes of viruses and bacteria contain mostly unique sequences with only a few repetitive regions. However, the proportion of repetitive DNA increases in higher organisms, for example sea urchins have only 38% unique sequences and human just over 50%.

Genes encoding the same protein in bacteria, plants, and humans often display similar genetic sequences and perform the same or similar function across the spectrum of organisms. Such homology between the sequences allows scientists to identify the genes in humans by using fragments of mouse or yeast genes to search for similar DNA fragments. Although most of the genes show some species-dependent differences, not all of them can be used to discriminate between organisms. Only a few genes can be used for this purpose. The two main groups are ribosomal (16S in bacteria and 18S in animals) and mitochondrial genes.

Ribosomal genes are useful for tracing evolution and relationships, especially in bacteria. However, mitochondrial genes have an advantage over the ribosomal genes as they are not encoded by the nuclear DNA, but are present as circular molecules in the cells. As such they are less likely to be degraded with time. This is advantageous for the forensic scientist, since genetic **identification** may be possible using bones, teeth, or tissue fragments even when death occurred a long time before.

The presence of unique DNA sequences allows forensic scientists to identify signature sequences that can be later used as probes to detect individual organisms or to detect a particular gene. Changes of even one base pair can be readily detected by most hybridization techniques and by **sequencing**.

Signature sequences are particularly important for diagnosis of viruses, which are the **pathogens** that lack ribosomal or mitochondrial genes. Their detection and identification is greatly simplified by

using these sequences, as traditional methods can take up to a few weeks.

The unique DNA sequences can also be used to design primers (short DNA fragments needed to initiate DNA amplification) for **polymerase chain reaction** (**PCR**). There are sufficient differences between all the genes within one organism, as well as between organisms from different species, to ensure that the selected primers will only amplify the target sequence even if a mixture of different DNA molecules is present. This allows forensic scientists to design diagnostic and identification tests for the common pathogens and diseases and for parts of pathogen's genome.

Although everyone except for identical twins has unique DNA, the identification of an individual is not based on the sequencing of the individual's genome. Instead, analysis of mitochondrial DNA in a region of a displacement-loop (D-loop or control region) or of short tandem repeats (STRs) is used for identification purposes.

D-loop analysis is used for individual identification in forensic analysis. This is possible due to the polymorphisms of such sequences resulting from substitutions of base pairs during DNA replication process (for example, instead of A, DNA polymerase incorporates T).

The D-loop region is 1274 base pairs long and is located between the genes encoding transfer RNA (tRNA) for proline and tRNA for phenylalanine. It contains the regulatory regions of the for replication other genes.

The main method used for the identification of the changes in this region is PCR amplification and sequencing. However, new microarray approaches that analyze patterns of gene expression in miniature environments such as glass slides or silicon wafers are also being developed.

SEE ALSO Biodetectors; DNA profiling; RFLP (restriction fragment length polymorphism); STR (short tandem repeat) analysis.

DNA typing systems

Deoxyribonucleic acid (**DNA**) typing is a way to categorize an individual's genetic makeup in order to distinguish one individual from another. This has been made possible due to the rapid acceleration of genomics-based technologies coupled with the fact that human genomic DNA, which is comprised of

3 billion bases (letters in the DNA alphabet), is unique in only 0.1% of its makeup. Therefore, approximately 3 million bases differ from one person to the next, allowing scientists to use these differences to perform identity matches with a high degree of certainty. These variable regions of DNA can be used to generate a DNA profile of an individual, using samples from **blood**, bone, hair, **semen**, and **saliva**, as well as other body tissues.

In DNA typing, there are several systems that can be employed to characterize DNA from a sample. These systems have different applications and purposes. For example, in forensics, scientists may need to obtain DNA from a crime scene in order to analyze a specific set of DNA markers (regions within the genome that are variable) rapidly, yet with good results. DNA typing systems that have previously been used or are currently being used in forensics include **restriction fragment length polymorphism** (**RFLP**) typing, short tandem repeat (STR) typing, single nucleotide polymorphism (SNP) typing, mitochondrial DNA (mtDNA) analysis, human leukocyte **Antigen** (HLA) typing, gender typing, and Y-chromosome typing. RLFP analysis was the first major DNA typing system used in forensics. All of the techniques that followed could not have been developed without the discovery of a revolutionizing methodology called the **polymerase chain reaction**, or **PCR**. PCR allows a scientist to amplify genomic DNA (small sequences up to a few thousand in length) extracted from a sample so that there are sufficient quantities to be analyzed.

RFLP analysis was first developed by Alec Jeffreys. RFLPs can be used to analyze the DNA directly in a way that is fairly inexpensive. In RFLP analysis, genomic DNA is digested with a molecular enzyme that cuts the DNA at specific sequences it recognizes, creating multiple fragments. These fragments can be variable depending on whether the enzyme cuts at a particular site in the DNA. Variable DNA that is inherited (and not mutated) at a site may or may not be cut by the enzyme depending on whether the sequence contains the enzyme recognition site. These sites can be highly variable based on inheritance patterns. For this reason, a pattern of fragments will be produced based on the number of cut sites, separated by gel **electrophoresis**, transferred to a nitrocellulose membrane, and using radio-labeled probes (short sequences of DNA that bind to the complementary sequence from the sample DNA) that bind to specific sequences of interest, they can be identified by audioradiography. Radioactively labeled probes are visualized by audioradiography, or what appears to be film that has burned bands, based on size, that run in the gel during gel electrophoresis. If there is a lack of a restriction site in an individual's DNA at a specific site, the enzyme will not cut it and the fragment will therefore be larger. RFLP analysis is not always applicable because it requires a large amount of high quality DNA. In forensics, samples obtained from a crime scene tend to be degraded. Although RFLP is one of the original applications of DNA analysis that forensic investigators used, newer, more efficient DNA-analysis techniques have replaced this technology.

PCR-based assays followed RFLP analysis because of their greater sensitivity, simplicity, and amenability to analyzing degraded DNA samples. PCR can amplify extremely small amounts of DNA (even DNA from a single cell) to large DNA concentrations (nanograms). Using PCR to amplify a specific sequence of interest, which contains a variable sequence within the amplicon (amplified PCR fragment), **STR analysis** can be performed. STRs are short tandem repeats of 2–5 base pairs that are repeated a few to dozens of times. Identification of the STR can be performed by direct DNA **sequencing**. However, it is most often analyzed using gel electrophoresis (if the difference in tandem repeat is large enough) with ethidium bromide, a carcinogen that inserts DNA and fluoresces with an ultraviolet lamp. As the size of the amplified STR loci is in the range of 200–500 base pairs, it makes it ideal for degraded DNA samples.

The Federal Bureau of Investigation (**FBI**) uses a set of thirteen specific STR regions for **CODIS**, a software program that comes from a database derived from local, state, and national agencies using information collected from criminals or arrested individuals. With these markers, it is estimated that there is approximately a one in one billion chance that two individuals will be the same at the thirteen different marker sites.

Another DNA typing system, which is used most frequently in forensics, is **mitochondrial DNA analysis**. Mitochondrial DNA (mtDNA) is DNA that comes from a source separate from the DNA found in the nucleus. It is much smaller (only 16.5 thousand bases) than nuclear DNA and is important for producing proteins that are important and specific to energy production within the cell. The advantage of using mtDNA is because many tissues (such as muscle) have a much higher copy number of mtDNA compared to nuclear DNA, which only has two copies of genetic information and two sex chromosomes.

For samples with little DNA recovered, mtDNA analysis is the preferred approach. It is also important for samples that do not have nucleus, such as red blood cells, rootless hair, bones, nail clippings, and teeth. For these tissues, STR and RFLP analysis cannot be used. Finally, mtDNA analysis is possible due to a highly variable region (by 1–2% in unrelated individuals) in the mtDNA genome called the "D-loop." Mitochondrial DNA is maternally inherited.

Y-chromosome analysis is only applicable in cases that test for identity matches in males. Y-chromosomes can only be inherited by sons from fathers. It can also be useful in testing male suspects when multiple sample sources have been identified at a crime scene. Gender typing can also be performed by analyzing the X-chromosome and determining if there is one allele (male) or two different alleles (female) at an informative site.

Another DNA typing system, used in particular by forensic scientists, involves designing small pieces of short DNA sequences called "probes" that bind to complementary DNA sequences extracted from a sample found at a crime scene. Much like the radiolabeled probes, these short sequences can be used to create a distinct pattern depending on the DNA source. These patterns can be compared to the sample from a crime scene and determined if a match exists between the DNA from the sample and the DNA from the suspect. These probes can be fluorescently labeled and used to identify Small Nucleotide Polymorphisms (SNPs), which are single base variations that are known to be variable within a given population, are not themselves disease-causing, do not represent spontaneous mutations, and are found throughout the genome. A marker is only informative if there is a difference between two samples. Although a single SNP may not be informative, combining several SNPs is useful and can easily be automated. The more markers that are used, the likelihood that the two samples are identical is greater.

Although six or more probes are usually used in forensics DNA typing, new, more advanced DNA typing systems are being developed. DNA-chip technology is the latest molecular advancement that will considerably speed up analysis and allow forensic scientists to study many sequences at one time in a fully automated manner. DNA chips (also known as microarrays) have small sequences printed or synthesized onto microscopic spots on a tiny chip. When DNA is added to the chip, binding of the sample to the probe occurs when there is a match. The probes are labeled with a fluorescent dye that fluoresces when it hybridizes to a sequence from the sample DNA. Different fluorochromes (colors) can be used to distinguish which DNA base is present in a variable position of the DNA sequence.

Despite its speed, this type of DNA technology is more expensive and probably better suited for applications where a large number of suspects' samples are required for DNA typing. It might also apply DNA typing to identify the remains of many different individuals from a natural disaster. For example, after the tsunami that developed off the west coast of the Indonesian islands in 2004, coastal regions in Thailand and other Asian countries were devastated by its destruction. Many visitors' and residents' remains were found but could not be identified. Microarray-based DNA typing would have been helpful in characterizing the DNA patterns from the remains and matching them to various samples.

After the discovery of PCR, a DNA typing system that was used in forensics was the HLA DQ a / HLA DQA1 system, or Human Leukocyte Antigen (HLA) system. This system is comprised of a 242 base area in the genome that is highly variable in the population. It can be detected using molecular probes that seek out complementary subregions within this genetic region. The probe for HLA DQa set started out with six common sites called DQ alleles that, when combined, produced 21 possible genotypes. With only one locus or region in the genome used, the predictive value was lower than RFLP analysis or other PCR-based assays. The HLA DQA1 system improved the analysis by detecting 28 possible genotypes. The AmpliType PM+DQA1, another HLA-related locus, was developed to expand the HLA DQ system. It uses several markers at different loci (the location of a particular **gene** on a **chromosome**), analyzed simultaneously (also called multiplexing). With five additional markers analyzed, the statistical power increases considerably.

SEE ALSO Analytical instrumentation; Chemical and biological detection technologies; DNA fingerprint; DNA profiling; DNA recognition instruments; DNA sequences, unique; Mitochondrial DNA typing.

Document destruction

Accounting, in particular **forensic accounting** (where accounting and investigative practices are used to trace the sometimes deliberately clandestine movement of finances from person to person and within an organization), can be concerned with paperwork and other documents that can be destroyed. The task of document reconstruction in a forensic investigation may be onerous but is not necessarily impossible.

Even documents stored on a computer may circulate as hard copy, and these, combined with other paper items such as phone messages, notes, memoranda, and other items, can be valuable forensic **evidence**. Those seeking to hide a paper trail have increasingly turned to document destruction, a security solution long applied by government agencies. Document destruction can be achieved with paper shredders, burn boxes, and other forms of technology, often in industrial facilities dedicated to that purpose.

Stories of document destruction by businesses and public officials regularly appear in the media. In 2002, as a scandal erupted around Enron Corporation for falsifying records of earnings, it was revealed that Arthur Andersen LLP, the accounting firm that had helped Enron falsify its books, had shredded literally tons of documents.

Forensic evidence can be obtained from a crude attempt at document destruction such as disposal of paperwork in the trash. Once garbage is placed on the curb for pickup, the discarded information is easily obtained by someone dedicated enough to pick through the garbage.

In the 1990s, garbage-combing thieves earned the colorful appellation of "dumpster diver." Private detectives, for purposes either laudatory or malign, also obtain a great deal of their information from trash. (So, too, do law-enforcement officers, including forensic specialists who take advantage of the fact that material an individual has discarded is open to search without a warrant.).

The best methods of document destruction take place on an industrial scale. The document destruction industry, which primarily serves corporate clients, is estimated to generate $1.5 billion a year in revenue. Whereas only about two dozen companies nationwide were in operation in the early 1980s, by 2002 that number had risen to about 600.

Document shredding, which particularly came to national attention in the wake of the Enron debacle, is only one of many methods of document destruction, though it is the one most frequently used. As a report in the *Wall Street Journal* noted, "For routine destruction work, many companies use shredding services because even heavy-duty office-model shredders tend to choke on anything thicker than about 50 pages—and can be stopped dead in their tracks by a binder clip."

By contrast, the shredders at a facility such as that of American Document Security Corporation (ADS) in Brooklyn, New York, are capable of chewing through 20 tons of documents an hour. Clients of such companies range from law and consulting firms to investment banks, hospitals, and many others.

Though document shredding is probably as old as the concept of written documents, shredding by machine dates back to the 1920s, when an American inventor developed the first shredder from a Bavarian noodle cutter. Today's shredders are far more efficient than those used even in 1979, when the students who took over the U.S. embassy in Tehran, Iran, were able to piece together documents shredded by embassy personnel.

Some shredders are known as disintegrators. Often used for destroying CD ROMs, circuit boards, and other items containing computerized data, the disintegrators chop up materials into a fine dust that can be sifted through a screen at the bottom of the machine. Another variation on the shredder, inasmuch as it destroys documents by purely physical (rather than chemical or electromagnetic) means, is a hammer-and-mill device, which beats paper quite literally to a pulp.

Paper that has been put through industrial shredders and hammer-and-mill devices often is recycled. Waste-to-energy plants burn paper waste at temperatures as high as 2,200°F (1,204°C).

For burning documents on a smaller scale—especially documents for which security is an extremely high concern—a burn box may be used. Actually, the purpose of the burn box is not to destroy documents per se, but to destroy documents discovered by the wrong people. Inside the box, a sturdy metal container, is a volatile chemical mixture attached to a tamper-sensitive switch. If someone opens the box in an unauthorized manner, the chemicals turn the pages to ash.

An intriguing variety of document destruction can be used for electronic media such as CD-ROMs, hard drives, floppies, and so on. This is a degausser, which applies electromagnetic energy to rearrange particles of information contained on a magnetic field. Used either in the form of a stationary box or a hand-held wand, a degausser removes information permanently, leaving the storage device free to be used again.

SEE ALSO Computer forensics; Document forgery; Product tampering.

Document forgery

Information can serve as **evidence** in a forensic investigation. Paperwork, computer files, notes, and more can help piece together the incident under study. However, it is not always guaranteed that the information is genuine. Identifying a deliberately altered document or identifying the manufacture of a fictitious, but convincingly real, document or file is a challenge for the forensic investigator.

Forensic scientists examine paper manufacturers' marks and, if necessary, use radiocarbon dating techniques to verify the age of a document. Handwriting and linguistic style analysis can help determine the document's author. Forgery specialists also make use of ultraviolet lighting and spectography equipment to determine whether a document contains evidence of tampering through erasure or added characters. Inks and dyes are examined through chemistry, and paper fibers are examined microscopically in order to validate or determine their source. When criminals create elaborate forgeries, such as counterfeit currency, sophisticated computerized printers are often used, and examining their encrypted computer files and printer cartridges can help determine the source of the forgery. Evidence from criminal cases of suspected forgery are probed by the Federal Bureau of Investigation's Questioned Documents Unit; the United States Secret Service investigates counterfeit currency.

On September 8, 2004, CBS News anchor Dan Rather aired a news report questioning the service record of President George Bush in the Texas Air National Guard during the Vietnam War. Several weeks later, when the authenticity of one of the key documents used by CBS News was called into question, Rather publicly apologized. CBS News has since been criticized for failing to follow basic journalistic principles; in essence by failing to properly conduct a forensic investigation.

The CBS debacle is one of literally hundreds of examples of forged documents passing scrutiny as the authentic item. On September 17, 1980, White House press spokesman Jody Powell announced that an unidentified group had sought to sow racial discord by circulating a forged Presidential Review Memorandum on Africa that suggested a racist policy on the part of the United States. The first surfacing of the forgery appears to have been in the San Francisco newspaper, *Sun Reporter* (September 18, 1980). The *Sun Reporter's* political editor, Edith Austin, claims in that issue of the paper to have received the document from an "African official on her recent visit on the continent." The forgery was replayed by the Soviet news agency TASS on September 18, 1980, and distributed worldwide.

Former United States Ambassador to the United Nations Jeanne Kirkpatrick was the target of more than one Soviet forgery. On February 6, 1983, the pro-Soviet Indian weekly, *Link* published the text of a supposed speech by U.N. Ambassador Kirkpatrick outlining a plan for the Balkanization of India. The speech was never given, but this forgery was replayed many times by Soviet-controlled propaganda outlets. Its most recent appearance was in the book, *Devil and His Dart*, published in 1986. The author, Kunhanandan Nair, was the European correspondent of *Blitz*, another pro-Soviet publication.

On November 5, 1982, the British magazine, *New Statesman* published a photostat of a letter supposedly from a South African official to Kirkpatrick. He was allegedly sending her a birthday gift. The U.S. Mission to the U.N. wrote the magazine on November 19, branding the letter a forgery. The *New Statesman* countered this by printing another photostat of the forgery with entirely different spacing between the lines. The magazine claimed that the letter was authentic and that they had received it from a source in the U.S. Department of State. A comparison of this forgery with a letter sent by the South African official to a number of U.S. journalists announcing his appointment as Information Counsellor at the embassy revealed that this letter was the exemplar. The real letter had been typed on a computer. The forgery based on it was typed on a typewriter and contained a number of misspellings.

In a particularly bizarre incident, two leaflets were mailed to African and Asian participants in the 1984 Los Angeles Summer Olympics, which were boycotted by the Soviets. Signed by the Ku Klux Klan, they threatened the lives of the athletes. These leaflets later proved to be Soviet forgeries, written in poor English. When the U.S. government exposed them and pointed out that there is no organization in the United States called simply the Ku Klux Klan (the organizations bear individual names like White Knights of the Ku Klux Klan or Invisible Empire of the Ku Klux Klan), TASS, the Soviet official news agency, responded on July 12, 1984, by claiming that the leaflets were signed "the Invisible Empire, The Knights of the Ku Klux Klan." TASS attempted unsuccessfully to correct the error on the leaflets made by the KGB. The forgeries were intended to preoccupy African-American and Asian-American athletes with intimidation, and negatively affect their performance.

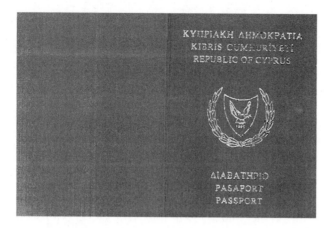

Forged Cypriot passport used by Turkish rebel leader Abdullah Ocalan before his arrest in 1999. © CORBIS SYGMA

In the 1980s, before the downfall of the Berlin Wall in 1989 and the Soviet Union in 1991, President Ronald Reagan's signature appeared on a number of forgeries. The last to appear was in May 1987. It was a supposed memorandum to the Secretaries of State and Defense, and the Director of the CIA. In this forgery, which bore the date March 10, 1983, the President was supposedly ordering the establishment of a U.S. military force called the "Permanent Peace Forces" to intervene in Latin America. This forgery received wide circulation in Latin America and was designed to inflame nationalist and anti-American feelings.

These and other examples serve to illustrate how effective a forgery can be. While a typical forensic investigation would likely not have such political ramifications, a forgery could undermine a legal case or lead the investigation in a wrong direction.

SEE ALSO Art forgery; Crime scene investigation.

Dog sniffers SEE Canine substance detection

Dosimetry

A forensic investigation could potentially involve the detection of radiation. In this situation, measuring the amount of radiation present is important, both as **evidence** and to discern whether the radiation presents a potential hazard to the investigators.

Dosimetry measures the amount of radiation energy absorbed over a given period of time by an object such as the human body or a part of that object (e.g., an organ or tumor).

A device that measures cumulative radiation exposure is a dosimeter. A Geiger counter is a radiation detector, but not a dosimeter, because it gives only a moment-to-moment reading of radiation intensity. A strip of photographic film, however, whose degree of exposure indicates how much radiation it has absorbed (up to its saturation limit), can act as a dosimeter. Filmstrip dosimeters are, in fact, still used to measure exposure to ionizing radiation. By grading the sensitivity of a specially formulated film strip from one end to the other, it can be made to indicate net, cumulative radiation exposure as a bar of darkening that grows from the most sensitive end of the film to the least sensitive end. Such "badge dosimeters" are common in the nuclear weapons and nuclear-power industries. However, they have the disadvantage that they must be developed to be read, and so do not give the bearer immediate knowledge of their exposure level.

Another type of dosimeter is the pen ionization dosimeter. These devices contain a long, narrow chamber filled with a few cubic centimeters of nonconducting gas. A metallic contact touches the interior of the chamber at each end. When the dosimeter is to be used, an initial electric charge is placed on the gas tube. This creates an imbalance of electrons between the two ends. Since the gas in the tube is normally nonconducting, electrons cannot pass through it to even out the charge imbalance. However, ionizing radiation passing through the gas forcibly frees electrons from atoms in the gas, and so partially ionizes the gas. The negatively charged electrons are free to flow toward the end of the tube having a positive charge. The more ionizing radiation the pen dosimeter is exposed to, therefore, the more of its initial charge is enabled to leak through the gas tube. The amount of charge lost is a measure of the amount of radiation that has passed through the tube. A pen dosimeter can be read by its bearer at any time, and so gives a current reading of exposure; however, pen dosimeters readings can be affected by mechanical shock or vibration.

A more modern dosimeter design is the thermoluminescent dosimeter (TLD). A TLD contains a tiny crystal of lithium fluoride (sometimes mounted in a finger-ring) that undergoes cumulative structural changes as it is exposed to ionizing radiation. When heated, the crystal glows, giving off an amount of light that is proportional to its radiation exposure. This light is observed by an electronic sensor in a readout unit and recorded digitally. This data can be stored in a central database, a convenient feature if an organization wishes to systematically monitor radiation exposure of a large body of personnel or share data in forensic investigations. Databasing of TLD data has been used, for example, by Canada to monitor the exposure of its troops to radiation from depleted-uranium munitions used by NATO in Bosnia. TLDs, unlike film badges, can be re-used; however, they must be inserted in a reader that heats the crystal and records the light emitted, a process that may take 20 to 30 seconds and erases the data in the crystal.

An even more recent dosimeter design is the optically stimulated luminescence dosimeter (OSLD). In this design, a thin film of crystalline aluminum oxide undergoes cumulative structural changes as it is exposed to ionizing radiation; when an exposure reading is desired, the crystal is exposed to green **laser** light. The amount of blue light emitted by the film in response is proportional to its radiation exposure. Unlike a TLD, an OSLD can supply an instant readout that can be repeated if necessary.

Solid-state devices that measure radiation by detecting ionization leakage current through a transistor device also exist. Radiation detectors and dosimeters based on such solid-state technology have been available since the 1980s, but have not edged out other dosimeter technologies in terms of cheapness, sensitivity, and accuracy.

Dosimetry for laser light, radio waves, and ultrasound is more difficult than dosimetry of ionizing radiation. One method of measuring dose delivered to a volume of tissue is to measure the temperature increase of the tissue; the more increase, the more radio or sound energy has been absorbed. However, these techniques do not work for tissue embedded in living organisms (where temperature measurement is difficult and where heat is rapidly conducted away) or for whole-body exposure, as biologically tolerable doses of laser, radio, and sound energy produce undetectably slight changes in body temperature. Absorption by the body of radio waves is particularly different from absorption of ionizing radiation; the body acts as a complex antenna whose performance is strongly affected by its posture and orientation and by nearby objects. Dosimetry for radio and ultrasound therefore relies heavily on computational models rather than on direct measurements.

SEE ALSO Analytical instrumentation; Isotopic analysis; Radiation damage to tissues; Radiological threat analysis.

John E. Douglas

AMERICAN
FORENSIC CONSULTANT

John Douglas, who retired from the Federal Bureau of Investigation (**FBI**) after a more than twenty-five year career, was the founder and head of the FBI's Investigative Support Unit (created in 1980). Douglas is a veteran of the United States Air Force, and he holds a Doctoral degree in Education.

Douglas is a renowned expert on criminal and behavioral **profiling**, and is a prolific and best-selling author on the subject. Among his publications are *Mindhunter: Inside the FBI's Elite Serial Crime Unit* (1996) and *The Cases that Haunt Us* (2001). He continues to be in considerable international demand, both as a public speaker/lecturer and as an expert consultant to police departments, law enforcement agencies, and to prosecuting attorneys.

During his tenure with the FBI, Douglas earned a reputation as a widely known expert on criminal personality profiling. He has been touted as one of the pioneers of modern criminal investigative analysis, and is credited with conducting the first organized study in the United States regarding the methods and motivations of violent serial criminals. As part of that research project, he interviewed such notorious killers as James Earl Ray, Richard Speck, John Wayne Gacy, Ted Bundy, Ed Gein, David Berkowitz, Sirhan Sirhan, and Charles Manson.

John Douglas describes the world of the criminal profiler as arduous, filled with lengthy periods of reading and studying case files, investigator's notes, **autopsy** and crime scene reports, examining crime scene photographs, poring over eyewitness statements, police reports, and, if possible, victim's statements. When the perpetrator's identity is unknown, these forensic scientists seek patterns in the **evidence** that suggest the offender's behavior and character style. They use their composite information to develop a profile of the unknown subject (UNSUB) that may be used to narrow the search for possible suspects.

Over time, the Investigative Support Unit became known as "The Mind Hunters," with John Douglas being the chief Mind Hunter. This elite FBI Unit was involved in some of the most notorious and high-profile serial and sadistic **murder** investigations in American history: the San Francisco Trailside Killer, the Atlanta Child Murderer, Robert Hansen (who hunted and killed prostitutes on his property in Alaska), the Tylenol Poisoner, and the Green River

Killer. John Douglas has been described as a profiler who is adept at understanding the way criminals think, getting inside their minds, understanding the workings of both the predator and his prey (the vast majority of serial and sadistic killers are male). Douglas uses this information, along with examination of the crime scene, to create a profile of the perpetrator, and to attempt to predict his future behaviors. Upon the criminal's apprehension, Douglas' profile could be used to aid in structuring the processes of **interrogation** and prosecution. John Douglas is both a pioneer and a legendary figure in the **forensic science** world of **criminal profiling**.

SEE ALSO Bundy (serial murderer) case; Careers in forensic science; Crime scene staging; Psychopathic personality; Ritual killings.

Arthur Conan Doyle

5/22/1859–7/6/1930
SCOTTISH
WRITER

The British author Arthur Conan Doyle is best remembered as the creator of the famous detective Sherlock Holmes. His fictional crime stories describe the law enforcement and forensic techniques used in crime investigations of his era.

Doyle was born in Edinburgh, Scotland, into an Irish Roman Catholic family of noted artistic achievement. After attending Stonyhurst College, he entered Edinburgh University as a medical student in 1876. He received a doctor of **medicine** degree in 1885. In his spare time, however, he began to write stories that were published anonymously in various magazines from 1878–1880.

After two long sea voyages as a ship's doctor, Doyle practiced medicine at Southsea, England, from 1882–1890. In 1885, he married Louise Hawkins and in 1891, moved his young family to London, where he began to specialize in ophthalmology. His practice remained small, however, and because one of his anonymous stories, "Habakuk Jephson's Statement," had enjoyed considerable success when it appeared in a magazine in 1884, he began to devote himself seriously to writing. The result was his first novel, *A Study in Scarlet*, which introduced detective Sherlock Holmes to the reading public in 1887. This was followed by two historical novels, *Micah Clarke* in 1889 and *The White Company* in 1891. The immediate and prolonged success of these works led Doyle to abandon medicine altogether and launch his writing career.

The second Sherlock Holmes novel, *The Sign of the Four* (1890), was followed by the first Holmes short story, "A Scandal in Bohemia" (1891). The instant popularity of these tales made others like them a regular monthly feature of the *Strand Magazine*, and the famous *Adventures of Sherlock Holmes* series was begun. In subsequent stories Doyle developed Holmes into a highly individualized and eccentric character, together with his companion, Doctor Watson, the ostensible narrator of the stories, and the pair came to be readily accepted as living persons by readers in England and America. But Doyle seems to have considered these stories a distraction from his more serious writing, and eventually grew tired of them. In "The Final Problem," published in 1893, Doyle kills both Holmes and his archenemy, Moriarty. Nine years later, however, Doyle published a third Sherlock Holmes novel, *The Hound of the Baskervilles*, but dated the action before Holmes's literary death. Then, in 1903, Holmes effected his mysterious resurrection in "The Empty House" and thereafter appeared intermittently until 1927, three years before Doyle's own death. All told, Doyle wrote 56 Sherlock Holmes stories and four novels (*The Valley of Fear* [1914], was the last).

Among the other works published early in his career, which Doyle felt were more representative of his true artistry, were *Beyond the City* (1892), a short novel of contemporary urban life; *The Great Shadow* (1892), a historical novel of the Napoleonic period; *The Refugees* (1893), a historical novel about French Huguenots; and *The Stark Munro Letters* (1894), an autobiographical novel. In 1896, Doyle issued one of his best-known historical novels, *Rodney Stone*, which was followed by another historical novel, *Uncle Bernac* (1897); a collection of poems, *Songs of Action* (1898); and two less popular novels, *The Tragedy of Korosko* (1898) and *A Duet* (1899).

After the outbreak of the Boer War, Doyle's energy and patriotic zeal led him in 1900 to serve as chief surgeon of a field hospital near the front lines at Bloemfontein, South Africa. His *The Great Boer War* (1900) was widely read and praised for its fairness to both sides. In 1902, he wrote a long pamphlet, *The War in South Africa: Its Cause and Conduct*, to defend the British action in South Africa against widespread criticism by pacifist groups. In August 1902, Doyle was knighted for his service to England.

After being twice defeated, in 1900 and 1906, in a bid for a seat in Parliament, Sir Arthur published *Sir Nigel* (1906), a popular historical novel of the Middle

Arthur Conan Doyle, British novelist who introduced the famous literary evidence-gathering character, Sherlock Holmes. © HULTON-DEUTSCH COLLECTION/CORBIS

Ages. A year after the death of his wife from tuberculosis in 1906, Doyle married his second wife, Jean Leckie. Doyle then took up a number of political and humanitarian causes. In 1909, he wrote *Divorce Law Reform*, championing equal rights for women in British law, and *The Crime of the Congo*, attacking the exploitation of that colony by Belgium. In 1911, he published a second collection of poems, *Songs of the Road*, and in 1912, began a series of science fiction stories with the novel *The Lost World*, featuring another of his famous characters, Professor Challenger.

After the outbreak of World War I, Doyle organized the Civilian National Reserve against the threat of German invasion. In 1916, he published *A Visit to Three Fronts* and in 1918, toured the front lines. These tours, plus extensive correspondence with a number of high-ranking officers, enabled him to write his famous account *The British Campaigns in France and Flanders*, published in six volumes (1916–1919).

Doyle had been interested in spiritualism since he rejected his Roman Catholic faith in 1880. From 1917 to 1925, he lectured on spiritualism throughout Europe, Australia, the United States, and Canada. The same cause led him to South Africa in 1928 and brought him home exhausted, from Sweden, in 1929. He died in 1930 of a heart attack, at his home in Crowborough, Sussex.

SEE ALSO Crime scene investigation; Literature, forensic science in.

Drawings, composite SEE Composite drawing

Driving injuries

In a disaster, natural or man-made, involving a blast or explosion and resulting in mass casualties, many serious or fatal injuries are caused by driven projectiles (also called driving injuries). Quite often, driving injuries are caused by shards of flying **glass**. The latter part of the twentieth century and the beginning of the twenty-first centuries documented significant increases in the number of terrorist activities resulting in massive serious injuries and loss of life. In the United States, the most notable terrorist activities resulting in driving injuries (among the myriad of other severe and lethal outcomes) occurring during that time period were attacks on abortion clinics, the Atlanta Olympic Park and associated area bombings, the bombing of the Murrah Federal Building in Oklahoma City, and the two attacks on New York's World Trade Towers, with the final attack on September 11, 2001, resulting in the collapse of the buildings. Explosive devices are commonly used both during times of war and in acts of terrorism worldwide. On a lesser scale, driving injuries may also be caused by industrial accidents, fireworks explosions, and motor vehicle accidents.

In the event of a blast, physicians and forensic examiners identify injuries of four types that occur: primary, secondary, tertiary, and quaternary or miscellaneous. Primary injuries are caused by the intense wave of excess pressure emitted immediately after a blast; this generally affects air-filled regions of the body, such as the tympanic membranes (ear drums and middle ear), gastrointestinal tract, and lungs. Secondary injuries are caused by driven objects; debris and shards of glass become high-speed projectiles that are driven into any part of the body. Driving injuries can result in blunt trauma (severe surface and underlying tissue injury that does not result in ruptured skin) or penetrating ballistic fragmentation injuries (shrapnel-like pieces of shattered glass or other blast debris make high-velocity impact with the body and lacerate it, causing surface and underlying tissue damage). A significant number, estimated at around 10% of blast survivors experience driving injuries to the eye. Tertiary damage is caused when humans become projectiles as a result of the concussive effect of a blast (the very strong wind caused by a high pressure explosive), and are injured or killed when they come into contact with other objects, including other humans. Miscellaneous or quaternary injuries are all other blast or explosion-related injuries or complications.

Driving injuries are the most frequent post-explosive occurrences. Blasts in buildings or motor vehicles typically shatter windows, creating driven glass, military **explosives** are generally designed to fragment and create shrapnel, and terrorist bombs often contain small metal objects such as screws, nails, and glass fragments that are designed to maximize secondary blast injuries.

SEE ALSO Bioterrorism; Blunt injuries, signs of; Explosives; Oklahoma bombing (1995 bombing of Alfred P. Murrah building); World Trade Center, 1993 terrorist attack.

Drowning (signs of)

A forensic examiner must consider that a body recovered from water may or may not have been dead when the water was entered. If the person died in the water, there are several possible causes of death, including drowning. It is actually difficult to prove drowning as a **cause of death** with 100% accuracy. The forensic pathologist cannot rely on **autopsy** or laboratory findings alone. Instead, the pathologist may focus on elimination of other causes for the death and on the circumstances surrounding the event.

Immersion of a body in water causes certain characteristic changes that are not necessarily signs of drowning. The skin on the palms and soles becomes white and wrinkled. A similar effect is seen on the tips of the fingers in someone who has their hands in water for extended periods of time. After a few days in water, this macerated skin will begin to separate, and after about a week, it will peel off from the body.

There may also be some evidence of **decomposition** when a body is pulled from water, although this occurs more slowly than it would on land. After about two weeks in water, the rest of the skin and the hair are sloughed, and the face, abdomen, and genitals become bloated with the gases of decomposition. This results in most bodies eventually floating to the surface, unless they have been weighted down to avoid discovery. Predators, such as fish and reptiles, will tend to prey on a corpse in water and this will accelerate decomposition. The body may also knock against objects in the water such as boats, piers, and rocks, and this may cause postmortem injury.

Drowning occurs when water enters the airways and blocks off the supply of oxygen to the body. When this happens, the person will struggle to breathe and will cough, which unfortunately sets off a reflex action that only draws more water into the lungs. The person will generally lose consciousness within a minute or two and then the heart will stop. The brain is the most vulnerable part of the body to oxygen deprivation and it can usually survive for less than four minutes before irreversible damage occurs, along with cardiac arrest. In some cases, however, **hypothermia**, or the chilling of the body that occurs in cold water, has protected the brain by slowing metabolic demands for oxygen, and allowed the person to survive.

The mechanism of drowning differs depending on whether the person was found in fresh water or salt water. Fresh water enters the circulation through the lungs rapidly and dramatically increases the blood volume, creating great strain on the heart. The massive dilution of the blood also causes substantial disruption to its normal chemistry and starts to break down red blood cells. Sea water has an opposite effect. It draws fluid from the blood plasma into the lungs. This does not have the effect of increasing the workload on the heart, so people tend to survive for longer before drowning in salt water.

Postmortem, there may be few obvious signs of drowning on external examination. There may be a copious (visible amount of) froth, perhaps blood-stained, that has come from the lungs and surrounds the nose and mouth. This is a mixture of water and protein from the blood plasma, which froths up as the person struggles to breathe. However, the froth is not always present in cases of drowning and should not be relied on as an indicator.

Internal examination may reveal froth in the windpipe and lungs. Although the lungs are usually swollen, spongy, and full of water on drowning, this can also be seen with other causes of death, such as drug overdose or cardiac arrest upon hitting the water. The struggle to breathe causes great pressure to the sinuses, which often bleed and sometimes leave evidence of hemorrhage.

Laboratory tests may reveal the presence of diatoms in the body. Diatoms are microscopic algae found in both seawater and fresh water. Their silica-based skeletons do not readily decay and they can sometimes be detected even in heavily decomposed bodies. If the person is still alive when entering the water, diatoms will enter the lungs if the person inhales water and drowns. The diatoms are then carried to distant parts of the body such as the brain, kidneys, and bone marrow by circulation. If the person is dead when entering the water, then there is no circulation and diatoms cannot enter the body. Diatoms do not occur naturally in the body. If laboratory tests show diatoms in the corpse that are of the same species found in the water where the body was recovered, then it may be good evidence of drowning as the cause of death. However, the diatom test is now considered very unreliable and would never be used, on its own, as evidence of drowning. The forensic pathologist has to rely on many other sources of evidence to determine cause of death when a body is found in water.

SEE ALSO Death, cause of; Death, mechanism of.

Drug Enforcement Administration SEE DEA (Drug Enforcement Administration)

Drugfire

Drugfire was an electronic database that contained digital images of fired bullets and casings. This system was equivalent to the **Automated Fingerprint Identification System (AFIS)** developed for fingerprints or the Combined DNA Index System (**CODIS**) developed for classifying and storing **DNA** profiles. This system allowed for law enforcement agencies to submit images of crime-related fired bullets and casings to the database. The database then classified the images based on the different characteristics exhibited by the bullet or casing.

The database returned to the submitting agency a list of bullets or casings that were present in the database, and could have been fired by the same firearm. The scientist then sorted through the list to identify any matches. This tool was a paramount improvement in the cross-comparison of **firearms**, bullets, and casings. There were 171 state and local law enforcement agencies that participated in the Drugfire program.

As an illustration, imagine that a firearm is used in a **murder** in Washington, D.C., and no suspect was identified in this crime. The crime scene investigators retrieve the bullets from the crime scene and submit them to the laboratory, which in turn, submits them to the Drugfire database. At that point, no hit (match) is found and the crime goes unsolved. Six months later, the same firearm is seized from a suspect in a completely unrelated crime. When the forensic laboratory submits the images to the database, the images from Washington, D.C. are listed as a potential match. The firearms examiner looks at the images and links the firearm to the homicide, which provides assistance to the crime-solving process.

Drugfire was developed by Mnemonics Systems, Inc. for the Federal Bureau of Investigation (**FBI**). It was first implemented by the FBI in late 1989. Similarly, the then Bureau of Alcohol, Tobacco, and Firearms (**ATF**) developed a system called **Integrated Ballistics Identification System (IBIS)**. In 1996 the **National Institute of Justice** assisted the FBI and the ATF in rendering both databases compatible with one another. In 1999 a memorandum of understanding between the FBI and ATF was signed, and the National Integrated Ballistics Information Network (NIBIN) was created to unite Drugfire and **IBIS** under one unique system. The system chosen for this database was IBIS, and Drugfire was then phased out.

SEE ALSO Caliber; FBI crime laboratory; Identification.

Drunk driving SEE Breathalyzer®

DUI SEE Breathalyzer®

DWI SEE Breathalyzer®

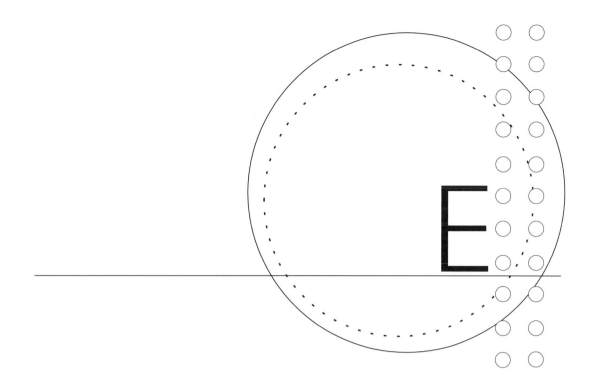

Ear print analysis

Ear print analysis is far more popular as a means of forensic **identification** in Europe than it is in the United States. The European Commission, a scientific arm of the European Union, has launched a program aimed at setting the worldwide standard for ear print analysis and identification research. The assumption among members of the EU **forensic science** community is that forensic analysis of ear prints is more economical than that of **DNA profiling**. It is also thought to be more reliable in legal proceedings, as it is virtually impossible to either tamper with, or accidentally leave at a crime scene, an ear print.

When a human ear is pressed against a surface, materials present on the ear's surface (waxes, skin oils, etc.) are left behind, forming a two-dimensional "ear print." Each ear print is believed to contain specific and individual (unique) anatomical markers, which can be used both to distinguish it from others found at the crime scene, and to compare it to other ear prints on file in forensic databases as a means of identifying suspects or linking crimes/crime scenes, much like occurs with **DNA** profiling at present. It is also possible to take ear prints from suspects under laboratory conditions (akin to those used for **fingerprint** or serological DNA testing and analysis), and compare those prints to ear prints recovered during the **crime scene investigation**. It is believed that ear prints are unique to each individual adult, and are considered difficult to tamper with (fingerprints can sometimes be altered).

It is not uncommon for a perpetrator to put an ear to a door or window prior to entering a crime scene in an effort to determine whether the area is occupied, or for an ear print to be left against a wall or other hard surface during a struggle or when a body is being positioned or moved. This **evidence** can be collected at the crime scene, using methods analogous to those used for the lifting of fingerprints. A benefit to the collection of ear prints along with other crime scene evidence is in its use as confirmatory data: the legal system typically requires two different types of corroborative evidence in order to confirm placement of a suspect at a crime scene. While it is possible to "plant" fingerprints or even DNA material, it is difficult to intentionally place an ear print, particularly before ear prints become a common form of forensic identification, at a crime scene.

At present, there is a paucity of scientific evidence supporting the use of ear prints in forensic investigations. There has not been incontrovertible research evidence that ear prints are unique to each individual; there is a lack of systematization in the collection and analysis of ear print data; and there has not been widespread development or usage of automated ear print matching technology. These issues are being addressed via the European Union's FEARID program, spearheaded by Cornelius van der Lugt at the ICR in the Netherlands, and the United Kingdom's National Training Centre for Scientific Support to Crime Investigation's systematic collection of ear prints in an effort to establish a comprehensive research-based database that is sufficiently large to be able to address the issue of uniqueness.

SEE ALSO Anthropometry; Crime scene investigation; DNA profiling; Evidence; Impression evidence.

Ebola virus

Since the mid-1970s, scientists from organizations that include the **Centers for Disease Control and prevention (CDC)** have periodically been pressed into action to help quell disease outbreaks caused by the Ebola virus. One facet of their responsibilities has been forensic investigations that involve determining the origins of the outbreaks.

Although naturally occurring, the swift and high lethality of the Ebola virus makes it an attractive potential **bioterrorism** agent. This high lethality characteristic can actually work against a large outbreak, as it limits the natural spread of the virus. Deliberate spread of the virus in multiple population areas could counteract the natural limiting factor.

The Ebola virus is one of two members of a family of viruses that is designated as the Filoviridae. The name of the virus comes from a river located in the Democratic Republic of the Congo. It was near this river that the virus was discovered.

The species of Ebola virus are among a number of viruses that cause hemorrhagic fever, which is typified by copious internal bleeding and bleeding from various orifices of the body, including the eyes. The disease can be swift and devastating, resulting in death in up to 90% of cases.

To date, four species of Ebola virus have been identified, based on differences in their genetic sequences and in the immune reaction they elicit in infected individuals. Three of the species cause disease in humans. These are Ebola-Zaire (isolated in 1976), Ebola-Sudan (also isolated in 1976), and Ebola-Ivory Coast (isolated in 1994). The fourth species, called Ebola-Reston, causes disease in primates. The latter species is capable of infecting humans but so far has not caused disease in humans. Ebola-Reston is named for the United States military primate research facility where the virus was isolated during a 1989 outbreak of the disease caused by infected monkeys that had been imported from the Philippines. Until the non-human involvement of the disease was proven, the outbreak was thought to be the first outside of Africa.

The explosive onset of the illness and the under-developed and wild nature of the African region of the virus's appearance has complicated forensic investigations into the origin and natural habitat of Ebola. The source of the Ebola virus is still unknown. However, given that filovirus, which produces similar effects, can establish a latent infection in African monkeys, macaques, and chimpanzees, it seems reasonable that the Ebola virus could reside normally in a similar host. However, direct **evidence** is so far lacking.

Almost all confirmed cases of Ebola from 1976 to 2003 have been in Africa. In the latest outbreaks, which persisted in Gabon through 2003, 122 people were known to have been infected and 96 died, according to data from the CDC. A smaller outbreak killed 7 of 17 infected people in 2004 in Sudan. In the past, one individual in Liberia presented immunological evidence of exposure to Ebola, but had no symptoms. As well, in 1976 a laboratory worker in England developed Ebola fever as a result of a laboratory accident in which the worker was punctured by an Ebola-containing needle.

The Ebola virus produces a high fever, headache, muscle aches, abdominal pain, tiredness, and diarrhea within a few days after infecting a person. Some people will also display bloody diarrhea and vomit blood. At this stage of the disease, some people recover. But for most of those who are infected, the disease progresses within days to produce copious internal bleeding, shock, and death.

Outbreaks of infection with the Ebola virus appear sporadically and suddenly. The outbreak rapidly moves through the local population and often just as quickly ends. The initial infection is presumably by contact between the person and an animal that harbors the virus. Subsequent person-to-person spread likely occurs by contamination with the infected blood or body tissues of an infected person in the home or hospital setting, or via contaminated needles. The fact that infected people tend to be in more under-developed regions, where even the health care facilities are not as likely to be equipped with isolation wards, furthers the risk of spread. The person-to-person passage is immediate; unlike the animal host; people do not harbor the virus for lengthy periods of time.

The possibility of air-borne transmission of the virus is debatable. Ebola-Reston may have been transmitted from monkey to monkey in the Reston military facility via the air distribution system, since some of the monkeys that were infected were never in physical contact with the other infected monkeys.

Mourners look on as Zairean men in protective clothing lower the coffin of an Ebola virus victim into the ground. The 1995 Ebola epidemic killed 245 people in the city of Kikwit over a period of a few months. © PATRICK ROBERT/SYGMA/CORBIS

However, if the other species of the virus are capable of similar transmission, this has not yet been documented. Laboratory studies have shown that Ebola virus can remain infectious when aerosolized. But the current consensus is that airborne transmission is possible but plays a minor role in the spread of the virus.

In the intervening years between the sporadic outbreaks, the Ebola virus probably resides in its natural reservoir. Whether that reservoir is an animal or plant, or resides in the soil or other environment is unknown, although scientists suspect the reservoir is a mammal.

Currently there is no cure for the infection caused by the Ebola virus. However, near the end of an outbreak of the virus in 1995 in Kikwit, Africa, blood products from survivors of the infection were transfused into those actively experiencing the disease. Of those eight people who received the blood, only one person died. Whether or not the transfused

blood conveyed protective factor was not ascertained. A detailed examination of this possibility awaits another outbreak.

The molecular basis for the establishment of an infection by the Ebola virus is still also more in the realm of proposal than fact. One clue has been the finding of a glycoprotein that is a shortened version of the viral constituent in the circulating fluid of humans and monkeys. This protein has been suggested to function as a decoy for the **immune system**, diverting the immune defenses from the actual site of viral infection. Another immunosuppressive mechanism may be the selective invasion and damage of the spleen and the lymph nodes, which are vital in the functioning of the immune system.

The devastating infection caused by the Ebola virus is all the more remarkable given the very small size of the viral genome, or complement of genetic material. Fewer than a dozen genes have been detected. How the virus establishes an infection and evades the host immune system with only the capacity to code for less than twelve proteins is unknown.

SEE ALSO Bioterrorism; Hemorrhagic fevers and diseases.

Electrical injury and death

The human body is a good conductor of electricity because it contains a large amount of water and dissolved salts in the form of blood and other body **fluids**. This means that an electric current may pass easily through the body, a process known as electrocution, causing various types of tissue damage and even death. Most cases of electrocution occur by accident, but still need a thorough forensic investigation. Homicidal electrocution, which used to occur mainly by putting an electrical appliance in a bath with the victim, is now relatively rare.

The amount of damage done by electrocution depends upon the size of the current and the length of time for which it is in contact with the body. According to Ohm's Law, the voltage of the source is equal to the current passing through the circuit—in this case, the body—and the resistance to the flow of current it offers. If the skin is wet, it offers lower resistance than dry skin and so currents passing through the body are higher and so cause more damage. Most cases of electrocution occur from contact with a live wire from the public power supply that has voltages of around 200 volts, depending on the country. Contact with overhead power cables,

Dogs being walked by a Lower Manhattan resident walk around a metal electrical service box cover. Many in New York City have become wary of walking over the city's metal manhole and electrical service box covers after the accidental electrocution death of a woman who stepped on one such plate while walking her dogs in 2004. © MIKE SEGAR/REUTERS/CORBIS

which carry thousands of volts, can be far more dangerous. The electricity takes the fastest route through the body which is, typically, from one hand to another or from a hand down to the ground.

If the hand comes into contact with a current of around ten milliamperes, then the person feels pain and usually lets go before any real damage can be done. This is known as an electric shock. Larger currents, up to 30 milliamperes, cause the muscles of the arm to go into spasm and then the person cannot let go of the source of the current. This longer contact could cause serious damage to the body. Fifty milliamperes is enough to cause ventricular fibrillation, a condition in which the heart's upper chambers beat irregularly, which generally leads to cardiac arrest, although it can sometimes be reversed by application of a controlled shock from a defibrillating machine.

Contact with high voltage power supplies does not cause cardiac arrest, but will lead to serious internal burns and organ damage. If the head touches an overhead power cable, a current may pass through the breathing control center in the brain stem, leading to respiratory failure and death.

At **autopsy**, the points of entry and exit of the current may be marked by a burn or a collapsed blister, the latter with a characteristic brown center and pale rim. The hands should always be examined with care, as this is the most common entry point for electrocution. There may, however, be little sign of either external or internal damage, even if the electrocution has been fatal. The pathologist's interpretation may therefore rely much more on the circumstances of the incident rather than on the autopsy findings.

Being struck by lightning is a special case of electrocution. It is always accidental and can give a wide range of findings. Some people do survive a lightning strike, but they are lucky—for they have been exposed to voltages of up to 200 million volts, albeit for just a fraction of a second. A lightning strike causes a range of electrical and thermal injuries to the body, as the victim is exposed not just to high voltage but also an accompanying thermal compression wave like an explosion. Although some people killed by lightning are completely unmarked, an electrocuted corpse may have a bizarre appearance. Sometimes the victim is stripped of clothing by the strike, which may lead investigators to suspect some kind of sexual or homicidal attack. There can be very severe burns, fractures, and lacerations. Metal objects worn on the body, like jewelry or belt buckles, may be completely melted. There is one telling sign of a lightning strike that does not occur in all cases and therefore, cannot be regarded as diagnostic. Lichtenberg figures consist of a red fern-like pattern on the back, shoulders, buttocks, or legs of the victim of a lightning strike. This pattern fades within 12–48 hours without leaving scars or discoloration. The cause of Lichtenberg figures is unclear and they are quite rare. When they are observed, however, it is clear to the pathologist that the person has indeed been struck by lightning.

SEE ALSO Death, cause of; Death, mechanism of.

Electromagnetic spectrum

The electromagnetic spectrum consists of all the frequencies at which electromagnetic waves can occur, ordered from zero to infinity. Radio waves, visible light, and x rays are examples of electromagnetic waves at different frequencies. Every part of the electromagnetic spectrum is exploited for some form of scientific or military activity; the entire spectrum is also key to science and industry. Forensic scientists often use ultraviolet light technologies to search for latent fingerprints and to examine articles of clothing. Infrared and near-infrared light technology is used by forensic scientists to record images on specialized film and in **spectroscopy**, a tool that determines the chemical structure of a molecule (such as **DNA**) without damaging the molecule.

Electromagnetic waves have been known since the mid-nineteenth century, when their behavior was first described by the equations of Scottish physicist James Clerk Maxwell (1831–1879). Electromagnetic waves, according to Maxwell's equations, are generated whenever an electrical charge (e.g., an electron) is accelerated, that is, changes its direction of motion, its speed, or both. An electromagnetic wave is so named because it consists of an electric and a magnetic field propagating together through space. As the electric field varies with time, it renews the magnetic field; as the magnetic field varies, it renews the electric field. The two components of the wave,

which always point at right angles both to each other and to their direction of motion, are thus mutually sustaining, and form a wave which moves forward through empty space indefinitely.

The rate at which energy is periodically exchanged between the electric and magnetic components of a given electromagnetic wave is the frequency, ν, of that wave and has units of cycles per second, or Hertz (Hz); the linear distance between the wave's peaks is termed its wavelength, λ, and has units of length (e.g., feet or meters). The speed at which a wave travels is the product of its wavelength and its frequency, $V = \nu\lambda$; in the case of electromagnetic waves, Maxwell's equations require that this velocity equal the speed of light, c ($\cong$186,000 miles per second [300,000 km/sec]). Since the velocity of all electromagnetic waves is fixed, the wavelength λ of an electromagnetic wave always determines its frequency ν, or vice versa, by the relationship $c = \nu\lambda$ The higher the frequency (i.e., the shorter the wavelength) of an electromagnetic wave, the higher in the spectrum it is said to be. Since a wave cannot have a frequency less than zero, the spectrum is bound by zero at its lower end. In theory, it has no upper limit.

All atoms and molecules at temperatures above absolute zero radiate electromagnetic waves at specific frequencies that are determined by the details of their internal structure. In quantum physics, this radiation must often be described as consisting of particles called photons rather than as waves; however, this article will restrict itself to the classical (continuous-wave) treatment of electromagnetic radiation, which is adequate for most technological purposes.

Not only do atoms and molecules radiate electromagnetic waves at certain frequencies, they can absorb them at the same frequencies. All material objects, therefore, are continuously absorbing and radiating electromagnetic waves having various frequencies, thus exchanging energy with other objects, near and far. This makes it possible to observe objects at a distance by detecting the electromagnetic waves that they radiate or reflect, or to affect them in various ways by beaming electromagnetic waves at them. These facts make the manipulation of electromagnetic waves at various frequencies (i.e., from various parts of the electromagnetic spectrum) fundamental to many fields of technology and science, including radio communication, radar, infrared sensing, visible-light imaging, lasers, x rays, astronomy, and more.

The spectrum has been divided up by physicists into a number of frequency ranges or bands denoted by convenient names. The points at which these bands begin and end do not correspond to shifts in the physics of electromagnetic radiation; rather, they reflect the importance of different frequency ranges for human purposes.

Radio waves are typically produced by time-varying electrical currents in relatively large objects (i.e., at least centimeters across). This category of electromagnetic waves extends from the lowest-frequency, longest-wavelength electromagnetic waves up into the gigahertz (GHz; billions of cycles per second) range. The radio frequency spectrum is divided into more than 450 non-overlapping frequency bands. These bands are exploited by different users and technologies: for example, broadcast FM is transmitted using frequencies on the order of 10^6 Hz, while television signals are transmitted using frequencies on the order of 10^8 Hz (about a hundred times higher). In general, higher-frequency signals can always be used to transmit lower-frequency information, but not the reverse; thus, a voice signal with a maximum frequency content of 20 kHz (kilohertz, thousands of Hertz) can, if desired, be transmitted on a signal centered in the Ghz range, but it is impossible to transmit a television signal over a broadcast FM station. Radio waves termed microwaves are used for high-speed communications links, heating food, radar, and electromagnetic weapons, that is, devices designed to irritate or injure people or to disable enemy devices. The microwave frequencies used for communications and radar are subdivided still further into frequency bands with special designations, such as "X band" and "Y band." Microwave radiation from the Big Bang, the cosmic explosion in which the Universe originated, pervades all of space.

Electromagnetic waves from approximately 10^{12} to 5×10^{14} Hz are termed infrared radiation. The word infrared means "below red," and is assigned to these waves because their frequencies are just below those of red light, the lowest-frequency light visible to human beings. Infrared radiation is typically produced by molecular vibrations and rotations (i.e., heat) and causes or accelerates such motions in the molecules of objects that absorb it; it is therefore perceived by the body through the increased warmth of skin exposed to it. Since all objects above absolute zero emit infrared radiation, electronic devices sensitive to infrared can form images even in the absence of visible light. Because of their ability to "see" at night, imaging devices that electronically create visible images from infrared light from are important in security systems, on the battlefield, and in observations of the Earth from space for both scientific and military purposes.

Visible light consists of elecromagnetic waves with frequencies in the 4.3×10^{14} to 7.5×10^{14} Hz range. Waves in this narrow band are typically produced by rearrangements (orbital shifts) in the outer electrons of atoms. Most of the energy in the sunlight that reaches the Earth's surface consists of electromagnetic waves in this narrow frequency range; our eyes have therefore evolved to be sensitive to this band of the electromagnetic spectrum. Photovoltaic cells—electronic devices that turn incident electromagnetic radiation into electricity—are also designed to work primarily in this band, and for the same reason. Because half the Earth is liberally illuminated by visible light at all times, this band of the spectrum, though narrow (less than an octave), is essential to thousands of applications, including all forms of natural and many forms of mechanical vision.

Ultraviolet light consists of electromagnetic waves with frequencies in the 7.5×10^{14} to 10^{16} Hz range. It is typically produced by rearrangements in the outer and intermediate electrons of atoms. Ultraviolet light is invisible, but can cause chemical changes in many substances: for living things, consequences of these chemical changes can include skin burns, blindness, or cancer. Ultraviolet light can also cause some substances to give off visible light (flouresce), a property useful for mineral detection, art-forgery detection, and other applications. Various industrial processes employ ultraviolet light, including photolithography, in which patterned chemical changes are produced rapidly over an entire film or surface by projecting patterned ultraviolet light onto it. Most ultraviolet light from the Sun is absorbed by a thin layer of ozone (O_3) in the stratosphere, making the Earth's surface much more hospitable to life than it would be otherwise; some chemicals produced by human industry (e.g., chlorfluorocarbons) destroy ozone, threatening this protective layer.

Electromagnetic waves with frequencies from about 10^{16} to 10^{19} Hz are termed x rays. X rays are typically produced by rearrangements of electrons in the innermost orbitals of atoms. When absorbed, x rays are capable of ejecting electrons entirely from atoms and thus ionizing them (i.e., causing them to have a net positive electric charge). Ionization is destructive to living tissues because ions may abandon their original molecular bonds and form new ones, altering the structure of a DNA molecule or some other aspect of cell chemistry. However, x rays are useful in medical diagnosis and in security systems (e.g., airline luggage scanners) because they can pass entirely through many solid objects; both traditional contrast images of internal structure (often termed "x rays" for short) and modern computerized axial tomography images, which give much more information, depend on the penetrating power of x rays. X rays are produced in large quantities by nuclear explosions (as are electromagnetic waves at all other frequencies above the radio band), and have been proposed for use in a space-based ballistic-missile defense system.

All electromagnetic waves above about 10^{19} Hz are termed gamma rays (γ rays), which are typically produced by rearrangements of particles in atomic nuclei. A nuclear explosion produces large quantities of gamma radiation, which is both directly and indirectly destructive of life. By interacting with the Earth's magnetic field, gamma rays from a high-altitude nuclear explosion can cause an intense pulse of radio waves termed an electromagnetic pulse (EMP). EMP may be powerful enough to burn out unprotected electronics on the ground over a wide area.

Radio waves present a unique regulatory problem, for only one broadcaster at a particular frequency can function in a given area. (Signals from overlapping same-frequency broadcasts would be received simultaneously by antennas, interfering with each other.) Throughout the world, therefore, governments regulate the radio portion of the electromagnetic spectrum, a process termed spectrum allocation. In the United States, since the passage of the Communications Act of 1934, the radio spectrum has been deemed a public resource. Individual private broadcasters are given licenses allowing them to use specific portions of this resource, that is, specific sub-bands of the radio spectrum. The United States Commerce Department's National Telecommunications and Information Administration (NTIA) and FCC (Federal Communications Commission) oversee the spectrum allocation process, which is subject to intense lobbying by various telecommunications stakeholders.

In summary, it can be said that the manipulation of every level of the electromagnetic spectrum is of urgent technological interest, but most work is being done in the radio through the visible portions of the spectrum (below 7.5×10^{14} Hz), where communications, radar, and imaging can be accomplished.

SEE ALSO DNA fingerprint; DNA profiling; Electromagnetic weapons, biochemical effects; Fluorescence; Laser; Ultraviolet light analysis.

Electromagnetic weapons, biochemical effects

Exposure to electricity and electromagnetic radiation, while relatively uncommon, can be a factor in a forensic investigation. Because the effects of exposure to electromagnetism leave no visible signs such as bruises or cuts, the cause of a disability or death can be difficult to unravel without knowledge of the phenomena.

Forensically, an encounter with electromagnetic radiation would likely be due to the deliberate use of an electromagnetic weapon.

Electromagnetic weapons—also known as E-bombs—are designed to release a high-power flash of radio waves or microwaves. Depending on the energy of the electromagnetic pulse, effects can range from the disabling of electronic circuitry to physiological effects in those exposed to the electromagnetic pulse.

The pulse released by an electromagnetic weapon lasts for an extremely short time, around 100 picoseconds (one ten-billionth of a second). The absorption of this blast of high energy by anything capable of conducting electricity, including nerves and neurons, overwhelms the recipient.

Research and development into the effects of electromagnetic weapons on human beings and animals was underway in the 1940s. The Japanese spent considerable sums of money on the development of a "Death Ray" between 1940 and 1945. A review of these studies by the United States military concluded that it was possible to develop a weapon that would produce an electromagnetic ray capable of killing humans five to 10 miles away from the source.

Animal studies have demonstrated the lethal nature of electromagnetic radiation. In the studies, wavelengths ranging from 60 centimeters destroyed the lung cells of mice and groundhogs. Wavelengths less than two meters also destroyed brain cells.

Electronic stimulation can have other, non-lethal effects on humans. Secret research conducted in the United States following World War II demonstrated that electronic stimulation of different regions of the brain of test subjects could produce extreme emotions of rage, lust, and fatigue. Another research program, dubbed "Operation Knockout," operated at the Allan Memorial Institute in Montreal, Canada, with funding from the Central Intelligence Agency. The study's director, Dr. Ewen Cameron, discovered that electroshock treatments caused amnesia. Memories could be erased, and the subjects reprogrammed. Once these "psychic driving" experiments became public, Cameron—then a pre-eminent psychiatrist—received harsh public and professional criticism.

In the 1960s, the U.S. Defense Advanced Projects Research Agency (DARPA) studied the health and psychological effects of low energy microwaves for weapons applications. The ability of microwaves to damage the heart, create leaks in blood vessels in the brain, and to produce hallucinations was demonstrated.

Many scientists assume that research into the debilitating effects of electromagnetic radiation has continued up to the present day. However, increasing restrictions on the information obtainable through the U.S. Freedom of Information Act have made verification difficult. A 1993 U.S. Air Command and Staff College paper entitled "Non Lethal Technology and Air Power" documented low frequency, "acoustic" and high power microwave weapons that could deter or debilitate humans.

Low frequency electromagnetic waves, also known as acoustic waves, have been commonly used for decades in functions such as ultrasound machines. However, acoustic waves can also cause internal organs of humans to vibrate. The result can be nausea, diarrhea, earache, and mental confusion. The discomfort increases as one gets closer to the source.

Shorter wavelength electromagnetic radiation produces different effects. A common example is microwave radiation, which in a microwave oven can be used to heat up foods and liquids. When directed at humans, a microwave weapon causes atoms to vibrate, which in turn generates heat. At 200 yards away, body temperature increases from the normal 98.6°F to 107°F. At closer range, the temperature increase can be even higher, and is lethal.

Microwave electromagnetic weapons can also stun a victim. This is the result of the stimulation of peripheral nerves. The simultaneous activity of many nerves overwhelms the capacity of the brain to process the incoming information, and can induce unconsciousness.

The biochemical effect of microwave exposure is dependent on the distance from the source, as electromagnetic fields become much weaker as the distance from the source increases.

Experiments with very low frequency electromagnetic radiation have demonstrated that the radia-tion can induce the brain to release chemicals that induce slumber, or to release a chemical called his-tamine. In human volunteers, the histamine release produces flu-like symptoms, which dissipate when the radiation stops.

Not all electromagnetic weapons are cloaked in military secrecy. A device called the Pulse Wave Myotron is commercially available. The Myotron emits rapid pulses of electromagnetic radiation. The pulses incapacitate the movement of voluntary mus-cles by overriding the electrical pulse that normally flows from nerve to nerve within the muscles. Invo-luntary muscles, such as the heart and the muscles that operate the lungs, are unaffected. Thus, a victim is rendered incapable of movement or speech. The effect lasts until the muscles can repolarize; approxi-mately 30 minutes.

SEE ALSO Electrical injury and death; Radiation, electromagnetic radiation injury.

Electrophoresis

Electrophoresis is a valuable approach to fight-ing infectious disease. Electrophoretic analysis allows the identification of bacterial and viral strains and is finding increasing acceptance as a powerful forensic tool.

Diseases caused by microorganisms are a threat to national security. One strategy is to examine the relevant microorganisms, particularly to find out the component(s) that are responsible for the infection. For many microbes, proteins are an important factor in the development of a disease. Proteins can func-tion as receptors, to allow the microorganism to adhere to the surface of a host cell. As well, the **toxins** produced by microbes such as *Escherichia coli* O157:H7 and *Vibrio chlorerae* are proteins. Methods that can dissect microorganisms into their components, and that can compare a non-disease-causing strain of a microbe to a disease-causing strain to see where they differ, are a valuable approach to fighting infectious disease. Electrophor-esis is especially well suited to this role. Further-more, specialized types of electrophoresis (i.e., pulsed field electrophoresis) allow the genetic mate-rial of the microorganism to be examined. Thus, electrophoresis can reveal much detail at the mole-cular level.

Electrophoresis is a sensitive analytical form of **chromatography**. Under the influence of an electrical

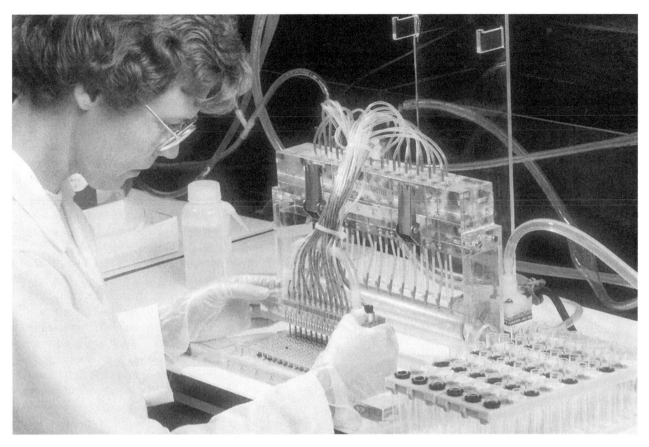

Lab technician performs electrophoresis. © ROYALTY-FREE/CORBIS

field, charged molecules can be separated from one another as they pass through a gel. Gel electrophoresis is a method that separates macromolecules—either nucleic acids or proteins—on the basis of size, electric charge, and other physical properties. The term electrophoresis describes the migration of charged particle under the influence of an electric field. Electro refers to the energy of electricity. Phoresis, from the Greek verb phoros, means "to carry across." Thus, gel electrophoresis refers to the technique in which molecules are forced across a span of gel, motivated by an electrical current. Activated electrodes at either end of the gel provide the driving force. A molecule's properties determine how rapidly an electric field can move the molecule through a gelatinous medium. Gel electrophoresis makes it possible to determine the genetic difference and the evolutionary relationship among species of plants and animals. Using this technology it is possible to separate and identify protein molecules that differ by as little as a single amino acid.

The advent of electrophoresis revolutionized the methods of protein analysis. Swedish biochemist

Arne Tiselius was awarded the 1948 Nobel Prize in chemistry for his pioneering research in electrophoretic analysis. Tiselius studied the separation of **serum** proteins in a tube (subsequently named a Tiselius tube) that contained a solution subjected to an electric field.

In electrophoresis, the electric charge often is passed through one of various support mediums. In general, a medium is mixed with a chemical mixture called a buffer. The buffer carries the electric charge that is applied to the system. The medium/buffer matrix is placed in a tray with molecule samples to be separated. As electrical current is applied to the tray, the matrix takes on this charge and develops positively and negatively charged ends. As a result, molecules that are negatively charged, such as deoxyribonucleic acid (**DNA**), ribonucleic acid (RNA), and protein, are pulled toward the positive end of the gel.

Intact DNA is so large that it cannot move through the pores of a gel (although the technique of pulsed field electrophoresis does allow very large pieces of DNA to be examined). When DNA is subjected to electrophoresis, the DNA is first cut into smaller pieces by restriction enzymes. Restriction enzymes recognize specific sequences of the building blocks of the DNA and cut the DNA at the particular site. There are many types of restriction enzymes, and so DNA can be cut into many different patterns. After electrophoresis, the pieces of DNA appear as bands (composed of similar length DNA molecules) in the electrophoresis matrix.

Electrophoresis can be combined with the prior addition of a radioactive food source to the **culture** of bacteria. The bacteria will use the food to make new proteins, which will be radioactive. Following electrophoresis, the gel can be placed in contact with x-ray film. The radioactive bands or spots will register on the film, and so will determine what proteins were being made at the time of the experiment.

There are many other variations on gel electrophoresis, with wide-ranging applications. These specialized techniques include Southern, Northern, and Western Blotting (blots are named according to the molecule under study). In Southern blots, DNA is cut with restriction enzymes, then probed with radioactive DNA. In Northern blotting, RNA is probed with radioactive DNA or RNA. Western blots target proteins with radioactive or enzymatically tagged antibodies.

Modern electrophoresis techniques now allow the identification of DNA sequences that are the same. They have become an integral part of research into **gene** structure, gene expression, and the diagnosis of heritable diseases. Electrophoretic analysis also allows the identification of bacterial and viral strains and is finding increasing acceptance as a powerful forensic tool.

SEE ALSO Chemical and biological detection technologies; Chromatography; DNA; DNA recognition instruments; DNA sequences, unique; DNA typing systems; Thin layer chromatography; Toxins.

Endothermic reaction

In a chemical reaction, reactants are converted into products by the breaking and making of chemical bonds. An example is the burning of carbon in oxygen to make carbon dioxide. Bond breaking requires energy, while bond making releases energy.

The balance between the two gives a positive or negative energy change for the reaction. Chemical reactions are classed as being either endothermic, with a positive energy change, or exothermic, with a negative energy change. In an endothermic reaction, more energy is taken breaking bonds than is released making them, so the reaction proceeds with a net absorption of energy. In an exothermic reaction, the reverse is true and energy is released. The issue of whether a reaction is endothermic or exothermic is important in the forensic investigation of explosions.

Endothermic reactions are in the minority—most chemical reactions release energy. An endothermic reaction usually needs some energy to get it going. However, some endothermic reactions occur without this boost; the dissolving of ammonium nitrate in water occurs spontaneously with a marked decrease in temperature due to heat being taken in from the surroundings. Compounds formed by endothermic reactions have stored or potential chemical energy in their bonds, which may be released spontaneously in an explosion. Such compounds include chlorates, perchlorates, and nitrates. These may explode spontaneously, which makes them dangerous to handle whether or not there is any criminal intent. If combined with other components, they will make a high explosive mixture. Explosions of endothermic compounds typically produce a lot of gas, creating a destructive pressure wave spreading through the surrounding area.

The explosion of an endothermic substance is in itself exothermic, with the chemical potential energy of the compound being released in the form of heat, light, and sound. Endothermic explosions are possible too, but need some kind of primer explosive to give them the energy required to set them off. A knowledge of the chemistry of **explosives** can help the forensic investigator understand the devastation that occurs at the scene of an explosion.

SEE ALSO Exothermic reactions.

Energy dispersive spectroscopy

Energy dispersive **spectroscopy** (also called energy dispersive x-ray spectroscopy) is an analysis technique that can be of great value in the forensic examination of samples. The technique utilizes a scanning electron microscope, a type of high magnification microscopy in which the sample is bombarded by electrons. The resultant pattern of electron reflection by the sample is used to generate a detailed three-dimensional appearing surface view.

At the heart of energy dispersive spectroscopy are x rays. During electron bombardment, electrons are also ejected from surface atoms of the sample. The resulting electron vacancy is filled by a higher energy electron. To maintain the energy balance of the atom, some energy must be released. The energy is released as x rays.

Released x rays are gathered by a detector positioned above the sample. Because the energy of the x rays will vary, depending on the element from which they were released, analysis of the x-ray spectrum can permit the various elements comprising a sample to be identified.

The x-ray spectrum is graphically displayed as a series of peaks. The pattern of peaks is a fingerprint of the specific elements in a specimen. Thus, **blood** will produce a different and characteristic pattern of peaks from gasoline.

Fluid samples such as the aforementioned cannot be examined directly. This is because the electron microscope operates in the absence of air, which would otherwise deflect the electron beam from the sample. During sample preparation, **fluids** can be dried down onto the surface. This residue is sufficient for analysis and **identification**.

Fluids can thus be identified and differentiated from each other using the spectroscopy technique. Furthermore, solids can also be analyzed, as the electron beam of the microscope can be focused to a small point on the sample surface. Indeed, various areas of a solid can be independently analyzed. This is advantageous when trying to identify the presence of a component on a solid object (i.e., blood on a knife tip). As well, different types of solid materials can be differentiated from one another.

Energy dispersive spectroscopy requires a dedicated laboratory equipped with a scanning electron microscope and ancillary equipment to conduct the x-ray analysis, as well as trained personnel. Thus, the analysis is typically done at regional or state facilities that will accept samples from local agencies.

SEE ALSO Analytical instrumentation; Fourier transform infrared spectrophotometer (FTIR); Scanning electron microscopy.

Entomological studies of time of death SEE Time of death, contemporary determination

Entomology

Entomology is the study of insects and their life cycles. Many insects live and feed on dead flesh, which is why entomology is relevant to **forensic science**. The forensic entomologist can help estimate **time of death** by looking at which insects are present on a corpse and where they are in their life cycle. Entomology can also shed light on the nature of injuries, whether a corpse has been moved, and whether drugs were involved in a death.

A newly deceased corpse attracts flies. Within minutes of a death, blowflies will start to lay their eggs in moist areas such as the nose, mouth, armpit, groin, or open wounds. The eggs hatch into larvae or maggots within 24 hours and these grow to around half an inch in length after about three days. Then, over the next six to ten days, they will develop into pupae with a hard outer case. Adult flies emerge about twelve days after this. If the corpse is not recovered by this time, the life cycle repeats itself so that flies at all different stages of development may be recovered from the corpse.

The forensic entomologist can use the life cycle of the flies found on a corpse as a kind of clock, giving the minimum time that elapsed since the time of death and the time of discovery. If eggs are found, it suggests death occurred less than 24 hours before discovery. The presence of maggots indicates the death occurred less than ten days ago. Pupae and mature flies will suggest a time of death one to three weeks before discovery of the corpse. However, the life cycle of flies is not an accurate clock. Flies are cold-blooded and their activities are dictated by the weather. Maggots may become dormant if it is cold and flies do not lay eggs at night. If someone is killed at midnight, flies will not appear till daylight, which means time must be added to the estimated time of death.

Because flies feed on human tissue, their own tissue can sometimes be used to measure levels of any drugs that may have played a role in the person's death. This is useful when the corpse itself does not yield tissue for analysis. Insect ecology varies from place to place and sometimes the species found on a corpse are not native to the place where the corpse is found. This may indicate that the corpse

A Thai health worker prepares to cremate hundreds of giant Madagascar hissing cockroaches seized as evidence in Bangkok in 2003. The cockroaches became the latest craze in pets in 2002, raising concern among health officials that the rapidly multiplying insects would spread diseases. © REUTERS/CORBIS

was moved after death. Furthermore, flies feed on open bleeding wounds and their presence may help distinguish between ante-mortem and post-mortem injuries.

SEE ALSO Time of death.

Environmental Measurements Laboratory

The Environmental Measurements Laboratory (EML) is a research laboratory located in New York City, first established in 1947, that is operated by the United States government. Research at the facility is coordinated by the Science and Technology (S&T) Directorate of the Department of Homeland Security. EML scientists are an integral part of the nation's

radiological incident emergency response plans. As such, they contribute to forensic investigations.

As a federal laboratory, EML supports The United States Department of Energy (DOE) National Security objectives. EML responsibilities include monitoring international compliance with nonproliferation treaties. EML is a part of the Homeland Security Monitoring Network (HSMN) and is also an official U.S. Radionuclide Laboratory with facilities dedicated to support of the International Monitoring System.

EML programs are designed to develop and train personnel in instruments and technologies capable of detecting radioactive substances and identifying nuclear threats. EML has advanced programs in radiation survey planning, radiological monitoring and assessment, and radiation measurements (including **dosimetry** measurements). EML also hosts high resolution gamma sensors and equipment dedicated to measuring environmental radiation and radioactivity.

Unique EML research capabilities include the ability to generate atmospheric conditions that allow experimental evaluation of instrumentation. EML scientific programs include collaborative research with global meteorological groups dedicated to developing more accurate atmospheric modeling programs. Since the Cold War, EML has maintained the International Environmental Sample Archive (IESA), a collection of atmospheric and other environmental samples containing isotopes present in the atmosphere during periods when nations still engaged in atmospheric testing of nuclear weapons. These samples can be used to test current samples for signs of nuclear testing and are a part of nonproliferation monitoring. The samples can also allow quantitative and qualitative standardization of monitoring instrumentation.

As part of HSMN implementation, EML scientists constructed a prototype monitoring platform on top of the GSA building in New York city that is capable of detecting radiological anomalies. Radiation levels can be measured by instruments utilizing a pressurized ionization chambers (PIC), comprehensive radiation sensors (CRS), and direct analysis of trapping filters via high-resolution gamma-ray analysis. The instruments are capable of distinguishing between natural radioactive sources and artificial or man-made sources.

EML programs include surface, air, and high altitude sampling programs, soil and sediment sampling programs, and fallout measurement programs.

EML scientists have developed particulate collection systems that utilize sodium iodide gamma detectors, and RAMPSCAN, a highly portable battery-operated gamma radiation detector.

Other EML facilities include pulse ionization chambers capable of measuring radon levels, a gamma ray analysis laboratory, and a thermoluminescent dosimeter reader facility.

SEE ALSO Analytical instrumentation; Electromagnetic spectrum; Meteorology.

Epidemiology

Epidemiology is the study of the occurrence, frequency, and distribution of diseases in a given population. As part of this study, epidemiologists—scientists who investigate epidemics (widespread occurrence of a disease that occurs during a certain time)—attempt to determine how the disease is transmitted, and what are the host(s) and environmental factor(s) that start, maintain, and/or spread the epidemic.

Epidemiology can be an important facet of a forensic investigation. A recent infamous example occurred in the fall of 2001, when a number of letters containing **spores** of Bacillus anthracis, the agent that causes **anthrax**, were sent through the United States postal system. The illnesses and deaths that resulted prompted the near shut-down of the postal delivery system, and an investigation to find the sender(s) of the letters and the source of the bacterial spores. These investigations were rooted in epidemiology.

The primary focus of epidemiology is on groups of persons, rather than individuals. The primary effort of epidemiologists is in determining the etiology (cause) of the disease and identifying measures to stop or slow its spread. This information, in turn, can be used to create strategies by which the efforts of health care workers and facilities in communities can be most efficiently allocated for this purpose.

In tracking a disease outbreak, epidemiologists may use any or all of three types of investigation: descriptive epidemiology, analytical epidemiology, and experimental epidemiology.

Descriptive epidemiology is the collection of all data describing the occurrence of the disease, and usually includes information about individuals infected, and the place and period during which it occurred. Such a study is usually retrospective, i.e., it is a study of an outbreak after it has occurred. The 2001 anthrax investigation is one example.

Analytical epidemiology attempts to determine the cause of an outbreak. Using the case control method, the epidemiologist can look for factors that might have preceded the disease. Often, this entails comparing a group of people who have the disease with a group that is similar in age, sex, socioeconomic status, and other variables, but does not have the disease. In this way, other possible factors, e.g., genetic or environmental, might be identified as factors related to the outbreak.

Using the cohort method of analytical epidemiology, the investigator studies two populations, one who has had contact with the disease-causing agent and another that has not. For example, the comparison of a group that received blood transfusions with a group that has not might disclose an association between blood transfusions and the incidence of a blood borne disease, such as hepatitis B.

Experimental epidemiology tests a hypothesis about a disease or disease treatment in a group of people. This strategy might be used to test whether or not a particular antibiotic is effective against a particular disease-causing organism. One group of infected individuals is divided randomly so that some receive the antibiotic and others receive a placebo—a "false" drug that is not known to have any medical effect. In this case, the antibiotic is the variable, i.e., the experimental factor being tested to see if it makes a difference between the two otherwise similar groups. If people in the group receiving the antibiotic recover more rapidly than those in the other group, it may logically be concluded that the variable—antibiotic treatment—made the difference. Thus, the antibiotic is effective.

In the process of studying the cause of an infectious disease, epidemiologists often view it in terms of the agent of infection (e.g., particular bacterium or virus), the environment in which the disease occurs (e.g., crowded slums), and the host (e.g., hospital patient). Another way epidemiologists may view etiology of disease is as a "web of causation." This web represents all known predisposing factors and their relations with each other and with the disease. For example, a web of causation for myocardial infarction (heart attack) can include diet, hereditary factors, cigarette smoking, lack of exercise, susceptibility to myocardial infarction, and hypertension. Each factor influences and is influenced by a variety of other factors.

Epidemiologic investigations are largely mathematical descriptions of persons in groups, rather than individuals. The basic quantitative measurement in epidemiology is a count of the number of persons in the group being studied who have a particular disease; for example, epidemiologists may find 10 members of a village in the African village of Zaire suffer from infection with **Ebola virus** infection; or that 80 unrelated people living in an inner city area have tuberculosis.

A fundamental underpinning of infectious epidemiology is the confirmation that a disease outbreak has occurred. Once this is done, the disease is followed with time. The pattern of appearance of cases of the disease can be tracked by developing what is known as an epidemic curve. This information is vital in distinguishing a natural outbreak from a deliberate and hostile act, for example. The appearance of a few cases at first with the number of cases increasing over time to a peak is indicative of a natural outbreak. The number of cases usually begins to subside as the population develops immunity to the infection

(e.g., influenza). However, if a large number of cases occur in the same area at the same time, the source of the infection might not be natural. Examples include a **food poisoning** or a bioterrorist action where the accidental or deliberate release of organisms will be evident as a sudden appearance of a large number of cases at the same time.

Any description of a group suffering from a particular disease must be put into the context of the larger population. This shows what proportion of the population has the disease. The significance of ten people out of a population of 1,000 suffering tuberculosis is vastly different, for example, than if those ten people were part of a population of one million.

Thus one of the most important tasks of the epidemiologist is to determine the prevalence rate—the number of persons out of a particular population who have the disease (prevalence rate). A prevalence rate can represent any time period, e.g., day or hour; and it can refer to an event that happens to different persons at different times, such as complications that occur after drug treatment (on day five for some people or on day two for others).

The incidence rate is the rate at which a disease develops in a group over a period of time. Rather than being a snapshot, the incidence rate describes a continuing process that occurs over a particular period of time.

Period prevalence measures the extent to which one or all diseases affects a group during the course of time, such as a year.

Epidemiologists also measure attributable risk, which is the difference between two incidence rates of groups being compared, when those groups differ in some attribute that appears to cause that difference. For example, the lung cancer mortality rate among a particular population of non-smoking women 50 to 70 years old might be 20/100,000, while the mortality rate among woman in that age range who smoke might be 150/100,000. The difference between the two rates ($150 - 20 = 130$) is the risk that is attributable to smoking, if smoking is the only important difference between the groups regarding the development of lung cancer.

Epidemiologists arrange their data in various ways, depending on what aspect of the information they want to emphasize. For example, a simple graph of the annual occurrence of viral meningitis might show by the "hills" and "valleys" of the line in which years the number of cases increased or decreased. This might provide evidence of the cause and offer ways to predict when the incidence might rise again.

Bar graphs showing differences in rates among months of the year for viral meningitis might pinpoint a specific time of the year when the rate goes up, for example, in summertime. That, in turn, might suggest that specific summertime activities, such as swimming, might be involved in the spread of the disease.

One of the most powerful tools an epidemiologist can use is case reporting: reporting specific diseases to local, state, and national health authorities who accumulate the data. Such information can provide valuable leads as to where, when, and how a disease outbreak is spread, and help health authorities to determine how to halt the progression of an epidemic—one of the most important goals of epidemiology.

Molecular epidemiology has been used to trace the cause of bacterial, viral, and parasitic diseases. This knowledge is valuable in developing a strategy to prevent further outbreaks of the microbial illness, since the probable source of a disease can be identified.

Molecular epidemiology arises from varied scientific disciplines, including genetics, epidemiology, and statistics. The strategies involved in genetic epidemiology encompass population studies and family studies. Sophisticated mathematical tools are now involved, and computer technology is playing a predominant role in the development of the discipline. Multidisciplinary collaboration is crucial to understanding the role of genetic and environmental factors in disease processes.

Much information can come from molecular epidemiology, even in the exact genetic cause of the malady is not known. For example, the identification of a malady in generations of related people can trace the genetic characteristic, and even help identify the original source of the trait. This approach is commonly referred to as genetic screening. The knowledge of why a particular malady appears in certain people, or why such people are more prone to a microbial infection than other members of the population, can reveal much about the nature of the disease in the absence of the actual **gene** whose defect causes the disease.

Various routes can spread infections (i.e., contact, air borne, insect borne, food and water intake, etc.). Likewise, the route of entry of an infectious microbe can also vary from microbe to microbe.

Laboratory analysis techniques can be combined with other techniques to provide information related to the spread of an outbreak. For example, microbiological data can be combined with geographic

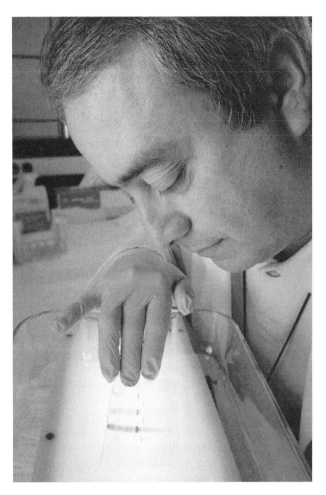

A CDC scientist examines the structural proteins (DNA) of a previously unrecognized coronavirus in a patient with SARS.
© CDC/PHIL/CORBIS

information systems (**GIS**). GIS information has helped pinpoint the source of outbreaks. In addition to geographic based information, epidemiologists will use information including the weather on the days preceding an outbreak, mass transit travel schedules, and schedules of mass-participation events that occurred around the time of an outbreak to try an establish a pattern of movement or behavior to those who have been affected by the outbreak. Use of credit cards and bank debit cards can also help piece together the movements of those who subsequently became infected.

Reconstructing the movements of people is especially important when the outbreak is of an infectious disease. The occurrence of the disease over time can yield information as to the source of an outbreak.

Epidemiologists were among the first scientists to effectively utilize the Internet and email capabilities to effectively communicate regarding disease outbreaks. The International Society for Infectious Diseases sponsors PROMED, a global e-mail based electronic reporting system for outbreaks of emerging infectious diseases and **toxins**, which is open to all sources.

SEE ALSO Anthrax, investigation of 2001 murders; Ebola virus; Pathogens; September 11, 2001, terrorist attacks (forensic investigations of).

Epilepsy

Epilepsy is a neurological disorder, usually characterized by either recurrent or sporadic seizures. Epilepsy presents a particular challenge for forensic scientists because sudden, unexplained death may occur in people with epilepsy, and up to 30% of individuals with epilepsy have no demonstrable **cause of death** at the time of **autopsy**.

Known as both sudden unexplained death syndrome (SUDS) and sudden unexpected death in epilepsy (SUDEP), the condition is often under-recognized. Deaths are sometimes attributed to other causes in people with epilepsy, such as drowning, when in fact, a seizure precipitated events leading to death. One study conducted in Australia in 2003 showed that SUDEP occurs in approximately one person per 200 people with epilepsy per year. Usually, a person with (SUDEP) dies in their sleep. With awareness of the condition growing and funding for research increasing, forensic scientists are assisting in collecting data and other research into unraveling the mystery of SUDEP.

Epileptic seizures are usually convulsive, affecting autonomic reflexes, as well as motor, sensory, and cognitive neuronal (nerve cell) functions. They are caused by the synchronous hyper-excitation of isolated groups of nerve cells in one of the brain cortical areas. Seizures can last from a few seconds up to minutes, depending on the intensity of neuronal excitability.

Epilepsy may be the result of inherited **gene** mutations, metabolic diseases, or brain malformation, or may constitute a major symptom of a neurological disease. When the epilepsy results from an identified cerebral condition, such as cerebral concussion or brain tumor, or is a clinical manifestation of a hereditary neurodegenerative syndrome, it is classified as symptomatic. Non-symptomatic epilepsies are those occurring in persons who do not present brain abnormalities or neurological disorders other than the seizures.

Other types of epilepsy may be induced through occupational damage, due to repeated exposure to acoustic or visual stimuli, or as a result of an isolated high-intensity auditory or visual stimulus. Whatever the case, the sensory stimulation induces chemical changes in the related brain areas, causing a kind of electrical short-circuit, with a group of neurons briefly firing in a synchronous rhythm. These stimuli-induced forms of seizures are known as acquired epilepsy. A dramatic example of seizures induced by repeated sensory stimuli happened in Japan on December 17, 1997, when hundreds of children suffered simultaneous epileptic seizures induced by the flashing red eyes of a Pokemon cartoon character. Epilepsies induced by sensory stimuli are also known as reflex epilepsies.

Absence epilepsy (e.g., non-convulsive epilepsy) occurs mostly in children between three and eight years of age, usually disappearing in adolescence. Non-convulsive epileptic episodes may happen one or more times a day, being characterized by a brief impairment of consciousness, absence of response to external stimuli, "stargazed" expression, and spatial disorientation. However, in contrast to reflex epilepsies, it cannot be induced by sensory stimulation. Convulsive forms of epilepsy are generally preceded by a brief state of dizziness, or external sensory shutdown, followed by convulsion. After convulsion, the person also experiences confusion, poor body equilibrium, and a few minutes of spatial disorientation.

Ignorance and prejudice in the past led to the popular and institutional belief that epilepsy was a kind of mental illness or disability that required institutionalization in psychiatric hospitals. It was also believed that some epileptic individuals entered in a state of somnambulism (unawareness) during the seizures and could commit crimes, which they could not recollect later. Thanks to the advances in neurosciences in the last fifty years, such assumptions have been disproved. However, popular prejudice and legal confusion still persist as to the degree of legal responsibility of epileptic offenders, both from the prosecution and the defense point of view. **Expert witnesses** in neurology and **psychiatry** are often requested to evaluate epileptic defendants and to inform the court about the nature of the disorder and the characteristics of seizures. In most developed countries, epileptic seizures are not considered a legal impediment for the full fruition of individual civil rights and liberties.

Epilepsy treatment usually requires the regular intake of controlled anti-convulsive medications. Law enforcement personnel are educated about the different intensities and types of epileptic seizures in order to prevent misinterpreting behavior, such as the appearance of intoxication, exhibited by persons experiencing a seizure or in the immediate recovery period.

SEE ALSO Brain wave scanners; Expert witnesses; Nervous system overview; Neurotransmitters.

Henry Erlich

6/4/1943–
AMERICAN
MOLECULAR BIOLOGIST

Since the early 1980s, Henry A. Erlich has been well-known in the forensic and medical communities for helping to pioneer the research and development of a **polymerase chain reaction** (**PCR**) technique that ultimately lead to a number of important forensic and clinical applications. As a result of the pioneering efforts of Erlich and his team of scientists, the first commercial PCR typing kit was developed specifically for forensic use. Currently, Erlich is the director of the Department of Human Genetics and vice-president of Discovery Research, both for Roche Molecular Systems, Inc.; and the co-director (and co-founder) of the HLA Laboratory at the Children's Hospital Oakland Research Institute—all three located in the San Francisco Bay Area of California.

Erlich grew up in Seattle, Washington. He began his bachelor's of art degree in 1961 at Harvard University in Cambridge, Massachusetts, where he completed his degree in 1965 with a major in biochemical sciences. That same year, Erlich was a research assistant at Yale University in New Haven, Connecticut. Erlich then began his advanced degree, completing his doctor's of philosophy (Ph.D.) degree in 1972 from the University of Washington (Seattle) with a genetics concentration. While working on his degree in 1967, Erlich also worked with street gangs as a Vista volunteer in New Mexico. Erlich did his post-doctoral work in microbial genetics (1972–1975) at Princeton University in New Jersey, where he was employed as a postdoctoral fellow at Princeton's Department of Biology. Erlich did further post-doctoral work in immunogenetics (1975–1979) at Stanford University (California), where he was employed as a postdoctoral fellow at Stanford's Department of Medicine, Division of Immunology.

After completing his postdoctoral studies, Erlich became a scientist at Cetus Corporation, an Oakland-area biopharmaceutical/biotechnology company located in Emeryville, California, where he held various teaching positions and served on the editorial boards of such industry publications as *Human Immunology*, *PCR Methods and Applications*, and *Technique*. Erlich was later promoted to senior scientist and director of the Human Genetics Department, both positions that he held until 1991.

During his early-1980s work with Cetus, Erlich led the human genetics group in the research of PCR techniques. He was especially interested in developing technology for the study of human genetic variation, and with it the applications in forensics and clinical medicine. In 1986, Erlich's research resulted in development of a PCR technique that ultimately produced a number of clinical and forensic applications. Also in 1986, in what is generally considered the first use of PCR-based forensic **DNA** (deoxyribonucleic acid) analysis in a U.S. court case, Erlich carried out the confirmation that two **autopsy** samples came from the same person in the case *Pennsylvania v. Pestinikas*. About two years later, Erlich and his scientific team saw the development of a commercial PCR typing kit as the first forensic application within the United States of DNA typing of HLA-DQA (human leukocyte **antigen** with a DQ alpha PCR test) locus.

Erlich transferred to Roche Molecular Systems, Inc., located in Alameda, California, in 1991 when the company acquired the rights of PCR technology from Cetus. Today, Erlich holds three important positions with Roche: director of Roche's Human Genetics Department, since 1992; co-director of the HLA Laboratory at the Children's Hospital Oakland Research Institute (CHORI), in Oakland, California, since 1996; and vice president of Roche's Discovery Research, since 2000. Erich's work at CHORI puts into clinical practice the technologies that he had developed for PCR-based HLA typing.

The primary research performed by Erlich in concert with Roche involves the analysis of molecular evolution and population genetics of HLA genes along with human genetic variation and genetic susceptibility to diseases, especially on autoimmune diseases such as type 1 diabetes. He also researches the analysis of polymorphism in HLA genes and the development of HLA typing for class I and class II loci within tissue typing and transplantation, anthropological genetics, and individual **identification**.

Erlich maintains an academic affiliation with the Stanford School of Medicines, where he is an adjunct professor of medical microbiology and immunology. In addition, he also sits on several editorial boards (such as *Human Mutation* and *Tissue Antigens*); participates on numerous human genetics committees

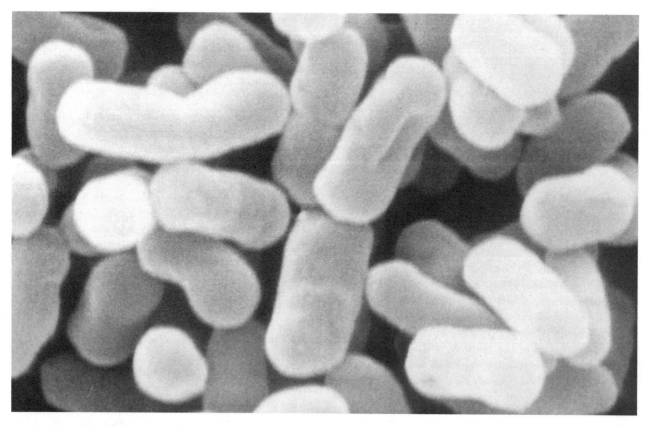

Scanning electron micrograph of Escherichia Coli (E. coli), irregular short tubes in shades of gold/yellow, resemble irregular soft medicine capsules. © 1997 CUSTOM MEDICAL STOCK PHOTO. REPRODUCED BY PERMISSION.

(such as the International Histocompatibility Council and the National Commission on the Future of DNA Evidence-Research and Development Working Group); and is a member of the American Society for Histocompatibility and Immunogenetics and the American Society for Human Genetics. Erlich has authored several books, with one of the latest titled *PCR Technology: Principles and Applications for DNA Amplification.*

Erlich has also been bestowed with many honors within genetic research and writing including such awards as the Gideon Goldstein Award (Walter and Eliza Institutes, 1989), the Biochemical Analysis Award (German Society of Clinical Chemistry, 1990), the Brown-Hazen Award (Wadsworth Center for Laboratories and Research, 1990), The Rose Payne Award (American Society of Histocompatibility Immunogenetics, 1990), the Advanced Technology in Biotechnology Milano Award (International Federation of Clinical Chemistry, 1991), the Award for Excellence (Association for Molecular Pathology, 2000), the Profiles in DNA Courage Award (**National Institute of Justice**, 2000), and the Colonel Harland

Sanders Award (March of Dimes Clinical Genetics Conference, 2000).

SEE ALSO DNA; PCR (polymerase chain reaction).

Escherichia coli

Forensic investigations of a food- or water-related outbreak of disease will often focus on select bacteria. One bacterium often associated with contaminated food is *Escherichia coli.*

Escherichia coli (*E. coli*) is one of the most well-known and intensively studied bacteria. It normally inhabits the intestinal tract of humans and other warm-blooded mammals. *E. coli* constitutes approximately 0.1% of the total bacteria in the adult intestinal tract.

Despite its intestinal habitat, some types (strains) of *E. coli* cause diarrhea and gastroenteritis (an inflammation of the intestinal tract) in infants. If these more infectious types are present in water or food that is ingested, then an infection can result. The vast majority of the many types of *E. coli* are harmless to humans.

When *E. coli* is excreted from the intestinal tract, the bacteria are able to survive only a few hours. This characteristic of rapid death was recognized at the beginning of the twentieth century, when the bacterium began to be used as an indicator of fecal pollution of water. The presence of large numbers of *E. coli* in water is a strong indicator of recent fecal pollution, and so the possible presence of other intestinal bacteria that cause serious disease (i.e., Vibrio, Salmonella, Shigella). Even today, *E. coli* remains one of the important tests of water quality.

In 1975, the United States **Centers for Disease Control and Prevention** identified a new strain of *E. coli* that was designated O157:H7. Strain O157:H7 was first linked to human disease in 1983, when it was shown to have caused two outbreaks of a severe gastrointestinal illness in the Unites States. This strain is capable of causing severe, even lethal, infection. Those who recover sometimes have permanent kidney damage.

The origin of O157:H7 is not known for certain. The consensus among researchers, however, is that O157:H7 arose when a strain of *E. coli* living in the intestine and which was not disease causing became infected by a virus. The virus carried the **gene** coding for a powerful toxin called Shiga-like toxin. Thus, the *E. coli* acquired the ability to produce the toxin.

The toxin can destroy the cells that line the intestinal tract and can enter the bloodstream and migrate to the kidneys and liver. Severe damage to these organs can occur. The intestinal damage causes severe bleeding, which can be lethal in children and elderly people. During the summer of 2000, *E. coli* O157:H7 contaminated the drinking water of the town of Walkerton, Ontario, Canada. Over 2,000 people became ill and seven people died. The source of the strain was the intestinal tract of cattle, a known natural habitat of O157:H7.

SEE ALSO Air and water purity; Bacterial biology; Food supply; Water contamination.

Ethical issues

Professional **forensic science** organizations promulgate codes of ethics for their members. An example is the code of ethics of the American Society of Crime Lab Directors (ASCLD), developed in 2004,

which states in part, "…as members of the American Society of Crime Laboratory Directors, we will strive to foster an atmosphere within our laboratories which will actively encourage our employees to understand and follow ethical practices. Further, we shall endeavor to discharge our responsibilities toward the public, our employers, our employees and the profession of forensic science in accordance with the ASCLD Guidelines for Forensic Laboratory Management Practices."

Any code of ethics articulates high ideals for its profession, but wide gaps can emerge between ideals and the reality of professional practice as it is carried out by fallible, and sometimes dishonest, human beings. Forensic science has not proven itself immune from these gaps.

For example, consider the performance of crime labs. The federal Clinical Laboratory Improvement Act established minimum standards for clinical laboratories in 1967, and the law was toughened in 1988. Both times, though, forensic laboratories remained exempt from the law, largely because it was assumed that such labs did not need such regulation. Under public pressure, though, the ASCLD in 1981 created an accreditation arm for the nation's some 400 crime labs. Fifteen years later, just 138 of those labs had earned accreditation, and the ASCLD refuses to release information about any labs that have applied for but failed to gain accreditation.

Meanwhile, studies have documented alarming levels of error in the nation's crime labs, leading molecular biologist Eric Lander to note: "Clinical laboratories must meet higher standards to be allowed to diagnose strep throat than forensic laboratories must meet to put a defendant on death row." While many of these errors result from simple human error, many represent a pattern of ethical lapses. In 1994, *USA Today* documented 85 cases over a 20–year period in which prosecutors had deliberately falsified **evidence**; during the same period at least 48 people were freed from death row when it was discovered that they were convicted on the basis of false evidence or that the prosecution had deliberately withheld potentially exculpatory forensic evidence.

Further, anecdotal cases of ethical lapses abound. A police forensic expert hired by the West Virginia State Police crime lab and later by the county medical examiner's office in San Antonio testified for 15 years, often in capital cases, about lab tests he had never run. A West Texas **medical examiner** faked over 100 autopsies and falsified **blood** and **toxicology** reports. An examiner in the **FBI** crime lab's

serology unit, who repeated lied under oath about his credentials, was found to have faked lab reports, including reports of blood analyses he never conducted, and to have issued reports confirming the guilt of suspects when he had ignored or distorted actual test results.

These ethical lapses could be dismissed as aberrations, but doing so does not erase the central ethical concern that confronts forensic science each day, the inherent conflict between science and advocacy. Scientists are dispassionate observers, not advocates for one side or the other. As scientists, forensic examiners are ethically obligated by the profession to follow the evidence wherever it leads, without bending to pressure from judges, prosecutors, the police, or the public to find results that serve their purposes. Scientists follow documented and widely accepted protocols in carrying out their work rather than working from an oral tradition that prevents outsiders from examining and questioning their methods. Scientists must follow the scientific method, which demands peer review so that other scientists can expose flaws in theories and procedures. At the heart of the scientific method is the criterion of "falsifiability." This criterion requires that for a theory to prove that X caused Y (e.g., that the defendant's gun fired the bullet), it has to state not only what is true (the markings on the bullet prove that it came from the defendant's gun), but also imply that other things could not be true (the markings could not have come from another gun). If those "other things" do in fact turn out to be true or could be true, the original theory has to be abandoned. All of this at the heart of the scientific method.

Forensic science is sometimes accused of being an arm of the prosecution—whose function is advocacy, not science—in large part because most forensic investigators are not independent experts. Estimates are that 80% of forensic examiners work in police laboratories, and most of the 80% and their superiors are law enforcement officers. As James Starrs, a law and forensic science professor at George Washington University, has noted, "They analyze material submitted, on all but rare occasions, solely by the prosecution. They testify almost exclusively on behalf of the prosecution... As a result, their impartiality is replaced by a viewpoint colored brightly with prosecutorial bias."

Rule 16 of the Federal Rules of Criminal Procedure states that all "results and reports" of forensic examiners are "discoverable" to the defense, meaning that the prosecution has to provide them to defense attorneys on demand so that they can examine the reports rather than having to accept the testimony of forensic examiners at face value. Some members of the forensic science and criminal justice communities consider Rule 16 problematic in two main areas. First, not all "results and reports" are written, or if they are, they are often brief and conclusory, sometimes deliberately so. Nothing requires forensic examiners to document their methods and procedures, so the defense sometimes has no meaningful way to examine "results and reports" that do not exist anywhere on paper. Some forensic labs have resisted inquiries into their methods and procedures; by committing as little as possible to paper they protect themselves from potentially damaging questions.

Another concern with Rule 16 is that it does not mention such items as notes, calculations, graphs, computer printouts, and other records made during testing. The courts have consistently ruled that these items are not discoverable because they do not represent the end product of forensic examination, "results and reports." During the 1983 trial of Wayne Williams, the Atlanta man accused of killing some 30 young African Americans, a hair and fiber expert testified for 11 days from bench notes, which the court ruled were not discoverable by the defense. Another expert testified about graphs produced during comparison of **fibers** from Williams's bedroom carpet and fibers found on the victims' clothing, but again the court ruled that those graphs were not discoverable. Further, defendants have no automatic legal right to test or retest evidence themselves, and labs have no legal duty to preserve records, including reports, bench notes, printouts, and the like, nor are they required to preserve **physical evidence** for later retesting.

In 1971, law professor James Starrs made proposals to solve these ethical problems at the institutional level. Among other things, he called for "full and complete disclosure of the entire case in a comprehensive and well-documented report," a requirement that forensic scientists "testify to the procedures undertaken and the results disclosed only when opinions can be stated in terms of reasonable scientific certainty," and a requirement that "a forensic scientist for the prosecution should permit the defense to interview him/her before the trial" without the need for the prosecutor's approval. In the years that followed, some of these proposals have been incorporated into forensic codes of ethics.

SEE ALSO American Academy of Forensic Sciences; Forensic science.

European Network of Forensic Science Institutes

Formed in 1992, The European Network of Forensic Science Institutes (ENFSI), aims to maintain a high level of forensic science throughout Europe. The initial meeting included eleven members of Western Europe's prominent governmental forensics institutes, who subsequently decided that membership into ENFSI should be open to forensic laboratories throughout Europe. To date, the organization has grown to include members of institutes from 32 European countries and the number continues to grow. Member organizations must fulfill stringent criteria to join and demonstrate high standards of forensic evaluation. Thus, ENFSI has become recognized as an expert group of forensic science institutes and thought leaders from the whole of Europe.

In order to fulfill its vision, "to ensure that the quality of development and delivery of forensic science throughout Europe is at the forefront of the world," ENFSI is structured into Standing Committees and Expert Working Groups. These groups meet on a regular basis and develop activities and guidelines to ensure that the goals of the group are achieved. ENFSI has several standing committees, The Expert Working Group Committee (EWGC), The Quality & Competence Committee (QCC) and The European Academy of Forensic Science (EAFS). The EWGC establishes and maintains the Expert Working Groups which may change in number and title but cover the spectrum of forensic science topics including **DNA**, forensic speech and audio assessment, and **firearms** and **explosives**, just to name a few. The QCC represents ENFSI on quality issues and supports the other committees and groups in terms of quality and international standards. They also develop and maintain laboratory proficiency testing programs for various forensic disciplines. Proficiency tests allow the laboratories to demonstrate the quality of their staff, assays, and organization. In addition, the EAFS establishes activities for the wide forensic community. These include seminars on forensic-related topics as well as annual meetings and other meetings for members of ENFSI. Through the EAFS, relationships are fostered with forensic colleagues worldwide to enable international networking and a true global forensic community.

ENFSI has several meetings a year, some of which are restricted to members only and others that are open to all forensic scientists. During these meetings, the latest forensic technologies are addressed, new standards are considered, and networking is a high priority. In addition to participating in such meetings, the Expert Working Groups meet to develop best practice manuals and guidelines to help to establish and maintain standards of expertise across European forensic laboratories. These documents also provide a framework so that laboratories can utilize common methods and means of considering forensic casework samples. The result is reduction in the complexity of comparing international crime data and samples and a means by which forensic laboratories can demonstrate their proficiency on internationally agreed comparable terms.

ENFSI members also strive to maintain close relationships with other forensic science bodies such as The American Society of Crime Laboratory directors (ASCLD), Senior Managers of Australian and New Zealand Forensic Laboratories (SMANZL), and Academia Iberoamericana de Criminalística y Estudios Forenses (AICEF). Thus, world-wide forensic laboratories have a means of communicating on a truly global and international level. Through these organizations, convergence of standard, common techniques is certain to continue.

One of the main goals of ENFSI is to maintain the highest standards of forensic work across Europe. Forensic laboratories are constantly under scrutiny to demonstrate the quality of their work. However, this is not always straightforward due to the confidentiality under which forensic casework samples must be evaluated. Furthermore, the lack of competition among many countries' government forensic laboratories, since they are commissioned, makes them susceptible to criticism and accusations of inadequate standards of evaluation. ENFSI gives these laboratories additional support by helping them maintain high standards. For example, the best practice manuals and ENFSI-approved guidelines detail the accepted methods and techniques. These materials are available to any laboratory, whether members of ENFSI or not. Utilization of these approved guidelines gives the laboratories additional confidence that they are performing to the standard accepted throughout Europe. ENFSI also helps labs with accreditation and best practices as well as the ongoing development of a system to assure competence for ENFSI laboratories.

As the forensic industry continues to grow and prosper, the ENFSI will continue to unite the forensic community across Europe. Their commitment to foster forensic standards and relationships with world-wide partners ensures that the industry as a whole is constantly assessing itself and improving.

SEE ALSO CODIS: Combined DNA Index System; DNA; DNA profiling; STR (short tandem repeat) analysis.

Evidence

Evidence is any item or information gathered at the scene of a crime, or at related locations, which is found to be relevant to an investigation. There are many different types of evidence, from **DNA** and tire marks, to bloodstains and fingerprints. Different kinds of evidence may require different types of expertise in interpretation. Analyzing DNA is a completely different discipline from understanding bite marks or bullet trajectories. However, there are some basic principles that apply to all forms of evidence. Perhaps the most important rule is that maintaining evidence is paramount; strict procedures must be observed by all involved in the investigation when it comes to collecting, labeling, and analyzing it. Above all, every effort must be made to ensure that evidence is not lost, damaged, or contaminated.

Evidence has many different roles in the investigation of a crime. It can link a suspect to a crime scene if, for instance, a footprint matching the shoe of the suspect is found. Evidence can also eliminate a suspect. If the shoe size of the suspect does not match that of footprint evidence, then those footprints cannot tie them to the crime scene. Evidence could also back up or contradict a witness statement, which may help guide the police in further investigations. Evidence such as DNA or fingerprints is also valuable in providing a firm **identification** of a perpetrator or suspect.

Forensic scientists place evidence into various categories. Direct evidence establishes fact without the need for further analysis. Perhaps the most important form of direct evidence is the eyewitness account. If someone saw a **murder**, then there may be nothing to add, although the witness could give false testimony and other evidence may be needed to prove this. **Circumstantial evidence** is more indirect and it is up to the forensic scientist to provide an explanation for it through his or her investigations. Most of the evidence handled in the forensic lab is circumstantial evidence. Although more objective than direct evidence, there is always the danger of losing or contaminating circumstantial evidence.

Forensic evidence is divided up into two basic classes, physical and biological. **Physical evidence** covers items of non-living origin, such as fingerprints, tire marks, footprints, **fibers**, paint, and **building materials**. Biological evidence comes from a living source, usually the victim or perpetrator. Biological evidence includes DNA extracted from **blood** or other bodily **fluids**, **semen**, hair, and **saliva**. Botanical items, such as pollen and plants, would also be considered as biological evidence. Fingerprints are probably the most valued type of physical evidence because of their ability to identify or eliminate a suspect. However, as DNA analysis technology becomes increasingly automated and rapid, it is likely that forensic investigators will place more emphasis on the collection of biological evidence.

In terms of the investigation as a whole, reconstructive evidence is relevant to understanding what actually happened at the crime scene and the sequence of events. Cast off blood, blood spatters and bullet holes can help determine exactly how the victim was attacked. Tool marks and broken **glass** can reveal how a perpetrator entered and left the scene. Associative evidence is used to create or eliminate a link between a suspect and a crime scene.

There are two kinds of associative evidence, class and individual. Class evidence relates to items that are, to some extent at least, mass-produced. In itself, class evidence cannot tie a crime to any one individual. For instance, a gun found at the crime scene will be of a particular make, but it will not be unique. Similarly, relatively new shoes all make similar footprints if they are the same brand and cannot be tied to any one person. However, if the shoe is worn, then the footprint may be particular to an individual, as people wear down their shoes in a unique way. Fingerprints and DNA are the most significant forms of individual evidence. In all investigations, it is individual evidence that provides the most information and is therefore, the most valued. Class evidence is also important but usually has to be taken in context with other evidence; the more, the better.

Trace evidence may fall into various categories and includes microscopic evidence such as hair, fibers, paint, and bloodstains. **Locard's exchange principle** explains that every contact between a suspect and people or objects at the scene of crime, including the victim, leaves traces. Evidence is transferred from suspect to scene and vice-versa. The suspect may leave their own hair behind and take seemingly invisible splashes of the victim's blood with them, for instance. Trace evidence can be a powerful form of associative evidence that can lead to identification of the perpetrator. Most often, trace evidence is found in the form of textile fibers and paint flakes.

When investigators arrive at the scene of a crime, they are faced with a wide range of evidence—from something as obvious as a body to the various kinds of trace evidence which may be present. All of it must be located, collected and packaged with the greatest care to avoid destroying or contaminated. The investigators will make a "fingertip" search to ensure that every part of the crime scene is searched for evidence. There are various ways of making this search. If a body is present, this will be searched first for trace evidence, like fibers, and swabs will be taken before it is removed. A further search will take place at the mortuary.

The investigators then might work outwards from a focal point, which could be where a body was found, or in towards it. Depending on the size and location of the scene, investigators will go over the ground in a systematic fashion in a specific pattern such as a grid or spiral. Usually two searches are carried out.

The first items to be collected are those which are fragile and could easily be damaged such as fingerprints, **shoeprints**, fibers, and hair. A systematic approach must be taken to ensure that the collection of one item of evidence will not destroy another. Taking casts of footprints is one example. The **casting** process will destroy any fingerprints present. Therefore, the location of the footprint must be dusted first for fingerprints. Some evidence may be invisible to the naked eye and may need special techniques for visualization. **Luminol** can reveal bloodstains and ultraviolet light shows semen stains. The investigators will also take **control samples** for use back in the laboratory to distinguish relevant from irrelevant evidence. For instance, if there are chemicals on a carpet, then samples of unaffected carpet must be taken for comparison. If a blanket was used to cover a corpse, then fibers must be taken to show that these do not have anything to do with the crime. The collection of individualizing evidence such as fingerprints and biological samples for DNA usually takes priority.

Each item of evidence is packaged separately to avoid contamination and damage. Every time an item is transferred from one person to another, it is signed and accounted for. The evidence is handled through a strict **chain of custody**, in other words. If it were not, then it could easily be challenged in court. Just one break in the chain of custody can invalidate the

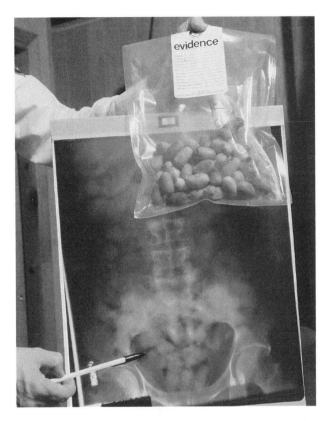

A U.S. customs agent shows x-ray evidence of a drug smuggler's stomach containing capsules of narcotics, along with the narcotics recovered from the smuggler.

claim that the item of evidence was present at the scene or on the suspect and is relevant to the crime.

Of course, the forensic service does not have the resources to investigate all crimes to the extent described above. Volume crime such as burglary is distinguished from serious crime such as rape or murder. In the former case, the search for evidence may be confined to fingerprints. In the latter case, all possible evidence will be collected. The investigators cannot usually go back a second time to collect evidence. Even if it were intact, they could not prove that it had not been placed there after the crime, so it would not be admissible in a court of law. For this reason, it is generally considered important to collect too much evidence rather than too little.

The forensic scientist is charged with answering various key questions about the evidence. First, and most obvious, is identification—what the evidence actually is. On its own, however, the identity of the evidence is insufficient to shed much light on the crime. The next stage is to carry out comparison studies, using the control samples that will be collected. For instance, if bloodstains are found in the suspect's car or on their clothes, samples of blood from the victim are needed so that comparison tests can be made. These can establish whether or not the blood associated with the suspect is that of the victim. Sometimes, however, the evidence will not be of sufficient quality to allow a clear result from the comparison test. The main thrust of the forensic investigators' work is to establish links through evidence—between a suspect and a victim, place, or object. Even if there is no link, then at least the suspect can be eliminated and the investigation narrowed down. Sometimes a link can be created between a suspect and one or more places. A footprint may be found at two or more scenes, for instance. Even if there is not a suspect at this stage, the very existence of this evidence may help police know more about the suspect they are searching for, or the crime they are attempting to solve.

SEE ALSO Analytical instrumentation; Animal evidence; Anthropology; Anthropometry; Artificial fibers; Autopsy; Ballistic fingerprints; Bloodstain evidence; Bite analysis; Crime scene investigation; Crime scene reconstruction; CODIS: Combined DNA Index System; Death, cause of; Decomposition; DNA fingerprint; Entomology; Exhumation; Fingerprint; Hair analysis; Impression evidence; Pathology; Trace evidence.

Evidence, chain of custody

Evidence found at the scene of a crime must eventually be presented and questioned in the courtroom. For the evidence to be of use in a trial, it must make the journey from crime scene to court in a validated and secure manner so that all involved can be assured that it has not been contaminated and that the evidence is relevant to the crime investigation. In order to insure validity, investigators must follow a routine commonly known as the chain of custody when it comes to collecting and handling evidence.

The first person to collect an item of evidence, be it a bloodstain or a bullet, will sign their initials and date either on the item itself or on its packaging. Clearly, marking an item ensures there is no ambiguity, as packaging could be separated from the evidence itself. However, some types of evidence, such as bullets, may be altered if marked and, of course, it is not possible to mark evidence like bloodstains or fingerprints directly.

Evidence usually goes from the crime scene to the forensic laboratory for examination where the receiving officer signs the evidence package and

dates it. Everyone who handles the evidence does likewise until the analysis is complete. At this stage, the evidence will be given to the police for storage until its presentation in court. The receiving police officer will sign for the evidence and it will be stored in a secure area to minimize the risk of interference or loss.

When the case is presented in court, the prosecuting lawyer takes over custody of the evidence and signs to that effect. If the chain of custody procedure is handled correctly, the case can proceed with all involved being aware of the precise journey the evidence took from crime scene to the court. This allows evidence to be admitted in court, and witnesses to have the assurance that the item of evidence was indeed present at the scene of the crime and testify accordingly. The judge and jury are then able to use the evidence, along with witness statements and other information, to guide their decision-making process.

SEE ALSO Crime scene investigation; Cross contamination.

Evidence, circumstantial SEE Circumstantial evidence

Exhumation

Exhumation is the removal of a body from a grave. It is a relatively rare occurrence and can be distressing for relatives. The most common reason for exhumation is need or desire to move the body to a different location. This may happen if a cemetery closing or if the family buys a new burial plot or wishes to re-inter the deceased elsewhere with other family members. However, some cases of exhumation occur because there is a request from a court to carry out or repeat an **autopsy** to gain new forensic **evidence**. This is more likely in countries where the autopsy rate is low. With cremation becoming increasingly common, exhumation is less important than in previous years.

Requirements vary from place to place, but it is usually necessary to obtain a license from the local or higher authorities to perform an exhumation. It is also usual to get the permission of the family of the deceased. The procedure is not without risk to public health, so an environmental health officer is usually present. If the body is buried in consecrated ground, it will be also necessary to obtain permission from

A forensic anthropologist excavates the grave of J. Frank Dalton in Texas. Dalton claimed until his death in 1951 that he was really the outlaw Jesse James and had faked his death 69 years earlier. DNA testing on the exhumed body proved inconclusive. © REUTERS/CORBIS

the church. Obtaining the necessary licenses may sometimes be time-consuming, and it is also very unusual to perform exhumations on people only recently buried.

The environmental health officer, or equivalent, will ensure that the correct grave is opened. If the grave cannot be identified, the exhumation is not carried out and nor is it if the body lies underneath another body which is not to be exhumed. In other words, anything that interferes with the respect due to the body to be exhumed or others buried on the site will be a reason to refuse permission for the exhumation. Proceedings must be carried out in daylight and are planned for a time of day to ensure maximum privacy; the area involved is usually screened. Protective and disposable masks, gowns, and gloves are worn by all involved to protect from any possibility of transmission of disease. Those concerned will take every care to show respect to the corpse. A medical officer should be present and will

examine the body before it is moved and take photographs. This is important because bones may become brittle after they have been buried for some time and may break when moved. The body is usually transferred into a new casket made of timber lined with zinc for security. Pieces of the old casket are transferred, along with the body, to the new casket. The area of exhumation is then thoroughly disinfected. The body is then transferred to its destination as quickly as possible.

There may have been some **decomposition** so any autopsy will need to be performed promptly. The results will rarely be as good as those from an autopsy on a fresh body. However, an autopsy on an exhumed body can still yield some useful information. Although the procedure of performing an autopsy on an exhumed body is basically the same as that for a fresh body, decomposition may mean some modification is necessary. There may be worms or insects present in the corpse, but they should not be sprayed with insecticide or other chemicals as this interferes with tests on the body. There may also be a strong odor when the body is opened, and the investigators might wear gauze masks dipped in potassium permanganate to minimize exposure to particulate matter in the air. Sometimes only bones are left in the grave if the body has been buried for some time. It is the usual practice to boil the bones before autopsy. They can still yield useful information about **cause of death**. However, autopsy on an exhumed body is generally a task for a skilled and experienced pathologist.

Should poisoning be thought to be a factor in the death of the person involved, samples of soil from above, below, and to the sides of the coffin should be taken and sent for **toxicological analysis**. A control sample would also be taken from another part of the cemetery. Many exhumation cases have involved investigation of possible arsenic poisoning, a less common cause of **murder** these days. Arsenic remains in the body for a long time, so it can be detected after burial. For example, it was long held by some historians that the twelfth President of the United States, Zachary Taylor, died from arsenic poisoning rather than by natural causes. Exhumation took place 141 years after his death. Extremely sensitive tests showed that levels of arsenic in his body were normal; poisoning was not involved in his death. Other exhumation cases have, however, proved the opposite. It is particularly important to take soil samples in the case of arsenic poisoning for comparison. Otherwise it is not possible to know if arsenic entered the body from the soil or by poisoning.

SEE ALSO Anthropology; Autopsy; Decomposition; Skeletal analysis; Toxicology; War forensics.

Exothermic reactions

An exothermic reaction is a chemical reaction that produces heat. The term exothermic is composed of the root *exo*, which is Greek for outside, and *thermic*, which means heat. Therefore, exothermic defines heat going outside. Exothermic reactions are important to forensic sciences and particularly to fire and explosion investigation. When a chemical reaction requires heat (rather than producing it) and results in cooling down the surroundings, it is conversely called endothermic.

Exothermic reactions occur in many phenomena and applications of every-day life. The speed at which

they occur can range from extremely slow to extremely fast. For example, an exothermic reaction occurs when a piece of steel rusts. Rust is iron oxide (Fe_2O_3), which is produced by the reaction of iron (Fe) with oxygen (O_2). This reaction releases heat and is therefore, exothermic. However, it takes place at such a slow pace that it is impossible to observe a difference of temperature on the piece of steel. Fire is an exothermic reaction that occurs much faster. When a fuel is burning, it releases heat, which can easily be felt. An explosion is also an exothermic reaction. Even if the end result of an explosion is the high pressure generated that pushes everything away from its seat, heat is first produced in great magnitude.

All combustion reactions are exothermic. In a **fire investigation**, it is important to know what kind of chemical reaction occurred and caused a fire. In order to do that, it is necessary to know the substances involved and how they react with one another. Some reactions also require a threshold amount of energy given to them before they can release (more) energy. This is called the energy of activation. For example, it is necessary to light wood on fire with a lighter or matches before it will burn and liberate heat.

Finally, it is possible to measure the amount of heat or energy liberated by a given chemical reaction. In order to do this, an instrument called a calorimeter is used. The calorimeter is a container placed in a well-insulated water bath. A known amount of the substance or substances that will react is placed in the container and the reaction takes place. Ideally, all the heat generated by the reaction is transferred to the water, whose temperature increases. By monitoring the temperature of the water, it is possible to accurately measure the amount of heat liberated.

SEE ALSO Chemical equations; Explosives.

Expert witnesses

Many criminal and civil investigations turn to expert witnesses in court to help resolve cases where the facts are unclear or in need of some explanation. An expert witness is a person who can provide information and opinion drawn from the body of knowledge that makes up their own area of expertise. An expert witness does not need to be legally qualified. Commonly the witness will be a forensic scientist or forensic pathologist providing information outside the realm of common knowledge about the circumstances of a crime. For instance, a scientist with knowledge of **paint analysis** or soil can help interpret **trace evidence**. A pathologist can help with the difficult questions such as the **cause of death** when a body is recovered from water or what **bloodstain evidence** might really mean in terms of how someone was killed.

Being an expert witness is not a profession in its own right. The expert witness is created and recognized as such by the judge and the court. There are many databases of people willing to act as expert witnesses in various specialties, and they also have their own professional organizations to represent their interests. The expert witness will have been vetted for suitability; they will also have undergone **training** in court procedures so that **evidence** may be given to the best of their ability to help the judge and jury come to a decision. Although many expert witnesses come from a **forensic science** or medical discipline, they can be drawn from any area of expertise, depending on the circumstances and background of the case. Document examiners and structural engineers may be called in to advise and give evidence, as may those from non-scientific disciplines as diverse as art history, mountaineering, or martial arts.

Either prosecution or the defense may call in an expert witness. He or she is expected to look at the evidence relevant to their discipline and put it in the context of the whole case. They will produce a report that can be taken up into the witness stand. First of all, the party who engaged the expert witness will ask questions that prove identity, experience, and background to the court. Then they will ask questions that generally take the court through the expert witness' report.

The expert witness can expect to be cross-examined by the opposing counsel. That is, an expert witness for the prosecution will be questioned by lawyers for the defense, and vice-versa. The other side may also engage their own expert witness. The purpose of cross-examination is to find flaws in the evidence and conclusions presented by the expert witness. Many people are experts in their own subjects, but it takes special skill and training to defend one's findings in public while still remaining objective and impartial.

The expert witness has a large responsibility, as the manner of giving evidence can influence the judge and jury—the decision makers in the case. Expert testimony is especially important when other evidence is insufficient to help come to a clear verdict. At the same time, in a stalemate situation, the expert

A forensic pathologist serves as an expert witness during the trial of convicted sniper John Allen Muhammad in 2003. © DAVIS TURNER/CORBIS

witness must remain completely unbiased. Expert witnesses have a duty to give concise, detailed, and clear answers to all the questions put to them. After all, the jury often consists of lay people who may have had little or no experience in **medicine**, building construction, or the many other subjects that are often relevant in a crime. The judge is, naturally, more knowledgeable about crime and its circumstances, from his or her experience. However, there will be cases in which the judge also needs more information about what may have occurred and how. The expert witness performs a vital role in helping judge and jury come to the right conclusions about what really happened at a crime scene.

The expert witness is the only one in court who is allowed to give opinion as well as facts. This is because the court has confidence in the facts and knowledge on which the opinion is based. Thus, the forensic psychiatrist is allowed to say, "I believe this man to be capable of this **murder**, with this degree of violence, based upon my assessment of his mental state." With other evidence, that opinion may be what is required for judge and jury to make up their minds in the case.

SEE ALSO Evidence.

Explosives

An explosive is defined as a substance or mixture of substances that is capable of producing an explosion by itself, without the need for an outside source of oxygen. An explosion is a rapid oxidation reaction that liberates a large quantity of energy and is accompanied by the evolution of a large volume of hot gases and a loud noise. Explosives are often used in criminal and, more particularly, terrorist activities. Crime scene investigators and forensic scientists are called to the scene of an explosion to determine if an explosive was used, and thus, what kind of explosive was used and how it was used. Therefore, knowledge of explosives and their characteristics is paramount for a forensic scientist involved in such criminal investigations.

In general, explosives are classified into two categories: low explosives and high explosives. Low explosives are characterized by a slow rate of reaction, also said to be rapid combustion, resulting in a deflagration. Deflagration is defined as an explosion whose resulting pressure wave travels at subsonic speed (less than 340 meters, or 1,115 feet, per second). These explosives are usually designed to produce a push or to heave a mass. These explosives are also referred to as propellants. Examples of such explosives are black powder, and single-, double-, and triple-base gun powder.

High explosives are characterized by a high rate of reaction resulting in a detonation. Detonation is defined as an explosion whose resulting pressure wave travels at supersonic speed (more than 340 meters, or 1,115 feet, per second). High explosives create a powerful blasting or shattering effect.

High explosives are further classified into primary and secondary explosives depending on their susceptibility to be initiated. Primary explosives are very sensitive to heat or shock and undergo a rapid transition to detonation. They are used to provide the minimum necessary energy to initiate the secondary explosives. Examples of primary explosives include lead azide, lead styphnate, mercury fulminate, and diazodinitrophenol (DDNP). Secondary explosives are much more stable and require a higher initiation energy to be detonated. They will only be detonated by an explosion, such as the one created by a primary explosive. Nevertheless, they are generally more powerful than primary explosives and are thus, mostly used as main charges. Examples of secondary high explosives are 2,4,6-trinitrotoluene (TNT), ammonium nitrate fuel oil (ANFO), cyclotrimethylenetrinitramine (RDX), cyclotetramethylenetetranitra-

mine (HMX), ethyleneglycoldinitrate (EGDN), and pentaerythritoltetranitrate (PETN). Secondary high explosives are designed to destruct by a shattering effect.

Most explosives are used in a combination of two or more explosives, adding the effects of the different types of explosives to the mixture. Dynamite was originally nitroglycerine absorbed into dry silica. Modern formulations of dynamite present some variations, but usually include a mixture of nitroglycerine, nitrocellulose, a fuel/oxidizer mixture, and sometimes EGDN. Semtex is a mixture of RDX and PETN. Amatol is composed of TNT and ammonium nitrate. C-4 is a plasticized composition of RDX. Pentolite is a mixture of TNT and PETN.

Detonating cords are plastic tubes filled with a powder form of explosive. These tubes are often wrapped with fibers to make them more solid. They are mostly used to link different charges by transmitting the shock wave of the detonation. They may also be used as an explosive charge by themselves. In such instances, they are typically used to perform small and accurate destruction. Detonating cords typically use PETN as their explosive content. In some instances, when the cord needs to be used in a medium with a high temperature where PETN would not be suitable, other explosives such as RDX or HMX may be used.

Boosters are defined as the components in the explosion train that propagate and amplify the shockwave from the detonator to the main charge. They are necessary with some secondary explosives that are insensitive and the shockwave created by the detonator would not be enough to initiate the main charge. Thus, the booster is placed after the detonator and amplifies this detonation, initiating the main charge. Examples of boosters are pentolite or tetryl (2,4,6-trinitrophenyl-methylnitramine).

The forensic analysis of explosives has two interests. On intact material, it is to determine if the material is an explosive. On explosive residues, it is to determine the nature of the explosive and to profile its origin. Identifying the nature of the explosive involved may lead to the author of the crime. Explosives are usually regulated and controlled by the government. Thus, they are not easily obtained by regular citizens. Explosives are often stolen or smuggled from one country to another. Once the nature of the explosives used is identified, it is possible to relate it to recorded thefts or smuggled activities. Some terrorist groups have been known to use one particular explosive consistently, thus allowing the investigation to head one direction or another.

Italian forensic officers carry out a search after a small package of explosives blew up at a language school in Rome on June 17, 2003. The package contained around 500 grams (1.1 lbs) of high explosive powder stuffed into a small metal cylinder. © REUTERS/CORBIS

Also, when several explosions occur over a certain time span, it is possible to establish links between them if the same explosives have been used.

SEE ALSO Air plume and chemical analysis; Analytical instrumentation; Biodetectors; Bomb damage, forensic assessment; Bomb (explosion) investigations; Gas chromatograph-mass spectrometer; Oklahoma bombing (1995 bombing of Alfred P. Murrah building); September 11, 2001, terrorist attacks (forensic investigations of); Unabomber case and trial; World Trade Center, 1993 terrorist attack.

Explosives (historical cases)

Some of the most significant and tragic events in the history of the last few hundred years have involved **explosives** in the form of bombs—devices used in a deliberate attempt to harm others. The forensic investigation of these incidents has often been a multi-disciplinary affair. Explosives experts and fire investigators are needed to analyze the event itself and discover what kind of device was used and where it may have originated. Bombs typically cause multiple injuries that can be challenging for the forensic pathologist to assess. There has also increas-

ingly been a role for the forensic psychiatrist, as some of those responsible for a bombing are clearly mentally disturbed.

Bombs are often planted by those with political motivations or grudges, working as a group or alone. Their actions, or even the threat of them, cause a great deal of public anxiety and are remembered for a long time. In Britain, one of the first major explosion attempts, the 1605 Gunpowder Plot, is now remembered in the annual celebration of Guy Fawkes, or Bonfire, Night on the fifth of November. Guy Fawkes and his co-conspirators were extremists who wanted to return England to the Catholic faith by blowing up the Houses of Parliament, killing King James I and his government. This bold plan involved rolling 36 barrels into the cellars of the Houses of Parliament. However, one of the group sent a warning letter to a friend in Parliament and this was intercepted and handed to the King. The group was arrested before they could ignite the gunpowder and put to death after trial.

On Bonfire Night, people in Britain burn effigies of Guy Fawkes on bonfires and set off fireworks to commemorate the would-be explosions. It is all harmless fun, many firework displays are now organized by local authorities in the interests of public safety.

In the twentieth century, Britain has suffered terrible losses of life through the bombings of the Irish Republican Army (IRA), a group wanting the re-unification of Northern Ireland and the Irish Republic. On November 21, 1974, bombs exploded in two pubs in central Birmingham, The Mulberry Bush and the Tavern in the Town, killing 21 people and injuring another 182. This was one of the worst IRA atrocities and of special interest because of some forensic issues it raises. The IRA at first claimed responsibility for the bombings, then withdrew their statement. It is widely assumed the group was behind the attack. Police arrested six men known to have associations with IRA personnel in connection with the bombings and they were convicted in 1975. However, the "Birmingham Six" were freed on appeal in 1991. Police and prison officers were found to have extracted false confessions and there was, in fact, no hard **evidence** of any kind linking the men to the bombing scene. Forensic evidence at the trial had included a positive Griess test for traces of explosives on the hands of two of the suspects. In fact, the results of these tests proved inconclusive and were the subject of some dispute between the forensic experts engaged on the case. No-one else has ever been convicted of the Birmingham pub bombings.

Letter bombs are often the work of one individual who wishes to terrorize others, for whatever reason. Perhaps the most famous case of letter bomb crime involved Theodore Kaczynski, also known as the Unabomber. In the first Unabomber incident, a package found in a University of Illinois parking lot in Chicago on May 25, 1978, exploded, injuring one person. Several similar incidents followed. The first fatality occurred on December 11, 1985, when the owner of a computer company picked up a bomb left outside his business.

A sighting of the Unabomber in 1987 led to a cessation of attacks until 1993 when Kaczynski revealed his anarchist views in a letter to the *New York Times*. After more bombings and fatalities, the Unabomber was finally caught on April 3, 1996. Forensic psychiatrist Sally Johnson declared Kaczynski fit to stand trial even though he was diagnosed as a paranoid schizophrenic. He was convicted and sentenced to life imprisonment without parole.

Britain's worst ever terrorist incident involved the placing of a bomb on Pam Am Flight 103 over Lockerbie, Scotland, on December 21, 1988. None of the 259 crewmembers and passengers on board survived. Forensic investigation revealed that the U.S.-based plane was brought down by a bomb placed in one of the overhead lockers. The plane disintegrated in mid-air, creating 1,200 significant items of debris needing to be investigated. Larger items, such as the engines and the aircraft wings, fell on the town of Lockerbie, producing a fireball and killing 11 people on the ground. Lighter debris was scattered for many miles.

Forensic scientists discovered traces of explosive material in the debris and were able to reconstruct the explosion and the impact it had on the plane. Post-mortem examination of the victims revealed they died of multiple injuries consistent with a mid-air explosion followed by impact on the ground. A former Libyan intelligence officer called Abdel Bassett al-Megrahi was convicted of the bombing and is serving a life sentence in Scotland.

The terror attacks of September 11, 2001, were not the first suffered at New York's World Trade Center. On February 26, 1993, a car bomb was planted in the underground garage below Tower One, killing six people when it went off and injuring over 1,000 others. Analysis revealed the 1300-pound bomb was composed of urea, nitroglycerin, sulfuric acid, aluminium azide, and bottled hydrogen gas. The device was placed in a van and attached to four fuses which the perpetrator, a Kuwaiti man called Ramzi Yousef, ignited with a cigarette lighter. He escaped to

Pakistan after the explosion and was involved in many other terrorist attacks before his capture in 1995. He is now held in the same prison as the Unabomber, the ADX Florence maximum security facility in Colorado.

ADX Florence is also the prison where the Oklahoma bomber Timothy McVeigh was held prior to his execution in 2001. Until the attacks of September 11, the **Oklahoma bombing**, in the nine-story Alfred P. Murrah local government building, was the worst terror incident on U.S. soil. It killed 168 people and injured more than 500 others. The homemade bomb was found to have 2,200 kilograms of ammonium nitrate and fuel oil packed into a hired van. McVeigh, a former soldier, was said to be obsessed with guns and mistrustful of authority. His motive was, apparently, to retaliate against the U.S. government for its part in a siege by the Bureau of Alcohol, Tobacco, and Firearms (**ATF**) in Waco, Texas, where 82 members of the Davidian sect were killed.

After September 11, there were two major terror attacks involving bomb explosions, one in Bali and one in Madrid, Spain. The Bali bombing occurred on October 12, 2002, in Paddy's Bar, in the town of Kuta, killing 202 people and injuring another 209, most of them foreign tourists. An electronically-triggered bomb ripped through the bar, driving the injured into the street. A few seconds later, a second, and much more powerful, car bomb went off in front of the Sari Club. This main bomb proved to be made of ammonium nitrate. In 2003, four men were sentenced to death for their part on the bombing, although the sentences have not yet been carried out as of March 2005.

On March 11, 2004, in Madrid, Spain, 191 people died when a string of ten bombs placed in backpacks and carried on four separate commuter trains went off. Later, three more backpack bombs were safely detonated; they had been timed to go off when rescuers and investigators would have been on the scene. More than 1,500 people were injured and many call the event "Spain's 9/11." It is certainly proving a challenge for forensic investigators and reveals how complex a business global terrorism has become.

Twenty-two suspects are being held in Spain and there is debate as to whether an Islamic fundamentalist group like Al Qaeda or the Basque separatist group ETA was responsible for the blasts. The explosive used in the train bombs was a type of dynamite sold in Spain and used in mining. The material resembles that previously used by ETA, although it is a more modern version. Analysis of the backpack bombs showed the explosive was reinforced with shrapnel, and investigators also found a detonator with a cell phone and a timer. The phones have proved a particularly useful source of evidence. Later, a similar unexploded bomb was found on a railway line at Mocejon, 40 miles south of Madrid. The devices had detonators of the type used in the mining industry, although they were made of copper, which is regarded as more sophisticated than the aluminum versions normally used by the ETA group.

The investigation of the Madrid bombings has covered other possibly related incidents, including the discovery in the previous month of a van with 500 kilograms of explosives, and the prevention of a similar attack where multiple bombs would have gone off simultaneously on the commuter trains system. Both of these incidents involved ETA. On the other hand, the near simultaneous attacks of the Madrid bombings were more typical of Al Qaeda. The attack was larger in scale than anything ETA has ever carried out before. Like the IRA, the group generally accompanies its attacks with warnings and claims responsibility for them. In the case of the Madrid bombings, ETA has denied involvement. It is up to the court, backed by expert evidence, to decide who is responsible and, it is to be hoped, convict the perpetrators. **Forensic science** can do much to help in the "war against terror" as experience is gained through the investigation of the dreadful events of recent years.

SEE ALSO Bomb damage, forensic assessment; Bomb detection devices; Bomb (explosion) investigations.

Facial recognition

Facial recognition is a biometric method of identifying a person based on a photograph of their face. Biometric methods use biological traits to identify people. The human eye is naturally able to recognize people by looking at them. However, it recognizes known people much more easily than perfect strangers. Moreover, concentration span for a human eye is limited. As a result, it is not useful in longer surveillance tasks or comparing hundreds of images to find a match to a photograph. Therefore, computerized methods have been developed to perform the facial recognition. **Identification** of faces is important for security, surveillance, and in forensics.

Biometric methods have been under development since the late 1980s. In the 1990s the first commercial systems appeared on the market. The first large trial of the technology was in 2000, during Super Bowl XXXV in Tampa Bay, Florida. Spectators were photographed, without their knowledge, as they entered the stadium. The images were then compared to a police database.

Currently, the technology is used by police, forensic scientists, governments, private companies, the military, and casinos. The police use facial recognition for identification of criminals. Companies use it for securing access to restricted areas. Casinos use facial recognition to eliminate cheaters and dishonest money counters. Finally, in the United States, nearly half of the states use computerized identity verification, while the National Center for Missing and Exploited Children uses the technique to find **missing children** on the Internet. In Mexico, a voter database was compiled to prevent vote fraud. Facial recognition technology can be used in a number of other places, such as airports, government buildings, and ATMs (automatic teller machines), and to secure computers and mobile phones.

Computerized facial recognition is based on capturing an image of a face, extracting features, comparing it to images in a database, and identifying matches. As the computer cannot see the same way as a human eye can, it needs to convert images into numbers representing the various features of a face. The sets of numbers representing one face are compared with numbers representing another face.

The quality of the computer recognition system is dependent on the quality of the image and mathematical algorithms used to convert a picture into numbers. Important factors for the image quality are light, background, and position of the head. Pictures can be taken of a still or moving subjects. Still subjects are photographed, for example by the police (mug shots) or by specially placed security **cameras** (access control). However, the most challenging application is the ability to use images captured by surveillance cameras (shopping malls, train stations, ATMs), or closed-circuit television (**CCTV**). In many cases the subject in those images is moving fast, and the light and the position of the head is not optimal.

The techniques used for facial recognition can be feature-based (geometrical) or template-based (photometric). The geometric method relies on the shape and position of the facial features. It analyzes each of the facial features, also known as nodal points, independently; it then generates a full picture of a face. The most commonly used nodal points are: distance between the eyes, width of the nose, cheekbones, jaw line, chin, and depth of the eye sockets. Although there are about 80 nodal points on the face, most software measures have only around a quarter of them. The points picked by the software to measure have to be able to uniquely differentiate between people. In contrast, the image or photometric-based methods create a template of the features and use that template to identify faces.

Algorithms used by the software tools are proprietary and are secret. The most common methods used are eigenfaces, which are based on principal component analysis (PCA) to extract face features. The analysis can be very accurate, as many features can be extracted and all of the image data is analyzed together; no information is discarded. Another common method of creating templates is using neural networks. Despite continuous improvements, none of the current algorithms is 100% correct. The best verification rates are about 90% correct. At the same time, the majority of systems claim 1% false accept rates. The most common reasons for the failures are: sensitivity of some methods to lighting, facial expressions, hairstyles, hair color, and facial hair.

Despite the differences in mathematical methods used, the face recognition analysis follows the same set of steps. The first step is image acquisition; once the image is captured, a head is identified. In some cases, before the feature extraction, it might be necessary to normalize the image. This is accomplished by scaling and rotating the image so that the size of the face and its positioning is optimal for the next step. After the image is presented to the computer, it begins feature extraction using one of the algorithms. Feature extraction includes localization of the face, detection of the facial features, and actual extraction. Eyes, nose, and mouth are the first features identified by most of the techniques. Other features are identified later. The extracted features are then used to generate a numerical map of each face analyzed.

The generated templates are then compared to images stored in the database. The database used may consist of mug shots, composites of suspects, or video surveillance images. This process creates a list of hits with scores, which is very similar to search results on the Internet. It is often up to the user to determine if the similarity produced is adequate to warrant declaration of a match. Even if the user does

not have to make a decision, he or she is most likely determining the settings used later by the computer to declare a match.

Depending on the software used, it is possible to compare one-to-one or one-to-many. In the first instance, it would be a confirmation of someone's identity. In the second, it would be identification of a person. Another application of facial recognition is taking advantage of live, video-based surveillance. This can be used to identify people in retrospect, after their images were captured on the recording. It can also be used to identify a particular person during surveillance, while they are moving around. It can be useful for catching criminals in the act, cheaters in casinos, or in identifying terrorists.

Most of the earliest and current methods of face recognition are 2-dimensional (2-D). They use a flat image of a face. However, 3-D methods are also being developed and some are already available commercially. The main difference in 3-D analysis is the use of the shape of the face, thus adding information to a final template. The first step in a 3-D analysis is generation of a virtual mesh reflecting a person's facial shape. It can be done by using a near-infrared light to scan a person's face and repeating the process a couple of times. The nodal points are located on the mesh, generating thousands of reference points rather than 20–30 used by 2-D methods. It makes the 3-D methods more accurate, but also more invasive and more expensive. As a result, 2-D methods are the most commonly used.

An extension of facial recognition and 3-D methods is using computer graphics to reconstruct faces from skulls. This allows identification of people from skulls if all other methods of identification fail. In the past facial reconstruction was done manually by a forensic artist. Clay was applied to the **skull** following the contours of the skull until a face was generated. Currently the reconstruction can be computerized by taking advantage of head template creation by using landmarks on the skull and the ability to overlay it with computer-generated muscles. Once the face is generated, it is photographed and can be compared to various databases for identification in the same way as a live person's image.

The use of facial recognition is important in law enforcement, as the facial verification performed by a forensic scientist can help to convict criminals. For example, in 2003, a group of men was convicted in the United Kingdom for a credit card fraud based on facial verification. Their images were captured on a surveillance tape near an ATM and their identities

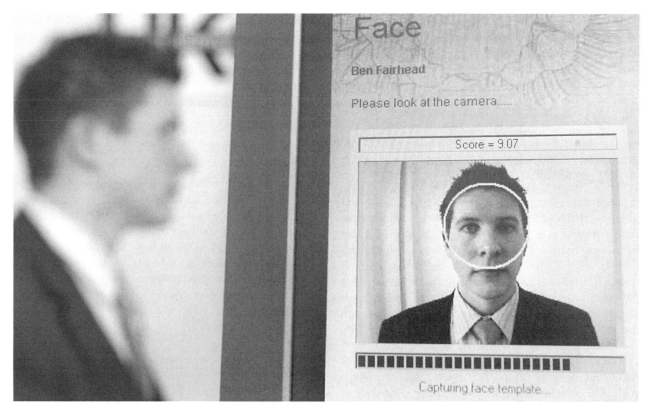

A British Passport Office volunteer has his face scanned for a biometrics enrollment card in London, 2004. © PETER MACDIARMID/ REUTERS/CORBIS

were confirmed later by a forensic specialist using facial recognition tools.

Despite recent advances in the area, facial recognition in a surveillance system is often technically difficult. The main reasons are difficulties in finding the face by the system. These difficulties arise from people moving, wearing hats or sunglasses, and not facing the camera. However, even if the face is found, identification might be difficult because of the lighting (too bright or too dark), making features difficult to recognize. An important variable is also resolution of the image taken and camera angle. Normalization performed by the computer might not be effective if the incoming image is of poor quality.

One of the ways to improve image quality is to use fixed cameras, especially in places like airports, government buildings, or sporting venues. In such cases all the people coming through are captured by the camera in a similar pose, making it easier for the computer to generate a template and compare to a database.

While most people do not object to the use of this technology to identify criminals, there are fears that images of people can be taken at any time, anywhere,

without their permission. However, it is clear that the ability of identifying people with 100% certainty using face recognition is still some time away. However, facial recognition is an increasingly important identity verification method.

SEE ALSO Biometrics; Composite drawing.

False memories

False memory syndrome (FMS), as defined by John F. Kihlstrom (**psychology** professor at the University of California, San Francisco) and utilized by the False Memory Foundation, is a condition in which a person's identity and interpersonal relationships are centered on a memory of a traumatic experience that is objectively false, but one that the person strongly believes. Note that the syndrome is not characterized by false memories as such. Almost everyone has memories that are inaccurate. Rather, the syndrome may be diagnosed when the memory is so deeply ingrained that it orients the individual's entire personality and lifestyle, in turn disrupting all sorts of other adaptive behavior. The analogy to personality disorder is intentional. False memory syndrome is especially destructive because the person diligently avoids confrontation with any evidence that might challenge the memory. Thus, it takes on a life of its own, encapsulated and resistant to correction. The person may become so focused on that memory that he or she may be effectively distracted from coping with the real problems in his or her life.

False memories are often of childhood sexual abuse (CSA) or satanic ritual abuse (SRA). The syndrome has been reported since the late 1980s; at that time, psychotherapeutic use of hypnosis and the concept of recovered memories were also becoming widely publicized. Persons with FMS typically report that they have suddenly remembered events of past abuse and, thus, feel compelled to confront their alleged perpetrators. The memories of the alleged abuse are typically reported to have been awakened during the course of some form of therapy. The response of the accused perpetrator is generally one of shock and disbelief, followed by adamant denial of its occurrence, and of the accusation. Adult children with FMS who accuse parents or other relatives (or other persons formerly close to them) often become estranged from their families. The accusers sometimes seek lawyers and the involvement of the legal system.

There is a cluster of characteristics associated with the development of FMS. Clients are typically adult females who seek psychotherapy because of significant negative life stressors, including relationship difficulties or dissolution, job dissatisfaction or loss, birth or death in the immediate family, addiction, or eating disorders. The nature of the presenting symptoms often prompts the therapist to search for memory of a childhood, or early life, trauma that could have acted as a catalyst for the current symptoms, generally at the expense of dealing with "real-time" problems while focusing on (real or imagined) past events. Patients experiencing FMS generally blame all current difficulties on the remembered past abuse, and adapt their identities to those of abuse survivors. They typically become increasingly dependent on the therapist, who professes belief in their abuse allegations, and they estrange themselves from those who either disagree with their new self-identification or attempt to prove them wrong.

One reported abuse survivor confronted her family with memories of repeated instances of incest occurring between the ages of three and eight with her father as the alleged perpetrator. She further asserted that the sexual abuse occurred in the attic of their home. She claimed she was taken to the attic via a back stairway. Her parents responded to the accusations by insisting that the home they lived in during that time had only one floor, no attic, and no staircase. They offered to bring the client (and the therapist) to the former home, to show her that the memory was incorrect. The daughter refused and cut off all further contact with her parents.

From a forensic **psychiatry** perspective, the issue of FMS is a challenging one. It is virtually impossible to distinguish between real and recovered or false or imagined memories, and it is difficult to validate early childhood memories via the use of objective data. Plus, it is difficult to base a legal or criminal case on recovered memory data as a result. The cost (both emotional and financial), when the memory is actually false, can be enormous, to the individual with FMS, to the accused family member (or other former close associate), and to the legal system.

SEE ALSO Crime scene reconstruction; Ethical issues; *Frye* standard; Physical evidence.

Fatherhood, determination SEE
Paternity evidence

Henry Faulds
6/1/1843–3/1930
SCOTTISH
PHYSICIAN

Henry Faulds was a Scottish physician who laid the groundwork for the scientific study of fingerprints in **criminology**.

Faulds was born in Beith, Scotland. His parents were initially quite prosperous but lost most of their money in the famous City of Glasgow bank collapse in 1855. Henry was withdrawn from school, employed as a clerk, and in 1858 he became apprenticed to a shawl manufacturer where one of his duties was to classify varied Paisley shawl patterns.

At the age of 21, Henry became conscious of his deficient education and took classes at Glasgow University in mathematics, logic, and classics. Then, at age 25, he decided that his true vocation was **medicine**, so he enrolled at Anderson's College, Glasgow, and became a licentiate with commendation in 1871. By this time, Henry had developed a strong religious faith.

In September 1873 he married Isabella Wilson. Following hospital posts at St. Thomas London and Glasgow Royal Infirmary, he took up a post with the Church of Scotland as medical missionary at

Darjeeling, India. He resigned a year later and then joined the United Presbyterian Church. In 1874, as their first medical missionary, Faulds went to Tokyo, Japan, where, in 1875, he established the Tsukiji hospital.

His reputation grew rapidly and he was offered a post as personal physician to the Imperial House. Faulds ran his hospital, lectured Japanese medical students, taught **physiology**, Darwinism, and Professor Joseph Lister's principles of antisepsis to Japanese surgeons, and trekked into the mountains to heal the bedridden. He became the first foreign doctor to be allowed to carry out post mortems, and was consulted by the authorities on the control of rabies, typhoid, and cholera epidemics. Provision for the blind was limited and Henry Faulds devised a bible for them to read using raised letters—a forerunner of Braille. By 1882 his hospital treated 15,000 patients annually.

While in Japan, Faulds and an American archeologist, Edward S. Morse, struck up a friendship. Morse's Japanese excavations were distinguished by cooking pots and other vessels made from clay. One day, Faulds noticed minute patterns of parallel lines impressed in the clay. Some months earlier, Faulds had lectured his medical students on touch and he had noticed the swirling ridges on his own fingertips. In a flash, he realized that the 2,000-year-old impressions he now examined in clay came from the ridges on the fingers of ancient potters.

Finding fingerprints on the ancient clay fragments of Japanese pottery led Faulds to study fingerprints with a scientific approach. Faulds and his medical students shaved off their finger ridges with razors until no pattern could be traced. They repeated the experiment, removing the ridges by any number of methods and each time the ridges grew back in exactly the same patterns.

Over a period of two years, he also examined the hands of large numbers of infants and children to see if growth affected their fingertip patterns. When an epidemic of scarlet fever swept through Japan, causing severe peeling of the skin, Faulds again studied the fingerprints and found no before-and-after change. He amassed a significant collection of prints and eventually found each person had a unique **fingerprint**. In an attempt to promote the idea of fingerprint **identification**, Faulds sought the help of the noted naturalist Charles Darwin in 1850. Darwin declined to work on the idea, but passed it on to his relative **Francis Galton**.

On October 28, 1880, while still in Japan, Faulds' first paper on the subject, entitled "On the Skin-Furrows of the Hand," was published in the scientific journal *Nature*. This included a remarkable forecast that fingerprints from mutilated or dismembered corpses might be of forensic importance in identification. Furthermore, Faulds anticipated the transmission of fingerprints by photo-telegraphy. He also suggested that criminal registers be kept of "the for-ever-unchangeable finger-furrows of important criminals."

Faulds' letter was the first in the scientific literature to suggest the basic concepts of the fingerprint system of identification as we know it today. Twenty years earlier, however, Sir William Herschel had begun collecting fingerprints, too. In the month following publication of Faulds' paper, Herschel published a letter, also in *Nature*, in which he explained that he had been using fingerprints as a means to identify criminals in jail since 1857. However, he had been using fingerprints merely as a means of signature and failed to mention the potential for forensic use. Later, Herschel published another letter in *Nature*, giving full credit to Faulds for his original discovery. This disclaimer was largely unnoticed and others had by this time usurped Faulds' place in history.

Due to his wife's illness, Faulds returned to Britain in 1885. He dispatched letters offering his fingerprinting system to the chiefs of the major police forces around the world, though he had little response. To make matters worse, a second system of scientific criminal identification, **anthropometry**, had been developed by the young Frenchman **Alphonse Bertillon**. In 1892 Francis Galton published a book on the use of fingerprints, with no mention made of Faulds' contribution. In 1901 Edward Henry, a former colleague of Galton and the Commissioner of Police at Scotland Yard, set up a fingerprint bureau.

It is to these three men—Galton, Herschel, and Henry—that credit is frequently given for the discovery of the use of fingerprints in criminology. Faulds became embittered and returned to the life of a police surgeon in the town of Fenton, Staffordshire. In 1922, he sold his practice and moved to Wolstanton where he died in obscurity in 1930.

SEE ALSO Criminology; Fingerprint; Medicine; Physiology.

FBI crime laboratory

The central premise of the Federal Bureau of Investigation's (FBI's) Crime Laboratory is that the successful solution of crimes, from investigation of an alleged crime scene through conviction of perpetrator(s), relies upon several factors: careful gathering of physical and **trace evidence**; preservation, delivery, and forensic scientific analysis of this **evidence**; presentation of forensic scientific analysis results; and demonstration of guilt or innocence of alleged perpetrator(s).

The FBI's Crime Lab, as one of the premier forensic research and analysis facilities, offers its expertise to law enforcement agencies across the nation and, at times, across the world, at no cost to the requesting entity. Teams of special agents and administrative staff offer on-site forensic and technical support, nationally and globally, in the event of disasters involving mass casualties or wide-ranging investigations.

Among the services currently provided by the Lab, both within its facilities and off-site, are: analysis of **blood**, tissue, and other biological evidence; analysis of **firearms**, weapons, and **explosives**; analysis of legal and illegal drugs; and courtroom expert witness testimony for cases involving **FBI** Crime Laboratory forensic investigations.

Under Director **J. Edgar Hoover**, the science of **criminalistics** in the United States became centrally located with the dedication of the United States Bureau of Investigation's Technical Laboratory in Washington, D.C., on November 24, 1932. The Technical Laboratory was located in room 802 of the Old Southern Railway Building, which had been outfitted with a newly purchased Bausch and Lomb microscope, an ultraviolet light machine, a machine designed to examine gun barrel interiors, moulage kits, wiretapping kits, photographic supplies, and various chemicals.

At its inception, the Technical Crime Laboratory was staffed by just one forensic scientist, Special Agent Charles Appel, whose area of special interest was in the area of questioned document examination (at the time, this consisted primarily of handwriting, typewriting, and printed document examination and authentication). The research capabilities and the assigned staff of the Lab grew over time, and the addition of subject matter experts broadened its range of expertise. Samuel Pickering, a specialist in chemical analysis, was the first such resident expert. Additional agents, specially trained in the areas of cipher analysis, research on infrared rays, use of dyes for **identification** of extortion packages, blood grouping, creating systems for the marking of ransom money, and the chemical development of latent fingerprints, were added to the cadre of scientists at the Lab.

In 1934, the Technical Laboratory moved to the Justice Department building. In 1935, the United States Bureau of Investigation was given the title of Federal Bureau of Investigation by Congress. In 1942, the Technical Laboratory became the Crime Laboratory, and was officially named a division within the FBI.

Both the Lab and FBI headquarters moved to the newly constructed J. Edgar Hoover Building in 1974. In 1981, the Lab's Forensic Science Research and Training Center (FSRTC) was created at the FBI Training Academy in Quantico, Virginia. This site gained worldwide acclaim as a training and research facility dedicated to sharing cutting-edge forensic and criminalistics knowledge and technology with the worldwide law enforcement communities. In April 2003, the FBI's Crime Lab moved to its fourth, and current, location at the Quantico Marine Corps Base. The new facility was seven years and $130 million in the making; it is comprised of three adjoining five-story towers, and contains 463,000 square feet of laboratory and office space. The glass-enclosed laboratory workspaces, spanning two-thirds of every floor of the towers, are sterile environments that contain 100% clean air. They are separated from the office areas by a walkway called the bio-vestibule.

At present, the FBI Crime Laboratory has two primary operating branches: Forensic Analysis and Operational Support. The Forensic Analysis Branch includes the Forensic Analysis and Scientific Analysis Sections. The Operations Support Branch is comprised of the Forensic Science Support, Operational Response, and Operational Support Sections.

The Forensic Analysis Section contains several units, including the Cryptanalysis and Racketeering Records Unit, tasked with examination of written communication and records related to terrorist and criminal organizations. This Unit has four program areas. The first is Cryptanalysis, which involves examination, analysis, and **decryption** of **ciphers** and **codes** embedded in all manner of written and electronic communications. Second, the Drugs program area analyzes and examines records related to illegal drug-trafficking operations. The third area, Racketeering, examines and analyzes records pertaining to all forms of gambling, loan-sharking, and prostitution. Fourth, the Money-laundering area analyzes a broad-range of criminally suspect financial records pertaining to the illegal movement of money both within and outside U.S. borders.

Also within the Forensic Analysis Section is the Firearms and Toolmarks Unit, which is charged with examining all aspects of the mechanical condition of various firearms and ballistic materials, as well as the examination of evidence toolmarks for identification of recovered or suspected tools.

The Latent Print Unit examines and analyzes latent prints on submitted evidence. Latent prints occur when the friction ridge skin of human palms, fingers, or the soles of the feet make contact with a surface and leave physical impressions thereon. Located within the Latent Prints Unit are the FBI Disaster Squad, which is composed largely of latent print and **fingerprint** analysis experts who are called to mass casualty scenes in order to assist in the identification of remains, and IAFIS (**Integrated Automated Fingerprint Identification System**), which was created and implemented by the FBI in 1999. IAFIS is a large database system designed to store and compare fingerprints (primarily in 10-fingerprint units) in order to facilitate identification or exclusion of suspects.

The Questioned Documents Unit is staffed with experts in the examination of printing, handwriting, typewriting, printing by hand, obliterated impressions, erasures, and alterations of written communications. Examiners in this unit are also proficient in the identification of edges, imprints, stamping, watermarks, **fibers**, and other components of writing surfaces, as well as analysis and identification of the media used to mark on them, such as photocopying and facsimile machines, and the media used therein (ribbons, cartridges, etc.). Databases within the Questioned Documents Unit include the National Fraudulent Check database, Bank Robbery Note database, Shoeprint database, Anonymous Letter database, and Watermark Files database.

The Scientific Analysis Section contains six functional units, the first of which is the Chem-Bio Sciences Unit, involved in extremely high-quality, standardized forensic examination of hazardous chemical, biological, and nuclear evidence, along with related materials.

Another functional unit is the Chemistry Unit, which contains six program areas.

- The first program area, General Chemistry, is used to analyze and characterize unknown materials in solid or liquid form. Chemists identify chemicals and dyes used in bank or other security devices and examine suspect cloth, clothing or currency for their presence; they compare stains, markings, and lubricants with possible sources; they also identify source inks by assessing and comparing the compositions of various types and forms of questioned and

known ink types. Program area chemists may also utilize various scientific means to determine the elemental composition, quantify and identity of suspected, but unknown controlled substances.

- Second, the Toxicology area is where toxicological analyses are conducted on food products or biological samples in order to ascertain the presence of poisons, drugs, or drug metabolites. This unit is also responsible for assessing claims of commercial **product tampering**.

- The third program area, Paints and Polymers, examines and analyzes paint specimens in order to make comparisons with suspected sources. These subject matter experts use obtained samples to identify automotive make, model and year; they also oversee the National Automotive Paint File and the National Forensic Tape File. Other forensic scientists in this unit examine plastics for comparison with suspected sources. Additional scientists examine caulks, sealants, and other adhesives and engage in chemical and material analyses of various types of tape in order to determine composition, construction, color, type and manufacturer, as well as to identify tape from torn or cut ends of suspected rolls.

- Fourth, Metallurgy experts examine and analyze evidence recovered from air, rail, and nautical calamities, along with product tampering, material strength assessments, structural damage and failure analyses, suspected fabrication and specification fraud, and appliance and device malfunction. Metallurgy experts also study material corrosion.

- Elemental section staff in the fifth program area perform examinations and chemical analyses of **glass** and light bulb shards, bullet contents, substrates and components isolated from biological or biochemical samples, and make materials comparisons in the investigation of **arson**, homicides, suicides, and accidents.

- The sixth program area, Instrumentation Operation and Support, provides oversight for maintenance of all unit instrumentation, databases, and reference libraries.

The third Unit, in the Scientific Analysis Section is **CODIS** (Combined DNA Index System), which utilizes advanced electronic computer technologies in tandem with cutting edge forensic science as a means of solving distant violent crimes. A computerized database and analysis system enables forensic labs across the country to share real-time data of

DNA profiles. Investigators use this information to evaluate and link crimes committed in differing geographical areas, serial crimes, and the comparison of known perpetrator DNA with DNA recovered from crime scenes.

The fourth Scientific Analysis Unit is dedicated to DNA Analysis. At crime scenes, DNA is extracted from questioned blood, tissue, and body fluid specimens. These specimens are compared with DNA analysis of known samples. By so doing, it is often possible to link victims, alleged perpetrators, and crime scenes.

Explosives, the fifth Unit, is staffed by scientists who analyze and compare samples from suspected explosions and evidence obtained from recovered explosives (or fragments thereof), in an effort to link the two. They also conduct on-site bomb scene investigations, search suspected bomb-making locations, and oversee the Terrorist Explosive Device Analytical Center (TEDAC).

The sixth Unit, Trace Evidence, provides expert identification and analysis of physical materials that may be transferred between victim, alleged perpetrator, and crime scene. Some common trace materials are fibers from cloth, ropes, ligatures, bindings, coverings or textiles, human and animal hair, wood or soil particles, glass fragments, and building or construction materials. This Unit archives samples of textiles, fibers, animal and human hair, different types of soil, wood, and feathers.

Housed with the Forensic Science and Support Section is the Counterterrorism and Forensic Science Research Unit, the mission of which is to continually research and broaden the security community's knowledge base in order to more effectively combat terrorism. This Unit has three subsections: (1) Biology, tasked with the automation of forensic DNA analysis; (2) a Chemistry Subunit which houses subject matter experts in the areas of chemical separations and mass spectrometry, who are equipped for field chemical research, evidence collection and analysis; and (3) the Physical Sciences Unit, which focuses on document analysis, imaging and **latent fingerprint** studies, and materials analysis.

The Evidence Control Unit is tasked with ongoing analysis of recovered evidence, as well as the oversight and management of the evidence control system, which tracks the movement of all forms of evidence throughout the investigational and judicial processes.

The Quality Assurance and Training Unit is responsible for the management and maintenance of all aspects of quality assurance and best practice standards within the FBI Crime Laboratory. It also coordinates and manages quality oversight training programs throughout the Bureau. In addition, this Unit maintains the FBI Crime Laboratory Library, which is responsible for the production and publication of the juried journal *Forensic Science Communications*, publication of the *Handbook of Forensic Services*, production of field and laboratory manuals and training materials, and has oversight and management responsibility for all forensic science training programs within the Bureau and among the field laboratories.

The Special Photographic Unit houses the FBI's entire forensic imaging and photographic continuum, from camera and equipment maintenance and repair, to technical assistance on concealment operations, to aerial and surveillance filming. There are three subunits: the Forensic Studio which is responsible for all FBI forensic photographic operations; the Field Support subunit, which processes film and produces hard copy and digital photographic images and trains Bureau and field personnel in photographic equipment use and image production; and the Training subunit, which is responsible for teaching new Special Agents and field support staff basic and advanced crime scene **photography**.

The Operational Response Section is comprised of the Bomb Data Center, in which specially trained forensic scientists create and implement advanced technologies designed to increase safety for those involved in bomb disarmament and disposal. The Hazardous Devices School is housed within this unit and its mission is to provide certification-level training to personnel involved with explosive device render-safe technology. Bomb Data Center staff are tasked with interface between the FBI and the law enforcement communities. It is the Center's responsibility to provide field technical support to the public sector on an as-needed basis. The Bomb Center Data Unit produces the *Special Technician's Bulletin*, the *Investigator's Bulletin* and the *General Information Bulletin*, as well as any other requested technical manuals, bulletins, and reports.

The Evidence Response Team Unit coordinates and supervises Evidence response Teams (ERTs) throughout the FBI. ERTs are comprised of specially equipped and trained Special Agents, support and administrative staff who are expert at planning, preparation, organization, and conduct of major evidence-recovery missions at disaster, crisis, and mass casualty sites. ERT staff are trained and experienced in leading techniques and have access to the most advanced scientific methodologies and forensic technologies available.

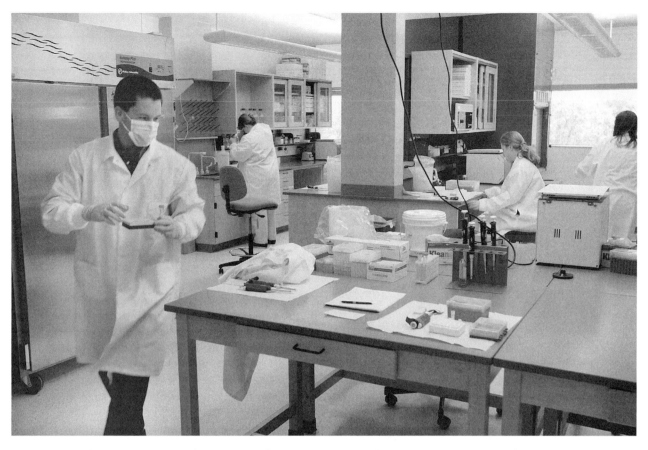

Lab workers perform the early stages of mitochondrial DNA extraction at the FBI's new crime laboratory in Quantico, Virginia, in April 2003. Forensic and evidence lab cost $155 million. Investigators from around the world use the academy, whose facilities are among the best in the world, for research. AP/WIDE WORLD PHOTOS. REPRODUCED BY PERMISSION.

The FBI Crime Laboratory's Hazardous Materials Response Unit is dedicated to countering terrorism in the nuclear, radiological, and biological realms, as well as to the investigation of environmental crimes. This Unit also provides training, equipment, and certification-level coursework for FBI central and field staff involved in hazardous materials operations.

Within the Operational Support Section, the Administrative Unit provides oversight, coordination, and adherence to published FBI and Crime Laboratory Policy and Procedural guidelines; the Facility Services Unit is responsible for assuring the safety and integrity of both the Crime Laboratory staff and the physical plant itself; the Investigative and Prosecutive Graphics Unit is responsible for the sub-areas of crime scene survey, documentation and reconstruction; forensic facial imaging; demonstrative evidence; and provision of the full range of FBI Director's Office Support, including the President and Presidential staff, the Attorney General of the United States, Congress, the Department of Defense, and various national and international officials and dignitaries.

The Planning and Budget Unit is charged with tracking, management, and financial oversight of the FBI Crime Laboratory budget as well as its federal funding and appropriations.

Finally, the Structural Design Unit plans, designs, develops, and implements actual physical models and evidentiary mock-ups for courtroom **crime scene reconstruction** and evidentiary clarification in support of expert witness testimony.

Vast in complexity and ever-broadening in scope, the modern-day FBI Crime Laboratory far surpasses the early vision of J. Edgar Hoover and his G-men; it continues to stand as one of the best known and most inclusive forensics research facilities in the world.

SEE ALSO Accident investigations at sea; Artificial fibers; Bacterial biology; Bioterrorism; Building materials; Crime scene staging; Cryptology and number theory; Fracture matching; Luminol; Mitochondrial DNA analysis; Mitochondrial DNA typing.

FBI (United States Federal Bureau of Investigation)

The United States Federal Bureau of Investigation (FBI) is the nation's primary federal investigative service. The mission of the FBI is to uphold and enforce federal criminal laws; aid international, state, and local police and investigative services when appropriate; and to protect the United States against terrorism and threats to national interests.

An important part of the FBI's mandate includes **forensic science**, both directly in the form of field investigations of accidents or deaths deemed of national interest, and in the maintenance of databases that can be accessed by local, state and federal law enforcement, and forensic investigators. An example of the latter function is the **Integrated Automated Fingerprint Identification System** (IAFID), which maintains millions of fingerprints for perusal.

The FBI employs nearly 30,000 men and women, including 12,000 special agents. The organization, headquartered in Washington, D.C., is field-oriented, maintaining a network of over 50 domestic field offices, 45 foreign posts, and 400 satellite offices (resident agencies). The agency relies on both foreign and domestic intelligence information, since the agency only has jurisdiction in interstate or federal crimes.

Origins and Formation of the FBI

In the nineteenth century, municipal and state governments shouldered the responsibility of law enforcement. State legislatures defined crimes, and criminals were prosecuted in local courts. The development of railroads and automobiles, coupled with advancements in communication technology, introduced a new type of crime that the contemporary legal and law enforcement system was unequipped to handle. Criminals were able to evade the law by fleeing over state lines. To combat the growing trend of interstate crime, President Theodore Roosevelt proposed the creation of a federal investigative and law enforcement agency.

In 1908 Roosevelt and his Attorney General, Charles Bonaparte, created a force of Special Agents within the Department of Justice. They sought the expertise of accountants, lawyers, Secret Service agents, and detectives to staff the ranks of the new investigative service. The new recruits reported for examination and **training** on July 26, 1908. This first corps of federal agents was the forerunner of the modern FBI.

When the federal bureau began operations, there were few federal crimes in the legal statutes. Federal agents investigated railroad scams, banking crimes, labor violations, and antitrust cases. The findings of their investigations, however, were usually disclosed to local or state law enforcement officials and courts for prosecution. In 1910, the federal government passed the Mann Act, expanding the jurisdiction of the investigation bureau by outlawing the transport of women over state lines for the purpose of prostitution. Granting federal agents the right to investigate, arrest, and prosecute persons in violation of the Mann Act solidified the interstate authority of federal investigative services.

The intervening decades, including the first World War, saw the FBI's mandate evolve. This evolution was particularly dramatic during the 1920s and 1930s, during the early tenure of director **J. Edgar Hoover**. Under Hoover's direction, the field office network grew from nine offices to over 30 offices within ten years. Agency personnel policy changed, requiring new agents to complete a rigorous, centralized training course. Promotions within the organization were secured through merit and consistency of service, not seniority. The agency still sought agent-recruits with training in accountancy and law, but expanded their search to include linguists, mathematicians, physicists, chemists, medical practitioners, and forensic specialists.

Technical advancements also changed agency operations. Basic forensic investigation began to be employed in FBI crime scene investigations. The Bureau established a **fingerprint identification** and index system in 1924. The national index assumed fingerprint records from state and local law enforcement agencies, as well as an older Department of Justice fingerprint registry dating back to 1905. The agency opened its first Technical Laboratory in 1932. The facility quickly expanded to cover a variety of forensic research, aiding investigators by comparing bullets, guns, **tire tracks**, watermarks, counterfeiting techniques, handwriting samples, and **pathology** reports.

In the 1960s, for example, the agency's forensic efforts helped prosecute criminals in several high profile civil rights cases. Field agents in Louisiana and Mississippi investigated the **murder** of three voter registration workers in Philadelphia, Mississippi, before turning the case over to FBI headquarters in Washington, D.C. FBI agents conducted crime scene, forensics, and extended investigations of the assassinations of civil rights leaders Martin Luther King, Jr. and Medgar Evers. They eventually arrested, aided in the prosecution of, and gained convictions for the assassins, although Byron De La Beckwith, who shot Medger Evers, was not found guilty until 1994.

Forensic accounting became an important part of the FBI's operations. Combating the rise of white-collar financial crimes and the drug trade were other priorities of the FBI during the 1980s. FBI investigations implicated high-ranking government officials in financial fraud and abuse of power scandals, including members of the Congress (ABSCAM), the defense industry (ILL WIND), and the judiciary (GREYLORD). Federal agents also investigated fraud cases during the savings and loan crisis.

To aid its current operations, the FBI embraced the use of several new technologies in its operations. Aid came with the advent of personal computers and Internet research, speeding up the **processing** of investigation information. Searchable databases now store information on suspects, crime statistics, fingerprints, and **DNA** samples. However, their use also created security risks that necessitated the creation of specialized information systems protection task forces. The agency created Computer Analysis and Response Teams (CART) to aid field investigators with the recovery of data from damaged or sabotaged electronic sources. In 1998, the establishment of the National Infrastructure Protection Center (NIPC) permitted the FBI to monitor the dissemination of computer viruses and worms.

Forensic use of DNA radically altered both the legal process and forensic research of FBI investigations. DNA analysis allows specialists to positively identify victims and perpetrators of crimes by comparing particular patterns in individual DNA. FBI forensic specialists created a national DNA databank in 1998 to aid ongoing investigations.

After the September 11, 2001, terrorist attacks on the United States, and subsequent **anthrax** attacks on national post offices and media outlets, the FBI expanded its counterintelligence and counter-terrorism operations to include anti-bioterrorism task forces. Various forensic techniques germane to the detection of biological agents are used in this effort, which continues to the present day.

SEE ALSO Anthrax; Bioterrorism; FBI crime laboratory; Integrated automated fingerprint identification system.

FDA (United States Food and Drug Administration)

Forensic science can involve the examination of foodstuffs and other items used by consumers. If contaminated or faulty, these items can cause illness or death.

Various federal government agencies participate in the regulation of consumer goods, which can involve the forensic determination of the circumstances surrounding accidents, illness outbreaks, or deaths. Principal among these is the Food and Drug Administration (FDA).

The FDA is an agency of the Department of Health and Human Services. Its mandate is the regulation of the development, sale, and distribution of food products, prescription and over-the-counter drugs, cosmetics, and medical equipment. The FDA's reach is extensive; one-fifth of all consumer dollars spent in the U.S. purchase a product regulated by the FDA. The goal of the FDA is to protect consumers by ensuring the safety of food and drug products sold in the U.S.

The FDA traces its history to 1862, when President Abraham Lincoln created a chemistry division under the Department of Agriculture. Congress created the modern FDA in 1906 with the passage of the Food and Drugs Act. The 1906 law gave limited power to the FDA to monitor the safety of food and drug products. In 1938, Congress expanded the power of the FDA by passing the Food, Drug, and Cosmetic Act. This act granted the FDA the power to test drugs and determine their safety and efficacy before allowing companies to sell the new drugs. The act also granted the FDA authority to regulate cosmetics.

While the FDA's primary task is to ensure food and drug safety, in recent years the agency has taken on an increased role in addressing the deliberate contamination of foods. The FDA is leading efforts to develop and produce **vaccines** and, in conjunction with agencies such as the **Centers for Disease Control and Prevention**, takes a role in the forensic investigation of foodborne outbreaks, especially if the outbreak can be traced to a breach in the food chain from the field to the consumer.

SEE ALSO *Escherichia coli*; Food poisoning; Pathogens; Toxins.

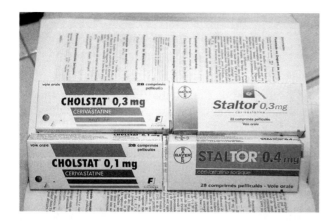

After the FDA received evidence of 31 U.S. deaths due to severe rhabdomyolisis, a condition resulting in muscle-cell breakdown in patients taking the cholesterol-fighting drugs Staltor and Cholstat, the drugs were withdrawn worldwide. © REUTERS/CORBIS

Federal court (forensic evidence)

The Federal court system creates the standards, rules, and procedures for use by all of the lower courts in the nation. Four **Federal Rules of Evidence** are of particular significance in the world of **forensic science**.

Rule 702 involves testimony by experts. The pertinent text of the Rule states "If scientific, technical, or other specialized knowledge will assist the trier of fact to understand the **evidence** or to determine a fact in issue, a witness qualified as an expert by knowledge, skill, experience, **training**, or education, may testify thereto in the form of an opinion or otherwise, if (1) the testimony is sufficiently based upon reliable facts or data. (2) the testimony is the product of reliable principles and methods, and (3) the witness has applied the principles and methods reliably to the facts of the case."

In 1993, a Supreme Court case entitled *Daubert v. Merrell Dow Pharmaceuticals* resulted in a ruling that when expert evidence based upon scientific knowledge is part of the evidentiary proceedings in a trial, and the testimony is questioned or challenged by the litigant, the judge is responsible for acting as a "gatekeeper" who must decide whether the expert testimony should be considered scientifically reliable or valid. The gatekeeping function extends to technical and other potential specialized knowledge as well as to scientific knowledge.

As a result of the *Daubert* decision, many of the lower courts had to examine whether the *Daubert* factors applied to decisions about the reliability of expert

evidence need also be applied to **expert witnesses** who were not offering opinions based strictly on scientific principles, but on specialized or technical knowledge. The general consensus was that the *Daubert* rules should be applied to all expert opinion testimony.

The *Daubert* rules were extended and clarified in 1999 by another Supreme Court decision, *Kumho Tire v. Carmichael*, in which it was mandated that trial judges act as gatekeepers who must make certain that only reliable expert opinion evidence and testimony be admitted, and that this rule apply to all possible forms of expert testimony. The text of the Committee Note following that decision is as follows: "The specific factors explicated by the *Daubert* Court are: (1) whether the expert's technique or theory can be or has been tested—that is, whether the expert's theory can be challenged in some objective sense, or whether it is instead simply a subjective, conclusory approach that cannot reasonably be assessed for reliability; (2) whether the technique or theory has been subject to peer review and publication; (3) the known or potential rate of error of the technique or theory when applied; (4) the existence and maintenance of standards and controls; and (5) whether the technique or theory has been generally accepted in the scientific community."

As a result of the *Kumho Tire* decision, the Court publicly stressed that these factors might not necessarily be fully applicable to all forms of expert opinion testimony, that the factors were more on the order of guidelines than rigid requirements, and that there might be specific situations or circumstances in which lower courts might give equal consideration to other factors that might best permit assessment of reliability or validity of nonscientific expert opinion testimony offered during a trial.

Among the procedural conclusions of *Daubert* was an assertion that the judicial decision regarding reliability for admissibility of evidence lay in the principles and methodology of techniques rather than on the conclusions reached by applying them. In the 1997 case *General Electric v. Joiner*, the Court partially reversed that language, by stating that it is not always possible to separate conclusions from the methods by which they were reached.

In its current wording, Rule 702 directs trial courts to determine not only whether an expert's analytic methods are based upon sound and scientifically accepted principles, but whether the expert used those methods in a reliable and scientifically appropriate manner, in order to reach the conclusions stated in testimony regarding the disputed facts of the case.

The relevant portion of Rule 703, regarding bases of expert opinion testimony, states: "The facts or data in the particular case upon which an expert bases an opinion or inference may be those perceived by or made known to the expert at or before the hearing. If of a type reasonably relied upon by experts in the particular field in forming opinions or inferences upon the subject, the facts or data need not be admissible in evidence in order for the opinion or inference to be admitted. Facts or data that are otherwise inadmissible shall not be disclosed to the jury by the proponent of the opinion or inference unless the court determines that their probative value in assisting the jury to evaluate the expert's opinion substantially outweighs their prejudicial impact."

In the original version of the Federal Rules of Evidence (1975), experts could base their opinions not only on facts brought into evidence, but also on facts not in evidence, and even on facts which would not under any circumstances be admissible as evidence, as long as the non-admitted or non-admissible facts were part of the aggregate body of knowledge that other experts in the same field of study would utilize in making professional judgments in situations not involving litigation. To clarify, the Federal Rules of Evidence sought to allow a subject area expert the latitude to use relevant and appropriate professional tools in order to render the most accurate and informed opinion possible, and to be able to communicate that decision to the participants of a particular proceeding in a court of law.

Rule 701 concerns opinion testimony given by lay witnesses. The significant portion states, "If the witness is not testifying as an expert, the witness' testimony in the form of opinions or inferences is limited to those opinions or inferences which are (a) rationally based on the perception of the witness, (b) helpful to a clear understanding of the witness' testimony or the determination of a fact in issue, and (c) not based on scientific, technical, or other specialized knowledge within the scope of Rule 702."

Members of the general public, as non-expert witnesses, may offer their personal opinions as evidence in situations where they have very strong recollection of specific events. They may testify as to what they observed or perceived: "he appeared to be drunk and his clothing smelled of beer," or "she was driving a great deal faster than the 15 mile per hour speed limit in the school zone." This rule does not permit expert witnesses to offer their perceptions, thoughts, or opinions in the guise of lay testimony.

Finally, Federal Rule 706, in relevant part, states, "(a) Appointment. The court may on its own motion or on the motion of any party enter an order to show cause why expert witnesses should not be appointed, and may request the parties to submit nominations. The court may appoint any expert witnesses agreed upon by the parties, and may appoint expert witnesses of its own selection. An expert witness shall not be appointed by the court unless the witness consents to act. A witness so appointed shall be informed of the witness' duties by the court in writing, a copy of which shall be filed with clerk, or at a conference in which the parties shall have the opportunity to participate. A witness so appointed shall advise the parties of the witness' findings, if any; the witness' deposition may be taken by any party; and the witness may be called to testify by the court or any party. The witness shall be subject to cross-examination by each party, including a party calling the witness...(c) Disclosure of Appointment. In the exercise of its discretion, the court may authorize disclosure to the jury of the fact that the court appointed the expert witness."

Federal Rule 706 essentially states that the court has the discretion to appoint or to deny appointment to any expert witness agreed upon by both parties; it also has the right to select its own expert witnesses, as well as the right to inform the jury that it has done so. In theory, a court-appointed expert is truly objective, as he or she is not employed by either party, the court-appointed expert has no potential loyalty to anything other than an unbiased assessment of the facts at hand.

These Federal Rules of Evidence are of particular importance for the forensic scientist: they inform the way in which expert witnesses may be used, the means with which the term "expert" must be defined, the role of the general public as trial witnesses, and the impeachability of expert witness testimony based on who is the employer of the expert.

SEE ALSO Ethical issues; Evidence; Expert witnesses; *Frye* standard; Pseudoscience and forensics.

Federal Rules of Evidence

The Federal Rules of Evidence are broad principles promulgated by the United States Supreme Court governing the admissibility of any evidence in a criminal or civil trial. As such, they are applicable in trials in federal courts, although most state courts have adopted them as well. From the standpoint of forensic evidence, which is gathered, examined, and interpreted by specialists who are often called on to testify as **expert witnesses**, the key rule is Rule 702, Testimony by Experts: "If scientific, technical, or other specialized knowledge will assist the trier of fact to understand the evidence or to determine a fact in issue, a witness qualified as an expert by knowledge, skill, experience, **training**, or education, may testify thereto in the form of an opinion or otherwise, if (1) the testimony is based upon sufficient facts or data, (2) the testimony is the product of reliable principles and methods, and (3) the witness has applied the principles and methods reliably to the facts of the case." A considerable body of case law applies this general principle to the facts of particular cases and defines standards for the admissibility of forensics evidence as interpreted by expert witnesses.

Historically, the courts relied on the *Frye* test, formulated by the Court in *Frye v. United States* in 1923. The case involved the admissibility of lie detector tests, at that time called "systolic blood pressure deception tests." This form of scientific evidence was then in its infancy and, at least according to the defendant, lacked what the Supreme Court would later call "sufficient facts or data" and "reliable principles and methods." The judge based his decision to admit the evidence on its "general acceptance in the particular field" (Frye, 293 F. at 1014). This was a key development, for it shifted the focus from the conclusions, even hunches, of a particular expert to an expertise recognized by other practitioners and gained from shared specialized training and experience. The Frye standard, however, had two principal problems: It failed to distinguish science from a pseudoscience such as astrology or, in the view of some legal experts, **forensic science**, and it rendered the court a passive observer, bound to accept expert testimony if it reflected "general acceptance in the particular field."

Accordingly, a new, more rigorous standard for the application of Rule 702 evolved from a 1993 case, *Daubert v. Merrell Dow Pharmaceuticals, Inc.* Under the *Daubert* standard, a trial judge can no longer defer to "general acceptance in the particular field" but must serve as a kind of gatekeeper by holding what are commonly called Daubert hearings, or pretrial hearings on the validity of the science in question using a five-pronged test: (1) whether the theory or technique can be and has been tested, (2) whether the theory or technique has been subjected to peer review and publication, (3) the known or potential rate of error, (4) the existence and maintenance of standards controlling the technique's operation, and (5) whether the theory or technique enjoys general acceptance within a relevant scientific community.

The relatively recent *Daubert* standard raised complex legal issues. Technically, it requires the courts to reexamine the validity and reliability of

such forensics tools as polygraph testing, **DNA** testing, fingerprinting, **handwriting analysis**, fiber comparison, and the **identification** of **firearms**, bite marks, tire marks, and **blood spatter** patterns. Many of these are staples of forensic testimony, and some, such as **fingerprint** comparison, have a venerable century-old history, so the courts are reluctant to exclude them. Yet many observers, especially defense attorneys, contend that the research base that supports them is often inadequate, and they are increasingly launching attacks. In *United States v. Havvard* (2000), for example, the defense filed a motion to exclude the government's expert fingerprint witness, arguing that "there is no reliable statistical foundation for fingerprint comparisons and no reliable measure of error rates in latent print identification, especially in the absence of a specific standard about the number of points of identity needed to support an opinion as to identification" (Havvard, 117 F. Supp. 2d at 850–51).

While the Court denied the defendant's motion, this type of challenge became more frequent after 1993 as defense attorneys become more sophisticated in their ability to assess and challenge scientific evidence. In the case of fingerprinting, for example, they are challenging the belief that a print match proves that the prints came from the same person. Defense attorneys note that fingerprint experts do not compare latent prints directly to known prints, but rather take points of comparison and then estimate the likelihood that the two came from the same person. More practically, defense attorneys challenge the reliability of forensics evidence (error rates), noting the many opportunities for error as evidence is found, bagged, labeled, transported, removed from storage, handled, examined, and re-stored.

SEE ALSO Evidence; Expert witnesses; Federal rules of evidence; *Frye* standard; U.S. Supreme Court (rulings on forensic evidence).

Felony

A felony, as applied to common law, is any crime generally punishable by more than one year in prison or by death. It is the second in seriousness of the three classifications of crimes: it is punished more severely than a **misdemeanor** (the least serious classification that covers minor offenses) but usually not as seriously as treason (the most serious classification). Examples of felonies are: assaults that cause serious bodily injury; **murder**; rape or sexual abuse in the first degree; grand theft; kidnapping; serious drug crimes; and racketeering.

The distinction between felonies and misdemeanors is not always clear, but generally any crime that has a sentence of only a fine or confinement in a local jail is not a felony. However, the offense may not be labeled a felony, but the punishment may make the offense a felony. For example, a state code could label a crime as an aggravated misdemeanor but provide for a sentence of more than one year in a state penitentiary, thereby treating the so-called misdemeanor as a felony.

Forensic science uses sophisticated laboratory techniques to solve felonies by detecting the presence of substances in the victim or suspected criminal, or at the crime scene. For instance, while investigating a murderous felony that involves a firearm, a scanning electron microscope can magnify objects 100,000 times in order to detect the minute gunpowder particles present on the hand of any suspect who has recently fired a gun. These particles can also be chemically analyzed to identify their ballistic origin from a particular bullet in order to match it with the bullet found within a victim.

In 1987, as an important example of using forensic **evidence** to decide a felony case, Tommy Lee Andrews became the first American ever convicted of a felony that utilized forensic **DNA** evidence. During the night of February 21, 1987, a break-in, burglary, and rape at knifepoint occurred at a Florida woman's home. During the next six months, law enforcement officials felt that the same man continued to commit over twenty felonious acts. In one case, Andrews' fingerprints were found on a window of a prowled house. Further, DNA samples of **semen** taken from several rape victims matched **blood** drawn from Andrews, while one rape victim made a positive **identification** of him. With overwhelming amounts of traditional and forensic evidence, Andrews was arrested and tried in court.

Since a DNA sample during the Andrews case was considered new scientific technology, it had to pass tests of acceptability in order to be used as testimony in the felony trial. That is, DNA analysis had to prove to be scientifically reliable in interpretation, method, and theory, and it had to be positively reviewed by peers. Passing all of these strict criteria, Andrews was initially sentenced to a twenty-two year prison sentence for the felonies of burglary, aggravated burglary, and rape. He was eventually tried for serial rape and convicted to a 115-year sentence.

In the 1980s no state had DNA databases, but after forensic evidence was shown to help convict felony lawbreakers, state courts and legislatures began to see how effective DNA was as evidence. They soon began to establish state DNA databases in order to assist law enforcement officials. Today, all fifty states require the collection of DNA samples into DNA databases for certain types of felons. Furthermore, in the first ten years of using forensic DNA evidence, the **FBI** reported DNA evidence being used in deciding over 6,800 felony cases.

SEE ALSO Misdemeanor.

Fiber evidence SEE Artificial fibers

Fibers

Fibers are one of the several pieces of forensic **evidence** known as **trace evidence**. Even though fibers are small and can be difficult to detect, their importance can be considerable. For example, textile fibers from an article of clothing can be influential in linking a suspect to the scene of a crime.

A fiber is the smallest portion of a textile material. Whether synthetic (i.e., rayon) or natural in origin (i.e., cotton), all fibers share the trait of being very much longer than their diameter. A short length of sewing thread is a good visual analogy of a fiber. The different origins of the materials that make up a fiber, and the differing ways that a fiber can be formed together to create the finished fabric, are all important in identifying the fiber.

Analysis of fibers that are found on a victim will involve determining the types of fibers present at the scene. For example, a fiber can be transferred from a carpet to a body. This fiber will not be as significant as a fiber found on a victim that is not present anywhere else at the scene. If a similar fiber is found on a suspect, this can be a powerful piece of evidence linking the suspect to the scene.

Fibers tend not to cling to other fabric tenaciously. Thus, forensic examiners must handle a victim with care, to minimize fiber loss. Retrieving the victim's clothing as soon as possible is a prudent step to preserving as many fibers as possible.

Fibers are typically collected using adhesive tape. The strips of tape are examined for fibers that match the fibers that are thought to be a normal part of the crime scene. This collection and analysis of fibers are tedious tasks.

Among the natural fibers, cotton and wool are the most popular. Other examples include flax, jute,

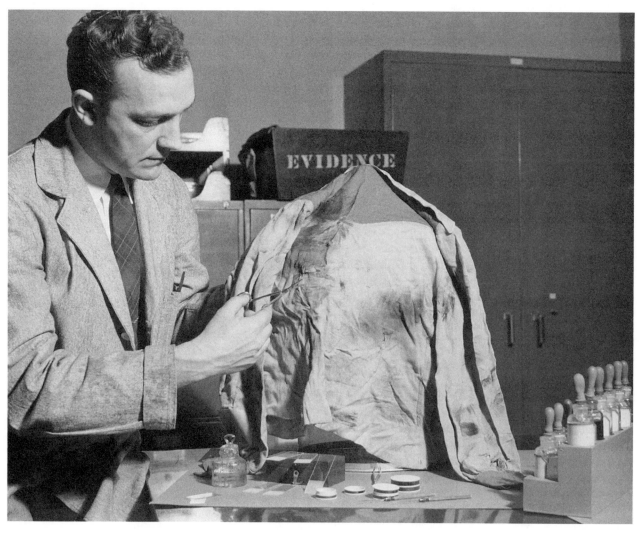

FBI lab technician cuts a sample of fabric from the clothing of a hit-and-run victim for comparison with fibers taken from the bumper of a suspect's car. © BETTMANN/CORBIS

hemp, and kapok. Each type can present a different appearance under an examination technique such as **polarized light microscopy**. Different fibers will refract light differently. Depending on a fiber's shape, the fiber can appear brighter along the edges or in the middle. Natural fibers tend to be circular when viewed in cross-section. In contrast, synthetic fibers can have a variety of shapes.

The number and location of fibers on a victim and a suspect are important in connecting the individuals together, especially if the fibers match. Matching fibers involves comparing the fiber type, color and type of dye used. The latter can be especially significant, given the nearly unlimited number of dye combinations that are possible.

Color is determined using a visible light microspectrophotometer or by thin-layer **chromatogra-**

phy, which separates the various dye components. Synthetic fibers can also be examined by infra-red **spectroscopy**, which can also yield information on the chemical makeup of the fiber.

SEE ALSO Bindle paper; Crime scene investigation; Filaments; Trace evidence.

Filaments

A filament is a thin wire made of tungsten that glows brightly when an electric current passes through. Filaments are found in light bulbs. A filament glows because the electrical current raises the temperature of the filament to about 4,000°F (2204°C). The study of lamp filaments can be important in accident reconstruction. In some instances, when a road accident occurs, it is not clear if the lights of a vehicle were on or off. One witness might contradict another one, and this question might be very pertinent to the outcome of the case. The forensic scientist can examine the remnants of the light bulbs and determine if they were on or off by looking at the filament.

Filaments are manufactured by extruding molten tungsten through a die, in a very similar process to the one used to manufacture spaghetti. The filament is then folded in a spiral and takes the general shape of a spring. The filament is supported by small steel arms placed inside the bulb. The filament is also connected at each end to electrical contacts, which will allow the current to pass through. The bulb is usually filled with an inert gas such as argon. If oxygen is present, the filament will burn as soon as it is switched on.

The determination of whether a light was on or off is based on the study of the breakage of the filament. Several situations can occur, each of them leading to a different phenomenon. If the filament was off, it is cold. If a shock is strong enough to break the filament, it will bear a neat break and a clean fracture surface will be present. If the filament was on and broke with the **glass** of the light bulb still intact, the fracture surface will show evidence of melting and the filament will be completely distorted. The reason is that the shock is fairly violent and when the filament is hot, it is easily deformed due to its spring shape. If the filament was on (hot) and the glass broke, it will burn in the air. Tungsten will react with oxygen to form tungsten oxide. If tungsten oxide is present on the filament or on the glass around the filament, it means that electricity was running through the filament while it was exposed to the air. If the filament was on at the time the glass broke, small particles of glass will be attracted toward the center of the light bulb, due to the slightly negative pressure inside the bulb, and would be deposited on the incandescent filament. At this point, the glass would melt and stick on the filament in the form of spherical glass beads. This could be the only evidence that a filament was on when the glass of the light bulb broke.

Examination of lamp filaments is performed under a microscope, so magnifications of 5–20 times can be achieved. If a light microscope does not allow the forensic scientist to conduct the examination properly, a scanning electron microscope (SEM) can

also be used. The SEM provides the examiner with a much clearer picture of the filament and particularly of the glass beads, if present.

SEE ALSO Accident reconstruction; Crime scene investigation; Physical evidence.

Film (forensic science in cinema)

Crime investigation has long been a favorite theme in film. **Evidence**, such as **blood**, weapons, and fingerprints, can provide fascinating plot twists and many films feature a detective as the protagonist. Crime labs, crime scene investigations, and autopsies often appear in such films. Some are based on true stories, such as the 1971 classic *10 Rillington Place* which is about the serial killer John Christie. Others are based on the work of famous crime authors, such as Agatha Christie or Raymond Chandler. If the filmmakers have consulted with police and forensic experts to get the details correct, then watching **forensic science** in film can be both educational and entertaining.

Film critics classify the detective-mystery film, the type that is most likely to feature forensic science, as a sub-genre of the crime-gangster or suspense-thriller movie. These are two of the major film genres, alongside horror, war, romantic comedy, and other genres. When talking about the history and development of film, genre is a term referring to a type of film with a specific theme, structure, content, subject matter, or filmic technique. Like other genres, the detective-mystery movie has undergone many developments and changes during the last century. Some are dark and haunting; others are action-packed, fast-paced, clinical, or even funny. What they all have in common is a narrative that follows an investigation—which is where the forensic science comes in to a greater or lesser extent, depending on the period—and a protagonist acting as a detective figure, be it a private investigator, a police officer, or a forensic expert. The plot of a detective-mystery film is often focused on the deductive ability and diligence of the central protagonist as he or she unravels the crime by gathering evidence, seeking clues, interrogating witnesses, and tracking down suspects.

The first significant detective-mystery films concerned the exploits of Sherlock Holmes, the private investigator created by the Scottish author

Sir **Arthur Conan Doyle** (1859–1930). There have been more than 160 Holmes movies, ranging from a 30 second silent film featuring the detective that was produced sometime between 1900 and 1905, and the 2002 made-for-TV version of *The Hound of the Baskervilles*. Perhaps the most famous portrayal of Holmes, with his Inverness cape, deerstalker hat, curved stem pipe, and magnifying glass, was by the British actor Basil Rathbone who appeared in 14 of the films between 1939 to 1946, including the classic *Hound of the Baskervilles*. The magnifying glass symbolizes the Holmes approach to detection: careful, painstaking, and, above all, scientific. The character was modeled on one of Conan Doyle's teachers at medical school, Joseph Bell, who always emphasized the importance of observation in making a diagnosis, advice that is equally applicable to criminal investigation.

Another classic series of detective-mystery films, appearing from the 1930s, featured the brilliant amateur detective Ellery Queen, based on the novels of cousins Frederic Dannay (1905–1982) and Manfred B. Lee (1905–1971), who used the character's name as a joint pseudonym. Ellery Queen was to become one of the most popular authors of the golden age of American mystery fiction between the 1920s and 1940s, although the radio plays and films did not, perhaps, have the same impact as the short stories and novels. Other detective heroes of this era include Charlie Chan, Bulldog Drummond, teenager Nancy Drew, and husband-and-wife team Nick and Nora Charles.

Several of the stories of the world's most famous detective writer, Agatha Christie (1890–1976), have been made into films. Her fussy eccentric Belgian sleuth Hercule Poirot appears in perhaps the best known of the Christie films, *Murder on the Orient Express* (1974). Directed by Sidney Lumet, the all-star cast including Albert Finney as Poirot. In the tale, a man is found murdered on the Orient Express and all the other passengers are suspects. It turns out they are all involved directly or indirectly in the case, and each one had a motive. Other Christie films feature a female investigator, the gray-haired Jane Marple, played by Margaret Rutherford, who was the protagonist in four films from the 1960s: *Murder She Said, Murder at the Gallop, Murder Most Foul,* and *Murder Ahoy*. Miss Marple has spent all her life in a sleepy English village where nothing much ever happens, but she has a remarkable eye for detail that serves well for crime investigation in any setting.

The history of the detective-mystery film can be traced through the evolution of the type of protagonist that, in turn, reflects changes in the pattern of crime and other societal factors. The gentlemanly approach of Sherlock Holmes, with his emphasis on logic and deduction seemed inappropriate for dealing with organized crime and gangs. Private investigator heroes became more physical, more likely to use violence in their pursuit of the criminal in films from the 1920s to 1940s. A significant development was the emergence of film noir, a film style characterized by moral and visual darkness, developed in the 1940s. Classics of the film noir era include *The Maltese Falcon* (1941), based on a story by Dashiell Hammett (1894–1961) and starring Humphrey Bogart as Sam Spade. The story has Spade investigating the death of his partner and being hounded by the police himself, while getting involved in the pursuit of a valuable statuette called the Maltese Falcon. *The Big Sleep* (1946) also stars Bogart, this time as as Philip Marlowe, the creation of Raymond Chandler (1888–1959). The complex plot involves seven killings, gambling, pornography, vice, and corruption. Both Spade and Marlowe are typical of the hard-boiled detective hero, preferring action, even violence, to analysis and careful investigation of evidence. These somewhat troubled heroes perhaps reflected the post-war mood in America, where men returning home often faced unemployment, disability, and a sense of alienation.

It was not until the late 1940s that the police and police procedure began to be a major focus in detective-mystery film. A major influence on the police procedural in film was the TV series *Dragnet*, which ran from 1951 to 1970. Dragnet emphasized the technical side of crime investigation, presenting it as rather less than glamorous. Details such as **ballistics**, surveillance, and forensic lab work soon began to find their way into film. The policeman hero was organized and methodical in his pursuit of the criminal. However, a new kind of protagonist began to emerge from the 1960s, as exemplified by *Dirty Harry* (1971), where a San Francisco cop, played by Clint Eastwood, tracks down a serial killer. Another classic from this era, *The French Connection* (1971), has Gene Hackman playing a New York City police officer pursuing drug smugglers. These heroes were tough and often angry and prepared to use controversial means of solving a crime. The action hero trend continued through the 1980s with films like *Lethal Weapon* (1987), starring Mel Gibson as a suicidal cop partnered with a more experienced officer as they investigate a drug smuggling racket in a blend of action and comedy.

However, from the 1990s to the present, there has been a return to the more intellectual, well-educated hero prepared to use observation and deduction rather than violence to solve a crime. One example is Clint Eastwood's *Bloodwork* (2002). Clint Eastwood plays a retired psychological **profiling** specialist, Terry McCaleb, who is recovering from a heart transplant. The plot twist comes when his new heart turns out to have come from a murder victim. Her death has been staged to look like a robbery gone wrong but is actually the work of a serial killer. McCaleb sets off in pursuit, an unlikely protagonist in comparison with the all-action hero.

Several aspects of forensic science also provide a background for *The Silence of the Lambs* (1991), directed by Jonathan Demme, in which the female protagonist, Clarice Starling (Jodie Foster), is a trainee **FBI** agent-investigator. The film concerns two **serial killers**, one of them, Hannibal Lecter (Anthony Hopkins), is behind bars while the other, known as Buffalo Bill, has just claimed a fifth victim whose **autopsy** is narrated in detail by Starling. The killer has kidnapped a sixth victim and the search is on to free her. To this end, Starling attempts to build a **psychological profile** of Bill, with Lecter's help. Lecter is a psychopathic psychiatrist who cannibalizes his victims and who has always been clever enough to avoid revealing his motives and inner fantasies to forensic investigators. Bill skins his victims post-mortem and also leaves an unusual signature. A forensic entomologist is brought in to identify the cocoon of the Death's-head moth, which is lodged in the throat of each victim. The film contains many other forensic and police procedural references.

Finally a forensic scientist himself becomes the victim in *Death of an Expert Witness* (1983), directed by Herbert Wise, which was the first film adaptation of the work of the English detective author P. D. James. It features Adam Dalgleish, a detective who writes poetry, and is set in a forensic laboratory in the East of England. The victim, as the title suggests, was also an expert witness. One of his colleagues may have killed him, a nice irony, given that forensic scientists are usually on the side of the law and are rarely under investigation themselves.

SEE ALSO Literature, forensic science in; Television shows.

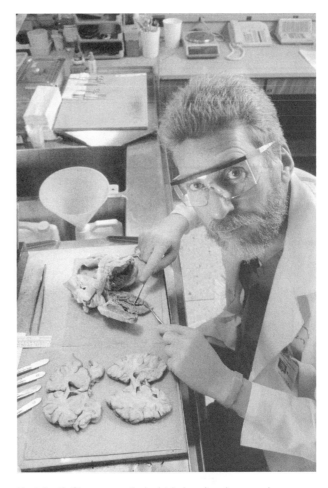

Dr. John E. Glassco, a pathologist in Los Angeles, examines a human organ in the hospital lab. Dr. Glassco also works to match up people in the medical industry for work in Hollywood feature films that require expertise in medicine. © JIM SUGAR/CORBIS

Fingerprint

Fingerprints are the impressions that are left behind by tiny ridges in the skin on the tips of the fingers and on the palms of the hand. The patterns left by these ridges, which are called friction ridges, are unique to every person. They are determined by the time a fetus is about six months old and they remain constant throughout a person's life. Even identical twins with identical **DNA** have different patterns of friction ridges on their fingers. Although many features of a person can be changed, fingerprints cannot. As a result, fingerprints are an extremely important tool for **identification** of individuals.

The outer layer of skin contains many microscopic pores that secrete sweat and oils. Sweat is mostly water, but it contains a very small fraction (1.5%) of salt, amino acids, and proteins. These

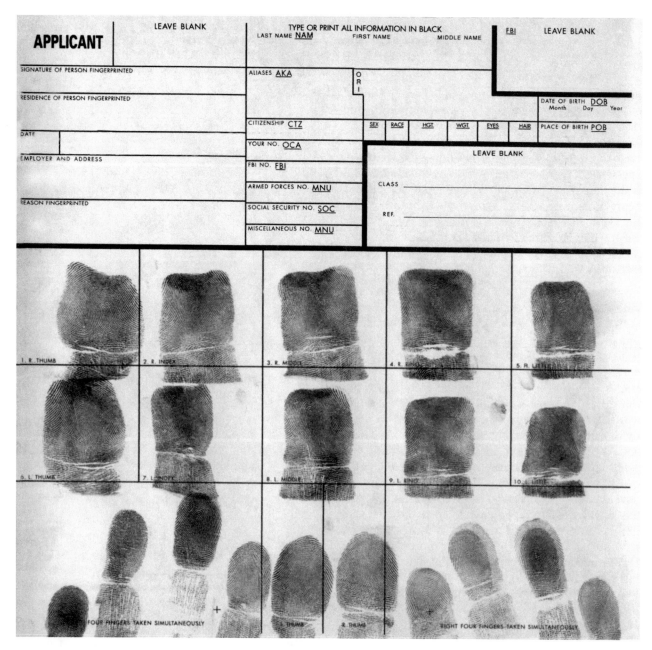

Fingerprints on a criminal record. © RANDY FARIS/CORBIS

chemicals remain on the skin after the water evaporates. The skin also contains sebaceous glands, which produce oils. Although the fingertips contain few sebaceous glands, the face and head contain many and people touch their faces and hair often, transferring oil to the fingertips. The oil and the residual chemicals from sweat cling to the surface of the fingers and attract dirt and other substances such as cosmetics and grease from foods and oils. Whenever a person touches something, these residues are transferred to that surface. Since people rarely commit crimes without using their hands, the prints from their fingers are often left on surfaces at the crime scene.

Detectives look for fingerprints at crime scenes in locations where things have been broken or disturbed. They also usually check the doorknobs and doorways, where a criminal may have entered or exited. Fingerprints can be found on a variety of surfaces including paper, human skin, smooth surfaces, painted surfaces, **glass**, the insides of gloves and **firearms**. They can last for a just a few hours in cold, dry weather or they may be visible indefinitely in warm, moist environments.

Fingerprints are classified into three groups. Plastic prints are prints that make an impression on a pliant surface like putty or tacky paint. Visible prints occur when someone has a material on their fingers that leaves a visible mark, such as **blood**, ink, or make-up. The most common fingerprints are called latent prints and they are formed from the oils and residues on the hands. Latent prints must be developed using one of many different chemical techniques.

Dusting for fingerprints is the most common technique for visualizing a latent print. This process begins by dipping a very soft brush into very fine powder. Most fingerprint kits contain black, gray, white, and red powders and the detective will choose a color of powder that contrasts best with the surface on which the print has been left. The detective carefully brushes the powder over the print and then blows the excess powder away. After the print becomes visible, it is photographed and then transferred onto special tape in a process called lifting.

Several other chemicals and techniques are commonly used to develop latent prints, and they are chosen depending on the surface and other environmental conditions. A chemical called ninhydrin, which is attracted to the amino acids that remain on the skin after the water in sweat evaporates, is used to develop fingerprints on paper. Iodine fumes can also be used to develop fingerprints on paper. The iodine vapors react with oils, turning them a brownish-violet color. Surfaces containing fingerprints can be dipped into or sprayed with silver nitrate, which turns black in the presence of salt. Superglue™ fumes, which produce white crystals in the presence of moisture in the fingerprints, are also commonly used to develop latent prints. In addition, specialized light sources, such as lasers and ultraviolet lights, can be used to make latent prints appear in situations where chemical techniques are impractical.

There are three basic classifications of fingerprints: arches, loops, and whorls. Of these, loops are by far the most common, next are whorls and a small fraction are arches. Arches are classified into plain arches, which are generally symmetric arched friction ridges, and tented arches, which become so

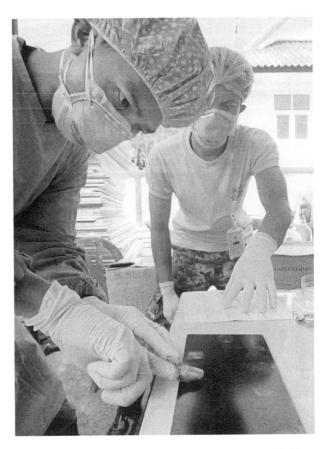

Forensic officials scan a fingerprint of a tsunami victim in Khabi province south of Bangkok on December 31, 2004. © CHAIWHAT SUBPRASOM/REUTERS/CORBIS

narrow that their core is a single friction ridge. Loops look somewhat like a cursive letter "e," but can be slanted either to the right or to the left. Loops are subdivided into radial loops, which flow towards the thumb, and ulnar loops, which flow toward the little finger. Whorls are circular or spiral shapes. They are subdivided into plain whorls, double loop whorls, central pocket whorls, and accidentals. As a result there are eight major categories of fingerprint patterns.

Fingerprint experts start with the basic patterns of friction ridges when they study fingerprints, but they depend heavily on the details called minutiae within fingerprints. These minutiae include ridge endings, dots, short ridges, bifurcations, and trifurcations. In addition, the location of sweat pores and the pores for oil glands serve as markers that can be used for identification.

SEE ALSO Bloodstain evidence; Crime scene investigation; Fingerprint; Superglue® fuming.

Fingerprint analysis (famous cases)

Forensic investigators have been using **finger-print evidence** as a source of **identification** of suspects for over a hundred years. Early work was by visual analysis of very obvious prints left at the scene of a crime. Modern forensic scientists now have a range of techniques for finding prints, cleaning up and enhancing print images, and rapidly finding a match from a database using computer technology. Fingerprint evidence is seen as one of the best types of **physical evidence** linking a suspect to an object or location or for establishing identity. Therefore, the forensic investigator will always search for finger-print evidence at the scene of a crime and at related locations, such as a suspect's home or car.

A fingerprint is the pattern of ridges and related characteristics found on the fingerpads, the fleshy parts of the fingers used for touching and gripping. Each person's fingerprints are unique and stay unchanged throughout life. According to Sir **Francis Galton**, the nineteenth-century English anthropologist, the chances of two fingerprints being identical are as small as 64 billion to one. In over a century of forensic fingerprinting, no two prints have ever been found to be the same, even those of identical twins.

Skin is never completely dry or clean; grime, oil, and sweat on the fingerpads create fingerprints whenever a person touches something. That is why criminals, unless they are wearing gloves, leave fingerprints behind. If their hands are bloodstained, then they will leave bloody fingerprints behind, an example of a patent (visible) print. Plastic prints are fingerprint impressions made in a soft material like soap or dust. Latent fingerprints are invisible, but the forensic scientist can visualize them though special lighting or with the application of chemicals. Fingerprints have been recovered from all kinds of surfaces, even plastic bags. It would be very useful to be able to reliably detect fingerprints on human skin. So far, this been very difficult to do if more than two hours have elapsed from the time the fingerprints were made. Potential methods are being developed to recover fingerprints after longer time periods have elapsed.

A fingerprint found at the scene of a crime can be dusted with chemicals to make it easier to see and then lifted or photographed. It is then compared with the fingerprints of known offenders stored in a computer database. In the past fingerprints were classified according to the specific features that make up the unique pattern of each print. With computerized storage and retrieval systems, however, classification is not really necessary as the computer can readily scan and match the whole pattern of thousands of prints. The image of fingerprints found at the scene of a crime can readily be enhanced and clarified with scanning and digitizing technology. This means that even partial prints can be of value in identifying someone at the scene of a crime.

In 1892 Francesca Rojas, an Argentine woman, became the first person ever to be convicted on fingerprint evidence. When her two young children were found beaten to death, she tried to blame a man called Velasquez who vigorously denied the charge and, in any case, had a firm alibi. Investigator **Juan Vucetich**, who was intrigued by the relatively new technique of fingerprint analysis, found a bloody fingerprint on a bedroom door in Rojas' house. He sawed the portion away and then had the woman give an ink-print of her thumb. Even with only a basic understanding of fingerprint analysis, it was obvious to the investigators that the bloody print belonged to Rojas. She confessed to the crime when confronted, and admitted that she committed the murders to improve her chances of marrying her boyfriend, who was known to dislike children. Rojas was sentenced to life imprisonment.

The brutal **murder** in 1905 of Thomas Farrow, manager of a shop in Deptford, near London, and his wife Ann was to become a milestone case in the use of fingerprint analysis in Britain. Money had been taken and a thumbprint was found on the cash box. The Criminal Investigation Department (CID) had already built up a file of fingerprints of known criminals, but this print did not match any of them. A witness led the investigators to two brothers called Albert and Alfred Stratton. A match was found between one of the men and the print found at the scene. The court battle over the evidence was, however, lengthy. Much hung in the balance as it was the first time fingerprint evidence had been used in a murder case in Britain. After two hours of deliberation, however, the jury found the two men guilty and they were later hanged.

In 1910, Thomas Jennings was arrested on suspicion of the murder of Clarence Hiller in Chicago. The main evidence against him was fingerprints, and four experts testified at his trial. However, fingerprint evidence was still relatively new and Jennings brought an appeal questioning its admissibility. In a landmark judgment, the Illinois Supreme Court upheld the conviction, saying that fingerprints were indeed a reliable form of identification. Jennings was sentenced to death and executed on February 16,

1912. He was the first person in the United States to be convicted of murder on fingerprint evidence.

Fingerprint analysis also played a role in convicting the man responsible for an audacious theft. On August 21, 1911, Leonardo da Vinci's *Mona Lisa* was stolen from the Louvre Museum in Paris. There was a clear fingerprint on the **glass** that had protected the painting. Fingerprint pioneer **Alphonse Bertillon** spent many months trying to match the print to samples in his collection but to no avail. Two years after the theft, police arrested Vicenzo Perugia in connection with the crime. His prints matched those from the crime scene. Ironically, Perugia's thumbprint had been in Bertillon's collection all the time, but it was of his right thumb. The one left on the glass in the Louvre was from his left thumb.

Criminals soon realized that fingerprints could be used to convict them and took evasive measures. Some used gloves but others, like John Dillinger, a gangster who terrorized the Chicago area in the 1930s, went further. While on the run from authorities, he had a plastic surgeon burn off the outer layer of his fingertips with acid, in the belief that this would erase his fingerprints for good. A tip off put the **FBI** on Dillinger's trail, they confronted him and shot him dead. In the morgue, they discovered Dillinger's attempts to burn away his this fingerprints. He had not succeeded. Fingerprints usually grow back and, in any case, go down through several layers of skin.

Early fingerprint investigators had a tough job sorting manually through print records. Today, matching is accomplished with the aid of high-speed computers. The FBI began to automate print analysis in the 1960s with **AFIS**, the **Automated Fingerprint Identification System**. The AFIS computer scans and digitally encodes fingerprint records into a database. It can match a sample, either a ten-print set or a single or partial print, by searching the database. Early versions of AFIS searched hundreds to thousands of prints a second; now the speed is up to 500,000 prints per second.

One notable success for AFIS was catching Richard Ramirez, a notorious killer known as the Night Stalker. He had committed a number of brutal rapes and murders throughout Southern California between 1984 and 1985, entering victims' homes at night and cutting the phone line. He would shoot any men present before raping their spouse, often in the same bed where the corpse laid. His final crime involved a couple in Mission Viejo, where he shot the man and raped the wife. Fortunately, both survived and the woman saw Ramirez' car, while another witness got the number of the vehicle. The stolen car was found abandoned and a partial fingerprint was recovered from the vehicle. The Los Angeles Police Department had just begun to use an AFIS system that could compare more than 60,000 prints per second and they found a match for the print in the car within minutes. A photo of Ramirez, a 25-year-old drifter from El Paso, went out in the papers and he was recognized within a day by residents in east Los Angeles, who overpowered him when he tried to steal another car. He was convicted by a jury and, on November 7, 1989, was given 19 death sentences.

Palm prints contain even more detail on them than fingerprints, and helped solve the kidnap and murder of 12-year-old Polly Klaas in 1993. The girl was enjoying a pajama party with friends at her home in Petaluma, California, when a man appeared through an open window with a knife and carried her off. The FBI used special light sources and fluorescent powder to locate an otherwise invisible palm print on a bunk bed. They also had a description of the intruder from the other girls. Torn children's clothing was found a few weeks later near a site where a man's car had rolled into a ditch. That man was Richard Allen Davis, who had two previous convictions for kidnapping. A fingerprint expert was able to match the FBI's palm print found at the scene of the crime to Davis, who then confessed and showed police where Klaas' body was. He was sentenced to death in 1996 for kidnapping and murder.

SEE ALSO Anthropometry; Fingerprint; Latent fingerprint; Ridge characteristics.

Fingerprints, ballistic SEE Ballistic fingerprints

Fire accelerants SEE Accelerant

Fire debris

Fire debris is a general term used to define the debris from a fire that is collected as **evidence** for laboratory examination. When a fire investigator suspects that a fire might have been deliberately set using accelerants such as ignitable liquids, it is possible to collect and analyze fire debris to see if such products are present.

When a person pours an ignitable liquid onto a substrate such as carpet, furniture, or clothing, that liquid gets adsorbed inside the substrate. When the liquid is set on fire, only the surface of the liquid burns and part of it is protected deep inside the substrate. If the fire department puts out the fire early enough, there are traces of this liquid left where the liquid was poured inside the burned debris. The fire investigator who collects the debris then sends it to the laboratory for analysis. The debris needs to be packaged in special containers that are sealed to prevent vapors of flammable or combustible liquids from escaping.

The forensic laboratory analyzes the debris using chemical techniques. First, the residues of the liquid are extracted from the debris, so they can be analyzed without the debris. For this step, different procedures can be used, but usually the sample is heated and the vapors are trapped onto a charcoal strip. This charcoal strip would then contain the residues of ignitable liquid. These residues are separated from the charcoal using a solvent. Once in the solvent, it is possible to analyze the residues with a gas chromatograph or **gas chromatograph–mass spectrometer**.

Once the analysis is done, it is important to interpret the results carefully. Modern furniture and clothing are composed of polymers that are based from petroleum products, the same petroleum products that are used to manufacture most of the flammable and combustible liquids such as gasoline, diesel fuel, charcoal starter fluid, and paint thinner. Thus, it is very important for the forensic scientist to be able to distinguish the presence of ignitable liquid from the chemicals that are produced by modern substrates. Only the proper collection, examination, analysis, and interpretation of the fire debris sample allow the forensic scientist to reach the proper conclusion.

SEE ALSO Arson; Canine substance detection; Chromatography; Fire investigation.

Fire investigation

Fire investigation is a field of forensic sciences dedicated to the determination of the origin and the cause of a fire. Determining the origin of the fire answers the question, "Where did the fire start?" Determining the cause of the fire answers the question, "Why did the fire start?"

In order for a fire to occur, three conditions must be met. There must be a combustible (fuel), an oxidizer (oxygen), and a sufficient heat energy source (source of ignition). The key elements that determine the cause of the fire rely on the determination of the first material ignited and of the source of ignition. Heat energy can be produced by mechanical, electrical, chemical, or radioactive means. The role of fire investigation is to identify the event that brought together the combustible, the oxidizer, and the source of ignition that started the fire.

Causes of fire can be natural, accidental, deliberate, or undetermined. Natural causes of fire include all the actions of nature that can cause a fire, such as lightning from the sky or lava from a volcano. Accidental fires include both fires that are caused by a negligent human intervention or by accidental occurrence without the necessary presence of a human being. Deliberate fires are caused by the intentional intervention of a human being. However, not all deliberate fires are arsons. For example, if one sets fire to backyard debris, it is deliberate but may not constitute **arson**. Arson is a legal term that can greatly vary from one country to another or from one state to another. In many instances, fire investigators will not be able to determine where and/or why the fire started, and the cause is classified as undetermined.

The determination of the origin of a fire is made based on observations of smoke, heat, and burn patterns at the fire scene. Fire evolves following the laws of physics and chemistry. While combustion is a complicated phenomenon that can be random in some instances, it is most often possible to determine the direction of fires. By tracing the direction backward, it is possible to find the origin of the fire. Once the origin of a fire is found, it is necessary to determine its cause.

One of the most important objectives in fire investigation is determining if a crime occurred in connection with the fire. If the fire is due to arson, it is extremely important to quickly determine that a crime occurred and gather **evidence**, so that an arrest may be made. If an accidental or natural fire occurred, it is important to determine how it started, so that the proper measures can be taken to prevent similar fires and to protect lives and property from future damage. In addition, in the case of accidental fire, it is important to determine the exact cause of the fire, because people or companies might bear a responsibility in the loss. The responsibility might be civil or criminal and carry an important financial burden. Many criminal laws also allow charges to be brought against people who accidentally created a fire.

Fires are investigated by fire investigators or criminalists. Fire investigators come from many

An arson inspector (foreground) in Los Angeles follows firefighters into a smoking fire scene to search for evidence of arson. © LAYNE KENNEDY/CORBIS

different backgrounds. In some European countries, fire investigators are commonly part of the police department, usually the crime scene unit. In English-speaking countries and in the United States in particular, it is often the fire department that employs fire investigators. Also, almost every state in the United States has a state fire marshal's office, which specializes in fire investigation. Furthermore, the Bureau of Alcohol, Tobacco, Firearms, and Explosives has a strong fire investigation practice and can dispatch the National Response Team within 24 hours almost anywhere in the United States to support state or local investigators.

In many instances, fire investigators need to rely on the knowledge of special experts such as electrical or mechanical engineers, forensic scientists, or chemists. For example, if the fire investigator suspects that liquid accelerants were used, he/she can collect **fire debris** to be sent to the forensic labora-

tory in order to search for such liquids. If an electrical apparatus is suspected to have caused a fire, an electrical engineer might help in the evaluation of the circuit or apparatus. If the failure of a shaft in a factory is suspected to have created the blaze by overheating, a failure analyst or mechanical engineer might be needed to determine the exact cause of the failure of the shaft.

Fire investigation is a harsh job, as it consists of working in dangerous conditions around burned structures or vehicles and in atmospheres containing many contaminants that are detrimental to the lungs and health. Fire investigators must often dig through debris from fire scene in order to see burn patterns. Often, it is necessary to reconstruct the fire scene in order to determine the pre-fire conditions.

SEE ALSO Accelerant; Exothermic reactions; Explosives; Gas chromatograph–mass spectrometer.

Firearms

A firearm is a weapon of attack or defense that expels a projectile via the action of the force exerted by the gases resulting from the rapid combustion of an explosive mixture. A firearm is often associated with the commission of a violent crime and is commonly found at crime scenes or on suspects. Also, many people who commit suicide use a firearm. An interest in firearms in forensic sciences is therefore, paramount. In **criminalistics**, the study of firearms consists first in the knowledge and **identification** of firearms and their ammunition, second in the internal, external, and terminal **ballistics**, and finally in the analysis of powders, primers, and their residues.

The birth and evolution of firearms is directly linked to the discovery of black powder. It is believed that the discovery of black powder dates from 1242, when the French monk Roger Bacon (1214–1294) wrote a letter describing the recipe for black powder. At that time, it was composed of about 40% saltpeter (potassium nitrate), 30% charcoal, and 30% sulfur. The first barrels, ancestors of the modern firearms, were developed at the beginning of the fourteenth century. At that time, the barrel was loaded from its end (muzzle), first with powder, and then with the projectile. The powder was ignited with a match, which was connected to the powder through the base of the barrel. Around 1800, mercury fulminate started to be used and the first primers were developed. In 1835, French arms manufacturer Casimir Lefaucheux (1802–1852) invented the first metallic cartridge. One year later, in 1836, American arms manufacturer Samuel Colt (1814–1862) invented the revolver. The pistol was invented prior to that time, however, it was loaded by the end of the barrel. The modern semi-automatic pistol (using a magazine) was invented after the revolver in 1893.

A firearm expels a projectile at high velocity. The projectile is part of the cartridge. The cartridge consists of a shell holding the primer at one end and the projectile on the other with powder in the middle. The cartridge is inserted either manually or automatically in the barrel of the firearm. The trigger of the firearm is then pulled, which arms the hammer. At some point, the hammer is released and hits the firing pin, which hits the primer. The shock to the primer starts its combustion, which, in turns, ignites the powder in the cartridge. The powder combusts very rapidly and produces gases, which increase the pressure inside the cartridge (and therefore the barrel) tremendously. This pressure is in the order of 2,000–4,000 atmospheres. This pressure is exerted on the base of the projectile, which is pushed into the barrel. The projectile then exits the barrel at high velocity, usually ranging from 250–1,000 meters per second (273–1094 yards per second).

Firearms are classified in two main categories: light and heavy firearms. Light firearms include handguns and shoulder guns. Handguns are then further classified into revolvers, pistols (semi-automatic, automatic, and machine), and Derringers (single-shot and double-barreled pistols). Shoulder weapons are divided into two subcategories: weapons with a rifled barrel, such as rifles and carbines, and weapons with a smoothbore barrel, such as shotguns. It is important to understand that some shoulder weapons may have more than one barrel. They can have two or more one-over-the-other barrels or side-by-side barrels. There are some shoulder weapons that have a combination of rifled and non-rifled barrels. Among the rifled shoulder weapons are the semi-automatic and automatic assault rifles and machine guns. Usually, heavy weaponry includes weapons that shoot calibers above 12.7 millimeter and are found on vehicles or armored tanks. These are specialized, usually military, weapons and are not encountered in the daily routine of a crime scene unit. Finally, there is the category of improvised or homemade weapons, which includes an enormous variety of different weapons of all calibers and functions.

Firearms are characterized by many variables, such as brand, model, size, length of barrel, shape, color, and functionality. Some of the most important variables of the firearm are the general rifling characteristics (when

Handgun confiscated as evidence. © RON SLENZAK/CORBIS

dealing with a rifled barrel), which include the **caliber**, the direction and degree of twist, and the number and width of grooves and lands. The caliber is correlated to the barrel's diameter and the power of the cartridges for which the firearm is designed. With few exceptions, a firearm is designed to use one given caliber. Upon shooting a projectile, the firearm leaves impressions on the projectile and the cartridge's casing. The observation of these impressions allows the forensic scientist to establish a link between the firearm and the elements of ammunition.

When dealing with a firearm found at a crime scene or on a suspect, the first security measure is to consider it as loaded and ready to shoot. Security with firearms is paramount and must be prioritized over everything else. If the firearm has just been found at a crime scene, it is possible to sketch, photograph, and take notes about it before touching it. Then, it is either placed in a container specifically designed to transport firearms and resist accidental discharges, or it needs to be secured. The firearm is then transported to the forensic laboratory where the firearms and **toolmarks** examiner can examine it.

SEE ALSO Ballistics; Crime scene reconstruction; Drugfire; Integrated Ballistics Identification System (IBIS); Microscope, comparison; Trajectory.

Michael First

AMERICAN
PSYCHIATRIST

Michael First is known as one of the world's foremost experts in the areas of psychiatric assessment and diagnosis. He is an associate professor of clinical psychiatry at Columbia University College of Physicians and Surgeons, and an associate attending psychiatrist at Presbyterian Hospital in New York City. His undergraduate degree, earned summa cum laude from Princeton University, was in computer science; his expertise in information technology has resulted in First's creation of a variety of quite popular computer-administered programs utilized for psychiatric interviewing.

First is well known as the text and criteria editor of the psychiatric diagnostic guide for the DSM-IV (Fourth Edition of the *Diagnostic and Statistical Manual of Mental Disorders*); he was the editor for the DSM-IV-TR (*Diagnostic and Statistical Manual of Mental Disorders*, Fourth Edition, Text Revision), as well as the DSM-IV-TR version developed especially for primary care physicians. The DSM is the universally accepted (as a valid and reliable research and diagnostic tool) diagnostic manual for psychiatry, **psychology**, and the behavioral health (mental health and substance abuse) professions.

First is the primary author of the Structured Clinical Interview for the DSM-IV (SCID). This is a longitudinally studied, highly reliable and valid diagnostic instrument employed by psychiatric, psychological, and behavioral health researchers, by the pharmaceutical industry, by clinicians and educators in many different settings, and by forensic clinicians and researchers as part of their psychodiagnostic and culpability assessments, as well as by those forensic psychologists and psychiatrists who make competency (to stand trial) assessments. The SCID is the most widely used diagnostic assessment tool in psychiatry.

First's **forensic science** expertise includes diagnostic assessment, differential diagnosis, and psychiatric interviewing. He is particularly noted for observing the subtle diagnostic underpinnings of the various personality disorders. First has published well in excess of thirty peer-reviewed articles on substance dependence, mood disorders, personality disorders, assessment, and psychiatric diagnosis. As a result of First's worldwide reputation as an expert in the fields of psychiatric and psychodiagnostic interviewing and assessment, he has been asked to act as a consultant to the Federal Bureau of Investigation (**FBI**) on the classification of violent crime. He serves also as a distinguished member of the professional organization the Forensic Panel, and he provides expert commentary to the journal *Forensic Echo*.

SEE ALSO Careers in forensic science; Computer modeling; Criminal responsibility, historical concepts; Mens rea.

First responders

It is usually a call to the emergency services that triggers the investigation of a potential crime. That is why the first person on the scene, known as the first responder, is usually a police, fire, or medical officer. His or her priority is always the safety of those who are at the scene, but the responder also has to be aware of the importance of preserving **evidence** that may be relevant to any crime that has been committed. After all, he or she is the only person to see the location in its original state. The actions and observations of first responders can therefore be crucial in terms of gathering and preservation of evidence that may eventually be presented in court.

On arrival at the scene, the first responder will carry out an initial assessment of whether a crime has actually been committed. If there is an obvious victim, the first priority has to be to offer first aid and any other assistance. In the case of a serious crime, the first responder will call for help so that the tasks of dealing with those present and preserving evidence can be delegated.

Although the first responder's first priority is assistance rather than looking for evidence, he or she will still keep the latter in mind in all their actions. However, the destruction of evidence is acceptable if it is needed to help a victim or even save their life. Whatever first responders do has the potential to affect evidence, and they need to be aware of this. Their first task is to assist any victims present at the scene of crime. They will also look for any suspects and arrest them if possible. Witnesses must be detained and kept separately. This is to stop them sharing from their stories and contaminating evidence. Should the first responder see suspects, victims, or witnesses trying to clean up or dispose of evidence, then they have a duty to stop them in the interest of preserving the scene.

The first responder will then secure the scene of crime by taping it off and taking careful note of who comes in and out. Entry is restricted to those who

Emergency workers attend to an 80-year-old woman involved in a single-car accident which caused her car to flip onto its roof in Berlin, Vermont, on August 14, 1998. AP/WIDE WORLD PHOTOS. REPRODUCED BY PERMISSION.

have a need to be there. Evidence outside this barrier may be easily contaminated, so the first responder should make the sealed-off area as wide as is practicably possible. The cordon should be policed and arrangements made to deal with the public and press, giving them information without allowing access that could otherwise disturb evidence.

When the first responder attends to a victim, he or she may need to move the person or any evidence. When this happens, a record should be taken of any actions that are performed. The original position and posture of the body and anything that is moved should be carefully recorded. The victim could need to go to the hospital and, ideally, someone would go with him or her. However, should the first responder be alone, the duty is to remain at the scene.

In the case of a serious crime, forensic investigators will be called to the scene. It is important for the first responder to mark out a common approach path for those coming to the scene later. This reduces the possibility of disturbing or contaminating the evidence at the scene, which can easily happen if people are moving at random through the site. Often the common approach path is from the cordon to the focal point of a crime, such as a body. Possible entry and exit points of perpetrators will also be avoided so that valuable evidence is not disturbed.

First responders must always minimize the impact they themselves have on the scene. They should attempt to minimize their own fingerprints or other trace left evidence behind and take special care to avoid areas and items that may contain suspects' fingerprints, such as doorknobs and light switches. Everything they do should be carefully recorded in case it alters the original crime scene. Sooner or later the first responder will be joined or replaced by others. It is particularly important that a record of what has been observed and carried out by the first responder is handed over by those who are next on the scene of crime. The **chain of custody** of evidence begins with first responders, even though they are not forensic experts. Their actions at the scene can be vital in the preservation of important evidence.

SEE ALSO Crime scene investigation.

Raymond M. Fish

AMERICAN
ELECTRICAL INJURY EXPERT

Raymond M. Fish has practiced emergency **medicine** for over two decades, and has become an expert in the study of electrical injury. As an instructor, researcher, lecturer, and author, Fish has spread his knowledge of treating electrical injuries and explaining the biological effects of electrical currents on the human body. He also has served as an expert witness and consultant in cases concerning electrical injury and related topics.

Fish earned his Ph.D. in biomedical engineering from Worcester Polytechnic Institute and Clark University. He is board certified in emergency medicine and has practiced this specialty since the 1980s. Fish also works as a professor, teaching bioengineering, surgery, advanced cardiac life support, advanced trauma life support, and electrical and computer engineering at the University of Illinois at Urbana-Champaign. At the university's Beckman Institute, Fish has conducted studies that combine engineering and medicine, such as the possibilities of using ultrasound to diagnose medical conditions. He is a fellow of the American College of Emergency Physicians, and a member of the Institute of Electrical and Electronics Engineers.

Fish is well known for his literary contributions to the treatment and investigation of electrical injury. He is a contributing author of *Forensic Aspects of Chemical and Biological Terrorism*. Written for public health and safety workers, the book addresses the roles and responsibilities of these officials in the event of a terrorist attack. Fish also co-wrote *Medical and Bioengineering Aspects of Electrical Injuries*, which serves as a reference manual for treating electrical injuries. He also has written many articles for trade journals and other periodicals, on topics including the effects of tasers and stun guns and physician and hospital responsibility.

Fish's interest in the interaction of law with medicine led him to work as a witness and consultant in legal cases involving electrical injuries and medical negligence. Through this involvement with attorneys and lawsuits, Fish has written books and articles related to medical/legal topics. He co-wrote *Electrical Injuries: Engineering, Medical and Legal Aspects*, which analyses electrical injury issues dealt with by litigators and investigators. He also wrote *Preparing for Your Deposition*, a book that outlines the deposition process and gives advice for dealing with deposition tactics.

SEE ALSO Death, cause of; Technology and forensic science.

Flame analysis

Some forensic analytical determinations rely on the separation of the various components in a mixture of compounds. One means of accomplishing this separation is to heat the sample using a flame.

The separated compounds can then be analyzed and identified. For example, when metals are burned, they can produce a characteristic color. The colors produced by the flame test are compared to known standards and the presence of certain elements in the sample can be confirmed. The color of the flame and its spectrum (component colors) is unique for each element.

Flame analysis or atomic emission **spectroscopy** (AES) is based on the physical and chemical principle that atoms—after being heated by flame—return to their normal energy state by giving off the excess energy in the form of light. The frequencies of the light given off are characteristic for each element.

Flame analysis is a qualitative test and not a quantitative test. A qualitative chemical analysis is designed to identify the components of a substance or mixture. Quantitative tests measure the amounts or proportions of the components in a reaction or substance.

The unknown to be subjected to flame analysis is either sprayed into the flame or placed on a thin wire that is then put into the flame. Volatile elements (chlorides) produce intense colors. The yellow color of sodium, for example, can be so intense that it overwhelms other colors. To prevent this, the wire to be coated with the unknown sample is usually dipped in hydrochloric acid and subjected to flame to remove the volatile impurities and sodium.

As useful as it is to forensic analysis, the flame test does not work on all elements. Those that produce a measurable spectrum when subjected to flame include, but are not limited to, lithium, sodium, potassium, rubidium, cesium, magnesium, calcium, strontium, barium, zinc, and cadmium. Other elements may need hotter flames to produce measurable spectra.

Other forensic analytical techniques are required to identify such substances. Typically, if there is enough of a sample, the sample can be divided into portions for testing by various techniques. This increases the likelihood of properly identifying the components of the sample.

Special techniques are required to properly interpret the results of flame analysis. The colors produced by a potassium flame (pale violet) can usually be observed only with the assistance of **glass** that can filter out interfering colors. Some colors are similar enough that line spectrum must be examined to make a complete and accurate **identification** of the unknown substance, or the presence of an identifiable substance in the unknown.

Flame analysis can also be used to determine the presence of metal elements in water by measuring the spectrum produced by the metals exposed to flame. The water is vaporized and then the emissions of the vaporized metals can be analyzed.

SEE ALSO Analytical instrumentation; Chromatography.

Flight data recorders

In the aftermath of an air crash, an extremely important task is to determine the cause of the disaster. This can be a daunting task, requiring patience and great attention to detail, since very little may be left of the aircraft. Eyewitness information, burn patterns, and the pattern of wreckage can all yield information as to the cause of the crash. The forensic work is greatly aided by the recovery of what is termed the "black box," or flight data recorder.

The flight data recorder is a repository of information about the operation of the aircraft. Sensors positioned throughout the aircraft relay information about the plane for storage in the data recorder.

In the earliest days of air transportation, plane crashes yielded few clues for safety investigators. Investigators would struggle to determine what happened immediately preceding the accident but often failed to come to any definite conclusions regarding the cause of the crash.

In June 1960, a Fokker F27 plane crashed while landing in Queensland, Australia, killing 29 people. Despite intensive investigations, the underlying cause for the accident was never determined. The mystery prompted the Australia board of inquiry to recommend that all airplanes be fitted with a flight data recorder (FDR) that would detail the flight crew's conversation.

Efforts to make the FDR a mandatory part of civil aircraft date back to the early 1940s. The idea, however, had one enormous technological challenge. Design specifications required that the unit survive the forces of an aircraft crash, as well as any resulting fire exposure.

In 1953, at a time when flight engineers were attempting to understand why a number of airliners had inexplicably crashed, Australian aviation scientist David Warren of the Aeronautical Research Laboratories in Melbourne invented a fully automatic "Flight Memory Unit." His prototype could record cockpit noise and instrument readings and remain intact following a crash or fire. Much to Warren's surprise, Australian aviation experts and pilots originally rejected the idea on the premise of privacy issues. Warren took the concept to the United Kingdom, where it was well received by aviation officials. By 1957, the FDR was in production. Australia then became among the first countries to require the device on commercial aircraft.

The common nomenclature for the FDR, the "black box," is actually a misnomer, since the unit is typically bright red or orange to facilitate visual location after a crash. The FDR is encased in heavy steel and surrounded by multiple layers of insulation to provide protection against a crash, fire, and extreme climatic conditions.

The device records actual flight conditions, including altitude, airspeed, heading, vertical acceleration, and aircraft pitch. A second device, the cockpit voice recorder (CVR), keeps tabs on cockpit conversations and engine noise. Both are installed in the rear of the aircraft.

In the 1970s, FDR technology was combined with a flight-data acquisition unit (FDAU), located at the front of the aircraft. The unit acts as the relay for the entire data-recording process. Sensors run from various areas on the plane to the FDAU, which in turn sends the information to the FDR.

In the early days, data were embossed onto a type of magnetic foil known as Incanol Steel. The foil proved to be destructible and FDR manufacturers began using a more reliable form of magnetic tape. Electromagnetic technology remained the data-recording medium of choice until the late 1990s, when solid-state electronics began to show promise. Solid-state recorders rely on stacked arrays of non-moveable memory chips. The technology is considered more reliable than magnetic tape, as the lack of moving parts provides a reduced chance of breakage during a crash.

Solid-state recorders also track a much greater number of parameters; 700 are tracked compared to the magnetic tape parameter recording potential of 100. Faster data flow allows the

A cockpit voice recorder, from crashed ValuJet Flight 592, drips mud after crash site searcher recovered it from the Florida Everglades. AP/WIDE WORLD PHOTOS. REPRODUCED BY PERMISSION.

solid-state devices to record up to 25 hours of flight data. In 1997, the United States Federal Aviation Administration (FAA) issued a requirement that all aircraft manufactured after August 19, 2002, record at least 88 parameters. The action came in the wake of two B-737 airplane crashes in which insufficient data was available to determine the cause of the accidents.

Modern day devices also track time, control-column position, rudder-pedal position, control-wheel position, horizontal stabilizer, and fuel flow.

Since its inception, the FDR has played a vital role in establishing the probable cause of a crash or other unusual occurrences and has allowed safety regulators to implement corrective actions. The value of flight data recorders was clearly evident in the investigation of the ATR-72 accident in Roselawn, Indiana, in October 1994. The FDR captured information on 115 parameters. Analysis of the data revealed a telltale, rapid wing movement that prompted the National Transportation and Safety Board to immediately issue urgent safety recommendations to improve flying in icy conditions.

SEE ALSO Aircraft accident investigations.

Fluids

Forensic analytical chemistry plays a crucial role in the **identification** of **physical evidence**, such as body fluids, tissues, and inorganic specimens (e.g., **artificial fibers**, accelerants, gun powder) found at crime scenes. Substance-specific metabolites, derived from the physiologic transformation of medications, **illicit drugs**, poisons, or alcohol, can be identified in **blood**, **saliva**, and urine. Blood and **semen** are also the preferred sources for **DNA** extraction from both victims and suspects, although saliva may also contain epithelial cells from the oral tract, from which DNA can be extracted. Therefore, body fluids may be used to detect drugs or other harmful chemicals present in the body or for DNA analysis.

Toxicological tests provide both qualitative results (the identification of substances present in the body) and quantitative results (amounts of substances present the body). Legal **medicine** also uses these tests for several other purposes related to public health, such as the determination of acceptable levels of **toxins** in the food and water supply, and determining the toxic potentials of prescription drugs and their interactions with other drugs.

Blood alcohol levels can be detected even after three or more hours after drinking. Metabolites of cannabis, LSD, and other hallucinogenic drugs persist in the system much longer, up to 72 hours, and are detected in cerebrospinal fluid, urine, blood, and other tissues. Blood levels of morphine derived from heroin injection and methamphetamine metabolites may be identified in several fluids and tissues, such as blood, urine, liver, muscles, and cerebrospinal fluids. The same is true for a variety of other chemicals and toxic gases as well as animal toxins, such as poison metabolites from venomous animals or insect bites.

Forensic investigators **processing** a crime scene must collect, condition, store, and transport body fluids, following strict technical and legal protocols to avoid contamination in order to guarantee credibility in courts. **Evidence** should be handled by the minimum possible number of personnel, preferably only two: the crime scene technician who collects it and the crime laboratory expert in charge of forensic testing. This is important because by law, all those who handled the evidence between the time of its collection and its analysis must be prepared to testify in court. This procedure is termed the "chain of custody." A **chain of custody** usually consists of the officer who seized the evidence and the forensic toxicologist, forensic chemist, or other officer who entered in direct contact with the substance before or after it was packaged (but not those who touched the outer sealed container). The validity and acceptability of the evidence may be questioned in court if this procedure is not properly followed and reported.

Biological fluids from victims and suspects are analyzed and compared for matches in cases of **murder**, rape, or in paternity tests. The first blood test involves usually ABO and other blood typing. Because this procedure only narrows the population of probable suspects, DNA analysis from blood, or semen, or other tissue may be necessary to establish a more precise match. Sometimes blood at a crime scene, especially near a victim, contains DNA from both the victim and the aggressor. DNA analysis is known as DNA typing or **DNA profiling**, and consists of several molecular techniques that screen specific segments of human DNA where certain characteristics are almost 100% unique in each individual.

DNA profiling is useful either to exclude a suspect or to identify one, through the comparison of the suspect's DNA with samples taken from the crime scene. In the absence of a suspect, the sample may be compared against DNA data banks such as **CODIS**, where thousands of DNA profiles of known criminals and suspects are recorded. DNA analyses do not always offer a 100% certainty in all cases, because DNA content in samples could have suffered degradation, or because the quantity of a sample is not large enough. However, the combination of several DNA tests, each one specific to a different segment or locus of the DNA molecule, may provide a unique pattern of matches that allows a high degree of scientific certainty as to whom it belongs. The probability that a person other than the suspect would display that same genomic pattern is about one in every five trillion individuals chosen from the population, with the exception of identical twins. Because the world population is around six billion, DNA profiling is a powerful identification tool.

SEE ALSO Assassination weapons, biochemical; Blood spatter; Bloodstain evidence; Breathalyzer®; Chemical and biological detection technologies; CODIS: Combined DNA Index System; Cross contamination; DNA evidence, cases of exoneration; DNA profiling; DNA sequences, unique; DNA typing systems; Luminol; Medical Examiner; Narcotic; Paternity evidence; Rape kit; Saliva; Serology; Toxicological analysis; Toxicology; Toxins.

Fluorescence

Fluorescence is an optical phenomenon wherein a material emits light in response to some external stimulus. Normally, the fluorescent light that is emitted is of a specific color or group of colors that is released when the material is bombarded with light in some other part of the color spectrum.

Certain **minerals** have a characteristic fluorescence pattern when hit with white light or ultraviolet light. Fluorite and calcite are two examples of fluorescent minerals. There are also many organic dye molecules with useful fluorescent properties. These molecules absorb light energy from external sources, and this energy causes some excitation of the electron orbitals in a process called pi-bonding. When the excited pi-bonds relax back to a lower energy state, photons of a specific wavelength are emitted in the process, giving rise to the fluorescent light. These organic dyes can be characterized by the wavelengths of light that they absorb (excitation wavelengths), and the wavelengths of light that they emit (emission wavelengths). The excitation and emission wavelengths are properties of each dye that are highly specific and reliable. Organic dyes tend to degrade over time as they are bombarded with light in a process called photodegradation. During photodegradation, the excited pi-bonds can break, rather than relaxing into their lower energy state. Organic fluorescent dyes have been in use for many years.

More recently, it has been discovered that very small particles of certain semiconductor materials also fluoresce, and the color of the fluorescence is dependent only on the size of the particles. These materials are referred to as quantum dots. Quantum dots absorb energy from a range of wavelengths, but the energy is not taken into pi-bonds. Rather, the fluorescence results from quantum mechanical interactions within the material. Smaller particles emit light on the blue end of the spectrum, whereas larger particles emit light on the red end of the spectrum. Because light energy is not absorbed into fragile pi-bonds, the rate of photodegradation is much lower for quantum dots compared with organic dyes, and thus the fluorescent signals are brighter and more durable.

There are a number ways in which fluorescence plays into forensic investigations. Biological materials sometimes have a characteristic fluorescent property that facilitates quick **identification** under UV examination. **Semen** stains, for example, may be identified by their characteristic fluorescence under ultraviolet light examination. Fluorescence of other biological samples can be brought about by chemical treatment to make their detection easier. Fingerprints can be treated with fluorescent powders to permit identification and detection even of relatively faint (latent) or degraded prints. Likewise, application of highly fluorescent materials, such as spy dust, permits tagging and tracking of suspects or agents across fairly wide areas by following the path of dispersal of the fluorescent agent as they drag and redistribute an unseen powder with their shoes or clothing. Certain chemicals, such as **explosives** and nerve agents, can sometimes be traced in the environment from their characteristic fluorescent spectral patterns. Examination of microscopic **fibers** for fluorescence can produce **evidence** linking suspects to crime scenes or other physical locations.

Fluorescence is a tool that allows evidence that would normally be invisible to come to light. It is a source of evidence only found with careful examination by those who are aware of its latent powers.

SEE ALSO Chemical and biological detection technologies; Confocal microscopy; Microscopes; Semen and sperm.

Food poisoning

Forensic investigations can involve determining if an illness or death was related to the contamination of food, along with the origin of the contamination.

Food poisoning refers to an illness that is caused by the presence of bacteria, poisonous chemicals, or another kind of harmful compound in a food. Bacterial growth in the food is usually required. Food poisoning is different from food intoxication, which is the presence of pre-formed bacterial toxin in food.

There are over 250 different foodborne diseases. The majority of these are infections, and the majority of the infections are due to contaminating bacteria, viruses, and parasites. Bacteria cause the most food poisonings. The United States **Centers for Disease Control and Prevention** estimates that 76 million Americans become ill each year from food poisoning. The cost to the economy in medical expenses and lost productivity is estimated at $5–6 billion per year. Infections with the common foodborne bacteria called salmonella alone exact about a $1 billion economic toll per year.

Aside from the economic costs, food poisoning hospitalizes approximately 325,000 Americans each year, and kills more than 5,000 Americans.

Staphylococcus is the most common cause of food poisoning. The bacteria grow readily in foods such as custards, milk, cream-filled pastries, mayonnaise-laden salads, and prepared meat.

Two to eight hours after eating, the sudden appearance of nausea, stomach cramps, vomiting, sweating, and diarrhea signal the presence of food poisoning. Usually only minor efforts need be made to ease the symptoms, which will last only a short time even if untreated. Over-the-counter preparations to counter the nausea and diarrhea may help to cut short the course of the condition. Recovery is usually uneventful.

This syndrome is especially prevalent in summer months when families picnic out-of-doors and food can remain in the warmth for hours. Bacterial growth is rapid under these conditions in lunchmeat, milk, potato salad, and other picnic staples. The first course of eating may be without consequences, but after the food remains at ambient temperature for two hours or more, the probability of an infectious bacterial presence is increased dramatically. The second course or mid-afternoon snacks can lead to an uncomfortable sequel.

A far more serious form of illness is produced by a toxin secreted by the bacterium *Clostridium botulinum*. Botulism, which is frequently fatal, is a hazard of home canning of food and can develop from commercially canned products in which the can does not maintain the sterile environment within it. Affected food has no tainted taste. Normal heating of canned products in the course of food preparation will neutralize the toxin but will not kill the bacterial **spores**. These will open inside the body, the bacterium will multiply, and sufficient toxin can be produced to bring about illness.

Ingestion of botulism-contaminated food does not lead to the gastric symptoms usually associated with food poisoning. Botulism toxin affects the nervous system, so the symptoms of botulism may involve first the eyes, with difficulty in focusing, double vision, or other conditions, then subsequent difficulty in swallowing and weakness of the muscles in the extremities and trunk. Death may follow. Symptoms may develop in a matter of hours if the tainted food has been consumed without heating, or in four to eight days if the food is heated and the bacterium needs the time to grow.

The most common foodborne bacterial infections are caused by campylobacter, salmonella, and a type of ***Escherichia coli*** (E. coli) designated O157:H7. The latter is the cause of "hamburger disease." A virus known as calcivirus or Norwalk-like virus also is a common cause of food poisoning.

Escherichia coli O157:H7 lives in the intestines of cattle. When it contaminates food or water, it can cause an illness similar to that caused by salmonella. However, in a small number of cases, a much more devastating illness occurs. A condition called hemolytic uremic syndrome produces bleeding, can lead to kidney failure and, in the worst cases, can cause death.

Food poisoning often affects numbers of individuals who have dined on the same meal. This enables forensic scientists to trace the contaminated food and, if needed, determine the specific type of bacterium that caused the illness.

SEE ALSO Poison and antidote actions.

Food supply

When investigating an illness outbreak or a death, one of the possibilities that a forensic investigator will assess is the involvement of food. The accidental or malicious contamination of food can be debilitating or, depending on the agent involved, fatal.

A variety of microorganisms or compounds produced by the organisms can contaminate food. As well, **inorganic compounds** in food can cause illness. Knowledge of the type of food and symptoms displayed can guide a forensic investigator in uncovering the source of the food contamination.

For example, if the nature of the last meal eaten and the symptoms demonstrated by the person affected are known, then forensic examination of the **blood** for the presence of a particular bacterial toxin may be a prudent step.

Food supplies can be compromised accidentally or deliberately. Since the terrorist attacks on United States soil in September 2001, much concern has focused on the susceptibility of food supplies to deliberate contamination.

Obtaining a strain of bacteria or virus that causes plant or animal diseases is much easier than obtaining a highly infectious human pathogen. Agricultural **pathogens** can even be obtained from the environment. For example, scraping the surface of infected leaves is sufficient to recover some disease-causing viruses. Both the former Soviet Union and Iraq are known to have experimented with agricultural pathogens.

Microorganisms can also be purchased from supply laboratories. An organization with convincing paperwork would be able to acquire microbes that are not considered to be highly infectious.

The advent of recombinant **DNA** technology in the 1970s—where a segment of genetic material coding for a protein of interest (i.e., a toxin) can be isolated and spliced into the DNA of a target microbe—holds the potential for the genetic modification of bacteria or viruses that are common in the environment. These genetic versions could spread quickly through the natural world.

Aside from deliberate contamination, food can harbor some types of harmful bacteria such as *Clostridium botulinum* and **Escherichia coli** O157:H7, and can cause illness when the food is eaten. Depending on the type of bacteria involved, the mere presence of the bacteria or its toxin may be sufficient to cause illness. Other bacteria need to grow to high numbers in the food before they become noxious. A well-known example is the bacterium *Staphylococcus aureus*, which has been identified in historical **food poisoning** outbreaks resulting from contaminated and improperly stored foods such as potato salad.

Different types of microorganisms contaminate different types of food. For example, the aforementioned *Clostridium botulinum* requires the absence of oxygen. Thus, improperly prepared (usually inadequately heated) canned foods are prone to contamination. The bacterium can produce a potent neurotoxin (a poison that acts upon the nervous system) that can paralyze and even kill a person who eats the contaminated food.

As well, *Clostridium botulinum* has the ability to form an environmentally resistant protective structure called a spore. The spore form of the organism can persist in a dormant state for very long periods of time. When conditions are more favorable for growth, resuscitation and toxin production can resume.

Following the September 11, 2001, terrorist attacks, the U.S. government moved to strengthen the country's defense against **bioterrorism**. This initiative culminated in the signing into law, on June 12, 2002, of the Public Health Security and Bioterrorism Preparedness and Response Act of 2002 (the Bioterrorism Act). The act authorized the Secretary of Health and Human Services to protect the nation's food supply. The U.S. Food and Drug Administration (**FDA**) is the lead agency in initiating the protective measures.

The U.S. measures are aimed at providing a system of accountability. For example, all businesses or growers who sell food for consumption in the U.S. must register with the government. As well, these firms will be required to maintain records of their food handling and processing activities. In the event of a deliberate contamination, this information would allow the source of the contamination to be traced.

The surveillance of food also must include inspection of food entering the country. This involves the manual inspection of foods arriving by air, sea, rail, and surface routes. Inspections typically consist of the visual examination of foods, although the use of portable devices that detect microorganisms or their products is being used experimentally. Other such devices are in the laboratory stage of testing, and have produced accurate results in laboratory settings.

Widespread alerts are often quickly recognized, and contaminated food sources are removed from the food supply, usually before many people will have consumed the contaminated food. Consumer vigilance is an additional important measure to protect the food supply. For example, even if raw produce has been doused with a poison or an infectious microorganism, careful washing will usually remove the threat. Canned foods that are damaged or swollen should be identified and discarded.

SEE ALSO Aflatoxin; Bacteria, growth and reproduction; Bioterrorism; Botulinum toxin; Food poisoning; Pathogens; Spores; Toxins.

Forensic accounting

Over the years, the role of the certified public accountant (CPA) has changed dramatically, with some of today's CPAs becoming quasi-private investigators in order to keep up with demands for fraud examinations. These specialized individuals use investigative procedures in an effort to uncover fraudulent activities being perpetrated on a business. Forensic accounting is a term used to describe the work being performed by accountants in advance of litigation and may include bankruptcy, valuation, fraud, and a variety of additional services. It is estimated that each year approximately $400 billion is lost due to employee fraud. To determine the depth and scope of the crime, a fraud examination is conducted in order to find where it is being perpetrated and by whom. Often the auditor must delve into the psyche of the suspect to find a motive for the crime. There are three main reasons why an employee generally steals from his employer, making up what is termed a fraud triangle.

The key elements that comprise most every fraud triangle include opportunity, pressure, and rationalization. The first and most important segment of a fraud triangle is opportunity. Often, companies unknowingly and unwisely offer their employees the opportunity to commit fraud. Typically it is a lack of adequate control and monitoring of employee actions that afford the chance to steal. An example to demonstrate opportunity would be a cashier or accounts receivable person being responsible for the daily collecting and depositing of payments. Without adequate control measures to authenticate the employee's accuracy, funds could easily be embezzled without notice.

Of course, not all employees will seize the opportunity to steal, so what additional factors also figure in to a fraud triangle? Succumbing to pressure is very often the reason why someone chooses to steal when others do not. Financial pressure can arise from a myriad of sources such as personal debt, business losses, and lifestyle standards. Therefore, employees with known financial trouble should not be placed in positions involving money transactions or other duties that would offer a chance to commit fraud. Even peer pressure can be a factor in an employee choosing to steal.

Rationalization is the third element of the fraud triangle. Regardless of the reason for taking money, the thief must then try to rationalize why he or she committed the fraud. The employee who steals often attempts to justify the crime psychologically. Such rationalizations might include thinking the company has so much money that the theft would not be noticed, or the money is for a worthy endeavor such as college tuition or emergency medical expenses. In this way, the perpetrator often attempts to ease a nagging conscience about stealing. In most cases however, the employee makes a mistake or error that places a cloud of suspicion upon them. This is when the fraud examination is conducted.

A fraud examination generally consists of four successive segments: analyzing the available data, developing a fraud theory, revising it as necessary, and confirming the theory. The first step is analyzing financial information culled from the books and records. The particular type of fraud that is being investigated will determine which documents, files, records, and other information are needed for studying. Once the information has been gathered, sorted, and processed, the examiner begins to review and analyze the data in order to develop a theory of what could have happened and who was the perpetrator.

Usually the theory addresses one of three types of internal or occupational fraud: asset misappropriation, corruption, or fraudulent financial statements. The examiner goes through a series of tests and retests in order to determine if there is sufficient **evidence** to proceed further. The evidence must be substantial enough to stand up in a court of law. If the examination is sound and has merit, then the corporate legal counsel is apprised of impending litigation, interviews are ordered, and third-party and corroborative witnesses are questioned. The examination must be detailed, in depth, and substantiated with indisputable evidence in order to move to the next stage, which entails confronting the suspect or target. This procedure is called an admission-seeking interview, and involves a deliberate process that lays out the evidence to the target in a specific order. The questions must be precisely phrased and the answers correctly interpreted so as to avoid any confusion or misunderstanding. While these procedures help detect and find fraud, the more practical solution would be to prevent fraud from occurring.

The problem with prevention is that certified fraud examiners and forensic accountants cannot affect the internal and external controls that tend to lead to fraud. The problem of company fraud is a social issue, not an accounting issue, and without effective punishment measures, the practice is expected to rise. Punishment is often neither swift nor certain when is comes to fraudulent crimes. It is also difficult for courts and judges to determine the punishment when an accounting crime ended with the destruction of a company that had employed many individuals who lost pensions and retirement investments as well as jobs.

The idea of prevention would seem like the correct response to an ever-increasing crime wave. However, given the current methods of detection of fraud, the fraud examination, and employing the methodology of the fraud triangle, prevention suddenly becomes closer to invasion of privacy and targeting of persons. If the manager of a clinic tells his employer about his spouse being laid-off from work, should the employer then keep a close eye and ear on the manager in order to prevent the possibility of an opportunity to defraud the clinic by the manager? The idea of **profiling** an employee for any potential of defrauding a company is not consistent with ethical standards of business.

Fraud examination and the fraud triangle are two of the most effective and important procedures a CPA or auditor can use when determining the existence of fraudulent behavior or activities in a company. Both of these concepts constitute the science of forensic accounting and help to uncover any illegal activities. The modern day accountant must have working knowledge of forensic accounting in order to be a success in the field. The government binds an accountant by various laws and statutes in order to

obligate them to report any financial mishaps or miscues on the part of the company.

SEE ALSO Document destruction; Document forgery; Evidence; Federal Rules of Evidence.

Forensic nursing

The field of forensic nursing has become increasingly popular since the last decade of the twentieth century, and is predicted to continue to be one of the fastest growing and most desirable nursing specialties.

In 1992, a group met in Minneapolis for the first convention of sexual assault nurses. One of the meeting's outcomes was the creation of the term, and the specialty, of forensic nursing. Another outcome was the inception of the International Association of Forensic Nurses (IAFN). The IAFN is the only international professional registered nurses' organization created with the specific goals of developing, advancing, and disseminating information about the science of forensic nursing. In 1995, forensic nursing was recognized as a clinical specialty by the American Nurses Association.

A growing number of schools of nursing offer **training**, certificates, or advanced degrees in the area of forensics. Some of the specialty areas within forensic nursing include: forensic clinical nurse specialist, forensic nurse investigator, nurse coroner/death investigator, sexual assault nurse examiner (SANE), sexual assault response team member (SART), legal nurse consultant, forensic gerontology specialist, forensic psychiatric nurse, and correctional nursing specialist.

Specialized forensic nursing coursework and practical training typically include advanced training in the identification of traumatic wounding, including training in recognition of patterned wounds, and injuries in various stages of healing (it is not uncommon in domestic violence situations to see victims with fresh, relatively new, and older healing injuries). Forensic nurses are trained to objectively, record a complete chronology of the injuries from the victim, patient, parent, legal guardian, or caregiver; they (forensic nurses) are often skilled at crime victim **photography**. This experiential combination makes them valuable **expert witnesses** in court proceedings.

In 2002 the Forensic Nursing Certification Board (FNCB) had its inception. The mission of the FNCB is to uphold the highest standards of both the science and the clinical practice of forensic nursing, via the creation, utilization, promulgation, and assessment of every aspect of the forensic nursing certification (and re-certification) process.

It is the stated philosophy of the FNCB that the clinical specialty of forensic nursing encourages attainment of the ultimate standards of nursing practice in order to deliver the best possible patient care. The FNCB seeks to standardize the coursework, training, and practice of forensic nursing in order to provide a common knowledge and experiential base. This, in turn, will lead to uniformly superior skill levels in the field. As a result of this professional standardization, the attainment of forensic nurse certification will be professionally (and legally) meaningful.

Quite often, work as a SANE or SART nurse provides an entry point into forensic nursing. Through the course of their work, SANE and SART nurses interact with coroners, members of law enforcement, judges, district attorneys, victims' advocates, criminal and civil attorneys; this is an ideal way to segue into forensic nursing. The SANE-A credential, a professional certification conferred by the FNCB, is given to sexual assault nurse examiners with adolescent and adult expertise. It indicates achievement of the most stringent standards of forensic nursing expertise in the field of sexual assault nurse examination, resulting in professional board certification.

Forensic nurses often interact with those involved in rape, child and elder abuse, domestic violence, and trauma associated with violent crimes. The work of forensic nurses can vary widely, from providing (typically emergency) care to both crime victims and perpetrators, to collecting or photographing **evidence** for law enforcement agencies, to performing death investigations, to providing support for emergency workers at crisis settings, to counseling schoolchildren who use weapons, to providing physical (and sometimes behavioral health) care in the correctional system, to acting as legal nurse consultants and expert witnesses in the court system.

They may provide direct nursing services to individuals, act as professional consultants to nursing, medical, legal, and law enforcement agencies, or provide expert witness testimony in court settings regarding trauma, questioned death investigations, adequacy, and appropriateness of service delivery, and offer diagnostic opinions on issues pertaining to specific nursing-related conditions.

Forensic nurses are particularly valuable in the emergency medical setting, as health care professionals are typically taught to clean and treat wounds and injuries, resulting in loss of valuable evidence and, sometimes, leading to an inability to prosecute crimes.

Nurse Lauren Guerira, who was involved with the investigation of the rape kit report of the alleged accuser, prepares to testify in the sexual assault trial of NBA basketball star Kobe Bryant in 2004. © ED ANDRIESKI/POOL/REUTERS/CORBIS

Forensic nurses are trained to photograph and meticulously document trauma and injuries, to collect, to preserve, and to properly package evidence.

Clinical forensic nursing involves applying standard clinical nursing theory and practice to the complex treatment of trauma, or to the investigation of death, of victims or perpetrators of criminal violence, child, elder, and domestic abuse, and traumatic accidents. Forensic nurses interact with the legal justice and law enforcement systems regularly.

Forensic nursing, a specialty field steadily gaining in both importance and popularity, is of significant importance whenever and wherever clinical nursing and the law enforcement (and legal) systems interact.

SEE ALSO Accident reconstruction; Careers in forensic science; Crime scene cleaning; Paternity evidence; Photography; Physical evidence; Rape kit.

Forensic science

Forensic science is a term used to describe the actions taken by investigators in multidisciplinary fields for the examination of crime scenes and gathering of **evidence** to be used in prosecution of offenders in a court of law. The main use of forensic science is for purposes of law enforcement to investigate crimes such as **murder**, theft, or fraud. Forensic scientists are also involved in investigating accidents such as train or plane crashes to establish if they were accidental or a result of foul play. The techniques developed by forensic science are also used by the U.S. military to analyze the possibility of the presence of chemical weapons or high **explosives**, to test for propellant stabilizers, or to monitor compliance with international agreements regarding weapons of mass destruction.

The main areas used in forensic science are biology, chemistry, and **medicine**, although the science also includes the use of physics, computer science, **geology**, or **psychology**. Forensic scientists examine objects, substances (including **blood** or drug samples), chemicals (paints, explosives, **toxins**), tissue traces (hair, skin), or impressions (fingerprints or tidemarks) left at the crime scene. The majority of forensic scientists specialize in one area of science.

The analysis of the scene of a crime or accident involves obtaining a permanent record of the scene (forensic **photography**) and collection of evidence for further examination and comparison. Collected samples include biological (tissue samples such as skin, blood, **semen**, or hair), physical (fingerprints, shells, fragments of instruments or equipment, **fibers**, recorded voice messages, or computer discs) and chemical (samples of paint, cosmetics, solvents, or soil).

Most commonly, the evidence collected at the scene is subsequently processed in a forensic laboratory by scientists specializing in a particular area. Scientists identify, for example, fingerprints, chemical residues, fibers, hair, or **DNA**. However, miniaturization of equipment and the ability to perform most forensic analysis at the scene of crime results in more specialists being present in the field. Presence of more people at the scene of crime introduces a greater likelihood of introduction of contamination into the evidence. Moreover, multi-handling of a piece of evidence (for example, a murder weapon) is also likely to introduce traces of tissue or DNA not originating from the scene of a crime. Consequently, strict quality controls are imposed on collection, handling, and analysis of evidence to avoid contamination.

The ability to properly collect and process forensic samples can affect the ability of the prosecution to prove their case during a trial. The presence of chemical traces or DNA on a piece of debris is also crucial in establishing the chain of events leading to a crime or accident.

Biological traces are collected not only from the crime scene and deceased person, but also from surviving victims and suspects. Most commonly, samples obtained are blood, hair, and semen. DNA can be extracted from any of these samples and used for comparative analysis.

DNA is the main method of identifying people. Victims of crashes or fires are often unrecognizable, but if adequate DNA can be isolated a person can be positively identified if a sample of their DNA or their family's DNA is taken for comparison. Such methods are being used in the **identification** of the remains in Yugoslav war victims, the World Trade Center terrorist attack victims, and the 2002 Bali bombing victims.

Biological traces, investigated by forensic scientists come from bloodstains, **saliva** samples (from cigarette butts or chewing gum) and tissue samples, such as skin, nails, or hair. Samples are processed to isolate the DNA and establish the origin of the samples. Samples must first be identified as human, animal, or plant before further investigation proceeds. For some applications, such as customs and quarantine, traces of animal and plant tissue have to be identified to the level of the species, as transport of some species is prohibited. A presence of a particular species can also prove that a suspect or victim visited a particular area. In cases of national security, samples are tested for the presence of **pathogens** and toxins, and the latter are also analyzed chemically.

A growing area of forensic analysis is monitoring non-proliferation of weapons of mass destruction, analysis of possible terrorist attacks, or breaches of security. The nature of samples analyzed is wide, but slightly different from a criminal investigation. In addition to the already-described samples, forensic scientists who gather evidence of weapons of mass destruction collect swabs from objects, water, and plant material to test for the presence of radioactive isotopes, toxins, or poisons, as well as chemicals that can be used in production of chemical weapons. The main difference from the more common forensic investigation is the amount of chemicals present in a sample. Samples taken from the scene of suspected chemical or biological weapons often contain minute amounts of chemicals and require very sensitive and accurate instruments for analysis.

Forensic chemistry performs qualitative and quantitative analysis of chemicals found on people, various objects, or in solutions. The chemical analysis is the most varied from all the forensic disciplines. Chemists analyze drugs as well as paints, remnants of explosives, **fire debris**, gunshot residues, fibers, and soil samples. They can also test for a presence of radioactive substances (nuclear weapons), toxic chemicals (chemical weapons), and biological toxins (biological weapons). Forensic chemists can also be called on in a case of environmental pollution to test the compounds and trace their origin.

The identification of fire accelerants such as kerosene or gasoline is of great importance for determining the cause of a fire. Debris collected from a fire must be packed in tight, secure containers, as the compounds to be analyzed are often volatile. An improper transport of such debris would result in no detection of important traces. One of the methods used for this analysis involves the use of charcoal strips. The chemicals from the debris are absorbed onto the strip and subsequently dissolved in a solvent before analysis. This analysis allows scientists to determine the hydrocarbon content of the samples and identify the type of fire accelerator used.

Physical evidence usually refers to objects found at the scene of a crime. Physical evidence may include all sorts of prints such as fingerprints, footprints, handprints, tidemarks, cut marks, tool marks, etc. Analysis of some physical evidence is conducted by making impressions in plaster, taking images of marks, or lifting the fingerprints from objects encountered. These serve later as a comparison to identify, for example, a vehicle that was parked at the scene, a person that was present, a type of manufacturing method used to create a tool, or a method used to break in a building or harm a victim.

An examination of documents found at the scene or related to the crime is often an integral part of forensic analysis. Such examination is often able to establish not only the author but, more importantly, identify any alterations that have taken place. Specialists are also able to recover text from documents damaged by accident or on purpose.

The identification of people can be performed by **fingerprint** analysis or DNA analysis. When none of these methods is viable, facial reconstruction can be used instead to generate a person's image. Television and newspapers then circulate the image for identification.

Pathologists and forensic anthropologists play a very important part in forensic examination. They are able to determine the **cause of death** by examining marks on the bone(s), skin (gunshot wounds), and other body surfaces for external trauma. They can also determine a cause of death by **toxicological analysis** of blood and tissues.

A number of analytical methods are used by forensic laboratories to analyze evidence from a crime scene. Methods vary, depending on the type of evidence analyzed and information extracted from the traces found. If a type of evidence is encountered for the first time, a new method is developed.

Biological samples are most commonly analyzed by **polymerase chain reaction** (**PCR**). The results of PCR are then visualized by gel **electrophoresis**. Forensic scientists tracing the source of a biological attack could use the new hybridization or PCR-based methods of DNA analysis. Biological and chemical analysis of samples can identify toxins found.

Imaging used by forensic scientists can be as simple as a light microscope, or can involve an electron microscope, absorption in ultraviolet to visible range, color analysis, or **fluorescence** analysis. Image analysis is used not only in cases of biological samples, but also for analysis of paints, fibers, hair, **gunshot residue**, or other chemicals. Image analysis is often essential for an interpretation of physical evidence. Specialists often enhance photographs to visualize small details essential in forensic analysis. Image analysis is also used to identify details from surveillance **cameras**.

The examination of chemical traces often requires very sensitive chromatographic techniques or mass spectrometric analysis. The four major types of chromatographic methods used are: **thin layer chromatography** (TLC) to separate inks and other chemicals; atomic absorption **chromatography** for analysis of heavy metals; gas chromatography (GC); and liquid chromatography (HPLC). GC is most widely used in identification of explosives, accelerators, propellants, and drugs or chemicals involved in chemical weapon production, while liquid chromatography (HPLC) is used for detection of minute amounts of compounds in complex mixtures. These methods rely on separation of the molecules based on their ability to travel in a solvent (TLC) or to adhere to adsorbent filling the chromatography column. By collecting all of the fractions and comparing the observed pattern to standards, scientists are able to identify the composition of even the most complex mixtures.

New laboratory instruments are able to identify nearly every element present in a sample. Because the composition of alloys used in production of steel instruments, wires, or bullet casings is different between various producers, it is possible to identify a source of the product.

In some cases chromatography alone is not an adequate method for identification. It is then combined with another method to separate the compounds even further and results in greater sensitivity. One such method is mass spectrometry (MS). A mass spectrometer uses high voltage to produce charged ions. Gaseous ions or isotopes are then separated in a magnetic field according to their masses. A combined GC-MS instrument has a very high sensitivity and can analyze samples present at concentrations of one part-per-billion.

As some samples are difficult to analyze with MS alone, a **laser** vaporization method (imaging laser-ablation mass **spectroscopy**) was developed to produce small amounts of chemicals from solid materials (fabrics, hair, fibers, soil, **glass**) for MS analysis. Such analysis can examine hair samples for presence of drugs or chemicals. Due to its high sensitivity, the method is of particular use in monitoring areas and people suspected of production of chemical, biological, or nuclear weapons, or narcotics producers.

While charcoal sticks are still in use for fire investigations, a new technology of solid-phase microextraction (SPME) was developed to collect even more chemicals and does not require any solvent for further analysis. The method relies on the use of sticks similar to charcoal, but coated with various polymers for collecting different chemicals (**chemical warfare** agents, explosives, or drugs). Collected samples are analyzed immediately in the field by GC.

SEE ALSO Computer forensics; Crime scene investigation; DNA; DNA recognition instruments; Document forgery; Gas chromatograph-mass spectrometer; Isotopic analysis; Thin layer chromatography.

Forensic science, careers SEE
Careers in forensic science

Forensic Science Service (U.K.)

The Forensic Science Service (FSS) is the largest supplier of forensic services to police forces in England, Ireland, Scotland, and Wales, commonly referred to as the United Kingdom (U.K.). The FSS is also a major forensic source of consultancy, **training**, and support throughout the U.K and overseas. Internationally, the FSS has assisted over 60 countries in various areas of casework, consulting, research, and training, especially with regard to

DNA research and development. In fact, its Research and Service Development unit is internationally acclaimed as one of the leading forensic science research organizations in the world.

The FSS was established as an executive agency of the Home Office of the U.K. government in April 1991 when several forensic laboratories in England and Wales were brought together. It was then merged with the Metropolitan Police Laboratory, London, England, in 1996 to become what is considered similar to the **FBI** (Federal Bureau of Investigation) Laboratory in the United States. Currently, the FSS is an executive agency of the U.K. Home Office with seven laboratories equipped with the latest technologies. Although the FSS is a critical part of the criminal justice system in the U.K., it performs all of its work independent from the police.

Although capable of providing an array of basic services for nearly any police investigation, the FSS has developed specialized solutions in the following important forensic areas: illegal drugs, high-technology crime, international crime, property crime (such as robbery and vehicle theft), road policing (including offenses of drinking-and-driving), and serious crime (such as **murder** and sexual offenses). In addition, the FSS pioneered the use of **DNA profiling** in forensic science when it set up in April 1995 the world's first national criminal intelligence DNA database, the National DNA Database (NDNAD). Under the guidance of the FSS for the Association of Chief Police Officers (ACPO), the NDNAD is a very successful international forensic database that contains well over two million individual DNA profiles and an excess of 200,000 crime scene profiles. In the years 2003 and 2004, personnel of the FSS have taken part in about 150,000 criminal cases, participated in approximately 1,700 crime scenes, and appeared around 2,600 times as **expert witnesses** in court cases.

SEE ALSO FBI crime laboratory.

Forgery, art SEE Art forgery

Fourier transform infrared spectrophotometer (FTIR)

A Fourier transform infrared spectrophotometer (FTIR) is an instrument used to examine specimens, both to detect the presence of target compounds and to measure the quantities of the compounds (quantification). FTIR can be an important analytical instrument in a forensic investigation.

A FTIR can be useful in detecting both organic chemicals (i.e., those that contain carbon) and inorganic chemicals. As with other forms of spectrophotometry, FTIR utilizes light. In this case, the wavelength of the light (the distance between a point of one light wave and the corresponding point of an adjacent wave) is in the infrared range. Infrared light lies in between the visible light and microwave portions of the **electromagnetic spectrum**. The infrared light that is nearest to visible light ("near infrared") has a wavelength of approximately 770 nanometers (nm; 10^{-9} meter). At the other end of the range, infrared light that is nearest to microwave radiation ("far infrared") has a wavelength of approximately 1,000,000 nm (1.0 millimeter).

The basis of FTIR is the absorption of the infrared light by various molecules in a sample. Depending on their chemical structure and three-dimensional orientation, the different sample molecules will absorb different portions of the infrared spectrum.

Depending on the nature of the chemical bond that absorbs the infrared light, a chemical bond will vibrate in varying ways. Reflecting the different types of bonds, a number of events can occur. For example, the input of vibrational energy can stretch the bonds between the carbon atom and the surrounding hydrogen atoms in CH_3. Also, the carbon-hydrogen linkages of CH_3 can remain the same length while the linked atoms are moved back and forth laterally to one another (rocking). Other chemical linkages, such as that between a silicon atom and CH_3 group, can be altered asymmetrically along their lengths, with some regions of the bond stretching and other regions contracting (asymmetric deformation).

The absorption of light by the sample will decrease the energy of the infrared light that exits the sample chamber or produce a wave that is "out of synch" with light that has not passed through the sample. A computational comparison of the frequency patterns of the incoming and exiting infrared light can be made as described subsequently and displayed as a series of peaks rising above the background baseline. The height of the peaks corresponds to the degree of absorption and/or to the nature of the chemical bond change (i.e., stretching, rocking, deformation).

Within the spectrophotometer, the incoming infrared light beam is split in two by a mirror. Half of the beam is directed through the sample. The aforementioned chemical interactions within the samples will produce an emerging light beam that is different in optical character from the portion of the light that has been directed away from the sample.

The two light beams will be out of phase will one another. Since light consists of waves, the out of phase waves can cancel one another or lessen the overall wave intensity through interference. The pattern that results from the interaction of the two beams is known as an interferogram.

The end result of the Fourier transform is the spectrum of peaks and valleys that is displayed to the analyst. The resulting absorption pattern can be compared to the millions of patterns that are stored in computer databases, both on-site and remotely via the Internet. If a matching spectrum is obtained, then the identity of the sample compound can be determined.

FTIR is a valuable forensic technique because of its detection sensitivity and versatility. Chemicals from a variety of sample types including **blood**, paints, polymer coatings, drugs and both organic and inorganic contaminants can be identified.

Liquid samples such as blood can be prepared for FTIR examination by placing a drop between two plates made of sodium chloride (salt). The salt molecules are transparent to the infrared light and so form convenient sandwiching layers to produce a thin layer of sample. Solid samples can be converted to a fine powder in combination with a carrier material like potassium bromide (KBr, which is also infrared transparent). Alternatively, solids such as polymers can be dissolved in a solvent such as methylene chloride and added to a salt plate. When the solvent evaporates, the sample forms a thin layer on the salt plate.

Solids as complex as soil have been successfully analyzed using FTIR in forensic studies.

FTIR is not a technique that can be done at the scene of a crime or accident. The spectrophotometer and ancillary computer equipment are too bulky and heavy for transport. Rather, samples need to be carefully collected and transported to a specialized laboratory that has the necessary FTIR equipment.

SEE ALSO Analytical instrumentation; Breathalyzer®; Gas chromatograph-mass spectrometer; Infrared detection devices; Micro-fourier transform infrared spectrometry; Spectroscopy.

Fracture matching

When an object has been torn, broken, or separated, one piece of it has the potential to match another piece of it when they are placed next to one another. In forensic investigations this is called fracture matching. Because both the composition of an object and the stress applied to break it are always unique, when something is broken, torn, or separated, the edges of the pieces will always have characteristics that identify them with each other. When the pieces fit together, an investigator can conclude they were originally part of the same object. For example, when a piece of paper is ripped in half the tear will never happen in exactly the same pattern twice. This is because each piece of paper has slightly different imperfections and the forces applied to the paper in order to rip it are never repeated identically. When the two halves of paper are put next to each other, it is obvious that they were originally part of the same object. Fracture match is such an important concept in collecting and presenting **evidence** that it is considered scientific evidence in courts of law.

Anything that can be torn, broken, or separated can fracture matched. Items commonly used for fracture match analysis include plastics, **glass**, metal, wood, metal, car parts, paper, currency, tape, cloth, and paint chips. Experts in fracture match examine the objects that are a potential match in either two or three dimensions, depending on the object. Paper, tape, and cloth are generally compared in two dimensions. Glass, metal, wood, and plastics are examined in three dimensions. The entire surface of the fracture, as well as the surfaces of the object, will be analyzed. There are four different fracture match criteria:

- The pieces have been broken apart.
- The pieces can be realigned.
- The pieces fit together along the fracture and the fit is verified by markings on the surface or within the three-dimensional structure of the fracture.
- The pieces contain unique shapes.

In order to fulfill these criteria, inspectors examine the shape of the break, any irregularities in the surfaces of the two pieces, and any striations that might have occurred during the break. They examine the composition of the pieces for similarities in age, texture, and deformation. They may also analyze the chemical composition of the pieces.

When working with glass, investigators can recover a considerable amount of information from reconstruction using fracture match. Glass pieces resist movement when they are placed next to pieces to which they were originally adjacent. Special ridges, called Wallner lines, are almost always aligned so that they curve in a concave manner towards the point of impact. When the impact is from a low-velocity object, the cracks in the glass will radiate out from the point of impact. If the object that breaks the glass is moving at higher velocities, the point of impact will be cone-shaped and the larger end of the cone indicates the exit side of the glass. Cracks that are smooth and curved and show no indication of a point of contact indicate that the crack was generated from thermal stress.

A variety of examples of the use of fracture match demonstrate its importance in solving crimes. An Iowa detective used fracture match with paper to identify the person who had made a bomb threat at a warehouse. The man claimed to have discovered a note on the windshield of his car that stated that a bomb was hidden in the warehouse. The note was on a piece of notebook paper from a spiral binder. The detective searched the man's car and found a spiral binder. When the note was ripped out of the spiral binder, pieces of paper were caught inside the metal spiral. The detective was able to make a fracture match to a piece of paper found inside the metal spiral and he arrested the suspect.

Tools are also often involved in fracture match. In Virginia, robbers stole the contents from night-deposit boxes in a series of crimes. In each case the boxes were forced open. At one crime scene, the police found a small piece of metal, which they saved as evidence. Eventually, the police identified suspects and searched their possessions. They found a variety of broken tools. One of these was a screwdriver that was a perfect fracture match to the piece of metal collected from the crime scene. The police were able to convict the criminals based on this evidence.

Fracture match of the ends of tape can also provide key information to criminal investigators. In 2003 in Florida, a woman was sexually assaulted and then murdered. Her body was wrapped in bed sheets, a shower curtain, and masking tape and dropped in the ocean. A man fishing off a bridge hooked the body on a line and pulled it up. After locating a suspect, police investigators fracture matched the end of the masking tape on the body to the end of masking tape on a roll in the suspect's house. The man was convicted of the assault and **murder** based on this fracture match as well as other corroborating evidence.

SEE ALSO Paint analysis; Tape analysis; Toolmarks.

Max Frei-Sulzer

1913–1983
SWISS
CRIMINALIST

Swiss criminalist Max Frei-Sulzer made many contributions to the field of **forensic science** in his lifetime, including founding the first Swiss **criminalistics** laboratory, and developing the tape life method of collecting **trace evidence**. He is also known for debatable findings he made in two high-profile **identification** cases, the authenticity of the **Hitler Diaries** and the Shroud of Turin.

Born in 1913, Frei-Sulzer worked as a freelance criminalist for many years in Switzerland. He also taught microscopical techniques at Zurich University, and in 1950, he was asked to create the first Swiss crime laboratory, the Zurich Police Scientific Laboratory. While director of the facility, he developed the tape lift method for **evidence** collection. By applying a piece of sticky tape to a surface, a scientist can collect particles that can then be examined under a microscope. The tape preserves the spatial relationship of the particles and fibers. This technique was a major advance in trace analysis, and is a method still used today.

In 1973, Frei-Sulzer served as a consultant to a commission investigating the authenticity of the famous Shroud of Turin, a cloth depicting the image of a crucified man that some believe to be the burial cloth of Jesus. Frei-Sulzer took samples from the cloth using the tape lift method, and studied the samples for two years. After analysis, he reported finding pollens originating from plants grown in Palestine during the time of Christ, thus supporting the theory of the Shroud being authentic. After Frei-Sulzer's report, however, other scientists conducted similar tests on the Shroud and disagreed with his findings. While many people now question Frei-Sulzer's credibility in the case, the debate regarding the authenticity of the Shroud still goes on. Frei-Sulzer's role in the Shroud investigation is documented in many books and journal articles.

Later in his career, Frei-Sulzer's credibility was again questioned when he performed a **handwriting analysis** of the Hitler Diaries, purported to be the personal writings of Nazi leader Adolf Hitler. Frei-Sulzer pronounced the diaries as genuine, but shortly thereafter the diaries were proved to be fake. It is believed that Frei-Sulzer's incorrect analysis resulted from him performing a comparison analysis with other forgeries, instead of actual Hitler writing samples.

SEE ALSO Ancient cases and mysteries; Document forgery; Locard's exchange principle; Palynology.

Friction ridge skin and personal identification: a history of latent fingerprint analysis

In 1904, the World's Fair was held in St. Louis, Missouri. A special exhibit of the British crown jewels sailed from London for exhibit at the fair, sent by Queen Victoria of England. Naturally, such valuable jewels could not travel and display in the exhibition unguarded. Sergeant John Kenneth Ferrier of Scotland Yard traveled with this British treasure to ensure that no theft would occur. However, he brought more with him than the crown jewels. Ferrier knew about a new concept that had not yet traveled to America; fingerprints, classifying them, and how they could be used for personal **identification**. Ferrier was so committed to the potential of **fingerprint** identification that he shared his knowledge by holding demonstrations of fingerprinting techniques for foreign police chiefs gathered at the fair, and training several American police officials afterwards.

By the mid 1880s, fingerprints had been studied by **Henry Faulds** (1843–1930), a Scottish medical missionary in Tokyo, Japan; by William Herschel (1738–1822), a British chief administrative officer assigned in Bengal, India; and by **Francis Galton** (1882–1911), an English biologist and cousin to the British naturalist Charles Darwin (1809–1882). These men considered fingerprints to be both individual to each person and permanent throughout life. Faulds even considered using fingerprints for identifying criminals at a crime scene and had successfully done so. By the time of the World's Fair in 1904, the industrial revolution had peaked, and the world was awash with new technologies. Telephones were fairly usual, automobiles were becoming more common, and the Wright brothers had just made their successful flight at Kitty Hawk less than a year earlier. New ideas and technologies excited Americans. Fingerprints became an important feature in this new technological world. Additionally, palm prints and footprints could also be used for personal identification

The skin on the palmar surface of the hands and plantar surface of the feet is specialized. It is called *friction ridge skin* because the skin occurs in a corrugated fashion with elevated ridges broken up by lower furrows. In other words, this skin is not flat and smooth like other skin. Friction ridge skin is slightly elastic in nature and assists in gripping objects and surfaces.

Friction ridges form in the uterus by the fourth month of fetal development and remain unchanged and absolute for a person's lifetime, only decomposing after death. These unique factors make friction ridge skin ideal for use in personal identification. Once friction ridge skin was recognized as valuable and reliable for personal identification, different people began to work on systems for taking these prints and then organizing them. Faulds had previously used printer's ink to take the fingerprints of his subjects. In the early twentieth century, American chemical engineer John A. Dondero (1900–1957) developed new inks for the purpose of recording prints, including special ink for footprinting newborns. Edward Henry, with the assistance of two Indian civil servants, developed a system for classifying and filing mass quantities of fingerprint cards. This system is the one shared by Ferrier and is still known today as the Henry System. With the advent of automated identification systems, use of Henry's system has declined.

While prints could now be documented for future identification, how would prints left at crime scenes be used? As with other technologies, an application of other sciences began to play an increasingly larger role. Prints left at crime scenes or on items are generally referred to as latent prints. The word latent is from Latin and means to be hidden or not visible to the naked eye. Such a print is left as a result of a person touching a surface and transferring oils, perspiration, and other materials to the surface; or by the touch actually removing material from the surface. A print that is visible is called a patent impression. Patent impressions can be found in substances such as **blood**, motor oil, grease, or other contaminants left, for instance, on a wall or door frame. Prints or impressions left in a semi-soft substance like window putty or butter are called plastic impressions because they are molded in the substance. The vast majority of crime scene impressions, however, are latent impressions, and must be developed in some manner to make them visible. In the early half of the twentieth century, much work was done in inventing different colored powders that could be dusted on a surface to develop the print and make it visible for **photography**. It wasn't until much later that latent prints were actually lifted with a special tape and placed on a backing card with documentation.

Initially, the study of friction ridge skin involved the science of embryology and anatomy. The practice of photography obviously became more and more important, as did the use of magnifiers and specialized lenses. Additionally, with the development of inks and powders, chemistry began to play an ever-larger role. By the 1950s, iodine was used for fuming evidential items in a chamber; and chemicals that reacted with amino acids (secreted in sweat) were used on porous items such as paper. This was only the beginning. By the 1980s, cyanoacrylate ester (more commonly known by the trade name of Superglue®) found its way into usage. Additional research brought the development of fluorescing chemicals that could be applied after cyanoacrylate ester. Next, physics found its place in **latent fingerprint** examination as lasers and other light sources allowed the application of different wavelengths of light to make such chemistry fluoresce (emit visible light), thus allowing for photography. Another role of physics involves utilizing high vacuum for coating items with metals such as gold and zinc in specialized vacuum chambers. Particular chemical and mechanical techniques continue to be developed each year for working with difficult surfaces such as adhesive tapes, human skin, distinctive plastics, and highly colored backgrounds. While some chemistry is especially effective on dry surfaces, other chemistry makes it possible to deal with wet surfaces. All these techniques optimize the opportunity to develop latent impressions on a wide variety of backgrounds and surfaces or substrates.

The 1990s firmly established the science of **biometrics**, which boomed with the improvement of computers and refinement of software programs. By the beginning of the twenty-first century, computers were able to scan fingerprints and palm prints, and store images of those prints in automated identification databases.

Once an impression is rendered visible, documented, and recorded; it must be compared with a known-recorded print of an individual in order to identify it. The recorded impression, whether inked or scanned, is considered an ideal impression. This is due to the fact that the print can be repeatedly documented to get the very best recording of the friction ridges. While computers can record and scan impressions, they can never make a positive identification. Computers only make tentative matches. Identification will always require a trained and skilled human being to make the physical comparison. Identification is established by analyzing, comparing, and evaluating the arrangement of friction **ridge characteristics** in the latent print to those in the known impression and finding a match to the exclusion of all other prints.

Forensic identification of latent prints is a specialized field of study that encompasses many sciences. Commitment to a career in this **forensic science** requires an understanding and application of the scientific method. Knowledge of the biological formation of friction ridge skin, the nature of this specialized skin, and an awareness of the various technologies and methodologies employed in developing latent impressions is also required. Of the utmost importance, a forensic scientist must have a solid sense of professionalism, including high personal ethics and integrity in assuming responsibility for forming qualified opinions of identification of individuals.

SEE ALSO Biometrics; Fingerprint; Fingerprint analysis (famous cases); Identification; Integrated automated fingerprint identification system; Latent fingerprint; Superglue® fuming.

Frye standard

The *Frye* standard is critical to the legal presentation of the findings of a forensic examination. Forensic **evidence** is based on science. Some of the scientific methods have been long-established and readily pass legal muster. Other, more modern techniques may potentially not have had the time necessary for rigorous evaluation and scientific debate. Generally, cutting-edge techniques will be used more in the research laboratory setting. But, if contemplated for a forensic examination, then the *Frye* standard can become very important.

The *Frye* standard rose out of a 1923 legal decision (*Frye v. United States*). The heart of the ruling was as follows: "Just when a scientific principle or discovery crosses the line between experimental and demonstrable stages is difficult to define. Somewhere in this twilight zone the evidential force of the principle must be recognized, and while the court will go a long way in admitting expert testimony deduced from a well-recognized scientific principle or discovery, the thing from which the deduction is made must be sufficiently established to have gained general acceptance in the particular field in which it belongs."

In the case of the ruling, the court found that an expert testimony to the jury on the use of a systolic blood pressure test at that time had not yet gained credibility in the scientific community, and so the evidence from the procedure was denied.

In modern times, the sophisticated molecular technologies that sequence deoxyribonucleic acid (**DNA**) and determine the DNA profile of an individual can be held up to the legal scrutiny of the *Frye* standard. Typically, observance of defined and accepted protocols of sample collection, handling and analysis are sufficient to ensure the legal admissibility of the evidence.

The *Frye* standard also applies to the testimony of someone deemed to be an expert in a field that is relevant to the case (i.e., a **ballistics** expert). If the information is not presented in a convincing fashion (including citing scientific literature on the approach, use of the procedure, limitations of the procedure and general acceptance in the scientific community) or if the qualifications of the expert can be called into question, then the evidence can be ruled inadmissible.

As an example, in the 2004 *Grady v. Frito-Lay* trial in Pennsylvania, an associate professor of chemical engineering testified that the shape of the manufacturer's tortilla chip was a hazard, which could inflict injury to the mouth. The state Supreme Court used the *Frye* standard to rule that the expert's testimony was not generally accepted in the scientific community, and in fact represented inadmissible "junk science."

SEE ALSO DNA; DNA profiling.

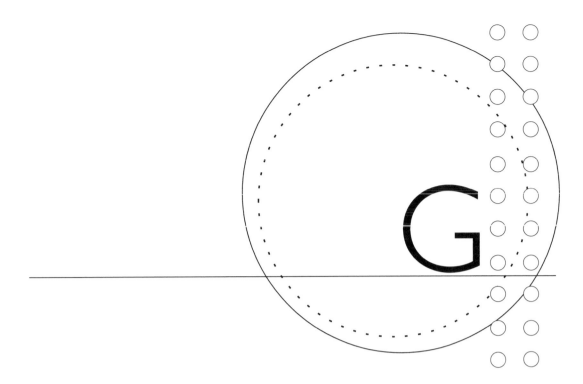

Francis Galton

2/16/1822–1/17/1911
ENGLISH
SCIENTIST, EXPLORER, BIOMETRICIAN

The English scientist, biometrician, and explorer Sir Francis Galton founded the science of eugenics and introduced the theory of the anticyclone in **meteorology**. **Forensic science** has benefited from Galton's pioneering anthropometric research. The system of fingerprinting in use today resulted from his work.

Francis Galton was born in Birmingham, England, the son of Samuel Galton, a businessman, and Violetta Galton. After schooling in Boulogne, he began to study **medicine** in 1838 and also read mathematics at Trinity College, Cambridge.

The death of his father in 1844 left Galton with considerable independent means, and he abandoned further medical study to travel in Syria, Egypt, and south West Africa. As a result, he published *Tropical South Africa* (1853) and *The Art of Travel* (1855). His travels brought him fame as an explorer, and in 1854 he was awarded the Gold Medal of the Geographical Society. He was elected fellow of the Royal Society in 1856.

Turning his attention to meteorology, Galton published *Meteorographica* (1863), in which he described weather mapping, pointing out for the first time the importance of an anticyclone, in which air circulates clockwise round a center of high barometric pressure in the Northern Hemisphere. Cyclones, on the other hand, are low-pressure centers from which air rushes upward and moves counterclockwise.

Meanwhile, Galton had developed an interest in heredity, and the publication of the *Origin of Species* (1859) by Charles Darwin won Galton's immediate support. Impressed by evidence that distinction of any kind is apt to run in families, Galton made detailed studies of families conspicuous for inherited ability over several generations. He then advocated the application of scientific breeding to human populations. These studies laid the foundation for the science of eugenics (a term he invented), or race improvement, and led to the publication of *Hereditary Genius* (1869) and *English Men of Science: Their Nature and Nurture* (1874).

Finding that advances in the study of heredity were being hampered by the lack of information, Galton started anthropometric research, devising instruments for the exact measurement of every quantifiable faculty of body or mind. In 1884, he finally set up and equipped the Biometric Laboratory at University College, London. He measured such human traits as keenness of sight and hearing, color sense, reaction time, strength of pull and of squeeze, and height and weight. The system of fingerprints in universal use today derived from this work.

The developed presentation of Galton's views on heredity is *Natural Inheritance* (1889). A complex work, it sets out the "law of 1885," which attempts to quantify the influence of former generations in the hereditary makeup of the individual. Parents each contribute one-quarter, grandparents each one-sixteenth, and so on for earlier generations. For Galton, evolution ensured the survival of those members of the race with most physical and mental vigor. By applying eugenics, he desired to see this come about in human society

Francis Galton (1822–1911). © BETTMANN/CORBIS

more speedily and with less pain to the individual. Evolution was an ongoing progression; the nature of the average individual being essentially unprogressive.

Galton's application of exact quantitative methods gave results which, processed mathematically, developed a numerical factor he called correlation and defined thus: "Two variable organs are said to be co-related when the variation of the one is accompanied on the average by more or less variation of the other, and in the same direction. Co-relation must be the consequence of the variations of the two organs being partly due to common causes. If wholly due … the co-relation would be perfect." Co-relation specified the degree of relationship between any pair of individuals or any two attributes.

Galton used his considerable fortune to promote his scientific interests. He founded the journal *Biometrika* in 1901, and in 1903 he established the Eugenics Laboratory in the University of London. He died at Haslemere, Surrey, in 1911, after several years of frail health. He bequeathed £45,000 to found a professorship in eugenics in the hope that his disciple and pupil Karl Pearson might become its first occupant. This hope was realized.

SEE ALSO Anthropometry; Fingerprint; Integrated automated fingerprint identification system.

Gang violence, forensic evidence

Organized street gangs are any social alliance in a group, usually consisting of juvenile and young adult members, whose primary purposes are for material gain for the group (often resulting in violence against the local community) and for retaliation or revenge against other groups (resulting in violence between rival gangs). To successfully learn more about gang violence, forensic experts must be aware of the different investigative approaches, especially with regard to forensic **evidence**, in dealing with both categories of gang violence.

Gangs were once loosely based groups of juveniles and young adults who committed minor crimes. However, such gangs have developed into powerful, well-organized groups. In fact, there was a dramatic increase in gang activity throughout the United States during the 1980s and 1990s, which caused an increase in violent crime along with extortion, harassment, and intimidation. By the beginning of the twenty-first century, street gang violence existed in nearly every suburban, metropolitan, and inner-city community in the United States.

When violence is involved, such gangs are classified as either violent or delinquent by forensic investigators in order to separate and identify evidence associated with each group. Violent gangs often contain members who have unstable and aggressive personalities, which can easily lead to violent disputes centered on territorial (turf) control or overall gang warfare, sometimes with deadly consequences. Delinquent gangs are usually small but cohesive groups who carry out minor criminal acts, such as muggings and petty thievery. When violence is used, it is usually not deadly or as serious in nature as with the violent groups. In most cases, material gain is the primary purpose of delinquent gang actions. In both types of gangs, criminal activities include dealing illegal drugs; performing assaults, extortions, robberies, and other felonies; and terrorizing neighborhoods.

Forensic evidence is often used to identify gang members when criminal activities are suspected within street gangs. Photographs, jewelry (along with badges, insignia, and other artifacts), stylized haircuts, and body piercing are among some of the more obvious physical traits that forensic investigators consider when **profiling** gangs. Other means of identifying gang members are by their tattoos and other types of burns and scars on their bodies, clothing (style, type, and color; and how it is worn), nicknames (or monikers), vehicles driven, common types of illegal activities, and communication styles such as graffiti, slang, and sign languages.

SEE ALSO Criminal profiling.

Gas chromatograph-mass spectrometer

In a forensic examination, some sample material can be evaluated at the scene of the accident of crime. Other material, however, needs to be collected and taken to a dedicated laboratory for more sophisticated analyses using a variety of analytical instruments. In 1976, scientists William Keith Hadley and J. A. Zoro, in the United Kingdom, first suggested the use of gas chromatography/mass **spectroscopy** for forensic purposes and the instrument is now used for a variety of forensic purposes.

The GC/MS instrument helps separate and determine the individual elements and molecules in a sample. The GC/MS provides forensic investigators the ability to identify individual substances that may be found within a very small test sample. Forensic applications of GC/MS include **identification** and detection of **explosives**; investigations of **arson**, fire, and blasts or explosions; environmental analysis; and drug detection. In recent years, GC/MS has begun to be used in airport security areas as a means of detecting dangerous substances in luggage, on animals who are traveling, or on human beings. Because of its great sensitivity, gas chromatography/mass spectroscopy can be utilized to identify trace elements in either minute amounts of substances or in substances that were believed to be contaminated or to be degraded beyond usability.

The GC/MS is comprised of two parts: the gas chromatograph and the mass spectrometer. The gas chromatograph functions by separating the molecules within the sample compound into their most elemental particles, allowing some types of molecules to pass into the mass spectrometer more rapidly than others. When the molecules move into the mass spectrometer, they are broken down into ionized fragments, and then each molecule is specifically identified based on mass and ionic charge.

Gas chromatography is a technique for separating closely related compounds (solutes) from a liquid or gaseous mixture. (Solids must be vaporized or liquefied before analysis.) Gas chromatography is most commonly used to separate and detect volatile and semi-volatile **organic compounds** (VOCs and SVOCs) with molecular weights less than 500 atomic mass units (amu). Although chemists have probably used rudimentary **chromatography** to separate mixtures since the Middle Ages, the modern chromatograph was not developed until 1941, when British biochemists Archer Martin and Richard Synge invented a chromatographic method that allowed for precise partitioning and detection. Martin and Synge were awarded the 1952 Nobel Prize in Chemistry for their efforts.

The GC component of a GC/MS system includes a carrier gas supply, a sample introduction inlet, a capillary column coated with a stationary liquid or solid, and an outlet to the detection system, in this case a mass spectrometer. To begin analysis, a GC/MS technician vaporizes the sample, or analyte, and introduces it into the chromatograph by syringe injection through a rubber septum. A flow of inert carrier gas like helium, argon, or nitrogen moves the analyte into the separation column. Partitioning occurs as the gaseous components of the original analyte assume different velocities when confronted with the column's liquid or solid coating. Partitioning behavior is temperature dependent, and precise temperature control is an important part of the GC process. A filter removes the separated compounds from the carrier gas at the end of the column before they are fed into the mass spectrometer for individual analysis.

Mass spectroscopy is a method of determining the molecular weights of a chemical compound's component ions. (Ions are electrically charged atoms or groups of atoms, and sub-particles of molecules.) The MS instrument, which has been called the smallest scale in the world, provides a graph, or mass spectrum, with peaks that indicate the relative amount of each type of ion within a compound. Today's MS systems are based on Sir J. J. Thomson's research at the Cavendish Laboratory at the University of Cambridge. Thomson discovered the electron in 1897, and went on to observe that the parabolic paths of ions traveling through electrical and magnetic fields vary according to the ions' mass-to-charge (m/z) ratios. His experimental instruments were the first mass spectrometers, and he was awarded the 1906 Nobel Prize in Physics for his discoveries.

Mass spectroscopy instrumentation has become increasingly accurate and complex since Thomson's time, but the principles of the technique and its basic components have remained the same. The MS component of a GC/MS system includes a sample inlet into a vacuum-sealed chamber that houses an ionization source, a mass analyzer, and an ion detector. In a GC/MS system, the input sample is always a chemically-homogenous gas produced by the GC component that can be introduced directly to the ionizer. Once ionized, the partitioned compound moves into the mass analyzer where the ions travel through an electrical or magnetic field that sorts them according to their m/z ratios. The detector measures the beam of now-separated ions arriving at the end of the analyzer, and converts changes in its intensity to produce the mass spectrum. A sample's mass spectrum is then displayed, catalogued, and compared to a library of known mass spectra by a computer data system.

Improvements in the individual GC and MS components, electronic automation, and computer data analysis and storage have led to machines that can analyze ever more complex, fragile, and tiny chemical components; GC/MS can now be used to quickly analyze proteins, **DNA**, and even viruses, and has become a common technique in molecular biology and medical science. GC/MS instruments are also becoming smaller and less expensive, and field laboratory and even portable, suitcase-sized systems that can be used to analyze forensic samples on site now exist.

One of the reasons that the GC/MS test has a great deal of value in the world of forensic substance identification has to do with its specificity: the GC/MS can positively identify the presence of a suspected poison or other substance. The portability of GC/MS test equipment allows it to be taken directly from a crime scene to the area where a suspect is detained to immediately perform tests on a suspect's tissue, **serology** (**blood**), clothing, etc.

SEE ALSO Accelerant; Analytical instrumentation; Arson; Breathalyzer®; Chemical and biological detection technologies; Control samples; Fourier transform infrared spectrophotometer (FTIR); Micro-fourier transform infrared spectrometry.

Gene

Molecular techniques that detect the presence and even the activity of genetic material are now a central part of **forensic science**. Exquisitely sensitive techniques can amplify and detect even small regions of deoxyribonucleic acid (**DNA**) that are present on objects such as cigarette butts or **glass**, or found underneath fingernails, as three examples.

Besides identifying the genetic material, modern-day forensic science techniques permit the detection of the fundamental unit of heritable genetic information (the gene), and can use genes to single out a person.

A gene is an individual element of an organism's genome and determines a trait or characteristic by regulating biochemical structure or a metabolic process.

Genes are segments of nucleic acid, consisting of a specific sequence and number of the chemical units of nucleic acids, the nucleotides. In most organisms the nucleic acid is DNA, although in retroviruses the genetic material is composed of ribonucleic acid (RNA). Some genes in a cell are active more or less all the time, which means that they are continuously transcribed and provide a constant supply of their protein product. These are the "housekeeping" genes that are always needed for basic cellular reactions. Others may be rendered active or inactive depending on the needs and functions of the organism under particular conditions. The signal that masks or unmasks a gene can come from outside the cell, for example, from a steroid hormone or a nutrient, or it can come from within the cell itself as a result of the activity of other genes. In both cases, regulatory substances can bind to the specific DNA sequences of the target genes to control the synthesis of transcripts.

In a paper published in 1865, Gregor Mendel (1823–1884), advanced a theory of inheritance dependent on material elements that segregate independently from each other in sex cells. Before Mendel's findings, inherited traits were thought to be passed on through a blending of the mother and father's characteristics, much like a blending of two liquids. The term "gene" was coined later by the Danish botanist Wilhelm Johannsen (1857–1927), to replace the variety of terms used up until then to describe hereditary factors. His definition of the gene led him to distinguish between genotype (an organism's genetic makeup) and phenotype (an organism's appearance). Before the chemical and physical nature of genes were discovered they were defined on the basis of phenotypic expression, and algebraic symbols were used to record their distribution and segregation. Because sexually reproducing, eukaryotic organisms possess two copies of an inherited factor (or gene), one acquired from each parent, the genotype of an individual for a particular trait is expressed by a pair of letters or symbols. Each of the alternative forms of a gene is also known as an allele. Dominant and recessive alleles are denoted by the use of higher and lower case letters. It can be predicted mathematically, for example, that a single allele pair will always segregate to give a genotype ratio 1AA:2Aa:1aa, and the phenotype ratio 2A:1aa (where A represents both AA and Aa since these cannot be distinguished phenotypically if dominance is complete).

In 1910, the American geneticist Thomas Hunt Morgan (1866–1945) began to uncover the relationship between genes and chromosomes. He discovered that genes were located on chromosomes and that they were arranged linearly and associated in linkage groups, all the genes on one **chromosome** being linked. For example, the genes on the X and Y chromosomes are said to be sex-linked because the X and Y chromosomes determine the sex of the organisms; in humans X determines femaleness and Y determines maleness. Nonhomologous chromosomes possess different linkage groups, whereas homologous chromosomes have identical linkage groups in identical sequences. The distance between two genes of the same linkage group is the sum of the distances between all the intervening genes. A schematic representation of the linear arrangement of linked genes, with their relative distances of separation, is known as a genetic map. In the construction of such maps, the frequency of recombination during crossing over is used as an index of the distance between two linked genes.

The molecular structure and activity of genes can be modified by mutations and the smallest mutational unit is now known to be a single pair of nucleotides, also known as a muton. Mutations used to be detected biochemically, typically by the failure of an organism to grow in a given food source due to the presence of the non-functional gene. Now, machines that automatically determine the arrangement of the nucleotide building blocks in the genetic material (a process called **sequencing**) allow mutations to be detected and, potentially, to match DNA with a victim or suspect.

SEE ALSO DNA; DNA fingerprint; Genetic code; PCR (polymerase chain reaction).

Genetic code

Some forensic **identification** techniques that detect living organisms or their products (e.g., **toxins**) rely on the detection of genetic sequences within the organism's genetic material. These tests can be exquisitely sensitive, allowing the detection of only a few organisms.

For example, tests have established that less than a dozen *Escherichia coli* bacteria can be detected in samples such as food and water. To put that in perspective, over a million bacterial cells will fit into the period at the end of this sentence.

A fundamental understanding of the genetic code is essential to understanding the molecular basis of advanced deoxyribonucleic acid (**DNA**) and the genetic tests that are increasingly important in **forensic science** and identification technology.

The genetic information that is passed on from parent to offspring is carried by the DNA of a cell. The genes on the DNA code for specific proteins that determine all aspects of the organism. In order for a **gene** to produce the proteins, the gene must first be transcribed from DNA to RNA (specifically, a type of RNA called messenger RNA; mRNA) in a process known as transcription. Translation is the process in which genetic information, carried by the mRNA, directs the synthesis of proteins from amino acids. The primary structure of the protein is determined by the nucleotide sequence in the mRNA.

The elements of the encoding system, the nucleotides, differ by only four different bases. These are known as adenine (A), guanine, (G), thymine (T) and cytosine (C), in DNA or uracil (U) in RNA. Thus RNA contains U in the place of C.

Proteins found in nature consist of 20 naturally occurring amino acids. One important question is, how can four nucleotides code for 20 amino acids? If a single nucleotide coded for one amino acid, then only four amino acids could be provided for. Alternatively, if two nucleotides specified one amino acid, then there could be a maximum number of 16 (4^2) possible arrangements. If, however, three nucleotides coded for one amino acid, then there would be 64 (4^3) possible permutations, more than enough to account for all the 20 naturally occurring amino acids. The latter, which was proposed by the Russian born physicist, George Gamow (1904–1968), was proved to be correct.

It is now well known that every amino acid is coded by at least one nucleotide triplet or codon, and that some triplet combinations function as instructions for the termination or initiation of translation. Three combinations in tRNA, UAA, UGA, and UAG, are termination codons, while AUG is a translation start codon.

The genetic code was solved between 1961 and 1963. The American scientist Marshall Nirenberg (1927–), working with his colleague Heinrich Matthaei, made the first breakthrough when they discovered how to make synthetic mRNA. They found that if the nucleotides of RNA carrying the four bases A, G, C and U were mixed in the presence of the enzyme polynucleotide phosphorylase, a single stranded RNA was formed in the reaction, with the nucleotides being incorporated at random. This offered the possibility of creating specific mRNA sequences and then seeing which amino acids they would specify. The first synthetic mRNA polymer obtained contained only uracil (U) and when mixed *in vitro* with the protein synthesizing machinery of *Escherichia coli* it produced a polyphenylalanine—a string of phenylalanine. From this it was concluded that the triplet UUU coded for phenylalanine. Similarly, a pure cytosine (C) RNA polymer produced only the amino acid proline, so the corresponding codon for cytosine had to be CCC. This type of analysis was refined when nucleotides were mixed in different proportions in the synthetic mRNA and a statistical analysis was used to determine the amino acids produced. It was quickly found that a particular amino acid could be specified by more than one codon. Thus, the amino acid serine could be produced from any one of the combinations UCU, UCC, UCA, or UCG. In this way the genetic code is said to be degenerate, meaning that each of the 64 possible triplets have some meaning within the code and that several codons may encode a single amino acid.

This work confirmed the ideas of the British scientists Francis Crick (1916–2004) and Sydney Brenner (1927–). Brenner and Crick were working with mutations in the bacterial virus bacteriophage T4 and found that the deletion of a single nucleotide could abolish the function of a specific gene. However, a second mutation in which a nucleotide was inserted at a different, but nearby position, restored the function of that gene. These two mutations are said to be suppressors of each other, meaning that they cancel each other's mutant properties. It was concluded from this that the genetic code was read in a sequential manner starting from a fixed point in the gene. The insertion or deletion of a nucleotide shifted the reading frame in which succeeding nucleotides were read as codons, and was thus termed a frameshift mutation. It was also found that whereas two closely spaced deletions, or two closely spaced insertions, could not suppress each other, three closely spaced deletions or insertions could do so. Consequently, these observations established the triplet nature of the genetic code. The reading frame of a sequence is the way in which the sequence is divided into the triplets and is determined by the precise point at which translation is initiated. For example, the sequence CATCATCAT can be read

CAT CAT CAT or C ATC ATC AT or CA TCA TCA T in the three possible reading frames. Sometimes, as in particular bacterial viruses, genes have been found that are contained within other genes. These are translated in different reading frames so the amino acid sequences of the proteins encoded by them are different. Such economy of genetic material is, however, quite rare.

The same genetic code appears to operate in all living things, but exceptions are known. In human mitochondrial mRNA, AGA and AGG are termination or stop codons. Other differences also exist in the correspondences between certain codon sequences and amino acids.

SEE ALSO Analytical instrumentation; Anthrax, investigation of 2001 murders; Bacterial biology; Biological weapons, genetic identification; DNA fingerprint; DNA sequences, unique; Mitochondrial DNA analysis; Pathogen genomic sequencing; PCR (polymerase chain reaction); RFLP (restriction fragment length polymorphism).

Geographic profiling

Criminal profiling is made up of psychological **profiling** and geographic profiling. The latter is a phrase coined by the Canadian criminologist Kim Rossmo in the early 1990s to describe the use of computers to generate predictions on a serial offender's place of residence or base of operations. The software used for geographic profiling—Rigel Profiler and Rigel Analyst (both created by Rossmo's Vancouver-based company), CrimeStat, and Dragnet—has changed the face of serial crime investigation in large urban centers.

It wasn't long ago that each briefing room across the country contained a map of the local detachment area and surrounding land, and on it crimes would be recorded by pins. Pin maps have a limited usefulness. If an area has heavy crime rates, the map becomes littered with holes and, with the exception of color-coded pins, essentially only one type of crime can be plotted. Updating the map means removing the pins and losing data from the past period of crime.

In the late 1980s, on the west coast of Canada, researchers at Simon Fraser University realized that humans follow patterns in their movements. People have mental maps of their surroundings, created through experience and familiarity with the location of sources for their daily needs. This mental map contains access routes to food, school, work, transportation systems, and at the heart of the mental map is their location of primary residence. Psychologists call this theory the principle of least effort.

Around the same time, Kim Rossmo, of the Vancouver Police, started to pursue his Ph.D. in Criminology at the same university. Through an interest in hunting behavior of animals, and his knowledge of the criminal field, Rossmo formed a theory that, like animals, criminal predatory behavior could be predicted. Offenders preferred to use familiar territory for their crimes. However, their anonymity was paramount and so there would be a buffer zone of no criminal activity around their place of primary residence for fear of being recognized. Rossmo also realized that the offender must have come across his victim at some point within his own mental map area. He developed a mathematical algorithm into which he could feed information on the crime and opportunities for interception between victim and offender, and obtain a rough prediction of the area in which the offender likely resided. This mathematical algorithm was subsequently patented by Rossmo and is at the heart of his geographic profiling software.

Geographic profiling brings the science of geography, criminology, mathematical modeling, statistical analysis, and environmental and forensic **psychology** into the realm of criminal investigation. It replaces the pin map and "hunches" on the whereabouts of the offender with a much more user-friendly, easy to read, and adaptable output map that uses science to indicate the most likely area that police agencies might focus their investigations in order to locate the serial offender. From the Rigel software, this map can be a two-dimensional or three-dimensional rendering of the geographical area under investigation. These maps are called jeopardies and use color-coding to indicate the area of highest probability to include the offender's place of residence.

Rigel system literature states that, "A Rigel analysis starts with a street map of the study area, the geographic coordinates of the crimes, and any database that the profiler wants to prioritize." Rigel is used in conjunction with **GIS** (geographic information systems) and is portable and usable in any mapped area in the world.

As well as its ability to predict the location of the offender's base (being able to "reduce the search area for a suspect's home by 90 per cent" states Kim Rossmo in his 1999 book, *Geographic Profiling*), Rigel software has gained enthusiastic responses from police agencies for its ability to help organize the vast amounts of data created when investigating a linked series of crimes. In the 1992 Washington DC

sniper case, Rossmo aided investigators by using geographic profiling. Although the profiling did not lead to the location of the offenders, it did aid the police to the point that Assistant Police Chief Deirdre Walker of Montgomery County, Maryland, released a statement saying, "The joint task force found geographic profiling a helpful and useful tool in strategically prioritizing information in this investigation." And indeed, that is what geographic profiling is, a tool. It is a tool to be used along with other aspects of police investigations and it relies heavily upon work already done by the primary investigation team. Elly Abru, in her February 2004 article "Coordinates of Crime" published in Australia's *Police News*, writes, "Yoking together the power of GIS and computing, geographic profiling has enormous potential as a tool for sifting, matching, clarifying and analyzing information. It has yet to reach its peak."

Geographic profiling is most useful in tracking serial criminals. As of 2005, it is not useful for solitary crimes, crimes where offenders travel great distances between offenses, or for small rural forces where major serial crimes are unlikely. There are areas for improvement in the software, but as the field of geographic profiling continues to develop and its software capabilities continue to improve, the demand for geographic profiling technology is expected to grow.

SEE ALSO Criminal profiling; GIS; Profiling; Psychological profile.

Geology

Geology, the study of planetary processes and histories, has applications in **forensic science** that date back to the 19th century fictional detective Sherlock Holmes. The principles and techniques of geology are most commonly used to identify the sources, or provenance, of rock or soil particles associated with a crime. Other applications include the use of principles borrowed from stratigraphy (the study of sequences of rocks) and structural geology (the study of deformed rocks) to infer a series of events that may be important in civil and criminal cases. Experts in the geology of specific regions can also help to identify locations using their knowledge of rock types and landforms.

Sherlock Holmes, the fictional detective created by the British author **Arthur Conan Doyle** (1859–1930), was able to distinguish different types of **soils** and use this information to infer the places to which suspects had traveled. The first known non-fictional use of geological techniques in a criminal investigation, however, did not occur until 1904. In that year, German chemist **Georg Popp** helped to identify a murder suspect by matching coal dust and particles of the mineral hornblende found on a handkerchief to the same substances at a coal processing plant and quarry that employed the suspect. Several years later, Popp matched layers of goose droppings, distinctive red sandstone fragments, and a mixture of coal, brick, and cement dust to materials at a murder victim's home, the place where the body was found, and the place where the murder weapon was found. Just as importantly, Popp determined that the suspect's shoes contained no distinctive quartz particles from field where the suspect claimed to be walking at the time of the murder. Popp's work, like the work of modern day forensic geologists, made use of the geologic concept of provenance, which is a description of the origin and history of a soil or rock particle, to place suspects in specific locations and disprove an alibi. His use of the sequence of layered goose droppings, sandstone fragments, and dust to infer the sequence in which the suspect visited those locations was an application of the principles of stratigraphy.

Geologists can often determine the geographic source and history, or provenance, of sand grains or soil particles found at a crime scene, especially if distinctive **minerals** or microfossils are found. This usually involves microscopic examination of soil or rock samples using magnifying glasses, reflected light **microscopes**, polarized transmitted light microscopes, and, in some cases, sophisticated instruments such as electron microscopes or microprobes. Even if details are not visible to the naked eye, microscopic examination can show that two seemingly similar samples of sand are composed of particles with different chemical composition, size, or shape. In some cases, the geologic details may be specific enough to place a suspect at a certain outcrop or in a specific watershed. This kind of information can be presented as **evidence** by geologists acting as **expert witnesses** in civil and criminal cases.

One of the most widely known uses of sand provenance studies in a forensic investigation involves balloons carrying explosive and incendiary bombs over the United States during World War II. Meteorological information was used to determine that the balloons were being launched in Japan and carried across the Pacific Ocean by the jet stream. The balloons carried sand-filled bags as ballast, some

of which were automatically released to maintain altitude as temperature dropped each night, and the U.S. Geological Survey was asked to identify the source of the ballast sand found at balloon crash sites. The sand contained an unusual mixture of mineral grains, diatoms, and foraminifera (single celled organisms that secrete siliceous and calcareous shells), and mollusk shell pieces but no coral fragments. Government geologists studied maps and reports published before the war, and determined that sand with that unique composition existed at only two places along the Japanese coast. Those locations turned out to be very close' to the actual launching points. **Identification** of sand grains and soil particles has been an important part of high-profile criminal cases such as the 1978 kidnapping and murder of Italian prime minister Aldo Moro and the unsuccessful attempt by Mexican federal police to cover up the 1985 kidnapping, torture, and murder of U.S. Drug Enforcement Agency operative Enrique Camarena Salazar and his pilot Alfredo Zavala Avelar.

Geologic details in images can also help investigators determine the locations in which photographs or video recordings were made. In the days after the September 11, 2001, terrorist attacks on New York City and Washington, D.C., for example, American geologists who had worked in Afghanistan were able to identify rock outcrops shown in video tapes of the terrorist leader Osama bin Laden, placing him in a certain part of that country. This use of geologic information was widely publicized and subsequent tapes were made against a cloth background in order to make identification more difficult.

SEE ALSO Forensic science; Geospatial imagery; GIS; Meteorology; Minerals; Physical evidence.

Geospatial imagery

Geospatial imagery depicts the locations and characteristics of features, both natural and constructed, on Earth's surface. The general term can encompass aerial photographs, multispectral or hyperspectral images based the response of a sensor to specific portions of the **electromagnetic spectrum**, shaded relief images produced from digital elevation models, and maps. Geospatial imagery can be combined with other kinds of information, for example databases showing the addresses of convicted criminals or hazardous chemical storage facilities, within geographic information system (**GIS**) software to visualize spatial patterns that may be important in civil and criminal investigations.

The first widely used type of geospatial imagery was aerial **photography**, which can now be obtained using **cameras** mounted in aircraft, spacecraft, or satellites. If the photographs are taken from a spacecraft or satellite, however, they are likely to be described as space or satellite images in order to distinguish them from photographs taken from aircraft. Aerial photographs can be taken either vertically or obliquely, and overlapping photographs taken from slightly different positions can be viewed stereoscopically in order to emphasize topographic features. Multispectral or hyperspectral imagery is created using instruments that are sensitive to specific portions of the electromagnetic spectrum, including portions that lie beyond the range of human vision. Multispectral images typically consist of several bands or ranges of information (in many cases infrared, red, blue, and green bands). Hyperspectral imagery, in contrast, can consist of 200 or more bands and can be processed to emphasize the occurrence of specific **minerals** or plant types. Bands that fall outside the range of human vision must be assigned visible colors in order to be seen, and the resulting images are known as false-color images. Like aerial photographs, multispectral and hyperspectral images can be obtained from instruments in aircraft, spacecraft, or satellites.

Publicly available geospatial imagery obtained from space was, for many years, not detailed enough to be used in most criminal and civil investigations because its resolution was too low. Landsat satellites launched in the 1970s, for example, had a maximum resolution of 30 meters per pixel. Because it takes many pixels to create a recognizable image of an object such as a building or an automobile, the smallest features than can be clearly seen in an image are many times larger than the maximum resolution. As of 2005, some modern commercial satellites had panchromatic (black and white) image resolution of less than 1 meter per pixel, which is at the limit of utility for forensic investigations in which individual buildings or vehicles must be identified.

One well known forensic investigation in which geospatial imagery played an important role was the search for the body of Xiana Fairchild, a 7-year-old girl who disappeared from her California home in late 1999. Her **skull** was found and identified using **DNA** analysis more than a year later, and investigators requested detailed maps and aerial photographs that could be used in the search for her body. Digital orthophotoquads, which are electronic versions of aerial photographs that are corrected to remove distortion (orthorectified) and then referenced to map coordi-

nates, were provided to searchers for use on laptop computers in the field. Although her body was never found, a suspect was arrested and charged in 2004.

After it was refused permission to revisit a Dow Chemical plant after an initial inspection during the 1970s, the U.S. Environmental Protection Agency (EPA) used aerial photographs to monitor activity at the facility. Although the company had concealed its activities from observers at ground level, many parts of the facility were visible from the air. The company argued that aerial photography constituted an illegal search that violated the Fourth Amendment of the U.S. Constitution, but the Supreme Court ultimately ruled in favor of the EPA. This case is often cited as a precedent because it gave a government agency the authority to use geospatial imagery to monitor potentially illegal activities. In a different case, related to a Superfund pollution cleanup investigation, the Nutra Sweet Company used a series of aerial photographs to show that contaminants had been dumped on nearby land owned by the X-L Engineering Company and transported beneath Nutra Sweet's property by groundwater. The photographs were one piece of information used to establish that X-L Engineering, not Nutra Sweet, was responsible for the groundwater contamination.

Geospatial imagery can also be used to resolve unsettled questions about international atrocities such as the Katyn Forest Massacre, in which 4500 Polish officers and soldiers were killed during the early days of World War II. German forces discovered mass graves near the Russian city of Smolensk in 1943, and the German government accused the Soviet government of mass murder. Soviet leader Josef Stalin refuted the charge and accused Germany of the atrocity. Despite evidence suggesting otherwise, the United States and Great Britain accepted Stalin's explanation and resisted further investigations. Aerial photographs taken by the German air force (Luftwaffe) during the war, which were captured and held as classified documents by the U.S. National Archives until 1979, provided important evidence in the form of images taken before, during, and after the area was occupied by German forces. A set of aerial photographs taken by the Germans in 1944, after the area had been recaptured by the Soviets, showed the bodies being removed and evidence of the massacre being destroyed by Soviet bulldozers. More recently, satellite images showing destroyed villages were used to assess the effects of civil unrest and document possible genocide in the Darfur region of Sudan in 2004.

SEE ALSO Cameras; Crime scene investigation; Digital imaging; Imaging; Remote sensing.

Gestational age, forensic determination

Estimating gestational age when a fetus dies is a specialized task in forensic **medicine**. Techniques for determining the gestational age of fetal or perinatal (around the time of birth) remains are mainly aimed at calculating the time since conception, and at determining if a specific disease could be the cause of fetal loss. In some cases, the time of conception cannot be known with certainty, as calculations based on last normal menstrual period may lead to an error of as much as two weeks.

The World Health Organization has set the viability threshold at 20 weeks gestation. Fetal death is defined as the death of a product of conception (fetus) before complete expulsion or extraction from its mother, regardless of the duration of pregnancy. Fetal death is divided into three categories: early, intermediate, and late. Early fetal death occurs at less than 20 completed weeks of gestation; intermediate fetal death occurs from week 20 through week 27 of gestation; and late fetal death occurs at 28 or more completed weeks of gestation. Proper classification of the fetal age into the correct classification has important ethical, legal, and also clinical implications.

Depending on the general condition of fetal remains, forensic specialists might face difficulties with age estimation. The whole skeletal length was probably the first marker used for fetal assessment and is considered valuable for diagnosing various syndromes and skeletal dysplasias (abnormal development) as well as for assessing fetal development. However, even if still considered a marker of developmental age, the whole skeletal length may be affected in post mortem (after death) assessment by the putrefactive (**decomposition**) process. In particular, body length increases slightly with maceration (tissue softening in liquid), whereas body weight and head circumference seem to be unaffected. For this reason, long bone length is considered a more stable and reliable marker than full-body measurements. Several investigators have produced linear regression formulas based on crown-heel length, crown-rump length, or body diameters to determine gestational age.

The advent of ultrasonography about three decades ago, especially high-resolution real-time ultrasonography, allowed a more accurate determination of fetal gestational age (crown-rump length or biparietal diameter and/or femur length). This technology is useful in forensic measurement of bones from standardized post-mortem radiographs in cases of questionable gestational age and can be compared with previous ultrasonographic measurements. Reference tables correlated with *in vivo* (in life) ultrasound measurements are widely available for complete fetuses and fetal remains including soft tissues, but the forensic specialist would also need methods for estimating gestational age estimation for osseous (skeletal, bone) remains.

One relatively accurate radiographic (x ray or other radiographic image) protocol for estimating fetal gestational age at death is based on femur (the long bone in the leg) diaphyseal (shaft) length, and compares images of fetal femur measurements with measurements of the same bones at **autopsy**. As several organs show major changes in developmental patterns throughout fetal development, maturation of fetal tissues and organs has been also proposed for gestational age estimation. One study evaluated the histological maturation of several soft tissues (skin, thymus, lungs, thyroid gland, kidneys, adrenal glands, and central nervous system) from 448 normal fetuses between 12–40 weeks gestation, and compared the estimated gestational age with that obtained by long bone measurement. Skin, lung, and kidney tissue (each with unique but distinguishable stages of development) were found to be useful for a more accurate assessment of gestational age when integrated with long bones measurements. In another study, the adrenal glands were found to be useful to define fetal age and maturation. Finally, another study reported that fetal development is constant and is not affected by intrauterine malnutrition and chromosomal abnormalities. Patterns of fetal skin development vary by site, with a range of 1–2 weeks in different regions of the body, and can sometimes give a rough suggestion of gestational age.

The growth of fetal long bones is affected by several conditions that might lead to growth retardation of the fetus in the womb. For this reason, many studies about estimating post-mortem gestational age have addressed the need for identifying new technologies and new targets to measure, aside from the long bones.

In conclusion, macroscopic examination (with the eye) or radiographic (x ray) examination are the most common methods used to estimate fetal age. Examination of the tissues and organs is also important for a better definition of fetal age.

SEE ALSO Autopsy; Coffin birth; Skeletal analysis.

GIS

GIS is an acronym for Geographic Information System, a type of computer software that stores, manipulates, and displays maps and other spatial data. In **forensic science**, GIS software can be used to display and analyze patterns in maps showing crime scene locations, transportation routes, and potentially important forensic information such as bedrock or soil types. Some proponents have expanded the original definition of GIS to Geographic Information Science in reference to the body of knowledge about the techniques and applications of GIS software in addition to the software itself, but this article uses the original definition.

The October 2002 sniper shootings around Washington, D.C., are a high-profile example of a criminal case in which GIS software was used as a forensic tool. As the shootings occurred, detailed maps of the shooting locations were created and concentric circles were drawn at 1/4 and 1/2 mi (0.4 and 0.8 km) radii around the location of each incident. This allowed investigators to inventory buildings and other features that may have hidden the snipers, identify roads that the snipers may have used to arrive at or leave the scenes, and analyze similarities and differences among the shooting locations. At the time that two suspects were arrested, there were plans to expand the use of GIS to quantify the ease of access to each crime scene, analyze demographic and economic information about the areas in which the shootings occurred, and create three dimensional renderings of the crime scenes in order to identify similarities and perhaps predict the likely locations of future shootings. One of the difficulties encountered in this case was that the shootings occurred in different counties and states, and much effort was required to combine data from the different jurisdictions. Similar techniques have been used to solve serial rape cases in several large cities.

The use of geographic information to help identify suspects is known as **geographic profiling**. Although it is sometimes portrayed in the popular media as a highly developed discipline, geographic profiling is an imperfect practice that is continually evolving. Geographic profiling computer programs available in 2005 were based upon the results of research conducted in the 1980s and 1990s. The results suggested that most offenders commit crimes close to their homes; crime patterns follow a distance-decay function (the number of crimes committed decreases with distance from the offender's home); juvenile crimes are more highly clustered

Dust and smoke in lower Manhattan, New York, is shown where the World Trade center towers once stood in an image taken by Space Imaging's IKONOS satellite on September 12, 2001. AP/WIDE WORLD PHOTOS/SPACE IMAGING. REPRODUCED BY PERMISSION.

than adult crimes (because juveniles lack easy access to transportation); and the distance traveled varies according to the kind of crime. The output of geographic profiling programs consists of so-called hit score maps that use colored contour maps or three–dimensional surface maps to indicate the likelihood that a perpetrator lives in a certain area. Hit score maps can be combined with additional information, for example the addresses of known offenders or other suspects, and displayed using GIS software. Because of the amount of information required, geographic profiling works best in large cities where many crimes are committed. It can also require officials to recognize that a series of crimes are related and have likely been committed by the same person. Geographic profiling may fail in cases where a suspect travels great distances to commit crimes.

GIS software is also used by many agencies for so-called hot spot analysis, in which the locations of crimes such as murder, burglary, and auto theft are plotted on maps. Specialized computer programs available to law enforcement agencies can then be used to find clusters of crime scenes, or hot spots, that may help to identify areas for undercover operations or increased police patrols. Although the two share some similarities, hot spot analysis is different from geographic profiling. Hot spot analysis identifies locations in which crimes are committed whereas a geographic profile is intended to identify the person committing the crimes that, like hit score maps, can be linked to the home or work addresses of suspects using GIS software. GIS analysts can then add other information such as the location of forested areas that might provide an avenue of escape or the occurrence of soil identical to samples obtained from a suspect's shoes. Some jurisdictions make crime location data available over the Internet, allowing citizens to interactively query databases and produce maps of reported crimes or the registered addresses of convicted sex offenders.

When combined with global positioning system (GPS) receivers and transmitters, GIS software can be used to track the movements of criminals released on parole or probation to determine if they are related to newly reported crimes. GPS receivers installed in police vehicles can likewise transmit their locations and help to more efficiently dispatch law enforcement officials in the minutes after a crime has been committed. In 2005, some transit police in San Francisco were equipped with wireless personal digital assistants (PDAs) that allowed them to use GIS information while on foot or in trains and laptop computers for use in patrol cars.

SEE ALSO Computer modeling; Crime scene investigation; Geology; Remote sensing.

Glass

Glass is a product of inorganic materials that solidified, but did not crystallize. Glass is mainly composed of silicon dioxide (SiO_2), and is extremely prevalent in everyday life. Often, windows are the most fragile elements of a building or a vehicle, and are thus broken by thieves or criminals in order to penetrate the premises or the vehicle. When glass breaks at the scene of a crime, small particles of glass are projected not only forward, but also backward, onto the perpetrator and into the immediate environment. These particles can later be retrieved and used to establish a link between a suspect and a crime scene.

Glass can be classified either by chemical composition or by use. There are four main chemical compositions of glass: soda-lime, lead, borosilicate, and special glass. While glass is mainly composed of silicon dioxide (SiO_2), it also contains modifiers that are used to vary the quality and properties of the glass. Soda-lime glass is obtained by adding a certain amount of soda (Na_2CO_3) and lime (CaO). It is this glass that constitutes most windows and bottles. Borosilicate glass is made by the addition of boron oxide and is much more resistant to heat. Different colors of glass are achieved by introducing small amounts of additives. For example, chromium (Cr) is used to give a green tint, cobalt (Co) for a blue tint.

Almost all types of glass are commercially available. Window glass is probably the most common type of glass, and is usually found as a flat, transparent piece composed of soda-lime glass. This type of glass does not resist high temperatures, quick temperature changes, or corrosive substances. Most of flat glass is now prepared using the floating process. This consists of laying the molten glass onto a bath of molten tin in an inert atmosphere in order to achieve a perfectly flat surface. Tempered glass is another type of glass that is much stronger than regular glass. This particular strength is achieved by introducing extra forces on both sides of the glass through rapid cooling and heating during the manufacturing process. This glass will shatter in very small pieces when it breaks. It is used on side and rear windows of cars. Laminated glass is a glass composed of multiple sheets of glass bonded together with a plastic film such as polyvinyl butyral.

When a criminal breaks glass during a criminal act, some small particles are projected onto his/her clothing, hair, or shoes. If the suspect is apprehended within a relatively short time span after the crime, these small particles of glass can be found on the hair, clothing, shoes, or inside pockets. At the crime scene, the crime scene investigator usually collects some of the broken glass as **evidence** for further comparison with any glass fragments found on a suspect. The comparison process might lead to the exclusion of a common origin between the glass from the suspect and the glass from the crime scene. Conversely, it might also show that the characteristics are similar and the two samples cannot be differentiated, thus supporting the hypothesis that the two samples of glass come from the same origin. It is important to apprehend the suspect shortly after the glass was broken, because the number of glass fragments on the clothing or shoes of the suspects diminishes very quickly after the activity. About 90% of glass fragments are shed from clothing within 24 hours.

Glass is characterized according to its physical and chemical characteristics. When investigating glass, the first examination is visual. The investigator observes its color, its thickness (if the fragments are big enough), its patterns, and its fluorescing (light-emitting) properties. Pieces of the glass can often be re-assembled, revealing patterns that can be compared to crime scene samples. Demonstration of origin by assembly is the only way the common origin between two fragments of glass can be clearly established. The refractive index of the glass fragments is then measured. This is typically achieved by immersion of the fragment in oil and observing the lines of refraction at different temperatures. Finally, elemental composition of the glass is determined.

The interpretation of glass is complicated by the fact that the characteristics exhibited by a large piece of glass (such as a window) might vary from one end to the other. Thus, the analyst needs to determine the extent of the intravariability (variations of characteristics within a same sample) before it can be compared to a different sample. If the variation exhibited between the two samples is greater than the variation exhibited within one sample, then the two samples can be excluded as having a common origin. On the contrary, if the two samples cannot be differentiated, then this supports the hypothesis that they have a common source. However, it does not indicate that they have the exact same common source. Again, the characteristics exhibited by the samples might be very common and found in many other pieces of glass. Thus, the analyst usually expresses his/her findings using statistics.

SEE ALSO Criminalistics; Minerals; Monochromatic light.

Calvin Hooker Goddard

1891–1955
AMERICAN
FORENSIC SCIENTIST

Over the course of his career, Major Calvin H. Goddard was responsible for a number of important advancements in the field of **ballistics**. With the aid of others, he created one of the most comprehensive ballistics databases of its time, and adapted the **comparison microscope** for use in bullet comparison. Goddard also helped established the first independent forensic crime laboratory in the United States. Because of his high level of knowledge, police often called for his help in investigations, including the high profile cases of Sacco and Vanzetti and the St. Valentine's Day Massacre.

Goddard earned a reputation as a **forensic science** pioneer because of his role in the creation of two major advancements in the field. He was especially interested in the research and study of ballistics, and, with the help of Charles Waite, began

to research and collect data from all known gun manufacturers. They compiled the results and created a database of the information, one of the most comprehensive ballistics databases of its time. About this same time, Goddard and fellow scientists Waite, Phillip O. Gravelle, and John H. Fisher adapted the comparison microscope so that it could be used for bullet comparison. This capability made it much easier for examiners to identify matching bullet striations.

As Goddard became known as one of the United States's foremost ballistics experts, the police sought him out to assist on investigations across the country. In 1927, Goddard was called to help investigators with the Massachusetts robbery/murder case of Sacco and Vanzetti. By using the comparison microscope to analyze bullets from Sacco's revolver and those found at the crime scene, Goddard confirmed that Sacco's gun was used in the robbery. His conclusions were upheld in a reexamination thirty years later. Goddard was also involved in the 1929 investigation following the St. Valentine's Day Massacre in Chicago. The case revolved around the murder of seven gangsters by men dressed in Chicago police uniforms. It was unclear whether the killers were actually police officers or rival gang members dressed as police officers. Goddard, working as an independent investigator, tested the machine guns used by the Chicago police and concluded that they were not used in the murders. Later that year, after a raid on the home of one of Al Capone's hit men, two machine guns were recovered. Goddard tested these weapons and proved that they were used in the murders.

As a result of Goddard's work in the St. Valentine's Day Massacre, he was asked to head the country's first independent forensic science crime laboratory, at Northwestern University. The lab provided testing of ballistics, fingerprinting, **blood** analysis, and **trace evidence**. In 1932, following the lead of Northwestern's lab, the Federal Bureau of Investigation set up its first crime laboratory, under the guidance of Goddard.

SEE ALSO Ballistic fingerprints; Sacco and Vanzetti case.

Hans Gross

12/26/1847–1915
AUSTRIAN
CRIMINALIST

Austrian professor and judge Hans Gross is often considered one of the founders of **criminalistics** for his research on the subject and the release of his 1891 book, *Criminal Investigation*. It was the first work of its kind to be published. Gross went on to publish other important research in the field of criminalistics. He also opened the first criminological institute in the world, at the University of Graz, Austria.

Gross was a driven young man, attending universities in Vienna and Graz, and earning his law degree in 1869. He worked as a magistrate for the criminal court at Czernovitz, Austria, and was also hired as a professor of criminal law at the University of Czernovitz. He later taught criminal law at both the German University at Prague and the University of Graz.

In 1891, Gross published his ground-breaking text *Handbuch fur Untersuchungsricter als System Der Kriminalistik*, with an English version entitled *Criminal Investigation* published in 1907. With this book Gross is credited for coining the term "criminalistics." The text provides the theoretical foundations for the science of **criminology**. He also founded and edited the *Archive for Criminology*, a journal that was continually published for more than one hundred years. In 1912, Gross opened the Imperial Criminological Institute at the University of Graz, the first of its kind. He considered it a major accomplishment in having criminology recognized as a serious academic discipline. The Hans Gross Criminological Museum, also part of the university, is still open today.

Gross is also known for a public conflict he had with his son, psychoanalyst Otto Gross. In 1913, Hans Gross ordered the arrest of Otto Gross because he considered him legally incompetent. Otto Gross was institutionalized then, and many times thereafter. One of Otto Gross's close friends was the writer Franz Kafka, who also was at one time a law student of Hans Gross. Kafka used information from *Criminal Investigation* in his notable novel *The Trial*. The book also makes references to Gross's arrest in the first chapter, and contains a character loosely modeled after Hans Gross.

SEE ALSO Careers in forensic science; Literature, forensic science in.

Gunshot residue

A powdery residue is created when a firearm is discharged. The residue can be helpful in forensically linking a suspect to the scene of the gunshot.

A bullet is propelled out of a gun or rifle at very high speed when the gunpowder in the barrel of the firearm is ignited. The ignition converts the solid gunpowder to a gas, which creates the pressure that propels the bullet outward. As the bullet emerges from the gun barrel, the gunshot residue is also propelled outward at high speed. The residue fans outward, forming a cone shape. Nearer the gun barrel, the residue is very concentrated. With increasing distance from the gun barrel, the residue becomes progressively less concentrated.

Gunshot residue can travel out from the gun to distances of 3–5 feet (0.3–1.5 meters) or even farther. At the farthest distance, only a few trace particles may be present. This information can be useful in determining if someone was involved in the firing of the gun. Close to the gun barrel, the residue deposits more heavily on surfaces like skin and clothing, to the point of being visible as a dark stain. Detection of a significant amount of residue, therefore, is a powerful piece of forensic **evidence** that the particular person was very near to, even holding, the gun when it discharged.

Residue can also be deposited on skin or clothing when a person briefly contacts a victim. In this case, only a light application of residue will be detectable.

This pattern can be critical in exonerating a suspect. For example, in 2005 actor Robert Blake, star of the 1970s television hit show *Baretta*, was found not guilty of the shooting **murder** of his wife. One of the important pieces of evidence was the absence of all but a trace of gunshot residue. It was successfully argued that the residue could have resulted from his handling of his wife's body or touching the interior of the car in which she was found.

Gunshot residue consists of tiny balls, flakes, or discs of the expelled gunpowder. The various shapes can be revealed by microscopic examination. The shape of the residue is governed in part by the composition of the gunpowder. Determining the type of gunpowder in the suspect firearm is a helpful step in a forensic investigation. In particular, the use of a scanning electron microscope equipped with an elemental analyzer permits the determination of the elemental composition of the residue.

Depending on the gunpowder, gunshot residue can contain lead residue, although lead-free ammunition is becoming more popular. As well, modern smokeless gunpowder residue can contain traces of nitrate, charcoal, and sulfur. Nitrocellulose and nitroglycerin may also be present.

SEE ALSO Ballistics; Firearms; Scanning electron microscopy.

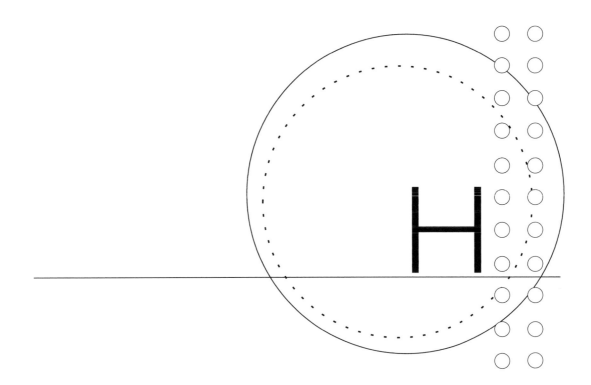

Habeas corpus

The formal term, writ of *habeas corpus ad subjiciendum* is Latin for "you shall have the body subjected to examination." Commonly stated as writ of *habeas corpus*, it is generally defined as a judicial order that is issued by a judge on the behalf of a prisoner, and directed to an official of a prison or other detention facility that has custody of the prisoner. The legality of the writ of *habeas corpus* is formally contained in state constitutions and within the United States Constitution: "The privilege of the writ of *habeas corpus* shall not be suspended, unless when in cases of rebellion or invasion the public safety may require it." [Article 1, Section 9, http://www.usconstitution.net/const.html#A1Sec9]

The writ of *habeas corpus* has a long history that probably originated in twelfth-century England as a way to release illegally detained persons. It was used over the next several centuries as part of common law within the English government. In 1679, the *Habeas Corpus* Act was passed by the English Parliament in order to guarantee this mandate in law. Today, in the United States and other countries around the world (in various forms), the writ of *habeas corpus* is a fundamental liberty that guarantees due process to prisoners without deciding innocence or guilt.

Before petitioning for a writ of *habeas corpus*, a prisoner must prove that all other available means have been attempted. In order to hold a valid writ of *habeas corpus*, the prisoner must demonstrate that a real or legal mistake was made by the court ordering the original detention or imprisonment. When approved, a writ orders a law enforcement official to deliver a detainee to a specified judge's court at a specific time in order to determine whether the prisoner should be released from custody or continue to be imprisoned. In most cases of present-day usage, the writ is used to appeal state criminal convictions to the federal courts. In some other cases, a writ may be used against a private individual detaining another private individual. For example, people who have been denied custody of children in divorce and adoption proceedings may file a writ of *habeas corpus* with the court system.

SEE ALSO Latin forensic terms.

Hair analysis

The scientific study of hair is called trichology and this field dates to the mid 1800s. Forensic scientists perform three major types of hair analysis. Chemical assays are used to assess the use of illegal drugs, to screen for the presence of heavy metals in the body, and to test for nutritional deficiencies. The root of the hair has cells that contain **DNA**, which can be used for DNA analyses. Microscopic comparison of hair collected from two different places is used to determine if the hairs are from the same person or animal.

Because hair can be moved from location to location by physical contact, the presence of a specific person's hair can link a suspect or a victim to a crime scene. If hair is transferred directly from the region of the body from which it originates, it is considered a primary transfer. Approximately 100 head hairs are lost per person per day. These hairs usually end up on clothing, furniture, or on other items in the environment. Transfer of hair from these items is called secondary transfer. Secondary transfer of hair is very common with animal hairs, which are commonly found on pet owners and in the environment of pet owners and can be used to link suspects to crime scenes.

Hair grows out of living cells in epidermis of mammals. It is almost entirely made up of the protein keratin. The club-shaped hair root is anchored in a follicle, which has associated muscles, called *arrector pili*. When these muscles contract, hair becomes oriented nearly perpendicular to the skin. The hair itself is composed of three layers: the medulla, the cortex, and the cuticle. The medulla is the innermost canal that extends through the hair. In humans it can be continuous or discontinuous, interrupted by a series of empty spaces. Surrounding the medulla is the cortex, which makes up the majority of the mass of the hair. The outermost layer is the cuticle, which is a single layer of scales. In humans these scales overlap quite a bit and cling tightly to the cortex.

Pigments are found in both the cortex and the medulla, but they are absent from the cuticle. In humans, the pigments tend to be distributed toward the outer edges of the cortex, but this can vary depending on ethnicity. In human hair, the medulla is generally narrow, taking up less than a third of the diameter of the entire shaft. In hairs from animals, the diameter of the medulla is larger than half the diameter of the entire shaft. The cross section of human hair is most often circular, but occasionally oval.

Using morphologic features, forensic scientists classify six different types of hair on the human body: head hair, eyebrow and eyelash hair, beard and moustache hair, body hair, pubic hair, and axillary hair. Biochemical studies show that there are no significant differences in chemical structure among the hair types. Animals also produce different types of hair. They often have coarse guard hair external to softer fur hairs. They also produce whiskers and longer hairs in such places as the tail and mane.

In humans, hair undergoes cyclical phases of growth (anagen), transition (catagen), and resting (telogen). During the growth phase, the cells of the follicle actively divide and grow upward. The average anagen phase lasts about 1,000 days. During the telogen phase, the cells of the follicle are dormant and hairs naturally fall out. This phase usually lasts for 100 days. At any time, between 10 and 18% of all the hairs on a human head are in the telogen phase; about 2% are in the catagen phase and the rest, between 80 and 90% are actively growing. There is no pattern to determine which hairs on the head are in any phase at a given time.

Because hair grows out of follicles in the skin, materials in the body are incorporated into the hair. Hair grows relatively slowly, so it takes several weeks for materials in the body to be reflected in the composition of the hair. Hair that is collected for the presence of drugs, heavy metals, and nutritional insufficiencies is usually clipped from the nape of the neck. About a spoonful is necessary for analysis.

Results from hair composition analysis are somewhat controversial. A variety of factors impact the results, including the location on the body from where the hair was removed, the color of the hair, and the person's age and race. Standards vary as to methods of washing, cutting, and collecting hair. Standards for analysis also vary and a single lab may report different results from subsamples of the same sample. False-positives for illegal drugs are not uncommon and can occur when someone is in the presence of second hand smoke from marijuana or crack cocaine. External substances such as air pollution, composition of the water used to wash hair, and materials used to treat hair such as shampoo, hairspray, and hair dyes may also skew results. Hair analyses that do report the presence of illegal drugs or heavy metals should be verified with **blood** or urine tests.

Microscopic hair analysis has two components. The first is to identify characteristic features of the hair in question. The second is to then compare these features in the questioned hair and hair from a known origin. In particular, the hair in question may be collected as **evidence** from a crime scene and the known hair may be collected from a suspect or from a suspect's possessions. Microscopic hair comparison in forensic laboratories usually involves the use of two compound **microscopes** that are optically connected so that the hair in question and the hair from a known origin are in the same field of view. The hair is usually magnified between 40x and 400x.

The first step of the examination involves verifying whether the hair in question is that of a human or an animal. If the hair is from an animal, the examiner can potentially identify the species from which it originated, but it is usually impossible to assign the identity of a hair to a particular animal. In the case of dogs, most examiners can attribute hairs to given breeds. If the hair is from a human, the examiner will

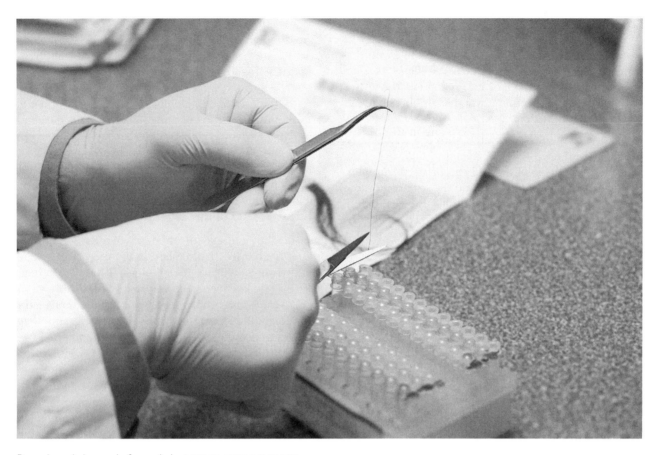

Preparing a hair sample for analysis. © JIM CRAIGMYLE/CORBIS

determine the part of the body from which it originated. Some of the features that the examiner uses include length, shape, size, color, stiffness, curliness, pigmentation, and the appearance of the medulla. The majority of hairs examined in forensic investigations originate from the head and the pubic areas.

Microscopic hair examiners can categorize hair into three different racial groups based on established models. These groups are European ancestry, Asian ancestry, and African ancestry. Hairs from people of European ancestry are generally straight or wavy, have cross-sections that are round or oval and have fine to medium-sized pigment granules that are distributed evenly. Hairs from people of Asian ancestry are straight, have circular cross-sections and have medium-sized pigment granules that are grouped in patches. They may also have a thicker cuticle than in the hairs of other races. Hairs from people of African ancestry are usually curly or kinky and they have an oval cross-section. The pigment granules are large and are found clumped in groups. The hair shaft may twist or buckle and commonly splits. Head hair shows the most distinguishing characteristics for determining race, however other body hairs also evidence identifying characteristics.

Complications with the assignment of race involve analysis of hair from infants and from people of mixed race.

The determination of age from hair is usually not possible by microscopic examination. Some general information may be surmised however, as the hair of infants is usually fine and contains few racial indicators. Hair of the elderly shows signs of pigment loss and often has variable diameter. The follicle of hairs contains chromosomes that can be stained to determine the sex of the individual. However, sex is usually determined from DNA testing.

Examination of the root can provide information as to the nature of a crime, especially if violence is suspected. If hairs fall out naturally during the telogen (resting) phase, the root will have a club shape. If hair is pulled out with force, the root will be stretched or broken and may have tissue attached. Examiners can also determine if hair has been burned, cut, or crushed.

A variety of factors influence the microscopic analysis of hair, including the experience and technique of the examiner. Because microscopic hair analysis is subjective, no statistics can be assigned to the probability that a hair belongs to an individual. The analogy often referred to is that an individual can recognize the face of a friend among a group of people even though all of them have the same features: eyes, nose, and mouth. In the same way, an experienced hair examiner can recognize those features of hair that determine whether or not it belongs to a specific individual.

DNA from cells associated with the root can be extracted and used for DNA analysis. Analysis of the DNA in the nucleus of the cell can be used for determining identity and DNA from the y-chromosome focuses on questions of paternity. Mitochondrial DNA is useful for establishing maternity. In theory, a single cell contains sufficient DNA to use for DNA analysis and so a single hair should provide the material required. In practice, a variety of complications make DNA testing of hair more complex. Roots of hair in the anogen (growth) phase contain more DNA than hairs from the telogen (resting) phase. However, hairs in the telogen phase are more likely to fall out passively. In addition, contamination issues are important as dead skin cells, which are also shed passively, contain DNA and may be collected from surfaces along with hair. If a hair from the telogen phase is collected, it may not contain enough nuclear DNA for analysis, but it might contain mitochondrial DNA. If the hair has been forcibly removed, then pieces of tissue may be attached and DNA analyses can usually be run easily on these tissue cells.

SEE ALSO Crime scene investigation; DNA fingerprint; Microscope, comparison; Mitochondrial DNA analysis; STR (short tandem repeat) analysis.

Handwriting analysis

The history of handwriting analysis to assess personality, today called graphology, could be said to extend back to Confucius, who wrote: "Beware of the man whose writing sways like a reed in the wind." The first extensive work on handwriting analysis dates to 1622, when an Italian physician named Camillo Baldi published *A Method to Recognize the Nature and Quality of a Writer from His Letters*. In this book, Baldi stated the fundamental premise that continues to guide handwriting analysis today: "It is obvious that all persons write in their own peculiar way ... Characteristic forms ... cannot be truly imitated by anybody else." In other words, like snowflakes, every person's writing is unique.

Over the following three centuries, Italian, French, and German investigators attempted to place the fledgling science of graphology on a firmer scientific footing. In particular, they linked graphology with Gestalt psychology, maintaining that handwriting originates in the brain and therefore betrays characteristics of the writer's mental makeup, even when done with a writing implement held in the other hand, the mouth, or the toes. They believed that the components of writing, such as pressure, speed, interruptions, variations in emphasis, the length and angle of upstrokes and downstrokes, and the upward or downward slope of writing on the paper, can be quantitatively measured and used to form a **psychological profile** of the writer.

In the context of modern **forensic science**, experts sharply distinguish graphology from true handwriting analysis. Graphology, scientists attest, is a pseudoscience, a fun but not scientifically valid parlor game, like palm reading, although many corporations take it seriously enough to hire graphology experts to profile job candidates. While graphology is not regarded as forensic **evidence**, it is still often used in combination with other techniques to profile criminals to aid authorities in their investigations. In the 1940s and 1950s, for example, graphology may have helped authorities track down George Metesky, the "Mad Bomber" of New York City. During the investigation of the **murder** of JonBenet Ramsey, a six-year-old girl found dead in the basement of her Boulder, Colorado, home in 1996, various experts closely examined the three-page, handwritten ransom note found in the home, attempting to provide a psychological profile of the note's writer and even to identify the killer. In 2002, graphologists had some success **profiling** the "D.C. sniper" who terrorized the Washington, D.C., area, but skeptics argue that the authorities resorted to graphology out of desperation in trying to break the case.

More commonly, forensic scientists use handwriting analysis for two more limited and defined purposes. One is to authenticate documents such as records, diaries, wills, and signatures. In 1983, for example, a German publisher claimed to have in its possession a collection of sixty-two notebooks that were the handwritten diaries of Nazi dictator Adolf Hitler. Handwriting analysts compared the writing in the diaries with known samples of Hitler's handwriting and concluded that the diaries were authentic. Later analysis of the paper and ink, though, showed that Hitler could not have written them, and investigation revealed that they were the work of a clever forger who was able to imitate Hitler's handwriting (so successfully that one of the known samples used by the handwriting experts was itself a forgery by the same person). A similar case involved the 1991 claim by a man from Liverpool, England, that he had in his possession a sixty-three-page diary and that its author, one James Mayrick, was the infamous Jack the Ripper, who brutally murdered five London prostitutes in 1888. While analysis of the paper and ink showed that the diary was not written with modern materials, handwriting analysts concluded that it was a fake, noting that most of the writing was done in just a few sittings and that some of the flourishes in the handwriting were added later, likely in an effort to make the document look more authentic.

The second purpose for which handwriting analysis is used is to link a specimen of handwriting with a crime suspect by comparing the suspect's handwriting with, for example, the handwriting on a ransom note or other communication linked to a crime. The purpose is not to profile the writer but to determine if the same hand produced a document known to have been written by the suspect, called an exemplar or standard, and the document in question. One of the first noteworthy cases in which handwriting analysis of this type was used was the 1932 kidnapping and murder of Charles Lindbergh, Jr., the infant son of aviation hero Charles Lindbergh. During the investigation, Lindbergh received fourteen notes from the kidnapper. Handwriting analysis later linked these notes to Bruno Richard Hauptmann, who was convicted and executed for the crime.

Handwriting analysts try to maintain a strict protocol with criminal suspects. They do not show the suspect the questioned document. They do not tell the suspect how to spell certain words or how to use punctuation. The suspect is to use writing materials similar to those of the questioned document. The dictated text should in some respects match the content of the questioned document so that the spelling and handwriting of certain words and phrases can be compared. The text the suspect is to write out should be dictated at least three times. And a witness should observe the procedure.

In either type of case—whether authenticating documents or investigating criminal suspects— handwriting analysts begin from the premise that while most people learn to write using a certain system, such as the Palmer or Zaner-Blosser system, they develop idiosyncrasies in the way they form letters and words. These idiosyncrasies become fixed and remain constant over time, even when the person is attempting to disguise his or her writing.

For comparison, analysts generally focus on four categories of factors that define a person's writing. The first is form: the shape of letters, their proportion, slant, lines, angles, retracing, connection, and curves. One writer, for example, might begin a *t* at the top and make a single straight line down, while another may begin at the bottom and form a loop. Similarly, a writer may form the vertical line of a *d* with an upstroke, then retrace downward to finish the letter, while another writer may form a loop rather than retracing. One person's capital *A* might be round and fat, another's thin and angular. One person's cross on a *t* may slope up, another's may be horizontal, and yet another's may slope downward. The second category is line quality, which results from the pressure exerted and the type of writing instrument and includes the continuity and flow of the writing. Thus, pauses can be discerned, and these pauses tend to take place in predictable patterns. The third category is arrangement, which includes spacing, alignment, formatting, and punctuation. Document examiners also look at a final category, content, which includes spelling, phrasing, grammar, sentence formation, and the like.

The central question is whether handwriting analysis is a valid forensic technique. The **Hitler Diaries** showed that even trained document examiners can be fooled, but for three decades it was regarded as valid and reliable evidence in court under the so-called *Frye* standard, which said that judges had to accept any form of expert testimony, including that of handwriting analysts, based on techniques generally accepted by scientists. The existence of such groups as the American Society of Questioned Document Examiners suggest that a community of scientists generally accepted the premises and techniques of handwriting analysis. Further, the U.S. Secret Service and the German law enforcement agency, the Bundeskriminalamt, maintain that their computer databases, the Forensic Information System for Handwriting (FISH), prove that among a large sample of writers, no two share the same combination of handwriting characteristics.

Since 1993, though, the admissibility of handwriting analysis has come under intense scrutiny. That year, the U.S. Supreme Court, in *Daubert v. Merrell Dow Pharmaceuticals*, created the stricter *Daubert* standard, which gives federal judges under the **Federal Rules of Evidence** more discretion in admitting or excluding scientific testimony. Specifically, it requires judges to determine whether a theory or technique has been tested, whether it has been submitted to peer review, whether standards exist for applying the technique, and what its error rate is.

Handwritten evidence in the case against Bruno Richard Hauptmann in 1934, who was convicted of kidnapping and murdering the infant son of the aviator Charles Lindbergh and writer Anne Morrow Lindbergh. © BETTMANN/CORBIS

Under this stricter standard, virtually any forensic technique, including handwriting analysis and even such venerable tools as **fingerprint** comparison, could be questioned and excluded.

One federal ruling dealt a severe blow to the admissibility of handwriting analysis. In *United States v. Saelee* (2001), a federal court ruled that handwriting analysis had never been adequately tested, raising "serious questions about the reliability of methods currently in use" (162 F.Supp.2d 1097 [D.Alaska 2001]). The court went on to say that "the technique of comparing known writings with **questioned documents** appears to be entirely subjective and entirely lacking in controlling standards." In later cases, however, such as *United States v. Prime* (220 F.Supp.2d 1203 [W.D. Wash., 2002]), the courts examined the issue and ruled that such testimony was admissible under the *Daubert* standard.

SEE ALSO Criminal profiling; Document forgery; Expert witnesses; Federal Rules of Evidence; *Frye* standard; Hitler Diaries; Howard Hughes' will; Lindbergh kidnapping and murder; Pseudoscience and forensics; Questioned documents.

Handwriting forgery

Handwriting forgery is the process used by criminals to fraudulently make, alter, or write a person's signature—so that in most circumstances it appears identical with the genuine signature—with the intent of profiting from the innocent party. Authentic signatures are included on such papers as checks, employment records, legal agreements, licenses, titles, wills, and any other type of personal or business transaction or agreement. Even slight handwriting alternations are considered as much a crime as the complete fabrication of a signature when the intent it to deceive. However, the consequences of being convicted of handwriting forgery are usually much less than many other major crimes in the United States, with the specific punishment generally being in the form of a **misdemeanor** and set by various state and federal statutes. As a result of these minor consequences and because most people are uninformed of the various tactics used by such skilled criminals, the illegal activity of handwriting forgery is growing at a higher rate than most other crimes.

There are several ways in which forgers commit handwriting forgery. The process of tracing is used when a real signature is possessed by a forger such as in a bank check. The signature is often placed under a pane of glass positioned over a light source while a blank paper is laid on top. The forger then traces the signature's outline onto the blank page, usually first with a pencil and later with a pen. This method will not produce a precise duplication of the original, but will be seen as acceptable for many uses of the forger. Sometimes forgers use freehand simulations, which involve copying a genuine signature until the forger can simulate its general style and characteristics without difficulty. In both cases, tracing and freehand, the forger is unable to exactly reproduce the various impressions and downward pressures used by the original writer.

Expert handwriting forgers, however, can more easily forge vulnerable signatures, such as those without complex characters. Absence of writing control, excessive use of variations, and weakly shaped character forms also contribute to vulnerable handwritings, making them easier to be forged by criminals. For all of these vulnerabilities, the forger will typically use personal checks as the preferred means of handwriting forgery.

The act of handwriting forgery annually takes many millions of dollars in cash and property from victims, primarily in the form of fraudulent checks, credit card purchases, invoices, identification papers, and passports. Within the field of **forensic science**, investigative experts use scientific **handwriting analysis** to examine the legitimacy of signatures and legal identifications. The latest of handwriting forgery detection methods used by forensic scientists involves a computer-generated hologram of a signature in order to analyze its tiny variations. Using the scientific techniques of image processing and virtual reality, the digital image makes it quite easy to analyze the differences between the forger's writings and those of the original writer.

SEE ALSO Document forgery; Identity theft; Impression evidence; Ink analysis; Misdemeanor.

Hanging (signs of)

Hanging is a form of strangulation where a noose is pulled tight around the neck by the person's own body weight. The noose compresses the airways, cutting off the supply of oxygen to the lungs. It also compresses the carotid arteries, which carry **blood** to the brain. Both mechanisms cause asphyxia, in which body and brain are deprived of oxygen. However, asphyxia is not always the cause of death in hanging. In some cases, the pressure on the neck causes vagal inhibition, a reflex that leads to cardiac arrest. The forensic pathologist has to try to distinguish between hanging and other forms of strangulation and between suicidal, homicidal, and accidental hangings.

Most adult hangings are suicides. In children, hanging may occur by accident if they get themselves tangled up in clothes or a harness. Homicidal hanging is very rare and the generally the victim needs to be unconscious or intoxicated for such an act to occur. The ligature, that is, the material used to make the noose and suspend the victim, usually consists of whatever is at hand. Ropes, belts, and electric flex are among the most common ligatures in hangings. Clothing, washing lines, and even dog leads are sometimes used. The victim may use a fixed knot or a slip knot, the latter being particularly efficient at compressing the airways and blood vessels because it tightens so quickly under gravity.

Some hangings take place from a high point of suspension, where the body swings freely under gravity with the feet off the ground. However, hanging can also occur with the person kneeling, sitting, or half lying, from a relatively low point of suspension such as a doorknob or bedpost. The weight of the chest and arms is enough to provide fatal pressure on

the neck; suspension of the whole body is not necessary. A tree is the most common suspension point in hangings occurring out of doors, but bridges or climbing frames have also been used. Indoors, there is a large range of suspension points including doors, banisters, rafters, and loft hatches, or practically any raised object. The circumstances of the hanging influence the signs on the body and the actual cause of death.

Suicide by hanging in prison is a particular problem. Obvious ligatures such as ropes or flex are clearly not made available. However, desperate people will fashion ropes out of bedclothes or their own clothes. Two of Britain's most notorious killers took their own lives by hanging in prison. Fred West hanged himself with a ligature made of strips of clothing in 1995, seemingly to avoid trial. In 2004, the serial killer Dr. Harold Shipman used bedclothes to hang himself from the window bars of his cell in Wakefield Prison.

An **autopsy** of a hanged body will often reveal neck markings. The nature of these depends on the type of noose. Few or no marks may be found with a noose made of a soft material like bed sheets. A rope or cord noose will, however, leave a deep furrow, often with accompanying abrasions and contusions. Hanging from a high suspension point leaves diagonal marks on the neck like an inverted V, which do not run around the full circumference of the neck. The point where the noose meets the vertical part of the rope is pulled up and away from the body and does not leave a mark on the neck. This can be used to distinguish a hanging from a manual strangulation. However, in a hanging from a low suspension point, the marks on the neck tend to be horizontal rather than diagonal and may look more characteristic of a manual strangulation.

High hangings are more likely to cause death by vagal inhibition, owing to the sudden pressure on the neck. The victim tends to be pale in such cases. A low hanging is more likely to lead to asphyxia and there may be some facial congestion and a purple protruding tongue. Asphyxia in hanging is usually related to the compression of the carotid arteries, rather than blockage of the airways. Petechial hemorrhages, caused by blood leaking from capillaries in the eyes owing to the pressure on the neck, are typical of many strangulations, but not often found in a hanging. Their absence can therefore help distinguish a hanging from other strangulations. The body may also show **lividity** due to pooling of blood in the legs, forearms, and hands.

In judicial execution by hanging, the body usually drops several feet, which causes disruption of the cervical vertebrae, which are the spinal bones in the neck. The cause of death, if the execution if correctly carried out, is disruption of the spine rather than asphyxia. Fractures of the cervical vertebrae are not often seen in suicidal, homicidal, or accidental hangings, unless the body has dropped through some distance.

In cases of suspected hanging, the pathologist will also carry out a **toxicological analysis** of the body. Drugs or alcohol sometimes play a role in hanging. It is not an easy form of homicide and a perpetrator may try to "knock out" or subdue the victim before applying the noose. In cases of suicide, the victim may drug himself or herself in an attempt to summon up the courage to carry out the act.

SEE ALSO Asphyxiation (signs of); Knots and ligatures.

Robert D. Hare

AMERICAN
FORENSIC PSYCHOLOGIST

Robert Hare has spent more than thirty years studying the concept of psychopathy, its assessment, its nature, its implications, and its amenability to treatment (or the lack thereof). Hare is the creator and developer of the Hare Psychopathy Checklist and the Hare Psychopathy Checklist-Revised, a reliable and valid assessment tool for determining the diagnostic presence of psychopathy, as well as risk for violence.

After completion of his master's degree in **psychology** in the early 1960s, Robert Hare realized that he needed to work for a while before commencing doctoral studies. Although he had no specific **training**, expertise, or interest in forensics, he accepted a position as the only prison psychologist at a men's maximum-security penitentiary near Vancouver, British Columbia (the British Columbia Penitentiary). His inexperience was immediately apparent to the inmates, and they commenced taking advantage of him by requesting favors, pushing boundaries, and manipulating him to the point of violation of prison rules. His interactions with a particular type of inmate (the psychopath), one who is endlessly manipulative, superficially charming, disrespectful of boundaries, a constant liar, and utterly unwilling to live within the standard rules and confines of society was, ultimately, one of the catalysts leading Hare to the study of psychopathy.

Hare's doctoral dissertation in psychology was concerned with the effects of punishment on human behavior. This led him to study the factors contributing to resistance to the effects of punishment, which, in turn, led Hare to research on psychopathy. He began publishing his empirical research on psychopathy in 1965, and published his first book, *Psychopathy: Theory and Research*, in 1970. This publication created the framework for Hare's future research in psychopathy.

Early in his work, Hare realized that a concept had to be quantifiable in order to be researched. He then set about creating an instrument with which to study the presence or absence of psychopathy in the criminal population. In 1980, Hare published his first 22-item psychopathy research scale. During this time period, the diagnostic criteria for antisocial personality disorder were being refined, and the psychiatric community paid little attention to Hare's work. By 1985, Hare had refined the assessment scale, pared it down to 20 items, and named it the *Psychopathy Checklist-Revised* (PCL-R). The PCL-R was to be completed during an in-person semi-structured interview, and used clinical chart data for corroborative information. Each checklist item was rated on a scale from zero (trait not present) to two (trait definitely present), making 40 the maximum possible score. The cutoff score for a diagnosis of psychopathy was 30. In 1991, Hare formally published the PCL-R, after having had validity and reliability data gathered as a result of the scale's use by his peers.

In addition to his groundbreaking research on the concept of psychopathy, and his development of the PCL-R, Hare has published books, articles, and book chapters on the subject of psychopathic criminal behavior. He belongs to the International Fellowship for Criminal Investigative Analysis, and is the recipient of numerous honors and awards, such as **FBI** citations, the Silver Medal of the Queen Sophia Center in Spain, the Canadian Psychological Association's Award for Distinguished Applications of Psychology, the American Academy of Forensic Psychology's award for "Distinguished Contributions to Psychology and Law," and the American Psychiatric Association's Isaac Ray Award for "Outstanding Contributions to Forensic Psychiatry and Psychiatric Jurisprudence." Robert Hare has made important and lasting contributions to the field and evolution of **forensic science**.

SEE ALSO Polygraphs; Profiling; Ritual killings; Training.

Robert (Roy) R. Hazelwood

AMERICAN
FORENSIC CONSULTANT

Former Federal Bureau of Investigation (**FBI**) agent Robert (Roy) Hazelwood retired from the FBI after serving for 22 years. When the Behavioral Sciences Unit (BSU) was created at Quantico, Virginia, Hazelwood was among the first criminal and behavioral profilers at the facility. He was a supervisory special agent with the Behavioral Science Unit at the FBI Academy, and his area of expertise was sexual crimes, particularly crimes involving sexual sadism. During his tenure with the FBI, Hazelwood taught courses at the FBI Training Academy, the University of Virginia, the University of Pennsylvania, the **United States Military Police** Criminal Investigation Division (CID), and the Southern Police Institute. He is a board-certified forensic examiner, an affiliate professor of administrative justice at George Mason University, vice president of the Academy Group, Inc. (a **forensic science** consulting firm comprised of former FBI and FBI BSU members), and an expert consultant, public speaker, lecturer, presenter, and published author of articles and books on forensic science (more than 40 journal and popular press articles, and co-author of five books). Numerous citations, certificates, and awards have been bestowed upon Roy Hazelwood by colleges and universities, law enforcement agencies, and criminal justice associations nationwide.

Prior to his career with the FBI, Hazelwood rose to the rank of major in the United States Army Military Police Corps, earned a master of science degree from NOVA University, and studied forensic **medicine** at the Armed Forces Institute of Pathology (AFIP).

Early in his career with the FBI's BSU, Hazelwood became interested in autoerotic fatalities, which led him to retrospectively study and amass data on more than 150 such cases. Another area of research interest he pursued involved a large-scale survey of the attitudes and beliefs held by law enforcement personnel (particularly police officers) concerning rape. In conjunction with scientists Janet Warren and **Park Dietz**, Hazelwood interviewed men convicted for sexually sadistic crimes; he personally interviewed perpetrators responsible for more than 800 rapes. They also extensively studied the wives and girlfriends of convicted sexual sadists. More recently, Hazelwood has conducted research in the area of juvenile sex offenders with scientists at the University of Virginia.

As vice president of The Academy Group, Inc. (AGI), Hazelwood continues his work in forensic science by acting as an expert consultant across North America, Latin America, and Europe in the areas of child abduction and molestation, rape, equivocal death, autoerotic fatalities, homicide, and sexual sadism. As an expert witness, he has testified in municipal, county, state, and federal courts, as well as before both houses of Congress and a presidential committee.

SEE ALSO Choking, signs of; Contact crimes; Criminal profiling; Hanging (signs of); Missing children.

Hemoglobin

As a component of **blood**, hemoglobin can be an important facet of a forensic investigation, especially to help detect the illegal practice known as "blood doping" in sports, and in helping to identify if a blood sample was from someone with a blood abnormality such as sickle cell disease.

Hemoglobin is a protein formed of two subunits (alpha and beta) that is found in red blood cells. The protein functions to pick up oxygen and distribute it throughout the body.

Both the alpha and beta subunits need to be present for the acquisition of oxygen, as does an iron molecule. Indeed, it is the presence of the iron that gives red blood cells the distinctive color that inspired their name.

The presence of iron enables hemoglobin to alternatively bind oxygen and carbon dioxide. As blood is pumped through the myriad of tiny channels that permeate the lung, oxygen can diffuse across the membrane of the channel to the red blood cell-containing fluid within the channels. There, the binding of oxygen to the iron-containing hemoglobin occurs. The oxygenated red blood cells pass out of the lungs and circulate throughout the body, transporting the oxygen along with them to cells.

Once oxygen has been released from hemoglobin, the vacated binding site is able to bind carbon dioxide and other waste products of cellular metabolism. This process is vital to maintain a body in a proper equilibrium. If otherwise allowed to accumulate, these products would reach toxic concentrations. The hemoglobin bound carbon dioxide is transported back to the lungs, where it is released from the red blood cells and expired. Completing the cycle, the once-aging vacant iron site can bind another molecule of oxygen.

The alpha and beta subunits of hemoglobin are encoded by separate genes. Normally, an individual has four alpha-encoding genes and two beta-encoding genes. Despite the different number of genes, protein production is coordinated so that precisely equal amounts of the subunits are made during red blood cell manufacture. The subunits are incorporated into the developing blood cells, where they remain throughout the days-to-weeks lifespan of the cells.

In the majority of people, both hemoglobin itself and the genes encoding the subunits are invariant. This aspect would seemingly rule out the routine use of hemoglobin as a tool to identify someone in a forensic investigation. However, in people with sickle cell disease (in which the abnormally-shaped red blood cell cannot easily pass through all blood vessels, producing an oxygen shortage) and thalassemia (a group of related maladies, in which hemoglobin production is low) the mutated hemoglobin **gene** that is the root of the malady can be detected in now-routine molecular biological test procedures such as gene **sequencing** (where the order of the bases that make up a gene is determined).

If a blood sample recovered from the investigation scene contains a mutated hemoglobin gene, the discovery of the same mutation in a blood sample of a suspect, for example, can be powerful, although not unequivocal, **evidence** tying the suspect to the crime scene.

In addition to the well-known hemoglobin disorders that underlie sickle cell anemia and thalassemia, there are several hundred other forms of abnormal hemoglobin. These forms, which usually do not cause harm to a person, can be detected using specialized molecular examination techniques, and so can be useful forensically.

In the case of a bloodstain at a crime or accident scene, determination of the amount of hemoglobin can be useful in indicating the approximate age of a person as well as their sex. Hemoglobin content can be determined in a less sophisticated fashion than hemoglobin disorders. Blood cells are broken apart in automated blood analyzers to free the hemoglobin. Upon exposure to a cyanide-containing compound, free hemoglobin binds the cyanide. The resulting compound (cyanmethemoglobin) specifically absorbs light at a wavelength of 540 nanometers, permitting the amount of hemoglobin to be determined. Normal ranges for hemoglobin (expressed as grams per deciliter; a deciliter being 100 milliliters)

are 17–22 for newborns, 11–13 for children, 14–18 for adult males and 12–16 for adult females, as a few examples. While not by itself definitive, hemoglobin content determinations of a blood sample can be another useful piece of forensic evidence.

When hemoglobin levels in blood or the red blood cells are low, as in the aforementioned cases of sickle cell anemia and thalassemia, an individual is described as being anemic. Anemia can also arise from loss of blood in a traumatic injury or internal blood loss, a nutritional deficiency, or compromised bone marrow. Thus, hemoglobin analysis can provide clues concerning the health of a victim or suspect.

Higher than normal levels of hemoglobin can be encountered in people who routinely live or work at high altitude, due to the increased production of red blood cells to maximize the blood's oxygen carrying capacity. Athletes who have artificially increased this capacity through blood doping by infusing their own previously collected red blood cells, or injecting the drug erythropoetin, which triggers the body to increase its red blood cell supply, can be found out in this way.

SEE ALSO Blood.

Hemorrhagic fevers and diseases

Hemorrhagic diseases are caused by infection with viruses or bacteria. As the name implies, a hallmark of a hemorrhagic disease is copious bleeding. The onset of a hemorrhagic fever or disease can lead to relatively mild symptoms that clear up within a short time.

Hemorrhagic diseases occur naturally, and are fortunately rare. However, the ferocity and lethality of their symptoms as well as the speed at which they render a person extremely ill has been exploited in weaponry.

This weaponization has made the use of **forensic science** in the detection of the use of the agents of hemorrhagic fevers and diseases very important. A recent example is the tremendous effort of United Nations inspectors to unearth **evidence** of biological weapons before the United States began the war in Iraq in 2003.

The viruses that cause hemorrhagic diseases are members of four groups. These are the arenaviruses, filoviruses, bunyaviruses, and the flaviviruses. Arenaviruses are the cause of Argentine hemorrhagic fever, Bolivian hemorrhagic fever, Sabia-associated hemorrhagic fever, Lassa fever, Lymphocytic chorio-meningitis, and Venezuelan hemorrhagic fever. The Bunyavirus group causes Crimean-Congo hemorrhagic fever, Rift Valley fever, and Hantavirus pulmonary syndrome. Filoviruses are the cause of Ebola hemorrhagic fever and Marburg hemorrhagic fever. Lastly, the Flaviviruses cause tick-borne encephalitis, yellow fever, Dengue hemorrhagic fever, Kyasanur Forest disease, and Omsk hemorrhagic fever.

Virtually all the hemorrhagic diseases of micro-biological origin that arise with any frequency are caused by viruses. The various viral diseases are also known as viral hemorrhagic fevers. Bacterial infections that lead to hemorrhagic fever are rare, though one example is a bacterium known as scrub typhus.

Few of the known viral hemorrhagic diseases occur naturally in the United States. Accordingly, a primary risk factor for viral hemorrhagic diseases is travel to areas where the virus is indigenous (e.g., portions of Africa, Asia, the Middle East, and South America).

Forensic investigations of hemorrhagic fevers and diseases are not routine operations because of the tremendous health risk posed by the infectious agents. Work must only be conducted in high containment (BSL-4) laboratories. As of 2005, there are four such labs in the U.S.; two in the Washington, D.C. area, one at the **Centers for Disease Control and Prevention (CDC)** in Atlanta, and the other in San Antonio.

All personnel who work with these highly infectious viruses must wear protective clothing (e.g., double-gloves, biohazard suits, shoe coverings, face shields, respirators, etc.) and must often work in negative pressure rooms.

While the viruses in the groups display differences in structure and severity of the symptoms they can cause, there are some features that are shared by all the viruses. For instance, all the hemorrhagic viruses contain ribonucleic acid as their genetic material. The nucleic acid is contained within a so-called envelope that is typically made of lipid. Additionally, all the viruses require a host in which to live. The animal or insect that serves as the host is also called the natural reservoir of the particular virus. This natural reservoir does not include humans. Infection of humans occurs only incidentally upon contact with the natural reservoir.

Hemorrhagic diseases can result in symptoms that can progress from mild to catastrophic in only hours. As a result, an outbreak of hemorrhagic disease tends to be self-limiting in a short time. In some cases, this is because the high death rate of those who are infected literally leaves the virus with no host to infect. Often the outbreak fades away as quickly as it appeared.

Hemorrhagic fever-related illnesses appear in a geographical area where the natural reservoir and human are both present. If the contact between the two species is close enough, then the disease causing microorganism may be able to pass from the species that is the natural reservoir to the human.

Although little is still clear about the state of the microbes in their natural hosts, it is reasonably clear now that the viruses do not damage these hosts as much as they do a human who acquires the micro-organisms. Clarifying the reasons for the resistance of the natural host to the infections would be helpful in finding an effective treatment for human hemorrhagic diseases.

The speed at which hemorrhagic fevers appear and end in human populations, combined with their frequent occurrence in relatively isolated areas of the globe has made detailed study difficult. Even though some of the diseases, such as Argentine hemorrhagic fever, have been known for almost 50 years, knowledge of the molecular basis of the disease is lacking. For example, while it is apparent that some hemorrhagic viruses can be transmitted through the air as aerosols, the pathway of infection once the microorganism has been inhaled is still largely unknown.

The transmission of hemorrhagic viruses from the animal reservoir to humans makes the viruses the quintessential zoonotic disease. For some of the viruses the host has been determined. Hosts include the cotton rat, deer mouse, house mouse, arthropod ticks, and mosquitoes. However, for other viruses, such as the Ebola and Marburg viruses, the natural host still remains undetermined. Outbreaks with the Ebola and Marburg viruses have involved transfer of the virus to human via primates. Whether the primate is the natural host or acquired the virus as the result of contact with the true natural host is not clear.

Another fairly common feature of hemorrhagic diseases is that once humans are infected with the agent of the disease, human-to-human transmission can occur. Often this transmission can be via body **fluids** that accidentally contact a person who is offering care to the afflicted person.

Hemorrhagic diseases typically begin with a fever, a feeling of tiredness, aching of muscles. These symptoms may not progress further, and recovery may occur within a short time. However, damage that is more serious can occur, which is characterized by copious bleeding, often from orifices such as the mouth, eyes, and ears. More seriously, internal bleeding also occurs, as organs are attacked by the infection. Death can result, usually not from loss of **blood**, but from nervous system failure, coma, or seizures.

SEE ALSO Ebola virus; Pathogens; Variola virus.

Edward Richard Henry

7/26/1850–2/19/1931
BRITISH
FINGERPRINT EXPERT

Over the course of his career, Sir Edward Richard Henry made significant advancements in the use of fingerprints as a tool to **forensic science**. He is responsible for developing the **fingerprint identification** system that is used throughout Europe and North America. In conjunction with his research, Henry published *Classification and Uses of Finger Prints*. As the head of Scotland Yard, he also led the transition from **anthropometry** to fingerprint identification.

Henry was born in London in 1850 and attended St. Edmund's College. He earned a degree from University College, London, in 1869, and a few years later began studying law at the Society of the Middle Temple. In 1873, Henry passed the examinations to join the civil service in India. It was in India where Henry first became involved in matters related to criminal identification and fingerprinting. He first worked in Allahabad, where he was an assistant magistrate collector, presiding over tax courts. Later, Henry was appointed as inspector general of the Bengal police.

While working as inspector general, Henry began to study how fingerprinting was and could be used as a way to identify criminals. He discussed the matter frequently with fellow English scientist Sir **Francis Galton** (1822–1911), and reviewed research conducted by William Herschel (1738–1822) and **Henry Faulds** (1843–1930). In 1896, Henry instituted the use of fingerprint impressions on criminal record forms in Bengal. Later that year, he developed a fingerprint classification system that allowed fingerprints to be filed, searched, and traced against thousands of others. Within a year, Henry's system was being used throughout British India. Within ten years, the system was being used by authorities throughout Europe and North America. Following the development of his system, Henry wrote and published a book detailing the subject, *Classification and Uses of Finger Prints*.

Henry returned to England in 1901, and became the assistant commissioner of Scotland Yard, overseeing the criminal investigation department. Later that year, under Henry's tutelage, Scotland Yard established its own fingerprint bureau. In 1903, Henry was appointed commissioner of Scotland Yard, a position he held for fifteen years. He was knighted in 1906.

SEE ALSO Fingerprint analysis (famous cases); Ridge characteristics.

William James Herschel

1833–1918
BRITISH
MAGISTRATE

William James Herschel is considered one of the first Europeans to recognize the value of fingerprints for **identification** purposes. He began using fingerprints and handprints, instead of signatures, in his work as a magistrate in colonial India in the 1850s and 1860s. He later collaborated with scientist **Francis Galton**, whose work led to establishing the first **fingerprint** classification system, implemented by Scotland Yard in 1901.

Herschel had always been fascinated by fingerprints. As a young man, he collected the fingerprints of his family members and friends as mementos, noticing that each impression was unique to each person, and that the patterns didn't change with age. In 1858, when he went to work in Jungipoor, India, as chief magistrate, Herschel found himself looking for a way to seal a contract with a local businessman. He asked for the man's handprint, and this unique method of signature secured Herschel's deal. Subsequently, Herschel began using handprints, and then fingerprints, on pensions, deeds, and jail warrants as a way to prevent fraud in a society where illiteracy was high.

At approximately the same time, Scottish physician and missionary **Henry Faulds** was studying the use of fingerprints in Japan. He wrote an article outlining his idea of using fingerprints to assist in criminal investigations for the scientific journal *Nature* in 1880. Herschel read the article and wrote a response to Faulds' piece in *Nature's* next issue. In it Herschel asserted that he had been collecting fingerprints since the 1860s, and was therefore the true inventor of this method.

In 1892, the debate caught the attention of Francis Galton, a British scientist and cousin of

Charles Darwin. Galton published *Finger Prints*, a work that established the uniqueness of fingerprints and suggested creating a classification system for them. Galton also publicly sided with Herschel, and thus Galton and Herschel became widely known as the two main innovators in fingerprint collection. Years later, Faulds' contributions were also recognized by the scientific community.

As one of the forefathers of fingerprint identification, Herschel's story and research has been well-documented in numerous books and journal articles, including the 2003 *Imprint of the Raj* by Chandak Sengoopta.

SEE ALSO Evidence; Fingerprint.

Hesitation wounds

Hesitation, or tentative, wounds are defined either as: any cut or wound that is self-inflicted after a decision is made not to commit suicide, or any tentative cut or wound that is made before the final cut that causes death. Such wounds are usually superficial, sharp, forced skin cuts found on the body of victims. These less severe cutting marks are often caused by attempts to build up courage before attempting the final, fatal wound. Non-fatal, shallow hesitation wounds can also accompany the deeper, sometimes fatal incisions. Although hesitation cuts are not always present in cases of suicide, they are typical of suicidal injuries. However, the presence of hesitation marks alongside or near to the final fatal mark usually indicates a forensic diagnosis of suicide over other possible causes of death.

Hesitation wounds are generally straight-line marks at the elbows, neck/throat, and wrists, although in a few cases they occur in the general area of the upper middle part of the abdomen (near the heart). Wounds made by people attempting suicide are typically made at an angle related to the hand that holds the weapon. The angle of such hesitation wounds is usually in a downward flowing direction because of the natural motion of the arm as it sweeps across the body. Hesitation wounds are often made under clothing, with particular parts of the clothing being parted to expose the target area of the body, a common feature seen by forensic experts examining suicidal wounds. Instruments used to inflict hesitation wounds are generally those found around the living quarters of the person attempting suicide. Such instruments include kitchen knives, single-edge and double-edge knifes, pocket knives, hatchets, razor blades, screwdrivers, and other sharp objects. People who have previously attempted suicide, but have not succeeded in their endeavor, will often carry visible scars from hesitation wounds.

Although usually used in association with attempted suicides, hesitation wounds are sometimes made in order to provide an alibi (a claim to have been elsewhere when a crime was committed) or to be seen as a victim (when in actuality the person was an active participant in the crime).

SEE ALSO Knife wounds; Suicide investigation.

Ludwig Hirszfeld

8/5/1884–3/7/1954
POLISH
SEROLOGIST

Ludwig Hirszfeld (also known as Ludwik Hirshfeld) is considered among one the most influential serologists and immunologists of the twentieth century. Along with the German physician Emil Freiherr von Dungern (born 1867), Hirszfeld discovered the inheritance of ABO **blood** types; these two scientists were responsible for naming the blood groups as such. Prior to Hirszfeld and von Dungern's work, the groups had been known as I, II, III and IV. Hirszfeld proposed the a and b designations for isoagglutinen (an **antibody** produced by one individual that causes agglutination of red blood cells in others of the same species. Agglutination is the clumping together of red blood cells, usually in response to a particular antibody.) In forensics, blood grouping and typing are critical for ascertaining whether bloodstains on weapons, tools, clothing, or elsewhere at a crime scene could have come from a particular victim or suspect; for matching fragmented human remains; and for assistance in resolving questioned paternity.

Another forensics contribution of Hirszfeld's was his establishment of serological paternity exclusion. This testing was the precursor to the modern-day use of **DNA** matching to establish criminal paternity—that is, establishing paternity in cases of unlawful sexual contact (particularly in the case of unlawful sexual contact with a minor). Serological blood testing can determine that an individual is not a biological parent of the offspring in question, hence the term paternity exclusion.

With R. Klinger, Ludwig Hirszfeld developed a serodiagnostic reaction test for syphilis, although this did not replace the Wasserman test for syphilis developed in 1906.

Ludwig Hirszfeld was born in Lodz, Poland, and studied **medicine** in Germany. After graduation from medical school he became a junior research assistant at the Heidelberg Institute for Experimental Cancer Research. There, his department chair was von Dungern, with whom he collaborated on studies of blood group heritability. In 1911, he accepted an assistantship at the Hygiene Institute of the University of Zurich; he was made an academic lecturer in 1914. The beginning of World War I led to epidemic outbreaks of typhus and bacillary dysentery in Serbia. Hirszfeld joined the Serbian Army as a serological and bacteriological advisor. While with the Serbian Army, Hirszfeld discovered the bacillus *Salmonella paratyphi C*, which has since been renamed *Salmonella hirszfeldi*. After the war ended, he and his wife (also a physician) returned to Warsaw, Poland, where he created a Polish **serum** institute; shortly thereafter, he was elected deputy director and scientific head of the State Hygiene Institute in Warsaw and became a professor there in 1924. In 1931, he was made a full professor at the University of Warsaw, and was asked to serve on numerous international boards.

After the occupation of Poland by the German Army, Hirszfeld was dismissed from his positions. He continued to do scientific work from his home until 1941, when he and his family were forced to move to the Warsaw ghetto. There, he was instrumental in organizing vaccination (against typhus and typhoid) and anti-epidemic campaigns. In 1943, he and his family fled the ghetto and remained underground until part of Poland was liberated in 1944. In 1944, Hirszfeld collaborated in the creation of the University of Lublin. In 1945, he became director of the Institute for Medical Microbiology at Wroclaw and dean of the medical faculty. He continued to teach at the institute, now affiliated with the Polish Academy of Sciences and named for him, until his death in 1954. Among the many honors bestowed on Ludwig Hirszfeld were honorary doctorates from the Universities of Prague (1950) and Zurich (1951); during his career, he wrote and published nearly 400 scholarly works in Polish, German, French, and English.

SEE ALSO Blood; Blood, presumptive test; Paternity evidence; Serology.

Hitler Diaries

In April 1983 Gruner and Jahr, the parent company of the West German publisher of the popular magazine *Stern*, announced that it had purchased for $2.3 million an astonishing set of documents: sixty-two notebooks that purported to be the handwritten diaries of Adolf Hitler, as well as an unpublished third volume of *Mein Kampf* (My Struggle), Hitler's autobiographical manifesto written while he was incarcerated in Landsberg prison in the 1920s. *Stern* began to serialize the diaries, which covered the period 1935–45, and sold publication rights to *Newsweek* in the United States and to the *London Times*.

The story surrounding the documents supposed that they had been on a plane carrying the Führer's personal archives out of Berlin when it was shot down in April 1945 near the village of Börnersdorf, in what would later become East Germany. The documents, which escaped destruction because they were housed in a metal box, were recovered by local farmers, who hid them until they were smuggled out of the country and came into the hands of a document collector and World War II enthusiast named Konrad Kujau.

The diaries sent shock waves throughout the world and touched off a historical controversy, for they portrayed a Hitler who was very different from the man who haunted the history books. In particular, they suggested that Hitler had no involvement in the 1938 riot against the Jews called *Kristallnacht* (Night of Broken Glass), that he knew nothing of the "final solution," or plans to exterminate Europe's Jewish population, and that his goal was simply to resettle western Europe's Jews in eastern Europe. If the diaries were authentic, they were the most significant historical find in decades, and the history of the Nazi regime of the 1930s and 1940s would have to be entirely rewritten.

Stern had initially been skeptical and reluctant to purchase the documents. In time, skepticism and reluctance turned into an almost fevered excitement about this apparent historical discovery. *Stern's* eventual willingness to accept the authenticity of the documents rested on two foundations. First were the memoirs of Lieutenant General Hans Baur, Hitler's chief SS pilot, who confirmed that a plane flown by one Major Friedrich Gundlfinger was indeed ferrying Hitler's private papers out of the country the month when his plane was shot down. Second, *Stern* sought confirmation from other sources. It submitted the papers to three handwriting experts: Dr. **Max Frei-Sulzer**, a former head of the police **forensic science** department in Zurich, Switzerland; American document verification expert Ordway Hilton; and a third expert in the employ of the German police. Comparing the writing in the diaries with known samples of Hitler's handwriting retrieved from Germany's Federal Archives, these experts concluded that both the diaries and the samples were written by the same hand, that of Adolf Hitler. Backing up their claims were prominent historians such as Britain's Hugh Trevor-Roper, although other historians noted historical inconsistencies in the diaries and denounced them as hoaxes.

The controversy prompted the German Federal Archives to conduct its own independent tests, focusing not on the handwriting, but on the physical documents themselves. On May 6, 1983, the archives held a press conference and announced that the diaries were forgeries.

The forensics **evidence** used to reach this conclusion was based on examination of the ink and paper, as well as seals affixed to the documents. Modern ink has different varieties of chemical composition, or "fingerprints," that fall into four groupings: (1) inks in which gallic acid is used to hold iron salts in suspension; (2) those in which gum arabic is used to hold carbon particles in suspension; (3) those that contain synthetic dyes, as well as a range of polymers and acids; (4) those that contain various solvents and additives such as chloride to hold synthetic dyes or pigments.

Ink samples, like any substance, can be tested using **chromatography**, a process by which the ingredients in the substance are held in a solution, then separated as they flow over a medium such as paper or silica gel that absorbs compounds at different rates. The bands created are then examined through micro-spectro photometry, a process of identifying substances from the light transmitted from the minute samples of them. In the case of ink, the results are then compared with a database of three thousand different inks maintained by the U.S. Federal Bureau of Investigation. The ink from the Hitler Diaries was subjected to these tests.

The chloride that was identified in the Hitler Diaries ink proved that the documents could have been written only in the previous year. Further, the paper, which had been "aged" by beating on it with a hammer and staining it with tea leaves, was examined under ultraviolet light. This examination showed that the paper contained an additive that had not been used in the papermaking process until 1954. The threads used to affix the seals to the documents, too, were suspect because they contained materials that were not available until after World War II. The **physical evidence** was conclusive: The documents were an elaborate forgery.

How could such a hoax be perpetrated on millions of people? At the center of the hoax was a sometime artist named Konrad Kujau (1938–2000), who was born into a middle-class family in Löbau, Germany. His father was an enthusiastic Hitler supporter, and the younger Kujau, who showed early promise as an artist, expressed his admiration for his father's hero by drawing sketches of the Führer. Kujau's early years are shrouded in some mystery; he worked in a number of short-lived jobs, and he later claimed to have studied at the Dresden Academy of Art. He surfaced near Stuttgart, West Germany, in 1957, where he had numerous brushes with the law and spent time in jail.

In the 1960s, Kujau decided to put his artistic skill to work as a forger, and he earned pocket change forging and selling the autographs of famous people. (In a bizarre footnote, it turned out that at least one of the documents the handwriting experts relied on was itself a Kujau forgery.) By the 1970s, Kujau was buying and selling Nazi memorabilia. He soon realized that he could enhance the value of the items in his collection by forging the signatures of prominent Nazi officials, as well as bogus documentation for them. Collectors snapped up the helmets, uniforms, flags, medals, and letters he sold in this way. Especially popular with collectors were paintings Kujau sold as Hitler's, but that were his own forgeries.

In the late 1970s, Kujau's criminal career took a more elaborate direction when he produced a handwritten manuscript purporting to be the third volume of Hitler's two-volume *Mein Kampf* (even though Hitler was known to have written the first two volumes with a typewriter). He went on to forge additional documents, including poems he sold to collectors by claiming they were from the pen of Hitler himself. Finally, he began producing the Hitler Diaries, which became a source of fascination among his gullible, but wealthy, clients.

The *Stern* saga began in 1979, when a journalist who worked for the magazine, Gerd Heidemann, himself a Hitler enthusiast, went to the home of one Fritz Stiefel to see his collection of Nazi memorabilia, including not just paintings and letters, but also a volume of Hitler's diary, supposedly one of six volumes extant. Heidemann smelled a major news story, but he knew that his editors would have interest only if he did further background work. He traveled to Börnersdorf, where he learned about the mysterious airplane crash and the metal box

A former reporter of West Germany's *Stern* magazine, Gerd Heidemann was convicted by a court of selling fake Hitler diaries to a West German magazine and sentenced to four years imprisonment in 1985. © REUTERS/CORBIS

containing papers that was retrieved from the wreckage. There Heidemann learned that there were not six but twenty-seven volumes of the diary, all in the hands of one Konrad Fischer, an alias Kujau commonly used. Based on his findings, Heidemann pitched the story to his editors, who agreed to pay two million German marks for the twenty-seven volumes. Kujau feared that selling the notebooks would lead to his exposure, but the money was just too much to refuse, so he began work on the diaries in earnest. Over a two-year period, Kujau wrote the diaries out in longhand Gothic script, sealing each notebook with special seals and black ribbon. For content, he relied on newspaper stories, medical documents, and reference books, including a book of Hitler's speeches.

After the documents were exposed as forgeries, Kujau fled, but he was arrested at the German border and tried in Hamburg in August of 1984. Kujau confessed to the forgeries, and during the trial he made no attempt to hide his guilt. Heidemann was tried as an accomplice, although he protested that he had also been duped. The pair was found guilty and sentenced to four and a half years in prison. The judge criticized *Stern*, stating the magazine "acted with such naïveté and negligence that it was virtually an accomplice in the fraud." After serving about three years of his sentence, Kujau was released. In the years that followed he created and sold art reproductions, ran unsuccessfully for public office, and was arrested in 1999 for forging his own driver's license. Kujau died in 2000. It has never been determined what happened to the total of five million marks *Stern* allegedly paid out for the Hitler Diaries.

SEE ALSO Chromatography; Handwriting analysis; Ink analysis; Micro-spectrophotometry.

Holocaust investigation

During World War II (1939–1945), an estimated total of 60 million people, including military personnel, paramilitary personnel, and civilians, had perished, whether in battle, by air raids or shelling of urban areas, village sieges, or in concentration camps. The term Holocaust refers to those ethnic populations who were persecuted and exterminated by the German Nazis in forced labor camps, death marches, inside ghettos, and rural areas. The International Military Tribunal in Nuremberg, Germany, conducted the investigation and trials of such crimes in the aftermath of World War II. In spite of strict secrecy kept by the Nazi authorities on their genocidal activities, thanks to several anti-Nazi paramilitary groups organized by civilians in the German-occupied territories, collectively known as the Resistance, testimonies of such atrocities were gradually gathered by the Allied Forces. Citizens from France, Italy, Austria, Poland, Norway, Denmark, and other countries formed a network of underground activity, supplying the Allies with intelligence, and smuggling targeted ethnic persons, such as Jews, Gypsies (Roma people), prisoners of war, and political dissidents from Germany and the occupied territories to the United Kingdom, southern France, and the Americas. In the face of the alarming amount of atrocities reported, the governments of the Allied Forces decided in early 1942 to thoroughly investigate and punish those responsible for such crimes. On December 17, 1942, the United States, the United Kingdom, and the Soviet Union signed a joint declaration acknowledging the mass murder of European Jews.

The Soviet Union issued the Moscow Declaration, on October 30, 1943, "Concerning responsibility of Hitlerites for committed atrocities" and the United Kingdom established, on August 8, 1945, the London Agreement, "Concerning prosecution and punishment of major war criminals of European Axis" (Axis meaning the Alliance of Nazi-Germany with Mussolini, then Dictator of Italy, and the Japanese Empire). Those two documents were combined into a body of laws to regulate the International Military Tribunal (IMT), created by the Allies (the United States, the United Kingdom, and the Soviet Union) in August of 1945. The IMT received jurisdiction to investigate and prosecute individual responsibilities concerning the following offenses: 1) crimes against peace, or "planning, preparation, initiation, or waging of wars of aggression, or war in violation of international treaties, agreements or assurances, or participation in a common plan or conspiracy for the accomplishment of any of the foregoing"; 2) war crimes, or "violations of

the laws or customs of war … shall include, but not be limited to, murder, ill-treatment or deportation to slave labor or for any purpose of civilian population of or in occupied territory, murder or ill-treatment of prisoners of war or persons on the seas, killing of hostages, plunder of public or private property, wanton destruction of cities, towns, or villages, or devastation not justified by military necessity"; and 3) crimes against humanity, or "murder, extermination, enslavement, deportation, and other inhumane acts committed against any civilian population, before or during the war … or persecution on political, racial or religious grounds in execution of or in connection with any crime within the jurisdiction of the Tribunal, whether or not in violation of domestic law of the country where perpetrated."

From October 18, 1945, until October 1, 1946, twenty-two Nazi officers were prosecuted on one or more of such charges. Under IMT law, American military tribunals had also tried another 12 high-ranking German Officials at Nuremberg. However, the vast majority of post-war trials concerned lower-rank officials, such as concentration camps commandants, guards, leaders of mobile killing units (Einsatzgruppen), police officers, and Nazi physicians who carried out gruesome medical experiments on both political dissidents and other prisoners (Jewish and Gypsy women, men, and children) in the concentration camps. These criminals were prosecuted in different courts and locations of the Allied-occupied territories, such as Soviet-occupied zones of Germany and Austria, British and American courts, and Italy. Additionally, other countries also tried those who committed crimes in their respective territories during Nazi occupation and those who collaborated with Nazi authorities. Poland, for instance, sentenced to death Rudolf Hess, the commandant of Auschwitz extermination camp, in 1947. In post-war decades, Israeli intelligence continued to investigate and hunt Nazi criminals who had fled to other countries under fake identities, such as Adolf Eichmann, who was finally tried in Jerusalem in 1961.

In spite of testimonial **evidence** and intelligence on Nazi crimes against humanity gathered by the Allies and the Red Cross during the war, nothing prepared the world for the horrors that were disclosed when troops finally reached the concentration camps. In addition to the on-site photographs, movies, **physical evidence**, and reports by officers of the liberation forces, as well as the individual testimonies of those who survived the Holocaust or the Nazi medical experiments, a great amount of Nazi documentation and material evidence was found in prisons, in the secret police archives, and local police administrative files, which the Nazis did not succeeded in destroying before the Allied invasion.

From the Nazi documentation, such as decrees issued by Hitler to the Gestapo (German secret police organization), ministry memos, and doctrinaire Nazi material, it became clear to Holocaust investigators and prosecutors that concentration camps had served initially as a tool of 1) political terror against Germans, Austrians, Poles, and other political dissidents; 2) as a means of exploiting slave labor; and 3), as places for mass extermination of Jews, Roma people (Gypsies), and others (Serbs, Russians, and Albanians). Soon after Adolf Hitler was nominated as Chancellor of the Third Reich, the Nazi party issued a presidential emergency decree, in February 28, 1933, establishing a so-called "protective custody" that gave the Gestapo unlimited power to arrest people without judicial proceedings.

The Nazi rationale behind ethnic persecution and extermination was twofold. First, according, to the head of the SS, Heinrich Himmler, in a speech to the SS Major Generals at Posen in 1943, the mass extermination of Jews was necessary, although it was a very difficult task, because Jews, due to their religion, were against the Nazi war efforts, acting "in every town as secret saboteurs, agitators and trouble-mongers"; and second, because of the Nazi racial theory about the existence of a pure, "superior" race, the Aryans (Europeans descended from the Saxons), which should be protected from miscegenation with non-Aryan "inferior" races, which were gradually polluting and degrading the Aryan race. Therefore, Jews in particular, and all persons having at least one Jewish grandparent, should be eliminated.

The Roma people, like the Jews, were for centuries victims of discrimination by Europeans in general, due to their traditional customs and nomadic behavior. Nazi killing mobile units were sent to assassinate tens of thousands of Roma in the occupied eastern territories, such as Poland, Hungary, Serbia, and Albania, as well as in the western territories of countries such as France and Italy. Like the Jews, the Roma were also imprisoned in concentration camps, forced to work in factories and mines, tortured, shot, hung, or gassed in the death chambers. An estimated 1 million Roma are thought to have died under Nazi oppression, approximately half of the existing prewar population.

Nazi documents on the number and location of concentration camps all over Europe, such as one signed by the SS General Pohl, compared quantities of prisoners between 1939 and 1942, as follows: "At the beginning of war (Dachau, 1939 = 4,000 prisoners, today, 8,000; Sachsenhausen, 1939 = 6,500, today, 10,000; Buchenwald, 1939 = 5,300, today, 9,000; Mauthausen, 1939 = 1,500, today, 5,500; Flossenburg, 1939 = 1,600, today, 4,700; Ravensbureck, 1939 = 2,500, today 7,500." The report continues, showing a list of new camps built between 1940 and 1942: Auschwitz (Poland), Neuengamme (Germany), Gusen (Austria), Natzweiler (France), Gross-Rosen (Germany), Lublin (Poland), Niederhagen (Germany), Stutthof (near Danzig), Arbeitsdorf (Germany). The War Crimes Branch of the Third U.S. Army (Judge Advocate Section), reported that "Concentration Camp Flossenburg was founded in 1938 as a camp for political prisoners ... and it was not until April 1940 that the first transport of prisoners was received. ... Flossenburg was the mother camp and under its direct control and jurisdiction were 47 satellite camps or outer-commandos for male prisoners and 27 camps for female workers ..." The SS police (Gestapo) established a program of "extermination through work" in these camps, alternating with torture, starvation, and mass execution in gas chambers and incineration in furnaces. A secret motion picture made by the Gestapo of these mass executions was presented as evidence in the IMT court. According to surviving witnesses, when bored, the camp guards also amused themselves by randomly shooting or hanging prisoners.

Physical forensic evidence presented at IMT included an exhibit of three tattooed parchments, identified as human skin by Lieutenant George C. Demas, U.S.N.R., of the United States Chief of Counsel for the Prosecution of Axis Criminality. The evidence was presented in support of testimonial by a former prisoner at the Buchenwald camp, as follows: "In 1939, all prisoners with tattooing on them were ordered to report to the dispensary ... but after the tattooed prisoners had been examined, the ones with the best and most artistic specimens were kept in the dispensary, and then killed by injections administered by Karl Beigs, a criminal prisoner. The bodies were then turned over to the **pathology** department, where the desired pieces of tattooed skin were detached from the bodies and treated. The finished products were turned over to SS Standartenfuehrer Koch's wife, who had them fashioned into lampshades and other ornamental household articles. ..."

The IMT and other investigation committees could never make an accurate estimate of the real numbers of the Holocaust victims. Although Nazis in general kept detailed records, and some concentration camp death lists have been retrieved, it is likely

A section of tattooed human skin preserved as ornament, found at Buchenwald. It was submitted as evidence by American prosecution at the Nuremberg War Crimes Trial of 21 Nazi leaders. © CORBIS

that they only represent the tip of the iceberg. However, due to the huge scale of concentration camps operations and facilities, it was evident they were designed as death factories for mass extermination. Mass graves were also found by the Allied troops in several locations, with hundreds of corpses inside many of them. From some interim reports to Himmler, issued by German officers, it is known that, only from Hungary, "Up to June 27, 1944, 475,000 Jews were deported" to concentration camps in Germany. One report also informs Himmler that between January 11 and 31, 1943, a total of 45,000 Jews were deported from Poland, Berlin, and occupied Dutch territories to Auschwitz: "... the figure of 45,000 includes the invalids (old Jews and children). By the use of a practical standard, the screening of the arriving Jews in Auschwitz should yield at least 10,000 to 15,000 people fit for work. ..." Those "unfit for work" were killed in the gas chambers. Auschwitz and the other camps were constantly receiving prisoners and discarding the unfit for work, and renewing their work forces as the fit quickly became unfit through disease, murder, or starvation.

Long after the confusion of war, work is underway to preserve sites where forensic evidence of the Holocaust might still be found. Most extermination sites were cleaned or deliberately bombed and machinery dismantled by the retreating Germans to attempt to hide the full extent of and motive behind concentration camp atrocities, but some relatively undisturbed sites still remain. In the Birkenau camp in Poland, parts of walls from the gas chamber and crematorium still stand. Preservation groups are consulting forensic scientists for methods to protect traces of chemicals or human remains that are still in the area.

SEE ALSO Hitler Diaries; War crimes trials; War forensics.

Holocaust, property identification

After Nazi leader Adolf Hitler (1889–1945) rose to power in Germany in 1933, the Holocaust and, ultimately, World War II began. During this era, the Nazis stole art, other cultural property, and money from Jews and other groups. Hitler took art theft seriously; he sent an advance team into The Netherlands to identify important collections before invading. Many of these stolen works are of major importance and great monetary value. Some were given to Nazi functionaries and others were sold at auction, while many more were stored. After the war ended in 1945, the Allies found more than 2,000 repositories of artworks in Germany and Austria. Efforts at returning property began soon after and continue to this day. Many works of art in museums around the world still need to be restored to their rightful owners or their successors. **Art identification** experts are helping many initiatives, both national and international, in this work. Similarly, investigations are ongoing into sums of money deposited in bank accounts that may belong to Holocaust survivors and their families.

The International Council of Museums (ICOM) and the United Nations Educational Scientific and Cultural Organization (UNESCO) have been involved in this restoration on behalf of museums around the world. They have encouraged many new initiatives; for instance, in 1998, museums in The Netherlands began an inventory to check the history and **identification** of all items received between 1940 and 1948. There are also a number of databases listing works of art of dubious origin or works known to be stolen. Such databases may help those in the difficult search for stolen items—which could be anywhere in the world, either in a private collection or in a museum—particularly if expert advice is available.

For example, the Museum Provenance List is a compilation of museums that have listed works of art of doubtful origin in their collections. The Art Loss Register is the world's largest private international database of lost and stolen art with a special section for items looted during World War II. Their dedicated team of art specialists check the thousands of missing art works on their database against those offered at art auctions and art dealer fairs; they also check museum collections. As of 2005, they have so far identified 21 missing paintings, including works by Claude Monet, Pierre Bonnard, and Alfred Sisley. Sometimes the detective work involves tracing the rightful owners of a looted painting, rather than locating the work itself. In 2002, the Register, with the help of a museum in the Czech Republic and a journalist in the United States, finally tracked down the descendants of the owner of André Derain's *Head of a Young Woman*. The painting had been stolen in 1941.

The Commission for Looted Art in Europe helps families, communities, and institutions with the identification and recovery of looted cultural property and works on some 100 cases at any one time. In one example, the commission was approached by the Glanville family for help in recovering a triptych called *Three Stages of Life* by German artist Count Leopold von Kalckreuth. The artwork had been looted from their home in Vienna in 1938. The work was quickly located in the Neue Pinakothek in Munich. Ten weeks later, the German museum agreed to return it to its rightful owners, who had relocated to London.

Many Jewish families also tried to hide cash from the Nazis by opening up accounts in neutral Switzerland and in Palestine (later, in part, to become the modern state of Israel). The banks involved have made some restitution; for instance, Swiss banks finally made payments of 1.25 billion U.S. dollars to Holocaust survivors and Jewish organizations in 2000, after many years of dispute.

The Nazis were also responsible for one of the biggest thefts ever perpetrated by a government. As they invaded European countries in the late 1930s and early 1940s, they looted central banks for gold to finance their war machine. That gold was then sold to Switzerland and other neutral countries. The Nazis also stole gold, coins, and jewelry from Jews and other victims of their persecution.

One of the more sinister ways the Nazis obtained gold was by removing the fillings from the teeth of their victims in concentration camps. The company that supplied the cyanide for the mass gas exterminations told the Nazis that they could melt down and reprocess the gold fillings into bars. Some of this gold ended up in the German and Swiss banks, but it is difficult for experts to determine, even with the most advanced modern forensic techniques, how much of it comes from concentration camp victims. The matter is under discussion again as of 2005, with the possibility that further reparation may be made to Holocaust survivors.

SEE ALSO Art identification.

Homogeneous enzyme immunoassay (EMIT)

Forensic **medicine** and hospital laboratories utilize several different types of biochemical assays (tests) for drug detection in body **fluids** and tissues, including liquid chromatography-mass spectrometry, high-performance liquid **chromatography**, and immunochemical techniques, among others. Immunochemical techniques identify chemicals in urine, **blood** plasma, or tissues through the reactions between body antigens and antibodies in the presence of a foreign protein or chemical.

Cells present fragments of intracellular proteins to T cell lymphocytes (a type of white blood cell) that scan tissues in search of foreign **pathogens** such as viruses, bacteria, or **toxins**. When a foreign protein (or toxin) is detected by T cells, an immune response is triggered and antibodies are produced by B-lymphocytes and sent to bind to these alien proteins. Antibodies are proteins that enhance **antigen** recognition by other cells of the **immune system**. Enzyme-Multiplied Immunoassay Technique (EMIT) was introduced in 1972 for the rapid detection of hormones and drug metabolites in human fluids.

Antibodies against abused drugs are synthesized in laboratories to make them recognizable as foreign entities by a B-lymphocyte (type of white blood cell). Drug molecules are attached to a high molecular weight protein to form an antigen conjugate. These antigen conjugates are then injected into a host animal, whose immune system will produce drug-specific antibodies. The resulting antibodies may be of two types, either monoclonal or polyclonal antibodies. Monoclonal antibodies are families of identical proteins that only bind to a specific site of an antigen molecule, whereas polyclonal antibodies are not identical and bind to more than one antigen site. Once the desired blood levels of **antibody** are obtained, antibodies are recovered from the animal blood and purified.

EMIT detects even small quantities of drugs and drug metabolites (drug-derived molecules) in biological fluids, such as blood and urine. EMIT assays can be run in two different ways: Competitive EMIT and Non-competitive EMIT. Competitive EMIT contains drug antigens which will compete for the same antigen sites with the drug under investigation that is present in the body fluid sample. In a non-competitive EMIT assay, the drug under investigation reacts with a labeled antibody protein to form a colored substance. The following drugs are detected by EMIT: cocaine and metabolites, cannabinoides, opiates, **amphetamines**, phentanyl, methadone, **barbiturates**, benzodiazepines, phenylciclidine, and propoxyphene.

SEE ALSO Amphetamines; Antibody; Antigen; Barbiturates; Commercial kits; DEA (Drug Enforcement Administration); Illicit drugs; Immune system; Narcotic; Toxicological analysis; Toxicology.

J. Edgar Hoover

AMERICAN
GOVERNMENT OFFICIAL

For more than forty-five years, J. Edgar Hoover served as the director of the **United States Federal Bureau of Investigation (FBI)**. Under Hoover's leadership, the bureau gained responsibility and importance within the U.S. government. A proponent of forensic investigation techniques, Hoover established the FBI's national **fingerprint** depository and crime laboratory. Hoover is also known for his aggressive anti-Communist and anti-radical actions and illegally investigating suspected individuals with wiretaps and surveillance.

Born in Washington, D.C., Hoover was active in the cadet corps and debate team in high school. He attended George Washington University, earning bachelor and master's degrees in law in 1916. In 1917, he joined the U.S. Department of Justice, working in the General Intelligence Division. When his division was moved to the FBI (at that time known as the Bureau of Investigation) in 1921, Hoover became the assistant director there.

Hoover became the director of the FBI in 1924, a position he would hold until his death in 1972. At the time, the FBI had been undergoing much criticism for a number of scandals under the previous administration. With Hoover in charge, the bureau rid itself of unqualified special agents, and implemented a new hiring process that selected only high-quality candidates. Hoover also ordered the creation of a crime laboratory, one that would provide forensic analysis on investigations across the country. In addition, he made the bureau's new fingerprint collection a national resource. The FBI thus became well known across the country, in particular because of its high-profile pursuit of gangsters like John Dillinger, Pretty Boy Floyd, and Baby Face Nelson. Hoover was honored for his contributions to the field of **forensic science** in 1959, when he was given the John A. Dondero Award from the **International Association for Identification**.

Over the course of his career, Hoover also became known for his relentless pursuit of Communists and other politically radical groups. He publicly attacked such figures as Martin Luther King, Jr., Robert Kennedy, and Ramsey Clark, and, in the privacy of the bureau, arranged such illegal investigative measures as wiretapping, surveillance, and the use of informers. Knowledge of some of these activities didn't become public until after Hoover's death in 1972.

SEE ALSO Bugs (microphones) and bug detectors; Careers in forensic science; FBI Crime Laboratory.

Howard Hughes' will

Howard Hughes, Jr. (1905–1976), an aviator, film producer, and manufacturer, died a multibillionaire. Unmarried and childless, Hughes left no clear heir. He had spent his final years as a mentally ill recluse and no one knew his intentions for his fortune. The fierce battle over the Hughes estate became a public spectacle involving dueling handwriting experts and neuropathology. The fight illustrates the difficulty of disproving hoaxes in the days before advanced forensic testing.

Hughes was born in Houston, Texas, to a mining engineer who devised an oil-drill bit that revolutionized the American oil industry. The family became wealthy, but the early death of his parents had a profound effect on Hughes. Always withdrawn, he became a hypochondriac fearful of germs. He ended his education in 1924 to enter the world of business. Not content with inheriting 75% of his father's tool company fortune, Hughes bought out the other 25% previously dispersed among relatives. The agreements with his relatives were bitterly arrived at and caused a permanent rift. After hiring executives to run his business, Hughes moved to Los Angeles and became a film producer. In 1933, he founded the Hughes Aircraft Company and it grew into one of the most profitable aircraft production companies in the world. Obsessive-compulsive by nature, Hughes became ever more eccentric as the years passed. Additionally, after sustaining serious injuries in an airplane crash, he became addicted to the painkiller codeine.

Hughes eventually refused to see people other than his closest business executives. Living behind closed curtains, he became best known to the public for his uncut hair and long fingernails. In November 1970, Hughes moved to the Bahamas to avoid taxes. He never returned to the United States. The last six years of his life were those of an itinerant exile, moving from one luxurious hotel to another. In his last years, Hughes refused medical treatment and did not eat properly. He became an emaciated wreck, weighing only ninety-four pounds at the time of his death. He denied his aides the right to tend him, until he finally lapsed into unconsciousness. They then flew him in an air ambulance to Houston, but he was dead of kidney failure by the time the plane landed, on April 5, 1976.

Hughes' death set off a stampede for his fortune. The assets of Summa Corporation, under which all of his businesses were governed, were valued at more than $2 billion. Probate was opened in Houston, Las Vegas, and Los Angeles. No one was certain if Hughes had left a will. George Francom, a personal aide, later testified that Hughes once mentioned he had drawn up a handwritten will. But when Francom asked about its whereabouts, the ever-suspicious Hughes refused to tell him where it was.

Summa conducted a worldwide search, but failed to turn up a signed document. The search did, however, yield an unsigned carbon copy of a 1954 will, written at the time Hughes set up the Howard Hughes Medical Institute in Florida. Stating his concern about germs and disease, Hughes declared that he wanted the institute to inherit most of his wealth and accomplish something good in his name.

The Summa representatives presented this 1954 carbon copy to a probate court as the best available **evidence** of Hughes' intentions. They argued that although a written will could not be found, Hughes' real and declared intent was to leave his whole fortune to the medical institute. Summa vice president Frank William Gay, attorney Chester Davis, and Hughes' former administrative assistant, Nadine Henley, wanted to continue to run the Hughes empire. Under their plan, as trustees of the medical institute, they would remain in command. They hoped to block the legal offensive of Hughes' former aide Noah Dietrich, with whom Hughes split in 1956, and who entered the fray with a new will.

The Mormon will, dated March 19, 1968, appeared days after Hughes' death as a public relations executive of The Church of Jesus Christ of Latter-Day Saints (Mormons) sorted through the mail on his desk one afternoon. A tattered yellow envelope, bearing a partly illegible Las Vegas postmark, was addressed to Spencer W. Kimball, president of the Mormon Church. Inside the first envelope was a smaller one that bore instructions written in a large scrawl. Kimball was directed to deliver the enclosed will to legal authorities in Clark County, Nevada. It was signed Howard R. Hughes.

The Mormons immediately doubted the legitimacy of the document. The three-page document, on lined legal paper identical to the type Hughes regularly used for memos to his staff, lacked the signatures of witnesses. Not wishing to appear foolish, Mormon Church leaders submitted the will to a Utah handwriting expert, Leslie King, who had studied Hughes' handwriting in an earlier court case. After a quick examination, she declared that Hughes possibly wrote the will. The Mormons then went to Las Vegas, the seat of Clark County, to file the testament.

The Mormon will gave one-fourth of the Hughes estate to the Hughes Medical Institute; divided one-eighth between the University of Texas, the University of Nevada, and the University of California; gave one-sixteenth to the Church of Jesus Christ of Latter-Day Saints; sent one-sixteenth to establish a home for orphaned children; gave one-sixteenth to go to the Boy Scouts of America; split one-sixteenth among Hughes' ex-wives, Jean Peters of Los Angeles and Ella Rice of Houston; gave one-sixteenth to cousin William R. Lummis (spelled Lommis in the will) and gave the last one-sixteenth to Melvin Du Mar (spelling incorrect) of Gabbs, Nevada. Dummar stated that he picked up the hitchhiking Hughes in 1968, loaned him a quarter, and never had any further connection with the old man after dropping him off.

The remainder of the estate went to the key men in Hughes' company. Dietrich was named executor of the estate despite the fact that he had not spoken with Hughes since 1956. Executors receive a portion of an estate for their services, giving Dietrich a financial interest in the case.

The will immediately became suspect because of the numerous spelling errors that filled its pages as well as suspect references. Hughes paid painstaking attention to detail throughout his life and never made vague statements. Dummar was suspected of forging the Mormon will, because no one could understand why Hughes would leave him one hundred and fifty million dollars or why the reclusive and germ-phobic billionaire would hitchhike. Dummar later admitted that his story was false. Lastly, lawyers who worked for Hughes found it inconceivable that he would have relied on a handwritten last testament. He had a deep fear that his handwriting could be forged and even tried to keep his signature secret.

In 1976 the technology did not exist for accurate forensic examination of the Mormon will. Ten handwriting experts, included well-known Bernard Bern, declared the document to be in Hughes' handwriting. One stated that the writing was typical of Hughes' consistent inconsistencies.

Hughes had three maternal second cousins who would become his heirs under Texas law if there was no will. Handwriting expert Spencer Otis, one of the most-respected analysts in the United States, examined the Mormon will and declared it to be a forgery. Hughes' relatives on his maternal side combined with his relatives from the paternal side to fight Summa. The heirs, who numbered twenty-three in all, were led by William Lummis. They wanted the estate to be divided according to a formula that would give nearly one-quarter to Lummis' mother and distribute the rest among the other heirs.

Meanwhile, a neuropathologist examined a portion of Hughes' brain that had been preserved in a jar on a shelf in Houston's Methodist Hospital. The scientist searched for evidence of disease or damage that could have impaired Hughes' judgment. Such a finding would throw into question anything that Hughes signed or said during his later years, but the neuropathologist found nothing significant.

By the end of 1976, the legal battle over the Hughes estate involved at least two hundred lawyers who pored over records in half a dozen

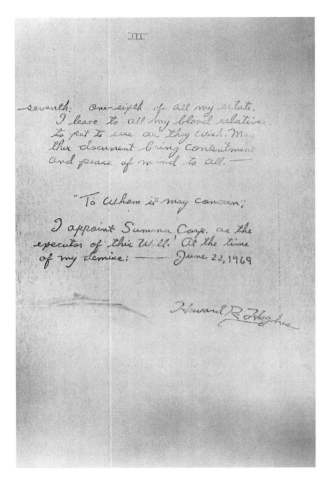

The last page of a purported handwritten will of the late billionare Howard Hughes, found to be a forgery by investigators. © BETTMANN/CORBIS

states to find clues as to Hughes' intentions for his empire. They found a key to a safe-deposit box among Hughes' belongings in his old Hollywood office in Hollywood and a 1938 registered letter to the First National Bank in Houston saying he was enclosing a will. Neither discovery produced results.

In June 1978, after a seven-month trial, a jury decided by unanimous verdict that Hughes did not author the Mormon will. In the absence of another valid will, the court awarded the Hughes estate to the billionaire's surviving relatives. Lummis, as the court-appointed executor, agreed to administer the estate. By this time, the value of the Hughes' estate had dropped into the millions, with much of the fortune going to attorney's fees.

SEE ALSO Document forgery; Handwriting analysis; Questioned documents.

Human migration patterns

One of the most heated debates in **anthropology** and **archaeology** involves the evolution of man and the subsequent migration of the species that led to humans populating the world. Scientists question whether humans evolved in Africa or somewhere else and if the human species did evolve in Africa, scientists have asked when they began migrating to other places. In addition, anthropologists wonder whether humans, as they began their migration, simply replaced pre-human species in a given location or interbred with them.

Traditionally, scientists trying to answer these types of questions have traveled throughout the world searching for the oldest human remains and artifacts in a given location. Then, using scientific dating techniques, such as carbon dating, they estimate when humans might have first lived in a location. This type of work is obviously painstaking and requires great amounts of experience. It is highly dependent on environmental factors that may or may not have preserved human remains in a condition that allows for proper dating. It also assumes that the materials found are actually the oldest.

Beginning in the 1990s anthropologists and archaeologists began using techniques similar to those used in **forensic science** to solve some of the questions relating to human migration patterns. Instead of collecting bones and artifacts, scientists began collecting **DNA** from people all over the world. The DNA contains information that can be used to determine when populations from different parts of the world arrived at their current locations.

The DNA found in human cells is an extremely long molecule that is made up of a sequence of four different nucleotides. Over time, small changes, called mutations, occur in the order of the nucleotides in this sequence. If a molecular biologist detects a particular mutation in the DNA of a population somewhere in the world and then detects the same mutation in another group, and this mutation is not found in any other populations, it can be assumed that the two groups are closely related. That is, they probably were at one time a single group and then one group migrated to a new location. By searching for mutations and mapping them to the locations of populations of people throughout the world, anthropologists can build a picture of human migration patterns. In addition, because the rate of mutations in DNA can be estimated, scientists can also estimate when the various waves of migrations took place.

Two major types of molecular analyses have been used to probe questions concerning human migration patterns. A large study of the Y chromosome, which is passed from father to son, shows that all humans share a common ancestor who lived in Africa about 60,000 years ago. Another study focused on mitochondrial DNA (mtDNA). Mitochondria, which are organelles that power the cell, contain DNA that is passed from mother to daughter. The mtDNA study agrees with the Y chromosome study in placing the origin of the human species in Africa, however it demonstrates that migrations began much earlier, around 150,000 years ago. Archaeological evidence suggests that a wave of migrations out of Africa and into the Middle East began around 90,000 years ago.

Evidence from studies of the DNA in the Y chromosome show that a second wave of migrations out of Africa began around 45,000 years ago. These people moved to the Middle East, India, and China. During a brief warming period between Ice Ages, humans migrated farther east, to Central Asia, 40,000 years ago and then a group of them reached Europe about 35,000 years ago. Somewhere around 20,000 years ago, a group from Central Asia migrated north toward Siberia and the Arctic Circle. At the end of an ice age around 15,000 years ago, a group from the Arctic Circle migrated across the Bering Strait and populated North America. While these patterns of migration generally agree with archeological data, the dates tend to be much more recent than fossils and artifacts suggest.

Similar to traditional archaeologists, researchers working with mtDNA believe migrations out of Africa occurred earlier than Y chromosome data suggest. However, **mitochondrial DNA analysis** indicates that a single wave of migration, rather than two major waves, left Africa about 80,000 years ago and moved through the Middle East and toward India and Asia. This research then indicates that humans populated Australia 60,000 years ago, and artifacts found there corroborate these findings. The mitochondrial DNA data also indicates that people reached Europe about 50,000 years ago. This means that they cohabitated with Neanderthals for about 10,000 years, but that there was no interbreeding between the two groups of hominids. Finally, about 25,000 to 20,000 years ago, mtDNA data indicates that people from Siberia crossed over a land bridge to populate North America. Tools dating to 16,000 years old have been found in current-day Pennsylvania in North America.

Although there are discrepancies between the results from the two molecular techniques and that of archaeological data, most scientists agree that as more disciplines become involved in answering the questions, new and better insight will arise. In particular, the types of investigations that allow forensic scientists to identify differences between individuals contribute greatly to the understanding of differences between populations throughout the world.

SEE ALSO Anthropology; DNA sequences, unique; Genetic code.

Hypothermia

An important facet of a forensic investigation into a death is the determination of the **cause of death**. In cases where outward signs of physical trauma (i.e., gunshot or stab wounds) are absent, a forensic investigator may be presented with more subtle indicators of death.

One example is hypothermia; the intentional or accidental reduction of core body temperature to below 95°F (35°C) which, in severe instances, is fatal. Humans are endothermic (warm-blooded) creatures, whose core body temperature is physiologically regulated at approximately 98.6°F (37°C), even in fluctuating environmental temperatures. An abnormal rise in this core temperature can cause heat stroke, with an abnormal decrease representing hypothermia.

Intentional hypothermia is used in **medicine** in both regional and total-body cooling. The body's metabolic rate (the rate at which cells provide energy for the body's vital functioning) decreases 8% with each 1.8°F (1°C) reduction in core body temperature, thus requiring reduced amounts of oxygen. Total-body hypothermia lowers the body temperature and slows the metabolic rate, protecting organs from reduced oxygen supply during the interruption of blood flow necessary in certain surgical procedures. In some procedures, like heart repair and organ transplantation, individual organs are preserved by intentional hypothermia of the organ involved. In open-heart surgery, blood supply to the chilled heart can be totally interrupted while the surgeon repairs the damaged organ. Organ and tissue destruction using extreme hypothermia −212 to −374°F (−100 to −190°C) is utilized in retinal and glaucoma surgery and to destroy pre-cancerous cells in some body tissue. This is called cryosurgery.

In contrast to these beneficial uses of intentional hypothermia, accidental hypothermia (i.e., falling into icy water, or exposure to cold weather without appropriate protective clothing) is potentially fatal and is of forensic interest.

Hypothermia is classified into four states. In mild cases, 95–89.6°F (35–32°C), symptoms include feeling cold, shivering (which helps raise body temperature), increased heart rate, and a desire to urinate, and some loss of coordination. Moderate hypothermia, 87.8–78.8°F (31–26°C) causes a decrease or inhibition of shivering, along with weakness, sleepiness, confusion, slurred speech, and lack of coordination. Deep hypothermia, 77–68°F (25–20°C) is extremely dangerous, as the body can no longer produce heat. Sufferers may behave irrationally, become comatose, lose the ability to see, and often cannot follow commands. In profound cases, 66–57°F (19–14°C), the sufferer will become rigid and may even appear dead, with dilated pupils, extremely low blood pressure, and barely perceptible heartbeat and breathing. This state usually requires complete, professional cardiopulmonary resuscitation for survival.

Normally, the body's core temperature represents a homeostatic balance between heat generation due to metabolic processes, and the loss of heat through conduction, convection, evaporation, and respiration, and radiation.

Conduction occurs when direct contact is made between the body and a cold object, and heat passes from the body to that object. Convection is when cold air or water makes contact with the body, becomes warm, and moves away to be replaced by another volume of cold air or water. The cooler the air or water, and the faster it moves, the faster the core body temperature drops.

Evaporation through perspiration and respiration provides almost 30% of the body's natural cooling mechanism. Because cold air contains little water and readily evaporates perspiration; and because physical exertion produces sweating, even in extreme cold, heat loss through evaporation takes place even at very low temperatures. When heat loss involves both evaporation and convection, for instance when someone is outdoors in wet clothes, body temperature can quickly plummet to dangerously low levels.

SEE ALSO Death, cause of; Death, mechanism of.

Hypoxia

Hypoxia is a condition in which cells of the body are deprived of oxygen. Despite the varying reasons for hypoxia, depending on the location within the body, the consequence is the same: tissues cannot survive for long without oxygen. Prolonged oxygen deprivation proves fatal to cells. When the brain is involved, the consequence for a person is coma and death.

Cells acquire energy from oxygen and glucose. Most cells can survive for a short period using an anaerobic (lacking oxygen) metabolic process. But brain cells cannot. The damage to brain cells when hypoxia occurs is immediate. Blood carries a limited amount of reserve oxygen and brain cell death can occur within minutes of falling below normal oxygen levels.

There are several types of hypoxia. One of the more common is hypoxic hypoxia; the reduction of the amount of oxygen passing into the blood because of a reduced oxygen exchange (i.e., reduced lung capacity) or high altitudes. Reduction in lung capacity may be a result of lung damage, disease, or removal of portions of the lungs. Smokers are particularly susceptible to hypoxic hypoxia. People who change altitudes can adjust to the lower oxygen pressure as the blood produces more red blood cells carrying additional **hemoglobin** (the oxygen-carrying molecule in red blood cells).

Hypemic hypoxia occurs when the number of hemoglobin molecules or red blood cells is reduced. Either condition causes a reduction in the oxygen carrying capacity of the blood. Hypemic hypoxia can result from hemorrhage or anemia. It can also be induced by drugs, chemicals, or an increase in carbon monoxide (a condition experienced by smokers).

Stagnant hypoxia occurs as a result of poor blood circulation. Blood flow is reduced by prolonged sitting in one position, cold temperatures, or being exposed to g forces (the inertial force produced by acceleration or gravity). People who fly in aircraft frequently, sit in a chair for hours, or are sedentary may experience this type of hypoxia. It is important for the elderly or those whose movement is restricted to be sure they get enough oxygen to avoid this type of hypoxia.

Histotic hypoxia is the inability of the tissues to use oxygen. When organ tissues are involved, they appear blue in color and are called cyanotic. The blue color associated with cyanosis, especially noted around the lips, is due to the build-up of high levels of deoxygenated hemoglobin in capillaries. Drinking alcoholic beverages, poisoning by cyanide or carbon monoxide, and certain narcotics can impair gaseous exchange in the tissues, and lead to hypoxia. Prolonged hypoxia can lead to tissue damage or death.

SEE ALSO Death, cause of; Death, mechanism of.

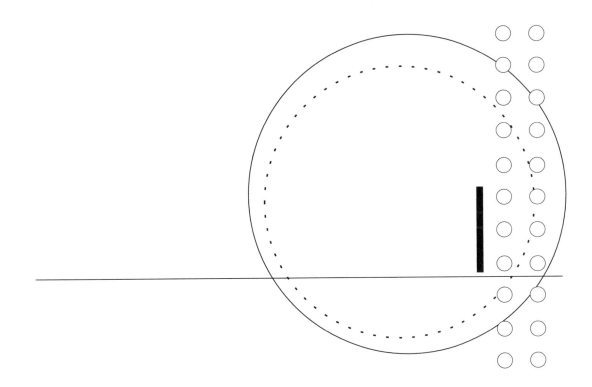

Identification

Identification means verifying that something or someone is a particular object or person. To a large extent, the field of forensics revolves around this task because, in many cases, laws revolve around the identity of objects or people. The United States legal system includes laws covering topics from voter identification to **identity theft** to eyewitness identification. Identity must be established before death certificates can be issued and before life insurance policies are redeemed. Forensic scientists may be called upon to identify the origin of objects found at the scene of a crime such as bullets, hairs, or documents. Their work often requires the identification of a person from **trace evidence** such as fingerprints, **blood**, or even teeth marks. Forensic scientists maintain a variety of skills and technologies, which aid them in identification.

Each human being has unique characteristics, both physical and social, and these characteristics are what allow for the identification of humans. The study of these characteristics is called **biometrics**. Biometric techniques attempt to quantify the unique characteristics of a person by measuring them in some way.

The most obvious biometric technique is identification by appearance. This includes a person's height, weight, skin color, hair color, and eye color. Other visible physical markings such as scars, facial hair, and wearing glasses can also be used for identification. Of course, most of these physical characteristics may be altered over time: weight can be gained and lost; hair can be colored; even eye color can change by wearing contacts. Such changes can make features of the appearance deceptive when attempting to identify a person.

Humans have a variety of different physical features that are not obviously apparent that make them unique from one another. These include **DNA**, the shape of the teeth, hand and fingerprints, and features of the eyes. DNA is an extremely long molecule found in the nucleus of all human cells, including the cells at the root of hairs, and in skin tissue, **semen**, and blood. DNA is made up of a sequence of four different nucleotides and particular regions of this sequence can vary in unique ways from person to person. These variations can be determined using different biochemical analyses, often called DNA typing or **DNA profiling**, and are used for identification. Forensic dentistry (**odontology**) is the study of the various features of teeth that allow for the identification of a person from his or her teeth. Usually identification is based on comparing teeth or bite marks to dental records from an earlier time. Often these comparisons look for the presence of dental treatments and reconstructions. In addition, DNA can be extracted from teeth. Each person's hand and fingerprints are unique, even those of identical twins who have identical DNA. The exact patterning of the ridges, sweat pores, and pores of oil glands has been used for identification in criminal cases since the end of the nineteenth century. Retinal scans rely on the pattern of blood vessels in the back of the human eye, which have a unique pattern in each person. Although somewhat costly, this form of identification is one of the most accurate available.

A third group of biometric features revolve around behaviors that are unique to an individual. These can be social behaviors such as how a person walks or moves, a person's speech patterns and voice inflection, and handicaps that may be apparent. Such features can be documented on video or audiotape and analyzed for identification. Other behaviors used in biometrics include signature analysis, keystroke dynamics, and digitally analyzed voice characteristics.

Finally, physical identifiers can be imposed on people. Examples include branding and tattooing, although these types of identification can be associated with socially repressive systems, such as slavery and racial subjugation. Other forms of imposed physical identification include wearing of jewelry with identifying information such as dog tags, ID bracelets, anklets, and badges. Some of these may even be equipped with radio transponders that not only identify a person, but also his or her location. Microchips have been developed that can be implanted under the skin of valuable breeds of animals so that they cannot be lost and under the skin of endangered species so that information about their migration patterns can be learned. As this technology develops, the application may be applied to the identification of humans in certain circumstances.

The forensic identification of objects spans a broad array of techniques and technology depending on the object in question and the reason for the identification. When fires occur, forensic scientists may be called upon to identify charred remains. In the case of **automobile accidents**, **tire tracks**, car parts, and even shards of **glass** may require identification. Incidents involving guns depend on **ballistics** experts to identify the bullet as well as the firearm responsible for discharging it. Recovered materials from thefts and forgeries often require the identification of valuables such as artwork, manuscripts, and jewels. Crimes involving breaking and entering require the identification of the tools used to force entry. The examples of investigation related to criminal activity and requiring identification are extensive.

SEE ALSO Biometric eye scans; Biometrics; DNA fingerprint; DNA sequences, unique; Fingerprint; Fracture matching; Hair analysis; Handwriting analysis; Odontology.

Identification of Beslan victims in Russia

The Republic of Chechnya in southwest Russia has been seeking its independence from the rest of the Russian Republic. During Russian Premier Joseph Stalin's reign from 1929–1953, he had many Chechens deported to distant regions, such as Siberia. Since that time, the Chechens have sought their independence from Russia. However, it was the proclamation of war on Chechnya launched by the Russian military in 1994, after failed attempts to oust the Chechen president, that launched the long and bitter fighting that has since ensued between the Republic of Chechnya and Russia. Armed conflicts and allegations of crimes against humanity by the Russians against the Chechens have resulted in terrorist attacks from the Chechen rebels. The escalating violence generated a devastating seizure and attack on a Russian school by Chechen terrorists, resulting in over 300 deaths. More than 100 of the victims required forensic **DNA identification**. Forensic analysis of the Chechen hostage takers also produced **evidence** that they were under the influence of narcotics at the time of the attack.

September 1, 2004, was the first day of school after summer break for the children of Beslan school number 1 in the North Ossetia region of Russia, which borders the Republic of Chechnya. However, shortly after arrival at the school, over 1,200 students, teachers, and parents were taken hostage by Chechen terrorists. The hostage takers demanded that Russian troops leave nearby Chechnya and continued to hold the hostages in the school gymnasium for three days. The world watched on television as parents and relatives of the hostages gathered outside the school. Conflicting reports on the number of hostages added to the confusion.

The culmination of the takeover was a series of explosions and gun battles between the Chechen militants and the Russian police. A massive fire broke out in the gymnasium, where the majority of the hostages were confined. Many were shot trying to escape as waiting relatives outside looked on in horror. When the violence was over, a total of 336 people had been killed, including 156 children and 31 of the Chechen rebels. Many of the bodies in the gymnasium were severely burned, charred, and unrecognizable.

Over 350 wounded were taken to nearby hospitals and the victims who had perished were transferred to the Vladikavkaz morgue. In the confusion, hundreds of people were missing. Desperate friends and family members clutched photographs and searched the hospitals hoping to find their relatives among the injured. They also went to the morgue hoping not to find their loved ones among the dead victims.

Initially, bodies of victims were identified physically, by their clothing, birthmarks or characteristics recognized by friends and family members. Because so many of the bodies were severely burned, the investigators turned to DNA analysis for identification of many of the victims. It was a difficult task, as the badly burned state of the corpses required multiple extractions and **PCR** amplification assays to obtain DNA that was able to produce a profile. Relatives of missing persons provided **blood** samples, which were also used to generate DNA profiles. Samples of both relatives and victims were taken to Moscow for analysis. Comparison of the profiles of the victims to that of the relatives provided definitive identification of all of the unidentified victims with the exception of one child. The DNA profile from the last child victim identified did not match the DNA profile of the parents, requiring many buried bodies to be exhumed and re-examined. Finally, all victims were correctly identified, enabling the families to bury and mourn their loved ones.

Forensic techniques were used in another means to investigate the tragedy at the Beslan school. Among the dead were 31 of the Chechen terrorists who had held the hostages in the gymnasium. Blood was taken from the Chechens and sent to Moscow for forensic analysis. Russian law enforcement officials reported that most of the militants were under the influence of drugs at the time that the school was seized. High levels of both heroin and morphine were found in many of the attackers' blood. Those without evidence of narcotics in their system showed signs of abuse of other drugs.

The forensic tests of the militants also indicated that some of them had been in withdrawal, and had not received drugs for several days. Such a state is often consistent with aggressive and abnormal behavior. The lack of drugs could account for some of the attackers' brutality. The suspicion that the hostage takers were probably long-time drug abusers is consistent with the suggestion that many leaders of groups that plan terror attacks coerce their followers into taking narcotics. Individuals in a drug-induced state may be more amenable to carrying out the grim tasks associated with many terrorist attacks.

Forensic analysis was paramount during the investigation of the tragedy at Beslan school number 1. Without these modern forensic techniques, the investigation would have required much more time, requiring those affected by the tragedy to wait for answers rather than begin the healing process.

Investigators gather IDs and personal belongings found in the debris of a school in Beslan, Russia, after a hostage seizure by Chechen separatists in 2004 ended in a bloodbath with at least 335 people killed, half of them children. © DENIS MARININ/ REUTERS/CORBIS

SEE ALSO CODIS: Combined DNA Index System; DNA; DNA profiling; European Network of Forensic Science Institutes; PCR (polymerase chain reaction); STR (short tandem repeat) analysis; Toxicological analysis; Toxicology.

Identification of Christopher Columbus' remains

DNA analysis could be used to solve an **identification** puzzle going back more than 500 years. The remains of Christopher Columbus are said to lie in Seville Cathedral, in Spain. However, bones buried in Santo Domingo Cathedral in the Dominican Republic

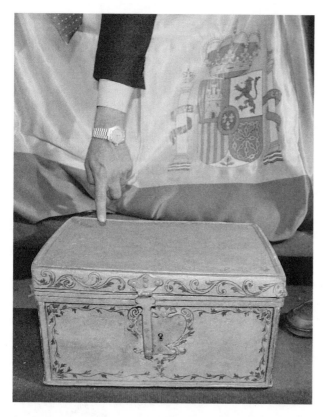

A scientist points to the box allegedly containing the remains of explorer Christopher Columbus, in Seville, Spain, 2003.
© REUTERS/CORBIS

are also said to belong to the famous explorer. In 2005, Spanish researchers are hoping to extract enough DNA from both sets of bones to allow an identification to be made.

Columbus died in 1506 in Valladolid, Spain, and was buried in a monastery there. His remains were later moved to Seville. However, he had always expressed a wish to be buried in the Americas. In 1537, the widow of his son Diego was allowed to take the bones of both her husband and his father to the Dominican Republic for burial in the cathedral of Santo Domingo. There they remained until 1795, when Spain lost control of the country. The bones believed to belong to Columbus were dug up and moved so they would not fall into the hands of foreigners. The remains finally arrived in Seville, via Cuba, in 1898.

These are the bones buried in Seville Cathedral next to those of Hernando Colon, Columbus' son. However, in 1877, workers digging in Santo Domingo Cathedral uncovered a box containing 13 large bone fragments and 28 smaller ones and inscribed with Columbus' name. It looked as if the Spanish had dug up the wrong bones in 1795.

Extraction of DNA from the bones in Santo Domingo and Seville and comparison with Hernando Colon's DNA could identify which set of remains is the genuine one. Preliminary DNA testing in 2004 used mitrochondrial DNA, which is passed down from the mother, rather than nuclear DNA, which was unavailable in the samples, and showed that the remains attributed to Columbus in Spain contain DNA that is similar to that of his brother Diego, who was also buried near Seville. Spanish researchers also traveled to Santo Domingo to carry out a preliminary assessment. They will study the condition of the remains and hope to take a sample of DNA for analysis. DNA can remain intact for hundreds of years, so there is a good chance that the analysis and identification can be confirmed.

SEE ALSO DNA fingerprint; Exhumation.

Identification of the son of Louis XVI and Marie-Antoinette

For more than two centuries, one of the most mysterious questions in history concerned the fate of the son of Marie-Antoinette and Louis XVI of France. Known as the "Lost Dauphin," official records claimed that ten-year-old Louis Charles, the heir to the throne of France, died in prison in 1795. Rumors, however, suggested that the child had escaped and the body found in prison was that of a double. In 2000 forensic techniques were applied to **DNA** from the remains of the heart of the purported Louis Charles as well as to locks of hair from Marie-Antoinette, her two sisters, and samples of DNA from two of the sisters' living relatives. These analyses confirmed that the heart was from a child with maternal relations to Marie-Antoinette.

During the French Revolution at the end of the eighteenth century, Louis XVI and his wife, Marie-Antoinette, were unseated from the throne. Louis XVI was killed at the guillotine and his wife and son were imprisoned in the Temple prison in Paris. Eventually, Marie-Antoinette, too, was beheaded and the son, named Louis Charles, was left in prison for two more years. He was treated poorly, left alone in a windowless room most of the time, and at the time of his death on June 8, 1795, his body was covered in scabies and tumors.

Official records show that Louis Charles died of tuberculosis, but many historians did not accept the official reports. Popular rumor supported the idea that the boy was taken from the jail cell and that another boy was left in his place. Others believed that members of the French Revolution had murdered him. Eventually, the idea that Louis Charles had escaped and was still alive found favor with the public. In 1814, the monarchy was restored to France and at this point many people came forward, claiming to be the lost dauphin.

Although he never claimed it himself, John James Audubon, the naturalist, was rumored to have been the escaped Louis Charles. He was born the same year as Louis Charles and lived in Paris as a child. He was adopted around the same time that Louis Charles was said to have escaped from prison. However, it was later shown that Audubon was born in Haiti, the illegitimate son of a French father. One Louis Charles impersonator was a man from Wisconsin named Eleazar Williams. Native American Mohawks kidnapped Williams at the age of seven. He went on to become an Episcopal minister in Green Bay and claimed to be the lost dauphin. He never presented **evidence** to prove his claim, and was eventually shown to have Mohawk genetic traits, proving that he could not have been descended from the French monarchy. A German clockmaker named Karl Wilhelm Naundorff also claimed to be Louis Charles. He convinced Louis Charles' childhood caretaker that his memories coincided with memories she had of the Louis Charles' youth. Naundorff moved to the Netherlands and there he convinced the government that he deserved the royal name of Burbon, which his descendents still use. In 1950, one of Naundorff's bones was exhumed and compared to DNA from Marie Antoinette. The DNA did not match, discrediting Naundorff's claim.

At the time of Louis Charles' death, a physician named Philippe-Jean Pelletan performed an **autopsy** on the boy who had died in the prison. As was custom for royalty, the doctor removed the heart so that it would not be buried with the body. The doctor then hid it in a handkerchief, brought it home and put it in a jar of alcohol where he kept it as a curiosity. Later, one of Pelletan's students was intrigued by the heart and stole it for himself. On his deathbed, the student admitted his theft to his wife, who returned the heart to Pelletan. Pelletan's wife then sent the heart to the Archbishop of Paris. In 1830, the palace where the heart was stored in a crystal urn was sacked and the urn was smashed. Pelletan's son, however, went to the palace and retrieved it from where it lay in a pile of glass. The heart was then sent to the arm of the Bourbon family that was in Spain. Later, the heart returned to

The heart of Louis XVII is displayed in a Paris church. DNA studies proved that Louis XVII, son of French King Louis XVI and Queen Marie-Antoinette (who were put to death during the French Revolution), did not escape as rumored, but died while imprisoned. © VICTOR TONELLI/REUTERS/CORBIS

Paris once again and was placed in a crystal vase in the royal crypt at the Saint Denis Basilica.

In April 2000, the Duc de Bauffremont requested that samples from the heart be removed for genetic testing. Two samples were taken: one from the aorta and one from the heart muscle. The samples were then split, and half was sent to the Center for Human Genetics of Leuven in Belgium. The other part was sent to the laboratory of Professor Ernst Brinkman in Münster, Germany.

The study focused on DNA from the mitochondria, the organelle responsible for providing energy to the cell. Each cell contains many mitochondria, and thus many copies of mitochondrial DNA. In contrast, each cell only contains one nucleus, and therefore only one copy of nuclear DNA. In addition, mitochondrial DNA is shorter and more likely to have survived intact over the centuries. Mitochondrial DNA originates from the egg, so the study could only determine the maternal relationships. The part of the mitochondrial DNA used in the study is called the D-loop, or displacement loop. It contains two regions that have considerable variability between people called HVR 1 and HVR 2. These two regions have been studied in a variety of cases involving very old tissue, including Neanderthal skeletons.

Mitochondrial DNA data from Marie-Antionette's family had already been collected from the Naundorff study in the Netherlands. These sequences were from hair from Marie-Antoinette and her two sisters, Johanna Gabriela and Mada-Josepha, and two living relatives, the Queen of Romania and her brother, Andre. The Center for Human Genetics found that the mitochondrial DNA from the heart of the putative Louis Charles varied from a standard in five nucleotide locations and these variations are identical to the variations found in the mitochondrial DNA sequences of Marie-Antoinette and all of her relatives. The laboratory in Germany found the same variations at four of the locations, but could not retrieve data from the fifth location because the DNA was degraded. The conclusion of both laboratories was that the boy who died in prison in 1795 was related to Marie-Antoinette and most likely was Louis Charles.

In June 2004 the heart of Charles Louis was removed from the crystal vase and buried alongside the bodies of Louis XVI and Marie-Antoinette and a funeral was held for the boy who would have been King Louis XVII of France.

SEE ALSO DNA fingerprint; DNA recognition instruments; DNA typing systems; Genetic code; Mitochondrial DNA analysis.

Identification of tsunami victims, Southeast Asia

On December 26, 2004, a tremendous earthquake measuring 9.0 on the Richter scale occurred under the sea near Southeast Asia. When the Australian and Eurasian tectonic plates under the Indian Ocean moved, a huge tidal wave was created that traveled thousands of kilometers across the ocean, causing a tsunami that devastated islands and coastal areas across the region. While the region is rebuilding after the physical destruction, teams of forensic scientists have taken on the immense task of identifying the victims of this tragedy.

The Southeast Asian tsunami is one of the largest natural disasters of modern times. The series of waves that emanated from the sub-oceanic earthquake off the shore of Sumatra claimed over 200,000 lives, as of February 2005, and the death toll continues to rise. In addition, thousands of people are still missing. Indonesia was the hardest hit and suffered the largest death toll. Also affected were regions of Sri Lanka, Southeast India and its Andaman and Nicobar Islands, Malaysia, Thailand, Bangladesh, Burma, and the Maldives. The devastation of the tsunami was far reaching; The Seychelle Islands as well as Tanzania, Kenya, and Somalia on the African mainland also suffered losses of life in the tragedy. In addition, because there are many tourist resorts in this region, the dead and missing include people from countries all over the world.

When the destruction was over, pictures of the missing were displayed at **identification** centers and family members gathered near the morgues, identification centers, and hospitals. Relatives of vacationers traveled to the region and assisted aid workers and the International Red Cross in their search for additional victims and wounded.

Identification of the tsunami victims is the largest forensic undertaking since the World Trade Center disaster of September 11, 2001. Over three years later, **DNA** profiles from the World Trade Center are still being analyzed, suggesting that the tsunami identification project will also continue for years.

After the tsunami, dead bodies lay strewn over beaches and required collection. Due to the force of the waves, dismembered body parts were also retrieved. Forensic specialists from all over the world rushed to Southeast Asia to assist with the task of identifying the victims, who were brought to makeshift morgues. Initially, physical identification was performed before the more complex task of using DNA. Corpses were photographed and compared to pictures displayed by friends and relatives. Physical characteristics such as hair or eye color, tattoos, and clothing were used initially to identify individuals. Dental x rays and fingerprints also proved useful. All of this information was recorded for each victim in makeshift, then organized, databases.

Once physical means of identification were exhausted, DNA samples were taken from the corpses for analysis. Identification of such a vast number of victims by forensic DNA analysis is a daunting task. Even though forensic companies and government agencies across the world are assisting with the process, the number of samples is overwhelming. Difficult samples of bone and skin often require multiple DNA extractions and analyses. Many of the dead were submerged in water then exposed to sun and heat while awaiting collection. High temperatures often degrade DNA, making it more difficult to analyze and requiring multiple attempts at extraction and amplification.

Each of the organizations assisting with identification and forensic analysis utilize their own

An American plastic surgeon prepares to repair facial injuries on tsunami victims in Thailand in order to help relatives recognize and identify the dead. AP/WIDE WORLD PHOTOS. REPRODUCED BY PERMISSION.

protocols and methods. This also causes complications when trying to compare victim data from several different organizations. In a meeting shortly after the tsunami, **Interpol** (a global police information organization) requested that a standardized means of forensic analysis be used by the involved scientific teams. Furthermore, DNA profiles and other information are entered into a computer database to make identification faster and easier amongst the various worldwide sites where DNA analysis is taking place. Thus, standardized methods such as those of Interpol and the European Network for Forensic Science Institutes (ENFSI) are extremely useful during a crisis such as the tsunami.

Forensic scientists are also extracting DNA from personal effects, such as razors, toothbrushes, and hairbrushes, of the missing. DNA profiles generated from these samples will be used for a reference database. This database is then compared to

the DNA profiles of those from victims in hopes of finding matches. In addition, relatives of the missing have given **blood** samples for DNA profiles. These can then be compared to the database of victim profiles to identify the victims based on the similarity of their DNA sequence to that of their parents, children, or siblings. In some cases, whole families were killed, requiring DNA profiles from more distant relatives to be used. While most identifications need about 10 DNA markers in the profile, up to 50 markers must be compared in these situations.

Automation of many of the steps of the DNA analysis is speeding up the identification process. Unidentified victims are buried in temporary graves and have been labeled with electronic chips that carry the information associated with the body that was obtained by forensic scientists. The use of forensic techniques has been instrumental in identifying

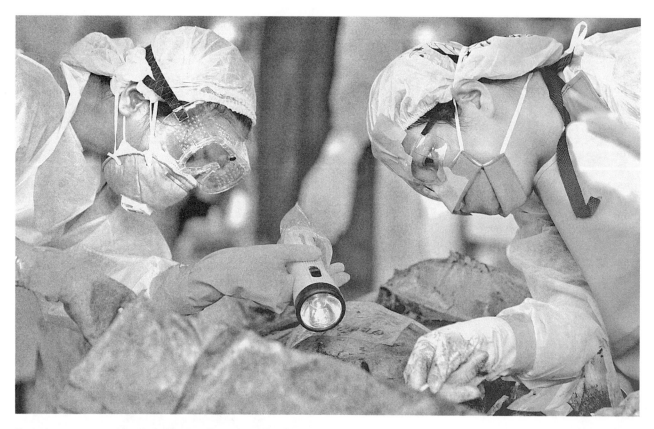

Forensic teams try to identify the bodies of victims of the December 26, 2004, tsunami at a makeshift morgue at Yan Yao temple in Takuapa in southern Thailand. AP/WIDE WORLD PHOTOS. REPRODUCED BY PERMISSION.

the victims of the Southeast Asian tsunami, however, it will be years until the project is complete.

SEE ALSO CODIS: Combined DNA Index System; DNA; DNA databanks; DNA fingerprint; DNA profiling; European Network of Forensic Science Institutes; Interpol; Odontology; September 11, 2001, terrorist attacks (forensic investigations of); Standardization of regulations; STR (short tandem repeat) analysis.

Identification of war victims in Croatia and Bosnia

Forensic analyses are used for many types of investigations, including those of wartime crimes against humanity, such as occurred in Bosnia and Croatia during the 1990s. A combination of forensic techniques, including forensic **DNA** analysis, forensic dental analysis, **ballistics** analysis, and others, were used to identify the victims of violence in these newly independent countries.

At the end of World War II, the communist country of Yugoslavia was formed and was comprised of multiple ethnic groups that were continually at odds. However, after the fall of the Soviet Union and communism in Eastern Europe, violence erupted in regions of now former Yugoslavia. Various regions declared independence in 1992, and others attempted to expand by invading neighboring territories. The diverse ethnic backgrounds of the former Yugoslav states added to the conflict and wars broke out amongst the different ethnic and religious groups. During several bloody years, more than 100,000 people were killed, a vast majority being civilians. Access to the region by the international press was limited, but reports from those who were present as well as Croatians and Bosnians alike, suggested that ethnic cleansing was rampant and mass executions were commonplace. Similar atrocities were committed in the Kosovo region of the former Yugoslavia, where ethnic Albanians and Serbians were both allegedly the victims of ethnic cleansing.

Many of the dead were buried in mass graves and survivors were forced to flee to neighboring regions for safety. When aid workers and forensic teams were allowed access to the war-torn regions of Bosnia-Herzegovina, Croatia, Serbia, and Kosovo, many of the mass graves were exhumed to identify the dead and determine the **cause of death**. As of March 2005, the **identification** of victims is ongoing. Most of the bodies were decomposed to mere skeletal remains when the teams arrived. However, this still allows for a significant amount of information to be gained about the individuals. Initial means of forensic identification include detailed examination of the clothing and belongings on and around the skeletons. Height is estimated and sex determined if possible. Unique skeletal features are then noted and x rays obtained. Then, dental records are used to compare the dead to the dental records of missing people.

Although some individuals may be identified using unique skeletal features, most cannot and require DNA analyses to be performed using DNA isolated from the teeth or bones of the skeletons. Multiple laboratories are currently performing DNA analysis corpses removed from mass graves. In general, commercially available molecular kits are used along with **PCR** techniques to amplify unique **gene** sequences, or STR (short tandem repeat) loci. In some cases mitochondrial DNA (genetic material in the mitochondria, organelles that generate energy from the cell and are inherited from the mother), is being used. The sequences obtained by these analyses are then entered into a computer and compared to a database. This database contains sequences of DNA determined from **blood** samples of relatives of missing persons. Comparison of the sequences and DNA profiles enables scientists to determine whether or not the skeleton in the mass grave was a relative of someone registered in the database. In addition to mass graves, thousands of bodies remain in refrigerators and morgues waiting to be examined and profiled.

In 1996, the International Commission on Missing Persons (ICMP) was created and given the responsibility of helping remaining family members find their missing relatives. The ICMP assists all victims in the former Yugoslavia, regardless of religion or ethnic background. Organized into four major areas: the forensics program, family association development, the political program, and the DNA program, the ICMP has the goal of **training** scientists and technicians around the region to set up a network of laboratories for victim identification and to help rebuild the war-torn communities.

Investigators have encountered many complications examining mass graves in countries that were once Yugoslavia. Because of the implication of war crimes against humanity, some of the mass graves have been disturbed by perpetrators. Bodies were often moved, mutilated, or other actions taken to attempt to disguise the cause of death. At The Hague, the International Criminal Tribunal for the former Yugoslavia (ICTY) is responsible for bringing criminal charges against those allegedly involved in the war crimes and ethnic cleansing. Forensic investigators are discovering **evidence** that some murdered individuals were killed execution-style or tortured. Physical forensic examination of the bodies is key to the ongoing trials, as evidence such as bullet holes in the **skull** and blindfolds may indicate execution-style shooting.

It is expected that the **war crimes trials** of individuals responsible for atrocities in Croatia, Bosnia-Herzegovina, Serbia, and Kosovo will continue for years. This is also the case with the identification of victims in mass graves found across the region.

SEE ALSO DNA; DNA databanks; DNA fingerprint; DNA mixtures, forensic interpretation of mass graves; DNA profiling; Odontology; STR (short tandem repeat) analysis; War crimes trials; War forensics.

Identity theft

A forensic investigation can involve tracing the whereabouts of a person or their finances (a facet of **forensic accounting**). Someone who is eluding capture can adopt a new identity or assume the identity of someone else. The mechanisms of identity theft must be familiar to a forensic scientist.

Identity theft is the most popular—and most profitable—form of consumer fraud, and is among the fastest growing crimes in America. It encompasses all types of crime in which someone illegally obtains and fraudulently uses another person's confidential information, most often for financial gain. A person's Social Security number is valuable to an identity thief. Armed with the Social Security number, a criminal can open a bank account or credit card account, apply for a loan, and remove funds from varying financial accounts. In some cases, criminals have assumed the victim's identity altogether, incurring debt in the victim's name and committing crimes that become a part of the victim's criminal record.

The rate of identity theft or identity fraud so escalated in the late 1990s that the Social Security Administration declared it a national crisis.

Advanced computer and telecommunication technologies have armed thieves with new ways to obtain large amounts of personal data from afar. Hackers can spy on e-mail and Internet users, silently stealing passwords or banking information.

Old-fashioned methods also remain effective. "Dumpster diving" thieves sort through garbage for telltale signs of identity such as cleared checks, bank statements, even junk mail, such as "preapproved" credit cards. A "shoulder surfing" criminal spies on someone as they type in a pin number or password at an automatic teller machine (ATM). "Skimming" occurs when a cashier receives a credit card for a purchase, then surreptitiously swipes the card through a portable device that records the card information.

The threat to privacy has prompted a number of new laws governing fraud. In 1998, Congress passed the Identity Theft and Assumption Deterrence Act. The legislation created a new offense of identity theft, making it a separate crime against the person whose identity was stolen. Prior to this legislation, identity theft was considered a crime only against the company the victim defrauded. Under the federal identity theft act, any person "knowingly transferring or using, without lawful authority, a means of **identification** of another person with the intent to commit, or to aid or abet, any unlawful activity that constitutes a violation of Federal law, or that constitutes a **felony** under any applicable State or local law" will be charged with a crime. Violators face a maximum term of 15 years in prison, a fine, and criminal forfeiture of any personal property used or intended to be used to commit the offense.

Identity thieves are often charged with other violations, including credit card fraud, computer fraud, and mail fraud. These felonies can carry substantial penalties and up to 30 years imprisonment. The Federal Bureau of Investigation (**FBI**), the United States Secret Service, and the United States Postal Inspection Service help prosecute identity theft cases. Many states have also enacted legislation regarding identity theft. Arizona led the way with a specific identity theft statute passed in 1996. As the crime's serious threat became evident, more states followed suit. In 1999, 22 states passed identity theft legislation. According to a U.S. General Accounting Office (GAO) report published in 2002, identity theft can be a felony offense in 45 of the 49 states that have laws to address the problem. Two years after the passage of the federal identity theft act, the justice department testified that it had used the statute in 92 cases, according to a GAO report.

Associated Press reporter Nedra Pickler displays the unauthorized credit card bills charged to her name in 2002, after she became the victim of identity theft, a growing crime. In a matter of a week, thieves charged $30,000 worth of merchandise on credit cards obtained using her identity. AP WIDE WORLD PHOTOS. REPRODUCED BY PERMISSION.

The Identity Theft and Assumption Deterrence Act requires the Federal Trade Commission (FTC) to "log and acknowledge the receipt of complaints by individuals who certify that they have a reasonable belief" that someone stole their identity. The act enabled the creation of the Identity Theft Data Clearinghouse, a federal database for tracking complaints. Consumers call a toll-free hotline (1-877-ID-THEFT) to enter their complaint, and have the option to do so anonymously. When established in 1999, the FTC logged about 260 calls per week. By 2002, the hotline was receiving more than 3,000 contacts a week.

Identity fraud complaints and related information are shared electronically between the FTC and other law enforcement agencies nationwide via the Consumer Sentinel Network, a secure, encrypted

Web site. The network was initially set up in 1997 as a way of tracking telemarketing scams. As of March 2005, more than 1,000 law enforcement agencies in the United States, Canada, and Australia had enrolled in the FTC's Consumer Sentinel Network collaboration. Accessing the Network allows police to analyze identity theft cases and determine if there is a larger pattern of crime. At this time, comprehensive results involving the number of cases prosecuted under the federal identity theft act and state statutes are not available.

SEE ALSO Codes and ciphers; Computer forensics; Computer hackers; Document forgery; Technology and forensic science.

Illicit drugs

Some chemical substances are dangerous to health due to their addictive nature, impact on the central nervous system metabolism, life-threatening side effects, and associate behavioral and mood changes. Drugs classified by the U.S. Drug Enforcement Administration (**DEA**) under Schedule I are considered illicit drugs when sold to or consumed by the public, except for some chemical derivatives with restricted and controlled medical applications. These are also known as psychoactive drugs of abuse, due to their effects in mood, sensory perception, and behavior. Substances of the following classes are considered illicit drugs: opiates, hallucinogens, depressants, and stimulants under Schedule I (tightly regulated use and supply), as well as the controlled substances under Schedules II, III, IV, and V, when used or sold without medical prescription. Among the most common illicit drugs in use are:

- cannabinoids (such as marijuana and hashish oil)
- hallucinogens (LSD, mescaline, peyote, MDMA)
- dissociative anesthetics (PCP, ketamine, dextromethorphan)
- stimulants (**amphetamines**, methamphetamine, cocaine)
- depressants (GHB, rohypnol, **barbiturates**, benzodiazepines)
- narcotics (opium, heroin, methadone, codeine)
- inhalants (nitrous compounds, glues, solvents, ether).

Drugs of abuse affect the brain structures that regulate feelings of reward, personal empowerment, and pleasure, which constitute an important component of their addictive properties, along with developed tolerance.

The initial effects of cannabinoids, such as relaxation, euphoria, and diminished concentration, are similar to alcohol. The active chemical of cannabinoids (the alkaloid THC or tetrahydrocannabiol) apparently interferes with nerve cells access to glucose (an essential source of energy for brain metabolism and function), inducing an aftermath sensation of acute hunger. Addiction is followed by increased tolerance, which leads to more frequent consumption and/or to increased doses. The speed of signal transfer between nerve cells (synapses) is reduced with long-term use, as a consequence of the loss of neurons (nerve cells) and components of nerve cells. Poor memory, learning difficulties, and a general apathy are the results of prolonged, frequent use of cannabinoids. Respiratory complications are also common, because cannabinoids are usually inhaled through smoking. High levels of THC in the brain may induce toxic psychosis and hallucinations, especially when the leaves are consumed in foods or infusions. In food or drinks, marijuana effects take about one hour to begin and last for approximately four hours. Flashbacks sometimes occur in some individuals in the three days following a high-dose intake.

Hallucinogens such as LSD, MDMA, mescaline, psilocybin, psilocin, and muscimol are drugs that interfere with neuronal pathways that process sensory information, and also affect the metabolism and levels of chemical messengers known as **neurotransmitters**, such as serotonin and dopamine. Hallucinogenic plants such as psilocybin, and peyote cactus, along with psilocin mushrooms have been taken by tribal medicine men in search of "visions" for centuries. Hallucinations are altered states of sensory perception that lead to all kinds of pleasant or unpleasant sensory experiences. They affect several functional brain structures that control emotions, behavior, body temperature, cardiac rate, blood pressure, sensory-motor coordination, and breathing. LSD (lysergic acid diethylamide) is a strong hallucinogen with unpredictable effects that may last for approximately 12 hours and create frequent occurrences of flashbacks in the following two days. However, it is not an addictive drug and most users stop using it over time. LSD induces tolerance in frequent users, however, leading to ingesting increased amounts of the drug. The results could include long-lasting mood disorders, psychotic episodes, severe depression, and suicide. These adverse effects may persist for years after the individual has stopped LSD consumption, suggestive of some forms of brain damage.

Mescaline is extracted from the peyote cactus, and also induces hallucinations along with physiologic changes similar to those caused by LSD. Effects last between 8 and 12 hours and its metabolites are detectable in urine for two or three days after use. Hallucinogenic mushrooms such as *Psilocybe cubensis* and *Amanita muscaria*, are highly toxic for liver and kidney cells. They induce drowsiness alternating with psychomotor agitation, distorted auditory and visual sensory perceptions, and lack of concentration, as well as nausea, paranoia, and chronic mental disorders.

MDMA, or ecstasy, is both a hallucinogen and a stimulant drug that dramatically increases the levels of serotonin in the brain, causing a sensation of immense joy, amplification of tactile sensations, altered body temperature, and increased sexual drive. MDMA interference with the metabolism of the neurotransmitter serotonin results in nerve cell toxicity that may cause brain damage. Cases of coma and death are also reported in association with MDMA. Frequent use of ecstasy has also indirectly influenced the spread of sexually transmitted diseases including HIV because of its ability to decrease sexual inhibitions and its frequent use in nightclubs.

Dissociative anesthetic drugs were first developed as pharmaceutical products for sedation or for general anesthesia. Dextromethorphan is a sedative of certain autonomous brain functions. Ketamine and PCP (or phencyclidine) are drugs for general anesthesia that present side effects of auditory and visual distortion, and sensations of "floating" above the environment or above oneself (out-of-body sensation). These two substances block glutamate pain receptors in the brain. The neurotransmitter glutamate is responsible for signaling pain sensation, and is also involved in memory formation, the learning process, and mood modulation. PCP inhibits dopamine, serotonin, and norepinephrine reuptake from cell receptors. These neurotransmitters control the modulation of feelings of reward, joy, euphoria, and physical energy. Phencyclidine is also a dissociative drug of potential abuse that induces dissociative anesthesia, a state in which the patient is conscious without feeling pain. In surgical centers, physicians carefully monitor the vital signals of a patient under PCP, ketamine, or other CNS depressant anesthetics, due to their dangerous and sometimes unpredictable side effects on blood pressure, elevation of body temperature, and heartbeat. When these drugs are illegally taken, users frequently end up in emergency rooms with convulsions, coma, hyperthermia (high core body temperature), or cardiac arrest. Addicts also undergo mood disorders, such as violent behavior, hallucination, panic episodes, paranoia, disorientation, memory loss, depression, and suicidal tendencies.

Depressant drugs, such as flunitrazepam (e.g., rohypnol) and gamma-hydroxibutyrate (or GHB) are frequently mixed with alcoholic beverages, a combination that is sometimes lethal. Rohypnol, often called the "date rape" drug, belongs to the family of benzodiazepines, drugs introduced in medical practice to control anxiety and nervousness. Because rohypnol markedly depresses the central nervous system (CNS), slows motor reflexes, causes disorientation and temporary amnesia, it is used by some who mix the drug in their victim's drink. As the drug is tasteless, odorless, and colorless, sexual assailants use it in nightclubs and parties, without the knowledge of their targets. GHB is now an illegal anabolic drug that was largely used by body builders between 1980 and 1992, when its use became forbidden in the United States. It has a sedative and euphoric effect, may induce coma, convulsions, breathing difficulties and vomiting, especially when mixed with alcohol or cannabinoids.

Stimulants affect the brain reward centers, inducing sensations of euphoria, boldness, and aggressiveness because they accelerate basal metabolism, cardiac rate, and increase blood pressure and sensory motor response. They also cause dizziness, insomnia, behavioral and emotional disorders, sexual inhibition, and lack of concentration. Cocaine is a strong stimulant and highly addictive drug that is trafficked in two chemical forms, hydrochloride salt (powdered cocaine), and freebase form (or crack). Powdered cocaine is inhaled into the nasal passages or diluted in water and intravenously injected, whereas crack is smoked. Cocaine and crack affect the dopamine pathways by attaching to the molecule that transports dopamine to cellular receptors, preventing dopamine reuptake from receptors. Therefore, it prolongs the effects of dopamine in the brain. Both forms of cocaine induce tolerance, leading to increased doses and more frequent consumption. Irritability, mood swings, restlessness, auditory hallucination, and violent behavior develop and tend to worsen through long-term cocaine abuse. Cardiac arrest or coma is a common cause of death when these and other stimulants are mixed with other drugs or alcohol, or taken in high doses.

constipation, and depression. Repeated use induces tolerance to the respiratory centers as well as decreased analgesia and euphoria, leading to dependency of higher doses and more frequent use, which increases the risk of accidental overdose.

Inhalants are chemical vapors derived from substances and solvents used in glues, wax, and domestic household products, as well as nitrous compounds and ether. They usually either depress the CNS or block oxygen access to the brain. Inhalants are often the first drugs that children experiment with. A study by the National Institute on Drug Abuse (NIDA) of 2003, named "Monitoring the Future," has shown that 12.7% of 10th graders and 11.2% of 12th graders had used inhalants at least once.

SEE ALSO Amphetamines; DEA (Drug Enforcement Administration); Hypothermia; Hypoxia; Narcotic; Nervous system overview; Psychotropic drugs; Toxicological analysis.

Imaging

High-tech diagnostic imaging techniques that have allowed physicians to explore bodily structures and functions with a minimum of invasion to the patient have been exploited for other uses. Forensic investigations have been one of the beneficiaries.

A forensic investigator may be faced with a body that displays no outward signs of trauma. Learning the **cause of death** may involve delving inside the body. Imaging techniques allow a detailed examination without the immediate need of a destructive **autopsy**.

The use of imaging techniques in forensics has followed the development of the techniques for other purposes. During the 1970s, advances in computer technologies, in particular the development of algorithms powerful enough to allow difficult equations to be solved quickly enough to be of real-time use in the clinical diagnostic setting and to eliminate "noise" from sensitive measurements, allowed the development of accurate, accessible, and relatively inexpensive (when compared to surgical explorations) non-invasive technologies. Although relying on different physical principles (i.e., electromagnetism vs. sound waves), all of the high-tech methods relied on computers to construct visual images from a set of indirect measurements. The development of high-tech diagnostic tools was the direct result of the clinical application of developments in physics and mathematics. These technological advances allowed the creation of a number of tools

Johann Muehlegg of Spain celebrates winning the gold medal in the men's 50-kilometer cross-country ski event at the Winter Olympics in 2002. Muehlegg was later stripped of his medal after testing positive in a drug test. AP/WIDE WORLD PHOTOS. REPRODUCED BY PERMISSION.

Narcotics are chemical derivatives from opium, such as codeine, morphine, and heroin, with very effective analgesic activity in relieving intense pain. However, because of their highly addictive properties and some dangerous adverse effects, a total of 23 opium derivatives are classified under Schedule I. Morphine is the most powerful analgesic found in natural opium, but both natural and synthetic opioid compounds are effective intense-pain inhibitors. Morphine causes analgesia without inducing loss of consciousness, along with a sense of wellbeing. Normal doses of morphine and other opioids depress the brain centers that regulate breathing by diminishing their sensitivity. With doses progressively higher, respiratory depression occurs, thus leading to death from acute overdose, a common result of opioid abuse. Other effects of chronic use of opioids are low blood pressure (hypotension), vomiting, that made diagnosis more accurate, less invasive, and more economical.

The use of non-invasive imaging traces it roots to the tremendous advances in the understanding of electromagnetism during the nineteenth century. By 1900, physicist Wilhelm Konrad Roentgen's (1845–1923) discovery of high-energy electromagnetic radiation in the form of x rays were used in medical diagnosis.

The development of powerful high-tech diagnostic tools in the later half of the 20th century was initially the result of fundamental advances in the study of the reactions that take place in excited atomic nuclei. Applications of what were termed nuclear spectroscopic principles became directly linked to the development of non-invasive diagnostic tools used by physicians.

In particular, Nuclear Magnetic Resonance (NMR) was one such form of **nuclear spectroscopy** that eventually found widespread use in the clinical laboratory and medical imaging. NMR is based on the observation that a proton in a magnetic field has two quantized spin states. Accordingly, NMR allowed the determination of the structure of organic molecules and, although there are complications due to interactions between atoms, in simple terms NMR allowed physicians to see pictures representing the larger structures of molecules and compounds (i.e., bones, tissues, and organs) obtained as a result of measuring differences between the expected and actual numbers of photons absorbed by a target tissue.

Groups of nuclei brought into resonance, that is, nuclei absorbing and emitting photons of similar electromagnetic radiation (e.g., radio waves) make subtle yet distinguishable changes when the resonance is forced to change by altering the energy of impacting photons. The speed and extent of the resonance changes permits a non-destructive (because of the use of low energy photons) determination of anatomical structures. This form of NMR is used by physicians as the physical and chemical basis of a powerful diagnostic technique termed Magnetic Resonance Imaging (MRI).

MRI scanners rely on the principles of atomic nuclear-spin resonance. Using strong magnetic fields and radio waves, MRI collects and correlates deflections caused by atoms into images of amazing detail. The resolution of the MRI scanner is so high that they can be used to observe the individual plaques in multiple sclerosis.

Principles of SONAR technology (originally developed for military use) found clinical diagnostic application with the 1960s development of ultra-sound. A sonic production device termed a transducer was placed against the skin of a patient to produce high frequency sound waves that were able to penetrate the skin and reflect off internal target structures. Modern ultrasound techniques using monitors allow physicians real-time diagnostic capabilities. By the 1980s, ultrasound examinations became commonplace in the examination of fetal development.

The advent of other imaging to supplant x rays provided for less potentially damaging forms of diagnosis. High photon energies found in x rays are ionizing and are thus capable of destroying chemical and molecular bonds in cells. In contrast, ultrasound relies not on electromagnetic radiation but rather on pressure waves that are non-ionizing.

Microscopes using ultrasound can be utilized to study cell structures without subjecting them to lethal staining procedures that can also impede diagnosis through the production of artifacts (extraneous bits of highlighted material). Ultrasonic microscopes differentiate structures based on underlying differences in **pathology**. Ultrasonic imaging devices are also among the least expensive of the latest high-tech innovations in diagnostic imaging.

During the early 1970s, enhanced digital capabilities spurred the development of Computed Tomography (derived from the Greek *Tomos*, meaning slice) imaging, also called CT, Computed Axial Tomography or CAT scans, invented by English physician Godfrey Hounsfield. CT scans use advanced computer-based mathematical algorithms to combine different readings or views of a patient into a coherent picture usable for diagnosis. Hounsfield's innovative use of high energy electromagnetic beams, a sensitive detector mounted on a rotating frame, and digital computing to create detailed images earned him the Nobel Prize. As with x rays, CT scan technology progressed to allow the use of less energetic beams and vastly decreased exposure times. CT scans increased the scope and safety of imaging procedures that allowed physicians to view the arrangement and functioning of the body's internal structures on a small scale.

American chemist Peter Alfred Wolf's (1923–1998) work with positron emission tomography (PET) led to the clinical diagnostic use of the PET scan, allowing physicians to measure cell activity in organs. PET scans use rings of detectors that surround the patient to track the movements and concentrations of radio-active tracers. The detectors measure gamma radiation produced when positrons emitted by tracers are annihilated during collisions with electrons. PET scans have attracted the interest of psychiatrists for their potential to study the underlying metabolic changes associated with mental diseases such as schizophrenia and depression. During the 1990s, PET scans found clinical usage in the diagnosis and characterizations of certain cancers and heart disease, as well as clinical studies of the brain.

MRI and PET scans, both examples of functional imaging (in addition to detailing structures they provide a view of dynamic functions), are the subject of increased research and clinical application. MRI and PET scans are used to measure reactions of the brain when challenged with sensory input (e.g., hearing, sight, smell), activities associated with processing information (e.g., learning functions), physiological reactions to addiction, metabolic processes associated with osteoporosis and atherosclerosis, and to shed light on pathological conditions such as Parkinson's and Alzheimer's disease.

During the 1990s, the explosive development of information technologies and the Internet allowed imaging data to be shared globally, both in real-time and by mining databases.

SEE ALSO Alternate light source analysis; Biometric eye scans; Confocal microscopy; Polarized light microscopy; Scanning electron microscopy; Ultraviolet light analysis; Visible microspectrophotometry.

Immune system

A staple in forensic investigations is the use of antibodies to detect a target **antigen**. **Blood** typing and the detection of bacteria, or their elaborated **toxins**, rely on the recognition of antigens by their corresponding antibodies. The production of antibodies is one aspect of the immune system, the body's biological defense mechanism that protects against foreign invaders.

The true roots of the study of the immune system date from 1796, when English physician Edward Jenner discovered a method of **smallpox** vaccination. He noted that dairy workers who contracted cowpox from milking infected cows were thereafter resistant to smallpox. In 1796, Jenner injected a young boy with material from a milkmaid who had an active case of cowpox. After the boy recovered from his own resulting cowpox, Jenner inoculated him with smallpox; the boy was immune. After Jenner published the results of this and other cases in 1798, the practice of Jennerian vaccination spread rapidly.

Louis Pasteur established the cause of infectious diseases and the medical basis for immunization. Pasteur formulated the germ theory of disease, the concept that disease is caused by communicable microorganisms. In 1880, Pasteur discovered that aged cultures of fowl cholera bacteria lost their power to induce disease in chickens but still conferred immunity to the disease when injected. He went on to use attenuated (weakened) cultures of **anthrax** and rabies to vaccinate against those diseases. The American scientists Theobald Smith (1859–1934) and Daniel Salmon (1850–1914) showed in 1886 that bacteria killed by heat could also confer immunity.

In 1888, Pierre-Paul-Emile Roux (1853–1933) and Alexandre Yersin (1863–1943) showed that diphtheria bacillus produced a toxin that the body responded to by producing an antitoxin. Emil von Behring and Shibasaburo Kitasato found a similar toxin-antitoxin reaction in tetanus in 1890, and von Behring discovered that small doses of tetanus or diphtheria toxin produced immunity, which could be transferred from animal to animal via **serum**. He concluded that the immunity was conferred by substances in the blood, which he called antitoxins, or antibodies. In 1894, Richard Pfeiffer (1858–1945) found that antibodies killed cholera bacteria (bacterioloysis). Hans Buchner (1850–1902) in 1893 discovered another important blood substance called complement (Buchner's term was alexin), and Jules Bordet in 1898 found that it enabled the antibodies to combine with antigens (foreign substances) and destroy or eliminate them. It became clear that each **antibody** acted only against a specific antigen. **Karl Landsteiner** exploited this specific antigen-antibody reaction to distinguish the different blood groups.

In the 1880s Russian microbiologist Elie Metchnikoff discovered cell-based immunity: white blood cells (leucocytes), which Metchnikoff called phagocytes, ingested and destroyed foreign particles. Considerable controversy flourished between the proponents of cell-based and blood-based immunity until 1903, when Almroth Edward Wright brought them together by showing that certain blood substances were necessary for phagocytes to function as bacteria destroyers. A unifying theory of immunity was posited by Paul Ehrlich in the 1890s; his "side-chain" theory explained that antigens and antibodies combine chemically in fixed ways, like a key fits into a lock. Until now, immune responses were seen as purely beneficial. In 1902, however, Charles Richet and Paul Portier demonstrated extreme immune reactions in test animals that had become sensitive to antigens by previous exposure. This phenomenon of hypersensitivity, called anaphylaxis, showed that immune responses could cause the body to damage itself. Hypersensitivity to antigens also explained allergies, a term coined by Pirquet in 1906.

Much more was learned about antibodies in the mid-twentieth century, including the fact that they are proteins of the gamma globulin portion of plasma and are produced by plasma cells; their molecular structure was also determined. An important advance in immunochemistry came in 1935 when Michael Heidelberger and Edward Kendall (1886–1972) developed a method to detect and measure amounts of different antigens and antibodies in serum. Immunobiology also advanced. Frank Macfarlane Burnet suggested that animals did not produce antibodies to substances they had encountered very early in life; Peter Medawar proved this idea in 1953 through experiments on mouse embryos.

In 1957, Burnet put forth his clonal selection theory to explain the biology of immune responses. On meeting an antigen, an immunologically responsive cell (shown by C. S. Gowans [1923–] in the 1960s to be a lymphocyte) responds by multiplying and producing an identical set of plasma cells, which in turn manufacture the specific antibody for that antigen. Further cellular research has shown that there are two types of lymphocytes (nondescript lymph cells): B-lymphocytes, which secrete antibody, and T-lymphocytes, which regulate the B-lymphocytes and also either kill foreign substances directly (killer T cells) or stimulate macrophages to do so (helper T cells). Lymphocytes recognize antigens by characteristics on the surface of the antigen-carrying molecules. Researchers in the 1980s uncovered many more intricate biological and chemical details of the immune system components and the ways in which they interact.

SEE ALSO Antibody; Antigen; Homogeneous enzyme immunoassay (EMIT); Vaccines.

Impaired driving SEE Breathalyzer®

Impression evidence

When an item like a shoe or a tire comes into contact with a soft surface, it leaves behind a pattern showing some or all of its surface characteristics known as an impression. The collection and analysis of impression **evidence** found at the scene of a crime can often be very important to an investigation.

The major types of impression evidence are **shoeprints**, **tire tracks**, tool marks and the marks that are found on a fired bullet. Impressions can be found in a variety of surfaces including dust, carpet, mud, and, very significantly, **blood**. Collection of an impression is a specialized forensic task because, unlike a hair or bullet, an impression cannot just be packaged and taken back to the lab. Impression evidence is often fragile; a tire track may deteriorate or even be destroyed by rainfall, for example. There is a need for the forensic scientist to retain as much information as possible when collecting impression evidence.

Impressions may be found in either two or three dimensions. An object like the sole of a shoe will leave a two dimensional impression on a hard surface such as a tiled floor. The impression comes from static charge on the sole transferring particles from the sole to the surface. Sometimes wet deposits on a sole will adhere to such a surface. A three-dimensional impression is made when the surface over which the shoe passed was soft and the sole actually sank into it. The method used to collect the impression evidence depends largely on how the impression was made and on what kind of surface. The impression is photographed on-site and then a plaster cast may be made, or the impression may be dusted with **fingerprint** powder. Dyes can be used to bring up impressions in non-porous surfaces, such as linoleum, although these are absorbed by a porous surface like carpet. Impressions made in dust can be very fragile. Contact with a brush or spray would destroy them. However, electrostatic treatment allows the impression to be lifted onto a more stable surface for transport back to the lab. Many new methods are being developed for the collection and enhancement of impression evidence so that the maximum information can be extracted.

SEE ALSO Casting; Crime scene investigation.

Indicator, acid-base

The forensic examination of tissues or other material can involve chemical testing. These tests help reveal the presence of contaminating chemicals and can help determine the cause of the incident or the death. Some tests rely on a color change to indicate the presence of the target compound. Acid-base indicators are often utilized to show this reaction.

An acid-base indicator is often a complex organic dye that undergoes the color change when the pH (a measure of the amount of acidic or basic components) changes over specific values. Many plant pigments and other natural products are good indicators. Synthetic compounds like phenolphthalein and methyl red are also good acid-base indicators.

Paper that has been impregnated with indicator chemicals and allowed to dry is a common site in laboratories that do acid-base testing. This paper, which is typically cut into thin strips, is called pH paper. The use of different chemicals allows the strips to detect different ranges of pH.

The pH at which the color of an indicator changes is called the transition interval. Forensic chemists use appropriate indicators to signal the end of an acid-base neutralization reaction. Such a reaction is usually accomplished by titration—slowly adding a measured quantity of the base to a measured quantity of the acid (or vice versa). When the reaction is complete and there is no excess of acid or base, but only the reaction products, this is called the endpoint of the titration. The indicator must change color at the pH which corresponds to that endpoint.

The indicator changes color because of its own neutralization in the solution. Different indicators have different transition intervals, so the choice of indicator depends on matching the transition interval to the expected pH of the solution just as the reaction reaches the point of complete neutralization.

The two most common pH indicators are phenolphthalein and methyl red. Phenolphthalein changes from colorless to pink across a range of pH 8.2 to pH 10. Methyl red changes from red to yellow across a range of pH 4.4 to pH 6.2. Other indicators are available through most of the pH range, and can be used in the titration of a wide range of weak acids and bases.

SEE ALSO Chemical and biological detection technologies; Inorganic compounds; Toxicological analysis.

Infectious disease research SEE USAMRIID (United States Army Medical Research Institute of Infectious Diseases

Inferior SEE Anatomical nomenclature

Infrared detection devices

Infrared detection devices are sensors that detect radiation in the infrared portion of the **electromagnetic spectrum** ($\cong 10^{12}$ to 5×10^{14} Hz). Often, such devices form the information they gather into visible-light images for the benefit of human users; alternatively, they may communicate directly with an automatic system, such as the guidance system of a missile.

Because all objects above absolute zero emit radiation in the infrared part of the electromagnetic spectrum, infrared detection provides a means of "seeing in the dark"—that is, forming images when light in the visible portion of the spectrum ($\cong 4.3 \times 10^{14}$ to 7.5×10^{14} Hz) is scarce or absent. Because the warmer an object it is the more infrared radiation it emits, infrared imaging is also useful for the detection of outstanding heat sources that may be invisible or hard to detect even when there is ample visible light. Many devices used by police investigators, including forensic examiners, exploit some form of infrared detection technology.

Infrared—"below-red"—light consists of electromagnetic radiation that is too low in frequency (i.e., too long in wavelength) to be perceived by the human eye, yet is still too high in frequency to be classed as microwave radio. Infrared (IR) light that is just beyond the human visual limit ($\cong 1.0 \times 10^{14}$ to 4.0×10^{14} Hz) is termed near IR, while light farther from the visible spectrum is divided into middle IR, far IR, and extreme IR.

All objects above absolute zero glow in the far IR, so no source of illumination is needed to image scenes using such radiation; to image scenes in near IR, illumination from a light-emitting diode or filtered light bulb must be supplied. Near-IR imagers, however, are still cheaper than passive, far-IR imagers.

There are two basic designs for electronic IR imagers. The first is the scanner. In this design, light from a tiny portion of the scene to be imaged is focused by an optical and mechanical system on a small circuit element that is sensitive to photons in the desired IR frequency range. The intensity of the signal from the IR detector element is recorded, then the mechanico-optical system shifts its focus to a different fragment of the scene. The response of the IR detector element is again recorded, the view shifts again, and so forth, systematically covering the scene. Many scene-covering geometries have been employed by scanning imagers; the scanner may record horizontal or vertical lines (rasters), spiral outward from a central point, cover a series of radii, and so on.

The second basic type of IR imaging system is the "starer." Such a system is said to "stare" because its optics do not move like a scanner's, scanning the scene a little bit at a time; instead, they focus the image onto an extended focal plane. Located in this plane is a flat (planar) array of tiny sensors, each equivalent to the single IR sensor employed in a scanning system. By measuring the IR response of all the elements in the flat array simultaneously (or rapidly), the system can record an entire image at once. Image resolution in a staring scanner is limited by the number of elements in the array, whereas in a scanning system it is limited by the size of the scanning dot.

Hybrid designs, in which partial or entire scanlines are sensed simultaneously by rows of sensors, have also been developed. Chemical films have also been developed for IR imaging, but these are rarely used today.

The earliest IR imagers, built in the 1940s, 1950s, and 1960s, were scanners. Starers were not technologically feasible until the early 1970s, when large-scale circuit integration made the manufacture of focal-plane arrays with good resolution feasible. As integrated-circuit technology has been refined, focal-plane arrays have become cheaper. Starers have many advantages, including greater reliability due to the absence of moving parts, quicker image acquisition, and freedom from internally-produced mechanical vibration.

The security of a building or area of land from intruders is often enhanced by **cameras** that image the perimeter of the secure area and can be monitored by personnel in a central office. At night, such systems must either be supplied with illumination or must be capable of IR imaging. Visible-light camera systems are cheaper and easier for human users to interpret; however, because excess illumination of an area by visible light ("light pollution") is sometimes a concern, and because security forces may wish to keep an area under surveillance without making their presence known, IR systems are widely used for perimeter security and other surveillance tasks. Scrutiny of the recorded data from such surveillance cameras can be useful in piecing together the course of nighttime events in a forensic investigation.

Aerial IR imaging can track vehicles, show which vehicles in a parking lot have arrived most recently, distinguish heated buildings, and locate buried structures (e.g., clandestine chemical laboratories) emit-

ting heat through vents. IR images can be used to determine precisely the **time of death** of a body less than 15 hours old or to detect **document forgery** by revealing subtle mechanical and chemical disturbances of the original paper and ink. The power consumption in a building can be estimated in real time by observing the IR radiation emitted by the power transformer on the pole outside; modifications to walls or automobiles are often obvious in IR images; and IR images can reveal such visually inconspicuous features of crime scenes as use of cleaning solvents to remove **blood**, drag-marks across carpets, fresh paint, and **explosives** residues.

SEE ALSO Analytical instrumentation.

Ink analysis

Ink analysis may be an important part of the investigation of **questioned documents**, including forged checks, wills, or altered records. Although all blue or black inks may look the same, there can be some important differences in their chemical composition. These can be revealed by laboratory analysis and the results can help assess whether there have been any additions or alterations to a document.

Analysis of documents under a microscope can be informative as a first step. The investigator may be able to see slight changes in ink color, not visible to the naked eye, that could be indicative of alterations, or there may be suggestions of obliteration and overwriting. The ink itself may be analyzed by non-destructive or destructive testing, depending on whether a sample needs to be taken from the document, a process that would alter it. It is preferable to try the non-destructive approach first, so that the document is left intact.

The main method of non-destructive ink analysis is **micro-spectrophotometry**. This involves scanning the ink with ultraviolet or infrared light to record its spectrum, that is, the wavelengths of light it absorbs. Some inks fluoresce, or emit light, on exposure to ultraviolet, while others disappear. Each ink should give a distinct pattern or spectrum on exposure to ultraviolet or visible light. Put simply, this is a way of discovering the true "color" of the ink. The spectrum of the ink on the document can therefore be compared with the spectra of standard inks. Other non-destructive or minimally destructive methods, such as Raman **spectroscopy**, can be used to supplement micro-spectrophotometry. It can be very informative to scan the document with infrared light because, at high frequencies, ink is invisible but pencil marks which may lie underneath will show up.

The main method of destructive testing of ink is known as **thin layer chromatography** (TLC). In reality, it is not very destructive to the document if done with care. However, a photographic record of the original document is taken before the procedure is started. A tiny sample of the inked paper is punched out using a thin, hollow needle; a hypodermic syringe is ideal. The investigator avoids places where the pen has changed direction or where ink lines meet. This avoids any interference with subsequent **handwriting analysis**. The sample is placed in a test tube with a solvent that dissolves the ink. Next, a tiny spot of the sample solution is placed onto a strip of paper, alongside spots from various reference ink samples. The paper is placed in a beaker containing a small amount of another solvent. It is positioned so that the paper dips into the solvent but the spots of sample remain dry. The solvent is drawn up the paper through capillary action and the sample spots move up with it. **Chromatography** means "writing with colors" and the chemical components of the ink, which are, of course, colored, travel with the solvent at a speed that depends upon their composition.

The end result with TLC is a pattern of colored spots, known as a chromatogram, for each ink. Different inks will have different chromatograms. If the sample ink has the same chromatogram as one of the reference inks, it suggests they are the same, and so **identification** can be made. The United States Secret Service has a reference ink database and the U.S. Treasury has a database of ink thin layer chromatograms which can be very informative.

Another technique called high performance liquid chromatography (hplc), which can be used as an alternative to tlc. Hplc involves injecting the ink sample onto a long thin metal column that is then washed over with a mixture of solvents, carrying the ink components one at a time to an electronic detector. Between them, non-destructive and destructive methods of analysis can identify more than 90% of ballpoint pen inks.

Just because a document appears to have been written throughout in the same ink does not mean it has not been altered or added to. The same ink fills many different writing implements. Pens, usually ballpoint pens, can be distinguished from one another by looking at the non-inked areas known as striae within a line of writing with a microscope. Striae arise from imperfections within the ball or ball housing of the writing pen.

However, it can be difficult to age an ink, unless it is known for sure that the ink did not exist when the document was said to have been prepared. From the 1990s, some ink manufacturers started to add a chemical tag to their products to indicate the year of manufacture. This enables chemical analysis to age the ink, but the tests to do this remain rather expensive.

SEE ALSO Document forgery; Questioned documents; Secret writing.

Inorganic compounds

There are two main classes of chemical compounds, organic and inorganic. **Organic compounds** are based on carbon (containing the element carbon as a structural backbone) and are found in living things. Inorganic compounds are those based on other elements. This distinction is a generalization. Some important inorganic compounds, like calcium carbonate, or lime, contain carbon. Carbon-based compounds need not come from living things; synthetic **fibers** like nylon and polyester are carbon based but not found in plants or animals. From the point of view of **forensic science**, both organic and inorganic compounds are found in items of **evidence**. The techniques used for determination of chemical composition of such evidence often depend upon whether the component compounds are organic (derived form living tissue or material) or inorganic.

Glass and paint are probably the most important types of evidence containing inorganic compounds. Glass is composed of silica, soda, lime and impurities that are usually mineral salts. The chemical composition of glass is often determined with the scanning electron microscope (SEM) in conjunction with energy dispersive x-ray analysis (EDX). The microscope ensures magnification of ten thousand times or more of the sample, using electrons rather than light. The item under the microscope will emit radiation that is characteristic of the elements of which it is made. The presence and proportions of these elements can be determined and then compared with reference types of glass. This allows not only the type of glass found at the crime scene to be identified, but also a comparison with glass fragments found on a suspect.

Paint is the other type of evidence that contains inorganic compounds, as pigments or extenders. The red, yellow, and white pigments of paint tend to be inorganic in nature. As with glass, XRD (x-ray diffraction) and EDX together are used to look at the inorganic content of a paint flake or smear. These are crossed against paint references or comparison samples. Atomic absorption **spectroscopy** is another technique that can be used to identify inorganic components of evidence. This relies on the emission of specific wavelengths of light when an inorganic element, such as a metal, is heated. Atomic absorption is used in a forensic context to determine the chemical nature of soil or mud samples found at the scene of a crime

SEE ALSO Glass; Organic compounds; Paint analysis.

Institutes

There are a growing number of **training** institutes and centers of professional excellence throughout the worldwide **forensic science** community.

In the United States, the American Society of Crime Laboratory Directors (ASCLD) is a nonprofit professional society whose mission it is to create and promote the highest standards of professional performance in forensic scientific analysis. This organization holds annual symposia and professional institutes designed to offer continuing education and training in forensic science, management, and leadership. In 1995, the ASCLD established the National Forensic Science Technology Center in order to create a centralized means of providing outstanding quality of education, systems support, and training for the forensic scientific community throughout the United States.

The United States Department of Justice's Bureau of Alcohol, Tobacco, Firearms and Explosives (**ATF**) Laboratory has a long and illustrious history of excellence in the worldwide forensic community in the areas of alcohol, tobacco, firearms, explosives, and **fire debris** analysis. A central facet of ATF's mission is to provide training to the worldwide forensic community, as well as to U.S. federal, state, and local investigators and examiners.

The **European Network of Forensic Science Institutes** (ENFSI) was created with the expressed intention of creating a world community of forensic scientists who would exchange ideas, and share knowledge as a universal group of experts, maintaining the highest standards of professional practice, without being bound by culture or location.

Interpol has a forensic section containing international working groups in areas such as **DNA**, fingerprints, and disaster victim **identification**. In

addition, Interpol hosts an international forensic science symposium every three years, the stated purposes of which are to provide a professional forum for forensic managers, to present an overview of the scientific advances occurring during the previous three years, and to create an environment conducive to the open exchange of information among all Interpol member states.

In Australia, the National Institute of Forensic Science was established as a national common police service whose purposes are: to sponsor and support forensic scientific research; to hold institutes for the sharing, support, and exchange of forensic training, education, and information; and to maintain system-wide standards of forensic scientific quality assurance. In addition, the NIFS works at continual professional forensic science quality improvement, both locally and worldwide, as well as at the promotion of environmentally responsible use of resources.

The Forensic Science Division, located in Hong Kong, provides comprehensive forensic scientific services to the criminal justice system. It contains two sections: the Criminalistics and Quality Management Group and the Drugs, Toxicology, and Documents Group. The Criminalistics and Quality Management Group has eight operational sections: Biochemical Sciences A Section, Biochemical Sciences B Section, Chemical Sciences Section, DNA Database Section, Parentage Testing Section, Physical Sciences Section, and Scene of Crime and Quality Management Section.

India's Central Forensic Science Laboratory was designed to meet the forensic science needs of the Indian Central Bureau of Investigation, the Delhi Police, the government of India, and various Indian central government agencies. In addition to the analysis of forensic, scientific, and evidentiary materials, the CFSL conducts research and development in all areas of forensic science, and provides forensic science training to investigating officers and others involved in the forensic sciences, and conducts institutes and educational symposia for police, professional, and public organizations.

Japan's Training Institute of Forensic Science is tasked with providing organizational staff, police professionals, and criminal laboratory personnel with training, education, and strategic technology in the theory and practice of forensic science. In addition to the five core training courses offered (Basic, Advanced, Specialized Technique, Research, and Management Courses), the Training Institute of Forensic Science is committed to the international exchange of forensic science information and technologies through its international research and training course.

The Netherlands Forensic Institute is part of the Ministry of Justice, and is responsible for ongoing forensic scientific and technical research. It is organized into the following technical units: **pathology**; toxicology; DNA-technology; hair and **fibers**; firearms and ammunition; shotgun residue; explosives; **toolmarks**, footwear, and tire impressions; forensic engineering and material science; **fire investigation**; fingerprints; environmental analysis; **illicit drugs**; general chemistry (excluding fire-accelerants and paint); hand- and machine-writing; speech; **questioned documents**; traffic accidents; vehicle identification; and digital technology. The NFI is one of the founding members of the ENFSI, and it maintains extensive contact, collaborative partnerships and projects, and professional networks with other countries' forensic laboratories, research institutes, and universities. The NFI is expressly committed to worldwide cooperation in the solution and prevention of international crime.

In Poland, the Institute of Forensic Research conducts forensic science research, prepares for and provides expert opinions throughout the country's legal system, and is tasked with professional development, advancement, and promotion of the forensic sciences, particularly within the legal and justice systems. The Institute conducts ongoing research in the areas of toxicology; illicit drugs; **DNA profiling**; road accidents; forensic engineering; paint; **glass**; fibers and textiles; gunshot residues; toolmarks, footwear, and tire impressions; forensic **photography**; handwriting; questioned documents; fingerprints; forensic **psychology**; and audio-speech analysis.

Singapore's Forensic Science Division of the Department of Scientific Services, Institute of Science and Forensic Medicine, claims world-renowned status for its forensic science services. It is the sole provider of forensic science expertise and services to the Central Narcotics Bureau, to the police, and to the Singapore judiciary. In addition, it provides expert forensic, medical, and legal services to hospitals and other requesting government agencies. Since 1996, the Forensic Science Division has achieved and maintained the distinction of being ASCLD accredited in the areas of DNA, **serology**, controlled drugs, firearms/toolmarks, **trace evidence**, questioned documents, and toxicology. The ASCLD accreditation is considered symbolic both of the achievement of international recognition and of consistent maintenance of the highest standards of professional excellence.

The Istanbul University Institute of Forensic Sciences is the only academic institution in Turkey to offer graduate degrees in forensic science. The Institute is a member of ENFSI, and it provides expert forensic scientific support to Turkey's criminal justice system.

This is by no means an exhaustive list of the most comprehensive or internationally respected forensic institutes in the world today; it is intended as a representative sampling designed to pique the reader's interest and, perhaps, to spark a personal exploration of the worldwide forensic scientific community.

SEE ALSO American Academy of Forensic Sciences; FBI Crime Laboratory; Law Enforcement Training Center (FLETC), United States Federal; Technology and forensic science.

Integrated automated fingerprint identification system

An important part of a forensic investigation is the **identification** of the victim or suspect. One of the most useful identification tools is the **fingerprint** pattern. An individual's fingerprint pattern is a unique identifier. This identification power was recognized long ago. On-paper impressions of fingerprint patterns stored in file cabinets have been a standard feature of law enforcement. In the Internet age, such information can be shared with the wider community. Computer databases can be made accessible to virtually any law enforcement agency, and to other forensic investigations who have the necessary authorization to access the database.

The most important fingerprint database is known as the Integrated **Automated Fingerprint Identification System** (IAFIS). The database—the largest in the world—is a national repository of fingerprint and other information on criminal history, which is maintained by the Federal Bureau of Investigation (**FBI**) Criminal Justice Information Services Division.

A user accessing the database can print out or download specified images. As well, images can be uploaded to the database. Indeed, the fingerprint image patterns in the database are voluntarily submitted by local, state, and federal law enforcement agencies. Over 47 million fingerprint patterns currently reside in the database.

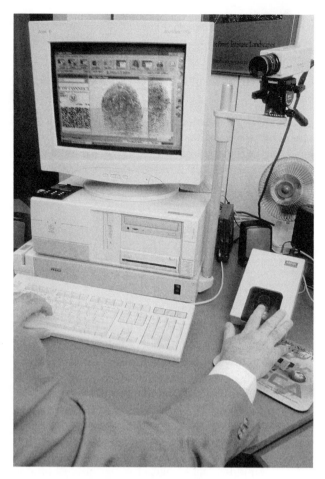

The project manager in biometrics for the state of Connecticut demonstrates integrated fingerprint identification software.
© NAJLAH FEANNY/CORBIS SABA

Many of the files in the database contain the digitized images of ten prints, the eight fingers and two thumbs, of an individual. Eight print patterns, which lack thumbprints, are also included.

The images can be downloaded directly to the database when submitted electronically. Fingerprints that are submitted by mail are converted to an electronic format.

Users can search the IAFIS database to compare a submitted fingerprint pattern with this tremendous number and geographically diverse repository of fingerprints. The submitted pattern is compared to those in the database. Any matching pattern is displayed, complete with the other information on the individual.

The IAFIS increases a forensic investigator's chance of identifying a subject or a deceased person. The electronic nature of the database facilitates rapid turnaround. Typically, in a non-criminal case, a response to a submission occurs within 24 hours. When a submission is concerned with a criminal or forensic investigation, the turnaround time occurs within two hours. Conceivably, a fingerprint pattern can be submitted and a response received within the same business day.

This rapid submission and turn-around capability has markedly accelerated forensic investigations. In the past, identifying a fingerprint from a national paper database took months. Indeed, it was this limitation that prompted the FBI to partner with law enforcement agencies in the 1990s to establish the electronic database. The IAFIS began operation in July of 1999.

SEE ALSO Automated Fingerprint Identification System (AFIS); Crime scene investigation; Digital imaging; Fingerprint; Fingerprint analysis (famous cases); Latent fingerprint.

Integrated Ballistics Identification System (IBIS)

When bullets and shell casings are shot from **firearms** they can leave unique marks, which when examined by forensic scientists can link a particular firearm to a specific crime. Before 1998, the U.S. Federal Bureau of Investigation (**FBI**) and the Bureau of Alcohol, Tobacco, Firearms and Explosives (**ATF**), both under the U.S. Department of Justice, developed independent **imaging** systems and databases to analyze and store ballistic images. The FBI system was called **Drugfire**, while the AFT system was named IBIS (Integrated Ballistics Identification System).

The Integrated Ballistics Identification System was purchased in 1993 by the ATF from its developer, Forensic Technology, Inc. (FTI) of Montreal, Canada. The project, which eventually turned into IBIS, was begun in 1990 in order to provide law enforcement professionals with the ability to use digital computer images of ballistic **evidence** and to assist crime laboratories with a growing number of firearm-related crimes.

The IBIS uses sophisticated electronic and optical technology to digitally compare evidence stored in the database. Initially, IBIS equipment photographs the surface of fired bullets and casings from crime scenes and laboratories. Upon entering a new image into the database, the system searches for a match by using advanced mathematical algorithms to correlate the new image against previously stored images. Using filters such as **caliber**, date of crime, date of entry, and rifling specifications, the correlations produce lists of possible matches. A forensic examiner then visually compares the matched images on a computer monitor. If a possible match is found, the images are compared with actual evidence by an examiner on a microscope for a final determination. Once an identification is confirmed in association with at least two different crimes, a unique identifier is assigned for future reference to that image.

Leaders of the FBI and ATF realized that their two systems (Drugfire and IBIS) were incompatible and agreed in the 1990s that both systems needed to transmit information between each other. In May 1997, the National Integrated Ballistics Information Network (NIBIN) board was created to develop a national imaging system. One year later, FBI and ATF officials agreed to pursue the joint development of one system, using only the IBIS, and created the National Integrated Ballistics Information Network. In December 1999, FBI and ATF leaders signed a memorandum that defined their individual roles: the FBI was granted responsibility for providing the communications network and the ATF was given responsibility for field operations. Forensic Technology was awarded the NIBIN Expansion Contract in 2002 for products and services relevant to IBIS. By the end of 2002, IBIS systems had been installed in 233 U.S. crime laboratories as part of the NIBIN and, as of the beginning of 2005, IBIS systems were used in over thirty countries by thirty-three local, provincial, state, and federal law enforcement agencies. The IBIS technology has allowed law enforcement officials to match over 32,000 pieces of evidence and has helped to open thousands of new investigative leads.

SEE ALSO ATF (United States Bureau of Alcohol, Tobacco, and Firearms); Ballistics; Computer forensics; Drugfire; FBI (United States Federal Bureau of Investigation).

Integument

The integumentary system includes the skin and the related structures that cover and protect the body. The human integumentary system is made up of the skin, which includes glands, hair, and nails. The skin protects the body, prevents water loss, regulates body temperature, and senses the external environment. Examination of the integument can also provide the forensic scientist with clues regarding the identity of a crime victim, the nature of the crime committed, and even the perpetrator of the crime.

The human integumentary system serves many protective functions for the body. Keratin, an insoluble protein in the outer layer of the skin, helps prevent water loss and dehydration. Keratin also prevents excessive water loss, keeps out microorganisms that could cause illness, and protects the underlying tissues from mechanical damage. Keratin is also the major protein found in nails and hair. Pigments in the skin called melanin absorb and reflect the sun's harmful ultraviolet radiation. The skin helps to regulate the body temperature. If heat builds up in the body, sweat glands in the skin produce more sweat that evaporates and cools the skin. In addition, when the body overheats, blood vessels in the skin expand and bring more blood to the surface, which allows body heat to be lost. Conversely, if the body is too cold the blood vessels in the skin contract, resulting in less blood at the body surface, and heat is conserved. In addition to temperature regulation, the skin serves as a minor excretory organ, because sweat removes small amounts of nitrogenous wastes produced by the body. The skin also functions as a sense organ as it contains millions of nerve endings that detect touch, heat, cold, pain and pressure. Finally, the skin produces vitamin D in the presence of sunlight, and renews and repairs damage to itself.

In an adult, the skin covers about 21.5 square feet (2 square meters), and weighs about 11 pounds (5 kilograms). Depending on location, the skin ranges from 0.02–0.16 inches (0.5–4.0 millimeters) thick. Its two principal parts are the outer layer, or epidermis, and a thicker inner layer, the dermis. A subcutaneous layer of fatty or adipose tissue is found below the dermis. Fibers from the dermis attach the skin to the subcutaneous layer, and the underlying tissues and organs also connect to the subcutaneous layer.

Ninety percent of the epidermis, including the outer layers, contains keratinocytes cells that produce keratin, a protein that helps waterproof and protect the skin. Melanocytes are pigment cells that produce melanin, a dark pigment that adds to skin color and absorbs ultraviolet light thereby shielding the genetic material in skin cells from damage. Merkel's cells disks are touch-sensitive cells found in the deepest layer of the epidermis of hairless skin.

In most areas of the body, the epidermis consists of four layers. On the soles of the feet and palms of the hands where there is a lot of friction, the epidermis has five layers. In addition, calluses, abnormal thickenings of the epidermis, occur on skin subject to constant friction. At the skin surface, the outer layer of the epidermis constantly sheds the dead cells containing keratin. The uppermost layer consists of about 25 rows of flat dead cells that contain keratin.

The dermis is made up of connective tissue that contains protein, collagen, and elastic fibers. It also contains blood and lymph vessels, sensory receptors, related nerves, and glands. The outer part of the dermis has fingerlike projections, called dermal papillae that indent the lower layer of the epidermis. Dermal papillae cause ridges in the epidermis above it, which in the fingers give rise to fingerprints. The ridge pattern of fingerprints is inherited, and is unique to each individual. The dermis is thick in the palms and soles, but very thin in other places, such as the eyelids. The blood vessels in the dermis contain a volume of blood. If a part of the body, such as a working muscle, needs more blood, blood vessels in the dermis constrict, causing blood to leave the skin and enter the circulation that leads to muscles and other body parts. Sweat glands whose ducts pass through the epidermis to the outside and open on the skin surface through pores are embedded in the deep layers of the dermis. Hair follicles and hair roots also originate in the dermis and the hair shafts extend from the hair root through the skin layers to the surface. Also in the dermis are sebaceous glands associated with hair follicles that produce an oily substance called sebum. Sebum softens the hair and prevents it from drying, but if sebum blocks up a sebaceous gland, a whitehead appears on the skin.

The skin is an important sense organ, and as such includes a number of nerves that are mainly in the dermis, with a few reaching the epidermis. Nerves carry impulses to and from muscles, sweat glands, and blood vessels, and receive messages from touch, temperature, and pain receptors. Some nerve endings are specialized such as sensory receptors that detect external stimuli. The nerve endings in the dermal papillae are known as Meissner's corpuscles, which detect light touch, such as a pat, or the feel of clothing on the skin. Pacinian corpuscles, located in the deeper dermis, are stimulated by stronger pressure on the skin. Receptors near hair roots detect displacement of the skin hairs by stimuli such as touch or wind. Bare nerve endings throughout the skin report information to the brain about temperature change (both heat and cold), texture, pressure, and trauma.

Some skin disorders result from overexposure to the ultraviolet (UV) rays in sunlight. At first, overexposure to sunlight results in injury known as sunburn. UV rays damage skin cells, blood vessels, and other dermal structures. Continual overexposure leads to leathery skin, wrinkles, and discoloration and can also lead to skin cancer.

SEE ALSO Crime scene reconstruction; DNA.

International Association for Identification

The roots of the International Association for Identification (IAI) extend back to 1915 when Harry H. Caldwell, an inspector with the Oakland (California) Police Department, identified the need to organize a criminal identification group. Consequently, twenty-two criminal identification operators formed the International Association for Criminal Identification in October 1915, with Caldwell as its presiding officer. Today, the IAI (web page http://www.theiai.org/) is the world's oldest and largest forensic organization, with over 5,000 members from the United States and numerous foreign countries. Through a network of products and services, the IAI is the primary organization engaged in the dissemination of information and support of **forensic science** professionals.

The word criminal was dropped from its name in 1918 because IAI bureaus were performing increasing amounts of non-criminal work. The newly named organization, International Association for Identification, was subsequently incorporated in Delaware on December 22, 1919. Throughout the twentieth century, the IAI grew in prominence as new state bureaus, divisions, committees, and other groups were formed. Indeed, the organization was recognized by the U.S. Federal Bureau of Investigation (**FBI**) and other government agencies as a valuable partner against crime; a status it maintains today.

Presently, the structure of the IAI, with headquarters in Mendota Heights, Minnesota (south of Minneapolis), consists of independent divisions and regions throughout the world. Two major IAI awards are presented each year: The John A. Dondero Memorial Award—established in 1958 and first awarded to FBI Director **J. Edgar Hoover** in 1959—recognizes people who make significant contributions to the field of identification; and the Good of the Association Award—first awarded in 1988—recognizes persons who make outstanding contributions to IAI goals, interests, and objectives.

The IAI runs six certification programs: Latent Print (the first program, established in 1977), Crime Scene; Forensic Art; Footwear and Tiretrack Analysis;

Bloodstain Pattern, and Forensic Photography/Imaging. A peer-reviewed IAI journal called the *Journal of Forensic Identification*, established in 1988, is an internationally recognized bimonthly journal that includes scientific articles on case reports, experiments, original investigations, reviews, tests, and other related subjects. The IAI also sponsors the Annual IAI International Educational Conference, which features educational presentations, field trips, general and advanced seminars, hands-on workshops, and vendor exhibits. Established in 1988, the Robert L. Johnson Foundation provides research and educational scholarships and grants to promote the advancement of professional forensic identification. A student membership category was created in 2000 so that full-time college students with majors in forensic science, law enforcement, and related fields could benefit from IAI information and **training**.

SEE ALSO Careers in forensic science; FBI (United States Federal Bureau of Investigation); Identification.

International laws and trials SEE
Trials, international

Internet tracking and tracing

Forensic science, in particular the process of **forensic accounting**, where the routing of finances, property, and other material items are traced, relies upon trails of **evidence**. The information that resides on the Internet can be tracked and traced, and so can be valuable in forensics.

Tracing is a process that follows the Internet activity backwards, from the recipient to the user. As well, a user's Internet activity on web sites can also be tracked on the recipient site (i.e., what sites are visited and how often, the activity at a particular site). Sometimes this tracking and tracing ability is used to generate e-mail to the user, promoting a product that is related to the sites visited. User information, however, can also be gathered covertly.

Techniques of Internet tracking and tracing can also enable authorities to pursue and identify those responsible for malicious Internet activity. For example, on February 8, 2000, a number of key commercial Internet sites such as Yahoo, Ebay, and Amazon were jammed with incoming information and rendered inoperable. Through tracing and tracking techniques, law enforcement authorities established that the attacks had arisen from the computer

of a 15-year-old boy in Montreal, Canada. The youth, whose Internet identity was "Mafiaboy," was arrested within months of the incidents.

Law enforcement use of Internet tracking is extensive. For example, the U.S. Federal Bureau of Investigation has a tracking program designated Carnivore. The program is capable of scanning thousands of e-mails to identify those that meet the search criteria.

Cookies are computer files that are stored on a user's computer during a visit to a web site. When the user electronically enters the web site, the host computer automatically loads the file(s) to the user's computer.

The cookie is a tracking device, which records the electronic movements made by the user at the site, as well as identifiers such as a username and password. Commercial web sites make use of cookies to allow a user to establish an account on the first visit to the site and so to avoid having to enter account information (i.e., address, credit card number, financial activity) on subsequent visits. User information can also be collected unbeknownst to the user, and subsequently used for whatever purpose the host intends.

Cookies are files, and so can be transferred from the host computer to another computer. This can occur legally (i.e., selling of a subscriber mailing list) or illegally (i.e., "hacking in" to a host computer and copying the file). Also, cookies can be acquired as part of a law enforcement investigation.

Stealing a cookie requires knowledge of the file name. Unfortunately, this information is not difficult to obtain. A survey conducted by a U.S. Internet security company in 2002 on 109,212 web sites that used cookies found that almost 55% of them used the same cookie name. Cookies may be disabled by the user, however, this calls for programming knowledge that many users do not have or do not wish to acquire.

A bug or a beacon is an image that can be installed on a web page or in an e-mail. Unlike cookies, bugs cannot be disabled. They can be prominent or surreptitious. As examples of the latter, graphics that are transparent to the user can be present, as can graphics that are only 1x1 pixels in size (corresponding to a dot on a computer monitor). When a user clicks onto the graphic in an attempt to view, or even to close the image, information is relayed to the host computer.

Information that can be gathered by bugs or beacons includes: the user's IP address (the Internet address of the computer) and e-mail address; the user computer's operating system (which can be used to target viruses to specific operating systems; the URL (Uniform Record Locator), or address, of the web page that the user was visiting when the bug or beacon was activated; and the browser that was used (i.e., Mozilla, Explorer).

Like cookies, the information provided by the bug or beacon can be useful to law enforcement officers and forensic investigators who are tracking down the source of an Internet intrusion.

E-mail transmissions have several features that make it possible to trace their passage from the sender to the recipient computers. For example, every e-mail contains a section of information that is dubbed the header. Information concerning the origin time, date, and location of the message is present, as is the Internet address (IP) of the sender's computer.

If an alias has been used to send the message, the IP number can be used to trace the true origin of the transmission. When the originating computer is that of a personally owned computer, this tracing can often lead directly to the sender. However, if the sending computer serves a large community—such as a university—through which malicious transmissions are often routed, then identifying the sender can remain daunting. Yet depending on the e-mail program in use, even a communal facility can have information concerning the account of the sender.

The information in the header also details the route that the message took from the sending computer to the recipient computer. This can be useful in unearthing the identity of the sender. For example, in the case of "Mafiaboy," examination of the transmissions led to a computer at the University of California at Santa Barbara that had been commandeered for the prank. Examination of the log files allowed authorities to trace the transmission path back to the sender's personal computer.

Chat rooms are electronic forums where users can visit and exchange views and opinions about a variety of issues. By piecing together the electronic transcripts of the chat room conversations, enforcement officers can track down the source of malicious activity.

Returning to the example of "Mafiaboy," enforcement officers were able to find transmissions at certain chat rooms where the upcoming malicious activity was described. The source of the transmissions was determined to be the youth's personal computer. Matching the times of the chat room transmissions to the malicious events provided strong evidence of the youth's involvement.

SEE ALSO Computer forensics; Computer hackers; Computer security and computer crime investigation.

Interpol

Interpol's main functions are to act as a global police communication system, to gather intelligence on activities of criminal international organizations and individuals, to provide its member states with several types of criminal databases and analytical services, and to give proactive support for police operations around the world.

The idea of founding an international police organization was initially conceived during the First International Criminal Police Congress, held in Monaco in 1914. Lawyers, magistrates, and police officers from 14 countries basically constituted the public present at the time. In that same year, World War I was initiated and the project was put aside until 1923 when the President of the Vienna Police, Dr. Johannes Schober, promoted the foundation of the International Criminal Police Commission (ICPC), which was the embryo of the modern Interpol. ICPC central office was located in Vienna, Austria, and when Germany annexed Austria to its territories in 1942, the Nazis moved the organization to Berlin. In protest, the vast majority of ICPC member-countries broke with the organization. Consequently, the ICPC was practically extinct at the end of World War II in 1945.

The reorganization of ICPC started in 1946, under Belgian initiative, and the name Interpol was created as a telegraphic address. The new headquarters were located in Paris, France, with new countries progressively seeking membership. The United Nations first recognized Interpol as a consultant agency in 1949. In 1971 the UN recognized it as an inter-governmental police organization, five years after the modernization process that created a new statutory regulation, administrative structure, and a new name, International Criminal Police Organization (ICPO-Interpol).

In the following decades, Interpol incorporated new technologies and organized its General Secretariat in Lyon, France, and the respective Interpol National Central Bureaus (INCBs) in each member-country. A communication system, X.400, was developed in 1990 for electronic exchange of information among the several INCBs around the world and the General Secretariat. Among other resources, an Automatic Search Facility (ASF data bank) was created in 1998 and in 2002, a web-based data system (I–24/7)

INTERPOL's database screen where all stolen artworks are catalogued, allowing cross-checking during inquiries. © DUNG VO TRUNG/ CORBIS SYGMA

was developed to optimize the access of INCBs to all available criminal records and new inputs.

The creation and consolidation of the European Union, as well as the new security challenges posed by terrorism and other transnational criminal activities such as international kidnapping and pedophilia, human traffic for labor, and narco-trafficking, make evident the strategic importance of Interpol. For instance, as an inter-governmental criminal police with law enforcement powers, Interpol is positioned to facilitate and coordinate the implementation of coordinated police operations simultaneously in several countries.

The administrative structure of Interpol consists of: 1) the General Assembly, composed of delegates appointed by each of its 182 member-countries; 2) the Executive Committee, whose members are elected by the General Assembly to represent the four Interpol regions (Africa, Asia, the Americas, and Europe) in Interpol affairs and decision-making; 3) the General Secretariat, along with the technical and administrative staff. Each member country main-

tains an Interpol National Central Bureau (INCB) that provides services to local law enforcement and institutions and functions as a liaison between the member state and the rest of the organization. The Interpol Executive Committee and the General Assembly have independent authority to appoint expert advisors.

SEE ALSO International Association for Identification.

Interpol, United States National Central Bureau

Forensic investigations at the local, state, and national level can be aided by the resources and data housed at international police institutions such as **Interpol**.

As the United States branch of Interpol, an international police organization, the United States National Central Bureau (USNCB) in Washington,

D.C., serves as a communications clearinghouse for police seeking assistance in criminal investigations that cross international boundaries. Directed by the U.S. Attorney General and representing sixteen law enforcement agencies under the Department of Justice in conjunction with the Department of the Treasury, the USNCB focuses on fugitives, financial fraud, drug violations, terrorism, and violent crimes. It can refuse to respond to any of the 200,000 annual inquiries from other nations and, as required by Interpol bylaws, does not assist in the capture of people sought for political, racial, or ethnic reasons.

Although Interpol dates back to 1923, the USNCB did not come into existence until the 1960s because of a lukewarm American attitude toward the organization. Hesitant about the benefits of international police work, the Federal Bureau of Investigation (**FBI**) in the Department of Justice did not post wanted notices with Interpol until 1936. When **J. Edgar Hoover** (1895–1972), head of the FBI from 1924 to 1972, observed Interpol's success in apprehending criminals, his subsequent support of the police force prompted Congress to order the Attorney General to accept Interpol membership in 1938. Hoover became the permanent American representative to Interpol with only the FBI authorized to do business with the group. In 1950, Hoover pulled the FBI out of Interpol for reasons that remain unclear. The Treasury, however, continued to maintain informal contact with the organization and became the official U.S. representative in 1958. When the U.S. decided to establish the USNCB in 1962 as part of Attorney General Robert F. Kennedy's fight against organized crime, the history of American involvement dictated a sharing of power between the two agencies with Justice as the dominant partner.

The USNCB became operational in 1969, with a staff of three and an annual caseload of 300. Agents are complimented by computer specialists, analysts, translators, and administrative and clerical support personnel drawn largely from the ranks of the Department of Justice. The agents operate in divisions dedicated to specific investigative areas while the analysts review case information to identify patterns and links. The law enforcement agencies represented at the USNCB include the Bureau of Alcohol, Tobacco, and Firearms; the Drug Enforcement Administration (**DEA**); the Environmental Protection Agency; the FBI; the Financial Crimes Enforcement Network; the Fish and Wildlife Service; the Immigration and Naturalization Service (INS); Internal Revenue Service; U.S. Customs Service; the Department of Agriculture, the Department of Justice, Criminal

Division; the Department of State; the U.S. Marshals Service; the U.S. Mint; the U.S. Postal Inspection Service; and the U.S. Secret Service. Additionally, each state, the District of Columbia, and New York City have established points of contact to receive international criminal reports from the USNCB.

The USNCB operates by linking the Treasury Enforcement Computer System, the FBI's **National Crime Information Center**, INS files, and DEA records to Interpol. In 1990, the U.S. and Canadian governments established an Interpol Interface between the USNCB and the Canadian NCB in Ottawa. This link allows police to tap into law enforcement networks across the border to verify driver registrations and vehicle ownership.

SEE ALSO European Network of Forensic Science Institutes; FBI (United States Federal Bureau of Investigation).

Interrogation

The aim of a criminal interrogation is to obtain information from a suspect that the suspect does not want to divulge. Interrogation must be carried out in a manner that does not violate the suspect's civil rights or compromise the legal admissibility of the obtained information. There is often confusion between the concepts of interview and interrogation. The distinction is this: an interrogation occurs when one person asks all the questions and the other gives the answers; an interview is a conversation where both people ask and respond to questions. A thorough interview should always precede an interrogation, providing a foundation for the questioner to gather essential information about the subject's feelings, motivations, fears, and belief systems, which can then be used to direct an interrogation. Through the course of the interview, the subject is asked questions about him/herself, others involved in the event, and the crime itself. The interview process should be conducted in an informal and non-threatening manner; the goal is to obtain verbal and nonverbal information about the subject while building rapport and determining whether an interrogation is warranted.

A cardinal rule in interrogation is that there one best chance at obtaining a confession or the desired information, and it occurs the first time a subject is interrogated. There are several facets of interrogation that significantly increase the probability of successful outcome. The first involves laying adequate groundwork and thoroughly preparing for the interrogation.

Iraqi cell used for interrogation where investigators with the U.S.-led coalition in 1990 found evidence of Iraqi torture of its own citizens and of Kuwaiti victims. © JACQUES LANGEVIN/CORBIS SYGMA

The interrogation must occur in an appropriate environment, where there is relative comfort but total freedom from distractions and interruptions. All potential distractions, such as cell phones, radios, beepers, etc. must be silenced; there should be no windows, telephones, or clocks in the room. The interrogator should be free to fully observe the posture, body language, and nonverbal cues of the subject throughout the course of the session. By eliminating other stimuli, the interrogator can be certain that all reactions stem from the line of questioning and the issues presented. An important aspect of environmental preparation entails prior preparation for documenting the information obtained. It is critical not to stop the process of interrogation. No matter what the means of recording the interrogation, it is imperative to obtain an signed, written summary statement of fact which will be admissible in a court of law. The interrogator must be certain to allot sufficient time to complete the interrogation, in order to maximize the likelihood of successful outcome.

The interrogator must be thoroughly familiar with the case facts, particularly those concerning the crime's commission. The interrogator gains immeasurable credibility and stature if he or she can communicate knowledge of how the crime was committed to the subject. Similarly, it is essential for the interrogator to become familiar with the subject's belief system, feelings, and attitude about the crime and victim. Psychologically, the interrogator must understand the subject's conflicts, needs, and goals in order to best elicit truthful information.

Interrogation is more direct than interviewing; its only goal is to elicit a confession or admission of guilty knowledge. The interrogator presents the subject with facts and information, and does not solicit new information. It is therefore critical for the interrogator to have previously amassed case facts and information with which to persuade the subject to tell the truth. The more experienced the interrogator and the more thorough the advance preparation, the more convincing the arguments will be.

There are several universal defense mechanisms that, if properly recognized and utilized by the interrogator, will greatly increase the likelihood of obtaining information: minimization, projection, and rationalization. Properly exploiting these defense mechanisms allows the subject to maintain a semblance of dignity while still being held accountable by the interrogator for their actions. If the interrogator minimizes the gravity of the incident by referring to it as an accident or an unfortunate mistake, the subject may also internally minimize the perceived impact of the incident and feel less resistant to talking about it By suggesting that someone else (often the victim) might share in the blame for the incident, the interrogator uses projection to allow the subject to feel that the incident is excusable. When an interrogator suggests that he or she can understand the subject's perspective (rationalization), it conveys empathy and allows the subject to feel like a decent individual who was in a bad circumstance at the time of the incident. By using careful wording, the interrogator can simultaneously decrease the subject's feeling of shame about the event and increase feelings of hopefulness about the ultimate outcome. The interrogator must be extremely careful not to mislead the subject into a belief in legal leniency or to in any way suggest denying the subject due process. Either event could lead to legal inadmissibility of the confession.

The interrogator presents a set of themes and arguments over the course of the interrogation, as many times and in as many ways as necessary to obtain a confession. In order to ensure a successful outcome, the interrogator must continually confront (degree and manner of confrontation must be person- and situation-specific) the subject with facts and information about the case and gradually limit the subject's ability to deny participation therein. One way to do this is by repeatedly stating the subject's participation in the incident(s) and questioning only the justification or motive for the event. Once the subject begins to acknowledge responsibility or participation in the crime, the interrogator can offer the individual reasons to confess without loss of dignity, such as an opportunity to tell his or her side of the story, to obtain psychological help, or to play a positive role in the ultimate outcome of the case. Successful interrogation outcome depends on maintaining a balance of the environmental, situational, and personality factors at play, while utilizing every available psychological technique and without compromising the legal integrity of the process.

SEE ALSO Criminal profiling; Ethical issues; Polygraphs; Profiling; Psychological profile.

Investigation, crime scene SEE
Crime scene investigation

Isoantibodies

Isoantibodies are antibodies (proteins that defend against foreign agents, such as bacteria) in **blood**.

Hemagglutination (clumping of red blood cells) reactions are used in the typing of blood. The presence or absence of antigens (a substance perceived as foreign to the body), designated A and B, located on the surface of red blood cells is determined by employing the use of specific antisera (antibodies). Since an individual possesses antibodies to the opposite **antigen**, when anti-A antiserum is mixed with type B red blood cells, no hemagglutination will occur. Similarly, persons of blood type A will have anti-B in their **serum**. Persons with type AB blood contain both A and B antigens on their red blood cells. Individuals with type O blood lack both A and B antigens, but they do have anti-A and anti-B in their serum.

ABO blood types are controlled by three alleles (versions of genes): IA and IB are co-dominant and both are dominant over the recessive i. The homozygous recessive condition (ii) results in type O blood. A person with blood type A may have either of the following genotypes: IAIA or IAi. The genotype IAIB results in type AB blood.

The Rh factor is a complex of over 30 different antigens on the surface of human red blood cells. The Rh factor that is routinely used in blood typing is the called the Rh, or D, antigen. The presence of the Rh factor is determined by a hemagglutination reaction between anti-Rh antiserum and red blood cells. Persons who have the Rh antigen are called Rh-positive. Rh-negative individuals do not naturally have anti-Rh in their sera.

Isoantibodies are present in human serum. An individual possesses isoantibodies to the opposite A or B isoantigen. For example, persons of blood type A will have serum containing isoantibodies to the B antigen. Rh-negative individuals do not normally have anti-Rh antibodies in their sera. When red blood cells with Rh antigen are introduced into Rh-negative individuals, anti-Rh-antibodies are produced.

In 1929, Kosaku Yosida established the existence of isoantibodies in body **fluids** other than blood (**saliva**, sinus secretions, etc.). By establishing the existence of serological isoantibodies in fluids other than blood, Yosida paved the way for far more sophistication in the forensic analysis of bodily fluids, along with the ability to use multiple means of **identification** of a single perpetrator of a crime.

SEE ALSO Antibody; Antigen; Secretor; Serology; Serum.

Isotopic analysis

Varieties of the same chemical element, but with different atomic weights, are called isotopes. Isotopic analysis (IA) is the analysis of the isotope composition of a sample. Samples in IA can contain almost anything: different objects of everyday life, pieces of rocks, pieces of wood, samples of tissue taken from a human body, chemical compounds, and so on. In general, IA is used for **identification** of a sample and for the determination of its age. Determining the age of an object can be important in a forensic examination, especially when examining human remains from cold cases, ancient sites, or mass graves. IA is based upon the use of mass spectrometers or radioactive radiation counters. A mass spectrometer is a device that determines the quantity and composition of different isotopes (of the same chemical element as well as various elements) in the sample.

The isotope composition of many objects is unique (relative to the composition itself as well as to the isotope concentrations), and because of this, isotopic analysis offers the possibility for identification of a sample. Isotopic analysis is also utilized in varying disciplines, including chemistry, **medicine**, biology, **geology**, archeology, and criminal forensics. Recently, isotopic analysis has seen use in the diagnosis of some diseases through analysis of air exhaled by the patient. Often, isotopic analysis permits the scientist to distinguish the genuine product from its imitation. For example, the technology is used to distinguish expensive types of wine and liquor from their imitations.

Isotopes can be both stable and radioactive. IA of radioactive isotopes permits scientists to determine the age of the investigated sample. Often the isotope ^{14}C is used for this purpose. This isotope itself is unstable and decays with time, and in the decay process, other stable isotopes are created. In nature, the concentration of ^{14}C is maintained because of cosmic radiation. While a tree lives, for example, the concentration of ^{14}C in its wood is equal to the ^{14}C concentration in the environment, because atoms of radioactive carbon penetrate the wood from the atmosphere with carbon dioxide (CO_2) molecules due to photosynthesis, and also through the tree root system. But when the tree dies, these exchange processes cease, and the ^{14}C concentration in the tree begins to decrease. The law of radioactive carbon concentration alteration in the sample is known, hence if its concentration is measured in the sample and compared with the concentration of the isotope in nature, the age of the tree itself can be determined (or more precisely, the time since the tree died). When the decay period of the radioisotope is considered, the age of the sample can be determined within an accuracy of several decades.

SEE ALSO Analytical instrumentation; Radiation damage to tissues.

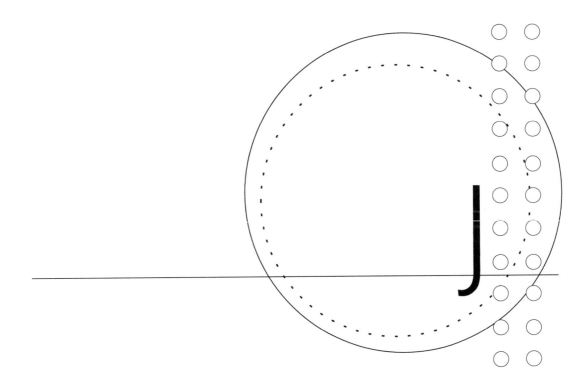

Jefferson, Thomas, paternity issue

Thomas Jefferson (1743–1836), the third president of the United States, has long been considered to have fathered children with Sally Hemings, one of his slaves. Slaveowners were notorious for taking sexual advantage of slaves and, if he did so, Jefferson would not have been unusual among the men of his time and place. A 1998 **DNA** test attempted to resolve the issue, but could not establish with certainty the paternity of Hemings' descendents.

Sally Hemings (1773–1835), one of Jefferson's slaves for most of her life and the probable sister of Jefferson's wife, gained notoriety when one of Jefferson's political opponents charged that she was also Jefferson's mistress. In 1787, Hemings accompanied Jefferson to Paris where he served as the U.S. minister to France. While in Paris, Hemings received a modest wage from Jefferson because the French did not permit slavery. Jefferson and Hemings returned to Virginia in 1789. Over the next two decades, Sally had six children, four of whom survived to adulthood. After Jefferson's death in 1826, his daughter Martha granted Hemings her freedom, and she lived with her sons Eston and Madison in Charlottesville, Virginia, until her death.

In 1802 Hemings became famous as the subject of a rumor promoted by a frustrated office seeker, James T. Callender. Angry because he had failed to secure a government appointment from Jefferson, Callender published a story in a Richmond, Virginia newspaper charging that Jefferson was the father of Hemings's children. Based upon gossip gathered in the neighborhood around Monticello, the story spread quickly as other newspapers reprinted the allegations. Although his friends and political associates denied the story and condemned Callender, Jefferson remained silent, unwilling to give further fuel to the controversy.

After a time, interest in the story flagged until Hemings's son Madison granted an interview in 1872 to an Ohio newspaper. Madison, who had been freed in Jefferson's will and subsequently moved to Ohio, contended that his mother became Jefferson's mistress while they were in France.

In 1998, Eugene Foster, a retired professor of **pathology** who taught at Tufts University and the University of Virginia, released the results of a study of Jefferson's DNA. Foster had decided to use DNA to resolve the Jefferson/Hemings controversy because historians had come to standstill with traditional sources.

Foster compared the Y-chromosomal DNA from the living male-line descendants of Jefferson and Hemings. He used Y-chromosomal DNA exclusively, because the Y-chromosomal DNA is passed unchanged from generation to generation, and is passed from father to son only. The rest of a person's DNA is diluted by at least half with every generation.

The DNA study was complicated by the shortage of male descendents. Thomas Jefferson did not have a son surviving long enough to reproduce, so it was necessary to locate the male-line descendants of Thomas Jefferson's paternal uncle, Field Jefferson.

DNA evidence is inconclusive whether Thomas Jefferson or one of his male relatives fathered the youngest son of his slave Sally Hemmings. THE NATIONAL PORTRAIT GALLERY/SMITHSONIAN INSTITUTION.

Five such descendants were found. Foster discovered three male-line descendants of Samuel and Peter Carr, the sons of Thomas Jefferson's sister, who also could have possibly been the fathers of Sally Hemings's children. Only male-line descendants of two of Sally Hemings' sons, Thomas Woodson (the oldest) and Eston Hemings (the youngest) were available. Madison Hemings had two sons who died without children and one who vanished into the western United States in the early twentieth century.

The DNA results showed that the five descendants of Field Jefferson have identical Y-chromosomal DNA alleles except for one microsatellite DNA. This difference is most reasonably accounted for by assuming that a mutation occurred. The descendant of Eston Hemings has the same set of Y-chromosomal DNA alleles as the descendants of Field Jefferson. The Carr descendants have similar DNA among them, but are clearly different from either the Jefferson or Hemings descendants. Four of the descendants of Thomas Woodson are quite similar among themselves, but different from Jefferson and Hemings although they do have similarities to the descendants of the Carr line. One of the Woodson descendants is quite different from all of the other individuals, which suggests that one of the genetic ancestors was not in the direct line from Thomas Woodson.

The DNA supports the claim that Thomas Jefferson could have been the father of Eston Hemings although it does not provide definitive proof, as the father could have been any male who had the same Y chromosome as Thomas Jefferson who was living in the Monticello region. Historical **evidence** implicates Randolph Jefferson, Thomas' brother, as the more likely father of Eston Hemings. With the paternity issue unresolved, the debate over Jefferson's relationship with Hemings continues, particularly among Hemings' descendents.

SEE ALSO DNA; DNA sequences, unique; STR (short tandem repeat) analysis.

Alec John Jeffreys

1/9/1950–
ENGLISH
GENETICIST

Alec John Jeffreys is a geneticist who is best known for the introduction of **DNA** analysis to **forensic science**. He discovered one of the most important tools for identifying human beings, genetic fingerprinting. This procedure analyzes each individual's **genetic code**. Each human being has about 100,000 genes in the chemical form of deoxyribonucleic acid (DNA). The genetic information coded in these genes—ranging from the color of hair to disorders such as hemophilia—varies greatly between individuals. No two humans, except for identical twins, have the same genetic code. Genetic fingerprinting has been used to catch criminals, establish paternity, and detect **gene** mutations.

Jeffreys was born in Oxford, England, to Sidney Victor and Joan Jeffreys. He attended Luton Grammar School and Luten Sixth Form College. Jeffreys went to Merton College in Oxford to study molecular biology, achieving a B.A. in 1972. He also earned an M.A. and D.Phil. at Merton in 1975.

At the University of Amsterdam, Jeffreys worked with Richard Flavell, another British molecular biologist, studying mammalian globin genes. From there, Jeffreys moved to the University of Leicester, where he made his most important contribution to science, discovering the unique genetic fingerprint in 1984. He found that the number of times sequences in DNA repeated seemed to vary from individual to individual, and that these repeated segments of genes were unique to each individual—just like a fingerprint.

Jeffreys devised a way to capture the distinctive fingerprint of each person's repeated fragments in an x ray. By taking x rays, Jeffreys could see the repeated segments of DNA as black images on film. He had, in essence, created the first **DNA fingerprint**.

In 1988, scientist **Henry Erlich** added to Jeffreys's work when he developed a method of DNA fingerprinting so sensitive that it could be used to identify an individual from an extremely small sample of hair, **blood**, **semen**, or skin. Erlich's technique used Jeffreys's traditional method and combined it with a technique called **polymerase chain reaction** (**PCR**), which was used to duplicate DNA and thus copy the genetic code. PCR multiplied the DNA from one single hair to an amount equivalent to that found in a million identical strands of hair. The amplified DNA was then used to obtain a DNA fingerprint.

Jeffreys continued to work in the field of genetic fingerprinting. In a famous 1989 **murder** case in Cardiff, England, PCR was combined with Jeffreys' traditional technique to extract and identify DNA from a miniscule amount of bone. A sample of bone from a skeleton found at an old house in Cardiff was sent to Erika Hagelberg, a scientist at the Oxford Institute of Molecular Medicine. Working with Jeffreys, Hagelberg found that the sample of bone had been in the ground so long and disintegrated so much that PCR could not generate the necessary lengths of DNA required for a fingerprint. So a different form of genetic fingerprinting had to be developed.

Working with Jeffreys, Hagelberg was able to find repeating DNA sequences other than the large ones usually present in a genetic fingerprint. They were finally able to show that the probability that the skeleton was Karen Price, a 15-year-old girl, was 99.9%. Two of Karen's acquaintances, Idris Ali and Alan Charlton, were put on trial for murder. It was the strength of the genetic **evidence** that finally sent them to prison, in Ali's case, for life.

At about the same time, Hagelberg and Jeffreys had been working on the new type of PCR typing to determine the identity of one of the most notorious war criminals of World War II, Josef Mengele. Known as the "Angel of Death" at Auschwitz, he sent thousands of Jews to the gas chambers as well as making thousands the subjects of medical research.

When the Soviets liberated Auschwitz in 1945, Mengele fled to South America. He was finally traced to a grave in southern Brazil in 1985. A sample of bone was sent to Jeffreys and, working with Hagelberg, he was able to identify a tiny amount of Mengele's DNA from the sample, which had been in the ground for six years.

The process of genetic fingerprinting can take as long as four to six weeks in a commercial laboratory today. Jeffreys made scientific history again in 1991 when he announced the development of a refined version of the test, allowing results to be obtained in as little as two days.

Jeffreys' technique of genetic fingerprinting has been used in a wide variety of ways, including to solve crimes like rape and murder, to identify the remains of soldiers, to identify people killed in Argentina by the military junta in the 1980s, and by biologists to protect endangered species. In a landmark study, Jeffreys and other researchers used the technique to assess the gene mutations apparent in children whose families had been exposed to radiation during the 1986 Chernobyl meltdown in the Ukraine.

Jeffreys is an international biomedical research scholar at the Howard Hughes Medical Institute, as well as working at the University of Leicester. Besides winning the Davy Medal from the Royal Society in 1987 and the Analytica Prize from the German Society of Chemistry in 1988, he became Wolfson Research Professor of the Royal Society in 1991.

In 2004 Jeffreys was awarded the Royal Society's Royal Medal "for his outstanding discoveries and inventions which have had major impacts on large areas of genetics. He is best known for the introduction of DNA analysis to forensic science, contributing not only the theoretical framework for application, but also the experimental method."

Jeffreys married Susan Miles in 1971. They have two daughters. His leisure interests include walking, swimming, postal history, and reading "unimproving novels."

SEE ALSO DNA fingerprint; DNA sequences, unique; PCR (polymerase chain reaction).

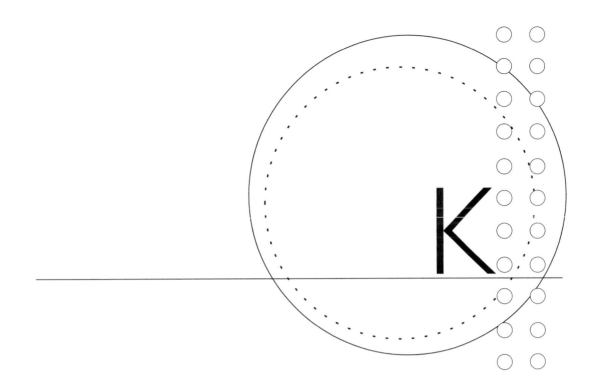

Kentaro Kasai

JAPANESE
FORENSIC SCIENTIST

Kentaro Kasai is a forensic scientist working in Japan who, in 1990, published the first scholarly paper proposing the use of the D1S80 locus (specific location on a **chromosome**) for forensic **DNA** analysis.

Every human somatic cell nucleus contains approximately 6.4 billion base pairs of DNA. Portions of that DNA encode more than 100,000 genes, the remainder of the DNA is non-coding. In the universe of humans, virtually 99.9% of all DNA is identical among all people, however, the remaining 0.1% makes critical distinctions, and allows for individual DNA typing. The scientific analysis of DNA, and the **forensic science** of **DNA profiling**, focuses on the highly variable regions of DNA. One form of that DNA variability is referred to as variable number of tandem repeats (VNTR).

Kentaro Kasai chose to focus his DNA analysis research on a variable number of tandem repeats locus labeled D1S80. D1S80 is located on human chromosome 1. It is composed of repeating units of 16 nucleotide long segments of DNA. The number of repeats can range from 15 to more than 40, depending upon the individual.

The D1S80 locus has been subjected to a variety of scientific tests in order to determine its specificity, reliability, and validity for use as a genetic identifying marker in criminal investigation and forensic science **identification**. Ethnically different samples have been used for validation (Native American, African American, and European American or Caucasian), using tissue and **serology** samples similar to those used in forensic settings: vaginal secretions, **saliva**, **semen**, **blood**, and hair, in order to ascertain whether there was uniformity of results across sample types within an individual. When the specimens were typed, there were found to be consistent and reliable results within each individual. The samples were each run twice, and also were sent to different (independent) labs for analysis. All typing results, from both laboratories, for each individual, were exactly the same. This is indicative of extreme reliability and validity of the D1S80 locus as a forensic science marker for individual identification.

The D1S80 locus was also tested for reliability through the use of restriction fragment length polymorphisms (**RFLP**) used as markers on genetic linkage maps, and through the use of polymerase chain reaction- (PCR-) based tests. In every analysis, the D1S80 locus has been proven to be a highly sensitive, reliable, and accurate marker for individual genetic (DNA) identification.

Through his pioneering the use of the D1S80 locus in DNA analysis, Kentaro Kasai has made an important and lasting contribution to the world of forensic science.

SEE ALSO DNA; DNA fingerprint; Mitochondrial DNA typing.

Sidney Kaye
AMERICAN TOXICOLOGIST

With a career that began in the 1930s, Sidney Kaye has worked both as a toxicologist and an educator. He is the founder of four major forensic laboratories, and a co-founder of the **American Academy of Forensic Sciences**. Kaye also has worked as a professor of pharmacology, **pathology**, **toxicology**, and forensic **medicine** at four major universities. In addition, he has written more than 120 articles for **professional publications**, and is the author of several books, including the popular *Handbook of Emergency Toxicology*.

Kaye grew up in New York City, and attended New York University, earning a bachelor's degree in chemistry in 1935 and a master's degree in toxicology in 1939. He then began his thirty-year involvement with the United States military, first, in 1941, as a toxicologist in the Army, and later as a toxicology consultant for the Army, Air Force, and Navy. Kaye also went back to school, earning a doctorate in pharmacology from the Medical College of Virginia in 1956.

While working as a toxicologist, Kaye was responsible for the founding and management of four major forensic laboratories. The first, in 1942, was the toxicology section of the Medical Laboratory of the U.S. Army, Antilles department. Later, in 1945, Kaye founded the St. Louis Police Laboratory, and in 1947, the toxicology laboratories of the Chief Medical Examiner's Office of Virginia. In 1962, he founded the toxicology laboratories of the Institute of Forensic Medicine at the University of Puerto Rico. In addition, Kaye was on the steering committee that was responsible for creating the American Academy of Forensic Sciences, one of the largest **forensic science** organizations in the world.

Kaye's involvement in forensic science extends beyond his contributions as a toxicologist. He has also worked for more than forty years as an educator, instructing hundreds of students in the theory and practice of analytical and forensic toxicology. His academic career led him to faculty posts at Washington University School of Medicine, the Medical College of Virginia, the University of Virginia School of Medicine, and the University of Puerto Rico Schools of Medicine and Public Health. Kaye is also the author of numerous articles for scientific publications, and is perhaps best known as the author of the *Handbook of Emergency Toxicology*, a widely used guide that instructs on the identification, diagnosis, and treatment of poisoning. The book's fifth edition was printed in 1988.

SEE ALSO Careers in forensic science; Toxicological analysis.

Leonard Keeler
AMERICAN POLYGRAPH EXPERT

American scientist Leonard Keeler is widely considered the developer of the polygraph machine. He, along with Berkeley police officer John Larson, was responsible for creating and using the modern version of the polygraph in the 1930s. Although there were minor changes to Keeler's machine since its advent, the basic composition and functions of the machine remained the same until the creation of the computerized polygraph in 1994.

Movement toward the creation of a machine to detect whether a suspect was telling the truth began in earnest around the turn of the twentieth century. In 1885, Cesar Lombroso began measuring the blood pressure of **murder** suspects. In 1914, two different methods of detecting truth were put into practice—one measured a person's breathing, and one measured the amount of a person's sweat. But it wasn't until the 1930s that work by Keeler and Larson produced what is considered the modern polygraph machine—one that records changes in blood pressure, pulse, respiration, and perspiration as an administrator asks the subject a series of questions. The machine then produces a four-line graph that is analyzed for fluctuations. Keeler, in particular, was responsible for adding a galvanometer to the machine, which measured the skin's electrical resistance. In 1948 Keeler began the first polygraph school, which instructed students on how to conduct and analyze the results of a polygraph test.

As a result of his invention, Keeler began to conduct polygraph tests for law enforcement officials across the country. Keeler used the polygraph on suspect Dr. Frank Sweeney in the Ohio serial murder case known as "The Mad Butcher." In that case he worked closely with well-known detective Eliot Ness. Keeler also tested suspects in the high-profile Colorado murder case of college student Theresa Foster in 1948. Keeler's role in **forensic science** was even documented in the 1948 film *Call Northside 777*. The movie is based on the true story of Chicago journalists James McGuire and Jack McPaul, whose series of articles in 1944 and 1945 shed light on the questionable conviction of Joe Majczek for the murder of a police officer in 1932. Keeler, who was involved in the Majczek case, played himself.

SEE ALSO Film (forensic science in cinema); Polygraph, case histories.

Kennedy assassination

On November 22, 1963, John F. Kennedy, the thirty-fifth president of the United States, was shot and killed while riding in the back seat of a limousine in a motorcade passing through Dealey Plaza in Dallas, Texas. The shooting occurred at 12:30 p.m. Central Standard Time, just after the president's limousine made a 120-degree left-hand turn off of Houston Street onto Elm Street in front of the Texas Schoolbook Depository. Also injured was Texas governor John B. Connally, who was riding in the limousine's front seat directly in front of the president.

The shooting took place over a period of six to nine seconds. Only after the driver of the limousine, Secret Service agent Bill Greer, turned and saw what proved to be the fatal wound to the president's head did he speed up to exit the plaza and head to Parkland Memorial Hospital, where the president was pronounced dead in Trauma Room #1 at 1:00 p.m. Just an hour later, after a fifteen-minute argument involving Secret Service agents who were cursing and brandishing their weapons, the agents removed the president's body, in violation of state law because no forensic examination had been conducted. They took the body to Love Field, where it was placed on Air Force One, the president's plane, and flown to Washington, D.C. There, an **autopsy** was conducted at the Bethesda Naval Hospital.

Eighty minutes after the **assassination**, Lee Harvey Oswald, an employee at the Texas Schoolbook Depository, was arrested for shooting a police officer. That evening he was charged with the **murder** of the president, but he was never tried for the crime because just two days later, while in police custody, Oswald was shot and killed by Jack Ruby. On November 29, a week after the assassination, President Lyndon B. Johnson formed a commission headed by Earl Warren, chief justice of the U.S. Supreme Court, to investigate the assassination. In September 1964, the Warren Commission issued its report, concluding that Lee Harvey Oswald, acting alone, was the assassin. The commission further concluded that Oswald fired three shots from a window on the sixth floor of the book depository, where three shell casings and the rifle were found; that one shot likely missed the motorcade; that the first shot to hit Kennedy likely hit him in the upper back and exited near the front of his neck, then caused Governor Connally's injuries; and that the second shot to hit the president struck him in the head. All three shots, the commission concluded, came from the same location, above and behind the president.

In the decades following the assassination, the forensic **evidence** was examined and reexamined by numerous experts, many of whom disputed the Warren Commission findings. They raised troubling questions, many of them focusing on the "grassy knoll," a small sloping hill in front of and slightly to the right (west and north) of the president. Numerous witnesses claim to have heard at least one shot come from the grassy knoll, and photographs taken by people in Dealey Plaza that day give some credence to the claim that another gunman was positioned behind a picket fence on the knoll. These claims appear to have been substantiated by the report of the 1976–79 House Select Committee on Assassinations (HSCA), which relied on acoustical evidence to conclude that indeed a shot came from the grassy knoll, that Oswald did not act alone, and that he was likely part of a larger conspiracy, although the reach and extent of that conspiracy remain the subject of passionate debate.

A major focus for forensic examiners was the number, sequence, timing, and direction of the fatal shots. Connally sustained his injuries virtually simultaneously with Kennedy having been struck in the neck, raising the question of whether one or two bullets, and hence one or two shooters, caused the injuries to the two men. Standing at the center of the Warren Commission's conclusion that Oswald was the lone gunman is the so-called single bullet theory, a theory generally credited to commission member Arlen Specter, later a U.S. Senator. According to the commission, a single 6.5 mm Western Case Cartridge Company bullet, Warren Commission Exhibit 399, caused all of the nonfatal wounds both to Kennedy and, an instant later, to Connally. The single bullet theory was crucial to the commission's conclusion because it precluded the existence of another shooter. Oswald was using a bolt-action rifle, so it would have been impossible for him to fire two shots virtually simultaneously. Two bullets would have meant two gunmen.

The bullet in question was found in Parkland Hospital Trauma Room #2 on a stretcher on which Governor Connally had lain, although even this detail has been disputed. The path the bullet followed was complex, leading critics of the Warren Commission to refer to it not as the single bullet, but as the magic bullet. The commission concluded that it traveled downward at a net angle of 25 degrees and entered the president's back 2 inches (50 mm) to the right of his spine and 5.75 inches (146 mm) below his collar line, leaving a small (4x7 mm) reddish-brown to black abrasion on his collar that suggested that the bullet was traveling slightly upward when it entered his body. It then slightly fractured the sixth cervical vertebra; passed through his neck, shedding fragments; passed through his throat; and exited his body at the bottom edge of the Adam's apple. The bullet then continued on its course, entering Connally's back just below and behind his right armpit. It destroyed a portion of his right fifth rib, exited his body below his right nipple, then entered the outside of his right wrist, possibly striking his cufflink, which was never recovered. It broke his right radius wrist bone, leaving behind metal fragments, then exited the inner side of the wrist, entered the front side of his left thigh, and buried itself 2 inches (50 mm) in his thigh muscle, leaving behind a tiny (1.5–2 mm) fragment in his thigh bone. This bullet, which had passed through several layers of clothing and flesh and struck two bones, was found in nearly pristine condition, having lost only about 1.5 percent of its weight, after having apparently backed itself out of Connally's thigh.

In **ballistics** tests conducted with the same type of bullet, the only bullet that survived in a condition similar to the bullet in evidence was one fired into a tube of cotton. These tests, combined with the zigzagging course that the bullet would have had to follow, have led some forensics experts to dispute the single bullet theory, though many others note that a bullet can behave in strange ways when it hits its target and rapidly decelerates. Further, some forensic pathologists assert that the official medical record, both at Parkland and at Bethesda, is a record of inconsistencies, in large part because it was based on testimony not from forensic pathologists with experience examining gunshot wounds, but by emergency room physicians at Parkland and general pathologists at Bethesda. They note, for example, that at least three times the emergency room doctors referred to the wound in Kennedy's neck as an entrance wound rather than an exit wound. Numerous other details

Cartridge case found on 6th floor of the Texas School Book Depository after the assassination of President John F. Kennedy. Included as an exhibit for the Warren Commission. © CORBIS

have been scrutinized, such as the path the bullet followed from Kennedy's back to his throat. Following this path, the bullet would have had to hit the president's spine, severely deforming the bullet. They note too that it was traveling upward when it exited the president's throat, but then downward when it entered Connally's body. Further, they note inconsistencies in testimony about where the bullet entered the president's back.

Forensic pathologists have also focused on the second, fatal bullet to the president's head. Their primary purpose was to determine the direction of the bullet and the angle at which it entered the president's head. Normally, a forensic pathologist relies on the beveling of bone, similar to the appearance of glass when a BB has passed through it, to confirm the direction of a bullet when it passes through bone. During the president's autopsy, pathologists had to reconstruct **skull** fragments, at least one of which is missing, to show that the beveling of the bone establishes that the bullet entered from above and behind, consistent with the conclusion at which the Warren Commission ultimately arrived.

One difficulty that forensics experts faced was reconciling this conclusion with the movement of the president's head and body captured on the so-called Zapruder film, a 26.6-second, 486-frame, 8 mm film shot by amateur cameraman Abraham Zapruder from Elm Street as the shots were fired. A frame-by-frame analysis of the Zapruder film suggests that when the president was struck by the first bullet, he was sitting

President John F. Kennedy slumps over after being hit by an assassin's bullet as the Presidential motorcade made its way through Dallas, Texas on November 22, 1963. © BETTMANN/CORBIS

in a position inconsistent with the bullet's supposed angle of entry (he would have had to have been leaning forward, but the film shows him sitting bolt upright). More significantly, the film suggests that when the second bullet hit him, the president was forced backward in a way more consistent with a shot from in front, not above and behind. Specifically, they note that when the bullet struck, the president's head moved slightly, about 1–2 inches (25–50 mm) forward and down. Then, as the wound in his head opened, his right shoulder twisted forward and up. Kennedy's torso then lurched quickly backward and to his left. He then bounced off the rear seat cushion and slumped lifelessly. If the autopsy findings and the Zapruder film are indeed inconsistent, this inconsistency raises for some the possibility that the source of the bullet was not Oswald's rifle on the sixth floor of the book depository, but elsewhere. For others, such an inconsistency represents unanswerable questions that may have arisen because of acceleration and deceleration of the limousine.

A sizable majority of Americans accept the crux of the Warren Commission's findings and regard inconsistencies as inevitable human error. Debate about these and other details suggest the monumental difficulty of establishing a clear, accurate, consistent forensic record of a crime that took place in front of hundreds of witnesses.

SEE ALSO Autopsy; Ballistics; Bullet track.

Kennewick Man

The remains of an ancient human found along a river in Kennewick, Washington, in 1996 set off a heated debate about the ownership and future of the skeleton. Scientists argued that the skeleton, dubbed Kennewick Man, could provide new information about human migration in North America, while Native Americans claimed him as an ancestor and wanted to bury him according to their rites. Forensic anthropological findings and cultural **evidence** were presented in court procedures over the course of nine years while the fate of the Kennewick Man was debated.

The story of Kennewick Man began in July 1996, when two college students watching hydroplane races found a human skeleton along the Columbia River. The young men turned the remains over to local police, who realized that they were probably very old. The bones were then given to forensic anthropologist James Chatters for evaluation. Chatters reconstructed the skeleton, which was 80–90% complete. He determined that it was from a man who was probably five feet nine or 10 inches and about 40–50 years old when he died. He showed little evidence of arthritis, indicating that he wasn't used to carrying heavy weights and that he might have been a wandering hunter. Dental examinations showed that the **skull** contained 30 of the 32 teeth and that they were in good shape, indicating that he probably had a diet that included lots of soft foods like meat. He was taller and thinner than most ancient Native Americans and the back of his skull was not flattened from a cradleboard as is commonly observed in skeletons of ancient Native Americans. In addition, the man had a stone spear point lodged in his pelvis and there was evidence of severe trauma to his rib cage that probably limited the use of his arm. Using computerized tomography (CT), Chatters determined that the spear point was serrated and leaf-shaped and typical of the types of spears used between 8500–4500 years ago. He hypothesized that the skeleton was either from a European pioneer who had been attacked by native people using stone-age weapons or from an ancient human. Chatters sent pieces of the bones to a laboratory for carbon dating, which determined that the age of the skeleton was between 9,200–9,400 years old, making the skeleton one of the oldest, and most complete, ever found in North America.

Once the age of the skeleton was determined, several groups came forward, vying for control of the remains. A group of five Native American tribes in the region, the Umatilla, the Yakama, the Nez Perce, the Wanapum, and the Colville, wanted to accord the remains the same rites given to any Native American, namely a speedy burial. They cited the legal authority of the Native American Graves and Repatriation Act (NAGRA), which requires the return of American Indian remains to tribes. As news of the unique find spread throughout the scientific community, a coalition of eight anthropologists and archaeologists petitioned for their right to study the ancient remains prior to burial. The scientists believed that study of the Kennewick Man could reveal important information about early human migrations into North America. The Native American group believed that any manipulation of the remains would show enormous disrespect to the dead and vehemently opposed scientific investigation of the skeleton, which they called the Ancient One. Because some of the features of the Kennewick Man, such as his height and the shape of his skull, indicated that he might not be of Native American ancestry but rather of European descent, a group of people representing the ancient Norse religion called Asatru also petitioned the court for the right to the remains.

The ensuing legal battle raged for more than nine years. One of the key questions of debate in the courts concerned whether or not the skeleton was subject to NAGRA. NAGRA requires that all Native American remains be returned to the tribe for burial, however it was unclear if the Kennewick man was of Native American ancestry. Eventually the court ruled that some scientific study was required in order to establish the origin of the skeleton and between 1998 and 2000, the Department of the Interior coordinated these studies. A 1999 physical examination of the bones established that the Kennewick Man shared most physical characteristics with people from Southern Asia. In April 2000, samples of bone from the Kennewick Man's skeleton were removed and sent to two different laboratories for **DNA** testing. Because of the age of the bones, it was impossible to extract sufficient DNA for analysis and the results of the study were inconclusive. After a series of appeals by all sides, in February 2004, a U.S. Federal judge ruled that it was impossible to prove that the Kennewick Man's ancestry was culturally affiliated to any of the Native American tribes in the region and gave scientists the right to go forward with their investigation. In 2005, plans were outlined for study three-phase study involving as many as 23 different scientists.

SEE ALSO Anthropology; Anthropometry; Mitochondrial DNA analysis; Odontology; Skull.

Kidd blood grouping system

Bloodstains left behind at the scene of a crime or found on a suspect's clothing can be a valuable source of **identification**. Red **blood** cells contain a number of proteins known as antigens on their surface. The exact biochemical nature of these antigens is inherited and so varies from person to person. An individual's blood can be typed according to several different classes of **antigen**. One of these is the Kidd system, which was discovered in 1951.

There are three major Kidd blood groups, depending on which combination of variants of a protein called Jk a person has on their red blood cells. The two variants of Jk are called Jk^a and Jk^b. The combinations are $Jk^a Jk^a$, $Jk^a Jk^b$, and $Jk^b Jk^b$. Blood from people in the first group may contain antibodies against Jk^b and that from those in the third group may contain antibodies against Jk^a. An **antibody** is a protein component of the **immune system**, which binds to a relevant antigen and plays a part in destroying foreign cells or bacteria. In blood transfusion, the first and third Kidd types would be incompatible, because antibodies from one blood type would bind to the matching antigen on the other blood type and the cells would clump together.

Antisera, that is, reference blood samples containing a specific type of antibody, are used to find out the type of blood present in a blood stain. They react with antigens and cause a clumping reaction that is measured by various techniques. In the case of Kidd blood typing, an antiserum containing Jk^a antibodies would bind to Kidd types containing Jk^b antibodies. The first blood type system identified was the ABO system, where people have one of four types of blood: A, B, AB, or O, depending on which combination of genes affecting these antigens they inherit.

Besides Kidd and ABO, other blood typing systems include Rhesus, MNS, Kelly, Duffy, and Lewis. They are all inherited independently. Therefore someone with blood group O could have any of the three different Kidd types. The more blood types that can be co-analyzed on one sample, the more individualizing it becomes as **evidence**. Coincidental matches of blood found at the scene of a crime with that associated with a suspect become less likely with the number of typing reactions carried out. However, the amount of blood present in a stain may limit the number of typing determinations that can be done. Forensic blood typing is perhaps most useful for eliminating a suspect than, on its own at least, identifying one.

SEE ALSO Serology.

Paul Leland Kirk

1902–6/5/1970
AMERICAN
CRIMINOLOGIST

Paul Leland Kirk is a leader in establishing **criminology** as an academic discipline. He worked as a professor at the University of California, Berkeley (UCB), for forty-three years, making advances to the university's program and conducting important research in the field. Kirk also wrote the groundbreaking textbook *Crime Investigation*. In addition, he consulted on many criminal cases, including the well-known murder trial of Sam Sheppard.

Early on, Kirk became known for his work as a microchemist. He found microchemistry had practical applications in two areas—tissue **culture** studies and **criminalistics**. Through his work at UCB, Kirk began to develop a more structured and scientific approach to the study of criminalistics. As a result, in 1937, he was selected to head the criminology program at the university. Eight years later, he established a major in technical criminology. Then, in 1950, he worked with Berkeley police chief **August Vollmer** to formally establish the school of criminology at UCB. He later advised other institutions about establishing their own programs. Kirk also worked with C. R. Kingston analyzing the statistical aspect of **fingerprint identification**.

In addition to his work in academia, Kirk was actively involved in providing professional consultation on criminal cases. Among other areas of expertise, he became known for his skill in **blood spatter** analysis. This knowledge came into play as Kirk became involved in the famous case in 1954 of Dr. Sam Sheppard, an Ohio osteopathic surgeon accused of murdering his wife. Sheppard was tried and convicted of the crime. Afterward, Kirk was summoned to investigate the crime scene, and through detailed analysis of the **blood** spatters, concluded that Sheppard could not have committed the crime. During Sheppard's retrial, Kirk's testimony became key to the defense. In the end, Sheppard was acquitted of the crime. His story was used as the basis for the popular television series and motion picture *The Fugitive*.

Kirk is also known for his contributions to literature on criminology. In 1953, he published *Crime Investigation*, one of the first **crime scene investigation** books to include both practical information and theory. Here Kirk presents techniques for examining **physical evidence** at crime scenes, including chapters on fingerprints, **fibers**, hair, blood, tracks and trails, **firearms**,

Jack the Ripper's knife and a framed drawing of one of his victims. © ALEN MACWEENEY/CORBIS

and vehicular accidents. Because of its popularity, the book has since been reprinted many times.

SEE ALSO Crime scene reconstruction; Television shows.

Knife wounds

When investigating an assault or **murder**, the pattern of injuries to a victim can provide clues as to the nature of the weapon used. For example, the angle of a gunshot wound and the deposition pattern of the **gunshot residue** can be valuable to a forensic investigator in determining the location from which the gun was fired. Similarly, for knife wounds, the pattern of injury can be a clue to the knife that was responsible.

The pattern of a knife injury can also be a clue to the nature of an attack. For example, a slashing motion can inflict long but superficial cuts, whereas a jab can produce a deep **puncture wound**. A forensic investigator may be able to gauge the timing of the blows, to determine which of the blows may have dispatched the victim.

Because a knife can retain some of the victim's **blood** (and even that of the assailant), and because the knife needs to be held to be effective, a knife can be a storehouse of forensic information. Blood types, skin cells that house **DNA**, and fingerprints may all be present on a knife recovered at a crime or accident scene.

Knives come in all shapes and sizes. At the extremely small end of the scale, for example, are thumb knives, lapel daggers, and coin knives. Developed by the British in World War II, the coin knife looks like an ordinary piece of pocket change. The blade itself is crescent-shaped, and attaches to the back by a small hasp so that it can rotate outward. It is too blunt to be used for inflicting grievous bodily harm.

Knives and daggers have been concealed in belts (that is, on the inside of the belt and parallel to it), in belt buckles, and even in the plastic arms of eyeglasses. But, when the aim is to attack someone, a large knife is desirable. Domestically, kitchen knives often become the preferred choice.

Most formidable-looking of all is the Fairbairn-Sykes fighting knife, developed in World War II by two British officers, W. E. Fairbairn and E. A. Sykes. Based on knowledge gained from their experience in close combat while serving with the Shanghai police, the knife would quickly dispatch a victim by striking at his vital organs. Its blade was long, but the handle was nearly as lengthy, so as to ensure great control on the part of the user. First produced in 1941, it was readily adopted by Allied forces. British commandoes carried it on raids into Norway, and the United States Office of Strategic Services (OSS), which employed Fairbairn as an instructor, developed its own version. Revised over the years, the knife remained in production through the 1990s.

SEE ALSO Crime scene investigation; Death, cause of; Puncture wound; Wound assessment.

Knots and ligatures

Ligatures are materials such as ropes or wire that are used to tie or bind; they have various roles in criminal acts. Knots and ligatures may be used are used to bind, restrain, strangle, or hang victims. Their analysis is a specialized branch of **forensic science**.

A ligature is an important form of **physical evidence**. Ligatures can be made from rope, electric flex, nylon, clothing, bedsheets, chains, dog leads, washing lines, luggage straps, or various other objects. The perpetrator may come prepared, armed with rope perhaps, or may use what is at hand. However, an assailant may carry traces of the ligature material away, and this can be used, if his clothing is examined, to link him with the scene of the crime. Ligature materials are class **evidence**, able to link a suspect to a type of material, rather than individualizing evidence, which can link a suspect to a particular portion of material.

A ligature is generally used by making a knot within the material. There are several different types of knot that can be identified by the forensic expert, such as slipknots, reef knots, and overhand knots. This may be revealing of certain characteristics of the person who tied it, such as knot-tying skill, trade, and hobbies.

Like the ligature from which it is made, the knot is an important item of physical evidence. When found at the scene of the crime, it must first be carefully photographed. When handled, the utmost care must be taken not to actually untie it. If a victim has been tied, then it will have to be removed, but will be photographed as this is happening. When it is cut away, the ligature is severed in a direction away from the knot so as better to preserve it. Great care has to be taken in handling loose knots so they do not disintegrate. Knots made in wire may be obscured by dirt or mud, but their intricacies can be revealed by fluoroscopy or x-ray analysis. The knot itself may bear important evidence such as fingerprints or hairs and this should be collected before the knot itself is removed.

Knot and ligature analysis may be especially important in the investigation of cases of strangulation, which are often homicide. The ligature is gradually tightened around the neck until compression on the airways and blood vessels in the neck produces asphyxia, where oxygen supplies to the body and brain are cut off. The mark on the neck in such cases tends to reflect the material used for the ligature. If wire or thin cord was used, there will be a clear-cut, deep mark with sharply defined edges. If a soft fabric is pulled tight around the neck, it will tend to fold up into a series of ridges that will show up as interlacing areas of bruising. Sometimes the mark reproduces the pattern of the ligature, such as a weave mark whose width may suggest its size. Sometimes the ligature is left on the neck and, if so, the position of any knots gives the investigator a good idea of where the attacker was relative to the victim.

SEE ALSO Asphyxiation (signs of); Hanging (signs of).

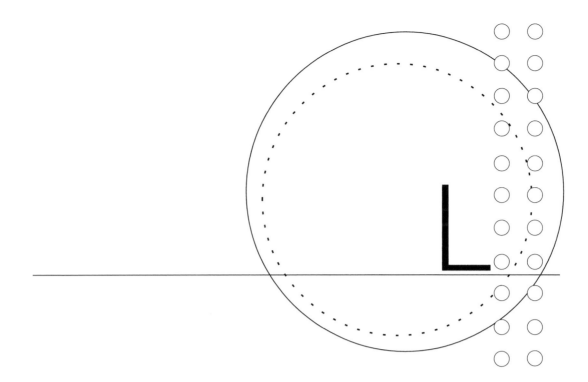

Alexandre Lacassagne

1844–1921
FRENCH
FORENSIC SCIENTIST

Alexandre Lacassagne devoted his life to the study, teaching, and advancement of **forensic science**. He worked for decades as a professor at the University of Lyons, France, participated in numerous forensic investigations, and served as a consultant and expert at many criminal trials. Lacassagne is also known as one of the first people known to conduct blood-stain pattern analysis and was the first scientist to study bullet markings and their relation to specific weapons.

For much of his life, Lacassagne worked as a professor of forensic **medicine** at the University of Lyons, France. Many up and coming forensic scientists had the opportunity to study under him, including Edmund Locard, the founder of the world's first forensic laboratory. At the same time, Lacassagne regularly participated in forensic investigations for crimes committed across the country. Along with forensic investigation, he also served as a consultant and expert in many high profile criminal trials in France. He played a significant role in the 1895 trial of Joseph Vacher, a man charged with the rape and **murder** of a local woman. At the trial Lacassagne testified that Vacher's behavior didn't indicate insanity but antisocial sadism, a concept not used previously in French courts. Vacher was found guilty of the crime.

Lacassagne is also known as being the first scientist to try to match an individual bullet to a gun barrel. He did this by examining the bullet's striations, counting and comparing the number of lands and grooves. In 1889, Lacassagne published the article *La Deformation des Balles de Revolver*, in the *Archive de Antropologie Criminelle et des Sciences Penales*, outlining his findings regarding bullet markings. While he didn't come up with a system to classify these markings, Lacassagne's research and study is considered the beginning of the science of **ballistics**.

Lacassagne also was one of the first scientists to study and report on the significance of bloodstains left at a crime scene, and what they could indicate about the nature of the crime committed. In particular, he conducted research on the relation between the shape of **blood** spots and the position of the victim.

SEE ALSO Ballistic fingerprints; Bloodstain evidence.

Karl Landsteiner

6/14/1868–6/26/1943
AUSTRIAN
IMMUNOLOGIST

Karl Landsteiner was one of the first scientists to study the physical processes of immunity. In the field of **forensic science**, he is best known for his **identification** and characterization of the human blood groups, A, B, and O, but his contributions spanned many areas of immunology, bacteriology, and **pathology** over a prolific 40-year career. He helped establish the science of immunochemistry.

Karl Landsteiner was born in Vienna on June 14, 1868. In 1891, he was awarded a medical degree by the University of Vienna. For the following five years he studied physiological chemistry in laboratories in Germany and Switzerland.

Landsteiner moved to Vienna's Institute of Pathology in 1897, where he was hired to perform autopsies. He continued to study immunology and the mysteries of blood on his own time. In 1900, Landsteiner wrote a paper in which he described the agglutination of blood that occurs when one person's blood is brought into contact with that of another. He suggested that the phenomenon was not due to pathology, as was the prevalent thought at the time, but was due to the unique nature of the individual's blood. In 1901, Landsteiner demonstrated that the blood **serum** of some people could clump the blood of others. From his observations he devised the idea of mutually incompatible blood groups. He placed blood types into three groups: A, B, and C (later referred to as O). Two of his colleagues subsequently added a fourth group, AB. In 1930 he received the Nobel Prize for medicine for his discovery.

In 1907, the first successful transfusions were achieved by Dr. Reuben Ottenberg of Mt. Sinai Hospital, New York, guided by Landsteiner's work. Landsteiner's accomplishment saved many lives on the battlefields of World War I, where transfusion of compatible blood was first performed on a large scale. In 1902, Landsteiner was appointed as a full member of the Imperial Society of Physicians in Vienna. That same year he presented a lecture, together with Max Richter of the Vienna University Institute of Forensic Medicine, in which the two reported a new method of typing dried blood stains to help solve crimes in which bloodstains are left at the scene.

In 1906, Landsteiner and Victor Mucha introduced the use of the dark-field method of diagnosis for the presence of the spirochete of syphilis. Landsteiner also determined the viral cause of poliomyelitis with research that laid the foundation for the eventual development of a polio vaccine. In 1908, Landsteiner reported the transmittal of poliomyelitis to monkeys from human material, thus substantiating the theory that the cause of the disease was a virus. In 1919, he went from his work as professor of pathologic anatomy at the University of Vienna to The Hague in

the Netherlands as pathologist at the R. K. Ziekenhuis. In 1922, he went to New York City's Rockefeller Institute and continued at the institute until his death. In 1929, he became a citizen of the United States.

In 1927, Landsteiner and **Philip Levine** announced the discovery of the M and N agglutinogens, and in 1940, Landsteiner and a colleague discovered still another group of agglutinogens called the Rh factors. Of fundamental importance to the rise of immunochemistry was Landsteiner's demonstration that serological specificity is based on the chemical structure of antigens. Although he officially retired in 1939, Landsteiner continued his work in immunology until two days before his death in 1943, at the age of 75.

SEE ALSO Antigen; Blood; Bloodstain evidence; Immune system.

Laser

Laser technologies are used for a wide range of purposes in laser-based products, including CD players, **DNA** screening machines, forensic tools, missile guiding devices, mapping and topographic instruments, and surgical devices. A laser is basically an intense beam of light. Ordinary light is scattered in variable wavelengths and frequencies, whereas laser beams are highly organized light with all photons traveling in the same frequency and wavelength. Laser (or light amplification by stimulated emission radiation) is a technology that allows controlled photonic release from atoms in specific wavelengths, thus producing a directional monochromatic (single-color) light beam of high coherence (e.g., tightly organized photons with synchronized wave fronts of the same frequency). **Forensic science** applications of laser technologies include a wide range of devices and techniques, such as laser **spectroscopy**, interferometric measurements (laser mapping systems), laser scanning, bullet **trajectory** projections, and laser **photography**.

Laser technologies are a growing market in forensics and crime investigation, with new tools designed specifically for this field. **Crime scene investigation** and reconstruction **ballistics** can be a time-consuming task, with crucial **evidence** such as trace fingerprints sometimes overlooked by the human eye. Bullet trajectory calculations with tapes and traditional reconstruction methods may take several hours in complex crime scenes. The use of bullet trajectory laser rods improves precision and saves time. Laser rods are used to determine the exact point of origin and distance from which a gun was fired, or, when more than one person was shooting, the exact original location and trajectory angle of each bullet fired. Laser rods are placed in each bullet hole found in the scene and activated to emit light. Laser beams flowing from each hole will reproduce the complete trajectory pattern of all bullets fired, making visible the entire exchange in a manner that can be photographed. Therefore, forensic technicians are able to track the trajectory of each bullet back to its point of origin, as well as to identify bullets that ricocheted from objects and changed direction.

Another useful application of lasers in forensic science is spectroscopy. Spectroscopy involves the analysis of materials by studying the reflection and absorption of light for the **identification** of traces of substance residues such as accelerants, illegal drugs, or poisons. Laser spectroscopy determine the molecular structure of materials and chemical compounds. Infrared laser spectroscopy can determine molecular structures of polymers on surfaces and gas phase ions, and is used to detect explosive components or illegal drugs in samples. Some portable spectrometers can analyze evidence at the crime scene, inside plastic bags or **glass** bottles, water solutions, as well as residual particles on surfaces.

Laser **fluorescence** is another method of analysis that can be used at the crime scene. One practical example is the small portable lasers in the shape of narrow flashlights, which are used to scan surfaces of a scene in search of fingerprints. As the beam travels on the surface of objects, furniture, walls, or doors, fingerprints become visible due to the rapid absorption and release of light by atoms present in the printed substance. This time-saving scan allows the location of fingerprints in places where they would otherwise be hard to find, as well as the quick location of fingerprints in an entire area. Once located and mapped, fingerprints can be dusted with fluorescent powder to be photographed.

Often more than one method is used to detect toxic industrial components present in the environment, such as coupling plasma mass spectrometry with laser spectroscopy. These techniques are used by the Federal Bureau of Investigation (**FBI**) to identify security dyes and gas residues in stolen cash. Laser desorption mass spectrometry (LDMS) is a technique used to identify substances in fabric, dyes, and security inks. Ink security systems are used to protect cash in ATM machines and bank safe contents. The ink is pressurized to release a concentrated red dye spray from the ATM cassettes when triggered by an anti-tampering electronic sensor, spraying an indelible stain on the currency. The skin and clothes of criminals are also marked, thus creating evidence. Other security systems use tear gas and red staining or smoke and dye for similar purposes. Smoke and dye in bank vaults release a hot cloud of red smoke that marks valuables and criminals, whereas tear gas and dye systems intend to stain evidence and temporarily disrupt the robbery, gaining time for the police arrival at the scene. LDMS is used to identify these markers in currencies and other items of evidence, and also facilitates tracking stolen currency in circulation.

Laser radars are law enforcement devices that measure the speed of vehicles. Laser speed guns are portable and can be pointed by police officers directly to a vehicle. A pulse infrared light is emitted towards the targeted vehicle, reflecting on its surface and returning to the gun where a sensor calculates the nanoseconds elapsed between emission and reflection, determining the distance to the car. As the car is in movement and the laser gun pulses laser light thousands of times per second, repeating calculations and comparing the many results, it can accurately determine the speed of the vehicle. Some laser speed devices are mounted on poles in strategic places by the roadside, in connection with high-speed photograph **cameras** that take a picture of the car and license number when triggered by the laser radar.

Other laser-based measurement tools, such as 3-D laser stations, are used to reconstruct the events underlying road accidents involving several vehicles or mass crime scenes such as nightclub or supermarket bombings. The scene is first photographed from all angles, and then 3-D mapping laser equipment is used to scan the entire area, registering several point positions. Some laser scanners have the capacity to capture 5,000 measurements per second, such as the one that was used in forensic analysis of the terrorist nightclub bombing in Bali in 2003. Photographs and mapping data are then downloaded into software that calculates point-to point distances and angles, automatically reconstructing three-dimensional images of the scene.

Some DNA typing machines also use laser fluorescence to identify certain molecules during the automated DNA **sequencing** process of certain DNA segments known as short tandem repeats (STR). STR sequences and lengths are so specific to individuals that they led to the expression "DNA fingerprinting." Another DNA technique is laser micro-dissection, used for **sperm** identification in **semen** samples. This method has high sensitivity,

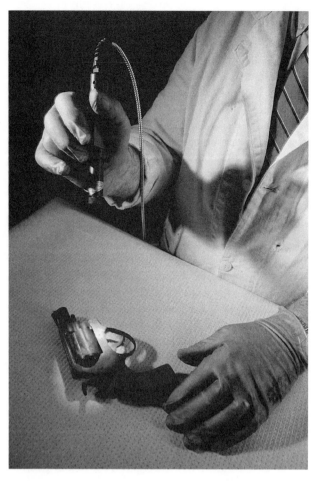

A technician at the San Francisco Police Department uses a laser to search for fingerprints on a gun. © ED KASHI/CORBIS

Laser ablation-inductively coupled plasma mass spectrometry

Laser ablation-inductively coupled plasma mass spectrometry (abbreviated LA-ICPMS) is a high technology device that analyzes trace matter samples within **forensic science** and other areas of science. In LA-ICPMS, a pulsed laser focuses on and vaporizes a very small amount of a solid sample (the LA within the acronym LA-ICPMS). A gas stream transports the resultant vapor into high temperature plasma (the ICP) where the vapor sample is ionized before being extracted into a mass spectrometer for analysis (the MS). Because of its advanced mechanisms, LA-ICPMS provides very reliable analysis of forensic **evidence** alongside strong improvements in sample size, sensitivity, and speed, when compared with traditional methods. For example, LA-ICPMS can detect microscopic samples such as clothing **fibers** and **glass** fragments at a level of parts per billion (ppb), providing forensic experts the ability to determine a material's origin often as precisely as to a particular manufacturer or brand. This expensive technology is an important part in countering domestic and international crimes that increasingly requires more innovative and systematic use of forensic science.

Before the availability of LA-ICPMS as a method for analyzing forensic samples and characterizing **physical evidence**, forensic scientists used such traditional techniques as Fourier transform infrared (**FTIR**) analysis, microscopy, refractive index, and X-ray fluorescence (XRF). However, these older techniques were not always able to analyze small samples or discriminate between chemically, physically, and visually similar materials. Some older techniques also required lengthy preparation times for the samples and used hazardous substances within the analysis, which both increased the potential for sample contamination and destroyed large amounts of samples.

On the other hand, LA-ICPMS is a valuable tool for analyzing elemental and isotopic characteristics of samples and accurately comparing samples with chemical, physical, and visual similarities. The ability to analyze microscopic samples can help investigators with the job of connecting a criminal suspect to a crime scene, where earlier technology was unable to do so. For instance, a sample that is very small in size is more likely and easily moved undetected by a criminal from a crime scene.

and permits the isolation of individual sperm cells from other cell types present in the sample. STR profiling can be accomplished from minute DNA samples with this technique, after DNA purification using high-sensitivity kits.

SEE ALSO Accident reconstruction; Alternate light source analysis; Ballistics; Biosensor technologies; Bomb detection devices; Bomb (explosion) investigations; Bullet track; Chromatography; Crime scene reconstruction; Digital imaging; DNA; DNA fingerprint; DNA sequences, unique; DNA typing systems; Electromagnetic spectrum; Energy dispersive spectroscopy; FBI crime laboratory; Gas chromatograph-mass spectrometer; Geospatial Imagery; Impression evidence; Ink analysis; Laser ablation-inductively coupled plasma mass spectrometry; Latent fingerprint; Metal detectors; Monochromatic light; Paint analysis; Radiation, electromagnetic radiation injury; Scanning electron microscopy.

Latent fingerprint

Chance impressions, or what is more commonly known as latent fingerprints, are the oftentimes invisible patterns made by fingerprints that are usually left at crime investigations or on objects recovered from crime scenes, and forensically analyzed by latent **fingerprint** experts with the application of chemical or physical methods.

The use of fingerprinting as a means to identify criminals spread throughout Europe and North America during the early twentieth century after British police officer Sir **Edward Richard Henry** introduced the use of fingerprints to solve crimes in the 1890s. As scientists studied fingerprint **identification** in more detail, they discovered that the ridge arrangement of fingerprints is unique and permanent, unless accidentally or intentionally altered. As crime-detection methods improved, law enforcement officers discovered that any hard, smooth surface touched by hands could produce fingerprints made by the oily secretions found on skin. When these so-called latent fingerprints were dusted with powders or chemically treated, the resultant pattern (or impression) could be observed, photographed, and stored for later use.

Latent fingerprints, which today are important pieces of forensic **evidence**, are created either artificially, naturally, or as a combination of the two. They are artificially created when fingers become covered with a foreign residue such as grease or oil. Latent fingerprints are naturally created when very small sweat pores on friction skin (that is, the top of skin ridges located on the inner surface area of fingers and hands) excrete perspiration. This perspiration, along with oils from touching other parts of the body and hair or from contact with external substances, remain on these ridges, so when an object is touched by a finger a duplicate recording of these characteristics is usually left on the surface. These hidden (or latent) impressions can be made visible when latent print examiners apply chemicals, lasers and other light sources, powders, or other physical means.

Latent fingerprint evidence is generally divided into two categories: porous evidence, such as cardboard, paper, and unfinished wood, that readily allows for the preservation of latent fingerprints because residue soaks into the surface; and nonporous evidence, such as **glass**, finished wood, and plastic, which does not easily permit the preservation of latent fingerprints because substances only lie on

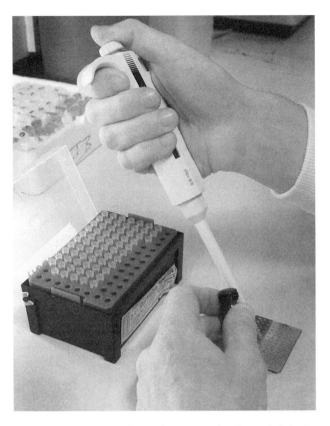

A laboratory worker loads samples onto a plate for analysis in the laser mass spectrometry machine at Manchester Metropolitan University in 2001. The machine, which can be used to detect anthrax spores, takes a mass-fingerprint of unknown bacteria which can be reliably matched in seconds against a database of quality-controlled reference spectra and then used for real-time detection of suspect bacteria. © REUTERS/CORBIS

Shattered glass, for example, produces small splinters, which can become attached to clothing, shoes, and other materials that can uniquely identify a criminal. Unlike traditional forensics techniques, such distinctive signatures can only be analyzed with LA-ICPMS.

LA-ICPMS is also far less destructive than traditional forensic techniques. LA-ICPMS requires only a minute sliver of a sample, often less than one microgram, which preserves the original sample and enables further measurements if authentication is needed. For this reason, LA-ICPMS is often described as an almost non-damaging technique with respect to the forensic sample.

SEE ALSO Chemical and biological detection technologies; Infrared detection devices; Isotopic analysis; Laser; Scanning electron microscopy; Scanning technologies; Spectroscopy.

the surface and can be intentionally or accidentally wiped away.

A positive identification of a latent fingerprint is normally achieved when, according to the expertise of a latent print examiner, the amount of similarity between the latent print (found at a crime scene, for example) and the inked fingerprint (taken from a suspect) is sufficient to make a corresponding match. Such matches are not based only on the degree of similarity (or number of matching points) between the two prints, but on various examinations made of the skin ridges. The resulting conclusion by the examiner is based on that person's experience, **training**, and understanding of the science behind latent fingerprint identification. A trusted latent print examiner must be knowledgeable in all areas of the science of fingerprint identification including classification methods, history, and procedures for locating, **processing**, and preserving latent prints at the crime scene or in the laboratory. As part of their duties, these examiners also give expert witness testimony with regards to latent fingerprints in all phases of the legal process.

New electronic procedures have been developed to detect and analyze latent fingerprints for crime detection. One such procedure is called **digital imaging**, the method of placing latent fingerprints into a digital format with the use of such equipment as digital **cameras**, computers, and scanners. Latent print examiners then use digital enhancement imaging software to adjust various features of the digital information such as brightness, contrast, and density in order to improve the quality of the evidence. Such electronic images are then input into an Automated Latent Print System (ALPS) computer, a database system that searches latent prints for possible matches. The ALPS computer assists the examiner in locating and retrieving records of known prints so that a list of possible matches can be made. Once a list is generated, another examiner (independent from the original investigation) conducts a scientific examination to verify the original identification.

On the federal level, the Latent Print Unit of the Federal Bureau of Investigation (FBI) conducts investigative work concerning the examination of latent fingerprints. When submitted as evidence to the FBI Laboratory, latent prints are input into the **Integrated Automated Fingerprint Identification System** (IAFIS) computer. The IAFIS then compares them against data from the FBI Criminal Justice Information Services (CJIS) Division, the largest international repository of fingerprint records.

Forensic technicians highlighting latent fingerprints. © MURIEL DOVIC/FRANCE REPORTAGE/CORBIS

Such efforts help to identify crime evidence involving latent fingerprints and solve serious crimes throughout the nation.

SEE ALSO Automated Fingerprint Identification System (AFIS); Chemical and biological detection technologies; Computer forensics; Digital imaging; DNA fingerprint; FBI crime laboratory; Fingerprint; Fingerprint analysis (famous cases); Ink analysis; Integrated Ballistics Identification System (IBIS); Ridge characteristics.

Latin forensic terms

Many Latin terms are used in the field of **forensic science** because forensics developed alongside the already established legal profession, which extensively uses phrases from the Latin language. The word forensic, itself, comes from the Latin word *forensis*, meaning of the forum. It originally applied to the marketplace areas within ancient Rome where many types of businesses and public affairs, such as governmental debates and actions by courts of law, were conducted. Entering the English vocabulary in 1659, the modern meaning of forensic is now limited to the areas of legal and criminal investigations.

Some commonly used Latin terms within the field of forensic science are listed below. A translation of the Latin appears in parentheses.

- *Aberemurder* (obsolete), willful murder
- *Abet* (to bait), to encourage another to commit a crime
- *Ab extra* (from outside), without
- *Actus reus* (guilty by act), wrongful deed performed with criminal intent

- *Ad hominem* (to the individual), relating to the preferences of a particular person
- *Amicus curiae* (friend of the court), person who is allowed to submit a point of view or intervene in a court case
- *Compos mentis* (of sound mind), legally responsible
- *Corpus delicti* (the body of the crime) fundamental facts that prove a crime
- *De novo* (new), trial that begins again without reference to previous trials
- *Fidei defensor* (defender of the faith), description of leaders especially with regards to British royalty
- *Flagrante delicto* (while the crime is blazing), caught in the act of a crime
- *Functus officio* (having served its purpose), expiration of someone's authority due to completion of duty or expired date
- *Habeas corpus* (that you have a body), writ issued to bring a party before a court or judge in order to release or continue to detain the party
- *In loco parentis* (in place of the parent), legal responsibility of a party to take on parental responsibilities
- *Indicia* (to point out), identifying marks or signs
- *In esse* (in existence), being
- *In extenso* (at full length), completely
- *In situ* (in its place), in its original position
- *Medias res* (the midst of things), middle of a series of events
- *Mens rea* (guilty in mind), intent or knowledge of performing a criminal act
- *Modus operandi* (**method of operation**), abbreviated M.O., particular way by which crimes are committed
- *Obiter dictum* (something said in passing), judge's observation on something not specifically before a court
- *Onus* (the burden), responsibility of governmental body or plaintiff to prove a case beyond reasonable doubt
- *Postmortem* (after death), **autopsy** performed after a person's death
- *Prima facie* (at first sight), **evidence** that appears to be sufficient to establish proof
- *Pro se* (on one's own behalf), person who presents their own case before a court without the use of lawyers

- *Res judicata* (the thing has been judged), case before a court that has already been decided by another court
- *Ultra vires* (without authority), outside the powers of legal authority.

In addition, many modern terms used commonly in forensic science have their roots in Latin. One such example is the word inquest, the term used for an inquiry into a death occurring under suspicious circumstances. The word comes from the Latin *in*, meaning into, and *quaro*, meaning to seek.

SEE ALSO Forensic science; Method of operation (M.O.).

Law Enforcement Training Center (FLETC), United States Federal

Many forensic investigators are police and other law enforcement officers. Thus, their **training** includes grounding in law enforcement. The Federal Law Enforcement Training Center (FLETC) is an organization, rather than a single facility, dedicated to training personnel from some 75 federal law-enforcement agencies. In addition, it provides training to personnel from state, local, and international agencies, and to those from federal agencies not immediately tasked with law enforcement duties.

FLETC is headquartered at Glynco, Georgia. Other facilities are located in Artesia, New Mexico; Charleston, South Carolina; and Cheltenham, Maryland. Founded in 1970, FLETC is now part of the Department of Homeland Security.

Studies of federal law enforcement training during the 1960s showed the need for a uniform system of training. Not only would this standardize the training process across the many law-enforcement branches of the federal government, but also it would prove most cost-effective. This would in turn make it possible to develop a center where a talented and educated cadre of instructors could provide comprehensive training using modern facilities and a course content that would ensure the highest possible level of proficiency among students. The result was the establishment, in 1970, of the Consolidated Federal Law Enforcement Training Center (CFLETC; the forerunner of FLETC) as a bureau of the Department of the Treasury.

The Glynco campus is similar to a town. Indeed, it has its own zip code. On the site is a practical exercise complex comprised of 34 buildings, including enclosed firing ranges; a driver training complex; numerous physical training areas; classroom buildings, which include laboratories and other specialized facilities; a computer resource learning center and library; and a television studio with the capability of broadcasting to field units throughout the United States and globally.

FLETC added a second major facility in 1989, when the former Artesia Christian College campus in Artesia, New Mexico, became the FLETC Artesia Center. Artesia remains the principal advanced training facility for the Immigration and Naturalization Service (INS), U.S. Border Patrol, Bureau of Prisons, and other organizations with headquarters or large concentrations of personnel in the western United States. Subsequent expanded responsibilities have led to the establishment of the other facilities.

The principal basic programs at FLETC are the Criminal Investigator Training Program (which has specific relevance to forensics); the Land Management Training Program, designed primarily for officers of agencies with a land management mission, such as the U.S. Forest Service or the National Park Service; and the Mixed Basic Police Training Program, which was created for uniformed services with a security or police mission, examples being the U.S. Secret Service Uniformed Division or the U.S. Capitol Police.

These and other programs provide a combination of classroom instruction on hands-on practical exercises. Areas of study include **firearms**, driver training, physical techniques, legal and behavioral sciences, marine operations, enforcement operations and techniques, and security specialties. There are also advanced courses in specialized areas ranging from law enforcement **photography** to seized computers and **evidence** recovery (which involves forensic analysis).

In addition to training for federal, state, and local agencies—in some cases through specially designed agency-specific courses—FLETC offers training to foreign agencies. This training focuses on three main areas: the Law and Democracy Program of the U.S. government, the Antiterrorism Assistance Program, and the International Law Enforcement Academy sponsored by the Bureau for International Narcotics and Law Enforcement Affairs.

SEE ALSO Careers in forensic science; Technology and forensic science; Training.

Roxie C. Laybourne

9/2/1910–8/7/2003
AMERICAN
ORNITHOLOGIST

Roxie C. Laybourne originated the science of forensic ornithology. Often called the "feather detective," Laybourne used feathers to identify bird-strike accidents in military and commercial aircraft, to solve crimes for the Federal Bureau of Investigation (**FBI**), to identify feathers unearthed by archeologists, and to recognize species of endangered poached or illegally killed birds.

In 1960, a Lockheed aircraft took off from Boston Logan airport, then crashed into Boston Harbor after flying through a flock of birds. Sixty-two people died on the crash. Laybourne gathered bits of charred materials from the engine intake areas, and by examining them under a microscope, suggested the cause of the crash was clogging of one of the engines with birds she identified as starlings. As a result of her work, aircraft manufactures made modifications to the fan blades of their engines, the military strengthened the cockpits of their aircraft, and airports took measures to discourage potentially hazardous bird species from nesting near airports. Laybourne continued to investigate bird strikes to engines or cockpits of commercial, private, and military aircraft, and became the world's foremost authority in identifying bird species by the remains of their feathers.

Laybourne later applied her skills to solve a **murder** case in conjunction with the FBI. Even though the victim was murdered, then thrown off a cliff into the sea, Laybourne matched a tiny portion of a down feather recovered from the suspect's truck with the down contained in the victims jacket. In another case, Laybourne matched feathers found at a murder crime scene with those in a pillow used to silence the fatal gunshot. Laybourne also worked with United States customs agents to identify illegally imported bird species.

Laybourne was born in Fayetteville, North Carolina, and raised in a rural area of the state near the town of Farmville. As a child, she climbed trees to get a better look at birds, especially owls, and spent hours watching turkey vultures flying overhead and catching thermal air currents. Laybourne earned an undergraduate degree from Meredith College in Raleigh, North Carolina, followed with a master's degree in **botany** from George Washington University.

After graduation, Laybourne worked for the National Fisheries Laboratory in Beaufort, N.C., and the North Carolina State Museum. In 1944, Laybourne joined the Smithsonian Institution, where she worked for over 40 years in the bird division perfecting her system for identifying birds and overseeing the institute's collection of over 650,000 bird specimens. Laybourne died at the age of 92 at her farm in Manassas, Virginia.

SEE ALSO Aircraft accident investigations; Trace evidence.

Henry C. Lee

11/22/1938
CHINESE-AMERICAN
FORENSIC SCIENTIST

As one of the world's most famous international experts in **forensic science**, Henry C. Lee has assisted law enforcement organizations in the investigation of over 6,000 major cases around the world, served as a consultant for over 300 law enforcement agencies, and served as an expert witness in over 1,000 high-profile criminal and civil court cases. In fact, during the latter half of the twentieth century and into the present century, the legendary investigator has figured prominently in many famous cases including the 1963 **assassination** of President John F. Kennedy; the 1986 Connecticut "Woodchipper" **murder** in Newtown; the 1993 death of White House Counsel (for President Clinton) Vincent Foster, the 1995 O.J. Simpson murder trial; the 1996 murder of JonBenet Ramsey in Boulder, Colorado; the 2001 murder of Chandra Levy, the former Washington, D.C. intern; and the 2002 kidnapping of Salt Lake City teenager Elizabeth Smart.

Lee was born in China and grew up on the island of Taiwan. In 1960, Lee completed his degree in police science from the Taiwan Central Police College. That same year, Lee gained his first professional job at the Police Department Headquarters in Taipei, the largest city on Taiwan, where he attained the rank of captain. In 1965, he and his wife, Margaret, moved to the United States in order to complete additional education. Seven years later, in 1972, Lee earned a bachelor's of science degree in forensic science from John Jay College of Criminal Justice in New York City. During this time, from 1968 to 1974, Lee was employed as a research technician within the biochemistry department at the New York University (NYU) Medical Center.

In 1974, Lee earned a master's of science degree in science, followed by a doctor's of philosophy degree in biochemistry a year later, both from New York University. Lee was promoted to research scientist within the biochemistry department for the NYU Medical Center, a title that he held from 1974 to 1975. After completing his advanced degree in 1975, Lee became employed by the University of New Haven at West Haven, Connecticut, where he created its Forensic Sciences program; became the director (1975–1979) of the Forensic Science Laboratory in Meriden, Connecticut; and worked as an assistant professor of the Criminal Justice Division (1975–1977).

Also, in 1975, Lee volunteered for the Connecticut State Police in order to develop its modern forensic laboratory and to introduce the concept of Major Crime Squad as a means for criminal investigation. In 1977, Lee became the director of the Center of Applied Research, a position that he held until 1980. He was promoted to associate professor of forensic science at the University of New Haven in 1977 and, in 1978, granted tenure as a full professor and chairman of the forensic science program. In 1979, Lee was appointed as the first chief criminalist for the state of Connecticut and then, a year later, became the director of the Connecticut State Police Forensic Science Laboratory; both positions that were held until 2000.

In 1996, Lee became the director and founder of the Henry C. Lee Institute of Forensic Science. Then, in 1998, Lee became the commissioner of the Connecticut State Police, Department of Public Safety, a position he held until 2000. Then, in June 2000, Lee became chief emeritus at the Division of Scientific Services within the Connecticut Department of Public Safety, a position he currently holds. Also in 2000, Lee became a research professor for the University of Connecticut and a distinguished professor of **criminology** at the Central Connecticut University.

Throughout his career, Lee completed various special **training** classes from the Federal Bureau of Investigation (FBI) Academy, Bureau of Alcohol, Tobacco and Firearms (**ATF**), Royal Canadian Mounted Police (RCMP), Connecticut State Department of Administrative Service, and other crime investigation organizations. Lee is also the recipient of many awards including the Distinguished Service Award from Taiwan National Police Administration (1962); the **American Academy of Forensic Sciences** Distinguished Criminalist Award (1986); the Distinguished Service Award from Connecticut Police Commissioners Association (1992), the Medal of Justice from the Justice Foundation (1996); and the Lifetime Achievement Award from the Science and Engineer Association (1998).

Lee and his team of forensic scientists have made seminal contributions to the advancement of forensic science such as the enhancement of bloody fingerprints, creation of new methods for extracting **DNA** from samples, and estimation of **blood** volume at a crime scene. For his achievements and contributions in criminal investigations, biochemistry, material science, forensic science, fire and **arson** investigation, home and industrial security, and law enforcement, Lee has received many awards, citations, commendations, and medals from civic groups, governments, police departments, and universities around the world. Lee is especially known within the forensic science industry for his knowledge, experience, dedication, humor, and common sense; and with the extraordinary ability for finding the smallest clues that decide crucial trial cases. In 1992, Lee was elected as a distinguished Fellow of the American Academy of Forensic Sciences.

Lee has either authored or co-authored about 30 books covering such areas as DNA, fingerprints, crime scene investigations, and **trace evidence**. His most recent books include *Henry Lee's Crime Scene Handbook* (2001), *Blood Evidence: How DNA is Revolutionizing the Way We Solve Crimes* (2003), and *Cracking More Cases: The Forensic Science of Solving Crimes: the Michael Skakel-Martha Moxley Case, the JonBenet Ramsey Case and Many More!* (2004).

Lee has also published over 300 articles in professional journals and conducted over 800 seminars and workshops covering such topics as DNA, fingerprints, **crime scene investigation** and reconstruction, criminal justice, and bloodstain pattern analysis. In addition, Lee has been the editor of several academic journals including being a member of the editorial board of the Journal of Forensic Sciences. In 2004, Court TV-The Investigation Channel premiered the new series, *Trace Evidence: The Case Files of Dr. Henry Lee*, which featured Lee discussing some of his most interesting criminal cases.

SEE ALSO Bloodstain evidence; Crime scene investigation; Crime scene reconstruction; DNA; Kennedy assassination; Simpson (O. J.) murder trial.

Less-lethal weapons technology

Knowledge of weaponry is valuable for a forensic examiner in determining the cause of injury. One group of weapons that can be encountered, and which can produce various injuries and wounds, includes those known as less-lethal weapons.

Less-lethal weapons are tools and techniques designed for riot control and other security functions with the intention of neutralizing hostile activity without killing or causing permanent bodily harm. Varieties of less-lethal weapons technology range from batons and beanbag rounds (non-lethal bullets fired from an ordinary or modified rifle or shotgun) to electric Tasers, pepper spray and tear gas, and equipment that emits loud noises, bright lights, or even bad smells.

As early as 1972, a report by the United States National Science Foundation identified no less than 34 varieties of less-lethal weapons technology then in the research or developmental stages. Among these were electrified water jets; stroboscopic light and pulsed sound weapons; infrasound weapons, which would use low-frequency noises inaudible to the human ear; guns for firing drug-filled rounds; "stench darts," which would emit a powerful and unpleasant smell; and a device called an "instant banana peel," designed to make pavement slippery. Less-lethal weapons technology in development at the beginning of the twenty-first century used sticky foam which, when fired at an attacker, made it impossible for that person to move.

Among the most well known of such devices is the M26 Advanced **Taser**, which can be used to neutralize an individual by means of electric shock. Similarly, electronic riot shields and electro-shock batons also use voltage to neutralize attackers. Manufactured since the mid-1980s, electrified riot shields make use of special plates fitted with metal strips. In the handle of the shield is a button which, when pushed, can send as much as 100,000 volts—twice the capacity of an ordinary Taser—through the metal, an act accompanied by the emission of loud noises and bright sparks.

Numerous varieties of less-lethal weapons are fired from an ordinary rifle or shotgun, or one that has been modified for that purpose. This technology originated with British colonial forces in Hong Kong, who used wooden rounds. Varieties of less lethal ammunition include baton rounds or plastic bullets; wooden bullets; hollow-point rounds; rubber balls; beanbag rounds; and nylon bags filled with lead pellets. All are capable of making a penetrating wound, but more likely result in deep bruising.

Less-lethal weapons technologies also make use of sounds, smells, or light. The basic idea behind such techniques is not new; biblical texts report that prior to attacking the city of Jericho, the Israelites marched around it seven times, shouting and smashing cymbals to intimidate the inhabitants. In World

War II, the U.S. Office of Strategic Services (OSS) issued to its operatives in Asia a "psychological harassing agent" called "Who, Me?" According to an OSS manual, the gas "is to be squirted directly upon the body or clothing of a person a few feet away. The odor is that of Occidental feces, which is extremely offensive..."

In the late twentieth century, a British government research project was tasked with developing means of using noxious odors for crowd control in Northern Ireland. Among the items in development, according to a *Financial Times* report, were chemical compounds intended to produce "transient symptoms of nausea and gagging." The principle is not different from that of tear gas and pepper spray (itself a variety of tear or CS gas), chemicals long used to quell riots or neutralize attackers.

Researchers at U.S. national laboratories are also reportedly in the process of developing various means for using sound and light as weapons. For example, ultra-sound generators, as well as microwave and acoustic disabling systems, may be used to disturb the inner ear, throwing an individual off balance. Another item of future technology is a radiator shell that would use superheated gaseous plasma, or ionized gas, to produce bursts of light.

SEE ALSO Crime scene investigation.

Philip Levine

8/10/1900–10/18/1987
PRUSSIAN
SEROLOGIST

Many of Philip Levine's greatest contributions to the fields of **serology** and **forensic science** occurred when he was working with the Nobel Prize-winning Austrian immunologist **Karl Landsteiner** (1868–1943). Together, they sought evidence in their research that there were more than the ABO blood groups previously identified by Landsteiner.

Levine was born in a small village in Polish Russia in 1900. He moved with his family to Brooklyn, New York, when he was eight years old. Levine grew up in New York, graduated from City College, and went to Cornell Medical School. After graduation from medical school and completion of a Master's Degree, he accepted a position at the Rockefeller Institute as an associate (eventually, assistant) to pathologist Karl Landsteiner, with whom he worked for seven years.

Landsteiner and Levine believed, based on blood transfusion reactions occurring when persons of the same blood type were transfused, that there were more blood groups than A, B, AB, and O. They embarked on research aimed at discovering additional blood groups. The pair immunized rabbits with human red blood cells from forty-one different types of human sera. Of those, four were found to have a distinctive agglutinin, meaning they caused reactions that were different than those of A, B, AB, or O blood groups. Through the course of their work, the distinct properties and inheritance patterns of M, N, S, s, and P were described.

The M, N, and S antigens are typically found on red blood cells. Antibodies to M are relatively common; they are the most often found antibodies in children who have never received transfusions. Antibodies against N are almost nonexistent. Anti-M antibodies can be found in individuals who have received multiple transfusions, as well as in women who have had more than one live birth; they are almost never associated with hemolysis of red cells. Antibodies against S and most of the M, N, and S antigens have been associated with both hemolytic transfusion reactions and with hemolytic disease of the newborn.

Landsteiner and Levine discovered the P blood group through their continuing search for additional blood groups. Most of the anti-P antigens they identified were only cold reactive, so were therefore not of major concern in transfusion. P system antigens are common and are naturally occurring. As a result, many of the antibodies to P system antigens result from immune response to other organisms.

Levine went on to become a bacteriologist and serologist, and in 1935 he accepted a position at Beth Israel Hospital in New York. There, he studied Rh factors; this was to become his greatest scientific contribution. His work on Rh incompatibility between mothers and newborns more fully explained transfusion reactions occurring in individuals transfused with their own blood type, and laid the groundwork for future successful organ transplantation surgery.

Philip Levine's discovery and detailed study of the M, N, S, and P blood groups, as well as his research concerning the Rh factor, has had a tremendous impact on the field of forensic science, due in large measure to the dramatically increased ability both to specify paternity and to pinpoint the connection between a blood sample and an individual crime victim or perpetrator via the use of progressively more refined (and defined) blood group typing.

SEE ALSO Antibody; Antigen; Blood; Paternity evidence.

L-Gel decontamination reagent

L-Gel is a coating that was developed at Lawrence Livermore National Laboratory (LLNL) in Berkeley, California. The coating is effective at decontaminating areas exposed to both chemical and biological agents. As such, L-Gel is potentially applicable to **forensic science**, both in the decontamination of a crime scene and in the pathologist's laboratory.

The need to decontaminate spills of liquid or powdered poisons or infectious organisms is potentially urgent. In order to prevent injury from chemical or biological warfare agents, for example, the source agent must be contained before anyone touches the material, or before the agents become dispersed in air currents.

The development of L-Gel began in the 1990s. Among those striving to develop a nonhazardous, portable, and inexpensive decontamination reagent were LLNL researchers. Their L-Gel formulation incorporates a chemical compound called potassium peroxymonosulfate into a material called silica.

Potassium peroxymonosulfate is an oxidant. That is, it contributes an electron to the chemical bonds of the target compound, which disrupts the bonds that hold the target together or make it active. Bleach is another oxidant. However, bleach produces noxious fumes, making its use in confined settings dangerous. Bleach is also corrosive, and could damage equipment and tissue that is being decontaminated.

The oxidant is incorporated into a gel. The thick gel is able to cling to surfaces better than water, and remains where it has been applied. A water-based solution will spread out and could even run down an inclined surface, which could further disperse the poison or infectious microbe. Another advantage of a gel is that the oxidant is kept in contact with the target longer than would be possible if the oxidant was dissolved in water.

L-Gel is effective at killing over 99% of populations of bacteria including *Bacillus anthracis* (the bacterium that causes **anthrax**) and *Yersinia pestis* (the bacterium that causes plague). Surfaces as varied as carpet, wood, and stainless steel are all efficiently decontaminated with L-Gel.

SEE ALSO Anthrax; Biohazard bag; Pathogens.

Lie detector SEE Polygraph

Lincoln exhumation

The story behind the 1901 **exhumation** of the body of Abraham Lincoln, felled by a bullet from the gun of assassin John Wilkes Booth in 1865, began nearly three decades earlier with the actions of a bumbling counterfeiting ring in central Illinois. The ring's master engraver, one Ben Boyd, was imprisoned, and the gang was running out of counterfeit bills. The gang's leader, "Big Jim" Kinealy, came up with a plan that would restore the gang's fortunes: stealing Lincoln's body and holding it until the government paid a $200,000 ransom and freed Ben Boyd. Initially, the plot was thwarted when one of Kinealy's conspirators had too much to drink and revealed the plot to a woman, who in turn revealed it to a number of acquaintances. Soon, the plot was known throughout Springfield, Illinois, and gang had to beat a hasty retreat from the city.

Kinealy, however, did not give up. In Chicago, he opened a saloon, where one of his regular customers was a man named Lewis G. Swegles. In time Kinealy admitted Swegles to the gang, not knowing that Swegles was a Secret Service agent on the trail of the counterfeiters. In concert with Swegles and other members of the gang, the plot to steal Lincoln's body was hatched anew and scheduled for execution on the night of November 7, 1876, election day, when the conspirators figured that Oak Ridge Cemetery in Springfield would be deserted because people would be preoccupied with the outcome of the election. The plan was to place the body in a sack, transport it by horse-drawn wagon to northern Indiana, and hide it amid the sand dunes there until the national furor over the theft died down, ransom demands could be made, and the ransom was paid and Boyd was released.

Accordingly, that night the gang went to the cemetery, cut the lock off of the door of Lincoln's tomb, raised the marble lid of the sarcophagus, and were in the process of lifting the casket out when Swegles, whose job was to have driven the wagon into position, alerted eight detectives in hiding. The detectives rushed to the tomb, weapons drawn, but the grave robbers escaped. After their capture ten days later, Lincoln's son Robert hired prominent attorneys to prosecute them. At a trial eight months later, two men, Terrence Mullen and John Hughes, were found guilty and sentenced to a year in Joliet State Prison, where they began serving their sentences on June 22, 1877.

By 1900, the monument at Lincoln's tomb was in need of major reconstruction. Over the fifteen months during which it was being rebuilt, Lincoln's pine coffin was laid in a temporary grave nearby. Finally, in August 1901, the monument was complete and the coffin was reinterred. But in September, Robert Lincoln visited the tomb and decided that the project was not complete. Remembering the 1876 incident, he wanted to ensure that no one would ever be able to disturb the resting place of his father. So he ordered that the coffin be placed in a cage some ten feet below ground and encased in concrete. He got the idea from the burial of George M. Pullman, inventor of the Pullman sleeping railroad car.

On September 26, 1901, the new tomb was ready. When it was time to transfer the coffin into the tomb, discussion arose about whether the coffin should be opened, for there were persistent rumors that Lincoln's body was not in the coffin, and this would be the last opportunity to put those rumors to rest. Some observers thought that opening the coffin would be disrespectful, while other believed that the remains should be identified. The decision was reached to open the coffin.

Accordingly, Leon P. Hopkins and his nephew, Charles L. Willey, both plumbers, carved a piece out of the top of the lead-lined coffin, exposing the fallen president's head and shoulders. Each of the twenty-three people present said that a choking smell emerged from the coffin. Then each passed before the coffin and looked down. All agreed that the features of the body in the coffin were clearly those of Abraham Lincoln. Still visible were the whiskers on his chin, a wart on his cheek, and his coarse black hair, although his eyebrows had vanished. Also clearly visible was his black suit, the same suit he had worn to his second inauguration, although it was covered by a yellow mold.

Afterwards, the section of the coffin that had been removed was soldered back into place, the coffin was lowered into the cage, and the whole was covered with two tons of cement. Lincoln's body had been moved seventeen times since his death, but it would be removed no more.

In 1928, one of the witnesses who viewed the body, J. C. Thompson, said: "As I came up I saw that top-knot of Mr. Lincoln's, his hair was coarse and thick, like a horse's, he used to say, and it stood up high in front. When I saw that, I knew that it was Mr. Lincoln. Anyone who had ever seen his pictures would have known it was him. His features had not decayed. He looked just like a statue of himself lying there." Another witness, Fleetwood Lindley, who was just thirteen when he saw the body, was the last of the twenty-three witnesses to pass away. Just before his death in 1963, he said in an interview: "Yes, his face was chalky white. His clothes were mildewed. And I was allowed to hold one of the leather straps as we lowered the casket for the concrete to be poured. I was not scared at the time, but I slept with Lincoln for the next six months."

Credit for the condition of Lincoln's body must go to undertaker Dr. Charles D. Brown, of the firm Brown and Alexander. Assisted by Harry P. Cattell, Brown embalmed the president's body, first draining Lincoln's blood through his jugular vein. Then, an incision was made in his thigh and the embalming fluids were pumped in, hardening the body like marble. Brown and Cattell then shaved the president's face, leaving behind a tuft on the chin. They set the mouth in a slight smile and arched his eyebrows. They then dressed the president in his suit. The condition of Lincoln's body supported the claims made in a Brown and Alexander advertising flyer, which touted the benefits of their patented embalming procedure over other methods of preserving bodies: "...the mortal remains will be kept in the most perfect and natural preservation, and that cherished countenance looked at once more, by those who may be led to remember and repeat these holy words of consolation: 'He is not dead but sleepeth,' until we meet again in a better world."

In a letter to his mother, Army Assistant Surgeon Edward Curtis, one of two doctors who performed the **autopsy** on President Lincoln, described to her what happened when he found the bullet that had killed the president: "There it lay upon the white china, a little black mass no bigger than the end of my finger—dull, motionless and harmless, yet the cause of such mighty changes in the world's history as we may perhaps never realize...silently, in one corner of the room, I prepared the brain for weighing. As I looked at the mass of soft gray and white substance that I was carefully washing, it was impossible to realize that it was that mere clay upon whose workings, but the day before, rested the hopes of the nation. I felt more profoundly impressed than ever with the mystery of that unknown something which may be named vital spark as well as anything else, whose absence or presence makes all the immeasurable difference between an inert mass of matter owning obedience to no laws but those covering the physical and chemical forces of the universe, and on the other hand, a living brain by whose silent, subtle machinery a world may be ruled." Lincoln's autopsy, burial, and reburial site in Springfield, Illinois, attracts over one million visitors a year.

SEE ALSO Exhumation.

Lindbergh kidnapping and murder

In 1936, Bruno Richard Hauptmann was executed after a jury found him guilty of the brutal kidnapping and **murder** of twenty-month-old Charles Lindbergh, Jr., the son of American aviation hero Charles Lindbergh. The elder Lindbergh had become a celebrity in 1927 when he electrified the world by making the first nonstop solo airplane flight across the Atlantic. After returning home to a hero's welcome, he married Anne Morrow, the daughter of the U.S. ambassador to Mexico, and the couple's son Charles, Jr., was born in 1930. The reclusive Lindbergh, who shunned the public and the press, was thrust back into the glare of the spotlight in 1932, when his son disappeared from the family's rural home near Hopewell, New Jersey, and was later found murdered. Americans followed with intense interest the investigation and the sensational trial of Hauptmann for what was dubbed the "Crime of the Century."

The Lindberghs generally spent the weekends on their isolated 390-acre Hopewell estate and returned to the Morrow family estate in Englewood, New Jersey, on Monday mornings. That weekend, however, young Charles had a cold, so the family decided to remain in Hopewell one more day. On the cold and rainy evening of March 1, 1932, sometime between 8:00 p.m., when the child's nursemaid went to the second-floor nursery to look in on him, and 10:00 p.m., when Lindbergh went to the nursery to check in on his son before going to bed, the child had disappeared. Lindbergh later reported hearing a thumping noise from upstairs at about 9:00 p.m. Both the local and state police, with Lindbergh's help, conducted an unsuccessful search of the grounds for the child. (The state police investigation was led by H. Norman Schwarzkopf, the father of General H. Norman Schwarzkopf, Jr., the U.S. commander of Operation Desert Storm in Iraq in 1991.)

The initial investigation turned up ladder impressions in the ground outside the nursery window, a carpenter's chisel nearby, and, about a hundred yards away, a broken ladder. Inside, a ransom note was found in the nursery, the first of fourteen notes that would be received during the investigation, all apparently written by the same hand on the same type of paper with the same blue ink:

> Dear Sir!
>
> Have 50000$ redy with 2500$ in 20$ bills 1500$ in 10$ bills and 1000$ in 5$ bills. After 2–4 days we will inform you were to deliver the Mony.
>
> We warn you for making anyding public or for notify the polise the child is in gute care.
>
> Indication for all letters are singnature and 3 holes.

The final line refers to a peculiar feature of all the notes: In the bottom right-hand corner of each was a pair of interlocking blue circles, each about an inch in diameter, with the overlapping area of the circles colored red and punched with three small holes.

A second note, delivered on March 5, upped the ransom demand to $70,000. A later note agreed to use the services of Lindbergh admirer John F. Condon as a go-between, with communication conducted through ads in a New York newspaper under the code name "Jafsie," from Condon's initials, J.F.C. Another included instructions for the type of box in which the ransom money was to be delivered. The first meeting between Condon and the kidnapper took place in Woodlawn Cemetery in the Bronx, where Condon insisted on proof that the kidnapper held the child before paying any ransom; soon the child's sleeping suit was delivered to the Lindbergh home.

At a second meeting, on March 31, Condon delivered to the cemetery two packages of unmarked gold certificates, whose serial numbers would later be widely circulated in nearly a quarter of a million booklets. Gold certificates were used to pay the ransom because the nation was just about to go off the gold standard for its currency and gold certificates, which had to be turned in by May 1, 1933, would be conspicuous if the kidnapper attempted to pass them. The first of the bills reappeared on April 2, and in the months that followed additional bills turned up. On May 1, 1933, $2,980 of the ransom bills were turned in at the Federal Reserve Bank in New York City by one J. J. Faulkner, but Faulkner was never identified or found.

The child, however, was not returned when the ransom was paid. Instead, another note indicated that he could be found on a boat near Elizabeth Island, but a search for the boat proved unsuccessful. Then on May 12, a truck driver named William Allen discovered the child's body, now little more than a skeleton, in the woods about four miles from the Lindbergh estate. The body's left leg from the knee down, as well as the left hand and right arm, were missing. An **autopsy** showed that the likely **cause of death** was a blow to the head, but it otherwise provided no clues, and the investigation languished. Finally, on September 15, 1934, a gas station attendant became suspicious when a customer with a German accent used a $10 gold certificate to pay for a 98-cent gas purchase. Thinking the certificate might be counterfeit, he recorded the car's license number and contacted the police. The police traced the car to Hauptmann, a German immigrant, who denied having any more of the bills, but a search of the garage at his home in the Bronx, New York, turned up over $14,000 of the currency. He was arrested, and after a six-week trial conducted in a circus-like atmosphere in Flemington, New Jersey, found guilty on February 13, 1935. He was executed by electric chair on April 3 the following year.

The prosecution built much of its case on the forensic **evidence**. One important piece of evidence was the ladder, which was examined by a number of wood experts, including Arthur Koehler of the U.S. Forest Products Laboratory in Wisconsin. Koehler examined slivers of the ladder sent to him and concluded that the ladder was made of pine from North Carolina, Douglas fir from the West, birch, and Ponderosa pine. He even traced some of the lumber to a mill in South Carolina and from there to a lumber dealer in the Bronx. The hand-made ladder in some respects showed the work of a skilled carpenter. Hauptmann was a carpenter, and in fact had constructed the garage in which the ransom currency was found. During the search of Hauptmann's home, one of the investigators noticed a missing beam in the home's attic. The pattern of the nail holes in one of the uprights of the ladder found on the Lindbergh estate matched the pattern of nail holes left when the beam was removed from Hauptmann's attic.

The most crucial evidence, however, was the ransom notes themselves. The notes were examined by several analysts, who all concluded that they came from the same hand. They noted consistent misspellings, such as *note* rather than *not*, as well as inversion of letters such as *g* and *h*. They also noted peculiarities in the way that *x* and *t* were written and the illegibility of the word *the*. The letter *o* was open, and *t*'s were uncrossed. Additionally, some of

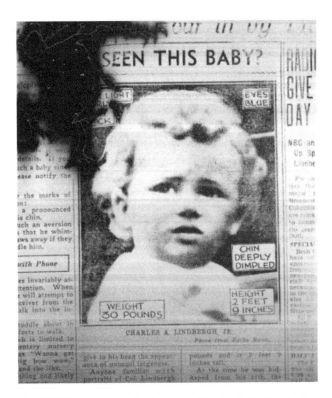

March 1932 newspaper clipping shows Charles A. Lindbergh, III, son of aviator Charles A. Lindbergh, Jr., who was kidnapped from his Hopewell, New Jersey, home on March 1, 1932. AP/WIDE WORLD PHOTOS. REPRODUCED BY PERMISSION.

the words in the ransom notes ended with incorrect *e*'s, a feature found in some of Hauptmann's other writing. The notes' grammatical errors and phraseology suggested that the writer was a native German speaker. In the original ransom note, for example, the word *gute* in the phrase "gute care" suggests a German speaker using the German word *gut* rather than the English word *good*.

During the investigation, one of the handwriting experts, Albert S. Osborn, wrote out a paragraph that the police could dictate to a suspect to write down to determine if he or she could have written the notes. The paragraph contained such words as *our* (*ouer* in the ransom notes), *place* (often spelled *plase*), and *money* (*mony*). Later, when Hauptmann was arrested, he was asked to provide samples of his handwriting, as well as to copy the ransom notes repeatedly over a period of hours. When Osborn and his son, Albert D. Osborn, first examined these writing samples, they were not convinced that Hauptmann wrote the ransom notes. The police then forced Hauptmann to write more notes, dictating the way he was to spell certain words. Again, the Osborns concluded that there were too many dissimilarities between Hauptmann's writing and that of the ransom

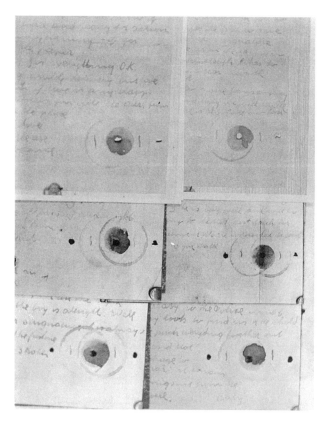

Ransom notes from the kidnapping and murder case of Charles Lindbergh, Jr. © BETTMANN/CORBIS

notes, as well as discrepancies among the writing samples themselves. Only after the cash was discovered in Hauptmann's garage did they change their opinion and conclude that Hauptmann's writing and that of the ransom notes matched. Meanwhile, at least one other expert believed that the writing was that of Isador Fisch, Hauptmann's business partner, who, Hauptmann claimed, had given him the money for safekeeping before leaving for Germany. Nonetheless, despite violations of **handwriting analysis** protocol, the state's handwriting experts convinced the jury that Hauptmann had written the notes.

SEE ALSO Handwriting analysis.

Linguistics, forensic stylistics

Forensic linguistics, or forensic stylistics as it is sometimes called, applies linguistic techniques to legal and criminal issues. This discipline subjects written or spoken materials (or both), to scientific analysis for determination and measurement of content, meaning, speaker **identification**, or determination of authorship.

In the analysis of a crime, it is important to study the written or spoken language of the perpetrator, as it can offer insight into the offender's age, race, gender, level of education, religious or spiritual beliefs, geographic and socioeconomic background, culture, and ethnicity.

Most adults' speech patterns retain vestiges of the geographic region, and sometimes of the local dialect, from the area in which they spent their childhood. Written communications provide fewer clues, although vocabulary and the use of colloquialisms (such as the variability in usage of "you" and "you all"; "pop," "soda," and "soda pop"; or "hot dog," "frank," and "wiener") may suggest geographic region. Written language stylistics generally reveals language of origin; the ordering of verbs, nouns and subject words in sentence structure is typically dictated by native spoken/written language. English speakers write in subject-verb-object order, non-English speakers more often write in subject-object-verb order ("You had better grasp the seriousness of my threat" versus "The seriousness of my threat you will be grasping").

Spoken and written nuances, grammar usage, generational characteristics, references to specific television shows, commercials, movies, music genre, or performers can all suggest general age. Although perpetrators sometimes attempt to disguise their gender, longer communications typically allow the individual to let down his/her guard sufficiently so as to reveal gender nuances. Females typically use more self-deprecating, more emotional, more polite, and less self-confident language than males. Females are more likely than males to overtly apologize for their actions, to utilize emotional words, and to use intensifiers.

Vocabulary, sentence complexity, abstract logic, and sophisticated word usage are likely to indicate higher levels of education. Use of technical or specific language can suggest occupation; biblical references may relate to religious or philosophical persuasion.

Forensic stylistics extends the principles of psycholinguistics to criminal, civil, law enforcement, or other legal venues. The field of psycholinguistics is concerned with the relationship between linguistics and the psychological processes underlying them. During the last third of the twentieth century, psychologists (in concert with other behavioral health professionals) studied and attempted to quantify linguistic features associated with character styles and personality traits, such as impulsivity, rage, anxiety, mania, depression, paranoia, sadism, narcissism, and the need to exert power and control over others, with the goal of utilizing this knowledge to understand or to predict criminal behavior.

Forensic linguistic analysis is utilized in cases involving assessment of threat, adjudication of authorship (submission of issues to a third party who has the power to deliver a binding decision), workplace and school violence, statement and confession analysis, and false allegations.

Specific word usage in spoken or written threats can give investigators a great deal of information concerning likelihood of action, suspect's motivation, personality characteristics, demographics, and degree of psychological stability (relates to the likelihood of impulsive action and the ability to safely manage stressful situations). The Behavioral Science Unit of the Federal Bureau of Investigation is engaged in a longitudinal research project concerning the relationship between language use in threatening communications and the likelihood that the author/speaker will act on the threats made.

In adjudication of authorship, forensic linguists compare specific characteristics of current communications (tone, sentence structure, idiomatic usage [unique to a particular style], vocabulary, punctuation, spelling, and grammar) with a known corpus (body or group) of writings from the suspect, to match for authorship.

There has been significant media coverage of workplace and school violence in recent years. Terminated or disgruntled employees have killed supervisors and coworkers, estranged spouses have taken mass revenge at job sites, and angry, depressed, or marginalized students have opened fire on classmates. Although these attacks are often characterized as "coming out of the blue," analysis by experts in forensic stylistics generally reveal that the perpetrators planned their actions, or at least contemplated them, far in advance of their occurrence. Disgruntled employees and chronically distressed students often express their discontent in the presence of others, and their vocalizations tend to escalate in intensity and specificity over time. It is not uncommon for them to talk about weapons they have, or plan to acquire, before the violent event occurs. These verbal threats are often minimized or ignored until the act occurs.

Confession and statement analysis are used to determine the truthfulness of the speaker's words,

the information communicated via word choices, and references to the information omitted. Forensic linguists can study these patterns to determine the best method of approach with individual suspects.

The study of false allegations is particularly interesting; this is the situation in which an alleged victim may be found either to be misrepresenting the facts or to be causing the circumstances in question. Specifically, a victim may intentionally accuse an innocent party in an effort to protect the true offender (or for myriad other reasons) or to punish the accused; an alleged victim may fabricate the reported event entirely (report being threatened when s/he is the actual author of the communications; or report the occurrence of a crime when none has occurred, etc.).

Forensic linguists also study the contents of suicide notes, to determine whether they were, in fact, authored by the deceased, or whether they might have been fabricated as a means of disguising a homicide.

The analysis of cybercrime is an emerging field of expertise for forensic stylists. Hackers use written code to break into, or to sabotage, programs and computer systems; sometimes the code can be linked to a particular individual, through the use of stylistics.

A key role in criminal investigations is played by forensic linguistics/stylistics. Analysis of the spoken or written words of the offender can greatly assist forensic scientists in identifying a perpetrator, in linking seemingly unrelated crimes, in determining authorship of disputed documents, in assessing the veracity (truthfulness) of statements and confessions, in preventing or understanding school or workplace violence, in uncovering false allegations, and in assessing the danger level, and potential for violence, in threatening communications.

SEE ALSO Computer virus; Criminal profiling; Document forgery; Geographic profiling; Identity theft; Lindbergh kidnapping and murder; Psychological profile; Psychopathic personality.

Literature, forensic science in

People have always been fascinated by detective fiction. Reading a well-written thriller or crime story can be a satisfying experience and, in many books, the details of forensic investigation can drive the narrative along and add drama to the plot. It can also be educational in explaining the role of science in solving a crime. Forensic laboratories and crime scenes can help create an atmosphere that will keep the reader involved. Some great investigator heroes and heroines have emerged from the detective genre, from Arthur Conan Doyle's Sherlock Holmes to Kathy Reichs's Dr. Temperance Brennan. They have different styles and approaches but they always solve the crime.

Sherlock Holmes, the private investigator created by the Scottish author Sir **Arthur Conan Doyle** (1859–1930), is probably the most famous hero in detective fiction. Holmes was inspired by one of Conan Doyle's teachers at medical school, Joseph Bell, who always emphasized the importance of observation in making a diagnosis, advice that is equally applicable to forensic investigation. Conan Doyle wrote 56 short stories and four short novels between 1887 and 1927. They are still in print today.

Holmes endures, while the exploits of some of the later fictional detective heroes have long been forgotten. Maybe Holmes continues to fascinate us because of his scientific approach to solving crime. Britain's Royal Society of Chemistry even made him their first fictional Fellow in 2002 to mark the way he used chemistry in his investigations and sparked people's interest in the subject. Holmes was always something of an academic; he explored the use of tobacco ash, the shapes of ears, the dating of documents, tattoos, and footprints as clues. These are all used today as **evidence** in modern forensic investigation.

The first Sherlock Holmes novel, *A Study in Scarlet*, was published in 1887. Here Holmes meets Dr. Watson, who is to become his assistant, for the first time. They talk of a test that can detect human **blood** with a sensitivity of one part blood to one million parts water. This was several years before the discovery of a test that could identify human blood and even longer before the routine use of **luminol**, a chemical that detects invisible blood by turning it bright green, at crime scenes. Another Holmes novel, *The Sign of Four*, published in 1890, refers to many forensic techniques including soil **identification** and the **toxicology** analysis of alkaloids on a poisoned dart. There is still much to learn from Holmes about **forensic science**, and many of the techniques he utilized came into use and are applicable today.

The figure of the gentleman private detective persisted with Lord Peter Wimsey, the creation of the English writer Dorothy L. Sayers (1893–1957). The classic novel *The Documents in the Case*

features forensic **botany** and chemistry. It depicts a death wherein the victim was first thought to have died by eating a poisonous mushroom mistaken for a nonpoisonous species. However, analysis of the residue of a mushroom stew reveals that muscarine, the active ingredient of the poisonous mushroom *Amanita muscaria*, is in the synthetic rather than the natural form, meaning the poison had to have been added by the perpetrator.

Death by arsenic poisoning is very common in crime fiction, much less so in modern life. In Sayers's novel *Strong Poison*, the villain tries to build up his tolerance to the poison by taking small, increasing, doses. This enables him to share an arsenic-laced omelet with his victim, Philip Boyes. The poison has little effect on the perpetrator but Lord Peter is able to discover the presence of arsenic in his nails and hair.

A Sayers short story, *In the Teeth of the Evidence*, features forensic **odontology**, the study of the structure and development of teeth. Lord Peter works with a dentist friend in the investigation of a concealed murder by looking at the teeth of the dead man and comparing them to his supposed dental records. The chart shows a fused porcelain filling done in 1923, but examination of the corpse reveals a filling material first used in 1928. The establishment of true identity hinges on the dental evidence, the rest having been destroyed in a fire, and leads to the arrest of the perpetrator.

In more recent times, there has been a clear shift towards the more professional kind of forensic hero. One popular example is Adam Dalgliesh, the hero of English author P. D. James's detective mysteries. Dalgliesh writes poetry, which perhaps gives him a flavor of earlier gentleman heroes. Of the several novels featuring Dalgliesh, perhaps one of the most compelling is *Death of an Expert Witness*. It is actually set in a forensic laboratory where, as the title suggests, the victim is a scientist. The book contains many examples of how forensic science is used in investigations and draws on the author's own experience in the Department of Home Affairs, working in the criminal and police departments.

Other modern crime writers feature the forensic scientist as protagonist. Perhaps the best known is Kay Scarpetta, the heroine in many novels by the American author **Patricia Cornwell**. Scarpetta is a **medical examiner** in Richmond, Virginia, and the novels draw on Cornwell's own experience of working in a medical examiner's office. In *Body of Evidence* (1991), many forensic techniques are on display as integral parts of the plot. A major character called Benton Wesley shows how to use psychological **profiling** to catch a perpetrator. There is also a detailed discussion on fiber analysis including how evidence is collected and its examination on a stereomicroscope.

Another Cornwell novel, *Post Mortem* (1990), discusses the latest techniques for gathering evidence at the scene of a crime. An **autopsy** description involves the use of a **laser** to find fingerprints on skin that could identify a perpetrator. There are also laboratory scenes involving blood grouping, **DNA** analysis, protein analysis, and other biochemical techniques. Scarpetta is a sympathetic personality, so the exposition of forensic science from her viewpoint is sure to engage the reader.

Another modern detective character in literature is Kathy Reichs's Dr. Temperance Brennan, who is a forensic anthropologist. The author is herself a forensic anthropologist with an international reputation working in the locations she describes, so her work feels authentic and teaches much about how crime investigation is actually carried out. In recent books such as *Bare Bones* and *Monday Mourning* there is much detail about the work of an expert witness, the dating of bones, **wildlife forensics**, and the discovery of the **cause of death**. There's an irony in the name, for Tempe, as she is known, is a recovering alcoholic. Therefore, a heroine is shown who, although an expert, is somewhat vulnerable. Another newcomer on the forensic science fiction scene is Tess Gerritsen, a writer of medical thrillers, whose medical examiner character Dr. Maura Isles autopsies her twin sister in *Body Double*. The story hinges on **serology**, the study of serums, and DNA evidence. As in Reichs's books, the heroine is also put at risk, a development that is a long way from the Holmes books, where the protagonist stays aloof from the action.

Karin Slaughter is another contemporary author working in the forensic investigation field. She writes about Dr. Sara Linton, who is a pediatrician working as a medical examiner, and about Linton's relationship with a police officer and the investigations they carry out together. In *Blindsight* there is a detailed description of **bullet track** analysis in a killing and of an old rape case.

The English crime writer Ruth Rendell writes from the point of view of the criminal, except in the Inspector Wexford novels where she writes about the police and the investigators. The novel *Adam and Eve and Pinch Me*, written in 2001, makes an interesting point about both **psychology** and forensic investigation. The killer, a woman called Minty, suffers from obsessive-compulsive disorder. She washes frequently and cleans up everything around her all the time. When she goes to the movies with her victim, she leaves no **trace evidence** behind after she stabs him to death, much to the frustration of the forensic investigators.

A novel drawing on forensic science is, of course, far more satisfying if the detail is there, and if it is correct. Authors who have worked in the forensic field, like Kathy Reichs, are naturally authentic. Many other authors want to write about crime and need to include forensic detail. Often they will consult a Web site organized by a forensic professional wanting to help writers. One such site is run by Douglas Lyle, a physician experienced in forensic work and also a writer of fiction. He maintains a Web site where he answers writers' questions and helps their work seem more believable.

SEE ALSO Film (forensic science in cinema).

Literature, popular

The field of **forensic science** initially developed as a scientific application to the legal profession in the nineteenth century. It is probably not a coincidence that the writings of popular fictional literature with regards to detective work also began that same century. E. F. Bleiler, Charles Dickens, Edgar Allen Poe, and **Arthur Conan Doyle** were among some of the nineteenth century writers who popularized established law enforcement and early forensic science theories and practices in the detective stories they wrote about. Further detective writings of this literature expanded into the twentieth century and now into the twenty-first century.

In the 1827 book *Richmond*, Bleiler wrote about **circumstantial evidence** that links a person to a crime when someone else is in reality the guilty person, as did Dickens in *Bleak House*. Like other writers in those early years of detective stories, Dickens employed **physical evidence** to implicate suspected criminals. Poe, who is generally credited with establishing the category of detective fictional literature, wrote numerous books involving fictional crime solution including *The Murders in the Rue Morgue*, where the crime centers on an unlikely location, and *The Purloined Letter*, which uses the principle of ratiocination (reasoned train of thought). Poe also introduced the detective C. Auguste Dupin, who is frequently considered the first fictional detective.

British physician and novelist Sir Arthur Conan Doyle created the famous detective Sherlock Holmes in four novels and fifty-six short stories that highlighted the sound deductive reasoning of the investigator. Among Doyle's books are *The Adventures of Sherlock Holmes* and *The Hounds of the Baskervilles*. Because of the popularity of Doyle's investigative hero, the detective-type story has remained a very popular form of storytelling. In fact, the brilliant detective stories of Doyle are generally considered the beginning point when discussing classic detective books.

Other detective writers who followed Doyle into the twentieth century include G. K. Chesterton (who created a series of detective stories relating the escapades of mild-mannered Father Brown, a Roman Catholic priest turned crime fighter), Arthur Morrison (who invented investigator Martin Hewitt), M. McDonnell Bodkin (who created the first detective family), and R. Austin Freeman (who introduced the first science-based detective, John Thorndyke).

Later on in the twentieth century, other writers weaved tales of detective work including Agatha Christie (who is remembered for her complicated plots and her memorable detectives, Miss Marple and Hercule Poirot, and for such books as *Curtain* and *The Murder of Roger Ackroyd*), Dorothy L. Sayers (who created the charming detective Lord Peter Wimsey featured in such books as *Whose Body?*), Raymond Chandler (who created the tough detective Philip Marlowe), Erle Stanley Gardner (whose lawyer-detective Perry Mason appeared in over eighty books such as *The Case of the Deadly Toy* and *The Case of the Duplicate Daughter*), Rex Stout (who created the stout detective Nero Wolfe), Dashiell Hammett (who wrote about private eye/detective Sam Spade in such books as *The Maltese Falcon*), and the collaborate writers of Frederic Dannay and Manfred B. Lee (who wrote under the pseudonym of Ellery Queen while writing about legendary detective Ellery Queen in such detective books as *The Roman Hat Mystery*).

A notable writer of 2005 is Kathleen (Kathy) Reichs, who has taken her experiences as a forensic anthropologist and turned it into another career writing best selling novels on real-life aspects of forensic **anthropology**. As one of only a select number of forensic anthropologists certified by the American Board of Forensic Anthropology, Reichs has traveled worldwide in order to assist critical forensic investigations on such incidents as the United Nations Tribunal on Genocide in Rwanda and the September 11, 2001 disaster in New York

City. With her lead character, Temperance Brennan, Reichs has published such popular fictional books based on forensic science as *Déjà Dead*, *Death du Jour*, *Deadly Decisions*, *Fatal Voyage*, and *Grave Secrets*.

SEE ALSO Literature, forensic science in; Television shows.

Lividity

The term lividity refers to an unnatural color of the skin. Lividity can be a useful reaction in determining the position of a body at the **time of death** and even whether a body was moved within the first few hours after death.

There are various forms of lividity. In a living person, a blow can result in the localized rupturing of cells and the pooling of **blood**. When the blood cells begin to decompose, the release of the blood forms a bluish-purple bruise.

In a living victim, bruising can be indicative of the nature of the trauma. For example, choking can leave a distinctive pattern of neck bruising that mirrors the pressure applied by the fingers.

Lividity can also result when blood flow ceases after death. The blood that was formerly flowing through the body can be drawn to the lowest point in the body by the influence of gravity. For example, if a victim was lying on her right side at the time of death, lividity would be evident on the right side of the face, hip, and on the areas of the right arm and leg that were closest to the ground.

As blood pools in a corpse under the influence of gravity, the lividity can become more intense in color. This trend has inspired attempts to correlate the degree of lividity with the approximate time of death. However, the development of lividity is too variable to be an accurate indicator of the time of death. Other indicators, such as **rigor mortis**, are more reliable.

Movement of a body in the first few hours after death can be evident by patches of lividity on different areas of the body. To continue the example cited above, the right-side pattern of lividity accompanied by a more intense lividity on the lower back and buttocks could indicate movement of the body onto the right side after death.

Typically, postmortem lividity appears as a bluish-purple or reddish-purple color in the regions of the body that are in close contact with the ground.

Areas that are further removed from the ground can be pink at the periphery of the discoloration.

Exceptions to these aforementioned colors can be important forensic clues to the **cause of death**. For example, in **carbon monoxide poisoning**, lividity can be cherry red in color. When a compound called methaemoglobin forms in the blood, as occurs in exposure to lethal concentrations of potassium chlorate, nitrates, and aniline, lividity tends to be a dark, chocolate-like brown color. Death due to intense cold (**hypothermia**) or the refrigeration of a recently deceased body will produce a bright pink lividity. The latter color can also be produced if the area of the body was covered by wet clothing.

Lividity typically appears as patches or blotches that coalesce over time to produce a more generalized area of discoloration. After about 12 hours, the lividity becomes fixed. Then, even if the body is shifted, the pattern of discoloration will remain the same.

SEE ALSO Blood; Crime scene investigation; Rigor mortis.

Living forensics

Forensic science has by tradition been identified with investigations of questionable and criminal deaths. However, only recently a new discipline, called living forensics, has begun as a way for forensic scientists to deal with survivors of traumatic physical injuries and illnesses. As a result, living forensics is defined as the part of forensic science that deals with the unbiased solutions to legal issues in cases involving living victims. (Forensic **pathology** is the other part of forensic science, which traditionally has involved only victims who are deceased.)

The application of living forensics deals with most of the wide range of subjects within forensic science, including the living victims of alcohol and drug abuse/addictions; domestic violence such as abuse of children, elders, and spouses; food, **medicine**, and drug tampering and poisoning; incest; medical malpractice; nonfatal assaults; pedestrian and motorized vehicle accidents; abuse while in the custody of law enforcement and correctional facilities; rape; suicide attempts; and work-related illnesses and injuries.

Forensic scientists who work within living forensics are trained to identify living victims of abuse, neglect, and violence in a wide variety of locations such as health clinics, correctional facilities, emergency centers, hospitals, occupational health centers, nursing homes and senior citizen living centers, schools, rehabilitation centers, and the community at large.

Forensic scientists, in addition to dealing with these subject areas, help to support the civil and constitutional rights of the living victim. Many of the important ways that these rights are guaranteed include recognizing **physical evidence** with regards to known or potential criminal acts, collecting and safeguarding such **evidence**, and preserving the overall **chain of custody** of this evidence.

Because living forensics is emerging as a forensic field, healthcare personnel and other people in positions to identify abuse, violence, and neglect of living victims are just now being made aware of such criminal acts so they can deal with the appropriate procedures to document and safeguard such evidence. As the field of living forensics matures, evidentiary materials (evidence) will be more properly detected, collected, preserved, and transmitted to appropriate authorities within law enforcement and the criminal justice system. These advancements will help to reduce the costs of prosecuting criminals and increase the protection that society needs for living victims of such criminal acts.

SEE ALSO Careers in forensic science; Evidence, chain of custody; Food poisoning.

Edmond Locard

1877–1966
FRENCH
CRIMINALIST

Edmond Locard had a paramount role in the European and worldwide development of **criminalistics**, the practice of gathering **evidence** for scientific examination and crime solving.

Locard was born in 1877 in the city of Lyon, France, about 300 miles southeast of Paris. In 1902, He obtained his doctoral degree in medicine. At that point, his interest in science pertaining to the law was already clear, as his thesis was entitled "La médecine légale sous le Grand Roy" (Legal Medicine under the Great King). After receiving his degree, he became the assistant of French medical doctor **Alexandre Lacassagne** (1844–1921), often referred to as the father of modern forensic medicine, of the University of Lyon. Lacassagne became Locard's mentor. A few years later, Locard decided to study the law, and in 1907, he passed the bar examination. Both a medical doctor and an attorney with a great interest for the study of sciences pertaining to criminal law, Locard had the right educational background and motivation to develop his passion and realize his dream.

In 1908, Locard began traveling the world. He first stopped in Paris, France, to study with French anthropologist **Alphonse Bertillon** (1853–1914), and to understand the anthropometric system of criminal **identification**. Locard subsequently visited the police departments of Berlin, Germany, Rome, Italy, and Vienna. His trip took him to the United States where he visited the police departments of New York and Chicago. He finally returned to Lyon in 1910 after a visit to Swiss criminalist Rodolphe Archibald Reiss in Lausanne, Switzerland.

After arriving back in Lyon, Locard's interest in modern and scientific investigation methods dedicated to police work was at its highest. In addition, Lyon was undergoing an increasing number of violent crimes, especially murders. In 1910, Locard was able to convince the Lyon police to establish a laboratory for collecting and examining evidence from crime scenes. They provided him with a few rooms in the attic of the court house in order to set up his laboratory.

In 1912, the laboratory was officially recognized by the Lyon police. Locard then headed the first official police crime laboratory in the world. This laboratory received world recognition and many great criminalists obtained their knowledge and experience under the guidance of Locard in the years that followed. One of these was the Swedish criminalist **Harry Söderman** (1902–1956), to whom Locard became a mentor.

In 1929 in Lausanne, Switzerland, Locard founded the International Academy of Criminalistics with Swiss criminalist Marc Bischoff, Austrian criminalist Siegfried Trkel, Dutch criminalist C.J. van Ledden Hülsebosch, and German criminalist **Georg Popp**. Unfortunately, this academy did not survive WWII. Several other police laboratories were created based on the model and influence of Locard. Even after WWII, the French police served as a model to many other countries. Locard was the driving force behind the development of modern scientific and technical police. He died in 1966. Subsequently, a significant decline occurred in criminalistics activity in France.

Locard published more than 40 works in French, English, German, and Spanish. His most famous work, still referenced daily, is the seven volumes of the Traité de criminastique (Treaty of Criminalistics), published between 1931 and 1935. Many of his books represent significant contributions to the field of criminalistics, and forensic scientists often still read his writings. His publications include several works about police investigations that he personally conducted. Locard was also passionate about philately (stamp collecting), and he wrote a few books on this topic.

Locard's contribution to forensic sciences is immense. His most important contribution is the principe de l'échange (principle of exchange). Locard stated "Toute action de l'homme, et a fortiori, l'action violent qu'est un crime, ne peut pas se dérouler sans laisser quelque marque." Translated, it means that any action of an individual, and obviously the violent action constituting a crime, cannot occur without leaving a trace. From this sentence, the whole principle of exchange of traces between two objects entering in contact was established. For example, when a car hits another car, paint from the first car will be deposited on the second one and vice-versa. Similarly, when somebody sits on a chair, **fibers** from his/her clothing will be deposited on the chair and fibers from the cloth of the chair will be deposited on the person's clothing.

Söderman later wrote of Locard, "He put the analysis of handwriting on a firmer footing, systematized the analysis of the dust in the clothes of suspects, invented a modified method of analyzing **blood** stains, and invented poroscopy, whereby the pores in the papillary ridges of fingerprints are used as a means of identification."

SEE ALSO Fingerprint; Handwriting analysis; Locard's exchange principle.

Locard's exchange principle

Edmond Locard (1877–1966) studied law at the Institute of Legal Medicine and worked subsequently as an assistant to the forensic pioneer **Alexandre Lacassagne** prior to directing the forensic laboratory in Lyon, France. Locard's techniques proved useful to the French Secret Service during World War I (1914–1918), when Locard was able to determine where soldiers and prisoners had died by examining the stains on their uniforms.

Like **Hans Gross** and **Alphonse Bertillon** before him, Locard advocated the application of scientific methods and logic to criminal investigation and **identification**. Locard's work formed the basis for what is widely regarded as a cornerstone of the forensic sciences, Locard's Exchange Principle, which states that with contact between two items, there will be an exchange. It was Locard's assertion that when any person comes into contact with an object or another person, a cross-transfer of **physical evidence** occurs. By recognizing, documenting, and examining the nature and extent of this evidentiary exchange, Locard observed that criminals could be associated with particular locations, items of **evidence**, and victims. The detection of the exchanged materials is interpreted to mean that the two objects were in contact. This is the cause and effect principle reversed; the effect is observed and the cause is concluded.

Crime reconstruction involves examining the available physical evidence, those materials left at or removed from the scene, victim, or offender, for example hairs, **fibers**, and soil, as well as fingerprints, footprints, genetic markers (**DNA**), or handwriting. These forensically established contacts are then considered in light of available and reliable witness, the victim, and a suspect's statements. From this, theories regarding the circumstances of the crime can be generated and falsified by logically applying the information of the established facts of the case.

Locard's publications make no mention of an "exchange principle," although he did make the observation *"Il est impossible au malfaiteur d'agir avec l'intensité que suppose l'action criminelle sans laisser des traces de son passage."* (It is impossible for a criminal to act, especially considering the intensity of a crime, without leaving traces of this presence.). The term "principle of exchange" first appears in *Police and Crime-Detection*, in 1940, and was adapted from Locard's observations.

SEE ALSO Criminal profiling; DNA; Fingerprint; Forensic science; Handwriting analysis.

Lock-picking

An important facet of a forensic investigation is the examination of the crime scene. Attention to all the details can be invaluable in determining the nature and course of the events. One telltale clue to a crime can be signs of forced entry. Crude means of entry, such as the breaking down of a door or smashing of a window, are easy to discern. Lock-picking is less evident.

One of the simplest types of lock to pick is known as a pin-and-tumbler design. This lock uses a row of pins, divided into pairs, which rest in a row of shafts running perpendicular to the clock's main cylinder plug and its housing mechanism. Insertion of the right key forces the top and bottom pins apart at just the right distance so that all of the upper pins rest in the outer housing and all of the lower pins rest in the plug. At that point, no pins bind the plug to the housing, meaning that the cylinder can be turned freely, releasing the bolt that holds the locking mechanism in place.

To open such a lock without a key, one needs a long, thick piece of metal with a curved end (a pick), which can be inserted carefully inside the lock as one would a key. Moving with finesse, it is possible to adjust all the pins into place so that the cylinder can be turned as though the key had been used. Or one can apply a sloppier variation, known as raking, in which a pick is inserted and pulled out quickly with a tension wrench, such as a flathead screwdriver, while the cylinder is turned.

Experienced lock-pickers use a wide array of tools. They are likely to go to work using an entire tool kit with picks, "rakes" (picks for raking a lock), and tension wrenches, all of which are small enough that a basic lock-picking kit could fit into a pocket. To be equipped for a greater range of eventualities, a lock-picker may use a kit that includes other tools, such as a burglar alarm evasion kit, a key-impression kit (for making a key based on impressions that a lock makes on a key blank), a key-pattern device (for copying old-fashioned warded keys, made to fit into lever locks), files, and other items.

Even more sophisticated is an electric lock-opening device, which is used in tandem with a pick to move the pins into the proper position. Additionally, a lock-pick gun can be used to open most pin-tumbler mechanisms. By squeezing the trigger, one strikes the pins with the pick, after which a tension wrench is applied to turn the lock cylinder.

There are other varieties of techniques and tools, just as there are variations in lock design, such as the wafer-tumbler lock, in which tumblers in the shape of wafers take the place of pins. Most aspects of lock-picking are simple in concept, but far from easy in application. It is the less than deft attempt at lock-picking that can leave telltale lock damage as a valuable forensic clue.

SEE ALSO Crime scene investigation.

Douglas M. Lucas

CANADIAN
FORENSIC SCIENTIST

In 1960 Douglas M. Lucas was the first forensic scientist to utilize the technique of gas **chromatography** as a means of **identification** of petroleum products used as accelerants in suspected cases of **arson**. In so doing, he recognized the inherent difficulties in attempting to minutely identify accelerants by brand type or commercial manufacturer.

In forensic fire investigations (suspected arson, acts of terrorism, etc.) it is extremely important to analyze the explosion, blast, or **fire debris** for the presence of small amounts of suspected volatile accelerants, which can be used to prove that the fire or blast was caused intentionally.

Accelerants are chemical fuels that cause fires to burn at higher temperatures, to spread exceptionally rapidly, or to be extremely difficult to contain or extinguish. **Accelerant** residue often remains at the crime scene. If identified, the presence of an accelerant can be used as forensic legal **evidence** of arson. However, even when it is collected immediately after the incident, carefully packaged, promptly transported, and analyzed by the best methods, test results have not always been conclusive or perfectly accurate.

Part of the difficulty in accurate analysis is that petroleum distillates, typically used as accelerants, typically undergo physical and biochemical changes as they burn or evaporate. In addition, arsonists generally use compounds of gasoline, kerosene, or diesel fuel as accelerants. Those crude oil products are made from mixtures that may contain thousands of different **organic compounds**, most of which contain only carbon and hydrogen atoms (hydrocarbons).

In order to identify volatile accelerants in a forensic scientific (laboratory) setting, it is first necessary to isolate the liquid suspected of being an accelerant from the surrounding fire or blast debris. It is then analyzed using gas chromatography, which results in the production of a graph called a chromatogram. The chromatogram is then computer analyzed and compared with chromatograms of known accelerants until a match is found.

Gas chromatography is one of the most effective techniques for detecting accelerants in explosion, blast, or fire debris. The basic gas chromatography technique utilizes uses a stream of gas (nitrogen or helium) as a carrier to move a mixture of gaseous materials along a long column or tube filled with a separating compound. Gas chromatography involves separating mixtures of gases into their individual chemical components based on the different boiling points of their hydrocarbons. Each gas in the mixture can then be identified, because each produces a distinct chromatogram.

Lucas set the worldwide standard for volatile accelerant identification in forensic arson investigations; gas chromatography remains considered among the most accurate scientific means of identifying flammable or combustible accelerant residues. In addition, Lucas authored "Ethical responsibilities of the forensic scientist: exploring the limits," published in the *Journal of Forensic Science* in 1989.

SEE ALSO Arson; Crime scene cleaning; Fire debris; Fire investigation.

Luminol

When investigating suspected crime scenes where the visible **evidence** of crime was removed by the perpetrator, nothing is more useful than luminol, a chemi-luminescent compound, which reacts to red **blood** cells (**hemoglobin**) and gives off a blue-greenish light. Luminol (5–amino–2,3–dihydro–1,4–phthalazine-dione) was accidentally discovered in 1928 by the German chemist H.O. Albrecht, and was first used at a crime scene in 1937 in Germany. Luminol is highly sensitive to bloodstains or residues, even to old stains, in walls, carpets, upholstery, wooden floors, or painted surfaces.

When a luminol solution is sprayed on surfaces, it reacts with metal ions, such as iron, which are stored and transported by hemoglobin cells (red blood cells). Very discrete iron concentrations on a surface, such as 1 part per million, are enough to catalyze luminol's chemi-luminescence (react and cause a glow). However, luminol sensitivity is not blood-specific, and the compound also reacts with other substances, such as **saliva**, rust, potassium permanganate, animal proteins, vegetable enzymes, and other organic **fluids** and tissues. Therefore, luminol tests are not conclusive for blood and cannot be admitted for evidence in court.

A biomarker (or a chemical marker) produces conclusive identification when it combines high sensitivity to a particular substance with high specificity, e.g., it is significantly more sensitive to that substance than to others. For instance, 100% sensitivity plus 95–99% specificity to a given compound number one, compared with 40–60% sensitivity and 30–40%

specificity to substance number two, would indicate strong evidence of the presence of compound number one. Luminol, however, only meets the first criteria, a high sensitivity to blood and to other protein-containing animal fluids, whether human or not. Another aspect of a luminol reaction is its different degrees of sensitivity from one substance to another. Luminol shows higher sensitivity to animal or human blood, organic tissues and fluids than to other compounds containing metal ions, such as paints, metallic surfaces, household products, or vegetable enzymes. Therefore, the light emitted by luminol has different intensities and time duration, depending on the material of contact. In other words, the lesser the sensitivity, the shorter the period of luminol chemiluminescence. Such variations constitute useful leads to experts investigating the scene.

In spite of the above-described limitation, luminol is very useful in **crime scene investigation**. The inside of an apparently clean room in which blood and other crime evidence is not visible can be sprayed with luminol over suspected surfaces. If a reaction occurs in a carpet, for instance, closer examination may reveal bloodstains or residues on the floor beneath it. It can also indicate direction of bloodstains, spatters, and reveal concealed bloody **shoeprints**.

When biological samples have to be collected for **DNA** or other tests, luminol should only be used after samples are seized. Luminol's chemical reactions with blood and other body proteins destroy some important genetic markers required for DNA fingerprinting.

SEE ALSO Blood; Blood, presumptive test; Blood spatter; Bloodstain evidence; Chemical and biological detection technologies; Crime scene investigation; DNA fingerprint; Fluids; Genetic code; Hemoglobin.